HOLMES-LASKI LETTERS
VOLUME II

HOLMES-LASKI

LETTERS VOLUME II

THE CORRESPONDENCE OF

MR. JUSTICE HOLMES AND

HAROLD J. LASKI 1916-1935

EDITED BY MARK DE WOLFE HOWE

ABRIDGED BY ALGER HISS FOR

ATHENEUM NEW YORK 1963

Published by Atheneum
Reprinted by arrangement with Harvard University Press
Copyright © 1963 by Atheneum House, Inc.
Copyright 1953 by the President and Fellows of Harvard College
All rights reserved
Manufactured in the United States of America by
The Colonial Press Inc., Clinton, Massachusetts
Published in Canada by McClelland & Stewart Ltd.
First Atheneum Edition

PREFACE

In February 1949, Harold Laski gave to the Harvard Law School the original letters which Mr. Justice Holmes had written to him between 1916 and 1932. At the time when they were delivered to the School I undertook, at Mr. Laski's request, to have the letters transcribed and to supply him with copies, in order that he might publish some or all of them. As work progressed on the transcription I was told by a common friend that Laski had stated that I need feel no haste in completing the work since, under the pressure of other duties, he had abandoned, at least for the time, his original intention of preparing an edition of the Holmes letters. Work on the transcription continued, however, and was virtually completed when Laski died on March 24, 1950. At that time I reminded Mr. Justice Frankfurter of the fact that the Harvard Law School had in its possession all of the letters from Laski to Holmes which the Justice had preserved—nearly all which Laski had written to Holmes. On the suggestion of Mr. Justice Frankfurter, Mrs. Laski quickly and most generously consented to the plan of publishing the correspondence between the two men and indicated entire willingness that all editorial decisions should be mine. The publication of these volumes is the outcome of that willingness.

The kindness of Mr. Justice Frankfurter in providing a Foreword reduces to a minimum my responsibilities for setting the background of the correspondence. It may be well, however, if I state briefly what the principal editorial problems have been and how they have been resolved.

Some readers, feeling that the first responsibility of an editor is to discard superfluous materials, will complain, perhaps, that the publication of virtually all of the surviving correspondence of Holmes and Laski showed a lack of judgment. It may be urged that a selection from the letters would have sufficed to record the essentials of an extraordinary friendship and to mark the course of the intellectual pilgrimage of the friends. Time may justify the criticism, yet it seemed clear to me that the editor should not pretend to possess prophetic powers, and make judgments for later generations. If this correspondence is destined to become an important chapter in intellectual history it would be arrogance in its editor to cut the chapter to comfortable proportions determined by his own predictive interpretation of the history of ideas between 1916 and 1935. If the correspondence has the major importance which I believe it possesses, it is manifestly better to have the whole produced today than to leave to others the task of correcting this editor's well-meaning sins of omission.

This basic decision in favor of completeness involves one consequence which should be squarely faced. That consequence may, perhaps, best be phrased in terms of taste. In the letters as published there are many harsh comments, doubtless some unfair reflections on persons still living. Feelings are sure to be hurt by the publication of these statements and the taste of an editor who permits private criticism to become a matter of public knowledge is sure to be impugned. To this charge there is no plea in bar but there is merit, I believe, in a plea in confession and avoidance. Those critical comments which are published relate to people whose careers were conducted in public and whose names are familiar to their own generation and will probably not be unknown to later generations. Comment on such men is, therefore, criticism of their times. To spare the sensibilities of a few persons now living would have been to deny to later generations the benefit of contemporary judgment and, if you will, contemporary prejudice. Discretion by the editor might have developed his own reputation for good taste but it would have deprived the correspondence of much of its vitality and produced an artificial propriety hardly characteristic of the two correspondents.

This editorial problem was not unrelated to another. That was the question whether the editor, while disregarding the sensibilities of persons now living, should endeavor to protect the memory of the correspondents themselves. It would be less than honest to pretend that the exuberant, the passionate, and the controversial strains in Laski's character were loved and admired by all who knew him and his work. Among those who did not admire, some will be quick to seek in his letters to Holmes justification for their distrust. There they may find exaggeration, distortion, and falsehood. Had the editor felt it to be his duty to safeguard the reputation of either one of the correspondents he might have followed the easy course and omitted all passages which raised doubts in his own mind or he might have pursued the hopeless task of seeking to uncover the "true" version of all reported incidents. The hopelessness of following the second course ruled it out. The first alternative seemed unacceptable in the light of my conviction that the two men are larger than their failings and that the record of their lives and thought is a record of their times which should speak for itself in its entirety if it is to be heard at all. Presuppositions and prejudice could find easy confirmation in editorial censorship; when the whole correspondence is laid before the reader he will be empowered, as he should be, to form his judgment of the character of the correspondents upon the basis of all of the relevant evidence. The result was the decision to omit no passage in order to protect the name of its author from either justified or unjustified criticism. Those omissions which have been made are indicated by the conventional symbols and mark the spots at which either my judgment determined that the matter was of no appreciable interest to the public or where the limits of fair comment, as those limits are set by the caution of British publishers, seemed to have been passed.

In translating the informality of the handwritten originals to the formality of the printed page—and none of the originals was typewritten—I have taken liberties which purists may condemn. Paragraphing and punctuation have been added when they seemed manifestly called for; abbreviations have, for the most part, been eliminated. In all other respects the transcription is as accurate as my industry could make it, though I am sure that there are errors which other readers will discover. A particularly perplexing problem concerned the order in which the letters were to be printed. My general rule was to prefer that order which makes each letter responsive to its immediate predecessor over a sequence based entirely on a letter's date. I believe that this preference, aided by cross references, is justified, yet the reader may occasionally be troubled by its consequence. Perhaps it will be well for American readers to remember, in this connection, that it was Laski's habit to date his letters by numerals alone and that his practice was to give the day of the month before the month of the year. Thus his 9.X.24 stands for October 9, 1924, not for September 10, 1924.

With respect to the slight scaffolding which my annotations and biographical appendix provide I should perhaps add one word of explanation. It will be quickly seen that a series of somewhat arbitrary editorial judgments lie behind the footnotes and the Appendix. In the notes I have sought to provide the minimum aid which an informed Anglo-American reader of ordinary cultivation might find helpful. For his further assistance, and for the special benefit of any person who does not fit the measure of this imagined reader, the Biographical Appendix seeks to provide the relevant materials concerning persons who are referred to by the correspondents with some frequency and who are not such familiar figures as to need no identification. Doubtless a more scientific division could have been made between that information which is contained in footnotes and that which is to be found in the Appendix, yet I have felt that such allocations as I have made are better justified by instinct than by science. I should add, perhaps, that the relatively full annotation at the beginning of the volumes is reduced in the later correspondence. That reduction is based on the hope that the reader's familiarity with the materials, supplemented by the Index and the Appendix, makes editorial assistance increasingly superfluous.

M. DeW. H.

Harvard Law School
September 1952

PREFATORY NOTE
TO THE ABRIDGED EDITION

———————

The decade which has passed since the publication of the two-volume edition of the *Holmes-Laski Letters* has naturally brought new interpretations of the two correspondents and their times. The letters themselves, of course, were kindling for reassessment. Now that I have looked into this skillful abridgment of the correspondence I have come to wonder whether I did not almost smother the flame of understanding by my extravagant use of kindling. In any case, I see in this selection self-portraits of Holmes and Laski no less revealing than those which appeared at fullest length ten years ago. I like to believe that a new generation of readers will find excitement in an extraordinary record of a remarkable friendship.

M. DeW. H.

THE METHODOLOGY OF
THE ABRIDGEMENT

———————————

It is appropriate to set out the criteria I have tried to follow in deciding upon the extensive excisions made necessary by limitations of space. First, I have sought to present without disfigurement the rich and varied contents of these widely-ranging, highly-civilized letters. Next, I have tried to preserve the tone of responsive dialogue which is the matrix for the self-portraits sketched by the two authors as they revealed to each other, through this prolonged correspondence, their personal tastes and traits.

With these major objectives in mind I have been guided by one further basic consideration. Justice Holmes's letters are an extraordinary historical and cultural heritage. As a boy he heard from his grandmother of the British entry into Boston. He thus spanned in his own lifetime and that of his familiars the entire history of our country. Brought up in a household of high culture, youthful officer in the Civil War, philosopher, eminent legal scholar and pre-eminent judge, he was a paragon without peer in American intellectual life. His letters are his major contribution to general literature, for his other writings ("The Common Law," judicial opinions, and collected legal papers and speeches) are principally concerned with legal subjects. Only the letters are fully accessible to the non-lawyer. And, despite the literary and intellectual power of his other writings, it was, naturally, in his letters that he most fully disclosed the style of his thought, the distinction of his personality, the mellow cultivation within which he was so fully comfortable, and the perceptive discrimination that had ripened during his long and privileged sojourn in the fairest fields of Western civilization.

Any conscientious editor, it seems plain, would want to preserve intact the corpus of Justice Holmes's letters. I have done just this with his letters to Harold Laski. The only excisions from Holmes's letters that I have made are of a few sentences that refer without expression of opinion to passages in Laski's letters omitted from this edition. These deletions from Holmes merely avoid the distraction that would otherwise have resulted from unconnected, dangling statements of no intrinsic quality.

My decision to make the required deletions almost exclusively from Professor Laski's part of the correspondence was the more easy to reach, and to adhere to, because the volume of his letters was by far the greater. Despite the 540 pages of Laski's letters that have been omitted, the representation of the two authors is in this edition nearly equal in volume—Laski's share taking up just under half the total number of pages. The Justice's frequent practice of restating Laski's points in replying to them has facilitated abridging the Laski letters without undue loss of that quality of interchange which characterizes notable collections of letters. My excisions bear down most heavily on Laski's numerous lists of rare works read, acquired or noted in dealers' catalogues, on conventional anecdotes, and on routine descriptions of scenery, paintings, notables, and well-known or unimportant books. These omissions do not, I hope, diminish the reader's opportunity to savor fully Laski's warmth, his dedication as a teacher, his vast scholarship, and the important part he played in the large events of his time.

One typographical point should be noted as to the Laski letters retained in this edition. Deletions were sufficiently great in number and varying in length to call for a simplified method of noting them in order to minimize interruption to the flow of the text. Three dots represent each deletion, slight or extensive, and where found at the beginning or end of a paragraph frequently replace material that is separately paragraphed in the original letters.

Professor Howe's footnotes and biographical paragraphs have been retained in view of their contribution to the general reader's understanding. Wherever the footnotes I have added do not readily disclose their authorship, by express reference to this edition, they are marked with my initials.

Alger Hiss

February 1963

CONTENTS

FOREWORD

The only justification for an extraneous foreword is the hope of drawing on one's good will with readers to secure their attention to an unknown author, or to assure them that a seemingly extinct volcano has again burst into flame. The crass absurdity that such could be the purpose of introductory remarks to the *Holmes-Laski Letters* precludes a misinterpretation of arrogance. When the public is offered two hefty volumes of correspondence neither revealing long-awaited secrets nor appealing otherwise to elemental curiosity, but preoccupied merely with things of the mind and the insoluble issues of man's spiritual quest, it may not be amiss to bear witness to the excitement these letters have stirred in one who has read every word of them.

This testimony is the more relevant since the public has already had two volumes of the *Holmes-Pollock Letters*, and since it comes from one who has read hundreds of unpublished letters of Mr. Justice Holmes and Harold J. Laski to other correspondents. How is it possible, we naturally suspect, that these *Letters* should not echo what we have already read? How can a correspondence so copious excite the mind from first to last? With full awareness of the treachery of superlatives, it becomes necessary to say that this correspondence surpasses all others from the pen—and it was the pen—of these prolific and extraordinarily endowed letter-writers.

One may ask in all soberness, was there ever another such correspondence? Consider its duration and continuity and range: high themes canvassed with enormous learning and a light touch, expressing deep convictions unmarred by intolerance, the exploits of two self-reliant adventurers in the world of ideas, passionately pursued but with gargoylish humor. Added to all this, are the striking differences between the two correspondents.

The outpour began with a bread-and-butter note from Laski, on July 11, 1916, following the first meeting of the two in the Justice's summer home at Beverly Farms, thirty miles north of Boston. This opening letter and the prompt, longer reply by Holmes foreshadow the essential characteristics of an exchange that lasted for close to twenty years—the last letter written by Laski on February 17, 1935, about a fortnight before the Justice's death. They found themselves drawn to one another at first sight by the magnetic attraction of two deep-ploughing minds full of disinterested zest for the adventure of ideas.

Consider the situation of the two men who struck up at once this deep, lasting friendship on that July day, 1916, at Beverly Farms. By that time, through his writings—a famous little book, a few essays, and his opinions—Holmes had powerfully changed ways of thinking about law and had thereby rationalized law. A few months earlier, his seventy-fifth birthday had been celebrated as a national event. His fame transcended the boundaries of his own country. He was acclaimed the preëminent judge of the English-speaking world. Indeed, Judge Cardozo, no mean authority, was inclined to the view that Holmes was the profoundest intellect who had ever dispensed Anglo-American justice. The gifts which nature had showered upon him—the handsome face and distinguished presence, the noble voice and charming manner— were accentuated by his long, dashing career which enveloped him as though in a romantic aura.

Neither David Belasco nor Max Reinhardt could have contrived a more dramatic contrast than Laski and Holmes when their friendship began. Facing one of the most impressive personalities of his day was a frail stripling of twenty-three. More than half a century separated them. Until he spoke, Laski was not particularly noticeable. But it was not the first time that Laski struck fire in an old man who was the leader of his profession. When Francis Galton, the famous geneticist, discovered that the author of an article which had attracted his attention was "a schoolboy at Manchester, aged 17!!" he wrote: "It is long since I have been so much astonished. The lad probably has a great future before him and he will make a mark if he sticks to Eugenics . . ."

The lad did not stick to Eugenics after he went up to Oxford. Probably through the influence of Sir Ernest Barker, then a don at New College, the problems of politics, especially how liberty was to be achieved, became for the rest of his life Laski's dominant interest. He left Oxford at the outbreak of World War I. Having been rejected for war service because of his physique, he spent two years as a tutor at McGill. At the time of his visit to Holmes he had just come to Harvard, an obscure junior instructor in the De-partment of Government, piecing out an academic pittance with which to support his wife and child (he had married at eighteen), by much writing during the summer, for Herbert Croly's *New Republic.*

Short as was his stay at Cambridge, only four years, the qual-ities in Laski that produced "the shock of recognition" between him and Holmes made a dent also on Harvard. Were there not a cloud of witnesses, competent and critical, it would not be credible that a young, unknown teacher could affect so deeply the life of a great university in so brief a time. For he taught his colleagues as well as his pupils as do all great teachers. In his case they were senior and distinguished colleagues. Professor Charles H. McIlwain, one of the glories of Harvard both as scholar and teacher, said of him: "His influence on students was greater than that of any other instructor I have ever known. His influence on me was pro-found . . ." One more bit of evidence must suffice. It is that of Professor Zechariah Chafee Jr., the eminent legal scholar and hu-manist: "There are few men with whom I have disagreed so often, and fewer still with whom I have passed so many happy hours and from whom I have learned so much."

It is not surprising that an ardent spirit with such diverse talents should have had his energy dispersed in many directions and his compassionate nature readily enlisted for all sorts of causes and individuals. But the main stream of his life was teaching. His central significance was that of teacher. To that calling he gave all he had—his learning (Holmes, writing to Pollock, called him "one of the very most learned men I ever saw of any age"), his elo-quence, his imagination, his fantastic feats of memory, his dialectic powers, his ever-ready kindness and generosity, above all, what has been rightly called his "quite passionate interest in young people." There can be few countries in the world where there is not some-one who will cherish for the rest of his days what Laski meant to him as a teacher. Not often can the function of teacher have been more completely fulfilled.

A temperament as swift as Laski's in reacting to any manifesta-tion of injustice was bound, on occasion, to be betrayed by an ex-cess of zeal on the side of the angels. He was not one of those, as R. H. Tawney said of him, who regard the omission from the beati-tudes of "Blessed are the discreet" a regrettable oversight. The world suffers less from knight-errantry induced by a passion for liberty than from prudence dictated by self-regard. The letters of both men contain flippant and heretical passages that may offend some sensibilities. Judgments upon Holmes and Laski are bound to be drawn from these letters. But fair judgment can rest only on the correspondence in its entirety.

One more thing ought to be said. Good talkers are apt to embellish their tales and Laski's stories often gained in the telling. Indeed, at times he reinforced history by fancy. Some of his anecdotes remind one of Landor's "Imaginary Conversations," except that they are gayer and more illuminating. More often, however, when his accounts seems to transcend common experience they do so because things happened to Laski that lay outside the experience of less extraordinary people. And if he appears to indulge in some tall tales about the great, he was in fact the intimate of men like Lord Haldane and John Morley and Lord Chancellor Sankey and eminent men on the Continent, in the United States, and in Asia. He did move in the center of affairs as well as among the notables in the world of learning.

Holmes and Laski were obviously men apart. Much about them was calculated to keep them apart also from one another. But the factors of divergence—antecedents, age, preoccupation, geography —were absorbed by the confluence of their feeling for one another and by the intensity and range of their intellectual interests.

Thus it came to pass that when Laski announced to Holmes, in the early stages of their friendship, his return to England, the Justice wrote: "I shall miss you sadly. There is no other man I should miss so much." And toward the end, as Laski kept up his flow of gay and sustaining letters, his venerable friend wrote: "One of the greatest pleasures of my waning life is a letter from you."

July 1952

HOLMES-LASKI LETTERS

VOLUME II

V

1925

Dear Laski: A letter[1] from you every word of which evokes a response has come this morning. I will do as well as I can with a lumbago that threatens to keep me from court tomorrow. 1. Reading proofs, on the whole I think a great pleasure. That chap has a way of saying what you think and hitting you where you live that is all his own. On the other hand are the chills that you mention and I well know. 2. When you write about Hardy you have me. His more famous novels I feared as disagreeable and never read. I imagine I should not care for his philosophy, as I do for that of but few. I read your "divinity that shapes our ends" first "divinity that *drapes* our ends" and thought you had imparted to him a decency not to [be] found in Shakespeare. 3. I have expressed my agreement with you as to Racine and Corneille heretofore. Only you are rather more extreme. I could see something but not a great deal. But what right have we to feel superior to our brothers because our sense of the beautiful is different? You do like beer or you don't, but how is either better than the other? I agree that we reach a point where we can say the difference marks inferior perception or less education but we hardly can say that to the French. 4. I am tickled about Barrett Wendell. I never could suppose he was important and have read little of him. He had some minor gifts and I believe was a good teacher. He was a student in my office and I remember discoursing to him on the philosophy of law and just as I was thinking this would put a heart into a brass monkey I saw his eyes roll in his head and he was going to sleep standing up. I believe he failed in his examinations and he

---

[1] Omitted from this edition.

3

gave up the law. But with all his peculiarities I think he was a good fellow. 5. Your argument with Jenks reminds of a talk I once had with Davey, when I was passing a Sunday with him. I put him a point, and some considerations to which he reflected, "That is not the law of England." I said, "I am perfectly aware of it, but I am considering whether it should be the law of Massachusetts." I felt as I often have that working with great ease and swiftness within a given system the English judges were apt to go no farther and did not readily bring their practical postulates into solution. But inside their limit they do work with great ease and swiftness. *Between ourselves* I agree with you as to Holland and Salmond. They do not sting. (You know my division of able lawyers into kitchen knives, razors, and stings.) You ask whether I have found a lawyer the worse for being a philosopher. I haven't known many who were. I don't think Langdell, or Ames, was in any important degree, and intimately as I knew Gray I didn't suspect him until his book came out. I have known some young lawyers who I thought were the worse for their liberal interests. It made them unwilling to tackle the details. 6. As to economic principles. I had a letter from Lepaulle (whom you remember?) saying he was writing a book in which the Jews had reversed the order of time and he was showing how 1200 was the inevitable development of 1925, and that the causal reasoning was just as good. It sounds as if a book would be too ponderous, but it is amusing. McKenna leaves the Bench tomorrow. I don't know whether the point will be marked at the time, but he has a sweet nature and though worn out we shall miss him.

Now I shall recumb with a hot bottle at my back, and read Lodge's *Life of Washington* till I slumber.

Affectionately yours, O. W. Holmes

16 Warwick Gardens, 30.XII.24
My dear Justice: . . . a lunch with Mrs. Asquith which was *very* amusing. . . . Charles Masterman who was there told me one good story. Curzon threatened to get the Lords to throw out the Labour housing bill.[1] There was great distress; but Haldane said if it was left to him he would arrange it. An hour later he came back and announced an agreement. "If you throw it out," he told Curzon, "we shall create peers; and our first peer will be Saklatvala,[2] the Parsee communist who sits for Battersea." Curzon was

---

[1] At this time Lord Curzon was President of the Council and Leader of the House of Lords. The Conservative party was committed to the policy of letting private enterprise deal with problems of housing.
[2] Shaphuiji Saklatvala (1874-1936); after a socialist beginning and the successes of the Russian Revolution he became an active organizer of the British Communist Party and a vigorous critic of British policy in India.

so appalled at that suggested profanation of the Temple of God that he surrendered without further ado.

. . . Of reading I have done a good deal. Of the elegant, all Jane Austen again—very pleasant but with a sense that she liked the littlenesses of mankind and was dead to the bignesses; but incredible to have written during the Napoleonic wars and to have seen the soldier as nothing but a silly animal who flirts. Of the serious, the first three volumes of Gibbon in the Bury edition— very fine indeed—the two chapters on Christianity and Roman law as admirable at the tenth reading as at the first. Also with much interest the *Federalist*—numbers X and 46 seem to me to put sensibly almost all there is of really permanent merit in Marxian theory. And as we have bought a pianola to celebrate the fact that we have known each other fifteen perfect years we have been giving each other Beethoven-Chopin concerts each night and revelling in it—and we are convinced that Beethoven is a universe better than Bach. The latter has the voice of an angel, but clearly the soul of a bishop.

Our best love to both of you.

Ever affectionately yours, H. J. L.

16 Warwick Gardens, 6.I.24 [sic]
My dear Justice: . . . the time has passed mainly in reading and in one amusing dinner with Churchill. He raised the question of a labour attack on him for intellectual inconsistency on account of his frequent changes of party and was much concerned to defend himself. I told him that I thought his only weakness was to think he needed a defence, that a wise man never feared inconsistency which was usually the result of mental growth or a changed environment; and I quoted to him Halifax's admirable dictum that ignorance maketh a man enter into a party and shame preventeth him from leaving it.[1] We talked about political science and he attacked theorists on the ground that their schemes never reached fruition. I said you might as well attack practical men on the ground that their schemes never last. I told him that the only difference between the theorist and the practical man was that the first tried to test his assumptions and the second never knew that there were assumptions he ought to test. He's an amusing and brilliant fellow who pursues an idea as a hound a hare, but with no *fond* of real ideas. He talks electrically and with the *aplomb* of the man who has moved amid great affairs; but he has none of the inner perceptiveness of Morley or the exquisite playfulness of

[1] George Savile (1633-1695), first Marquess of Halifax, in *Political, Moral and Miscellaneous Thoughts and Reflections* (2 Foxcroft, *Life and Letters of Sir George Savile, Marquess of Halifax*, 1898, p. 507).

Birrell which make them, in my experience, the two best talkers I
have met in England. . . .

My love to you both.   *Ever affectionately yours, H. J. L.*

16 Warwick Gardens, 18.I.24 [sic]
My dear Justice: I have two letters and a postscript to answer;
for last week, with its endless little jobs which always proliferate
around the beginning of term, made letters impossible. First let
me answer some of your questions. Russell told me that he thought
Morris Cohen quite the best critical mind among American philosophers, but a mind which would not do justice to its powers
because it found the business of being negative too interesting.
And I must say I agree, for dearly as I love Morris, he is, I think,
of that combative type which regards a head as something to be
hit, and, if possible, to be hit really hard; and while what he
has written I always find arresting, I don't find that it leaves me
satisfied. The sceptic is, of course, invaluable, but the universal and
professional sceptic seems to me to miss the things the universe
offers. . . .

Our love to you both.   *Ever affectionately yours, Harold*

Washington, D.C., January 11, 1925
Memorandum
Dear Laski: Within is a case that I believe I mentioned.[1] I have
kept in the house by lumbago for two days—so the C.J. delivered
it for me. I returned to the Bench on Wednesday but am still
rather stiff and find it a little hard to get up. The papers have had
rumors that I intended to resign—of course unfounded. I thought
the wish was father to the thought but F. suggests that perhaps it
was due to confounding me with Hughes, which has happened
very often. Love to all three of you.   *Aff'ly yours, O. W. H.*

Washington, D.C., January 15, 1925
Dear Laski: Whether you like to put me in a hole or not you often
do—I confessed a little while ago my ignorance of some—many—
of the illustrious chronicled in *These Eventful Years.* Now I am
gravelled by your best of American historians. Years ago when a
good man painted my portrait at Beverly Farms I met an aesthetic
dame on the street just as he finished and asked her into the barn
studio to take a look—She: "Oughtn't there to be a shadow under

---

[1] Enclosed with the letter was a copy of Holmes's opinion in *Sanitary
District of Chicago v. United States, supra,* p. 459, Vol. I.

the moustache?" He: "I paint standing up and don't see it." She: "Very interesting—but I think it would have a little more *Brio* if there were a shadow under the moustache." Exit. Painter, who knew Paris like his hat, to me—"What in Hell's Brio?" So I, "Who in Hell are F. J. Turner and Carl Becker?" I must add though irrelevant, the painter presently went on [to] damn people who say *interesting*—in which again I agreed with him.

In what you say of Jane Austen you come nearer to the difficulties that I have expressed from time to time. I believe I wrote that I don't like to read about snobs and fools unless they are more transfigured than they are by Pollock's Saint Jane. (Of course I don't mean that that is all there is in her.)

You interest me by what you say of Gibbon. When one reads him one feels a great man—but he told me nothing that I wanted to know—and I remember distinctly my disappointment at the chapters on Christianity and the Roman law. That was ten or more years ago—perhaps I should be wiser now. But apart from the pleasure of dead greatness I could get a good deal more from Fustel de Coulanges—who I suppose is not the last word.

You gravel me again by your musical talk—I didn't know that you could speak critically of Bach and Beethoven—as you do of Rembrandt. I hope some day in a flush of conscience you will confess to faking a little—*pour épater les bourgeois*. I sent you an opinion the other day that cost me some sweat, simple as it sounds. I stop short hoping this will go early tomorrow morning.

Affectionately yours, O. W. Holmes

16 Warwick Gardens, 27.I.25
My dear Justice: . . . You question my musical knowledge. Admittedly it is not great. But my replication is that (1) I have a sister who is pretty nearly first-rate at the job so that I was brought up with the breed in and out of the house. (2) That I love, have loved, and am like to love it. (3) That on my pianola I can test any piece by the simple expedient of seeing it played by any pianist of the first order. This with my humble submission to the court. Of news not overmuch. Felix sent me a telegram from which I gathered that Pound was likely to go to Wisconsin.[1] I am deeply sorry; but I did not feel (between ourselves) that I could myself or get Haldane to urge him not to go. Those are things about which a man must make up his own mind; and no one else can help very much. . . . I met J. G. Frazer[2] the anthropologist at his

---

[1] The presidency of the University of Wisconsin had recently been offered to Dean Pound.

[2] Sir James George Frazer (1854-1941); author of *The Golden Bough* (1st ed., 1890).

house—a most charming creature but, I should say, for a great observer singularly unobservant. He greeted me with the remark that I looked much older than he expected me to be; and his next was that Haldane's sister (who looks her 62 years) was not a day more than 45. But in his field he talked greatly and with a quite perfect choice of words—something almost French in the elegance of phrasing, and yet without a trace of affectation. . . .

My love to you both.   *Ever affectionately yours, H. J. L.*

Washington, D.C., February 1, 1925

Dear Laski: There has been rather a longer gap than usual in our letters—due I imagine to pressure of work on both sides. In your last, telling of talk with Churchill, I see that you got on to what I have called the inarticulate major premises of business men. I should think that your account of him hits him accurately. I think the last time I saw him, at a dinner when I ventured some remark in reply to what sounded to me rather blunt discourse of some Philistine I noticed his eyes brighten, and set it down to his credit. I remember years before he made me chuckle with his talk to old Harcourt. I am entirely with you against the man who said begin with Plato and Aristotle. I did with Plato with no modern advantages to be sure, but it was Plato. I always say whether it be philosophy or law, or what you like, begin with the latest. The modern book starts from your *milieu,* emotional and intellectual, and of course, whatever they say, has enormous advantages also from the advance of science. I shouldn't tell a law student to begin with Coke, Littleton, or even with Blackstone. I did with Blackstone and had infinite trouble from details and language that I didn't understand, and that no one could understand until he had made some progress in the history and philosophy of law. As I said of Montesquieu, to read the great books of the past with intelligent appreciation is one of the last achievements of a studious life.[1] Oh—I am fierce on that theme. The philosophically least consideration, perhaps, is practically very great. Ideas rarely are difficult to grasp. The difficulties come from the language and emphasis. The language, even if English, and the emphasis, of a different time, to some extent also of a different place, are strange and puzzling to a neophyte. To this day I am troubled as I hear arguments in patents, or mining, or admiralty or railroad cases, by the slang of the specialty. The thoughts behind the words rarely require a colossus. Of course I agree with you as to morality and have uttered my barbaric yawp on the subject from time to time. It is amusing to see in the law how in a century what was thought natural and wholesome may become anathema—like rum and the

---

[1] *Collected Legal Papers* (1921), 250, 253.

lottery—but they generally are argued about as if the present view was an eternal truth.

February 4. I thought another letter would come, and it has, bringing the usual pleasure. . . . On my side I have a letter this morning asking leave to translate my *Common Law* into French, which gives me pleasure. Of course I assent. The writer whom I suppose to be a mussoo who came here with a letter a year or so ago says this proposed translation is competent and even a bad one would tickle me.[2] I don't know the merits or demerits of the Italian and German versions of the past. This is the first week of a four weeks adjournment. My opinions are written and distributed and I am *vacuus* for the moment. I have begun at once Bradley's *Essays on Truth and Reality*. The first pages on the Good left me cold, but presently, when he falls foul of Pragmatism and chops it into mincemeat, he gives me glee. I feared that I had missed something until I was confirmed in my criticisms by him. I should think he was an admirable example of Oxford tone. I have been relieved of one anxiety this morning. My secretary thought he had discovered underpayment on my income taxes for some years past and I was frightened. So I saw the Commissioner and he sent an expert who reports this morning that it was all right. The uncertainty is worse to me than the actual payment would have been. The expert in addition is cutting down my return for this year—so the sun shines.

Perhaps after a few days of culture I shall offer to relieve some of the judges who have arrears but I don't commit myself to it yet, as I am tired and want to see how I feel. Now (11:45 a.m.) I will take a walk. I haven't walked but twice for a month, then philosophy and slumber.   *Affectionately yours, O. W. Holmes*

Washington, D.C., February 6, 1925
Dear Laski: Just after my last to you another from you arrived which I must begin to answer at once. Frankfurter telegraphed to Brandeis for him and me to write to Pound. I wrote that of course I couldn't advise but that I should feel much sorrow if he left. I also was of opinion, which I didn't state, that probably he would make a great mistake in going into a new field—and that probably also unless he has more executive ability than I suppose it would not be a success. I am happy to read in the papers that (after considerable wobbling, I suspect) he has declined the offer.

. . . I have fallen upon Bradley—*Essays on Truth and Reality* —as I believe I mentioned—a pontifical gent, I suspect with all his soft airs—also amusing for his declaration that he doesn't understand abstract reasoning, when much of his discourse is so

---

[2] No French translation of *The Common Law* has been published.

abstract, so unillumined by illustration, that in matters that I don't care about he is hardly intelligible. He presupposes familarity with his special lingo and as usual I am concerned that the unintelligibility consists not in the difficulty of his ideas but in his damned language. I deeply agree with him in believing that you can't take the individual apart from the whole—but when he thinks he has the absolute I think we all of us have simply ignorance and a *ne plus ultra* for speculation. When a man talks of Goodness and Beauty and Truth as cosmic and as more than human superlatives—and even thinks that human beings are the means by which the Absolute knows itself—I say goodbye. When, however, once a man has begun to spin in the Hegelian system, he never will get out—but will go on circling and circling. Hegel seems to me, whatever good he may have done, to have blighted the spontaneity of his followers. They talk Hegel over and over and I wish they were dead.

February 7. Bradley is finished. I take it that he thinks no one a philosopher who hasn't a closed system—a cosmos that accounts for and sustains itself and is seen as necessary. As I don't believe he or Hegel or anyone else has made or found such a structure, or is likely to. I regard philosophy as simply the broader generalizations of thought that can't lift itself by the slack of its own breeches. I see not the slightest reason for believing that our reason and our truth are cosmic ultimates or anything more than our own *flammantia moenia*. We end with an arbitrary can't help and if we believe that we are part of a universe bigger than ourselves, I see no ground for imposing our can't helps upon it. So far as we think we must think in those terms—but I see [no] objection to modest silence when we reach the veil of the temple. I am sad today— for my friend Rice—of the Print Department, Congressional Library, died suddenly in the hospital. I saw him rarely—but the possibility of seeing him gave me a vista—where now is a blank wall. I think that perhaps after reading one or two cases submitted for decision I will follow you with another glance at Molière. I find, though in a less degree, the same difficulty with him that I have with Racine *et al.*—a good deal of classic formalism in his characters, but even I recognize an element of delight. Again *adieu* for the moment.   *Affectionately yours, O. W. Holmes*

16 Warwick Gardens, 3.II.25

My dear Justice: . . . I have discovered Pascal. Have you ever read the *Pensées* deliberately and slowly, in the proper manner of eating caviar? All other psychology seems petty and mean before the almost feverish insight of that poor, tortured soul. I have been literally swept away by the power he had to know the things

that move one. Granted that their ultimate purpose is all wrong
(though I note how amazingly it anticipates the religious side of
James's philosophy) still the *verve* and range are extraordinary.
It's at once and everywhere the clearest proof of the highest genius.
The hunger to believe is so extraordinary, the crushing down of
reason because it dares to suggest doubts he cannot suppress, like
a man who will not believe, despite the evidence, an evil tale of
his wife.

. . . You will have seen the news of Asquith's surrender—a
great pity in every way.[1] But I imagine he could not stand the
physical strain of another election and a peerage is a dignified
method of cremation. But I wish he had not taken so grandiose
a title. In these things I have a passion for simplicity.

Our love to you both.   *Ever affectionately yours, H. J. L.*

Washington, D.C., February 14, 1925
Dear Laski: After a fitful fever once again repose—with nothing
in the world to do but answer your last. I took some extras this
week but put them through at high pressure and have had them
returned by all but two, already.[1] I have not read the *Pensées*
slowly as you say they should be read, but I think I appreciated
the heights, while I thought a good deal of them past any usefulness. Trollope must wait for better days with me. . . . I went on
Monday to a funeral of my friend Professor Rice—the head of the
Print Department in the Congressional Library. His death closes,
at least for the time, one of the few vistas that remained to my
old age. I didn't go often to see him but the possibility lightened
every adjournment of the Court. When I had sent out my three
new opinions I took up the delight of my boyhood, Lamb's *Dramatic Authors* and am reading it at odd moments. He praises
things that I should not praise so highly—doesn't seem to care
much for the best of them, Marlowe; but his gusto delights me
and there is enough to interest if not greatly to excite. I again
realize that *sound* is the half of immortality. The song of Shakespeare's words counts, I think, as much as their meaning to keep
them remembered—and in reading *Troilus and Cressida* I was
struck anew by what I often have remarked before that when
[he] gets the shakes over life or the world or any other damn
theme for tall talk, he shoots it off through the mouth of whoever
happens to be on the stage without much bother about dramatic
fitness. And (I have said it before) as we'd rather hear Shakespeare than Achilles or Richard II or Macbeth we thankfully ac-

---

[1] On January 20, Asquith had accepted a peerage, becoming Lord Oxford
and Asquith.

[1] On March 2, the next sitting of the Court, Holmes delivered the Court's
opinion in four relatively unimportant cases; 267 U.S. 222-232.

cept it and don't trouble ourselves about the cup into which the
nectar is poured. I reread *Le bourgeois gentilhomme* with undi-
luted pleasure—though what will happen after the play when
Monsieur Jourdain finds out, one wonders. But my days are so
broken up by odd jobs that as you see I don't do much. Yet I get
through a good deal of business *per diem*. Perhaps I will take
another look at Pascal—but I doubt it. How about Bosanquet's
Logic? Bradley refers to it often but somehow I don't hanker—

Till next time *adieu*.   *Affectionately yours, O. W. Holmes*

16 Warwick Gardens, 10.II.25

My dear Justice: . . . I have spent the last week on Bossuet, and
I think not unfruitfully. I have read all his important controversial
works, and the most famous of the Sermons. I'm convinced that he
does not deserve, except as a writer of ornate prose, anything like
the reputation he has. I omit such considerations as the facts that
he was a snob, a persecutor and a time-server; they are relevant
to, but not final in judgment. What impresses me is that he has
no originality, no power to think ahead, that his learning is merely
skill in citation, and that most of the results his generation deemed
fatal to Protestantism are by his own methods fatal to Catholicism
also. I add that his highly praised political theory is simply
Hobbes's own adorable pithy commonsense. . . . A young American from Virginia comes to the School and desires to write a book
on Jefferson as a political thinker. I explain that it is a good subject, that Jefferson was a shrewd, but windy, *tâcheron*, with a real
gift for rhetoric and lies. "Ah," he said, "I perceive you have been
misled by the malice of Beveridge's *Life of Marshall*. I shall prove"
(I wish I could give you these words in their startling emphasis)
"that he is not only the greatest American, but stands only below
the pre-eminence of Aristotle!" I told him as best I could some
of the weaknesses of Jefferson to which his response was that
neither Virginia nor Woodrow Wilson thought that way. *O sanc-
tissima simplicitas!*

. . . The more I go on, the more certain I am that a broad and
humane education is by all odds the best training for life, whether
in business or politics or anything else. A man who begins to
specialise at twenty in the economics of wool will never do work
of any magnitude. But, indeed, I do not like specialism in education at all. After ten years I remain convinced that the most valuable part of a university training is the chance it offers to explore
great subjects with more or less adequate teachers; and the kind
of material you have to work at in a business school is not a
mental discipline qualified by its nature to make the universe peep
through the little problem. Do I seem to you to be talking nonsense?

. . . Did you know that the children or grandchildren of Renan, Hugo and Taine are all leaders of the younger monarchical Catholics? It is a comic irony.

Our warm love to you both. *Ever affectionately yours, H. J. L.*
I transcribe a poem (for Mrs. Holmes) of Leigh Hunt's which has delighted the three of us.

> Jenny kissed me when we met,
> Jumping from the chair she sat in,
> Time, you thief, who love to get
> Sweets into your list, put that in.
> Say I'm weary,
> Say I'm sad,
> Say that health and wealth have missed me
> Say I'm growing old, but add,
> Jenny kissed me.

Washington, D.C., February 20, 1925
Dear Laski: Your letter comes apropos as usual. The lines of Leigh Hunt seemed an answer to a question my wife was asking two nights ago whether there was anything of Leigh Hunt's that any one remembered. I mentioned "Abou Ben Adhem," but I ought to have recited this—so I rushed to read it to her. He came up as she was reading Amy Lowell's *Life of Keats.* I was playing solitaire as I listened and may not have done Miss Lowell justice—but it seemed to me rather thickfingered—bad expressions, such as "ghastly" to express disapproval, that seemed to me unpardonable in a literary dame, and on the whole an undesirable theme for a woman. *Endymion* when I reread it last summer struck me as what Little Abbott[1] (who was killed in our regiment) used to call cocktalk. Keats needed to let off a little of his energy into a woman—of course that is not all I have to say about it, but it is an aspect that a woman imperfectly understands and cannot talk about pleasingly. However, I have not reached her comments on that poem. Lady Bryce sent me the *Memorials of Dicey* so if you haven't sent it, don't. I read it at once—surely he was the most *naif* and ingenuous of men—and really too modest about himself. The only qualification that I should put in to his greatness is that he could not think like a devil and therefore could not touch the deepest complexities of the exquisite.

In these last moments of unexpired leisure, in which there still are daily jobs, I have been reading Hind's *Short History of En-*

---

[1] Henry L. Abbott (1842-1864); intimate friend and fellow officer with Holmes in the Twentieth Regiment, Massachusetts Volunteers; killed in the Wilderness, May 6, 1864.

graving and Etching—and renewing my youth when I pored over
a dictionary of engravers by one Shearjashut Spooner—"Phoebus,
what a name"—until I could recognise prints by their remembered
description. It is a very pleasant pursuit of useless knowledge—
most of which I shall forget forthwith. Now I miss Rice (of whose
death I wrote to you lately). I put the magnifying glass on to my
Dürers and Mantegnas—(school of—if the elephants and two
others were by his hand according to current judgment they would
have cost many more hundreds than they did tens). But I don't
try to follow in detail the minute distinctions of method that these
conoshures take.

Adieu pour le momong.   *Affectionately yours, O. W. H.*
No, I must add a word or two. How characteristic of the Virginian
(generally provincial) to think more of Jefferson than of Washington. Washington had the nation in his belly. It is many years
since I read Bossuet but my recollection is of really moving eloquence. You don't expect to be moved by the thought of anyone
of that time. If I remember rightly, Jhering at the beginning of his
Geist d. R. R. has remarks on the dangers of specialists, but I
always have thought it best to get at the universe through some
definite door. I am surprised at what you say of those who have
joined the monarchical Catholics. Unless this is merely a political
move I should think it threw a very discrediting light on the faculties of the youth in question.

16 Warwick Gardens, 17.II.25
My dear Justice: . . . Reading has been mostly in the 17th century. . . . what interests me enormously is the question of why
it should be called the age of Louis XIV. In philosophy there was
no one of real eminence came to maturity in his reign. In theology,
Bayle and Jurieu lived abroad, Richard Simon,[1] a great pioneer, if
ever there was one, was killed by Bossuet. In letters, Molière's
great plays are all prior to 1640, Boileau, La Rochefoucauld, Pascal,
Corneille, are all mature before he really began to rule personally.
He has the right to Racine, to La Bruyère (whom he disliked) and
La Fontaine. But apart from these, and, if I remember aught
Malebranche, there isn't a first-rate thinker or writer to whom he
can lay claim. Whatever the merits of patronage, it is, I think
pretty clear that his reign shows all its demerits in a most striking
light. Of course he has the preachers, but God knows he is welcome to them. I think most French excitement over the virtue
of the 17th as against the 18th century is almost wholly misplaced
and because Faguet, Brunetière, *et al.* disliked the Revolution the

---

[1] Richard Simon (1638-1712); Biblical critic; author of *Histoire critiqu
du Vieux Testament* (1685), which was banned and destroyed through th
energetic intrigues of Bossuet and the Port Royalists.

transferred their hatred of the period to the philosophers and
exalted the 17th century as a consequence. It's all intensely interesting. The relativity of criticism, as soon as you note what environment the critic lived in simply leaps to the eyes; and he turns
out, on examination, to be about as impartial as say McReynolds,
J. examining a bill for the limitation of the hours of labour. . . .

Ever yours affectionately, H. J. L.

16 Warwick Gardens, 1.III.25
My dear Justice: . . . I must not forget to tell you my two stories
of Sir Frederick Pollock. First, he was met the other day by his
cousin Ernest Pollock M.R. at the Temple. They walked up Chancery Lane together and in the ten minutes despite eager efforts by
E.P., F.P. could not be induced to say a word. The M.R. was
rather angry and cherished a grudge; but four days later he met
Leslie Scott who said to him "I met F.P. the other day, and he
told me he had a delightful chat with you." Can't you see that
happening. The other comes from Jenks who has known F.P. thirty
years. He writes to him on some matter and gets back a curt note
signed "yours truly." Jenks writes and says after thirty years'
friendship he is entitled to a warmer signature. He gets back a
truly delightful four pages from F.P. on the charm of friendship
with Jenks, his delight in his company, the true fellowship common studies bring with them, and then signed "yours truly,
F.P.". . .
     My love warmly to you both,

Ever affectionately yours, H. J. L.

Washington, D.C., March 5, 1925—8 p.m.
Dear Laski: Only a word or two this *time* in answer to an interesting one from you, as we are sitting and I have a case to examine before Saturday that will take *time*. (How, having once used
a word one is sure to repeat it.) Also I am beginning to receive
letters about my birthday which comes on Sunday—(84)—and I
can't let them accumulate or I shall be swamped. I agree with you
in not wishing to concede more to Louis XIV than I must. Sainte-
Beuve's admiration only prejudiced me the more. I think I told you
of my latest books—Hind's *Engraving and Etching,* & then a
Primer of Modern Art. Since then nothing except short pages of a
diary of P. Loti—published by the *Illustration.*[1] I think Pierre
Loti's prose has more charm than that of any other Frenchman I
know—qu. if not more than that of any other in any language. I
see his limits better than I did on first reading—but having been

---

[1] *"Journal intime," La petite illustration,* no. 221-224, 226 (1925).

induced by the above to begin again *Le pêcheur d'islande*—the old impression remains. I should think he might perhaps have been a dirty dog in some of his ways, but I guess that at bottom he was simple as he says of himself with overlayers from varied sampling of his kind. Yesterday the Inauguration—always dreaded by me as a bore and a chance to die from sitting in the open air while the President speaks. The Vice-President[2] talked what I dare say was sensible enough but on the wrong occasion and making it grotesque by extravagant emphasis and gesticulation. Afterwards my wife and my secretary and his wife had our luncheon in the Supreme Court room and on the whole as the weather was ideal we got out of it very nicely. In the p.m. I had a call from Beck, Solicitor General that made me feel sympathy for him as a human being—avowedly disappointed in his ambitions, and *naïf* beyond belief. I felt sorry that I had criticized him and if I could have thought of a compliment that I could pay him honestly I would have paid it. We talked literature in which he takes an interest, though I should suppose hardly to be called a cultivated man and certainly having gaps in his education. I inferred that his ambitions were external—to be on our Court or Ambassador or something of the sort. But I have little sympathy with any ambition except to do something that first rate judges will pronounce first rate. . . . We have been having some cases under the Sherman Act,[3] which I loathe and despise—and I am pleased to know that Brandeis who used to uphold it, doesn't think it does any good. I am wondering whether I shall be in a minority. I don't mean to let my disbelief in the act affect my application of it—but I think it has been enlarged by construction in ways that I regret. Ah—I ran through a little *Anatole France en pantoufles*—which at first gave me the impression of a secretary making up after death for his subordination in life—but soon I thought I was wrong and that it was an honest and rather interesting account of his talk— a little dirtier I think than ours would be—but a picture that seemed true. Animals who ask this and that, "an autographed photograph," often add to their offense by "thanking you in advance" but I will send in advance the blessing of a veteran of an additional year.   *Affectionately yours, O. W. Holmes*

16 Warwick Gardens, 14.III.25
My dear Justice: . . . I reread Maitland's *Life of Leslie Stephen* and fell in love with him all over again. I add the footnote (for

---

[2] Charles G. Dawes (1865-1951).

[3] See *Maple Flooring Manufacturers Association* v. *United States,* 268 U.S. 563; *Cement Manufacturers Protective Association* v. *United States, id.* 588 (June 1, 1925). In each case a majority of the Court found that the Sherman Act had not been violated. Taft, C.J., and Sanford and McReynolds, JJ., dissented.

you to comment on) that I don't understand James Russell Lowell and that I don't like Charles Eliot Norton. There is a core of queer hardness about the first (it is in his poetry too). The second I always feel made friendship by playing on the vanity of his correspondents—a kind of super-bagman for European letters—the thing I dislike so intensely in Henry James. Is that utterly unfair? I don't doubt that Norton genuinely cared for literature, but I feel also that if I had sent him a book he would have felt it was a good book because it was sent to him. Did he ever do anything of his own? Probably I have missed something since Leslie loved him and he knew quality when he saw it, but I am frankly very puzzled. It looks like mythology.

I was greatly relieved to hear from Felix that Pound is to stay at Harvard after all. And Felix writes of a book he is doing which pleases me immensely. As did his opposition to the Child Labour Amendment, which I keenly share.[1] For while I think child labour is an outrage, I am convinced that the process of constitutional amendment was not intended to be a substitute for gaining conviction. People who live under a federal system ought to accept its implications. See *e.g.* Holmes, J. in *Noble State Bank* v. *Haskell* which I take to mean that it isn't the business of the Supreme Court to prevent a state from playing the fool if the Constitution leaves room for foolery. There are far too many American reformers eager to legislate the U.S. into their own peculiar nostrums. I don't like that type of procedure. For if what I preach is right ultimately decent-minded people will come to see it as I do; and the slow process of persuasion always ultimately makes for greater permanence than legislative fiat. . . .

My love to you both.   *Ever affectionately yours, H. J. L.*

Washington, D.C., March 26, 1925
Dear Laski: A letter from you today and one of about a fortnight earlier unanswered! Well, you have been busy and I have been rather miserable. I couldn't write or do anything more than I had to and even stayed away from Court for two days. I don't know how far it was the disturbance of a very violent cough and how far the upset caused by heroin pills taken to relieve me. However,

---

[1] In the spring of 1924, following the Supreme Court's invalidation of Congressional statutes dealing with child labor first under the commerce clause and later under the taxing power, Congress had approved a proposed amendment to the Federal Constitution by which Congress was granted the power to regulate and prohibit the labor of children. Sufficient ratifications of the amendment were never received. Ultimately the position of Holmes, dissenting in *Hammer* v. *Dagenhart*, 247 U.S. 25 (1918), became the majority view in the Supreme Court and it was held that the congressional power to regulate commerce among the states could reach the employment of children in producing goods for interstate commerce; *United States* v. *Darby*, 312 U.S. 100 (1941).

it is over now and I am back at normal, only a little languid and tired. Your prejudices in this letter, as is apt to be the case, coincide with my own. I always found James R. Lowell hard and rarely touching me in the depths. His *Biglow Papers* are A-1 and his chaff on England ditto. As to poor Norton it is hard to be exactly just. He had a fine side to him. He was cultivated and gave of his cultivation to those who needed it. When I was in college I got him made an honorary member of the Hasty Pudding unless my memory deceives me, but he was only a parasite of literature. Bill James once said that in another century they would think Norton the great dark sun around whom the eminent of his time revolved, as he published the letters to him and had the intelligence not to print his replies. On the other hand Woodberry,[1] a somewhat more than local poet, told in teaching verse how Norton opened to him a world of beauty and cultivation that otherwise would have been closed. Let us be just to him while not expecting him to say anything to us. It is said that he began a lecture once—"probably none of you ever has seen a gentleman." He had a good Boston tradition as a speaker, and in his later years certainly spoke like a gentleman, with a certain personal distinction. In middle life I found it hard to be just to him, but age has mellowed my revolt just as it has brought back kindly feelings to Charles Eliot[2] of whom at one time I might have complained—we are good friends now. I wrote to him on his 90th birthday and got back a regular schoolmaster's letter in which he considered and summed up his former pupil. What you say about H. James in connection with the others perhaps has in view the same thing that I had when I used to say that I thought it underbred to discourse on and make literary capital out of the social position of the important American in Europe. That is a matter solved by the individual and best not made a matter of consciousness. A man of intellect ought to take society *de haut en bas, i.e.,* recognizing its value and charm, and at the same time its unimportance as compared with his superlatives.

Frankfurter is here, giving some lectures next door. I haven't seen him yet, but he and his wife dine here Saturday and I hope he will come in before that. I think he is taken under Brandeis's wing, at Stoneleigh Court. I am just finishing my work and there are two weeks' adjournment after this but I lack energy to make the most of it.

I glanced over Ovid's earlier poems last Sunday and decided that he could wait until I was ready to read Seneca for companion prose. More and more do I articulately affirm that it is waste of

[1] George Edward Woodberry (1855-1930); biographer, poet, and literary historian; Professor of Comparative Literature at Columbia, 1891-1904.

[2] Charles William Eliot (1834-1926), President of Harvard University, 1869-1909.

time to give much of one's life to past literature except when it is a theme for your own discourse. You can get more ideas and later ones with less trouble except in the way of intellectual effort from the moderns. A dame said, "Oh, but the New Testament. Where was ever such a standard of life?" etc. I said I think my club of the jobbists has a sound standard—that *love* for one's neighbors is a good thing no doubt, but that few do or can feel it while destiny and human nature concur in making a sound man put his life into his work. . . . Of course I agree with you about Constitutional Amendments. Your tales of F.P. *et al.* are delightful. One from Taft's schoolmaster's brother[3] via the C.J.—a freshman translating comes to *pax in bello*—he hesitates and then, "freedom from indigestion." I am glad the lines are open again.

Affectionately yours, O. W. Holmes

16 Warwick Gardens, 22.III.25
My dear Justice: With characteristic stupidity I find that I forgot to post that book of essays to you.[1] But it goes off, with my apologies, by the same post as this letter. The essay I am eager for you to read is the one that gives its title to the book. I used to know •
Ingram Bywater, its subject, at Oxford. He was Regius Professor of Greek there, and every bit the same as Chapman paints him. I remember his showing me an Aldine (I think it was a Homer but am not sure) and telling me with a pride and gravity that no words can depict that it was by four milimetres the tallest copy known. I remember vividly also his comment on my praise of Ferrero's *Greatness and Decline of Rome*. "Ah! Laski, so you like romantic fiction?" Gilbert Murray told me that he was probably the most perfect Greek scholar since the Renaissance—which means that he was the first in modern times. I have always regretted the margin drawn since the end of the 17th century between the Grecian and the Latinist. Men like Scaliger and Casaubon who made philology part of the inheritance of rationalism were mighty men; and the application of their results to the sacred not less than the profane was a thrilling adventure. But I suppose it would be impossible today for a new Richard Simon[2] to provoke a scandal by a book on the New Testament. Our withers are, more's the pity, permanently unwrung. . . .

The week since I wrote passed very pleasantly. First a dinner at the Asquiths which I enjoyed though it was difficult to be

---

[3] Horace Taft (1861-1943); founder and headmaster of the Taft School.
[1] R. W. Chapman's essay, "The Portrait of a Scholar," in the volume of essays under that title, was a study of Ingram Bywater (1840-1914), Greek scholar and bibliophile, successor to Jowett as Regius Professor of Greek, and distinguished editor of Aristotle.
[2] See, *supra*, p. 14.

polite when Margot performed as the political virago. He spoke
very happily about his Oxford days and told me that he has gone
on the Judicial Committee where he hopes to sit sometimes in
constitutional cases. I speak as an amateur on these matters, but I
cannot easily believe that a man who is 72 and has been out of
the law for over twenty years can make the effort that efficiency
requires. I was interested, by the way, to discover the depth and
reality of Asquith's Christianity. He goes to church regularly, takes
the Communion once each month; and he told me that except for
a brief period at Oxford, he never remembers being seriously puzzled by doubts. He takes things like the miracles as irrelevant to
an essence which you either have or don't have; and he said that
James's *Will to Believe* was philosophically final for him. I said
it was an attractive piece of special pleading which neglected every
scientific canon of evidence, but he clearly found doubt disturbing
and I did not persist. Second, I had a dinner with Birrell at which
J. M. Barrie told us one pleasant story. When he first came to
London he wanted to buy a volume of Swinburne's which was six
shillings. In the shop he discovered that he had only four and six,
and since he did not look fashionable and the shop was Hatchard's,
he was in agonies as to what he would do when the shop man
came to him. When at last he approached "I turned to him," said
Barrie, "and said in a cool nonchalant voice, 'Have you a first
edition of Keat's *Endymion*?'" As there are only a dozen copies
of this in existence he retired in honour. . . .

Reading I have divided between my Frenchmen and detective
stories. . . . Of the French I am enthusiastic still about Bayle, and
that even after the labour of reading him in a folio edition. His
rival Jurieu merely seems to me a Protestant Bossuet and I have
no liking for that kind of animal. But Bayle has a power of words
and a happy if sometimes pointless erudition I find superb. . . .

Ever affectionately yours, H. J. L.

Washington, D.C., April 5, 1925
Dear Laski: Again your letter finds me at peace with life and the
world. I have been rather seedy for a day or two with another
cold and coughing at night, but there is a lull—and I hope it
means that some doctor's stuff has real effect. I also am visiting
the dentist but it isn't very bad except as an interruption. I have
done an extra case or two amounting to nothing and I have been
thrilled by the greater than ever beauty of the cherry trees around
the Potomac basin and the magnolias. I know an alley of magnolias that rivals the cherry trees. Then I took up Volume 4 of
Holdsworth's *History of Law*, with the illusion that I had read 3
—and finished it today with profit. He is not a vivid writer, or a

very good one—but he makes you feel the growth and the relation
of law to general conditions which I thought such a merit in Brissaud.[1] I doubt if I shall go on unless I come to a dull moment—
I don't suppose it is worthwhile for me to be ambitious for improvement—the end is too near, though I only partially feel so.
And yesterday came your little book—*Portrait of a Scholar*—I read
it through with delight. I don't believe with him, however, that
the writing of English has gone down hill. There are more writers
and therefore more bad writing but I should think that there was
a good deal that was as good as ever. Holdsworth led me to look
into Bodin for something or other and I am skimming through his
Réponse aux paradoxes de Malestroit which I should suppose
showed originality in realizing that gold and silver had not fixed
values that were a starting point for everything else. I think I
shall not bother about the *République*. I feel about that as I do
about Suarez, *De Legibus* etc. I like to know that there are big
dull time-taking books on which one could fall back if the time
should come when one didn't know what to do with oneself. It
hasn't come yet. I am glad you told me who the scholar was—and
I wonder how Gilbert Murray dared to say that he was the most
perfect Greek scholar since the Renaissance. No doubt he had his
reasons and it is a subject on which I know nothing—but I immediately asked myself whether he had the data for comparing him
with Gildersleeve[2]—or Sophocles[3] (my old Greek professor) to
mention only men I knew but have no means of ranking. I agree
with you that I should think it is a perilous adventure for Asquith
to sit in law cases. I have generally found that less than 20 years
of politics made men blunt in the law, but it wasn't so with Senator
Hoar[4]—a dispassionate testimony as he didn't like me and I didn't
care much for him. He thought his nephew Sam[5] ought to have
filled my last two places—which I humbly think he couldn't have
done with special advantage to the world. The Senator was just, I
have been told, when my name came up—but I think there had
been something, I don't know what—that gave him a prejudice
against me—just as I think there was with Ames—although we

---

[1] *Supra*, p. 23, Vol. I.

[2] Basil Lanneau Gildersleeve (1831-1924), Professor of Greek at the University of Virginia and at the Johns Hopkins University; friend of Holmes.

[3] Evangelinus Apostolides Sophocles (ca. 1805-1883); Greek-born classicist
who taught Greek at Harvard from 1842 until his death.

[4] George Frisbie Hoar (1826-1904); lawyer and Republican Senator from
Massachusetts, 1877-1904. Concerning his opposition to Holmes's nomination
to the Supreme Court of the United States, see Garraty, "Holmes's Appointment to the U.S. Supreme Court," 22 *New England Quarterly* 291 (September 1949).

[5] Samuel Hoar (1854-1904), railroad lawyer, had been seriously considered
for the Chief Justiceship of the Supreme Judicial Court of Massachusetts in
1899 and was proposed as an appointee to the seat on the Supreme Court of
the United States to which Holmes was named in 1902.

got on very well together. What have you read of Bayle? All I
have ever read of or from him impresses me as he does you—but
I couldn't recite on the subject. I must stop and go down to solitaire—as I am still a little careful—but I could jaw on with joy.

Affectionately yours, O. W. Holmes

Felix and his wife dined here the other day much to my joy. I
opened for him a prize bottle of champagne that I had been keeping for a great occasion—and we had much pleasant talk though
I get tired sooner than I used *to*. Item—Some of Chapman's criticism of modern English opened my eyes to things I never had
noticed—but I think it permissible to end a sentence with an insignificant word.[6] Not a paragraph, however. That should end with
a blow of the axe.

16 Warwick Gardens, 1.IV.25

My dear Justice: I have been voyaging in the North giving some
lectures to working men, and though it is interesting and enjoyable it is a little tiring and doesn't make writing easy. But the
thing that chiefly prevented my usual letter was being near Newcastle in a town where there was a mine-explosion and some forty
dead. I cannot describe the scenes to you, first because they are
too horrible and I want to forget them; and second because they
do not go into words. But I was immensely moved by two things.
Above all the Stoic courage of the miners; some of them en-
trapped for three days, come up to the surface, greet their wives
and ask casually for a cigarette—no repining, no complaints, even
a tendency to jest about their adventures, and to tell how queer
it was to find that their lamps were out; then the heroism of the
rescuers who go down time after time with their lives in their
hands. It is startling to find that they expect to go and are expected to go; to battle with death is simply a part of the day's
work. Men like these make you believe in man. The other side is
the women. Joe isn't dead, can't be dead, until the last body has
been recovered. There is an optimism, a faith, that I cannot describe. They seem to smile at their fate rather than give you the
sense that they're near a breakdown. They set their teeth and
when their dead are buried they take counsel with their neighbours as to how to carry on as John or Bill or Harry would have
liked it. I spent a day with two young fellows whose injuries made
hospital necessary, reading to them, discussing things with them.
All that the accident meant to them was that they'd not be down

---

6 In the original letter Holmes drew a curved line, with terminal arrows,
between the last word of this sentence and the last "to" in the preceding
sentence.

the pit for a month. It was part of the daily job. Probably it's due (in fact) to failure properly to stop up some old workings from which gas escaped after a shot was fired. The newspapers show a tendency to criticise the manager; I never heard one word said against him by any of the men who had been down the pit at the time. They spoke only of his courage in going down first of the rescuers and keeping at that task thirty-six hours on end. You can guess how things like these catch hold of one. Their very dumbness is the most eloquent thing I know. One poor fellow with an arm lost through fall of roof said to me with a smile—it was worse in the trenches! A woman who lost her husband (he was sixty-three) said that he'd 'done her proud by giving his chance to a younger man.' One comes away feeling that these people are entitled to the richest life civilisation can offer them. And it makes me feel intensely humble to get letters of thanks from them for sitting by them or visiting them or sending them a book to read. You will sympathise with what I am feeling and realise to what thoughts it gives rise.

From Newcastle to Burnley—thence to Manchester. There I had a happy day with Alexander the philosopher whom I have known from childhood. We discussed men—agreed that Bradley was powerful but wrong-headed, James a man of insight but not logic, Morris Cohen easily the best intelligence in contemporary American philosophy. Alexander had a higher opinion of E. B. Holt[1] than I have, and made much of an American (Montague?)[2] whom I do not know. He told me one good story which bears repeating. When Rashdall[3] was appointed Dean of Carlisle, Alexander said to the Archbishop of York that he was surprised that a man was appointed who believed in a limited God. "Ah," said the Archbishop, "you forget that it is a limited Deanery." He told me of a visit to Bergson this winter, the latter surrounded by the wealthy and the beautiful who acted as Delilahs upon his intelligence; of a dinner at Croce's when the latter's Italian was unintelligible as he insisted on speaking very fast with his mouth full of hot macaroni and the other guest had a cleft palate which made the translation two years behind the text; and of a dinner with the King who asked him what he taught—"Philosophy, your Majesty." "Oh! Yes. A fascinating subject, I suppose?" "Your Maj-

---

[1] Edwin Bissell Holt (1873-1946); philosopher of the realistic school; author of *The Freudian Wish* (1915), *The Concept of Consciousness* (1914); and contributor, with William Pepperell Montague, to *The New Realism* (1912).

[2] Presumably William Pepperell Montague (1873-1953); Professor of Philosophy at the University of California; author, *inter alia*, of *The Ways of Knowing* (1925).

[3] Hastings Rashdall (1858-1924); churchman, philosopher, and historian of universities; Dean of Carlisle, 1917-1923; author of *The Universities of Europe in the Middle Ages* (3 vols., 1895).

esty is very good to say so." "Personally, Professor, I find it very
boring." You can imagine that I had some happy hours there.

In reading, mainly novels, Montaigne and Lamb. The latter superb—a play of gentle and lambent humour untouched in English
letters. I found a workman in Burnley who had known Carlyle
who told him that Emerson and Increase Mather (!) were the two
greatest Americans who had ever lived; two days later Carlyle
sent him a postcard withdrawing Emerson and substituting George
Washington. The old fellow had met John Stuart Mill who told a
great story of Bright on the glories of the American Constitution.
Mill said that Marshall had been able to make himself a fundamental figure in the history of the law. Whereupon Bright asked
who Marshall was. He told me that as a boy of eighteen he attended a meeting in memory of Lincoln the day after his death.
There were three thousand cotton operatives there, most of whom
had been near starvation during the Civil War. Each of those who
spoke, he said, indicated a personal loss such as, among English
statesmen, he knew only in the cases of Bright and Cobden. He
told me also of a railway porter who when Judah Benjamin[4] was
on circuit in Liverpool refused to handle his luggage because he
had been in the Confederate Government. I hope these tales do
not bore you, for, at the moment, they are all I have to tell. But
I go on Sunday to Paris when I hope to proffer fare of a different
kind.

My love to you both, in which Frida joins,

Ever affectionately yours, H. J. L.

Washington, D.C., Sunday, April 19, 1925
Dear Laski: The chief news is a letter from you nearly a week
old and still unanswered. I have been too hard driven. The past
week of the last long sitting and the dentist together have kept
my hands (and mouth) full. Your account of the miners is very
moving and your tales are amusing, but I am a tired old man and
have just finished writing an opinion in the case assigned to me
last night. I had a pleasant call from a colleague of yours to whom
you gave a letter to Brandeis and meant to give one to me. We
had a jaw that I enjoyed. I hope he did. Herman Finer[1] by name.
I received yesterday "A Request for Aid in Formulating a State-

---

[4] Judah P. Benjamin (1811-1884); American lawyer and statesman, who
was successively Attorney General, Secretary of War, and Secretary of State
in the Confederate States; following the Union victory he fled to England,
studied for the bar, and quickly rose to the top of the profession; author of
Treatise on Sales (1868).

[1] Herman Finer (1898-   ), author of many books on government, was
lecturer in Public Administration, London School of Economics, 1920-1942,
and in 1924 was the holder of a Rockefeller Fellowship in the United States.

ment of Basic Processes in Society" from L. C. Marshall, Department of Political Economy, University of Chicago. Some pages of
print with margins for comment and suggestion. The generalities
seemed to me well enough but one can't tell until one gets to
particulars. I am too tired to bother with it and shall send back
virgin sheets in a few days. Absolutely the only thing I could tell
you about is the spring and the flowers, which would bore you,
or some matters of law on the right of the papers to publish income taxes paid.[2] We had a Senator who delivered a stump speech
on the freedom [of] the press—beginning before the invention of
printing. Between ourselves I can't imagine what such men think
they are doing—whether it be simply earning a fee or whether
they think they could affect the mind of a rational or at least a
competent being by such drool. Yet he seemed like a man of force.

Keep on writing, dear boy, some day I may have something to
say.

Affectionately yours, O. W. Holmes

16 Warwick Gardens, 15.IV.25
My dear Justice: I came back yesterday from a most exhilarating
ten days in France. People, weather, book-hunting were all as
good as could be; and my companion, Gregory (an economist-
colleague) had almost as voracious an appetite as I for the book-
shops. We visited a number of people. Lévy-Brühl the philosopher,
a charming fellow with that *justesse* of mind which some Frenchmen have; Aulard, the historian, a wonderful old fellow, the lineal
descendant of the Jacobins who gave us great joy by a brilliant
dissection of Taine's utter worthlessness as an historian; Maxime
Leroy, the lawyer, whose books I once persuaded you to read—
an admirable person with the proper reverence for Dicey and
Maitland. We visited the Chamber and saw the government fall,
on Good Friday;[1] which provoked François Albert, the Minister of
Education,[2] to say to me that an anti-clerical government which
fell on Good Friday was sure of a Resurrection. Of *les jeunes* I saw
a number; but only one, whom, curiously, I had known at Har-

---

[2] *United States* v. *Dickey*, 268 U.S. 378 (May 25, 1925), held that under
existing statutes it was not a punishable offense to publish the names of
federal taxpayers and the amount of taxes which they had paid. James A.
Reed (1851-1944) was a Kansas City lawyer, a Democratic Senator from
Missouri from 1911 to 1929, and was of counsel for the defendant in the
Dickey case.

[1] On April 10 the Herriot ministry fell, after it was revealed that, despite
pronouncements that inflationary tendencies would not be permitted to develop, the Bank of France had issued bank notes largely in excess of the
authorized amount.

[2] François Albert (1877-   ), journalist and politician, had been leader
of the anticlerical movement in the Herriot government.

vard, impressed me much. The others were mainly interested in
form, or were engaged in that philosophic process called eating
their own insides on the ground that all other nourishment is inadequate. But the main joy was bookhunting. I brought back a hundred volumes, almost all in my private domain, and many of them
perfect copies. I did not find the two things I wanted supremely,
but I got things of Bossuet, Bayle, Jurieu, contemporary attacks
on Rousseau and Montesquieu, which were all of them on my list.
I found a copy of Dupin's attack on Montesquieu on the *Quais.*
There are only twelve copies in existence as all the others were
destroyed by order of the Pompadour, and there is none in any
library in this country. I also got a very pretty copy of the first
edition of the *Provincial Letters* (50 fr) and Sainte-Beuve's *Port-
Royal* on the good principle that, as S-B said, he who knows not
P-R does not know humanity. The list of all I bought would be
too long to reproduce, but I have had two happy days in arranging them, and the pleasure that comes in finding that of certain
authors I can now say *e.g.* of Rousseau that I have all the attacks
and comments starred by the bibliographers as important.

I came back to a very jolly letter from you, which tells me of
Felix and champagne and a cough that has, I hope, disappeared
now. You speak of spring on the Potomac, and I can only retort
with English broom against your cherry-blossom; but when Frida
and I motored yesterday to the Surrey hills the hedges were one
flame of gold, and I confess that even I was tempted to hold books
of little account alongside of them. I am glad that Chapman's book
tickled your palate. Parts of it, *e.g.* the linguistics, were caviare to
me, but the essay on Bywater did hit me where I live. I agree
with your remark on Murray's eulogy of him; but it was one of
those sudden tributes that has, one feels, the inside of truth in
them. You ask me what I have been reading of Bayle that I found
impressive. Mainly (1) *Commentaire philosophique* which I
thought as good a defence of religious freedom as I know; (2)
Avis important aux refugiés—that difficult task of being moderate
and understanding in an age of extremism on both sides. (3)
Critique générale de l'histoire du Calvinisme de Maimbourg which
is a masterly piece of historical dissection. These and the *Dictionary* all give me a mind I know I should have liked instinctively
—balance, sanity, hatred of shams, dislike of ecclesiastical preten-
sion, and refusal to admit that the infliction of pain is justified by
enthusiastic faith. Above all, I like the method of scepticism by
the accumulation of tiny facts. All Voltaire is there; and I think
Bayle only of all the 17th century Frenchmen can truly claim a
faith in toleration. Jurieu, his great rival, merely wants toleration
for his own sect, which is fairly easy. I was amused, by the way,
to find on the French bookstalls that Beck on the U.S. Constitution

had been translated with a puff from Birkenhead saying that it
was the best thing ever.[3]. . .

Our warm love to you both.   *Ever affectionately yours, H. J. L.*

Washington, D.C., May 8, 1925

Dear Laski: At last I have a breathing moment and can write to
you. The end of our sittings kept us breathless and crowded for
a week or ten days. However only your last is unanswered. You
surprise me by what you say of Taine's worthlessness as an historian. I haven't read his history or -ies and have no opinion of my
own. As to *les jeunes* eating their own insides I got the impression
that that was the nourishment of some of characteristic modern
artists—and I thought it made damned poor food. I am amused
also by your finding Beck—translated, and puffed by Birkenhead.
Poor Beck, he has resigned and gone to Italy—avowing his ambitions disappointed—as they were bound to be. They were all external—and according to reports I heard of a speech of his he
thinks he has just missed being Secretary of State, Ambassador,
and a Justice of our Court—of no one of which do I believe there
ever was the least chance; he is kindly and likeable personally but
of a vanity *naif* beyond belief. He has put much energy into
blowing his own horn. F.F. sent me Bertrand Russell's little book
What I Believe which in the main is what I believe also! I think
him a sentimentalist about war—and in his willingness to criticize
the cosmos—which I regard always as damning the weather—and
simply evidence of maladjustment. Also I now have taken up with
vast interest and satisfaction Tawney's Introduction to Wilson's
Discourse upon Usury. It illustrates the superiority of the modern
to the old books whereof I have spoken heretofore. Also my wife
is reading to me a study by Francis Hackett,[1] I assume the same
one, as it has the old F.H.'s capacity for penetrating and exact
expression—though perhaps not the charm I have felt in earlier
things. I can't imagine how he was interested to make this study
of a conventional and ordinary young American couple—but it is
keen. It is a comfort too to have a man tackle his job in the old-
fashioned way and recognize that there is no short cut instead of
trying to storm the public by a mannerism. But except at the
solitaire hour I have been all law—and may get a little more after
our conference tomorrow. At this moment my work is done, and I
am open to suggestions for summer reading independent of your
immediate interests. I think I haven't written since I had a delightful evening with Learned Hand—who both thinks and is
amusing. This p.m. I had a call from a dame introduced by a

---

[3] The French translation of James M. Beck's *The Constitution of the United
States* (1923) had introductory comment by Balfour and Sir John Simon.
[1] Francis Hackett, *That Nice Young Couple* (1925).

London friend of mine with the suggestion that I might help her.
I wish to God that no one ever would expect me to help anybody
—I will fork out—under extreme compulsion—but I am not a
man of affairs—I have no wires that I can or would pull. I don't
know any of the things that people who can help you know—and
it drives me frantic. The lady wanted to deliver a course of lectures here and there—and believed, I judge, in all that I don't.
Luckily in a fetch about her name and in finding her yesterday I
met another dame who said she knew about the matter and would
talk to my bugaboo. She has gone and for half an hour my nerves
were a wreck. I restored them by going to the dentist, and then
taking a short walk. I don't get a walk once a fortnight in these
days—and now soon I shall go through the torment of trying to
eat with this addition that the dentist has made to my outfit. It
hurts. May the fiend gripe his entrails. (This is a shame for he is
a good little man.) Love to you both.   *Aff'ly yours, O. W. H.*

16 Warwick Gardens, 28.IV.25

My dear Justice: A crowded fortnight since I wrote to you; but
now, happily, term has begun, and I am in the leading-strings of
routine once more. The first event was a day in Oxford where I
went with two of my younger colleagues. We did the bookshops
thoroughly, and I found a magnificent copy of Bayle's *Oeuvres
diverses* in four folio volumes which I brought away in pride; and
I found half a dozen out of the way economic treatises of the
eighteenth century, mainly economic, which I was glad to have.
We lunched with Joseph,[1] the philosopher, and talked life over
with him. I had not seen him since I went down in '14, and I
was amused to find how very little he had changed. Psychology
was still a non-existent subject; jurisprudence meant Maine's
Ancient Law; an undergraduate not compelled to read the *Republic*
and the *Ethics* was definitely illiterate. I mentioned new names like
Morris Cohen's—all in vain. He stopped at William James whom
he regarded as a clever journalist splashing in philosophic puddles.
I felt that I could not go back to Oxford as a don even if I were
paid two thousand a year. It literally does not know that the
world moves. I spoke of America and found that it meant only
Babbitt to him. Where, he asked, are its scientists? I mentioned
Franklin, Agassiz, Gibbs,[2] Michelson,[3] Morley;[4] no response. Where

---

[1] H. W. B. Joseph (1867-1943); fellow of New College; author of *An
Introduction to Logic* (1906), *The Concept of Evolution* (1924), and *Some
Problems in Ethics* (1931).

[2] Josiah Willard Gibbs (1839-1903); Yale's mathematical physicist.

[3] Albert Abraham Michelson (1852-1931); Chicago physicist, best known
for his determination of the velocity of light; Nobel Prize winner, 1907.

[4] Edward Williams Morley (1838-1923); physicist, some of whose most
important work was done in collaboration with Michelson.

are its philosophers? The same result. As one of my young colleagues said, one got converted at once to the idea of compulsory
travel for dons. Clearly, there is no adequacy in purely mental
travel, despite the example of Kant.

Then Frida and I spent a week-end with Christopher Turnor[5]
and his wife at Stoke Rochford. His family has been at the hall
since Coke's time and he is the best kind of Tory democrat. I wish
I could describe the house. A library with a first folio bought as
it appeared *et hoc omne genus* to the tune of ten thousand volumes; and a copy of Bozzy presented to the Turnor of 1794, from
the handwriting after a merry night at a tavern. The gardens would
have made Mrs. Holmes green with envy—especially the golden
barberry bushes on great grey boulders, and the fields literally
massed with double daffodils. And the pictures, Dutch interiors
by Maas and Snyders and Ostade—these, on the small side, went
to my heart; a divine picture of Robert Cecil [6] by Zucchero with
all his crafty caution written all over him; a bust of Newton by
Roubillac, and a letter from I.N. to the Turnor of the day begging
his acceptance of *Principia* and, oh glory, hoping it will be approved. Other things a-plenty, Rubens, Jordaens, Hoppner, Rae-
burn, not much in my line, though a Reynolds of a little Turnor
who died early was quite charming. The house, vast as it was,
had a wonderful air of happy friendliness, and the talk was good.
Turnor himself says he did not know it in its glory; but his father
remembered keeping fifty servants and fifteen turned out in crim-
son plush knee-breeches and white gloves to wait on the Duke
of Wellington at lunch. I wish you had been there; it was really
like living history, especially when he showed me a letter written
to his g.grandfather just gone to Oxford warning him against one
Percy Shelley since the latter's father avers that his son has become "a blasphemous Atheist void of all principle." Turnor himself, without great powers, has the love of the place in him, and
I the Socialist liked his being there as he was there. Can I explain
better my pleasure in those days?

Back to London and a dinner (*entre nous*) with Baldwin. I like
him the more, the more I see of him. Simple, straight-forward, with
a certain quick shrewdness of judgment about men. Balfour was
there, a little too determined to charm and shine, and talking about
things with an assumed air of ignorance which I found boring.
But I had one happy moment. The Marquess of Salisbury had sent

---

[5] Christopher Hatton Turnor (1873-1940); Canadian-born great-grandson
of Edmund Turnor (1755?-1829), the antiquary. In 1903 he had succeeded
to Stoke Rochford Hall in Lincolnshire and there developed new and progressive methods of agricultural development; he was a leader in movements for
educational reform and author, *inter alia*, of *The Land and its Problems*
(1921).

[6] Robert Cecil (1563?-1612), first Earl of Salisbury.

him some bacon, and Balfour complained that his own lacked the quality of Salisbury's. "Ah," said I, "blood will tell"; and I was amused to find that Balfour was not quite easy in being pricked.

. . . Did I, by the way, tell you that I picked up for sixpence, in Charing Cross Road Holbach's volume on Christ, being Huxley's own copy with his annotations. A good sixpenworth, especially as an early and devout owner notes, in perfect charity, that while the blasphemies are horrible, the *esprit* is so superb, that he cannot help wishing him a better fate than he will receive.

My love to you both. I am buried in proofs and an index.

Ever affectionately yours, H. J. L.

Washington, D.C., May 9, 1925

Dear Laski: A ripping good letter from you this morning—after yesterday's one dispatched to you—*per* my secretary—who can't remember what he did with it but hopes he deposited it mechanically in a box. It was no loss if you don't get it—for I am only gradually emerging from the law. I suspect that even you don't know of the later generation of American men of science. My wife's nephew Gerrit Miller[1] I think has a very high standing. Years ago the British Museum came to him to make a catalogue of European vertebrates or mammalia or something which I believe was a *magnum opus* &c, &c. Your account of the old house at Stoke Rochford is enchanting. I got so far before going to a conference—which resulted in the Chief's saying he should assign the only two cases requiring written opinions to me—so I am not out of the woods yet. We seem to be rather a damaged Court. The only ones who seem to me all right are Butler, Stone (the newcomer and a good man), and also, I might add, Brandeis so far as appears, but I privily suspect that he is tired. I don't like to ask him but I am told that his wife is still broken down in nerves and hysterical—which must be very wearing. So I am not yet far from the preoccupations and the cramp of the job. I told you in my yesterday's letter how much I liked Tawney's introduction to the *Discourse upon Usury.* It is amusing to see in him and elsewhere little echoes of Maitland's style. My only criticism is one that I have made upon you once or twice—that probably because of his own familiarity—not, as if it were a New York woman I should suspect, to *épater les bourgeois*—he refers in an offhand way, and without explanation, to facts that I for one don't know—so that I don't get his point. However, this is on only few occasions. . . . My mind sags back to legal matters. The cases that I expect are

---

[1] Gerrit Smith Miller, Jr. (1869-1956); zoologist, son of Mrs. Holmes's sister; author of numerous scientific monographs and of *Catalogue of the Land Mammals of Western Europe in the British Museum* (1912).

not very closely allied. One is a question of a priority claimed by the U.S. in bankruptcy,[2] the other, extradition of a man charged with peculation (embezzlement) in Mexico from Vermont where he now is.[3] You have said nothing of your family relations for a long time. Are you, as I suppose, all right with your father now? I think I need not ask for I heard of him sitting in your library with evident pride in you, the better part of a year ago. Your reading drives me mad. For even if I had as much time you would be through six volumes while I was laboriously nibbling on Volume 1. And I am afraid you remember much more accurately than I do, even when I take my time. For one thing I easily am blurred by words. When Tawney describes familiar commercial doings in the language of the business I often get but a confused notion of what it is all about. I can't conceive why some people think I am quick, unless it is that when I am locked in with a case that I have got to understand it does clear up in twenty-four hours. I believe that yesterday I asked you what I repeat, that you send me some suggestions for the approaching leisure. I don't promise to follow them but I am sure to profit by them—if I keep well. Nowadays I say to myself so often, "Thou fool, this night thy soul shall be required of thee"—as I believe Scripture hath it. Do you remember how I always drove around in a *coupé* with an old horse? Charley, my driver, one day turned up with an automobile, which was scornfully refused until the winter months made it almost necessary—and now we have collapsed—to our great advantage.

Affectionately yours, O. W. Holmes

16 Warwick Gardens, 9.V.25
My dear Justice: . . . But I have read a little—most interesting of all, I think, the Roosevelt-Lodge correspondence. I enjoyed the letters far more than I expected. Lodge repelled me a good deal. I was baffled by the contrast between his obviously aristocratic temper and his willingness to immerse himself in mean schemes with mean men. Moreover, I was astounded at the simplicity which mistakes a political speech for an historic event; and some of the judgments on books seem to me curious in relation to the man who, at any rate in the late 'seventies, had real claims to be regarded as a scholar. T.R.'s part I liked enormously. What a gloriously simple world he lived in. If you agreed with him, you were a noble fellow; if you disagreed you were a low blackguard. His letter to Lodge on your appointment to the Supreme Court amused me much.[1] In

---

[2] *Davis* v. *Pringle,* 268 U.S. 315 (May 25, 1925).

[3] *Fernandez* v. *Phillips,* 268 U.S. 311 (May 25, 1925).

[1] See 1 *Selections from the Correspondence of Theodore Roosevelt and Henry Cabot Lodge* (1925), 517. Writing to Senator Lodge on July 10,

its light, I reread the speech on Marshall which seemed to me to say quite rightly that great powers need great events to reveal themselves and that Marshall was fortunate in his epoch. What exactly was criminal in that I do not know. But perhaps there are shades and shadows about which I have no knowledge. I realised after reading them why Morley said of Roosevelt that he could not avoid the belief that his convictions sprang rather from physical energy than from mental exertion. Of other things, in memory of old times, I read Francis Hackett's novel. It seemed to me a not very original pendant to Sinclair Lewis, with a brilliant piece in it—the description of the Democratic Convention of 1912—but, otherwise, I didn't think it first-hand observation, and the minor figures weren't at all clearly sketched. A derivative knack rather than an original talent.

. . . At Haldane's there were mainly Shaw, Barrie and pretty women who treated Barrie as a kind of dear lapdog who must be stroked. Shaw said one brilliant thing. Barrie was explaining that most of his inspiration came at night in bed, and Shaw said that clearly in that case Barrie accepted the ideas of which the consequences were hidden from the light. He told us an amusing story of Wells sending William Archer[2] a book with the inscription "to the last Atheist" and getting one back with the inscription "to the latest humbug" apropos of Wells's *Soul of a Bishop*. Shaw told us how when he defended Henry George at the British Association in '89 Sidgwick got up and said that the taxation of land values was confiscation, that confiscation was robbery and he could not stay in a meeting where robbery was preached. Balfour, his brother-in-law, was sitting next to Sidgwick and apologised to Shaw saying, "I don't know why Sidgwick feels it so keenly as all his money is in consols?" . . .

Our love to you both.   *Ever affectionately yours, H. J. L.*

Washington, D.C., May 21, 1925
Dear Laski: A delightful letter from you finds me in the right spirit for it and talks of things I have been thinking about. I have listened to parts of the Roosevelt-Lodge correspondence, with the

---

1902, President Roosevelt, who was then considering the nomination of Holmes to the Supreme Court of the United States, had expressed some distress that Holmes in a speech which he had delivered on John Marshall (Holmes, *Speeches*, 87) had shown "a total incapacity to grasp what Marshall did." In that address Holmes had stated that if he were "to think of John Marshall simply by number and measure in the abstract" he might hesitate in his superlatives, for "a great man represents a great ganglion in the nerves of society, or, to vary the figure, a strategic point in the campaign of history, and the fact of his greatness consists in being there." *Id.*, p. 88.
    [2] William Archer (1856-1924), journalist, dramatic critic, and dramatist was an ardent rationalist in religious controversies.

same or greater interest that you express, in view of my knowledge of Roosevelt and having been rather familiar with Cabot since he was in College. R.'s talk about my attitude to Marshall seemed to me unintelligent if he had read the whole. I still think what I said was just. R. was a more or less great man no doubt but I think he was far from having a great intellect—in the sense in which we ordinarily use that word. Perhaps I have not heard enough but I don't as yet recognize what you say of C.L.'s willingness to enter into mean schemes with mean men. I haven't either come across his judgment of books, but I shouldn't expect him to reach any great penetration. However, I suppose I owe my appointment to him or Mrs. Lodge and I think he generally was kind in his judgment of me, except perhaps when Roosevelt was so angry at my dissent in the *Northern Securities* case (about which you probably know little and care less). Of F. Hackett's book you think as I do. I believe I mentioned some keen observations and I was thinking of the description of the Democratic Convention which you pick out. Apropos of the Henry George incident, did you ever read his book? I thought it took to rhetoric just when argument was needed, and made the very usual assumption that ownership instead of being a method of distribution meant consumption of the products of the thing owned. I speak from a recollection of 30 or 40 years ago. . . . Why does Barrie seem to be a teacup storm-centre? I should think, again from old memory, that he had done pleasing and touching things—not calling for vehemence. I remember that I rather liked the little man when I knew him in the dim past. I recur to Cabot Lodge to say that I thought the letters that I heard were very pleasing and showed the affectionate side of his character which usually was not visible. I have just begun an article in the *Yale Law Journal* by Frankfurter and Landis[1] who I hear is to be with Brandeis next year. It promises to be very good. The newspapers seem to want a Massachusetts vacancy in our Court. On Sunday or Monday there was a statement that I was going to retire at the beginning of next term, and a day or two later a statement that Brandeis was just returning from a week at a sanatorium. I hear that the present C.J. (Rugg) of Massachusetts wants a place here and he is a friend of Coolidge's, I have heard, a classmate. Whether the President desires a vacancy I know not. But I presume that somehow the wish is father to the thought. Both statements were untrue so far as present knowledge goes. I got a mighty good little monograph on the Historic Origin of Trade Marks—I suppose a thesis for a new degree from Columbia of D.J. The author, Frank I. Schechter, has gone outside the law to the early gild practices etc., etc., as a man must to throw real light—and has

---

[1] Frankfurter and Landis, "The Compact Clause of the Constitution—A Study in Interstate Adjustments," 34 *Yale L. J.* 685 (May 1925).

made a good job of it. I received it one day, a letter from him the next, and finished it and wrote to him the next (yesterday) but I have undertaken no mighty labors, and go out every morning with my wife to see monkeys, woods, roses or River, get back just in time for luncheon and per chance a snooze afterwards and the days rush by. To be sure there is a folio lying open here but if inspected it is open at A. Dumas's *Crimes célèbres.* On Sunday I looked into Mather's *Magnalia,* a few copies of which with the map descended to me from my grandpa. It is truly amazing to see what people believed two centuries and a quarter ago. The old boy doesn't want in vividness, though it has been thought that only one man ever read the *Magnalia* through.

Affectionately yours, O. W. Holmes

16 Warwick Gardens, 16.V.25

My dear Justice: . . . Also I had a great book expedition in the East end of London—a queer old place in the Minories. No order, no shelves; all books on [*sic*] heaps on tables; put in your hand and pick out what you can get. So I did. Shaftesbury's *Characteristics*—3 volumes, first edition, three shillings; Pithou's *Libertés de l'église gallicane*—a real rarity in perfect condition (1594) 1/–; Huxley's copy of Gladstone's *State and Church* with a footnote explaining that Mr. G. was a humbug; from Huxley to Leslie Stephen who annotates with characteristic moderation—"Perhaps he was, but there were moments when he did not know it." . . .

Of reading . . . at Frida's orders, some George Sand of which *Consuelo* struck me as very fine. . . .

For the rest, a dinner with H. G. Wells and a fight over Henry James. Wells thinks him big in a limited sphere; I maintain that no man can be big who thinks, as James did, (I) that American civilisation is on the whole no place for a gentleman; and (II) that the only ideas worth examining are those of the leisured classes and (III) that the insignificant becomes universal by looking at it through a microscope. Wells retorts that life is like that and that Henry James got a real glimpse of a corner of it. I don't believe it, for I think he had a mind much too tortuous and involved ever to see anything straight. Did you ever really enjoy anything he wrote—friendship for him apart? And did you ever read such a monument of artificiality as his letters? But I grow profane. . . .

Our love to you.   *Ever affectionately yours, H. J. L.*

Washington, D.C., May 28, 1925

Dear Laski: Your letter (16th) has several things whereof I would speak, but first a word on a book sent to me by the C.J.—Morgan's about Morley.[1] Perhaps as another friend of Morley's you don't like it but I found it very interesting and not without charm—a charm that begins with the portrait at the beginning. The face has a look of holiness about it that reminds me of the portrait of Newman. It is beautiful and yet—somehow it suggests to me that not from such faces does one expect or get the fierce electric high light that I think Pascal but not Newman had. My secretary, apropos, brought me Morley's *Compromise*. I have read just six pages but they seem to me polite English crumbs. A man with the gift of volubility could fill a loaf—*i.e.* a volume, with discourse of that degree of intensity and be unexhausted while the consumer might fill his stomach without delight. This is not a general judgment but what I said at the outset is, so far as I know Morley's writings. I suspect that Morley, like men who believed a little more, never got out of the atmosphere of belief and therefore perhaps (but I don't know him enough to affirm it) could not think with full force and effect in another air. England with all its beauties and powers is Little Pedlington. The dominant interests there as elsewhere are determined by proximity. As a politician M. necessarily was interested in Gladstone, as a thinker I don't see how he could have been interested by him.

I turn to your letter. A translation of *Consuelo* made a deep impression on me as a boy. I never have read it since. I think there was something big in H. James, but I think with all his preoccupation he wanted something of the gentleman and that it tells in his choice of subjects and sometimes in his writing. This is a thing that I wouldn't say except in confidence and I will not develop it. His letters I haven't read but you don't surprise me by what you say.

29th/ I envy you your bookshop—it is like my feeling when I came as a boy on dirty portfolios of old prints in seedy print shops —but I should not have your eyes for rarities (in books) and should not buy them if I did. I am too old to collect—even in prints. Although I have bought a few, I don't collect, and now that Rice is dead I buy nothing for the present. I hope I may live long enough to get a few more.

I am rather up in the world just now from various superlatives that have been applied to me but I am rather worried by my young Chinese friend Wu. He is *tête montée* about me and has a scheme for an institute to be named for me where the different systems of law will meet in China. He actually has sent on the plans for a building before which I am helpless, and I fear expects his enthusiasm to be shared in this country. I wrote to him some time ago cautioning him as he is not a businessman, and telling him he could get little aid from me. Naturally I can't boost a thing to be called after me and I told him I could give very little. This bothers me and also it frightens me to be put very high as one fears that before one is dead or out of it there will come disappointment. Luckily he bid me forward the plans to Frankfurter and I shall get them off my hands. I didn't dare open them for three days having the excuse of work that was pressing—about 35 *certioraris* to be considered before a meeting today.

I am cut short unexpectedly and have to wind up. I am sorry as I felt like talking.   *Aff'ly yours, O. W. H.*

16 Warwick Gardens, 23.V.25
My dear Justice: Two delightful letters from you arrived simultaneously during the week, and I take the first bit of leisure to answer them. First, anent my father. In general, we are on excellent terms. He cannot bear my insistence that I will not have a parliamentary career, but tries to assume that it is a form of madness; nor can he understand why I will not take money from him. But these trifles apart, I think he is happy in our reconciliation, and I, certainly, have a good deal of pleasure in his faith in me. Then, a list of books for your summer reading. I think these would tickle your palate. (I) Vaughan—*Studies in the History of Political Philosophy*, 2 volumes, Longmans. (II) Cole, *The Life of Cobbett* (Harcourt and Brace). (III) Sainte-Beuve, *Port-Royal*, especially Volumes III-IV, dealing with Pascal. (IV) La Rochefoucauld, *Maximes* and La Bruyère, *Caractères*—these would, I think, really give you immense pleasure. (IV) [*sic*] Brunetière, *Études critiques sur la littérature française*—Series II—essays on Bossuet and Fénelon, Massillon, *La librairie sous Malesherbes*. Series III—essays on Descartes, Pascal, Voltaire and Rousseau. Series IV—essays on Pascal, *Jansenistes et Cartesiens*, Molière, Voltaire. Series V—Bossuet, Bayle, *Idée du progrès*. . . .

My love warmly to you both.   *Ever affectionately yours, H. J. L.*

16 Warwick Gardens, 7.VI.25
My dear Justice: . . . We spent a delightful week-end in the country with the Webbs and Bernard Shaw. Talk in plenty, particularly from Shaw and Mrs. Webb. Shaw insistent that for clear homespun no one has ever equalled Cobbett in style and that Swift is the supreme master of savage irony in any tongue. . . . I read down there Mrs. Webb's ms diary of the eighties, full of most interesting glimpses of Spencer and Galton and Huxley. I was especially impressed by the fact that she greatly admired the first two and found something inexplicably vulgar in Huxley.

. . . I reread Maitland's *Leslie Stephen* which left me with the firm and immovable conviction that it really is the best *personal* biography in our tongue—in the sense I mean that you see the man *au naturel* and recognising faults, even great faults, you must love him. . . .   *Ever affectionately yours, H. J. L.*

16 Warwick Gardens, 14.VI.25

My dear Justice: . . . Since I wrote last week I have had two happy days in Scotland. . . . I add a talk with an assistant in one shop [in Edinburgh] whose grandfather was Scott's bookseller and he told me the family legend of Scott reading Hazlitt for the first time and saying "the rascal may be a radical, Mr. Thompson, but, by God, he writes like a man," which is, I submit, as fine a tribute as one big fellow can pay to another. In Glasgow I heard one of those charming academic stories that tickle one's palate. Professor A., a mathematician, is troubled by the work of Professor B., a logician, who writes on the foundations of mathematics. How can B. who was not a wrangler, know anything about the matter? B. writes an essay on first principles and sends it to A for criticism, omitting to state, since it is obvious, that he has written it himself. He gets back this letter from A. "Dear B. I have read the student's essay you sent me. I cannot speak upon the metaphysics of which I know nothing. But in the mathematics I am clear that he lacks the ability which would justify you in urging him to continue at this work." What, if you were B., would you reply? Actually, to his infinite credit, he told me the story. . . .
                          Ever affectionately yours, H. J. L.

Beverly Farms, June 14, 1925

Dear Laski: A grub that has split his skin but not yet emerged as a butterfly greets you. We got here last night. Washington was hell, the worst I have ever known it, only mitigated by dining on the roof of the Powhatan and watching darkness fall on the great landscape and in the distance the Arlington bridge over the Potomac suddenly become a glow-worm. The last day of Court I let out a page of slack on the right of an ass to drool about proletarian dictatorship but I was alone with Brandeis.[1] Free speech means to most people, you may say anything that I don't think shocking.

In passing through Boston I went to the Athenaeum and caused them to produce Sainte-Beuve, *Port-Royal* and promise to send it to me. I am disappointed that it has not yet arrived, but I have not so fully recovered from the exhaustion of Washington and the journey on as to aspire to an idea. I have got through the term better I think than most of the judges (I mean in the way of health) and I am well, but I still feel like an animal in the repair shop.

[1] *Gitlow* v. *New York*, 268 U.S. 652, 672 (June 8, 1925).

I meant to go to Schoenhof about Brunetière but time was short and I didn't fetch it. It will keep, especially as I haven't an enormous appetite for Brunetière. Vaughan *Studies &c.* tempts me more but I bet the later editions are more than two volumes. Why should I read the life of Cobbett? Doesn't that belong to the local gossip of England?—and I rarely read lives—though I have a few under your compulsion of late years.

For the moment, to breathe living air is joy enough—or almost. I walked to the postoffice this morning which was long for me, and food tastes good once more. Washington empties you of everything except what you wanted to get rid of and made everything an effort.   *Aff'ly yours, O. W. H.*

Beverly Farms, June 19, 1925

Dear Laski: Your delightful letter of the 6th has just reached me and has been read this minute. Before anything else I must refer to Mrs. Webb's view of Huxley. I met him at dinner, I think at Fred Pollock's, and thought him an objectionable boor. Also as to Maitland's *Stephen* (which is not here). When I read it I wrote opening my heart to him, only to receive a line from Mrs. Maitland that he was dead. I remember only the exalted impression I got of the writer from the book. Now I am striving simply to abandon myself to life—the joy of the air, the trees, the ocean but it is almost impossible for me not to erect something into a duty and a task. Your damned *Port-Royal* comes near being that. I have nearly finished volume 1 enchanted with St. Francis de Sale from the quotations, and disliking Sainte-Beuve—whether he is a mealy-mouthed hypocrite, as I hope, or at that date really believed, as his ever present sense of the requirements of the religion would seem to indicate. Surely he didn't continue a Christian did he? (Answer.) So far, although I have got interested, I rather wonder why you put me on to the book. Do you know anything of Count H. Keyserling *Travel Diaries of a Philosopher* as the translation is advertised? I have seen much praise yet suspect it wouldn't talk to me.

20th/ I say I wonder at your recommending *Port-Royal.* I mean that while the position of Saint Cyran is very intelligible to me on his postulates, those postulates were a wholly uncritical assumption of historical facts and doctrines, which seem childish nowadays even if they make one tremble. I suppose that it was as a picture of literary conditions that you thought of it and I wait for Pascal. I am wondering whether *Travels in Arabia Deserta* by Doughty is necessary to salvation. I think he was spoken of as a great poet and this book as the greatest book of travels that ever was in *These Eventful Years*—but I am not given to travels. I think I must read

(reread) the second part of *Don Quixote.* Fitzgerald prefers it,
but he read it in Spanish and said, probably truly, that you must
read it in the original. The first part did not greatly delight me a
year or two ago. But I recur to my wish that I could be content
with simply living as I am when I play solitaire, but rarely otherwise. I believe I quoted Pliny, that it is better to be idle than to
do nothing. In a few minutes I shall go out for a drive and that
pretty well fills the bill. Also if I don't go out in the morning I take
a nap to recover from the fatigue of getting up, and if I do go out,
I do it *nolus volus* over my book in the afternoon. So it is a pretty
relaxed old file that sends you both his love.

Affectionately yours, O. W. Holmes

Beverly Farms, June 26, 1925

Dear Laski: Let my first word of answer to yours of the 14th, a
joy to me as usual, be one of justice to Sainte-Beuve. In an appendix to volume 2, as very likely you remember, he states the succession of his studies and interests, and explains that his effort to get
to the bottom of his subjects has led different people to think him
a hopeful case, whereas he is engaged in a course of moral physiology. This, coupled with a certain amount of dramatic imagination, may account for his speaking as one imbued with the doctrine
of grace. I think I got my prejudices against him from some
marginalia printed in one of the late volumes of the *Causeries,*
where he is malicious if not malevolent to those whom he treated
as friends. Perhaps also I got a slant from a dirty little book I
saw at the Athenaeum 1000 years ago depicting him in an unpleasing light. . . . Beveridge and his attractive wife called last
Sunday and he discoursed copiously about the Ku Klux and other
matters. He told my wife when I was out, the next day, that he
would like me to read two chapters of his *Lincoln.* I haven't yet
answered him as I waited to finish volume 2 of Sainte-Beuve and
take 1 and 2 back to the Athenaeum when I go to town today, but
I shall be glad to.

You have a great advantage in England that you are all so near
together that you can find intellectual companionship on every
side. Whereas here it is nearly solitude outside my wife. However,
one gets a spark here and there. I am afraid that letters giving one
a puff, a natural incident of old age, hardly takes the place of talk
with people who keep you up to the mark. Brandeis is a great comfort in the winter, but he is not here. I have got my volume of
opinions from the binder after anxieties due to the delay of the
Post Office and am indexing it, a job of some hours. The cases
seem to me more interesting than those of last year and I am
rather pleased as I reread—subject to the eternal misgiving

whether I have not been too speedy with them. I console myself
by thinking of the immediate decisions common in England, but
they are pretty certain that the case has been adequately argued,
and are not bothered by masses of irrelevancies as we are. You
see that I haven't much to tell and that I am slow with my reading. If only I could waste time comfortably I should think better
of myself. I sometimes flatter such waste by calling it the leisure
of crystalization but I don't know whether anything really happens
or whether it is not better to be content with nothing happening
and to live on the fat of one's guts. Give me another filip soon. If
I had your eye for a rare pamphlet it would be another joy.

Affectionately yours, O. W. Holmes

16 Warwick Gardens, 30.VI.25

My dear Justice: I ought not to have allowed a fortnight to elapse
without a word, but you will, I know, forgive me when you hear
the reason. A Canadian professor whom I used to know at McGill
University came to see me and went suddenly insane in the house.
I had the ghastly job of getting him medically examined, certified,
taken to a home, communicating with his people, and making all
the financial arrangements. Today a relative came over from
Canada, and took things off my hands, so that my responsibility
has ceased. But as you can imagine, it was a hectic time and I feel
a little worn as a consequence. However, term is over and I can
take things easily. . . .

I have seen various people these last days whom you know. Item,
Norman Hapgood,[1] who, as always, talked well anent the surfaces
of life; Manley Hudson, item, who was fine on things in general,
but inclined to get the League of Nations mixed up with God;
item Felix Adler[2] whom I'm afraid I thought a quite dreadful old
bore. I went also to dinner to Birrell and had three joyous hours
with him over books. He showed me a Bozzy annotated by Coleridge and an unpublished ms (belonging to Rosebery) of Jane
Austen. And I went to a philosophy meeting at which Balfour
spoke where F. Pollock turned up, a little lame, but as spruce and
dryly caustic as ever. As Balfour talked I could guess each emotion
from Pollock's face. Alexander, the philosopher, proposed a vote
of thanks, and I was tickled by a phrase of his that "Bolshevism
would have left Lord Kelvin unruffled but the Quanta theory would
have seemed to him impiety." Balfour in his way was very remarkable. He never said anything that touched the *fond* of things,
and there were places where prettily devastating footnotes might

---

[1] Norman Hapgood (1868-1937); journalist, man of letters, and biographer of Webster, Lincoln, and Washington.

[2] Felix Adler (1851-1933); lecturer and founder of the Society for Ethical
Culture.

have been added. But the form and manner of delivery were exquisite, and odd phrases such as "philosophers must learn that to be nebulous is not necessarily to be profound," and that "the cult of simplicity usually involved complexity of statement" were very happy. . . .   *Ever affectionately yours, H. J. L.*

Beverly Farms, July 9, 1925

Dear Laski: It is a relief to hear from you again. I hope your book will come to Beverly Farms which it will not if sent to Washington. I want a relief from that damned *Port-Royal* on to which you put me for my sins. I have still volume 5 to read, as I have not your lightning pace and read only a small part of the day, alleviated by slumber. I am glad of course to know more about Pascal, though I don't lie awake nights loving him. I can imagine writing a work on prevenient grace but as to the biographies of men who wrote forgotten books on such themes two centuries and a half ago, it is a mitigated joy. It is in the line of your studies but not of mine. Also, as I have said, I dislike Sainte-Beuve. After which abatements I get an appreciable pleasure from his literary *finesse* and am more or less amused by the gossip. But again I detest Louis XIV and his court—that is the spirit of it. I wonder if your future world is coming to pass when people will regard my postulates of self-justification in the comfort I take, as I think of those of the courtiers and theologians of the sixteen hundreds. It may be, so I will snatch a fearful joy from my creed and have the present while it lasts.

We motor about the Cape for about two hours nearly every day and see many beautiful things. I doubt if you ever went to the old graveyard of Marblehead from which one looks out on a wonderful stretch of sea. With the old and new gravestones of the sea captains, sailors lost on the Banks, revolutionary heroes and pre-revolutionary divines all round one—or to Bass Rocks at the furthest point of Gloucester, where we saw a perfect rose garden, with a long pool at the end dug from the rock, and a glimpse of the sea hard by. (It was constructed by the dame who runs our two little beds at the *impense* of, I believe, the Vice President of Heinz's pickles, said to be a simple, amiable, and generous man.) One day we went again to an old house toward the further end of the stream that connects Gloucester Harbor with the ocean on the other side and makes Gloucester an island. The house looks across to the white sands of Ipswich and out to sea. Nice people in it, and by the by it always pleases me to see that one always finds some of the natives of Marblehead on the benches of the graveyard, having climbed the hill seemingly to take in the view once more.

I see very few people but a few drop in. Beveridge again, in my
absence, and again asking that I read some chapters of his inchoate
work, which, I shall be happy to do. I heard from Frankfurter at
Cornell, seemingly happy, and intending to read Keyserling's
Travel Diary. I believe I asked you whether you could pronounce
on it. Somehow I shrink. He and his associate Landis have an
article in the June *Harvard Law Review*,[1] received by me this
morning which I shall read forthwith and expect to profit by.
("The Business of the Supreme Court of the U.S." to be continued). Also I hear of an article by Cardozo in the July *Yale Law
Journal* [sic] which I have not seen.[2] What with occasional matters
like these, checks to be drawn, casual letters to be answered &c,
my days keep filled without too much improvement from Sainte-
Beuve. I gave letters (to Leslie Scott and Fred Pollock) to Dodge[3]
of the Boston Bar for help in studying the English civil procedure
with a view to its possible adoption in Massachusetts. This at the
request of Judge Loring.[4] I am not sure that I know Dodge—partner of Moorfield Storey[5] and successful jury lawyer. Enough to tell
you my uneventful story and send you my love.

Affectionately yours, O. W. Holmes

16 Warwick Gardens, 6.VII.25
My dear Justice: Last week there went off to you a book and a
pamphlet of mine. I hope they will arrive safely, and pass pleasantly
some of your leisure hours.

I have two attractive letters from you to answer. First about
Port-Royal. I do not like Sainte-Beuve personally. He had a mean
mind, at times a dirty mind, and he was a *poseur.* But he had
exquisite scholarship, a genius for the *mot juste,* and a wonderful
power to paint a broad canvas. He interested me profoundly in
Port-Royal for three reasons. First Fontaine, Saint-Cyran and Pascal, in a lesser degree Arnauld, seem to me people whose secret
it is worth while to penetrate. They are full of charm, and they
have that life on the heights which always leaves me baffled and
wondering. Second they represent the last effort of religion in
France before the Revolution to make a decent society. They were
beaten, and to know the causes of their defeat is, I think, to under-

---

[1] 38 *Harvard L. Rev.* 1005 (June 1925).

[2] "Law and Literature," 14 *Yale Review* (N.S.) 699 (July 1925).

[3] Robert G. Dodge (1872-   ) was a member of the Judicial Council of
Massachusetts, 1924-1930.

[4] William Caleb Loring (1851-1930); Associate Justice, Supreme Judicial
Court of Massachusetts, 1899-1919; friend and North Shore neighbor of
Holmes.

[5] Moorfield Storey (1845-1929); political reformer and leading member of
the Boston bar.

stand as well as one can, why the Revolution came. Third they
were the last effort to keep back the full tide of free enquiry, and
to keep it back on the only terms ever likely to prevail in the long
run: that you can set over against it men who really, without it,
are living noble lives. So that it really does seems to me that Sainte-
Beuve took a great streak of human experience when he selected
that subject; and the art with which the whole thing is made to
lead up to, and away from, Pascal, seems to me consummate. Is
this all wrong?

. . . I suppose next term you will have this incredible Tennessee case.[1] I envy any judge the opportunity to pronounce on
that. Sankey said to me yesterday that Bowen would have surrendered his hope of immortality for the chance to pronounce
upon it.

I was most interested that your recollection of Huxley was much
the same as Mrs. Webb's. I think the vulgarity comes out even in
the *Life;* but, of course, toned down by skilful filial affection. Mrs.
Webb told me that the difference, at a dinner-party, between Spencer's grave courtesy and Huxley's beak and claws was an object
lesson in manners. Which somehow reminds me of a new story of
J. H. Thomas,[2] the labour leader, and the King. The latter asks
Thomas what he thinks of X. "Does your Majesty want me to be
frank?" "Certainly, Mr. Thomas." "Well, Sir, 'e's a bloody 'ell-
'ound." I will not comment.

. . . a visit to Oxford to vote (vainly, for he was beaten) for
Asquith as Chancellor against Cave. I wish you could have seen the
sight. Oxford, more lovely than I can depict, belittered by old and
decrepit clergymen, who had come up to save the Church by voting
for Cave. I lunched with Fisher at New College and while we
walked in the garden an old vicar came up to denounce him for
supporting Asquith. "That man," he said with a furious gesture,
"has done graver injury to the Church than any man since Judas
Iscariot!" Here I ought possibly to explain that the reference is to
the Welsh Disestablishment Act[3] . . .

Ever affectionately yours, H. J. L.

---

[1] *Scopes* v. *State,* 154 Tenn. 105 (1927) was at this time being heard in
the trial court, with William Jennings Bryan as the fundamentalist champion.
The case presented the question whether the Tennessee statute prohibiting
the teaching of evolution in public institutions of learning was constitutional.
The state decision that the statute was constitutional was never reviewed by
the Supreme Court of the United States.

[2] See, *supra,* p. 432, Vol. I.

[3] Asquith had never been forgiven by some for his efforts, ultimately successful, in favor of Welsh disestablishment in 1894-95, 1909, and 1912. The
Disestablishment Act was not adopted, however, until 1914, and then only
by virtue of the Parliament Act which made it possible for the statute to be
enacted over the opposition of the House of Lords.

Beverly Farms, July 17, 1925

Dear Laski: Your letter (6th) came with the book[1] and the pamphlet.[2] I shall begin the book in a day or two—the pamphlet seems to me to be somewhat in the air—to exaggerate the evils peculiar to capitalism—and to take a good deal for granted as to socialism. One can change institutions by a fiat but populations only by slow degrees and as I don't believe in millennia and still less in the possibility of attaining one by tinkering with property while propagation is free and we do all we can to keep the products, however bad, alive, I listen with some skepticism to plans for fundamental amelioration. I should expect more from systematic prevention of the survival of the unfit. However, I shall read the book with serious attention.

I have finished that scourge of a *Port-Royal*—yet helped by your letter. I will not say that I have not had my money's worth (especially as I didn't buy the five volumes). It tickled me to think of a possible meeting of Cotton Mather and Arnauld—agreeing in so much and each, I suppose, devoutly believing the other damned. As a counter-irritant I have a little book by a doctor—*Post Mortem*—accounting for the conduct of eminent historic persons on medical grounds. I have just looked into it—the view is promising. I can't yet judge adequately the performance. He begins by saying that Henry VIII had the pox and Joan of Arc suppressed menses ∴ ——————— Also *The Constant Nymph* on which also I am unprepared—it suggests to me the remark of an old English housekeeper, "Them P————s is the most fornicationest lot" but I may be wrong. Some type-written chapters of Beveridge show the same care for details—squalid in themselves and the same power of showing the development of a character as before. He is coming for a jaw later this afternoon. I shall give him your message. I always seem to end in a hurry—but so far I have been [illegible] so —I hope to be less in the future. I want this to sail tomorrow if it may—and so must shut up in a minute. I really am impressed by what you say of *Port-Royal* as I was by your political article in the *New Republic*.[3] I have motored by Rockport and sighed.

Affectionately yours, O. W. H.

Beverly Farms, July 23, 1925

Dear Laski: I started to write to Fred Pollock but I must say a few words to you first. Your book came the day before yesterday, or so, and I am in the middle of it—the last chapter, 7, of Part 1.[1] I

---

[1] *A Grammar of Politics* (1925).

[2] Presumably *Socialism and Freedom* (Fabian Tract, No. 216, July 1925).

[3] "English Politics Today," 43 *New Republic* 171 (July 8, 1925).

[1] Chapter VII in *A Grammar of Politics* (1925) was entitled "Authority as Federal."

like that best so far. I like very much your realization of the dependence of a large part of what you would like to see upon a
world movement. Being old I don't expect to see it. As you will
have expected I don't sympathize very greatly with your dream.
You think more nobly of man than I do—and of course, you may
be right. But I look at men through Malthus's glasses—as like
flies—here swept away by a pestilence—there multiplying unduly
and paying for it. I think your morals (I am struck by the delicacy
of your feeling) are not the last word but only a check for varying
intensity upon force, which seems to me likely to remain the ultimate as far as I can look ahead. I was hearing only a day or two
ago a traveler's report that every French boy was brought up to
think of licking Germany and every German to look forward to
revenge upon France. I think I perceive at critical moments a tacit
assumption that papa Laski, or those who think like him, are to
regulate paternally the popular desires. If a man makes a great
fortune by selling some patent medicine to the crowd, that shows
that in those circumstances the crowd wants it—and I can see
no justification in a government's undertaking to rectify social
desires—except upon an aristocratic assumption that you know
what is good for them better than they—(which no doubt you do).
I don't think you succeeded in smashing the legal conception of
sovereignty from the legal point of view. Of course I agree that
looked at from the outside it is subject to all sorts of limitations.
As to the *right* of citizens to support and education I don't see it.
It may be a desirable ideal to aim at, but I see no right in my
neighbor to share my bread. I mean moral right of course—there
is no pretense of any other, except so far as he in combination has
power to take it. I always have said that the rights of a given crowd
are what they will fight for. I once heard the older Agassiz say
of some place in Germany that there would be a revolution if you
raised the price of a glass of beer. If that was true and believed
they had a right to beer at that price. We don't here, alas (I say
alas, but don't greatly regret the social experiment, though not
scientifically conceived and though it kills much joy). I won't
attempt to go into details. I wondered what you meant by saying
that here the rich have possessed themselves of the means of education, p. 175 [*sic*].[2] On the same page, I doubt if the injunction
is used here to the advantage of the rich at the present time—
barring what some foolish single judge may do . . . I admire the
knowledge—I admire the feeling—very possibly the prophecy is
nearer fulfilment than I realize—but in my ignorance—I feel that

---

[2] At p. 176 Laski had stated that under the existing social system the rich
"may possess themselves, as in America, of the educational instruments of the
community" and that the law confers special advantages upon preferred
classes in varying ways—"as in the United States, by the use of the
injunction in labour disputes."

I am reading a richer and more profound *Oceana*—and have to make reserves even in wishing that your dream may come true.

To jump to a different theme—Sainte-Beuve heartily agrees with *Port-Royal* as to the native badness of man. I wonder if that belief is not easier to a Frenchman than to us because I wonder if he has not more of the subterranean meannesses than the average Englishman and if the consciousness of them does not lead to his assent. Sainte-Beuve showed that he had, at all events.

Of course I am not yet in a position to criticize your book as a whole. I have told you some of my difficulties. I think Chapter 7 impressive and fine. I am midway in it and return to it.

Affectionately yours, O. W. H.

16 Warwick Gardens, 20.VII.25
My dear Justice: You talk of being tempted (I hope in vain) towards Keyserling's *Travel Diary.* I read parts of it in German through Redlich's fervour, and found it portentous nonsense . . . Of other things, I have read (to review) a vast book by Willoughby on *The Fundamental Concepts of Public Law*[1] which was much ado about nothing . . . Also I went through, with judicious skips over the Greek period, Lange's *History of Materialism* which has just been reprinted. I found it not without *longueurs,* but, on the whole, repaying the price of admission.

What else have I done! . . . a black barrister from Nigeria, who wishes to write a book on justice. On what aspect? "On the grand general conception, Professor Laski, by which the bowels of humanity have been stirred." Do you wonder that I look forward a little eagerly to Wednesday when we go to the country?

. . . I have parted with my Bentham. A young man came to see me bound for an Australian professorship. Writing a book on Bentham. Did I know where a copy of the *Works* was to be had? I didn't see what I could do as there are no copies in Australia; so I sent him away rejoicing, and with a sense of private wonder as to whether I was not a damned fool. But he won my heart by praising Leslie Stephen and I suppose I shall find another some day.

I must tell you of one of God's own creatures I met at lunch. We have a friend, a niece of the Webbs, whose husband is a distinguished solicitor. He is a high Tory with no interest in his wife's pursuits. I went with Frida to lunch a little dreading it. I found he had a passion for French engravings of the 17th century. He'd begun by collecting any he could. Then he found he only wanted

---

[1] Laski reviewed Westel W. Willoughby's *The Fundamental Concepts of Public Law* (1924) in 40 *Political Science Quarterly* 618 (December 1925).

portraits. Then only portraits by one man. Then the margins became vital. Then he got to the stage where there were three only left that he didn't have. Came a catalogue from Paris with one in. He couldn't wait but went by the first aeroplane to get it. Came back, however, by ordinary transit—"I couldn't risk anything with that engraving in my trunk." . . .

I envy you journeys round the Cape. Bass Rocks used to be a favourite resort of ours at Rockport. But do you know Paradise Rocks? They were beyond Rockport and most charming. I remember well finding a pool there which was a perfect sea-garden full of anemones and tiny fish-like creatures—a real paradise. . . .

Our love to you both.   *Ever affectionately yours, H. J. L.*

Beverly Farms, August 1, 1925

Dear Laski: A delightful letter from you this morning . . . I am worried by this letter—because I have read your book and it does not command my sympathy and I hate to have any words but praise for you. Of course I recognize that it may mean that I am finished—an old fogey no longer able to keep the pace—all the more that I appreciate the ability and great knowledge with which you write. I never read so penetrating a socialist book—but I told you the other day that I don't believe your premises and I must add that the elaborate construction of an imaginary society seems to me premature and like the constitution makers of the 18th century. Yet here again I recognize that what you say may have a more practical significance for England than it has for me. But just as I said the other day that I take no stock in abstract rights, I equally fail to respect the passion for equality. I think it an ignoble aspiration which only culminates in the statement of one of your Frenchmen that inequality of talents was an injustice. I do not presume to think that even if I am right your book may not be a benefit to the world—but, in its immediate effect to encourage what I think mistaken views and desires, I feel sorry. If, as you say, the alternative is the ruin of civilization I think that more likely to come—but I do not accept any prophecy with confidence. The unforeseen is generally what happens. There—I have done my duty—and I hope I have not hurt my friend.

I have turned to literature. After reading Lemaître's *Racine* I sent for Racine's plays and yesterday read *Andromaque* twice in the light of Lemaître's critical praise. No doubt I appreciated more than before, the measure and elegance of the verse—the absence of empty declamation—the appropriateness, in very low relief, of what was said, to the person and situation—but that which delights the French *"gout de l'intelligible,"* seems to me to exclude the result from the superlative degree. There is in man and in life a residue of mystery, and that is what Shakespeare and many less than he make us feel—and that it is to my mind by which poetry enchants. Racine does not enchant—at least not me. If he does it for the French I see no way out except to recognize national ultimates—*de gustibus non est disputandum*—except to remember how much one may miss by not having the language in one's bones. I believe Jusserand (the Ambassador) thought that anybody could write "Hark, Hark the Lark at heaven's gate sings"—and that the translation was just as good. On the other hand I much doubt if Racine could have written *"Jeu sui Arnaut, que plor, e vau cantan"* (the poet in purgatory who weeps as needs he must but goes singing even in the flames that are refining him) *Purg.* xxvi. 142. I shall read some more—but as I whispered to your, I doubt not, unsympathetic ear, the literature of the past is a bore. The good of it comes later as from a cathedral where at the moment your shoes hurt and you are wondering whether you should give the young woman a shilling or half a crown. I read Lange 50 or 60 years ago—and can't recite on it now. I am specially tickled by your black barrister. He ought to get more from you than he would from me. I lost my humanity with my abolition days in college and in the army. I am sorry you gave away your Bentham. Never give what you really want—you will regret it—as I have more than once. Yet I think the occasion justified the gift. I went through Rockport again yesterday afternoon and saw new places. I don't know Paradise by name—but I must have seen most of it. You don't mean great pools in old quarries, evidently—I love the whole region. Was it Nanteuil that the solicitor you lunched with collected?   *Affectionately yours, O. W. Holmes*

                                    Churt, Farnham, Surrey, 28.VII.25
My dear Justice: . . . A brief but charming letter from you tells me that my book arrived safely; you know how eager I shall be to hear of your opinion. Agreement I don't expect, for I have convictions built on faith while you (forgive me!) have doubts built on fears. That, I think, explains your feeling about my pamphlet.[1] In prosperous America where you have not yet reached the point of diminishing returns, great schemes of social reconstruction rather naturally seem a mirage. Here, in the midst of industrial gloom, their need is a grim reality, and not the least task of social science is to discover the basis upon which they are to be built. Nor, at your distance, can you (I think) easily appreciate how outworn the war has made almost all the primary assumptions of classical

---

[1] *Socialism and Freedom* (Fabian Tract, No. 216, July 1925).

economics. The one thing I grant you freely is the urgent need of
controlling population. But that, I think, is a three-fold problem.
First it is a matter of gaining a permanently higher standard of
living. For statistically it is clear that a certain level of comfort
brings with it voluntary limitation of offspring, as Webb showed
years ago in his comparison of birth-rates among different sections
of the working-class.[2] But there cannot be a higher standard without greater productivity; and there cannot be greater productivity
until we enlist new motives to effort from the workers. Hence my
second assumption that a change in social direction is essential.
And thirdly, there must be unfettered distribution of knowledge
about birth-control. I believe this is increasingly important. The
power voluntarily and with prevision to restrict numbers seems to
me the greatest weapon placed in the hands of man since the discovery of fire. To prevent its use on what are either sentimental or
theological (perhaps they're the same) grounds seems to me as
near a betrayal of the future as one can easily conceive. I believe
Holmes, J. (whom you may know) pointed to the same thing in
his speech of 1913 to the Harvard Law Review [sic] Association.[3]

. . . Do you remember Meredith on Leslie Stephen in (I think)
The Egoist—the man who never made a century and never made a
duck, but could always be relied on for thirty or forty runs? That
seems to me a first-rate description of Trollope. He never touches
the heights. But he always has a good story to tell and he never
lets your interest flag; moreover his people are really flesh and
blood. . . .

In the way of writing there is nothing much of which I can write
proudly. A brief introduction for an English translation of Roustan's
book on the Encyclopedists;[4] a couple of book-reviews; and part
of an article on the coal situation which you will see later in the
New Republic.[5] But I really haven't tried to take life seriously. The
sun and the wind have been the main items of existence. And even
the coal-strike which may do terrible damage—seems as remote as
an event on Jupiter.

My love to you both.   *Ever affectionately yours, H. J. L.*

---

[2] Sidney Webb, *The Decline in the Birth-Rate* (Fabian Tract, No. 131,
March 1907).

[3] "Law and the Court" (a speech at a dinner of the Harvard Law School
Association), *Speeches*, p. 98; *Collected Legal Papers*, p. 291.

[4] Marius Roustan, *The Pioneers of the French Revolution* (Whyte, tr., with
Introduction by Laski; 1926).

[5] The article referred to does not seem to have been published. Current
disputes in the coal industry were at a critical stage; a major strike, however, was forestalled by government action early in August.

Beverly Farms, August 7, 1925

Dear Laski: Your ever welcome letter tells me that you are or were in the country. I know not for how long and shall direct to London. Your reply to my remarks on your pamphlet nearly echoes what I quoted from a young lawyer in my little piece on "Ideals and Doubts" [1] and I accept it as just. Also, as you will have seen in my letters about your book, I recognize that in my retreat from the world I can't judge about England. The only thing that I am competent to say from the experience of my youth is that I fear your getting into the frame of mind that I saw in the Abolitionists (and shared)—the martyr spirit. It is apt to be wrongheaded. I say this very timidly and with proper reserves, but I cannot forbear a word of apprehension. I value enthusiasm but not enthusiism. I cannot write at length because I want this to catch the 5 o'clock from here and possibly get off tomorrow—though why this anxiety to catch a mail I can't say. My study of Racine is drawing to an end with his first play—the last for me to read. I must repeat what I said to a dame the other day and that seemed to me a just criticism. He makes intelligent statements of woe—innuendo, that the great ultimate cry is not there. The niceties of the verse and the music (to a French ear) I get but imperfectly—but that is subordinate. The French don't get ours. . . .

I have had another talk with Beveridge about his book, making various minor criticisms about style—words &c. but I think it will be beyond comparison *the* life if he persists to the end—a frightful task. He is a truffle dog for the true details and after he has got them knows how to subordinate them. I gave him your message that he should leave politics for literature—and he said he accepts it and had told them to look over the younger men and not bring him forward unless they really couldn't find anyone else. But I fear that "unless" means a hankering. [2] I wonder if he has the presidential bee in his bonnet. I hope not for I think he will get more permanent honor from his present work. Your steady pleasure in Trollope gives me a slight prick but not a spur. I remember reading *Phineas Finn* with a good deal of pleasure—but I shy at him. I can't read the vital words in your letter—Meredith on Leslie Stephen "the man who never made a (?) and never made a (duck?) but could always be relied on for thirty or forty (?)" I am glad we agree about population—but there as elsewhere you need world control. If France doesn't produce Frenchmen people

---

[1] "But it is a pleasure to see more faith and enthusiasm in the young men; and I thought that one of them made a good answer to some of my sceptical talk when he said, 'You would base legislation upon regrets rather than upon hopes!' " "Ideals and Doubts," *Collected Legal Papers*, 303, 307.

[2] Beveridge's last political campaign, an unsuccessful one, was for the Senate in 1922.

of some other nation come in to fill the lower places—and you
have new troubles. I remember how I used to envy London when
I saw Englishmen in the poor streets and not a different race. And
I can remember the time when it was mentioned that in a certain
block in Broad Street (Boston) there were Irish—supposed to be
a bad lot, the rest of the population was Yankee. Now an old
Yankee like me is a *rara avis*—except in some country regions. The
Catholic Church here, which I once contributed to for the servants,
is now the dominant one and the old Baptist Church barely keeps
alive with contributions from the summer people—I bow my head
and feel not the simoon pass. Must stop.

Affectionately yours, O. W. H.

Beverly Farms, August 7, 1925

P.S. Immediately after posting the letter to you we drove over to
Gloucester and thence from near Bass Rocks by a new road, finished I think since you were here, to Rockport. As we reached your
little street by common consent we turned down (or up) it in
honor of you. Your house is as it was though perhaps newly painted
an unobjectionable green. Everything else much as it was except
that the breakwater is I think extended so as to leave rather a
narrow entrance to the little harbor. It diminished the picturesque-
ness a little. We went on a few steps up to the common and I got
out and took a view. The road was rough and just after we passed
your house returning we blew out a tire and sat and gazed on
everything till the new one was in—and so back to B.F. I hope this
report will reach you a week later and justify my haste for the mail
this p.m. Homage to your missus.   *Aff'ly, O. W. H.*

Churt, Nr. Farnham, 15.VIII.25

My dear Justice: If I had been a friend of Rousseau's and he had
sent me the *Contrat social,* I should have written to him that he
had published a brilliant book with every word of which I disagreed. You—to compare the great with the minute—say much
the same to me and I am joyfully and gratefully content. Indeed,
how could I expect much more? You are living in a new country
where, quite largely, the career is still wholly open to the talented,
and the point of diminishing returns is hardly within sight. I
write in an overpopulated Europe, devastated by war, full of bitter
social conflict, and beyond the point of diminishing returns; and,
in general, there is too much social stratification to make the talented easily find their careers. So, since all political speculation is
autobiography, we not unnaturally take different roads. I'm pretty

sure that the ultimate end—with one exception—is the same; and
I am equally sure that we are both sceptical enough by temperament to be willing to revise all our conclusions. The exception I
note is your view of equality as an ignoble ideal—the adjective is
yours. On that I make two remarks. First you write of equality as
identity, which we are far from doing; and second that I see no
reason whatever why it is ignoble to desire that the differences
between men should have their social connotation rather on the
intellectual and spiritual plane than on the material. I want a judge
of the U.S. Supreme Court to be more highly regarded than a
door-keeper in the court; but I want him more highly regarded because the one is a judge and the other a door-keeper and not
because one earns ten times the wage of another. And I do not
want the judge to have ten times his salary unless and until the
door-keeper is paid at a level which assures him social adequacy.
I don't think that you would seriously differ from that as a principle, whatever the difficulties of application. But, apart from all
this, I have no more pain in accepting your disagreement than you
will have in my feeling that your decision in *Kawananakoa* v.
Polyblank is unsound.[1] Friendship goes deeper than all these things.
You, apart from Frida, have been the great thing in my life in
that realm, and my main sentiment is one of profound gratitude
for it. . . .

People, we have hardly seen since I wrote last. A ride over to
the Webbs, a talk there with Ramsay MacDonald who was so full
of selfrighteousness that I wanted to vomit; . . .

Ever affectionately yours, H. J. L.

Beverly Farms, August 27, 1925
Dear Laski: A lovely letter from you starts my answer as soon as
I have read it. Of course you are right as to our disagreements, and
although a little nervously, I relied upon your magnanimity as you
can rely upon mine as to *Kawananakoa*. Of course what I said as
to the passion for equality didn't mean you—and with what the
passion means to you I hardly disagree. We agree as to Racine. Do
you not find the same abatement in Tennyson and Stevenson—
the feeling by the reader that the writer has searched for a happy
phrase? Whereas Shakespeare just naturally sings it out? Even
Kipling will tear the word from the guts of the dictionary or from

---

[1] In *Kawananakoa* v. *Polyblank*, 205 U.S. 349 (1907), Holmes had
written of sovereignty. In the course of his opinion he said: "A sovereign is
exempt from suit, not because of any formal conception or obsolete theory,
but on the logical and practical ground that there can be no legal right as
against the authority that makes the law on which the right depends." *Id.* at
p. 353. Laski had criticized Holmes's opinion on several occasions; see, *e.g.*,
Foundations of Sovereignty (1921), p. 126; review in 40 *Pol. Sci. Qu.* 618,
620 (December 1925). See, *supra*, p. 5, Vol. I.

speech and make it his own. I have not an event. On Monday
last we went to Gloucester to see a statue unveiled the day before.
It stands on the edge of the water just beyond the bridge that you
face coming from B. F. On the pedestal is "They that go down to
the sea in ships." The figure suitably above life size is a sailor
bending to his wheel, upon a slanting deck, his eyes fixed on the
sea ahead. He embodies all the men that ever died on the Banks
—yet without melodrama. It simply is The Man. I don't remember
any American work, unless perhaps the Confederate of the lost
cause in Alexandria (which moved my wife more than it did me
but made men weep) that has moved me so much. I cried when
I saw it. My wife and I inquired about the artist, Leonard Craske,[1]
whose name I had never heard, at the City Hall, and found he
had a studio on one of the wharves—(headquarters in Boston) so
I left a card to express my admiration of his feeling work—and
have received a nice letter from him this morning. I am in a sympathetic humor as I have gone back to the *Odyssey* and am powdering along in it slowly but with more pleasure than I used to feel.
Decidedly this year I am more hospitable to the past than I have
been—perhaps because I think of death as impending although I
don't feel it imminent. Indeed if I cross the line of 85 I shall set
90 for a goal. But in reading such books we don't feel as the
author did or as he meant us to feel. Homer speaks of Ulysses
looking often at the sun to see if it was not setting, he longing to
start from Alcinous for home. It made me think of the Seven Days
in '62—when I would wonder if that damned sun ever would go
down—a dispirited army fighting by day and marching for the
James by night. Homer says he was like the ploughman who longs
for his supper after ploughing fresh land all day until his legs are
stiff—and with no thought of bathos. Their happy moment was to
eat flesh and drink wine from morning till night. Ours is a dilet-
tante appreciation not exactly sympathy. Dante meant us to believe and tremble—we disbelieve and admire. You mention so
many books that even with your swift eye I think you must skim,
relying on intuition to stop at anything important—as I should
skim through a legal document without understanding it, feeling
sure that any material passage would arrest me. It would be unusual if I finished a book of the *Odyssey* in a day. But I don't give
it very much time. I saw Winchester with a charmer, once, and
was pleased to hear the bedesman who conducted us contemporize
the Wars of the Roses. He spoke with the feeling of one telling
of the *bôches* in the late war. Tacitus I thought of as one of my
exceptions when I said the literature of the past is a bore. I went
through Rockport yesterday and saluted your street—the last time
we went by the house and even on to the rocky hill far enough to

---

[2] Leonard Craske (1882-1950); Boston sculptor of British birth.

puncture a tyre. Every acre of this Cape is an incident—I begin
to feel the approach of next term. My love to you both.

Affectionately yours, O. W. Holmes

Beverly Farms, September 6, 1925

Dear Laski: 1. The account of your bookseller at Portsmouth is
heavenly.[1] I am glad that such a man is left on Earth. 2. Arthur
Hill lends himself easily to criticism, but I think he is a very
devoted and faithful friend, with something of the difficulties common to many descendants of Roger Sherman in not [*sic*] saying
sharp rather than soothing or flattering things. 3. Miss McNaugh-
tan[2] was a friend of my friend Lady Castletown[3] and I met her at
Lady C's. She wrote me a little, I can't remember what, and I
remember did me the honor to praise a few sentences or lines from
one of those *Speeches* for a magazine article. I don't recall much
about her. I think she was cleverish and that I liked her better
when she turned up in Washington than I had in London or Ireland. 4. My literary appetites have changed somewhat with old age.
Endymion impressed me with the need of Keats for a woman.
Browning I don't care so much for as I once did. On the other
hand I get unexpected pleasure from the *Odyssey*. Obvious faults
and tiresomeness made up for by the extraordinary felicities, the
songs, the occasional tenderness (alongside of a good deal that is
far from sentimental) and one touch of mysterious terror that you
expect from the Greeks hardly more than from the French, Odyssey
XX(Υ) 345ff—when after Telemachus has spoken and the trouble
is near the suitors laugh with faces not their own, and the flesh
they eat is blood bedabbled, their eyes fill with tears, and their
hearts feel anguish. But there are a number of things to be said
about the *Odyssey* still. I am in the 23rd book and but for many
interruptions should polish it off by tomorrow. We have just had
a call from Charley Curtis[4] and his wife that gave us much pleasure.
He seems to have a prosperous destiny—I should fear too surrounded by popularity and praise to achieve great things. F.F. sent
me Haldane's review of your book which gave me great pleasure.
Not much more liberation ahead as on the 28th I go to Boston and
on the 30th to Washington. However we will interchange a few
words before then. I forget whether I held forth to you about a
statue at the head of Gloucester Harbor that moves me mightily.

Yours ever, O. W. H.

---

[1] The letter to which this is a reply has been omitted from this edition.
[2] Perhaps Sarah Macnaughtan (?   -1916); English novelist, traveler,
and war-worker.
[3] Lady Castletown (1853-1927), daughter of the Fourth Viscount
Doneraile, was an intimate Irish friend of Holmes.
[4] *Supra*, p. 20, Vol. I.

16 Warwick Gardens, 6.IX.25

My dear Justice: I have waited two or three days before answering your letter in the hope of being able to tell you that Richardson's *Milton* is found.[1] But so far, it has evaded me. I found a copy at Quaritch but without the portrait, and he told me it ought not to be difficult to find at about ten shillings. So I hope to be able to report next week that it is on the way.

. . . an afternoon with Wells and Arnold Bennett. The last was really interesting, for each was finishing a novel and they spent an hour comparing their methods. It was most interesting to hear Bennett insist that all detail is significant and that no true effect can ever be produced except by the accumulation of details. Wells on the other hand was insistent that if you want to produce your effects you must get a broad canvas and it is by painting broadly upon it that you get the impression. People, he argued, have not time for details and the things they see are the outstanding events. No, Bennett said, people appreciate in novels what they appreciate in their own lives. What happens is that they give significance to certain details; if those you select in your novel are significant then they recognise them and admire your work, *e.g.* if Tom kisses Amy and then proposes, Jones reading the book says, "Ah, I remember doing that to Joan" and straightaway gets an affection for the book. Afterwards Masterman joins us and we had a gossip about politics. From that three remarks stand out in my mind. 1. Mrs. Asquith on John Simon, "he has a sandy soul"; 2. Haldane on Winston "his heart is not equal to his mind, and his mind is not equal to his desires"; 3. Asquith on Birrell's failure in politics —"He thought it was like writing an essay in which the next page begins a new subject in a new way. In politics you never begin a new subject, and only a dictator can afford to treat it in a new way." Masterman gave a most interesting account of Asquith as head of a cabinet—lawyer-like, stating the case with such admirable balance on both sides that he was unable to convince himself on what side the decision should be made; or when a new choice of colleague had been made feeling strongly that all the under-secretaries had worked so hard that all ought to be promoted. He told also an amusing tale of Asquith and Lloyd-George. Asquith turns up at a dinner party at Downing Street during the Budget campaign of 1909 and at a dark hour for the cabinet, full of good humour. L-G complains that he looks unduly happy. Asquith impressively insists that this is one of the great days of his life. L-G (eagerly) "Have you persuaded the King to create peers?"

[1] It is probable that the reference is to Jonathan Richardson's *Explanatory Notes and Remarks on Milton's Paradise Lost* (1734) in the first edition of which was included a portrait of Milton by Jonathan Richardson, senior. (See, *supra*, p. 228, Vol. I.

Asquith—"No, but I have found the Plantin Macrobius in large-paper." L-G afterward remarks to Masterman that he had never seen such absurd pleasure in a quite irrelevant topic. Masterman also told a pleasant tale of L-G being asked to make Pollock (Sir F.) an O.M.J. "Has he been a judge?" "No." "Has he done well at the bar?" "No." "Has he been in the House?" "No." "Well, then, what on earth has he done?" Altogether, I assure you, a most pleasant afternoon. . . . *Ever affectionately yours, H. J. L.*

Beverly Farms, September 19, 1925
Dear Laski: Another good letter from you—I was much interested at the controversy between Wells and Bennett. It sounds like an echo of the old one between the French notion, also accepted in England, that elegance required statement in universals, and the later desire for local color. Probably I have called your attention to Johnson's talk about Dryden in his edition of the poets. He quotes a passage and thinks that every reader will recognize the bad taste—not, as I understand, because it is indifferent poetry but because of its mention of such things as Oakum in speaking of repairs after a battle with the Dutch. I have been wont to contrast with it, Brownell in "The Bay Fight." [1]

> "Ha, old ship! Do they thrill,
>   The brave two hundred scars
>   You got in the River Wars?
>   That were leeched with clamorous skill,
>   (Surgery savage and hard),
>   Splinted with bolt and beam,
>   Probed in scarfing and seam,
>   Rudely linted and tarred
>   With oakum and boiling pitch,
>   And sutured with splice and hitch,
>   At the Brooklyn Navy-Yard!"

Which seems to me fine. Legouvé in his recollections says that they feared that there would be an outburst in the theatre when his father in one of his plays made a character answer the question what o'clock it was: *"Minuit."* To this day the French like abstract figures, even in sculpture, of Commerce, Fame, etc. You remember the handsome figure of the Republic on their postage-stamps. I might add St. Gaudens' angels—one over Bob Shaw in his *bas relief* in Boston—one leading Sherman in New York—a striking contrast to the Sailor at the Wheel I was telling you about at the head of Gloucester harbor. I doubt if there is any formula. A man

[1] Reprinted in Henry Howard Brownell, *Lines of Battle* (Howe, ed., 1912), pp. 29, 32.

of genius hits you, whether he paints with a camel's hair brush or his thumb. This is all repetition, but I cannot resist it.

As I believe I said, I resolved not to let anything in the way of books become a duty during my last fortnight. So I am idling through Pliny's letters with renewed amusement and pleasure. R. Hale the other day gave me *Rules for Compositors and Readers at the University Press* which contains many things as to punctuation, capitals, &c. &c. that I should like to remember—I recommend it. Don't put yourself to trouble about Richardson's *Milton* with the portrait. Only remember me if you come across it. I am much entertained at the stories of Lloyd George and Asquith and am glad of your scruples at selling books you have wanted enough to buy. I am glad also at the sale of your book, and hope it will let you see Venice—but fail to convince the readers. After I get to Washington I fear that I shall make even poorer returns than I do now for your letters. Age continues to advance and I know that I shall find it hard to write much when the mosquitoes and wasps swarm around my head. My return will be a jump from as complete repose as I am capable of into a whirl of buzzing machinery. I think I told you—?—of my visit to a house in Pigeon Cove built of newspapers—made into boards by pasting and varnishing. When I was inquiring about it in Gloucester and I mentioned that I always went to Rockport from the Beverly Farms end (via Pigeon Cove) an old fellow said the other way is better. You naturally look to the right as you drive and going from Rockport you look upon the sea. Certainly going that way revealed new delights. One of the quarry holes was positively awe-inspiring. I rather hope for a drive around by Bass Rocks this afternoon. *Macte virtute puer.*

Ever yours, O. W. H.

Washington, D.C., October 13, 1925
Dear Laski: Even after this long time it is only by neglect of duty that I can write a word. The work has been more pressing than ever. On Saturday last our Conference lasted from 12 to after 7 —we disposed of 60 *certioraris* as well as 7 argued and submitted cases and outside matters. This week there are 50 *certioraris*. I have written an opinion—and there are a lot of cases to be examined. Everybody seems in fair condition but I think it has been a mistake to press things so hard. It wouldn't matter if we disposed of only 20 *certioraris* a week as far as I see. Of course I have read nothing but cases and have seen nobody. Felix and his wife supped with us before we left and seemed cheerful and well. I have had two delightful letters from you[1] since I last wrote and hope for more—but I can't earn them while things are as they are now. An

---

[1] Omitted from this edition.

adjournment will come before long. This is only an explanation.
I don't see but I stand it as well as any of the others but if this
kept on long at this pace some one would break down.

Aff'ly yours, O. W. H.

16 Warwick Gardens, 4.X.25
My dear Justice: . . . a visit to Cambridge where I had to speak.
. . . I saw in the Library of Trinity with great reverence the mss
of Newton, and Thomson pointed out to me that, broadly speaking, he had laid down the outlines of all his great discoveries by
the time he was thirty. It is, I think, an interesting fact that
whereas in literature, politics and philosophy the great discoveries
are usually made by men of middle age, in physics, mathematics
and music the big steps are taken, even if they are not proved, by
comparatively young men; and these spend their later years in
working out the consequences of a big early intuition. So, also,
lawyers usually bloom late. Maitland was forty before he had
achieved anything of consequence; Montesquieu was fifty-four
when he published the *Esprit*; Savigny was in middle age when
his great book appeared; and Holmes, J. was forty when he published *The Common Law.* Is it because in humanistic studies the
factor of personal experience is an inescapable ultimate? Yet with
the poets the flash of insight seems unrelated to age. Keats was
scaling Shakesperean heights at twenty and so was Shelley. It is a
fascinating business on which the psychologist ought to embark. . . .   *Ever affectionately yours, H. J. L.*

Washington, D.C., October 18, 1925
Dear Laski: It still is impossible to write a decent letter or do
more than send a bulletin and thank you for yours. I am interested
by your comparison of the ages of production in different regions.
I should be inclined to qualify. I think it is very unusual, if a
man has original ideas of life, or some branch of it, for him not to
have shown them before 40. Kant and Montesquieu whom you
mention I think both had, although they got out their big books
later. Of course, something must be allowed for the fact that by
40 a man's direction and occupation generally are found. I know
that I was superstitious enough to hurry to get my book out before
my 40th birthday. When later I wondered whether it was coward-
ice to stick to the job when I had got my general ideas, (one chap
said it was), I reflected that it takes ten years to master a new
subject and that one could not bargain that at 80 one would still
have vivid reactions. Also, I remembered (I am not sure that I
quote correctly) *"une pensée de jeunesse executée dans l'age mûr,"*

and the need to make a living. No doubt similar considerations
keep others from new fields. I am glad I stuck to the law for I
think part of the business is to apply one's general mode of thought
to details. Apropos of your talk of Hazlitt and his times (I will try
to remember to get the book you name) I think that the most tremendous two lines that were written by any man jack of them
came from the second-rate (as commonly thought) Southey:

> Four gentlemen in a parlour
> All silent and all damned.

DeQuincey quotes it somewhere, I don't know where, or where it
is in Southey, but my memory can't be wrong about the author.[1]
Identify the place and be blessed by me—(as you are anyhow).

> *Affectionately yours, O. W. Holmes*

Have you seen W. Lippmann's new book? Very vivid and I think
full of sense and insight.

> *16 Warwick Gardens, 1.XI.25*

My dear Justice: . . . I have lived fast and furiously this last
fortnight. A visit to Sheffield to lecture to the civil service there;
a visit to Manchester as a member of a board to choose a new
professor of history; a lecture to the Fabian Society; the writing
of a long memorandum for Slesser, the late S-G, on sedition for
his guidance in the present communist case;[1] and a long and difficult notice to do of the life and letters of Marshall the economist[2]
—these in addition to the normal routine have been a big job. But
at least I am out of the wood and for six whole weeks now, I
have a perfectly free time outside the university. Also (very privately) the university has now decided to create, for the first time,
a full-time university chair in political science which will go to
me as of next August. I am rather happy about this as it will put

---

[1] See DeQuincey, "Dinner, Real and Reputed." The reference is to the
stanza in the first published version of Wordsworth's "Peter Bell" (which
was dedicated to Southey). This stanza Wordsworth deleted from later editions of the poem. The lines in question were as follows:

> "Is it a party in a parlour?
> Cramm'd just as they on earth were cramm'd—
> Some sipping punch, some sipping tea,
> But as you by their faces see,
> All silent and all damn'd."

[1] In mid-October twelve leading Communists had been arrested, charged
with a conspiracy to publish seditious libels and to incite mutiny in the
armed forces. In late November the case came to trial before Mr. Justice
Swift, and was concluded with a conviction of all the defendants and the
imposition of sentences of six months and twelve months imprisonment. Sir
Henry Slesser (1883-   ), who became Lord Justice of Appeal in 1929,
was one of counsel for the defendants in the case. See Slesser, *Judgment
Reserved* (n.d.), 175 *et seq.*

[2] The review has not been identified.

in my hands the organisation of political teaching through all the
universities and also (no light boon) add nearly forty per cent to
my salary and so free me from the need to review books and such
like. To which I add the joy (to me) of the fact that my *Grammar
of Politics* is to be translated into German. Forgive my song of
petty triumphs; but if these things are not shared with friends
what is the good of them?

    . . . Walter Lippmann sent me his new book[3] and I read it
with appreciation. Its style I thought exquisite, but the thesis
seemed to me merely a repetition of his *Public Opinion* and, like
all he writes, strong only on the analytic side. When he comes to
synthesis and positive suggestion he seems invariably to break
down. Also I read in ms a book by Bertrand Russell on education[4]
which with much wrongheadedness seemed to me very suggestive.
He has sheer genius for getting at the heart of a subject and
though there is something impish, like Puck, about his mind, he
really is a most attractive fellow.

    My love to you both. Take care of yourselves so that we can
talk at length next March.   *Ever affectionately yours, H. J. L.*

                         Washington, D.C., November 13, 1925
Dear Laski: Your letter relieves me from what was becoming an
anxiety, it was so long since I had heard from you. We had a
month of very hard work followed by a three weeks' adjournment
just drawing to an end and to be followed by sitting for a month.
But I think it unlikely that the rest of the time should be as hard
as the beginning, unless possibly the very end. I have had only
three opinions to write in the recess[1] and not much outside business
and therefore have had a little leisure though less than it sounds
as there are a good many things to attend to including the examination of the opinions sent round. I haven't been able to read
much. Charley and Richard Curtis's book on *Hunting in Africa*—
very prepossessing—a posthumous publication of papers by Emerson, Natural History of the Intellect &c—the old man still charms
me, and a queer book that I haven't quite finished *Michael Neo-
Palaeologus, his Memoirs, by his Father Stephen N. Palaeologus.*
You may call it an analysis of talking and thinking, very amusing
in its illustrations and not without some keenness, though he
touches themes that I imagine the philosophers have handled better, and when he criticizes, his examples I think seem to neglect

----

[3] *The Phantom Public* (1925).

[4] *Education and the Good Life* (1926).

[1] On November 16 Holmes delivered the Court's opinion in *Old Dominion
Land Co.* v. *United States,* 269 U.S. 55; *Western Union* v. *Georgia, id.* 67;
and *Hicks* v. *Guiness, id.* 71.

what he insists on, that you read in some particular atmosphere, generally taken for granted, and that makes what he finds fault with plain enough—but a stimulating, tickling book. I hope you will go slow if you write about political appointments. The political appointments here, those most obviously so, have been Marshall, Taney and Story, and I suppose Chase.[2] Your Chancellors don't make a bad showing. The chances are, I am afraid, that men who are of the abstract type only exceptionally prove wise in practical affairs. I used to think that it raised a presumption against a young man if he was predominantly interested in the philosophy and theory of the business, which you will admit was a disinterested judgment. Going back to appointments, I suppose you might call Taft's a political appointment, and taking everything into account it was the best that could have been made. He works hard, keeps everything moving, and gets the work done with good temper and humor. His political associations I suppose made it easier to get passed a bill remodelling our jurisdiction (drawn by the judges)[3] that was very important and I think will work well. I don't know what the influences were that led Taft to name White. I never have ventured to ask him. White certainly was an unusually powerful man though not a good writer and I hardly think as well fitted for the bench (where Cleveland put him) as for the Senate which he left. I suppose the Catholics were behind him. I know nothing about Watson whom you name except the name. I didn't know that he was to be regarded as one of the greater figures. I was driven years ago to the conclusion that political considerations had not hurt the character of appointments here and probably not with you. (Even as I write an opinion is handed to me from the C.J. on which I must be ready to recite before the conference tomorrow.)

I have had a few motor drives that have let me see the foliage and the River and Rock Creek—low three days ago and today a boiling torrent and generally I have got into condition for another bout. I get so soaked in law while I am here that I feel as if I had no ideas outside of it. I am delighted by what you tell me of your prospects and that your book is to be translated into German. You needn't fear that I don't sympathize with your triumphs. The better part of a year ago some one wrote proposing on behalf of another Mussoo to translate my *Common Law* into French but I have heard no more of it. Perhaps they expected me to fork out something. Then a man writes to me requesting in soapy terms what he calls an autographed photograph. I reflect that I am not

---

[2] Salmon P. Chase (1808-1873) was Lincoln's appointee as Chief Justice, succeeding Taney.

[3] See Frankfurter and Landis, *The Business of the Supreme Court* (1928), Chapter VII.

willing to pay a dollar for a compliment and, if I answer, regret
my inability. Don't you think it damned cheek? It is not uncommon. Well, dear boy, if I am to work I must go out now as it looks
threatening. My homage to your wife.   *Aff'ly yours, O. W. H.*

Washington, D.C., November 29, 1925
My dear Laski: Your letter[1] came this morning. Obedient to duty
I spent the day in writing my opinion in a case assigned last night,
and that being done I turn to you. *Imprimis.* After some delay I
received Hazlitt's *Spirit of the Age* which I ordered as directed
by you weeks or months ago. I am taking great pleasure in reading it, but I wonder if you don't a little overrate him. He is cultivated, discriminating and very clever but he hardly, it seems to
me, has the *ut de poitrine* which in one way or another a man
must have to live long. I mean either some important originality or
charm. That said to clear my conscience, I repeat that here as in
former books he gives me great pleasure—especially perhaps, here.
It is quite moving to read such account of men whose books are
well known but whom he seems to have known in person. He
sometimes seems like a superior interviewer and goes a little beyond good breeding, but it is mighty interesting to look even
through a keyhole on such great men. *Secundo.* Don't make a mistake about Stone. He is a mighty sound and liberal-minded thinker.
In the case to which I suppose you to refer he thought as I did
but also that that no countenance should be given to the notion
that the decisions of the Court were subject to a change of personnel and therefore refrained from joining in my declaration.[2] I
certainly am not prepared to say that he was wrong. *Tertio.* I am
interested by your having fallen in with Mark Rutherford. I can't
recite on him now, but I remember being a good deal stirred by
him I suppose forty years ago when he first appeared, at least
among us. Unless I am mistaken a man confined to the deadening
job of writing in ledgers somehow drew even from that experience
a theory of life—but what, I now know not. You also interest me
very much by saying that Hobbes did much to form Bossuet, but
it is Orphic to me. I remember too little even to understand.

I will take a big envelope and enclose a newspaper reproduction
of a photograph we just have had taken. My wife thinks that I
look sick and bored. I don't know that I was either, especially—
but I do not think it a great success. Still, it is the latest news such

---

[1] Omitted from this edition.
[2] On October 10 the Court, in a *per curiam* decision, had affirmed the
decision of a lower federal court that the Arizona minimum wage statute was
unconstitutional. Holmes had concurred solely because he considered the
Adkins case (261 U.S. 525) controlling. Brandeis, J., dissented. Mr. Justice
Stone evidently concurred with the majority. *Murphy* v. *Sardell,* 269 U.S. 530.

as it is. I have listened with amusement to an autobiography of Marshall,[3] the late Vice President, a very kindly and rather humorous man—not great, but sensible and good, with perhaps a touch of the bitterness that seems more characteristic of Democrats than of Republicans. I used to spot them by that when I was student in the Law School. I dunno but I mentioned a life of Lord Timothy Dexter[4]—a half or wholly cracked man of Newburyport who bought my great-grandfather's house there, as the Jackson fortunes went down and the Dexter ditto went up. He made money by sending warming pans to the West Indies and cats to some oriental cat centre, and there are many queer things that tickle one who has my local interest. *Neo-Palaeologus* I know I mentioned. That really did amuse me, but I am all law now and for three weeks to come. I hope your letters will come regularly to save a remnant of my soul.   *Affectionately yours, O. W. Holmes*

16 Warwick Gardens, November 21, 1925
My dear Justice: . . . I have been out a little since I wrote to you last. First a dinner at Haldane's, where we discoursed much about current topics and, a little, about philosophy. Bertrand Russell was there, and I was glad to hear him say that Morris Cohen was, in his view, quite the ablest philosopher now writing in America. He did not seem to think very much of John Dewey whom I have been told to admire, but find unreadable. And we had a fine set-to over Keyserling's *Diary* which Haldane and Dean Inge praised and Haldane especially. . . .

In between whiles I have been several times to the Communist trial.[1] The government, I think, has a very poor case unless the jury is passionately prejudiced. Most of the exhibits are simply translations of official Russian documents, reproduced without comment; others are appeals not to shoot the workers, of the usual sort; in no case could one apply your *Abrams* test[2] and get a verdict of guilty. But I doubt whether that test is applicable to the English law of sedition which, since 1852, has had little or no chance

---

[3] *Recollections of Thomas R. Marshall* (1925).

[4] By John P. Marquand.

[1] Laski wrote of the trial in 45 *New Republic* 183 (Jan. 6, 1926), and the Manchester *Guardian*, Dec. 11, 1925.

[2] Dissenting in *Abrams* v. *United States*, 250 U.S. 616, 628 (1919), Holmes had urged that "it is only the present danger of immediate evil or an intent to bring it about that warrants Congress in setting a limit to the expression of opinion where private rights are not concerned." He had gone on to say that "we should be eternally vigilant against attempts to check the expression of opinions that we loathe and believe to be fraught with death, unless they so imminently threaten immediate interference with the lawful and pressing purposes of the law that an immediate check is needed to save the country." *Id.* at p. 630.

of making effective criteria. The judge is handsome but ignorant and I think will not affect the case a great deal. I will firmly believe all my life in the glory of the jury-system if only these men get off. I hate their doctrines but they are as harmless as men could be. And it might make our Home Secretary,[3] who wants to be another Sidmouth, resign.

Our love to you both. Please give me an hour of your first real leisure.   *Ever affectionately yours, H. J. L.*

Washington, D.C., December 5, 1925

My dear Laski: A delightful letter from you made me feel badly about my enforced silence, but you will have received two letters at least from me before this—written when the anguish abated. I am rather pleased at what you say about John Dewey—whom I have supposed myself bound to revere, and have revered, but have not read—except in matters of no great moment or impressiveness. I have not read a word of Keyserling—F.F. praises him —I know that you are capable of prejudice and you sent me a rather Philistine notice of him—so I suspend my judgment (but shall not read). I respect your stomach for long-winded books. I fear that even Boswell would have a hard time with me in these days. Mrs. Piozzi's little book[1] is good reading however. The only thing that I have had time for since Hazlitt is a little *Manual of Year Book Studies* by Bolland—no giant I should judge but a pleasant discourse on his theme. Maitland, whom I do not mention with hushed breath as you do, but whom I think I sufficiently appreciate, among other effects, has made writers on the lesser mercies of history attempt at least a certain spriteliness unknown in earlier learned. I listen at night to various things that I hardly feel authorized to add to my list of books read but that give me a smattering—the autobiography of Vice President Marshall (a good little man not without sense—but a democrat, bitter I should think, as too many democrats are). I believe I spoke of this before —just now it is the last novel by the author of *Main Street.* It grow harder every day for me to remember names—*Arrowsmith,* it comes back just in time. I write my weekly opinion this week delayed a little by Einstein, our minister to Czechoslovakia, coming to luncheon and the British Ambassador calling later. He puts

[3] Since November 1924, Sir William Joynson-Hicks (1865-1932), later first Viscount Brentford, had been Secretary of State for home affairs. His action against the Communists was reminiscent of many of the efforts which Henry Addington (1757-1844), first Viscount Sidmouth, had taken as Home Secretary from 1817 to 1819 when he sought to bring the law of seditious libel to bear upon the disgruntled laboring classes.
[1] Hester Lynch Piozzi, *Anecdotes of the Late Samuel Johnson* (1786).

us on to *Arrowsmith* and I have squared it by directing a copy of
Leave It to Psmith to be sent to him with my card. Last night
Lepaulle (do you remember him at the Law School?) dined here
(alas I have come to hating to have to put on a boiled shirt and
togs)—he was very pleasant and suggestive—*inter alia* made a
striking presentation of the French procedure in the trial of facts
—that made it sound far superior to ours. Though Brandeis doesn't
believe it.

Frankfurter in a recent letter spoke of having to have an operation on his knee. I couldn't exactly make out what—he spoke
lightly of it but it made me uneasy. As to the *Life of Lincoln* why
not wait for Beveridge? If he could get any encouragement to
chuck it for politics I believe he would, in spite of his wife and
me, but happily his fellow citizens don't seem to need him just yet.
He gets cast down on his job, and I don't know whether it is worth
doing—but I think that if he does it he will make a pretty big
thing of it. My assignment of a case to write has come since the
last word.[2] It will be easy. It grazes the matter of sovereignty that
you have such difficulties in grasping—but unfortunately not so
as to raise any question that might let in a little light. As you
may gather from this, I am well and cheerful in spite of cheerless
weather. I assume that you are when you don't say the contrary
but I should like to have you state it as I always am afraid you
run your machine too hard—but I have great confidence in your
wife—to whom my homage. *Affectionately yours, O. W. Holmes*

                                        16 Warwick Gardens, 1.XII.25
My dear Justice: Your delightful letter[1] and the photograph of the
Court greeted me this morning to cheer up the worst fog I have
ever known in London. I agree with Mrs. Holmes. It makes you
look wan and tired. But even more was I impressed by the change
in Brandeis who appears thin and sad. Have you noticed that, or
is it my imagination? . . .

Since I wrote last week I think the most interesting thing I have
done was to take the chair at a discussion of a philosophical society on Criminal Responsibility. The protagonists were Travers
Humphreys,[2] one of our best criminal lawyers, and a Dr. Hislop
[*sic*],[3] a great mental specialist. There was no doubt in my mind
that the lawyer had the best of it. The medicals spoke passionately

---

[2] *White* v. *Mechanics Securities Corp.,* 269 U.S. 283 (Dec. 14, 1925).

[1] *Supra,* p. 62.

[2] Sir Travers Humphreys (1867-1956) became Judge of the King's Bench
Division in 1928.

[3] Theophilus Bulckeley Hyslop (1863-1933), distinguished practitioner
and author of numerous works on abnormal psychology and medicine.

of "uncontrollable impulses" and such like; Humphreys always drove them back to the the vital point of getting definitions which could be explained by a judge to an average jury, and I thought he showed admirably that the refinements of psychological analysis are not yet ripe for legal use. I suggested that their results might be made available to the judge for the purpose of sentence. Humphreys warmly agreed; but the doctors wanted to dictate from the witness box and the idea of advice did not seem to them adequate. . . .

I have picked up some pretty trifles this last week, though nothing to set the Thames on fire. But what did please me much was an attic adventure where the old bookseller, who was quite blind, was assisted by his daughter. I told him the names of things I wanted and if he had it he told me the shelf on which I could find it, the approximate place on the shelf, and the price marked on the fly-leaf. He was a wonderful old boy; had been a bookseller for fifty years, and every Sunday in the seventies used to stand at the corner of Cheyne Walk in the hope of seeing Carlyle set out on his Sunday walk. Once the old sage was accompanied by Fitzjames Stephen and the latter, said my friend, was so vehement in his gestures that Carlyle had to walk slightly behind in order not to be hit. Another good tale he told me was of Austin Dobson coming in and asking if he had a really bad novel, badly written. "Why a bad novel, Mr. Dobson?" "Oh! I have just read Henry James's latest and I want to recover from perfection of style." And he told me of Dobson's remark to James when the latter said he had been lost in the Maze at Hampton Court. "I am surprised at that," said Dobson, "I should have thought you would have felt that you were in the middle of one of your own sentences." I had, as you can guess, a delightful time with the old fellow. I found a common chord in his joy in quite useless knowledge. I promised to go again as he has stories of Ruskin he wants to revive.

My love warmly to you both. *Ever affectionately yours, H. J. L.*

Washington, D.C., December 17, 1925

My dear Laski: In answer to your last I don't think Brandeis seems otherwise than well and cheerful in these later days. As to your doctors and judges on uncontrollable impulse I think the short answer is that the law establishes certain minima of social conduct that a man must conform to at his peril. Of course as I said in my book it bears most hardly on those least prepared for it, but that is what it is for. I am entirely impatient of any but broad distinctions. Otherwise we are lost in the maze of determinism. If I were having a philosophical talk with a man I was going to have hanged (or electrocuted) I should say, I don't doubt that your act was inevitable for you but to make it more avoidable by others we propose to sacrifice you to the common good. You may regard yourself as a soldier dying for your country if you like. But the law must keep its promises. I fear that the touch of sentiment that I notice in your political writing will be revolted at this, but personally I feel neither doubt nor scruple. I delight in your account of your old bookseller and also at Dobson's remarks to Harry James apropos of being lost in the maze. We adjourned on Monday for two or three weeks and my work is done except some further study on a postponed case. I have had real intellectual pleasure with my cases this term. They have been sufficiently interesting and to write them shortly and compactly with a hint at general theory when possible is good sport. The Chief called me up by telephone to know if a case that he proposed to assign to me would be too troublesome. I told him that if he spared me in that way I ought to leave. He gave me the case and I polished it off in short metre. I always say, and probably have said to you, there is no such thing as a hard case. There may be bothers from complex facts but when you have mastered them one question of law is much like another. I wish you were here to tell me just what book I want, to fill the approaching vacuum. That vacuum is always tomorrow for each day brings a lot of jobs. This p.m. I am to have a call from Miss Elizabeth Shepley Sergeant on a letter from Frankfurter.[1] I know that she has written for the *New Republic* but I can't recite. She says she wants to talk of something. I know not what. If it is for me to do anything, I won't. I am interrupted by a telephone from my secretary who is attending a meeting as to the proposed inclusion of I Street between 17th and 18th in the commercial zone, which of course, I oppose. It hasn't been reached yet. I wrote a letter saying that I hoped to die here where I have lived for twenty years, that we were too old to establish a new residence and that I thought making this business would be bad for health and the official work I do at home. Whether I shall soften the heart of that Commission in cooperation with neighbors I know not. These realtors, as they call themselves, I presume are influential. My wife thinks they want to drive us all up Cathedral way but I expect to hang on here, business or not. I have listened to *Arrowsmith* at first with *ennui*, then with interest, in the end with admiration—a pretty big chap, the author seems to me. But, Oh dear me, I wish I knew the quintessential book that would give me vital juices.

Affectionately yours, O. W. Holmes

[1] The fruit of this first meeting was the biographical sketch by Miss Sergeant, "Justice Touched with Fire," first published in the *New Republic,* later in her volume *Fire under the Andes* (1927), reprinted in *Mr. Justice Holmes* (Frankfurter, ed., 1931).

16 Warwick Gardens, 12.XII.25

My dear Justice: . . . I enclose a brief note of mine from the Manchester *Guardian* which, I think, has its points.[1] We are having big demonstrations all over the country against the Communist conviction, so that at least the idea of free speech is not dying easily. And we end on Monday with a vast demonstration here in London. I, heaven be thanked, have just finished term, and can sit down to a month of peace. I want to write two articles for Harvard and Michigan—the first on the *Poplar* case[2] and the second on judicial appointment.[3] . . .

Our warm greetings and love to both of you. Three months from the time you receive this I hope to be embarking at Southampton.

Ever affectionately yours, Harold J. L.

Washington, D.C., December 27, 1925

Dear Laski: Your last letter had the slip from the Manchester *Guardian* in which you express views that I need not say I also take with devout conviction. Of course I am pleased with your reference to what I have said. It is almost superfluous to send my wishes for a happy new year to you and yours as I have the same wish all the time. You mention Gray's letters. I read them some years ago with a certain pleasure—few letters give a great deal, to me, at least. Your other books (on Walsingham and Ogg and Ray) I know not. Lives of great men or others I don't read when I can help it. I prefer the abstract. I wrote to F.F. the other day that Brandeis had an insatiable appetite for facts and that I hate them except as pegs for generalizations, but I admire the gift and wish I had a barn in which I could store them for use at need. I hope they manure my soil but they disappear in specie as soon as taken in. Have I ever given you my ultimatum on human speculation? We begin with an empirical fact—that is gossip. We go on to make it part of philosophy by formulating laws. At the end we have more or less of a system, showing that the Universe acts thus and not otherwise. But the universe so given is only an empirical fact. Why it should be as it is—why there shouldn't be two stars more in a vacant space—why it should be at all, we know not, and so

---

[1] The December 12 issue of the Manchester *Guardian* published a short paper of Laski's "What is 'Sedition'?" in which he urged enactment of a pending bill which, adopting Holmes's principle of "clear and present danger," sought to make seditious utterances punishable only if they threatened immediate harm.

[2] "Judicial Review of Social Policy in England: A Study of *Roberts* v. *Hopwood*," 39 *Harv. L. Rev.* 832 (May 1926). In the *Poplar* case the House of Lords sustained the determination of a District Auditor that wages of municipal employees should be reduced as the cost of living declined.

[3] "The Technique of Judicial Appointment," 24 *Mich. L. Rev.* 529 (April 1926).

we end as we began, with gossip. Just now I am filling the crevices
of leisure with *Why We Behave like Human Beings,* by George
A. Dorsey (previously unknown to me), a stimulating summary
of man, but one of the things worth doing but not worth doing
well. There is so much technical language, so much that needs
diagrams to make it clear, that I satisfy myself with the general
drift and don't bother about details. Still I don't know when I
have read a book that seemed so effectively to put man in his
right place. Also vivid to the point of slang and very colloquial.
I would far rather read a book like that than the life of anybody.
I hope to finish it today and then to take up a book sent to me by
Walter Lippmann, *Science and the Modern World,* by A. N.
Whitehead, which I hope will stir up my monkeys, though the
titles to chapters suggest some reserves. But I haven't much time
left. Tomorrow (Monday) a conference (as Saturday was a holiday) probably a lot of opinions coming in to be read and a week
from tomorrow a month or more's sitting begins. I learn from
Dorsey that Watson argues that thinking is action in a certain
motor mechanism, and later, that he calls it *laryngeal itch,* which
tickles even if it doesn't illuminate. I have finished the volume
since this letter began. While he freely criticizes what is, his suggestions or exhortation for the future I find a little vague beyond
perhaps cultivating a free spirit in yourself and other people. At
least he does not afflict me with the shuddering *ennui* that I feel
at many ideals of the day.

I have peeped into Whitehead. I see on the title page that he
is professor of philosophy in Harvard College. I know not exactly
why but that diminishes my expectation of being hit where I live.
I think it is the Professor of Philosophy and not the Harvard College that raises the doubts. Yet Cohen is a professor of philosophy
and he can hit me where I live. I am so glad to hear all the good
things you say and quote about him. I firmly believe that he deserves them, yet I still wonder whether he will adequately articulate himself. As to the Whitehead I await developments. Chapters
entitled God, and Religion and Sciences excite my suspicions. I
read a political article of yours in the *New Republic* that impressed me.[1]

    Macte virtute puer.   *Affectionately yours, O. W. Holmes*

16 Warwick Gardens, 20.XII.25
My dear Justice: First of all, the happiest of possible New Years
to you both. I shall, I am almost certain, see you before its first
quarter is over. I expect to sail on March 20th on the *Berengaria.*

---

[1] "Mr. Baldwin's First Year in Office," 45 *New Republic* 103 (Dec. 16,
1925).

I shall stay just three weeks and have a week each, or thereabouts, in New York, Boston and Washington. In your city, I propose to stay at the Cosmos Club, and to be invited by you to dinner each night except once which I must devote to Brandeis. But I think it will be far less bother to you to say definitely now that I shan't stay at 1720 as that will only cause Mrs. Holmes much and un-necessary worry. Is this agreed?

. . . I had a visit to Oxford to poor Vinogradoff's funeral. I liked him a good deal, though he was absurdly pompous and a little like Pound in the possession of an omnivorous appetite for useless or repetitive learning. But his *Villainage in England* was a good book and, *après tout*, he started Maitland on the great jour-ney. But he never did enough to justify his learning and he had the bad habit of putting people on to little problems which stunted their imaginations at the stage where it ought to be luxuriant. I remember when I was an under-graduate, he offered to get me a research fellowship if I would devote three years to a statistical study of the Derbyshire Domesday and was indignant when I refused. But he was a real stimulus to legal research in this country and will be sadly missed. I must not forget to tell you that I went on Tuesday to hear Sir F. Pollock on the need for a philosophy of law. He was really admirable, not easy or fluent in delivery but always suggestive and with the grace of charm in the pushing of his ideas. He put some people high who bore me, *e.g.* Kohler, and some men higher who are, I think, just good pedestrians *e.g.* Holdsworth, but in general he was very stimulating and for a man of 75 the freshness and vigour of his mind were really remarkable. I add the note of a pleasant lunch with John Burns who told me that Cave, J. after his acquittal for sedition in 1886 wrote to him to say that politicians spent their lives in a moral sedition which only did not become legal because the Attorney-General was ex-pected to have a Christian temper. . . .

My love to you both. Please be fit and well *circa* the Ides of March.   *Ever affectionately yours, H. J. L.*

VI

1926-1927

Dear Laski: A happy New Year to you. It is delightful to think that you will be here. I agree with you that it would not be best for us to attempt to put you up. Among other reasons, you would have to climb so many stairs, but you will share our victuals at convenient moments and we will talk. And you shall have one more chance to see light on sovereignty. In actual fact I wouldn't think it possible for us to disagree had you not said that you thought *Kawananakoa* v. *Polyblank*[1] wrong. That chap Zane said that no one who thought it right could hope to be a lawyer,[2] while I categorically and brutally think that one who doesn't think it right (I mean in the general aspects) simply doesn't understand what he is talking about.

Your friend Smellie[3] called yesterday and took luncheon here today. I enjoyed seeing him very much and learned only by accident that he was a "thin red 'ero" and had lost both feet in the war. Another man, Gates,[4] was here just before, from Frankfurter, whom also I liked greatly. But I have spasms of shame after I have seen these fellows to think of having repeated all my old chestnuts to them. Yet if we worried about repeating ourselves who should escape?

I didn't know Vinogradoff was dead. I don't think him a great loss to the world of thought, judging by what I have read of his

---

[1] *Supra*, p. 52.

[2] *Supra*, pp. 132-33, Vol. I.

[3] Kingsley Bryce Speakman Smellie (1897-   ), political scientist at the London School of Economics, was a Rockefeller student at the Harvard Law School, 1925-26.

[4] Sylvester Gates, an Oxford graduate, was currently a special student at the Harvard Law School.

writing, but I agree that his *Villainage in England* was a good book. He was the first to print what I had noticed, the reappearance of the *festuca* etc.[5] in the manorial ceremonies.

I should have liked to hear Pollock on the need for a philosophy of law. You speak of him as a man of 75, or, qu. Ms? 78. He has just celebrated his 80th birthday and I have congratulated him as an infant just appearing through the trap door in the upper story of the old.

I haven't had time to read Warren's volume 4 about our Court.[6] The other three I thought as good as could be from anyone except a very superior and penetrating intellect which I hardly think Warren has. I should call them first rate.

I read Whitehead's *Science and the Modern World.* It seemed to me obscurely written, perhaps not so to mathematicians and it did not change my view of the universe. He's a clever man, but I doubt if he wields a thunderbolt. . . .

Smollett I haven't read since you were born. I thought him rather dull I believe in former days.

Tomorrow morning we take a dry dive into a longish sitting, with its concomitant prepossessions. On looking at the schedule I see that we sit during the first three weeks of March. March 22 begins a 3 weeks recess, which I hope will be propitious for your visit. I can almost say *à bientôt.*   *Yours ever, O. W. H.*

---

16 Warwick Gardens, 9.I.26

My dear Justice: . . . Maurice Amos and I dined the other night with Haldane and the latter was recounting with a somewhat serene air the things that had made him contented with life. He had read philosophy; he had met the best minds of his generation; he had helped in some big events; and he had never passed an important dish at a public dinner. I wish I could picture to you the smile of happy benevolence on Haldane's tubby face as this grand climax came out. Amos said he felt that he ought to recite the *nunc dimittis.* Since I came back I have done but little beyond these things; but a bookshop adventure may interest you. I am talking to its owner, a man of about fifty. Suddenly a white-haired old fellow certainly around eighty approaches him. "Are you Mr. Bailey?" "Yes." "Mr. Angus Bailey?" "Yes?" "Don't you know me?" "No." (a little doubtfully). "I'm your Uncle Ezra who went to Australia fifty-eight years ago; and if your father's still alive

---

[5] Vinogradoff had noted the similarity between the rituals of enfeoffment in manorial courts with those observed in Frankish law. *Villainage in England* 372 *et seq.*

[6] Charles Warren's *Congress, the Constitution, and the Supreme Court* (1925) was not a fourth volume of his *Supreme Court in United States History* (3 vols., 1922).

I'm not coming into the shop." Luckily the father was dead and
so the old man did come in. But the nephew later told me the
history. The two brothers were members of the same Baptist chapel
and quarrelled violently (about 1865) about anti-paedobaptism.
They dissolved partnership and one went to Australia. They never
spoke or wrote to each other in the interval. Their sons and daughters met, and the English nephew's son was actually married to
the granddaughter of the old Australian gentleman. I had a chat
with him—utterly bewildered by London, amazed and chagrined
to find that Darwin (whom he regarded as a blasphemer) was
buried in Westminster Abbey. The greatest man in 19th century
England was Spurgeon, Australia was morally a bad country; the
Presbyterians and Romans have it in their grip. He wasn't keen to
stay in England. He had heard that in Iowa the Baptists were
very powerful and he thought he would go out there and start a
religious bookshop. He was a game old boy who asked me what
I was and when I told him at once said with fierce simplicity
"Another of them mucky Atheists?" He regarded research into
natural science as sin. Poverty was one's own fault and Herbert
Spencer (just dawning when he left England) ought to have been
living. He was as young in spirit as when he left England and he
fought at the crack of the pistol. Once I said that things change
—"Yes, young man, but God's truths don't change." I left him
walking back to his lodgings like an old Covenanter—a magnificent spectacle.

My love to you both.   *Ever affectionately yours, H. J. L.*

16 Warwick Gardens, 17.I.26
My dear Justice: . . . two books I have read with great pleasure,
both by the same man. One is a *History of Political Science since
Plato* (R. H. Murray) and the other the *Political Consequences of
the Reformation*. They are both what I should call informing
books, written from a full mind and a large heart, and the second,
especially, has the great merit of making things clear that otherwise seem entangled and complex. Also he is a devout Austinian
who accepts as obvious the conclusions of Holmes, J. in the *Polyblank* case, so he will give you especial comfort, even though,
thereby, he reveals to me the one channel of weakness in his mind.
And I have been reading for the first time Burton's *Anatomy of
Melancholy* and really liking it as an ideal book for bed-purposes.
Queer and distorted that world is, but there is an ability pungently
to reflect which is impressive. Also Vauvenargues, whom I find
delightful and I pray you to procure a volume of his *Maximes*,
preferably without editorial embellishments, and ask yourself if he
was not the wisest man since Bacon. I admire endlessly that

French gift of packing a lifetime's experience into a phrase; and he certainly had it in full measure. Also he is one up to Voltaire; for when the young and unknown army captain sent a sheaf of mss to the great man he struck the table with his fist and proclaimed genius on the spot. I mentioned this to Birrell who at once retorted that it is dangerous; he had done it once and the man next year got penal servitude for embezzling from his female admirers. Whence, said Birrell, I have been led to demand proofs of a sober life, preferably married, before I eulogise unduly in the public press. . . .

I lunched yesterday at his kind suggestion with Lewis Einstein and found him entirely delightful. He gave me a good report of you, and I forgot time in the energy of discussion. He reminded me much of a balanced and more cultured Arthur Hill; and I was charmed by the interest he retained in what ought to have been his life-work. . . .

You notice that I have changed the format of these letters,[1] in the belief that it may give you aid and comfort in reading them. I'm glad my general American plan fits your views. I begin to get really excited about it, even to the point of anger when cynical friends say that the State Department will not give me a *visé*. But I shall be in America on March 27 if I have to swim over.

My love warmly to you both,   *Ever affectionately yours, H. J. L.*

Washington, D.C., January 29, 1926

Dear Laski: Two letters from you, delightful as usual, this week. The last this morning. I could not answer at the drop of the hat because I was so busy with the work here. But a recess comes on Monday, and all my opinions are written, up to date. Do you know I really am bothered by the old difference between us, if there is one, as to sovereignty, because as I understand the question it seems to me one that does not admit of argument. The thing to which I refer has nothing to do with the difficulty of finding out who the sovereign is, or the tacitly recognized *de facto* limits on the power of the most absolute sovereign that ever was. The issue is on this decision that you criticize, and even narrower than that. If you should say that the Courts ought in these days to assume a consent of the U.S. to be sued, or to be liable in tort on the same principle as those governing private persons, I should have my reason for thinking you wrong, but should not care, as that would be an intelligible point of difference. But what I can't understand is the suggestion that the United States is bound by law even though it does not assent. What I mean by law in this

---

[1] In this letter and the two succeeding letters Laski widened the space between the lines.

connection is that which is or should be enforced by the Courts and I can't understand how anyone should think that an instrumentality established by the United States to carry out its will, and that it can depose upon a failure to do so, should undertake to enforce something that *ex hypothesi* is against its will. It seems to me like shaking one's fist at the sky, when the sky furnishes the energy that enables one to raise the fist. There is a tendency to think of judges as if they were independent mouthpieces of the infinite, and not simply directors of a force that comes from the source that gives them their authority. I think our court has fallen into the error at times and it is that that I have aimed at when I have said that the Common Law is not a brooding omnipresence in the sky and that the U.S. is not subject to some mystic overlaw that it is bound to obey. When our U.S. Circuit Courts are backed up by us in saying that suitors have a right to their independent judgment as to the common law of a State, and so that the U.S. Courts may disregard the decisions of the Supreme Court of the State, the fallacy is illustrated. The Common Law in a State is the Common Law of that state deriving all its authority from the State, as is shown by Louisiana where it does not prevail. But the late Harlan, Day, and a majority of others have treated the question as if they were invited to speculate about *the* Common Law *in abstracto*. I repeat that if you merely mean that we ought to imply a consent until it is denied in terms, I should think you were wrong and that I was better fitted to judge of that than outsiders, but that would be a specific question for a given situation, a difference about which could create no concern.

Wednesday I had to preside *vice* the C.J. absent at a funeral and again today as he had caught a cold and was advised to keep to the house. The newspapers laid hold of it for a paragraph, and even one chap got a photograph in the literal five minutes that I gave him. It came out in the evening paper—good but looking very old. It made me realize what a hungry lot the reporters are —every trifle that will make a paragraph is, I suppose, cash to them. The other day there was a railroad accident here and they were ferocious with the doctors and the nurses in a hospital who wouldn't let them interview the damaged engineer although they were told that it was a matter of life and death to keep him undisturbed. Queer, the way in which Beck has made an impression in Europe. I am rather sorry for him. He avows disappointed ambitions, I believe. A kindly man, but of an incredible egotism. I am not sure whether he has a *naif* belief in his own misfortunes, as some think, or asserts it to keep up his courage. He is clever, too, if he would only master something. Your account of the old Scotch quasi Covenanter was fine, also your anecdote of Haldane, also what you say of Burton and Vauvenargue's *Maximes*. . . . I rejoice that you and Einstein took to each other. And I am much pleased by your discerning touch as to what "ought to have been his life work."

Your suggestion of possible trouble about coming here worries me a little. They have made troubles that seemed queer, but I have assumed (in perfect ignorance) that the exclusions came from some hint on the part of a government. If I were you I would make sure beforehand that there will be no trouble. I was remarking to Brandeis the other day that speech was freer in England than here, now, whereas in 1866 or 7 it was freer here and he mentioned some writer who had made this same observation. I noted it as the striking of a bell when under Morley's editorship the Pall Mall spoke in a matter of course way of those who did not believe in Christianity. Much later I noted the complete change since my first visit when a lady whom I took down to dinner, having just been introduced to her asked me if I believed in it, and she turned out to be a Catholic. On the other hand when my friend Henry Cowper[1] was here in '67 he said I notice that you *say* you don't believe.

Let me return for a moment to the matter of actions of tort. I hesitate as to what government should do because among other things I think the action has been a doubtful good in these days. Lawyers are on the look-out to trump up claims, which they prosecute on shares. I suspect that the substitution of a regulated insurance is a great improvement so far as it goes. With the government as it is here the trouble would be greater even than it is with the railroads. Of course the abstract proposition of justice is plain. On the general theme you must remember that I criticized Austin and dwelt on the independent sources of actual authority, before you were born, and that therefore it is no novelty to me. (The approach of 85 makes me pose as an old man. Pray for me.)

Affectionately yours, O. W. Holmes

The President is getting to be recognized as a man of wit. I have heard several things of his saying that prove it. Long ago his remark that diplomas were not wolves in sheeps clothing looked that way. Stone, a good man, told me how he wished he had made a note of some of his sayings that he heard when Attorney General.

16 Warwick Gardens, 23.I.26

My dear Justice: . . . I also have been to see the memorial exhibition of Sargent—an amazing show. It's quite clear when you see the things *en masse* that his methods were French—Manet comes to my mind. But I think there is a lot of trickery in them; the paint is so put on that there is little or no inner coherence in

---

[1] See, *supra,* p. 253, Vol. I.

them. I take it that a picture ought to be a complete whole; it
seems to me that his are rather a catalogue, brilliant, insolent,
but without emotion or inwardness and with little delicacy of perception. I hope I do not insult one of your idols; broadly I felt
impressed but disappointed.

Also I have been reading Ambassador Page's letters.[1] He produces on me the same kind of impression that Lowell does, a
competent man of the world, not very profound, too often taking
ignotum pro magnifico for his standard of judgment, a little prone
to believe idle gossip, a tiny bit of a snob, and self-conscious of
it, yet on the whole a thoroughly good fellow who cared deeply
about America without having any great grasp of what it
meant. . . .

My love to you both.   *Ever affectionately yours, H. J. L.*

                                        16 Warwick Gardens, 6.II.26
My dear Justice: . . . I must not omit the story I heard the other
day of Bradley the metaphysician. Brodrick, the head of Merton,[1]
was a notorious talker to whom a two-hour monologue was a
normal incident. One day he came into the common room with
a broken arm. "How did he do it?" Bradley was asked. "Trying
to hold his tongue" was the retort.

Of other things. A jolly lunch with the Swedish minister at
which, *inter alios*, Alfred Noyes, the poet, and Baldwin were
present. The former, I thought, a self-conscious fool. He acted
the poet. "There are moments when I feel uplifted . . . perhaps
three of my things will live . . . one is conscious of persons as
colours. ΚΤΛ"; but it was good to see the professional aesthete in
action. Baldwin as always was simple and interesting—particularly
so on Lloyd-George. "It would be easy," he said, "to deal with him
if he merely thought he was Napoleon, but he insists that he is
the Twelve Apostles." He thought Asquith easily the finest speaker
he had heard in the House, but Bonar Law much the most successful in holding it. He said the House in his experience is always
kind to error and always ruthless to cleverness. He told us that on
the average five hundred people in a year ask directly for knight-
hoods and peerages, and he had one delightful letter from a business gentleman beginning, "Appreciating as you must do my services to the Empire." I like his simplicity enormously. He doesn't
set up to be a great man; and to a lady who made a remark imply-

---

[1] Burton J. Hendrick, *The Life and Letters of Walter H. Page* (3 vols.,
1925).
[1] George Charles Brodrick (1831-1903); his career as lawyer, journalist,
and liberal politician was followed by more than twenty years as Warden of
Merton College and amateur historian.

ing that he was he said "Madam, I know myself in my bath to be as naked as most. . . ."

I am very grateful for your kindness to my young colleague Smellie; he writes most happily of his visit to you. I have now booked my passage and *paid for it* on the *Berengaria* on the 20th of March. I shall, I think, go direct to Boston and spend ten days there; then on to Washington; and a few days in New York before I sail again. I need not say that the mere thought of talk once more gives me joy.

My love warmly to you both,   *Ever affectionately yours, H. J. L.*

Washington, D.C., February 7, 1926

My dear Laski: This is after having been shut up for a week with a cold—the grasshopper is a burden—but luckily all my work is done. Following your suggestion I telephoned the Congressional Library for Vauvenargues, and, on my own motion, for Benjamin Constant's *Adolphe*. By and by I received an English novel with a name (I forget it) dimly approximating Vauvenargues and a note saying they would send *The Constant Nymph* the next day! Later I got what I wanted. Yes, Vauvenargues has some merit, but it was a misfortune to have his *Maximes* bound up in the same volume with La Rochefoucauld. Once in a while he seems to be ahead of his time and to hit the eternal, but in the main he is a gentle joy, not too pungent for the sick room. French talk about virtue and envy, etc. etc., doesn't nourish me greatly. *Adolphe* interested me to reread—interested me by the reflections it suggested as well as by its acute analysis. How deeply concerned are the parties to the drama, and how little you care about them. The woman, of no intellect, could not expect to keep the man long, the man taking so seriously an absorption springing from the lumbar region. But I grow too detached with age. Perhaps I am too averse to any over-serious treatment of the personality as a definite indivisible unit, needing self-respect and striving for God's respect, instead of a shifting nebula of uncertain outline and content varying with the [aurora?]. I swear I believe many errors and much unhappiness are due to the view generally taken, recommended by religion as a duty, felt by good breeding as a foundation, which in my opinion is the true sin against the Holy Ghost. But I am so much alone in my thinking that if I grew very articulate they would shut me up.

I have spoken of the sickroom—I am doing very well and have nothing to complain of, only am not much good for a few days. I am not making the most of my time but dozing and dawdling, and trying to feel irresponsible. *À bientôt.*   *Yours, O. W. H.*

16 Warwick Gardens, 13.II.26

My dear Justice: Everything now is arranged. I have my passage booked, a *visé* from your consul on my passport, and nothing to do except wait for March 20. I assume that I shall not be detained at Ellis Island, as I have never been divorced, am not an anarchist or a polygamist, and do not believe in the violent overthrow of established governments. I need not tell you how the prospect of talk with you both heartens me. It will be a great adventure.

My chief news will, I think, please you. I have been given the chair of political science in the university. That means 33% on my income, the chief say in the teaching of the subject in the university as a whole, and the consequent chance, about which I care much, to make the department really important. . . .

I must not forget to tell you of the death of a fellow of Trinity Cambridge aged 97. His funeral was attended by a brother of 99. The latter was much distressed and said he had always told his junior that theological research was not compatible with longevity. "God," he solemnly told Rutherford, "does not mean us to pry into these matters." After the funeral the old man went back to Trinity and solemnly drank his half-bottle of port. He was asked his prescription for health and said with great fervour "Never deny yourself anything." He explained that he had never married as he had found fidelity restrictive as a young man. "I was once engaged, when I was forty," he said, "and I found it gave me very serious constipation. So I broke off the engagement, and the lady quite understood." He was very anxious not to be thought past the age of flirtation. The vicar, he said, found his presence very helpful at evening parties. I thought he was sheer delight for it was all so absolutely unconscious, but, to my amusement, two deans were shocked beyond words. I took the old man back to London and put him on his way to the Midlands and have rarely had a better journey. Twice he refreshed himself lustily from a flask of claret and once insisted on my sharing it with him. He told me he still had his pint of champagne for lunch but that it did not mean to him what it used to do.

Our love to you both, and every good wish,

Ever affectionately yours, H. J. L.

Washington, D.C., February 21, 1926

My dear Laski: This ought to be the last or the last but one from me before your welcome coming. I hope, I repeat, that you have made sure that there will be no obstacle to your entry here. I am ignorant as a child about it, beyond a vague notion that one is liable to be surprised. I don't know either of the books you men-

tion[1] (*Religion de Jean Jacques* and Cliffe Leslie), and I vainly
tried, though wobbly in my memory, for those volumes on the
history of politics and the influence of the Reformation. It didn't
matter much, for after getting away from the flabbiness of a cold
I walked into the dentist's trap and am no free man. I have, however, touched off two little dissents so far as to get them in proofs
—one concurring in a few words with a colossal piece of work by
Brandeis,[2] and the other on my own, concurred in by him, for
not applying the XIV Amendment to a state case that is
before us.[3] Also I have read one or two books, the most notable
Symonds's translation of Benvenuto Cellini, not read since boyhood
when Roscoe's version was all we had. I could not but chuckle
to think that I saw under Symonds's would be cosmopolitanism the
inner domination of the "We don't do that in England," which is
so apt to be the Briton's last word. I dare say the same local
standards prevail elsewhere but I am more conscious of it with the
English, although even Montesquieu taught one to associate Little
Pedlington with the Boulevards.

   . . . Yesterday p.m. I went to my shelves and took down two
volumes nearly at random. One was a life and sermons of White-
field, interesting mainly because he is buried at Newburyport. I
think you prostrated to his coffin when we went over there one
day. I didn't read much but was reminded of Sainte-Beuve and
Pascal by his discourse on election and reprobation and of what
is said of Edwards by his satisfaction in believing that most of us
are eternally damned. I found his language rather surprisingly
modern and direct. Soon I put him down and turned to the other,
which was Volume 1 of an old 4 volume edition of Horace Walpole's letters which began with his remembrances of the Courts of
George the First and Second. I find that so delightful for an irresponsible moment that I think I shall keep on. Hang it, one
can't be seeking improvement all the time. Mostly I avoid books
that don't help to strengthen the foundations or at least add a
flying buttress, but if I ever am to be allowed any levity it is time
for it now. Yet it doesn't come natural to say, My time for expecting
to contribute anything is over—serious amusement is all that is left.
I dunno—one goes up and down. I think that I will go forth and
walk an inch and a half. I did so yesterday for the first time for a
fortnight. If one has rather a nervous doubt it is astonishing how

---

[1] The reference is to a passage in Laski's letter of February 6 omitted
from this edition.

[2] Not identified.

[3] Probably in *Schlesinger* v. *Wisconsin*, 270 U.S. 230, 241 (March 1,
1926). The majority of the Court condemned a state statute, under the
Fourteenth Amendment, which created an absolute presumption that gifts
inter vivos made within six years of death were made in contemplation of
death. Mr. Justice Stone joined with Brandeis, J., in concurrence in Holmes's
dissent.

it gets on your nerves—as if it made any difference if he knocked all my remaining talk down my throat. However, one must accept one's irrational interest in oneself as a way in which the cosmos keeps up the circulation in its extremities or secures local [illegible]. So fare you well for a time. I am a little anxious about your dates. From March 22 to April 12 we are adjourned, then we sit till May 10. I hope for the best.   *Aff'ly yours, O. W. H.*

16 Warwick Gardens, 21.II.26
My dear Justice: A delight of a letter from you (29.I.26) warmed my innards. I don't think myself that there is much essential difference between us on sovereignty except differences of emphasis. I agree (I) that the Courts must enforce law and take law to be a command of the U.S. or a similar authority competent to act; (II) that it is not possible to go behind that ultimate source of reference at present. I think myself that any state, the U.S. or other, should be responsible for the tortious acts of its agents, and I should ultimately like to see large functions *e.g.* immigration, tariffs, colonial control, in the hands of an international and not a state authority. And, internally, I should want to do all I can to make the *de jure* limits of the state coincide with the *de facto* limits. Indeed, I suggest that if you will, wherever the word "state" is used substitute the word "government" and think of actual persons issuing orders that movement to concreteness makes the notion of a limit laid down by law quite intelligible *e.g.* I don't want the King in Parliament to be able easily to suspend *Habeas Corpus;* I want it to pay if its agents in the Admiralty invade a patent granted by the Board of Trade; I don't want a man of war to be able to evade paying damages if its captain has handled it carelessly, and so on. I gather that you would not vehemently dissent from all this even if you doubted its wisdom.

. . . Are you a Wordsworthian to the hilt? He always seems to me in temperament what Harriet Martineau would have been if the latter had been dowed with poetic talent. Also I had a shot at some Proust, but I was bored to tears. It was like living in a hot house in which the residents compare notes on their paleness and measure their birth in terms of the delicacy of their skins. I do not believe that the analysis, however consummate in power of handling detail, of people who have no real human value or significance can possibly be as important as is made out. I believe in fact that great subject-matter as well as great formal skill is necessary to great art. If Rembrandt paints a peasant woman the history of the ages of land tenure is there; it is the power to universalise an idea in miniature that gives it significance. But you read Proust and watch a lot of silly marionnettes doing silly things in great detail and solemnity and there is no significance of moral or intellectual value in what they do. *Nitchevo!* as the Russians say, and I go back to Dickens or George Eliot with a sense that they really knew how to amuse or to illuminate and that one or the other is the story-teller's job.

I imagine that this letter ought to reach you round about your birthday. You know with what eager affection I send you good wishes. Now the calendar must be set for 90. It is great to have you alive. But please take care; for I expect to absorb your energies for a relentless week of talk.

Our love to you both,   *Ever affectionately yours, H. J. L.*

Washington, D.C., March 4, 1926

My dear Laski: (I always remember that damned *My* just too late. I am told that to omit it is like omitting the personal pronoun, as when one says "Have been very busy" etc. I don't believe it, but am bullied by the suggestion.) This is just a word to say how I am looking forward to seeing you and hoping this will catch you before you start. I have been mad with work, and distributed another little 14th Amendment dissent in which I shall have Brandeis and I think Stone, this morning[1]—an opinion distributed Tuesday on patents that I hope I shall be allowed to announce on my birthday next Monday.[2] You warm my heart with your good wishes. No, I am not a Wordsworthian to the hilt, but I do think that whereas Mill spoke of him as the kind of poet that a man might learn to be, he had by flashes the power to utter the unutterable quite as much as Shelley. He stumps along by your side, a bore in a brown coat, and suddenly he goes up and you find that your companion was an angel. Proust gave me pleasure that I should find it hard to analyze, but he brought back the feelings of youth and the romance that gilds it. Your general remarks I agree with, but Rembrandt could make not merely a peasant woman but a beef carcass sublime. I agree, however, in substance. You must see the infinite, *i.e.* the universal in your particular or it is only gossip. Did I ever remark to you that philosophy after its flights ends in a return to gossip? It goes ahead and formulates as far as it can the laws of the cosmos, but it ends in the purely empirical fact that the cosmos is thus and not otherwise—an unrelated, unexplained datum, which is gossip and nothing else. I believe I saw

---

[1] *Weaver* v. *Palmer Brothers,* 270 U.S. 402, 415 (March 8, 1926). Brandeis and Stone, JJ., concurred in Holmes's dissent urging that Pennsylvania could constitutionally forbid the use of sterilized shoddy in the manufacture of bedding.

[2] *Alexander Milburn Co.* v. *Davis-Bournonville Co.,* 270 U.S. 390 (March 8, 1926).

the statuette of Voltaire of which you speak at an 18th century exhibition in London once. It had just the *diablerie* of which you speak and made a deep impression on me.

Your old man seems a companion to an old woman I heard of who was asked what she had done to live so long and said, "Oh, I lived human." *À bientôt.*   *Aff'ly yours, O. W. H.*

192 Brattle Street
Cambridge, Massachusetts, 29.III.26
My dear Justice: I have been here since Saturday, and the days with Felix and Marion are, literally and figuratively, bathed in sunshine. *Haec olim meminisse juvabit.*

I propose next Saturday night to travel to Washington. So, if I may, I will come in to lunch on Sunday. Will you send me a line to say that is convenient?

Ever affectionately yours, Harold J. Laski

Washington, D.C., March 30, 1926
My dear Laski: It is rejoiceable that you are here—I did not realize it until your letter came just now—I certainly shall expect you at luncheon next Sunday 1:30 o'clock, 1720 I Street.

À bientôt.   *Aff'ly yours, O. W. Holmes*

On Board the Cunard R.M.S. "Berengaria"
April 23, 1926 [1]
My dear Justice: I literally have no words to tell you what those days in Washington meant to me. I did not need to revise beliefs, or renew allegiance; those had been made *in aeternum.* But I found that all I had treasured as a great memory had the old beauty and more. I put it in the treasure house of remembrance as among the great things I have experienced. To you both my old homage and affection made deeper and more intense by new richness.

America has been a great adventure. To find Felix not less electric than ever, and to take up talk with him as though it ceased but yesterday was superb. And I am so much in agreement with many of the results of Brandeis's thinking that I had from him (apart from the fresh sense of his compelling charm) the satisfaction of guessing that my own diagnosis was not entirely wrong. New York was especially kind to me. Mack, J. especially helped me to meet Cardozo and Hough: [2] the former a nature as exquisite as his mind is perceptive, the latter a fine, masculine mind with

---

[1] A brief note from Holmes, dated April 5, 1926, is omitted.
[2] *Supra,* p. 418, Vol. I.

something of the nature of Bluff King Hal at its base. I saw your ex-secretary Benjamin,[3] and his charming young wife. Morris Cohen I had a great evening with. He has mellowed greatly, and I was particularly glad to find that he and I (like you, I believe, too) had not dissimilar views on Pound. I met also a young physiologist from the Rockefeller Institute, Alfred Cohn,[4] whom you must sometime meet. He has, I believe, a big reputation; but even more important, he has a wonderfully tempered mind. And the *New Republic* gave me a dinner at which the talk was quite thrilling; I learned much of an America too often hidden from the sojourner of so brief a moment as mine. I felt, again, too that with many limitations and a certain heaviness of method, Croly is really a big fellow, patient, curious, sincere and penetrating. So long as there are people of his quality around, your future as a nation is not without its guarantees.

But this is not a letter so much as a salute. I need not tell you both how warm is my affection and how eagerly it greets you. I shall resume writing so soon as I am straight at home.

Ever affectionately yours, H. J. L.

Washington, D.C., May 13, 1926
My dear Laski: Your letter from shipboard moved me in my marrow, but I have delayed in writing from day to day owing to the uncertainty and anxiety I have felt and feel as to your public affairs.[1] I suppose you are in the thick of it—I have much confidence in the business sense of the nation but one can't talk freely while things seem to hang in the balance. I shall say but a word or two therefore. (1) I also met Cardozo the other day and thought his face beautiful with intellect and character. I had only a limited chance to talk during the short time he was here—with others.

(2) I read with surprised satisfaction Murray's *History of Political Science,* etc. His slight whiff of the parson or the Hegelian at moments did not prevent my finding it most interesting and compactly instructive.

(3) I am reading out of regard to my friend Wu, Stammler's *Theory of Justice.* I have read 228 pages and though he seems a noble-minded moralist, I confess so far it has been simply marking time, and with tedious iteration impressing upon the reader the difference between an abstract scheme regarded as applicable to all possible controls of the law, and the empirical contents. As I don't believe the postulate—and think morality a sort of higher polite-

---

[3] *Supra,* p. 338, Vol. I.

[4] Alfred Einstein Cohn (1879-1957), distinguished and creative research physician; author of *Medicine, Science and Art* (1931), *No Retreat from Reason* (1948).

[1] See, *infra,* p. 85, note 1.

ness, that stands between us and the ultimate fact—force—I am not much edified. Nor do I see how a believer in any kind of evolution can get a higher formula than organic fitness at the given moment.

(4) Your impression of Croly is like my own, but he can't write —and he tends to give a pedagogic tone to his discourse that makes me shrink from it.

I tremble as I send this off—but affectionate thoughts and hopes go with it. *Yours ever, O. W. H.*

---

16 Warwick Gardens, 2.V.26

My dear Justice: . . . I came back to find Frida and Diana both very fit; but we tremble on the verge of terrible events here and I do not know what will happen.[1] I have a deep sense within me that before the general strike begins on Tuesday, Baldwin will somehow have found means of accomodation [*sic*], for, as I wrote to him last night, the breakdown seems to me rather the misunderstanding of tired men than any ultimate difference. I hope so; for a general strike, if at all prolonged, would loose forces of a kind that make for changes too vast to come rightly or wisely without deliberate plan. . . . *Ever affectionately yours, H. J. L.*

---

16 Warwick Gardens, 23.V.26

My dear Justice: A grand letter from you yesterday was like a fragrant scent in a dismal world. You can imagine that it has been a time of immense strain, made, I think, the worse by the fact that it was all perfectly unnecessary. . . . You will not, I am sure, have been deluded by all the talk of revolution and challenge to the government. From first to last it was a purely industrial dispute

---

[1] Since mid-April the crisis in negotiations between the miners, the employers, and the government had developed with mounting intensity. Since April 30 there had been a total stoppage in the production of coal and on May 1 the Trade Union Congress announced that a general strike would begin on May 3. Mr. Baldwin, and even more vigorously, Mr. Churchill, Chancellor of the Exchequer, treated the action of the Trade Union Congress as a lawless, revolutionary effort to upset the constitutional system. The Government, when the general strike took effect, stood by the proposition that it would not participate in negotiations concerning the shutdown of the mines while the general strike continued. On May 12 the general strike came formally to an end on the understanding that negotiations with respect to the coal dispute would be reopened forthwith. Those negotiations, however, fruitlessly dragged on, the miners stanchly refusing to accede to the employers' demand, supported by the Government, that wage reductions and longer hours were essential. The coal stoppage continued throughout the summer, and it was not until November that the miners finally returned to work, on terms far less favorable than those which had been offered to them in April. Laski wrote of the coal strike in 122 *Nation* 578 (May 26, 1926) and of the general strike, *id.* 663 (June 16, 1926). See also 56 *Survey* 416 (July 1, 1926).

carried out with amazing good temper and orderliness by millions
of men who could not without shame see the miners' wages reduced to between ten and twelve dollars a week. I speak whereof
I know; for I carried out the earlier private negotiations with the
government on behalf of the unions, and the ultimate settlement
was upon a draft I had written. This, of course, is strictly between ourselves; I have not even written it to Felix. And you will
not need me to say that, on this issue, had the question of a challenge to constitutional government been in question, I should not
have tried to help the trade unions. My own feelings were put
admirably by Keynes in the *New Republic* of May 19th.[1] It was a
piece of bungling, due to hotheads in the cabinet who wanted to
"teach labour a lesson." I come out of it with intense respect for
the qualities of the working-man. And of those in high place with
whom it was my business to deal, Baldwin and Birkenhead won
new esteem from me. The first isn't able, but he really has character and an absence of vindictiveness, though he lacks strength of
will. Birkenhead was amazing. Once you broke down his oratorical
habits, he was resourceful, quick, full of intelligence, and with
a great flair as a draftsman. . . . Well, it was a fortnight's grim
labour, which ought, at least, to enable me to write a much better
book on communism than I could have done before. It also convinces me that there really isn't much to be said for "muddling
through." You may win your end, but you pay a heavy price. The
miners are still out, and unless there is a return to my basis, they
will stay out. . . . Now we are trying to get the parties together
on the old basis. But the miners having seen the basis thrown over
once the general strike was called off were naturally suspicious,
and it will, I fear, be a long job. The suffering in the mining dis-
tricts is intense and I cannot find words to tell you what I feel
about their powers of endurance. They have five and ten shillings
a week strike pay, and they just set their teeth and bear it. In an
ultimate sense, they are unbeatable people; for, as I told the Prime
Minister yesterday, even if they lose this fight, they will strike
again as soon as the tide of trade turns. They are Cromwell's Iron-
sides, and they do not know what it is to be beaten. . . .

Our united love,   *Ever affectionately yours, H. J. L.*

Washington, D.C., May 15, 1926

My dear Laski: This is a postscript to my minuscript of the other day,
and is written to acknowledge your first letter from home—as you
say, on the verge of terrible events. My anxiety still makes it hard
to write. The papers speak as if a settlement were coming, but I

---

[1] Keynes, "The End of Peace by Negotiation," 46 *New Republic* 395
(May 19, 1926).

feel no security until the fact is accomplished. That Baldwin is on one side and MacDonald on the other seems to promise a rational result. I think I have told you before of going, 60 years ago, with Mill to a dinner of the Political Economy Club and finding the subject for the evening discussion to be whether the financial policy of England should be shaped to meet the predicted exhaustion of the coal in 90 years.

My *ennui* with Stammler continues, although some of his laborious applications of the Golden Rule have a little novelty in form. Lord, Lord, I wonder if you would get nourishment from him. I believe men have prolonged life by boiling their brogans.

I am a wreck this evening, though somewhat restored by slumber, from having got up half an hour or more earlier than usual, hurried through dressing, and going and sitting in the sun on the steps of the capitol to see the Hopi Indians do their dances, winding up with the snake dance, though it was said they were not allowed to bring the full-fanged rattlesnakes that they played with at home, and had harmless serpents squirming about on the stage, around their necks and in their mouths. Again I say to myself, the joy of life is the neglect of opportunities. However, this one is over and I am tolerably serene now.

Do you know Miss Elizabeth Shepley Sergeant? She writes intimating a call by and by. We had a clever chat once and I think she will be better than Stammler. I have read some good pieces of hers, using superlatives about people I did not know. I slightly suspect her of hyperaesthesia (not speaking pathologically), and yet she was very rational about Amy Lowell who was a friend of hers. Here the mere fact that a person is at ease with the more delicate allusions and assumptions of intellectual or literary interest distinguishes him. It may not go very deep. Many years ago Haldane said that the clever young ladies who seemed so on the hair trigger got their knowledge from reviews, not from the books. But I always have remembered what one of them said to me: "You Americans wait for us to finish our sentences."

The evening paper is calming. It seems to indicate that the worst is over. Also it says that the chap that started to fly over the pole in a dirigible has landed in safety after a silence that made one fear that he was lost.[1]

My wife has read a very engaging book to me, Pupin, *From Immigrant to Inventor*. He is a Serb now at Columbia and Stone promises to bring him in some day. He speaks with a reverence for the saints of science that gives joy to my heart.

My love to you and yours—and may this find you all in peace.
Affectionately yours, O. W. Holmes

---

[1] Roald Amundsen (1872-1928) on May 11 had started from Spitsbergen on his dirigible flight over the Pole. He landed on the 14th at Teller on the Bering Sea.

Washington, D.C., June 4, 1926

My dear Laski: An absorbingly interesting letter from you gives
me the only light I have on the recent great affairs except an
article by Keynes, no doubt the one you refer to. I received a
letter from one of a different mode of thought speaking contemptuously of MacDonald, but I don't know why. I have no comments
except my already expressed general impression that England as
a whole appeared to great advantage. I have nothing to tell. I
am in the details of approaching departure—on Monday we adjourn. There were 29 *certioraris* to be examined this week, of course
many opinions coming in at the last minute—one dissent by me,
concurred in only by Brandeis, though I think it pretty plain.[1]
One dissent from me by MacReynolds [*sic*], *solus*, concluding that
the argument sustained by him "cannot be vaporized by gestures
of impatience and a choleric 'obviously' " [2] which makes me smile,
the more that I don't think it hits or is aimed at anything in my
opinion but rather at my attitude at the last conference—which I
am afraid was not as respectful as it should have been. Poor
MacReynolds is, I think, a man of feeling and of more secret kindliness than he would get the credit for. But as is so common with
Southerners, his own personality governs him without much
thought of others when an impulse comes, and I think without
sufficient regard for the proprieties of the Court. I don't mind the
above a bit so far as I am concerned, but I think it improper in
an opinion. Formerly, according to my recollection, he was really
insolent to Brandeis, although now there is at least a *modus vivendi.*
When I was in the hospital he wrote a charming letter to me,
which I shall not soon forget. I have had also business matters
to attend to—tax return, probate return, etc., but thanks to my
secretary they are polished off. If left to myself I get balled up by
some detail every time. I have read nothing. I had a call the other
p.m. from Miss Elizabeth Shepley Sergeant. At parting she renewed the statement that she made on a previous occasion some
months or more ago that she wanted to write about me. What a
dame not learned in the law can find to say I don't know. I said
that so long as I took no part in it people were to write or not as
they liked. . . .

The dentist has let me loose with his blessing—and in short
the waters are accumulating in the dam for a bust toward Boston

---

[1] *Frost and Frost Trucking Co.* v. *Railroad Commission,* 271 U.S. 583,
600 (June 7, 1926).

[2] *Morse Drydock and Repair Co.* v. *Steamship Northern Star,* 271 U.S.
552 (June 7, 1926). The dissent of McReynolds, J., as published concluded
with the assertion that he agreed with the trial judge and ventured "to
think that the argument in support of his conclusion cannot be vaporized by
mere negation." *Id.* at 557.

next Wednesday evening. I expect that my next to you will be
from Beverly Farms.   *Aff'ly yours,* O. W. H.

                                        16 Warwick Gardens, 30.V.26
My dear Justice: A delight of a letter from you is a landmark in
these grim days. The miners are still out, and industry, as a result,
is inflicted with a kind of creeping paralysis. We have won a remarkable bye-election in London, in which a government majority
of two thousand was transformed into a labour majority of four
thousand. It has given the government a fright, and we cherish
a hope that it will persuade Baldwin to act, instead of standing
idly by, doing nothing. It is all very well for him to protest that
he loves the good and the beautiful, but that doesn't butter any
parsnips. I gather that the nigger in the woodpile is the good
Winston, who is never happy unless there is a fight. The other big
event of the week is the new quarrel between Asquith and Lloyd
George.[1] I never thought I should live to sympathise with the
latter, but here I think that Asquith has made a profound mistake
by trying to set up standards of party orthodoxy to which no man
can possibly be asked to conform. I don't know if you saw the
correspondence? I don't suppose that since the Russell-Palmerston
row over Louis Napoleon, one distinguished statesman has ever
so written to another. It doesn't seem possible that they should
ever collaborate again; and it means, I should imagine, the definite
disappearance of liberalism as a force in party affairs. It is a tragic
ending for Asquith's career, but he has proved so utterly incapable
of adjusting himself to the demands of a new age that the collapse
was inevitable. Yet I am enough of a traditionalist to see with
regret the end of power which goes back directly to 1832 and the
great epoch of reform, and, indirectly to the Revolution of 1688.
The funerals of historical entities are melancholy events.
    Frida and I used to know well the Miss Sergeant whom you have
been seeing, and to like her well. She had one or two aspects, *e.g.,*
admiration for Mexican Indians, which I thought a little *ennuyant,*
but in general a woman of real taste and insight, without a trace
of humbug, like that intolerable Gertrude King who struck philosophic attitudes for the applause of a group of young lawyers all
of whom were totally ignorant of philosophy. I cannot stand a
certain pretentious Anglo-American type of woman who has all

---

[1] On May 20, Lord Oxford, supported by other leaders of the Liberal
Party, had written a letter to Lloyd George severely reprimanding him for
his defection from Party policy in the matter of the general strike. The
letter led to an acrimonious dispute between the principals and their sup-
porters and finally in mid-June the controversy sputtered out with Lloyd
George the clear winner.

the latest "culture" on her lips, and is steeped in the latest slang
of the market-place. The other day I was at tea with Birrell, and
he had a visitor from Chicago who put him (and me) through a
catechism about our "reactions" to this and that fashionable figure
in letters. At last I told her frankly that I was a purely passive
recipient of sensations who never dared to examine their meaning;
and that the last biography I had read was Boswell. She looked
at me in pure amazement and said that I must be very "out of
things" at parties. I said that I very rarely went to parties. "Good
heavens," she exclaimed, "what do you do with your time?" . . .

I hope that my articles in the *Michigan* and *Harvard Law Reviews*[2] will have come safely to you. . . .

Of reading, a good deal in a quiet way. First the translation of
Stammler, which I do not find very impressive. He seems to me
to be platitudinous and in the air, and to lack precision both of
statement and ideas. I doubt, indeed, whether one can get a satisfactory theory of law deductively from a set notion of justice.
Analyse what judges do, explain why you don't like it, and make
a skilful argument to show that your personal preferences had
better be mine. But to dress it all up in categorical imperatives and
universality is, I think, to give very big names to very small
beer. . . .

Our love to you both. I think I shall risk sending my next letter
to Beverly Farms.   *Ever affectionately yours, H. J. L.*

Beverly Farms, June 17, 1926

My dear Laski: Your delightful letter met me here, forwarded
from Washington. We stopped at the Touraine from last Thursday
until Monday p.m. and then motored down with the faithful
Beverly man—cold, and the furnace in pieces, but electricity and
wood fires kept us going until the furnace was up and started. I
was really impressed in Boston by two things—the South Boston
Marine Pond and Aquarium and some of the harbor structures,
and the Franklin Park Zoo. There was a sort of bigness of conception that reminded me of what Borglum[1] the sculptor recently
said to us of a new class of young engineers with conceptions
worthy of the country. Also I brought down from the Athenaeum
a book by Carver, professor of political economy at Harvard, *The
Present Economic Revolution in the United States,* which cheers
my optimism. He, like myself, thinks the talk of class war is humbug and that we are finding a solution by the working men becoming capitalists, as illustrated by the Labor Banks and greatly

[2] See, *supra,* p. 68.
[1] Gutzon Borglum (1871-1941), American sculptor, best known, perhaps,
for his heads of Washington, Jefferson, Lincoln, and Theodore Roosevelt
carved on the face of Mount Rushmore in the Black Hills of South Dakota.

increased deposits, stock purchases, etc., etc. He defends capitalism which I still believe in, well. I was interrupted at this point and must hurry more than I meant to. You give me joy by what you say of Stammler—you must now have received a letter from me expressing similar views. I thought Wu's appendix the best thing in the book and excellent. I shall read to my wife what you say of Gertrude King. It will make her chuckle. I can't say that I made much of her essays, as I remember them. God forgive me if I acknowledged them with soap.

I have written to you how good I thought your essays, and my reservations as to political appointments here—although I always should be fearful of the effect of such considerations. I never have ventured to ask Taft what led him to make White C.J. I think that Hughes (whom I take it politics defeated) would have been fitter for the place. At the time I told McKenna, I believe, that he and I were the only two who didn't have booms going for us.

One of my interruptions was 10 essays by children of 13 on Saving the Ship Constitution, which I agreed to judge. I am now going to the post-office to return them with my adjudication, and shall post this hoping that it will go promptly. Beveridge called yesterday. He is taking infinite pains with his *Life of Lincoln*, and has the sound notion that what is wanted is not opinions but significant and authoritative details, so massed as to tell their own story. I expect some chapters to read, anon. My love to you both.

Affectionately yours, O. W. H.

16 Warwick Gardens, 13.VI.26

My dear Justice: . . . yesterday, McIlwain and I went down to Oxford and had a great time book-hunting all day. I can't say we made any epoch-making discoveries, though we seem to have spent eight or ten pounds between us; but we had that peculiar thrill which comes from going into a room redolent with the faint mustiness of old calf and feeling that almost any volume may turn out a treasure. We lunched with some of the younger history dons, and it was amusing to find how well they played up to the theory of what an Oxford man ought to be. At least, to me, the contrast between McIlwain's fine and intense seriousness, and the Oxford man's air of avoiding the only subjects of which he knew anything made lunch something that only Charles Lamb could describe adequately. . . . Did I, by the way, speak to you of Declareuil's *Histoire de droit français?* There's a truly admirable book which makes even Esmein and Brissaud look pretty thin by his side. He has got the flair for ideas that Maitland had and I read every word of him with interest. . . .

My love to you both.   *Ever affectionately yours, H. J. L.*

Washington, D.C., June 6, 1926

My dear Laski: This is an extra, slipped in between two storms, to say that I have read your two articles in the *Michigan Law Review* and *Harvard Law Review*[1] respectively, and think them both admirable. Of course I don't know the H. of L. decisions except by your report, but the attitude and general principle that you show has my sympathy and assent. One slight qualification. The political appointments here that I best recall have been good. I think Taft is all the better Chief Justice for having been President. Story, Taney and Chase were all good—and I might add one or two more. I don't know many as political appointments but I am ignorant. Also I think that Presidents, if there is a large preponderance of their own party on the bench try to get one of the [other] side—but it is not always easy.

The C.J. has telephoned to me that he does not expect to be present tomorrow, so I shall have a number of odd jobs on my hands as soon as I get some papers from him. It is the adjournment for the term and on Wednesday I hope to leave for the north.

Affectionately yours, O. W. Holmes

Beverly Farms, June 24, 1926

My dear Laski: One of your ever delightful letters came this morning. Your account of the Oxford dons avoiding their theme in contrast with McIlwain reminded me of how Bowen, when I tried to get him on serious subjects, dodged them with an anecdote. Following your order, I haven't read those biographies by Leslie Stephen. Perhaps I may this summer. I have obeyed your injunction and got Declareuil's *Histoire de droit français* from the Law School and begun it. So far it is preliminaries that I imperfectly understand without special maps and don't care much for, and forget, but *le bon temps viendra,* as old Fitzroy Kelley[1] said to my wife. I agree in your high valuation of Maitland's *Life of Leslie Stephen.* As to Spengler, I must have written when I was wrestling with volume I in German last summer. He stimulates with propositions that one doesn't believe when one understands them, but finds no less stimulating on that account. A new untruth is better than an old truth. As to Bodin's notion of sovereignty, he certainly states the proposition that the law-maker is superior to the law he makes —which doesn't seem to require much genius. If he believed, as McIlwain says the English did, in fundamental, unalterable law, I should guess that that was rather an unconscious assumption than a theory. I never read Richardson *in extenso,* nor the *Nouvelle*

[1] See, *supra,* p. 68.
[1] Sir Fitzroy Kelly (1798-1880), lawyer, politician, and Lord Chief Baron of the Exchequer, 1866-1880.

Héloïse at all. My wife won't read murder stories but we should finish tonight *Hangman's House* by Donn Byrne. I don't see how it can end as well as it began, but the first half at least is superlative, if you like Irish stories. I told you last week of my best experiences in reading down here.

We motored round Rockport this morning and I thought of you. I saw no changes since last year. Probably not enough has been done yet to amount to anything, but I hate to see them cutting out and carrying off the granite. I feel (with less justification) as the author of *The Wheel of Wealth* says of England's selling coal—it is the workman selling his tools, or at least cutting out the foundations of his house. The automobile somewhat takes the wonder out of things by bringing them so near. In the days of horses this Cape would be full of remote mysteries that I might hope to pry into one by one. Now you can go round half the show in two hours. But the charm to me is too great for familiarity to blunt it. It goes back to my first impressions as a child.

This is a mean looking sheet to write on—I shall try to get something better in Beverly. But there is such comfort in a block. Frankfurter has written, and I hope to see him and his wife next week. I can't offer to put up a married couple in these days—we should have to give up our room and be at more bother than is reasonable for old people, but I am sorry. I dare say I forgot to mention that the Chief Justice, as the result of too much physical exercise, was kept in bed for the last week of the term. So I bossed the funeral. I have written to him, but it is too early for an answer. I hope and have little doubt that it was only a set-back requiring caution as he has to take care of his heart. I suppose all old people have to—(I am not including him in that category).

I have seen Beveridge—full of his work. The trouble that he will take to verify a detail is admirable, the more so that details don't master him. His idea is to mass them so as to make them tell the story without comment. I should be surprised if he didn't supersede all that has been written about Lincoln before.

Aff'ly yours, O. W. H.

16 *Warwick Gardens, 19.VI.26*

My dear Justice: . . . This has been a really peaceful week. The only engagement I have had was a party at the Russian embassy, where I had some good talk with one or two old friends. A reception there is a very amusing thing to see. The *hauteur* of a normal diplomatic affair is entirely absent. One sees many who would not appear in the *entourage* of the older embassies and many who are always at the latter never appear there. Our Foreign office always scrupulously sends a junior clerk, but the mighty most carefully

absent themselves. The person there who interested me most was a
Russian jurist with an unpronounceable name. He talked fluently
eleven languages. The people I respect on the continent like
Ehrlich and Duguit he recited on with great insight and common-
sense. And he told me much that was illuminating and helpful
about the working of the present legal system in Russia. It seems,
if I followed him, to be a combination of executive justice and
justice without law. In all political cases the problem rests entirely
with the court, which means that, especially in matters like treason,
the accused has very little chance. In smaller cases, the jury acts
much more like a jury in medieval England in that it reproduces
the atmosphere of trying a neighbour from personal knowledge. He
himself was, I gathered, very opposed to the first, and well satisfied
with the second. He told me that the new Russia has produced a
remarkable literature about these things; but I had to take this
for granted as it is not even translated into German. . . .

I must not forget (how could I forget) to tell you that since I
wrote last I have met God. I was at a committee for the relief of
the miners when Mrs. Besant turned up with the young man whom
she announced as the new Redeemer.[1] I have never met a God
before and it was a little embarrassing to talk to him. I did not like
to mention the weather, as a comment on continuous rain seemed
like an attack on his will. So I asked if he remembered any of his
previous incarnations (he represents the Theosophists) and he told
me thirty-three. He was a simple and unaffected creature who, I
gather, has a gospel composed of a mixture between the Sermon
on the Mount and the Veddas [sic]. What turned my stomach a
little was the greasiness of his chief bishop who came with him;
. . . Gods, in my own view, should be more careful in the selection
of their prophets. But I grow blasphemous.

I had a pleasant adventure in a café yesterday. I was having
some morning coffee with my friend Siegfried Sassoon and we were
having a heated argument about some modern men of letters. An
old boy with a cloak, velvet jacket, flowing tie, and all the other
appurtenances of the literary movement of the nineties sat near,
listening with all his ears. Presently he came over, and in a booming voice asked to take part. We bowed and he made a long speech
ending, "Sirs, I have not had such a happy hour since I first came
here with Aubrey Beardsley, thirty years ago." The waiter told us
he was an old journalist of the Wilde-Beardsley set who still was
faithful to his haunt and, I dare say, peopled it still with the wan
ghosts of memories. . . .

---

[1] Mrs. Annie Besant (1847-1933), theosophist, had recently announced
that Jiddu Krishnamurti, her *protégé*, was the new Messiah. Shortly thereafter Krishnamurti repudiated these claims.

You I expect, are enjoying delicious sunshine. Here it is cold and wet, and the coal lock-out hangs over us like a dread spectre. Mr. Baldwin's new plans[2] proclaim him a typical Pecksniff, who has given way to all the worst influences in the cabinet. I am afraid peace is far away.

Our love to you both.   *Ever affectionately yours, H. J. L.*

16 Warwick Gardens, 3.VII.26

My dear Justice: . . . I am going with Frida and Diana to the Ardennes, thence for a little to Geneva, and ending up with a week of bookhunting in Paris. . . .

Yet, as I say, I have had diversions. I went to All Souls for an examination and spent a night there—dinner on Sunday is, I gather, a great event and I can boast of having contradicted (very gently) an Archbishop. But he said that Montaigne was foul-minded and I count the provocation ample. Dons, I add, are a queer breed. Their conversation is either the interchange of inept and slightly malicious *personalia,* or gossip about the passing daily events such as a careful reader gets from the *Times* before breakfast. Or the state of the college cellar; or the probability that X will get a certain chair. I was not impressed, though I don't deny a certain mellowness in the atmosphere. Then a dinner with Haldane which was amusing as Bernard Shaw and Austen Chamberlain got on each other's nerves and the claws came out. The latter, I thought, gave the provocation by trying to be the Minister of State; whereupon Shaw, with incredibly brilliant insolence, began to prove that Foreign Secretaries are by definition cynical and corrupt. Poor Austen, of course, tried to riposte; but he was like an elephant trying to catch an extremely agile wasp. And what complicated matters quite gloriously was the presence of an old society dame of the Gladstonian epoch, who backed up Shaw by recounting the *amours* and infidelities of the Victorian foreign secretaries since her girlhood. Altogether an evening such as one rarely gets outside a French salon. . . .

I think, if I may say so, that you attach overmuch importance to Carver's book. For your Trade Commission has just published a most interesting account of American income[1] from which it appears that one percent of your population holds over sixty percent of the wealth, and the total value of employee holding of corporation stock is less than two percent of common and preferred. Moreover nothing of this touches the problem of control.

---

[2] On June 15 Baldwin had announced the purpose of the government to take action to lengthen the working day in the coal mines.

[1] *National Wealth and Income* (1926).

I don't doubt that America will postpone longer than any other country the problems that come when one reaches the point of diminishing returns; but I don't doubt also that then your problems will be more serious, because of the degree to which your wealth is concentrated, than they have been elsewhere. . . .

Our love as ever to you both.

Yours always affectionately, H. J. L.

Beverly Farms, July 4, 1926

My dear Laski: If I could have a letter from you with no duty to answer except when I felt like it I should like to get one every day. Pretty often too, I want to write but not always. The languor of age I suppose makes one lazy. I have had various odds and ends of a business nature, including paying bills, that have taken time and energy. To draw a single check and dispatch it properly takes an appreciable moment. In one way and another Declareuil has had to wait. I am much tickled to note the Frenchman in him and am pleased for other reasons also to see him pronounce a hobby of the great Sohm pure imagination. Sohm was the fashion when I was younger and I even then thought that there were reserves to be made. His vogue led me to realize that there is fashion in ideas as well as in bonnets. Then Tawney's *Religion and the Rise of Capitalism* came along—the publishers said by his direction—and I have just finished that. A charming and handsome piece of work. I wrote to him this morning and said, as bound, after an appreciative word, that I was an old skeptic and thought capitalism better than any thing likely to replace it but that I got more intellectual companionship from you young prophets than from the older orthodox sages. Now I have typewritten chapters of Beveridge's *Lincoln* to criticize—and at first reading I am afraid that I shall have to say that one, which must have cost much time, seems to me of questionable value to the story—but I must read the rest and then go back before I can speak.

I am delighted with your old fellow in the cafe with the reminiscences of Aubrey Beardsley. I think I once was told to call and called on Beardsley's sister, but I am not sure, it may have been merely an actress who recalled meetings with him, and the French woman who wrote queer stories and reviewed those of other people in the *Mercure de France*—*Rachilde*[1]—that was what she called herself. Her book notices were good stuff, as I remember. I have not derived bliss from my encounters with actresses. I remember going with John Gray to call on one—lamenting over the rest—and as we came away he said consolingly, well, she wasn't so *damned* respectable. Ellen Terry I thought insufferable.

---

[1] Rachilde (Mme. Marguérite Vallette; 1862-1953), novelist and critic.

I had a letter from Leslie Scott who seemed to think Baldwin was doing well.

Let this brief despatch count me one

As ever aff'ly yours, O. W. H.

Beverly Farms, July 16, 1926

My dear Laski: An expected and appreciated letter comes today. Your account of the dons' conversation reminds me of Baliol [*sic*] in '66 when I was there with Edwin Palmer.[1] The dons spoke French after the school of Stratford atte Bowe and believed the formula that one Englishman could lick three Frenchmen. I probably have told you of Goldwin Smith[2] coming in at breakfast (I think) and saying, "I hear that Matthew Arnold is going to lecture on Celtic literature. I should like to know what Matt Arnold knows about Celtic literature." I read *Caleb Williams* when a boy—my father telling me it was the best novel he ever read, or to that effect. DeQuincey I think says that it was impossible to disclose in the finale the contents of the chest as no possible disclosure would be adequate. But all my memories are over half a century old. I can't believe that you really read all the books you mention. I don't doubt you read them as a good reader does, skipping by instinct, but I bet you didn't plod through every word of Declareuil as I am doing. I don't give much time to him, and for the first 300 pages, with some mitigations that I believe I have mentioned, I couldn't imagine why you had put me on to him. Now that I am in the Kingdom I begin to see, and although there still are details that I hardly pick enough long enough to forget, I am getting pleasure and instruction. I don't accept your comparison with Brissaud to the disadvantage of the latter. I couldn't recite on him, but I thought he brought the doctrines of private law into relation with life in a way that I never had seen equalled. So far, there is nothing of that here. Declareuil deals only with institutions. Some amusing explanations, *e.g.* the responsibility of ministers for the King, and a general impression going further than anything I knew before that England was a sort of provincial follower of French fashions in the origin of her institutions.

As to Carver's book, I can't control his facts. He pleased me because he thought as I do that the capitalist regime was better than the proposed substitutes and didn't believe in class war.

One of my few links with the living goes with the death of Miss Gertrude Bell—not that I had heard from her or seen her but once for I know not how many years—but there was a time when I

---

[1] Presumably Edwin Palmer (1824-1895), Fellow of Balliol, classicist and archdeacon of Oxford.

[2] Goldwin Smith (1823-1910), Cobdenite controversialist, who left Oxford for Cornell and Cornell for Toronto.

knew her pretty well and got some remarkable letters from her.
I sadly see Pepys drawing to his end—unfortunately I have nothing but a little cheap expurgated ten cents a volume edition here,
but it is an ideal book for idle days. Some things that I had forgotten come up, especially in the use of words, such as mad for
angry, which I should have supposed a modern Americanism. But
there is always less modern than one thinks, as philosophers have
observed since Solomon. I greet the budding laureate in you,[3] as
I do the historian in Beveridge. He is working along faithfully,
and really wants criticism. When I said cut out a number of pages
that had cost a lot of work, he argued his case but showed no
vanity or anything but a wish to get it right—which I think creditable. He gets the Roosevelt Memorial Medal this year which I am
glad of. I think there will be more trouble with his style than with
his conception or his work.   *Aff'ly yours, O. W. H.*

16 Warwick Gardens, 15.VII.26

My dear Justice: . . . on a barrow in the Caledonian market I
picked up a first edition of the *Lettres provinciales* in perfection
as to state for sixpence and sold it to Quaritch for ten pounds. So
I go to Paris with a good conscience. Did I, by the way, tell you
that my graduate students presented me with the 1557 folio of
Sir T. More's *Works.* Ten of them this year got their doctorates, by
way of being a record for one teacher in one year; and this was
their very charming salute in passing. . . .

I am sorry to hear your scepticisms anent Beveridge's *Lincoln.*
I take it that he lacks conciseness and sacrifices the perspective to
the love of trifling detail. . . .   *Ever affectionately yours, H. J. L.*

Beverly Farms, July 29, 1926

My dear Laski: Your latest calls for two or three counter memos.
1) I saw Trotsky's book[1] at the Athenaeum when by exception I
went to Boston to try on some clothes—wondered if I ought to
read it, but noticing that it was written more than a year ago
thought it could wait. I am glad to know that he has been answered, and will let the two books cancel each other. 2) But I
haste to correct a seeming impression that I am sceptical about
Beveridge's *Lincoln.* I confidently believe that he will write the
final life. I forget what I said, but it cannot have been more than
that I wanted him to cut out some pages that I thought irrelevant,
and thought that he possibly had been getting too high an opinion
of the South before the war (our war). 3) Sanborn is a distin-

---

[3] The reference is to four lines of rhymed verse in Laski's letter of July 3,
1926, which have been omitted from this edition.

[1] *Whither England?* (1925).

guishable Circuit Judge. I think I heard when I came on to the Bench that he had his name before the White House as a candidate for a place. I should think he was as good as some that have been promoted, but I should be inclined to speak as did the King in the ballad of Chevy Chase when he heard of Percy's death.[2]

Now for my turn. Thrice accursed man, why did you put me onto Declareuil? He does his work well I don't doubt, but out of his damned 1061 pages, all read by me, not more than 100 have anything that I want (the account of the development of French law and the relation to it of the Roman and Frankish law). His decent but universal denial of anything that any German ever said gives me pleasure, but I do not understand your great enthusiasm. I should as soon get hot in praise of the Almanac. However, since then I have turned off some *certioraris* against next term, and incidentally have tucked in Pepys and some small matters and now am happily at leisure. Miss Sergeant indicated the possibility of calling here this afternoon but as it is rainy and she is in Brookline I doubt. Whether her calls have an ulterior motive in a notion that she once entertained of writing about me I know not, but I believe I told her that I didn't see that there was anything to say for a writer not in the law. My wildest excursion was to Gloucester last night to hear a master play on the carillon of Our Lady of Good Voyages—a Portuguese church. It moved me, though somewhat impaired by the interjection of Three Blind Mice and the like. I have seen Bob Barlow and Palfrey—but know no personalities that would interest you. I turn from Declareuil to *Nize Baby,* Dryden's *Dramatic Essays,* Dorothy Osborne's *Letters to Sir William Temple,* and Frankfurter's admirable article, which I shall finish as soon as I have signed this. It is on Petty Federal Offenses and the Constitutional Guaranty of Trial by Jury.[3] I envy you your trip which I hope has come off satisfactorily. I envy also the *Provinciales* which I wouldn't have sold—yet I dare say you were right.   *Affectionately yours, O. W. Holmes*

16 Warwick Gardens, 25.VII.26
My dear Justice: . . . Then I read a good book by one Cru (an American of whom I know nothing) on Diderot and English influence of Shaftesbury in the 18th century. Did you ever read the *Characteristics*? I have tried twice and each time failed pretty completely. . . . I thoroughly enjoyed, too, McTaggart's *Hegelian*

---

[2] The words were those of King Harry when news of Percy's death reached London:

"'I've a hundred captains in England,' he said,
'As good as ever was he.'"

[3] Frankfurter and Corcoran, "Petty Federal Offenses and the Constitutional Guaranty of Trial by Jury," 39 *Harv. L. Rev.* 917 (June 1926).

Cosmology which, if you have it at hand, would, I think, give you real pleasure. The essays especially on sin, punishment, and society as an organism, are really first-rate. And I greatly enjoyed also (have I spoken of it to you before?) Höffding's *History of Modern Philosophy*. I don't know if you have read it. No other book I know is nearly so good for the purpose of discovering the sweep of the subject.

. . . I also had a most amusing lunch with Glenn Frank,[1] the new President of Wisconsin University. He is, I should guess, what Felix calls a faker—really charming *au fond*, but terrified of not being thought the real intellectual, with the result that statements such as "London is full of Americans just now" are made with a grim tensity such as might be used in announcing the discovery of the law of gravitation. He was most anxious to go to the King's garden party, So I wangled an invitation for him. It was most amusing to see him take the most infinite pains over the right clothes, even to the purchase of a white top-hat and white spats, which I dared him to wear in Wisconsin. . . .

Our love to you both. I hope the heat wave of which I read has not troubled you.   *Ever affectionately yours, H. J. L.*

Beverly Farms, August 5, 1926
My dear Laski: Pleasures are ultimates and in cases of difference between oneself and another there is nothing to do except in unimportant matters to think ill of him and in important ones to kill him. Until you have remade the world I can class as important only those that have an international sanction in war. Therefore I pass without further remark your raptures over Jane Austen (well enough if you don't make too much row about her). She shines in the firmament of your world—along with Declareuil. You are God of that, but the religion of taste is polytheistic.

I wonder whether McTaggart's Hegelian book is one that Haldane recommended to me when we crossed together and that I purchased and read with much pleasure. I can't remember definitely. As to Shaftesbury, I can't say whether it was his *Characteristics* or somewhat else of his that I read in times past. As the *Characteristics* have stared me in the face for years I am pretty sure it was they (them)—anyhow I remember spotting modern [vistas?] and thinking that I saw a man ahead of his time. Höffding perhaps I will send for.

I have been browsing and idling for a few days. G. Moore turned me to Synge's *Well of the Saints* and I can't say how much I admired the genius of that play. The Irish more than any others

---

[1] Glenn Frank (1887-1940), journalist who in 1925 had gone from the editorship of the *Century* to the presidency of the University of Wisconsin, where he remained in office until 1937.

have the poet's gift of uttering the unutterable, I think. I read
Twelfth Night to see if a little girl was right in thinking S. long
in coming to the point. Some twaddle, some unintelligibilities, the
treatment of Malvolio brutal and tiresome, but as always a precious
jewel in the head of the toad. I have spent two days in rereading
The Moonstone, and still found it absorbing. Yet it has no other
merit that I can see, except the *coup de théatre* at the end where
the three men part for their pilgrimage and the moonstone shines
once more from the forehead of the idol. That does truly tickle
my melodramatic soul. I read in Everyman's, Dryden's *Dramatic
Essays, i.e.*, his prefaces, with much pleasure and some surprise. It
made me feel that there were some who twigged Shakespeare from
his own time. Also he is more than a razor—he is a sting and says
poignant things. But as you see I am not deeply engaged. When
I read a book I read every word—a bad sign—and so am slow to
tackle a new one. I hope you are having a happy vacation.

Aff'ly yours, O. W. H.

Walsort-sur-Meuse, 4.VIII.26

My dear Justice: . . . One or two social observations will, I think,
interest you. Practically all the local peasantry are profoundly
Catholic, and so far as the countryside extends, the deputies in
the chamber are Catholic. But as soon as you move to the outskirts even of a small industrial town like Dinant, the church is a
dead force and the deputies become socialist. . . . One visitor here
is a Dutch professor of history with whom I have had some talk.
The other day I approached him while at dinner with a question,
only to be met with the stern remark that he never spoke at meals!
I must add that life among a small nation is most interesting. Their
sense of national feeling is much more intense than in a great
country like America or England. A writer of local reputation
assumes the proportions of a world-figure. The Dutch historian
was shocked beyond words that I did not know of a Dutch dramatist whose name, I think, was Wondel.[1] Surely I knew his *Lucifer*.
I asked if he had been translated into English or German. No; I
did not know Dutch. Ah! but he is the first dramatist of our time.
I hinted gently that a word might be said for Shaw. This was
waved gently aside. Shaw, of course, was a big man, but Wondel.
—So an historian who had written a history of Java was pointed
out to me with the same solemnity and reverence as I might show
in asking you to notice Gibbon on the other side of the street.
    . . . Of reading I have done but little that would interest you,
I fear; mainly communist pamphlets which have been chiefly noise,

---

[1] Joost van den Vondel (1587-1679), poet, translator, and dramatist;
his play *Lucifer* (1654) was translated into English in 1898.

except one or two by Lenin and Trotsky, in which one detects
at once the hand of the really big man. . . .

And I must not forget to tell you that on the way here Frida and
I celebrated the fifteenth anniversary of our wedding-day by buying ourselves two etchings by James Ensor, whose work I expect
you know. One of them is the cathedral at Antwerp—a large one
(12 x 8) with the square in front alive with a crowd, and as you
look closely, you see that about every person in it is doing some
little task with a gesture or an expression that gives them life.
The other is a study of the quay at Ostend, and is a delicate piece
of witchery rather in the manner of Whistler. The man we got
them from had a collection of Ostades that made my mouth water,
as also one of Rembrandt's which was in finer condition than any
I have seen at a dealer's. But this last was not for sale as the town
has bought it. While in Antwerp I stopped again to look at the
Platin Museum and sat on the chair were Justus Lipsius[2] used to
correct his proofs, and saw the letter to him from Casuabon regretting L's conversion to Rome. . . .

Our love to you both.   *Ever affectionately yours, H. J. L.*

                              Beverly Farms, August 20, 1926
Shall I direct to you as Professor or Esquire?
My dear Laski: Your account of the Dutch trencherman delighted
me—and what you say about small places. Did you ever read
Little Pedlington? If not, do make a note of it. It is what my
father used to call a seed book. The Vondel you mention, the
author of *Lucifer,* which was supposed to have given Milton hints
for *Paradise Lost,* suggested Wendel so far that my father bought
his portrait. I have it, it is engraved by Janus Lutma who in turn
(or his father—I think himself) was etched by Rembrandt, you
may remember the etching, a third state hangs in my dressing
room. Vondel is called *Olor Batavus.* I think I also have his works!
Ensor I know only by name—if by that. A few of Ostade's etchings I love. I have poor states of those that I like, but many I
don't care for.

Well, I have finished Höffding, and thank you as much for
recommending that as I damned you for putting me on to Declareuil. The book is already a little old, but really excellent, and
his brief criticisms are pungent. He has the best short account of
Kant that I remember. Eminent persons who have counted and
have disappeared I (unlike you) forget as fast as I read about

---

[2] Justus Lipsius (1547-1606), Belgian Latinist best known for his edition
of Tacitus. His early fluctuations in faith came to an end in 1590 when he
returned, forgiven, to the Catholic Church.

them, but I get the movement. One thing that bothers them all, I suppose from theological presuppositions, strikes me as twaddle —the "problem of evil." Of course the universe is a mystery— and its manifestation of life in seemingly isolated fractions—but, given that, evil is simply death—the end of a transitory manifesta- tion. The withering of a leaf, the sickness of man, the struggle for life, all are normal sequences of the datum—as are frauds and murders. The philosophers seem to me to put their mystery in the wrong place, as spiritualists and Catholics do their miracles. I consider the above remark good, and with that and the end of Höffding propose to pass to lighter themes. I mean to begin by sampling Guedalla's two books which lie upon my table—*Fathers of the Revolution* and *The Second Empire*. If they amuse me enough not to count the pages I may read them. I notice that Höffding refers to *Memories of Old Friends* from the Journal of Caroline Fox (Tauchnitz) which sounds as if it might be interest- ing. I may send for it. (Of the Mill-Carlyle period, converse of eminent persons, noted rightly by the journalist.) To one who reads every word articulately, as I do, it is a more serious job to tackle these histories, etc. than to you who read down the page instead of across. I suppose I could drool along over other sheets, but I drive out in a few moments and as it is possible that by stopping now I catch tomorrow's (?) boat, I stop—anticipating your next adventure.   *Affectionately yours, O. W. Holmes*

Beverly Farms, August 27, 1926

My dear Laski: You renew my job by another letter from Waulsort sur Meuse,[1] the precise place of which on the map I know not. I readily accept the judgment that Declareuil's work is first rate. My howl was only because the greater part of it concerned facts that I am not studying and forget at once. You ask in connection with Pepys whether I find pleasure in Horace Walpole. I should be surprised if I hadn't written or said that Pepys and Walpole were the two books that would occur to me first when I didn't want to be bothered with ideas and yet didn't want to waste my time. Not that I have read more than a volume or two of Walpole —but I wish I had him here now. . . . Your account of your Paris experience makes me feel envious and old. I have little to tell of myself—I think I mentioned reading Guedalla's two books, *Fathers of the Revolution* and *Second Empire*—the latter much the fitter subject for his pen. Since then only a mystery tale—by

---

[1] Omitted from this edition.

E. Wallace: *A King by Night*—good of its sort. I hung over it for a day.

Yesterday my leisure between driving, etc. was taken up with an article that my dear Wu sent me from China.[2] I wrote three opinion-size pages to explain why I didn't think it a source of new light—but one hates to do that kind of thing to one who commands all one's affection and esteem. I told him that I thought his studies in Germany had affected him a little with their own systematizing habit, that Kant's and Hegel's systems had gone into the waste paper basket and that they would have done better if they had confined themselves to their profound *aperçus*. Their systems, *pace* Haldane, have burdened and bored the world to get rid of them. Now for a few odd moments I have taken up to read a third time Lethaby's admirable little book on Architecture in the Home University Library. If I can find another story I shall read it—but I think it just as well to idle a bit. The other day I went again around your adorable Rockport, stopping to look at the house built wholly of newspapers that I must have told you of last year. The papers are glued together into boards, and now chairs, tables, etc. adorn, also made of newspapers rolled into tubes. I believe the man, whom I didn't see this year, is an expert electrician—building this house was his amusement. . . .

Affectionately yours, O. W. Holmes

As From 16 Warwick Gardens, 22.VIII.26
My dear Justice: I came back from two thrilling days in Geneva[1] to find your letter. . . .

The League itself was not especially impressive. I saw some old American friends—Manley Hudson, Herbert Feis,[2] Raymond Fosdick;[3] and I met James Brown Scott[4] who, I whisper quietly, did not seem to be a great man. I met also Zimmern, but he is now a crusader for the League and nothing but the League and to a

---

[2] Probably "Scientific Method in Judicial Process," 3 *China Law Review* 7 (July 1926), reprinted in Wu, *Judicial Essays and Studies* (1933) 26. Holmes's letter to Wu concerning the article is printed in *Justice Oliver Wendell Holmes, His Book Notices and Uncollected Papers and Letters* (Shriver, ed., 1936), 186.

[1] In Geneva Laski had delivered an address, "International Government and National Sovereignty," before the Geneva Institute of International Relations. It is printed in *The Problem of Peace* (1927) 288.

[2] Herbert Feis (1893-   ), economist and public servant, was associated for many years with the International Labor Office of the League of Nations.

[3] Raymond Blaine Fosdick (1878-   ), lawyer, man of affairs, and authority on police administration.

[4] James Brown Scott (1866-1943), energetic administrator of, and prolific writer on international law.

sceptic that does not help discussion. The place itself, as the centre
of the League, has become the most amazing medley of nationalities; and one finds oneself continually searching for an interpreter
to find out what some Czech or Pole is trying to say. On the other
hand the International Labour office *does* impress. One has the
sense that fertile thinking is on foot and that really effective work
is being done. The real genius of the place is an Irishman named
Phelan,[5] who has a good deal of Felix's quick, nervous charm. He
has a power of speculation that kept me up till four one morning
and a hatred of organised religion that gave me immense pleasure. . . .

Our love to you both.   *Ever affectionately yours, H. J. L.*

Beverly Farms, September 3, 1926
My dear Laski: Your account of Geneva and your book adventures
there move my envy—but I too have had my adventures, although
on a less impressive scale, both external and literary. One Wednesday, two days ago, we went to Plum Island and sat upon the
white beach, longer than the old Hoffman House bar, stretching
out of sight, with the black-blue ocean illimitably in front, and a
few mackerel gulls zigzagging swiftly overhead—infinite space and
air. Then returning we stopped at the old house that you will
remember in Newburyport, which was hard by, and renewed the
old sensation of the yard thick walls, and the daughter of the
house, now its mistress, came out (as there were a lot of girls
inside whom we didn't want to disturb) and made me proud of
the old Yankee race—though I horrified her by saying that I believed in "My country right or wrong." Yesterday we went to a
noble old house in Marblehead of which I spare you the description but found there an elderly Marblehead woman in charge who
again made me proud of the Yankees. Returning I found a woman
with proofs of a photograph that I weakly let them take the other
day. I expounded that it was not my job, but my wife liked the
photographs so well that she let me in for $74 before the short
seance ended. This p.m. we have been at the studio [of] Kraska
[*sic*][1] in Gloucester to see a model he has made for a companion
piece to the fisherman that stands at the head of Gloucester harbor
of which probably I wrote to you last year. This is of the Gloucester woman and again moved me. Also I liked the man. He said
he came from England (Norfolk).

---

[5] Edward Joseph Phelan (1888-   ), British economist of Irish birth;
after many years with the International Labor Office, he became its Director General in 1946; author, *inter alia*, of *The British Commonwealth
and the League of Nations* (1931).
[1] Leonard Craske, *supra*, p. 53.

In the way of reading, not much, but impressing. I've read, in a translation, not having the French, *Le père Goriot*—an odious story. I don't think the reproduction of ugly or hateful things always justified by the genius it may display—justified aesthetically, I mean of course. When I got enough for the moment I turned for a tooth wash to the little excellent book on Rome in the Home University series and the Plutarch's *Lives* referred to there. It is an ever fresh surprise to see how many of the axiomatic media got from life by men of the world you find in the old books. My father quoted Tom Appleton,[2] a noted wit, for "Give us the luxuries of life and we will dispense with the necessities"—which is Menger's[3] *"les gens pour qui le superflu est le nécessaire,"* previously hinted at by Balzac, and now in the life of old Cato I read of Scopas, a rich man, saying "It is just these useless and unnecessary things that make my wealth and happiness"—which comes pretty near, etc. etc. Now I have nothing on hand and have taken up the *Antigone* in the intervals of paying bills, and leisurely preparations for the return to Washington at the end of the month. Did you ever read Leacock's account of a Greek play given by college boys? It is balm to a wounded soul. It is in *Over the Footlights,* a book I recommend—"Oroastus, a Greek Tragedy, attributed to Diplodokus."

A day or two ago I received a parcel marked "Personal, Confidential and Urgent" and in another place "From Society for the Propagation of the Word among the Heathen; Subcommittee for the Illustrious Heathen"—and began to swear to myself, noting only the first words of the last. I opened and found *Gentlemen Prefer Blondes* (which, like Emerson's cannon shot, seems to have been heard round the world). I suspect an ex-secretary who was here with his wife a few days ago.

And so *adieu* for the moment.

Affectionately yours, O. W. Holmes

16 *Warwick Gardens, 1.IX.26*

My dear Justice: We got back here yesterday from Belgium, and are to spend a week in Manchester with my people before serious work begins. Meanwhile I am arranging new books, and finding out what is happening to the world. . . .

We spent a day also just outside Antwerp with friends. A perfect scene—flat dunes with the old Flemish houses fading into them, and good talk. One of the houses was Camille Huysmans',[1]

---

[2] Thomas G. Appleton (1812-1884); Boston man of letters.

[3] Carl Menger (1840-1921), founder of the so-called Austrian school of economics which emphasized the factor of subjective value in the explanation of economic phenomena.

[1] Camille Huysmans (1871-   ), Socialist statesman, was Prime Minister of Belgium from 1946 to 1947.

the Socialist Minister for Education in the present Belgian government and a very attractive fellow. He told me remarkable stories of Lenin, whom he knew well in the days of exile; and he took me to see a most interesting survival of the old common system where the Flemish peasant still has a right to fish, wood, and pasturage for one cow or two sheep. I talked to some old peasants there and found, to my amazement, that one of their deepest convictions was absolute loathing of Spain. Why, I could not understand until further talk revealed that it was the memory of Alva and the Spanish infantry which had been handed down as a legend of hate; and Huysmans told me that Alva still exists throughout Flanders as the nursery bogy for naughty children. . . .

Eliot's death, I suppose, was expected.[2] I take it for granted that he was a great man. I only saw him twice, when I found him impressive but harsh. Your father, if I remember aright, held him in great esteem. He must have done much for Harvard, and certainly he makes Lowell dwarf-like. But I am not sure that a smaller, more intense Harvard would not have been finer; at least I always feel that in the Law School which I respect above all other educational places.

My warm affection to you both. I shall write once more to B. Farms and then try you in Washington.

Ever devotedly yours, H. J. L.

Beverly Farms, September 15, 1926

My dear Laski: Your last letter tells of your return and among other things of a book by Sartaux[1] [*sic*] which you call a modern footnote to Hauréau. I read Hauréau once with interest, although I believe I was assured that there was a better book by someone else, and I wish I might read this, but we leave here at the end of next week. I wonder what you mean by saying that it is going to lead you further than you ever intended to go. Do you mean in reading? I remember that Hauréau impressed me by showing Descartes more indebted to the scholastics than I had supposed. As to a book on Plato's theory of law, it seems to me that that can wait. I saw the other day, possibly in Höffding, a reference to the *Antigone* (Don't you always say Antígone although the Greek accent is Antigóne? I am aware that the *o* is short) for the statement that no one knows where the law comes from. As the reference suggesting it did not give the lines I am rereading it, though I find the chorus a difficulty even with Sir G. Young's translation alongside. I find that Antigone is speaking of the divine law—

<hr />

[2] Charles William Eliot (1834-1926), President Emeritus of Harvard, had died on August 22.

[1] In a passage omitted from this edition Laski had praised Félix Sartiaux, *Foi et science au moyen âge* (1926).

1.456.457: ἀλλ' ἀεί ποτε ζῇ ταῦτα κοὐδεὶς οἶδεν ἐξ ὅτου 'φάνη,[2] but it fits pretty well the notion of the common law as pictured by McIlwain in Coke's time even. I shall try to reread *Sur la pierre blanche,* but my rather vague recollection is that I didn't like it. A. F. does not always hit me—although I bow to *Les dieux ont soif.*

I am not doing any serious reading, but give the best two or three hours to admirable drives, and have done a little more Balzac with continued dislike for the pictures of envy and malice and thirst for luxury. I imagine that I still should get pleasure from the *Contes drolatiques* but I have them not here. I bought them during our Civil War with Doré's illustrations, and have them on my shelf of horrors in Washington. Speaking of the Civil War, I believe that I am becoming a sort of mystical hero to two or three small boys, cousins or neighbors, as a survivor who was in that show. The grandmother of one asked me for an autograph for him, and an aunt stipulated that I should give it to her so that her boy could stick the addressee for a quarter, to get it. So I wrote telling the lad that 64 years ago on the 17th I was at Antietam and nearly killed. I like to boast of my grandmother who died at about that time and who remembered moving out of Boston when the British troops came in. I think Lord Percy occupied her father's house as my father told me that probably he had had his head powdered before a looking glass that is now in my parlor at Washington—but Rice, late of the print department, Congressional Library, knocked it out by saying that his grandmother with whom he had talked remembered the old French war which was earlier than the Revolution. An epitome of (my) life: my first book ends (designedly) with the word "explained" [3]—my last with the word "unknown." *Sat prata biberunt.* I close the gates.

Affectionately yours, O. W. Holmes

16 Warwick Gardens, 19.IX.26
My dear Justice: You must forgive my long silence, but I have been overwhelmed since I last wrote to you. First there was a visit of a week to my people in Manchester, which was not unattractive, but very exhausting. You see the atmosphere is so strange to Frida that I have to be, so to say, on duty all the time to see that she is comfortable. It isn't that they don't like her, on the contrary. But it is the meeting of two quite different worlds, and my job is to be the medium of adjustment. So while I am there I neither

---

[2] "[For their life is not of today or yesterday] but from all time, and no man knows when they were first put forth." (Jebb, tr.).

[3] In fact, the final word of *The Common Law* is not quite as its author's memory had it. It ends with the word "understood."

read nor write, but simply talk hard from morning till night. Then we had the problem of this house. The landlord had the option to terminate the lease next March, which he has done; and he offered to renew it only on terms which no professional salary could cope with, in addition to wanting us to take on a studio at the back at 150 pounds a year. As he offered to renew the lease only for 14 years we should have been paying a heavy rental for nothing at the end. So we decided that the path of wisdom was to find a new house and if possible a little freehold so that all we spent on it would still leave us with a ποῦστὼ we knew to be ours. After wearisome hunting we have found and bought a delicious little Georgian house (1796) about five minutes from where we now live. It has one disadvantage—a railway in the front. But it has beautifully proportioned rooms with Adam ceilings and fireplaces, an attractive little garden, and we think that with some five hundred pounds spent on it, we can make it a real joy to us. So sometime in the next few months we shall move there and you will have to accustom your envelopes to a new address.

As you can imagine, this has taken time and energy and I have done little else. But we managed a delightful dinner with Redlich at the Francis Hirsts' just before he set sail for America. (You know, I expect, that he is to teach jurisprudence in the Law School for three years.) He is a great conversationalist, and we wandered easily over the universe. We agreed in liking Jefferson more than Hamilton, in thinking that Destutt de Tracy[1] was a wrongly neglected figure, and in elevating Tocqueville above any similar person in the 19th century. I had to fight both him and Hirst over Leslie Stephen, whose books they rated low; and over you whom they accused of undue contempt for Aristotle and Plato. I argued (I hope fairly) that your "contempt" was simply an insistence that you must see with your own eyes first and adjust your scheme in the light of their criticism rather than bow the knee a priori. I wonder much how Redlich will fit into Harvard. He has great incisiveness and is very "European." On the other hand he has warm affection (who could not?) for Felix and I think he is counting much on that friendship as the certain basis of content while he is in America. But you will, I gather, be seeing him in October, I hope, and I shall look forward to your impressions. . . .

Ever affectionately yours, H. J. L.

---

[1] Antoine Louis Claude Destutt de Tracy (1754-1836), father of "ideology," a science of ideas sufficient, according to its author and disciples, to bring certainty to the political and moral sciences; his admiration for American ideals was reciprocated by Jefferson, who sponsored the publication of Destutt de Tracy's work as *A Treatise on Political Economy* (1817).

Washington, D.C., October 3, 1926

My dear Laski: Your letter telling of your visit to your father's and your hunt for a house was forwarded to me here, and gives me unusual pleasure even for a letter of yours. The simplicity with which you tell of domestic circumstances and your assumption of my interest and sympathy delights me. Perhaps it is rather late in the day for me to remark on such things and not take them for granted, but still they give me a happy pleasure.

I wonder what can have given Redlich or your illegible host (Francis Hust?) whom I do not recognize, the notion that I had a contempt for Plato and Aristotle? I revere them, and have reread Dialogues of Plato and read Aristotle (whom I know less well) of recent years. I simply apply to them what I apply to all the past, my belief that the present conception of the universe and man's place in it is more delicate and profound than ever before—which I think is obvious. Don't you? Apropos of Redlich, you call him a great "conversation*al*ist"—a common phrase. I always wonder why the adjective termination *al* is put into the noun. Galsworthy I mainly pass by on the other side and can't criticize in detail. I think I remember having read very beautiful descriptions of nature by him.

We got here Wednesday morning and things now are in pretty good shape for tomorrow's beginning. I have gone over (now and in the summer time) 57 *certioraris* and have a big stack of them still awaiting examination. I have called on the C.J. but have not seen him, and have missed a call from Brandeis who came when I allowed myself the let-up of a drive in the park yesterday morning. I did have a call from Hough (L. Hand's colleague) which gave me much pleasure. He has praised and criticized and chaffed me in articles in which, as in his opinions, he has a spicy tongue. I liked him greatly. He talks simply and straight—one was willing to trust him at once. Also he spoke with affection and appreciation of Felix, which went to my heart.

No reading for some time, I expect. I took advantage of the time saved by the C.J.'s being out to whisk over to the Congressional Library to look at an article to which I had been referred on Leibl [1]—whom Spengler—*Untergang des Abendlandes*—cracks up as one of the last of the great, and about whom (partly because I couldn't remember the name) I have been vainly curious since 1924. There was only one reproduction of an etching, but there were others of drawings and paintings. I couldn't make up my mind off hand on what I saw whether he was more than a man who thoroughly knew his job. That is, I didn't clearly detect a great poet, or one who had profoundly new things to say. And I

---

[1] Wilhelm Leibl (1844-1900), German painter who passed from an imitative phase to a more forthright and self-sufficient realism.

don't think that we yet have exhausted what man can learn of, or feel about, the universe—which you fellows, who propose to reshape it, will admit, I think.

I forget whether I have mentioned an excursion into Balzac, in translations that happen to be in the house at Beverly Farms, *Père Goriot, Chouans, Un grand homme de province à Paris,* and a popular French life of him. I don't like him or enjoy his books. Bob Barlow was talking about him, said in substance, You don't find what we call a good fellow outside our crowd, which has a certain truth. Their damned envies, jealousies, and mean tricks make me tired. But perhaps I should qualify Barlow by saying that one who does not know London or Paris but only this country, cannot quite realize the fierce temptations of social ambition. Still, there is too much of the boor and the snob about Balzac with all his genius. I prefer the British laugh from the guts.

One of the most universally applicable of quotations, which comes up to me in many places, is Caesar's *et superest ager*—but I will plough no more today.   *Affectionately yours, O. W. Holmes*

16 Warwick Gardens, 30.IX.26
My dear Justice: This letter is written on the verge of term, with all the tensity which comes therewith. . . .

Since I wrote last I have had a good deal to do. A week-end in Cambridge for an adult education conference with the extra job of finding a successor to Haldane as its president.[1] . . . Rutherford had a great German physicist staying with him who had never read a line of Goethe, the ancient classics, alternative sciences, did not know anything of history, abstained from the study of politics, and relaxed by reading the higher mathematics. He was a Nobel prizeman, obviously a genius in his line, and, as I said to Haldane, he cared nothing for ⅞ of the heritage of mankind. I added (Haldane dissenting strongly) that apart from physics I refused to regard his pronouncements on life as having any more interest or importance than those of a bricklayer or a waiter—less perhaps. But of course he had views about everything and could not be made to grasp the possibility that *e.g.* a knowledge of liquid hydrogen did not entitle one to judgments upon how a civil servant should be chosen. . . .

One other adventure I must record, but for your private ear only. I drafted some letters for the miners in their struggle with the government, as a result of which I went with them to Downing Street the other day. The change in Baldwin since I saw him last was quite tragic. He had become hard and a little cynical and

---

[1] Mr. Justice Sankey succeeded to the presidency. An account of the Cambridge conference is in Haldane's *Autobiography* (1929), 319-322.

impatient of all criticism. We had some private talk and I found
that he was a most curious mixture of the sentimental phrase and
the hard act. Churchill who was there was bigger and more skilful
in every way—he knew how to negotiate, Baldwin merely blun-
dering uncouthly. . . .   *Ever affectionately yours, H. J. L.*

                                    16 Warwick Gardens, 9.X.26
My dear Justice: . . . I have had all the documents to study for
my first case as a member of the Arbitration Court, and as I
cannot, like you, look into my docket and find 2000 cases, I have,
as Felix would say, sweated blood over it. It's a good case, I add,
with room for the display of ingenuity; but we don't sit until next
Tuesday so I have little notion of how these things work out as
yet.[1]

Of reading but little . . . the second volume of Wells's new
novel, *Clissold,* which, with some bits of bad taste, I thought quite
masterly. He has an amazing power of vivid insight, and a courageous frankness which it is impossible not to admire. People complain of his attack on the King; yet if I may whisper it, I think
the things he attacks the King for are justly put and have exactly
the incidence on social affairs that he indicates. Certainly, in my
own experience, the people at the top are helpless mentally and
morally before royalty; I have seen even a girl of brains and
courage like Elizabeth Bibesco[2] tremble with excitement at a
garden-party because the Duchess of York asked for some words
with her; and at the Institute of Philosophical Studies the largest
attendance we ever had at its executive was when the Prince of
Wales, who is its patron, took the chair. People of real distinction,
like Balfour, stood by him with an air of religious deference which
was frankly nauseating. . . . I have (with Frida's approval) definitely finished the purchase of the house, to which I think we shall
go in about Xmas time.

For the rest I have been hard at my book on communism which
moves slowly on its way.[3] I emerge as an admirer of Lenin who
was a master of courage and strategy. But I emerge also with the
conviction that toleration and good will, bourgeois as they are, out-
weigh in virtue all the other qualities in the world. And the dogmatism that is the price of a communist scheme seems the more
unlovely the more one examines it. However you shall judge for
yourself in the spring of next year when the little book comes out.

---

[1] The Case of Postmasters and Assistant Postmasters (#1256), 8 Industrial
Court Decisions 306. Laski had recently been appointed a member of the
Industrial Court, a post which he filled until his death.

[2] Princess Bibesco was Asquith's daughter, Lady Elizabeth Asquith.

[3] *Communism* (Volume 131 of Home University Library, 1927).

I have been rather baffled by receiving a number of circulars from the Harvard Law School asking for money. I don't like their scheme. A professorship of legislation seems to me merely foolish, and one of criminology dubious because likely to give a myopic view; and I don't want the Law School to grow bigger—it's already over-big. Accordingly with some doubts I have decided to do nothing for the scheme and send a gift to the library instead. I'd like much to know what your views are about this. To me it looks as though Pound had been trapped by the illusion of size.

Our love to both of you.   *Ever affectionately yours, H. J. L.*

16 Warwick Gardens, 16.X.26

My dear Justice: . . . This week Frida came along with me to Edinburgh and Glasgow, where I had to give some university lectures. . . . It was queer to meet one emeritus professor of law (aged ninety-three) whose grandfather had been a student of Adam Smith at Glasgow which takes one straight back to the middle of the eighteenth century; and the old gentleman told me of Carlyle's visit to him in the sixties when he asked C. what he thought of J. S. Mill and was given a scornful "He has nae roots in his mind" for an answer. . . .

Our warm love to you both,   *Ever affectionately yours, H. J. L.*

Washington, D.C., October 13, 1926

My dear Laski: You were harried and bothered about writing your last—and I am about answering it. The Lord knows when I can finish the few words I begin now. Before I refer to what you say and before I forget it: Do you remember Zane whom you ran against in some criticism and who has had whacks at me and I believe Pound?[1] During the war he excluded by one stroke all consideration of any work by German jurists—another wiped out Hobbes, Bentham and Austin, and in short left one to suppose that there was nothing worth considering except what he as yet did not see fit to reveal. Incidentally he said that anyone who thought my *Kawananakoa* case was law might give up all hope of ever being a lawyer—which was rather hard on me. I saw a notice by him of Vinogradoff's *Custom and Right*,[2] in which at last he praised and seemed to think Vinogradoff the greatest jurist of the last 50 years. I have sent for the brochure . . . and though I have had no time to read it yet I have a deep inward conviction from V's book in the Home University Library[3]—poor—and his book on Villenage

---

[1] See, *supra*, pp. 132-33, Vol. I.

[2] 35 *Yale L. J.* 1026 (June 1926).

[3] *Common-sense in Law* (1913).

—good—(I forget the title) that Vinogradoff was a distinctly finite being—not I should think to be named in the same year with Ehrlich. You know more about him. Am I wrong?

I agree with you, *totis viribus*, as to mathematics. Postulates depend on insight, man's greatest gift—one man having it in one direction, another in another. Mathematics like other reasoning starts from postulates, and in my very limited observation, mathematicians show little insight in the postulates that they accept. Of course I can speak of them only outside their special province, but it has struck me with mathematicians here—and I might add Bertrand Russell, and Haldane [illegible] in philosophy, although I was not thinking of them when I began. They say math teaches accuracy of thought. I should think it was the last thing to have that effect, as it is the place where an undistributed middle is almost impossible. A is always A and X, X. You learn accuracy where you have to do the quantifying. How I should like to run on—but I can't, and must go to work—it is Friday now. We have an off day and I am more busy than ever in the moment of leisure.

Affectionately yours, O. W. Holmes

Washington, D.C., October 23, 1926
My dear Laski: Imprimis congratulations on your purchase of a house. I think it adds to the pleasure of life to own your own headquarters. For although when I first came to Washington I was in another man's house with his furniture, without my books, and working in a room where his marriage certificate, sporting and other prints, occupied the walls, and yet had a good time, it wasn't near so good as it could have been if I had been here. *Secundo* —What is it about your being member of the arbitration court? What is the Court? and all about it? This is your first mention. If I may venture a hint, I hope you won't be too keen after the display of ingenuity that you mention. I was afraid from your account that you rather overdid it when you were on a jury. 3. As to the contribution to the Harvard Law School I have shared your impression so far that I have not forked out, and talking with Brandeis today found that he was even more decidedly of the same mind. I don't remember the proposed professorships now, but several of them struck me as more than doubtful. Beside what you mention, wasn't there one on the History of the Law. I wouldn't endow that. 4. As to the attitude toward royalty, of course I have been struck by the same thing. I remember in the middle of an interesting talk at a garden party at (Buckingham?) palace the lady I was with broke off to rush and adore as some royal children went by. But I don't think you should call it nau-

seating. It may be, and I don't doubt often is not snobbish, but just a kind of religious exaltation, an ideal of loyalty, really to England, personified. It is not relevant but I add that I think Thackeray quite wrong in assuming that it would be discreditable to be pleased to walk down Pall Mall arm in arm with a couple of dukes. It very probably would mean only satisfaction at evidence of one's own importance—which it is not base to feel, only foolish to believe (unless you are a Christian).

I have just been impressed with the doctrine of relativity in a different sphere from Einstein's and one that doesn't require a knowledge of mathematics although much used. At our conference yesterday p.m. (for now it is Sunday) we had some rate cases, the question being whether the rate fixed by the N.Y. legislature for gas companies in New York was confiscatory and so, unconstitutional.[1] We solemnly weigh the valuation of the property and all the tests and decide pro or con—but really it is determining a line between grabber and grabbee that turns on the feeling of the community. You say the public is entitled to this and the owners to that. I see no *a priori* reason for the propositions except that that is the way the crowd feels. I tell them that if the rate-making power will only say I have considered A. B. & C., all the elements enumerated, we accept the judgment unless it makes us puke. It is like the ideal of woman—on one end you have the dames of the *Decameron* who care only for God and man, at the other a peaked, elbowed school marm who talks on high themes and thinks man a superfluity of nature. A given community fixes its conception somewhere midway according to the dominance of companionship or dimples.

As to the communists I have little doubt that I shall agree with what you say. I take no stock in any scheme for remaking society that begins with property instead of life. And that means that I don't care much for any scheme that could be thought of now. I utterly disbelieve all postulates of human rights in general. Those established in a given society stand on a different ground. But I grow like my school marm above in what I am writing.

Things have gone pleasantly with me so far, and the constant over-pressure of the last three weeks will abate somewhat with our short adjournment tomorrow. I shall fire off an opinion[2] and have only one to write—on a matter that interests me much and will let in about an inch of theory *contra* some English intimations in your cases.[3]   *Affectionately yours, O. W. Holmes*

---

[1] *Ottinger* v. *Consolidated Gas Co.*, 272 U.S. 576; *Ottinger* v. *Brooklyn Union Co.*, id. 579. In each case the Court held that the rates established by the legislature were confiscatory.

[2] *Palmetto Fire Insurance Co.* v. *Conn*, 272 U.S. 295.

[3] *Deutsche Bank Filiale* v. *Humphrey*, 272 U.S. 517 (Nov. 23, 1926).

16 Warwick Gardens, 23.X.26

My dear Justice: . . . Your mention of John Zane comes to me a
little faintly down the years as of one who wrote boisterously but
without learning in the *Michigan Law Review.* I should not, as
now informed, take anything he said very seriously. I have that
little book of Vinogradoff's about which there isn't, I think, any
reason to get excited. I knew V. pretty well. He had immense
learning of which he always made a great parade; but I never
thought he had an incisive mind, and apart from that famous
paper on folkland [1] and the admirable preface to his *Villainage in
England* I never could get really excited by him. . . . I went, too,
to dinner with Jaeger,[2] the great German classic[ist] who has succeeded Wilamowitz[3] in Berlin. He was most attractive and his
hostility to Aristophanes for daring to satirise Socrates was one of
the most charming things I have seen. He told us one great story
of Mommsen hearing that Max Müller[4] had been appointed professor in Oxford. "Have they then no humbugs in their own country" said Mommsen, "that they must deprive us of grounds for
grumbling." He was the old-time German *gelehrte,* modest, interesting, eager to exchange ideas, and with a pride in his job
that was impressive. Yesterday, I gave my inaugural lecture at
the School, a copy of which I shall send you as soon as it is
printed.[5] . . .

We are having a fascinating time getting our new house put
into order; and I think Mrs. Holmes would enjoy our hunts round
for the oddments of Georgian furniture which give the note of
completeness to the rooms. At the moment we are searching for
the perfect Chippendale sideboard—not an easy thing. We have
a perfect 17th century carved oak chest for the hall; you would,
I think, endorse it as a work of art. And for my study I have had
a large photograve taken of the National Gallery Portrait of old
Hobbes—a most noble head with a mouth that is a marvel of obstinacy. And a small one of old Prynne which I have bought not
because I like him but because, as Maitland said, old Prynne

---

[1] "Folkland," 8 *English Historical Review* 1 (1893); reprinted in 1
Vinogradoff *Collected Legal Papers* (1928) 91.

[2] Werner Wilhelm Jaeger (1888-1961) was at the University of Berlin
from 1921 to 1936. Professor Jaeger then moved to the United States and
from 1939 was University Professor at Harvard; his best known work is
Paideia: The Ideals of Greek Culture (3 vols., 1939-44).

[3] *Supra,* p. 35, Vol. I.

[4] Friedrich Max Müller (1823-1900); comparative philologist and ori-
entalist who from 1848 until 1894 taught at Oxford and did much to
popularize the theory of Aryanism.

[5] *On the Study of Politics: An Inaugural Lecture Delivered at the London
School of Economics and Political Science on 22 October 1926* (1926); reprinted in *The Danger of Being a Gentleman and Other Essays* (1940), 33.

munching crusts in the Tower while he copies out records is an
heroic figure.

My love to you both. Do not do too much. Life is more even
than the largest possible number of *certioraris*.

Ever affectionately yours, H. J. L.

Washington, D.C., November 1, 1926

My dear Laski: Is it that you are more suggestive—Is it that when
I am swimming in the law I have few ideas outside of it? Is it—?
Why is it that I so often write half my letters in answer to questions that your letter evokes? I don't know what Carlyle's remark
about Mill meant to Carlyle, but it seems to have an obvious truth
in it. Carlyle's thoughts were rooted in his temperament, his prejudices, and his imagination—Mill's were detached by reason. People
pay higher for luxuries than for necessaries and Carlyle's pictures
may outlast Mill's thoughts but I doubt if Carlyle gave the world
as great a shove as Mill. I have forgotten what I said about Plato
but I believe I have given him his dues of love for the things you
mention.

I feel much as you do about Aristophanes, bar passages no
longer remembered by me when he says beautiful things—but the
fun of the ancients! Excuse *me*. Plautus I thought not as good as a
circus or on a higher level—when I peeked into him a year or
two ago. Why you snub Mencken in that connection I don't quite
see. I have read what I didn't care for in him but I took much
pleasure in a volume of *Prejudices*. Xenophon I haven't looked
into except the *Memorabilia* since I was young, except that a
glance at one of the translations at our house at Beverly led me
to wait for better days.

You tell me of a new judge—but as yet nothing of my dear
Leslie Scott—I do want to see him on the Appellate Court. We
adjourned this morning. My last opinion—a case assigned to me
on Saturday—has come back in proof from the printer and after
I have sent it out I have no duties to speak of except a trifle of 8
certioraris that came in this morning. I mean to read Wallas's *Art
of Thought*—though I believe you did not care much for it and
his antecedent synopsis did not look like a flash of lightning—
and a brochure of Vinogradoff's [of] which I hope to think lightly
for reasons of personal malevolence as I explained the other day.
It was so very highly cracked up by your friend John M. Zane.

Tuesday 2d. I mean to go out presently to look for some witch
hazel which my wife always gets on this day. I don't know what
the day is, (it should have been before Halloween), or why, except
for the flower of a bush that blossoms at this time. Returning to

the fun of the past, it dies quicker than the tragedy, I suppose
because more generally dependent on circumstances or special
powers of mind. Artemus Ward I found last summer had little
that lasted—a few memorable things based on the eternal, but
largely mannerisms that no longer please and make one wonder
that they ever did. Ditto of a good deal of Shakespeare. The fun
of the middle ages is generally, so far as I know, the dirty talk of
boys. All of which I believe I have said before.

Beveridge has sent me another chapter which I now have opened
and begun to read. It is interestingly told but I hate to go over
the squalid preliminaries to the war as I hate to reread of the
blunders and worse of the war itself and its sequel. I don't see
any great good to Beveridge in my reading, beyond a few corrections of English and some occasional point when my memory or
local knowledge helps—but I think I have encouraged him a little
when he has been feeling down. Brandeis wishes that he had taken
Taney (Marshall's successor) instead of Lincoln—but as he had a
stomach for it I think Lincoln was the better choice. It is not the
kind of undertaking that would have tempted me, but no biography—simple or auto—would. I like more abstract themes. I get
letters from time to time suggesting everything from my views of
life to my recollections of my father which move me only as bores
to answer. I believe this sums me up. My opinion has gone forth
—and when the irritation of the remaining small matters is over
I shall look out on a blank world and try to take my ease.

Affectionately yours, O. W. Holmes

Washington, D.C., November 5, 1926
My dear Laski: Your letter October 23 came just after your Inaugural on the Study of Politics and I have just read both, with
equal pleasure. The address seems to me admirable both in its
specific suggestions and in its exaltation of the service of thought.
I notice with interest that you have added affection for Sankey to
admiration of him.[1] I wish I knew more of his work. I am delighted
at what you say about Vinogradoff as it confirms the prophecy of
my soul. I shall read him directly.

My work is over for the moment, but leisure comes, never. When
law and life run short of chores—the wondrous tale's filled up by
bores. However, I have had some enchanting drives and yesterday
p.m. went to my first and only show for years—*The Barber of
Seville*—to see Chaliapin, but alas he filled only a subordinate part
and didn't give my wife the impression that I wanted her to get
—that I got in London from *Ivan the Terrible.*

---

[1] Laski's Inaugural lecture (*supra*, p. 116) was dedicated to "my friend
Mr. Justice Sankey with enduring affection."

I sympathize with the preparations for a house of your own, but there is a feeling of money in the background that makes me doubt if you know how we felt at Mattapoisett when we decided to invest in a wheelbarrow for manure to take the place of a [illegible] drawn by a bit of rope—or the joy we used to have when we lived in rooms next the Athenaeum and would skip off to the Museum to take 50 cent seats and sneer at the nobs. You talk of Chippendale—I was devilish glad to get pine boxes for my books. Not, though, that I don't believe you have shown more resolution in that way than ever I was called on to show. I don't forget that.

My secretary,[2] a very nice lad, has taken some walks with me. This morning I showed him the Soldiers' Home with the blue sky seen through the gold of the tulip trees, then over to the Adams Saint Gaudens statue in the Rock Creek cemetery, then whisking across the town to Arlington in the uncertain effort to tread the turf under which I shall lie before long. I found a spot, but whether it was *like* it or *it* I know not. I have returned Beveridge's chapters with some general criticisms that I hope were not unjust. I think he seems unduly impressed by the Southern point of view, which I imagine is new to him, before the war—an unfortunate atmosphere, if I am right, for a book on Lincoln. However he honestly and sincerely wants to get the facts and let them tell the story. Of course I was nearer to the events than he, and I don't think I'm prejudiced—although in my day I was a pretty convinced abolitionist and was one of a little band intended to see Wendell Phillips through if there was a row after the meeting of the Anti-Slavery Society just before the war. How coolly one looks on that question now—but when I was a sophomore I didn't like the nigger minstrels because they seemed to belittle the race. I believe at that time even *Pickwick* seemed to me morally coarse. "Now his nerves have grown firmer," as Mr. Browning says, and I fear you would shudder in your turn at the low level of some of my social beliefs. With which, *adieu* for the time. I suppose this will just miss a boat, but will muddle through in time.

Aff'ly yours, O. W. H.

16 *Warwick Gardens, 11.XI.26*
My dear Justice: A perfect delight of a letter from you warmed the cockles of my heart. It came after ten days in which I had been peculiarly driven, and gave me a sense that there are things behind the endless *paperasserie* in which I seem to have been deluged. Let me first answer some of your questions. Leslie Scott, I gather, is talked of for a lordship of appeal when a vacancy

[2] Thomas G. Corcoran (1900-   ); later renowned for his role as anonymous counselor of President Roosevelt and thereafter private practitioner in Washington, D.C.

comes; but the proposal to create a place for him which was, I believe, privately made failed because the Lords are well up to their cases and there would have been opposition. But the talk says that he will certainly get the next big post. I hear, poor fellow, that he needs it, as he has lost a good deal of money in Russia. As to my own Court. It deals with disagreements between the government and its employees and means sitting with a permanent president and one other person about once a month. So far I have sat on five cases and thoroughly enjoyed them. It is an invaluable experience to me as I learn a good deal not otherwise knowable of the inner workings of the civil service; and I see its results reflected in certain alterations of previous judgments which at least proves that my mind has not yet closed!

. . . The misery has been the packing of my books with a view to having that ready the day we move in. So I write with not a dozen books in this room, and, consequently an indefinable emptiness in the heart. And I have sat on myriads of committees—at the School, the Labour Party, and what not which were all necessary, but built on the basis of a world in which there is no time. Also, as chairman of the mediation board of the co-operative societies,[1] I had to settle a dispute about the wages of some 1000 men; and four nights of evidence plus the writing of a reasoned decision is not done with a flick of the eye. And I had to give a lecture to a conference of workingmen which, following one by Hugh Cecil,[2] I took rather special care to make informative and found, as a result, that it was more laborious than I expected. Finally, having been elected a corresponding member of the *Deutsche Gesellschaft für Sociologie,* I had to compose a rather elaborate address of thanks for their proceedings. The result has been that both reading and writing from my own standpoint have rather gone by the board. . . .

My love warmly to you both. Don't spend too much time on *certioraris;* and remember Birrell's advice to me for leisure periods —while there is life there is Dooley.

Ever affectionately yours, H. J. L.

Washington, D.C., November 23, 1926
My dear Laski: Your letter (Nov. 11) is most interesting, and tells me about what I didn't know before, your appointment to the Industrial Court, although I still have no idea beyond what you give me of its and your functions. I should think it would be a very valuable experience to you. I appreciate your sitting in the

---

[1] Laski was one of a panel of chairmen of the National Conciliation Board of the Co-operative Wholesale Society.

[2] Lord Hugh Cecil (1869-1956), who became Baron Quickswood in 1941, was the author of *Conservatism* (1912).

empty room. I worked in one for my first year here, as I believe I have told you, with the marriage certificate of the lessor and pious, relieved by sporting, prints.

We began sitting again yesterday, adjourning at 2 for luncheon and McKenna's funeral—a truly kind soul. The clergyman said that when his daughter told him a few days ago that he had been a perfect father, he said, "only a decent gentleman." I suppose like the rest of us he had his vanities but I think he also had humility. Some of the brethren took so long with their discourses that we shall take some time this morning in finishing—I am not reached yet. I have one case that interests me much, on the time at which the mark is to be valued in a suit here against a German bank, when the demand was made at a time when the mark was worth much more than when the suit was brought here (to reach money in the hands of the Alien Property Custodian).[1] It interests me because the dissent by Sutherland—McReynolds, Butler, Sanford, accord—seems to me to illustrate, as so many cases do to my mind, the notion that the law is a brooding omnipresence in the sky, as I once put it. When a man asserts a legal right he must refer to some law that creates it, and I say that the only right that the plaintiff had was a right created by the German law —and that was a right to so many marks and nothing else—not to the value of so many marks in other commodities at a given time—but to so many marks when the suit was brought. The tendency of some English and other cases is *contra,* but they none of them that I have seen seem to me to go to the bottom of the business. I think the same thing turns up on the question of rights against the sovereign, or center of legal authority however you name it. Borchard has a long article on this last theme in the last *Yale Law Journal*[2]—interestingly learned but to my mind helpless when he comes to this proposition. Also I have just reread Bacon's *Essays*—many shrewd thoughts and some noble language. I think I wrote the other day that great works survive largely by sound. Style seems to me fundamentally sound. But you could get more intellectual stimulus from a current number of the *New Republic* or the *Spectator*—why read him then? I think the question not entirely easy—and I should advise a young man to read mainly books of his own time until his views begin to be settled. Then he will begin to extend his boundaries. There is philosophy in knowing the vicissitudes of thought through which one's crowd has gone before getting to where it is—and it is pleasant to be cultivated, and so forth and so forth. At the same time every summer when I read a few pages of classics I have an anxious sense that

---

[1] *Deutsche Bank Filiale* v. *Humphrey,* 272 U.S. 517.

[2] Edwin M. Borchard, "Governmental Responsibility in Tort" (Part I), 36 *Yale L. J.* 1 (November 1926).

it would be easy to waste time upon them. Of course pleasure is self-justifying—but to me reading of old literature is but a moderate joy—a nutpicker and a shagbark—when you might have a slice of something better with less trouble.

I had a line from Beveridge rather gloomy over his work. It is not the kind of job that I should care for—but I have no doubt that it will be *the* life and the only one when he has done. Also this evening a letter from Wu.   *Affectionately yours, O. W. H.*

16 Warwick Gardens, 21.XI.26
My dear Justice: A grand letter from you was an oasis in the midst of a heavy week. But now, thank heaven, things will go more quietly until the end of term. Last week the outstanding thing was a paper at the Sociological Club by Sir M. Amos (whom you may remember) on the need for scientific jurisprudence.[1] I wish he would print it, for especially its analysis of the sins of Pound was a masterpiece. His argument was that a good many of Pound's "objective" results turn out on investigation to be derived either from an unconscious expression of need he feels, or from the way in which he classifies his material, the assumptions of classification not being tested. The whole paper was a superb *tour de force,* witty, eloquent, and full of curious knowledge. I was particularly struck by a devastating attack on Stammler which in general seemed to me unanswerable. . . .

Coventry was a great experience. I spoke there in a lovely 14th century hall with a piece of tapestry at its back which simply defies description. That had some perfect Tudor portraits, one, especially, of Mary Tudor by Zucchini which explains the Elizabethan reaction against Catholicism better than most histories. It was, by the way, amusing to see the satisfaction of the Mayor in an horrific picture of Lady Godiva, their patron saint. For fear of libel, my memory suppresses the name of the artist; but he made Lady Godiva a giantess with breasts like mountains, a fit mate for Gog or Magog; and she sits on a poor little palfrey which would certainly have invoked the Society for Preventing Cruelty to animals, could it have spoken. But the Mayor pointed it out to me with rapture and the Tudor portraits, I gathered, were nothing by the side of this gem. I spoke there with my friend Oliver Stanley,[2] a young Tory M.P. who is Derby's second son. He told me some amusing stories of an ancestor who held a cabinet post in the six-

---

[1] See Sir Maurice Sheldon Amos, "Some Reflection on the Philosophy of Law," 3 *Cambridge Law Journal* 31 (1927) which is evidently a portion of the paper referred to.

[2] The ancestor of Oliver Stanley (1896-1950) would seem to be Edward Stanley, fourteenth Earl of Derby (1799-1869), three times Prime Minister and always the sharp-tongued critic of those with whom he disagreed.

ties. The old boy lived in Westmoreland and was passionately
fond of shooting. From August to February he stayed in the North
and not even the Franco-German war brought him to town for a
cabinet meeting. All the departmental papers were sent him there,
and when Palmerston who was Prime Minister, protested at the
expense of (I) a daily messenger in a reserved compartment (II)
a special coach to the minister's country home, 14 miles from a
railway, Stanley replied "One must have some return for serving
the country." Certainly those were spacious days; the old gentleman, by the way, got a cabinet minister's pension and on his death
it was discovered that he had assigned it in equal parts to (I) his
wife (II) his favourite ballet-dancer and (III) the head-waiter at
his London club so that a certain port was reserved for himself.
His elder brother remonstrated with him for his loose ways of life
to which he replied, "Damme, my dear brother, look at Pam; I
can't let the P.M. down by being better than he is." He left a will
in which a thousand pounds was put aside for the son who could
guess which Prime Minister in his period (1830-68) had not committed adultery; and the answer was Peel, who, he said, was "too
damned proud to break the commandments; it would have given
God a hold over him and Peel never asked a favour from anyone."
He really must have been the perfect 18th century nobleman,
brought up on the principles of Chesterfield and convinced that
the world was made for his personal amusement. Yet extraordinarily shrewd. Charles Greville disliked him greatly and would
never go to the Privy Council when the old fellow was Lord President. Stanley said nothing about it and Greville was piqued that
his absence was not commented on. He sent an emissary to investigate to whom Stanley replied, "Tell the puppy I never look
at my footman's face." But I must not fill this letter with anecdotes. . . .

I had a long note from Felix yesterday, full of his crime survey
of Boston[3] and the incredible Sacco-Vanzetti case.[4] I hope the latter
is settled, for, otherwise, the working-classes will disbelieve in
Massachusetts justice.

Our love, as always, to you both.

Ever affectionately yours, H. J. L.

Washington, D.C., December 4, 1926
My dear Laski: A long desired letter meets me on my return from
conference this Saturday p.m. I am enchanted with your talk and

---

[3] The Harvard Survey on Crime and Law in Boston was currently under
way under the guidance of Felix Frankfurter.

[4] On October 23, Judge Webster Thayer, before whom Sacco and Vanzetti
had been tried and convicted of murder, had denied the motion of the
defense for a new trial. A few days later an appeal was taken to the Supreme
Judicial Court of Massachusetts.

wish that I could match them—but I have little except personal
news. I am worried about my Chinaman Wu who wants to come
here for a year or two and get 3 or 4,000 a year, delivering a few
lectures. I wrote to Frankfurter who doesn't hold out much encouragement. Wu wants it for his soul's sake connecting it also
more or less with me. I have an honestly disinterested desire to
help him. I can't help fearing that he may waste himself in deserts
of philosophizing—under the, as I fear, too great influence of
Stammler—out of whom as yet I have got devilish little—not of
course that philosophizing is not the chief end of man—but it is
only useful when expended on a copious supply of crude facts—
which I fear he may not be in the situation to accumulate. Perhaps having to stick it out, if he has to, will be a good test for
the fire in his belly, and if he comes through, his greatest lesson
and his greatest triumph. Just as I begin this letter I am shown a
long screed about me by Miss Sergeant in the *New Republic*.[1]
I rather wince at having a woman talk about me (in public)—but
I am surprised at some of the things she had got hold of—*e.g.* a
letter to Bill James giving some notions that later I expressed in
print. As to the rest I say no more than that women's rhetoric is
different from that of men—and that I hope my friends won't
laugh at the praise. I tried a little to turn her from the plan a year
ago—and until recently didn't suppose she was pursuing it.

I am reading a book by John Dewey, *Experience and Nature*.
Wu put me on to it saying that it was a great book and mentioning
that it had amiable words about me. I give you my word that it
was this former remark that set me to reading it—and I think Wu
was right. It is badly written in the sense that the style makes it
more difficult than the thought—but even in the writing it gives
me the feeling that Walt Whitman gives of the symphonic. Few
indeed, I should think, are the books that hold so much of life
with an even hand. If you asked me for a summary I couldn't give
more than a page of ideas, but the stimulus and the quasi-aesthetic
enjoyment are great—and the tendencies those which I agree with.
I have read but half of it as yet for my time is limited. My legal
life goes on serenely—a little while ago I wrote a case in which
I expressed the result in terms to suit the majority of the brethren,
although they didn't suit me. Years ago I did the same thing in
the interest of getting a job done. I let the then brethren put in a
reason that I thought bad and cut out all that I thought good and
I have squirmed ever since, and swore that never again—but again
I yielded and now comes a petition for rehearing pointing out all

---

[1] "Oliver Wendell Holmes," 49 *New Republic* 59 (Dec. 8, 1926); later
reprinted in *Fire Under the Andes* (1927).

the horrors that will ensue from just what I didn't want to say.[2]
I think the opinion will be altered by a few words that satisfy the
majority and that I privately think really mean my principles, and
all is serene again. I wish very much I could see Amos's paper that
you tell me about. I am afraid that I should agree with it more
than I want to—though I have no unwillingness as to Stammler
—good man though he be. My love to you all.

Affectionately yours, O. W. Holmes

16 Warwick Gardens, 4.XII.26

My dear Justice: . . . We have been out a little. A grand dinner
with Sankey to meet the C.J.[1] He's a good classical scholar, but a
mean little soul, who lives on trivialities and has no intimate zest
for the law. He praised Dunedin much and Sumner a little ("an
able dog") but otherwise had nought but jeers for the weakness
of X or C. I frankly disliked him, even though he had flattered
me by asking to meet me; for I respect fidelity to colleagues even
thought they are fit for the hangmen. But Sankey more than atoned
—especially when he had a great fight with Dean Inge upon
Christianity. The Dean isn't very good at personal controversy and
between ourselves he doesn't know his texts any too well. And he
uses big phrases like "economic law" without any real knowledge
of their meaning. The result was a grand massacre which I quite
thoroughly and deservedly enjoyed. Then a good party with Charles
Trevelyan,[2] to meet his father, the historian, Sir George. I like the
old gentleman hugely. It was a first-rate experience to hear tales
of Macaulay from the angle of the favourite nephew; and memories of Palmerston in his prime. He put Pam higher than I should
have done and Peel lower; and he was very interesting in his
tremendous admiration for Alexander Hamilton. He seems to read
very widely, and I was amused at the vehemence with which he
trounced one Nock for a bad life of Jefferson he had just read.
Then a good dinner with the Webbs whom I find more and more
satisfying in their thoroughness and receptivity. They are at work

---

[2] It seems likely that the recent case referred to was *International Steve-*
doring Company v. *Haverty,* 272 U.S. 50 (Oct. 18, 1926), the one case at
the October 1926 term in which Holmes had written an opinion and in
which a petition for rehearing was filed. It appears that no action on the
petition was taken. In its decision the Court held that stevedores engaged
in loading operations were to be treated as seamen within the meaning of
that word as used in the Jones Act. There is good reason to believe that the
earlier opinion mentioned by Holmes was that in *The Pipe Line Cases,* 234
U.S. 548 (1914).

[1] Gordon Hewart (1870-1943), Lord Hewart, was Lord Chief Justice from
1922 until 1940; author of *The New Despotism* (1929).

[2] Sir Charles Trevelyan, Bart., politician and civil servant.

on the history of the poor-law 1689-1835 [3] and had much of interest to me to communicate. Frida started the hare of who was
the best talker they had ever known and I was astonished to hear
them say with great emphasis that it was Mrs. J. R. Green. They
rated Bernard Shaw very high, but said he was too obtrusive and
sulked if he was talked down. I put all this to Birrell last night,
and he said he would put Dean Church[4] first for charm in talk
and Liddon[5] for eloquence; then Birrell-like he added reflectively
—"Those judgments must be true for they come from a Nonconformist." I add a tale Birrell told me which I like. He dined at
Trinity, Cambridge in 1902 and Butler,[6] the Master, proposed the
health of the College. He referred to the great part Trinity played
in the world and added that "it was well to remember that, at
this moment, both the Sovereign and the Prime Minister are Trinity
men." Birrell replied for the guests. "The Master," he said, "should
have added that he can go further; for it is obvious that the affairs
of the world are built upon the momentous fact that God also is
a Trinity man." Butler, says Birrell, never forgave him that. . . .

I am not disinclined to agree with what you say about reading.
But I am pretty sure that the essence of the scholar is to see the
roots of his period pretty far back and to travel along the road.
When I get a student who wants to do political philosophy seriously I like to pick out a modern problem of some size and ask
him to explain how it came to be a problem. But I find, also, that
knowledge of Plato and Aristotle doesn't compensate for ignorance
of yesterday's Hansard. I'm not, however, altogether sure that I
agree with you about style. I used to revel in Pater; now I find
him unreadable and I imagine that many have gone through my
experience. Yet it is a great style in its way. On the other hand
few things are as ugly as the style of Kant or Hegel and yet the
mind of each is irresistibly big once you sit down to them. Admitting all the glories of simplicity and clarity, isn't it true that
there are things so complex that one can't be either simple or
clear about them without violating the material? I tend more and
more also to the view that the big man in each age is the man
who asks the new questions it is in a position to answer if asked.
Literature ought to be divided into what pleases and what de-

---

[3] The fruit of their labors was *English Poor Law History* (3 vols., 1927-
29).

[4] Richard William Church (1815-1890), friend of Newman, select preacher
at Oxford, Dean of St. Paul's, and historian of the Oxford Movement. He
was noted for his telling style as writer and as preacher.

[5] Henry Parry Liddon (1829-1890), canon of St. Paul's and lecturer at
Oxford, who was an intimate and devoted admirer of Dean Church.

[6] Henry Montague Butler (1833-1918); before becoming Master of
Trinity he had been headmaster of Harrow, and dean of Gloucester. See,
infra, p. 383.

stroys. The first is eternal if it deals with ultimate things; the
second passes; but it is bigger because it clears the path.

But I must end and go to bed. Our warm affection to you both.
Ever yours as ever, H. J. L.

Washington, D.C., December 15, 1926
My dear Laski: Your letter just arrived worried me a little as it
seems to impute to me views that I cannot have meant to express
as I never entertained them. 1. When I speak about the literature
of the past in flippant terms I expect to be taken humorously, of
course. Because, although I think that if we are sincere with ourselves we get much more first hand pleasure, yes, and profit, from
the books of our own time, I deem it almost essential to our own
thinking to understand its genesis, so far as may be. Certainly I
have spent a good deal of time on books of other centuries and I
don't know what I should be without it. Also I am far from denying real pleasure derived directly from past literature—apart from
thinking about it. I am inclined to say that the greatest literary
sensation I ever had was in reading Dante (with a translation
along side)—in spite of all that I disbelieve, smile at or abhor.
2. As to style—never can I have said or implied that simplicity
and clarity were what I most or even very highly value as compared with other things. I quite agree with what Harry James said
to me in our youth—that many things have to be said obscurely
before they can be said clearly. When a man is perfectly clear he
is talking what is commonplace to him—when the effort of thought
to him is over. I think I said and I think that the main element of
style properly so called is sound—but that is a different matter—
and may be no more than a question of how one uses words. As
to clearness—I have just read a book by John Dewey—on Wu's
recommendation—*Experience and Nature*—of which I could not
have summed up a chapter or a page—and which I should find it
hard to give any intelligible account of, yet which—to my surprise
—I thought truly a great book. I mention that he quotes me in it
as one of our great American philosophers, and pleased me thereby
no little, only to say that that was not why I read it and is not
why I think it great. I think it so because with all its defects of
expression, he seems to me to hold more of existence in his hand
and more honestly to see behind all the current philosophers than
any book I can think of on such themes. But after him Henderson
on *The Federal Trade Commission* is an easy task—although I
golluped up the former with enthusiasm and do the latter as a
useful task.

I shouldn't think Birrell would have dared to make his joke

about God being a Trinity man in a speech such as you describe.
I am delighted at what you say was said about Mrs. J. R. Green.
I am very fond of her—although I haven't seen her since I last
was in England and have heard from her but only rarely. I stayed
with her a week when she lived facing the Thames above the
House of Parliament and had an adorable time. She is a heroine
as well as a very gifted woman. Dean Church and Liddon are only
names to me—but I suspect they could not be the types of what
I admire. Bowen was a good talker—but he turned off serious subjects with a story. Wm. and H. James were pretty near superlative
in their respective days—Bill more especially I think.

We sat on Monday to accommodate lawyers who had come
from a distance—and then adjourned for three weeks. I had but
one opinion to write—which I circulated this morning and my
other work is done. If I don't feel bound to go to the dentist to
be looked over I have some happy leisure ahead. I mean to make
my wife inspect me and see if she can see any reason for my going.
Dentists should be treated as I read in my youth that embalmers
were in Egypt when their dirty job was over—pursued with stones.
But on the whole I seem to have reached for the moment a sleeping equilibrium—too soon to be upset I fear. The army taught me
some great lessons—to be prepared for catastrophe—to endure
being bored—and to know that however fine [a] fellow I thought
myself in my usual routine there were other situations alongside
and many more in which I was inferior to men that I might have
looked down upon had not experience taught me to look up.

Ever aff'ly yours, O. W. H.

Devon Lodge
5 Addison Bridge Place, W. 14, 29.XII.26
My dear Justice: A joyous letter from you was a relief in the turmoil of moving house. In the last ten days I have arranged over
five thousand books on shelves, and I never realised how impish
they are until I tried to unpack them. The third volume of Montaigne insists on hiding itself behind the fourth volume of Gibbon;
and it is impossible to recognise the eleventh volume of Carlyle
upside down. However, they are done, and my room is almost in
working order. But I never, no never, want to move again. . . .

Since I wrote last week not much has happened. The most interesting thing was a dinner at Haldane's when he and the Prime
Minister and I talked confidentially for a couple of hours. You
can't help liking Baldwin. He is far from intellectually first-rate,
but he is *good*—a kind of Colonel Dobbin to whom you could
turn with your troubles and be comforted. He interested me much
by saying that Churchill was quite the ablest, and Bonar Law the

shrewdest, mind he had encountered in politics. He had a high
opinion of your present Ambassador Houghton; and an amazingly
low opinion (this between ourselves) of his predecessor Kellogg.[1]
. . . I declare with my hand on my heart that no one with any
brains is entitled to *ennui* in a world as interesting as this one is.
. . . I reread, too, in bed *Felix Holt*. Have you read that in
recent years? It is really very moving. Also a delectable story by
one P. G. Wodehouse called *Piccadilly Jim* which I urge you and
Mrs. Holmes to chuckle over.

. . . I have two most wonderful pictures of Hobbes—about
6 x 6; would you like one? They are quite small, essentially things
to stand on a mantlepiece. But I know few heads quite so massive
or so inspiriting. . . .

Our love as always to you both.

Ever affectionately yours, H. J. L.

Washington, D.C., January 1, 1927

My dear Laski: A happy New Year to you and yours. Your last
letter[1] has some remarks about Wu that please and relieve me. I
had felt and written to him in the same general direction. I cannot
see the profit that Stammler has been to him except as he may
have introduced him to other philosophic reading. I don't tell him
that, but I did hint that contact with actualities might be better
for him than easy philosophizing in comfortable circumstances. I
am a little afraid that he may feel as if he had more to say than
he yet has in fact, as some of the things he has sent to me seemed
to be statements of the well known with a feeling of discovery.
When a man *realizes* a truth he feels as if he had discovered it.
I have seen the same thing in others—and am not sure but I
haven't caught myself in the same illusion. I say your judgment
relieves me, for I much desire Wu's welfare and have asked myself
whether I ought not to bring out some appreciable sum to help
him to his desires. I don't think so—but one is suspicious of oneself.

I have little to report in the way of reading. Since finishing
Dewey's book and a law book by Henderson on the Federal Trade
Commission so many things have come in to be done including an
opinion to write and many to read, that I haven't had much time.
A *Life of Loyola* by Sedgwick is the only item I think of. Very
well done I should think, but beyond the desirableness of not being
blankly ignorant I don't care a damn for Loyola. A martyr's efficiency on postulates blindly held that today one doesn't even re-

---

[1] Frank Billings Kellogg (1856-1937), American Ambassador to England
in 1924 and Secretary of State in the Coolidge cabinet.

[1] Omitted from this edition.

spect. There is something of that even in Pascal, but with Loyola it seems too childlike and childish. Loyola was a hero. Hell is full of heroes. I feel as I did when the late McCabe (a friend of mine from Richmond)[2] began to talk about gentlemen. I told him nobody could know whether he was a gentleman or not. The question was whether he was a breech or a muzzle loader. If the latter he might get on a pedestal and feel as large as he liked but the world would pass him by. I mean by the world the few thousand men in the principal cities who as Bourget says constitute the civilized world.

On Monday we begin to sit again and I expect a hard month. But everything is done up to now and the year opens pleasantly and hopefully. I hope my brethren don't make allowances for me as an old man, but they are very pleasant and kind to me, and I feel happy with them. Also conscience made me go to the dentist and after worrying me and doing some work he let me go and I don't mean to go near him again until I have to. I believe Congress has increased our salaries, which I am glad of although I have enough now.[3] I couldn't live as I do on my salary. And as no doubt I have said before I think an intelligent and regulated avarice is one of the vices to be recommended to the old. There is no headache in it. But the great thing is not to have to think about the matter, and I don't. I couldn't tell you with certainty what my present salary is, and I never on either bench stirred a finger in the matter of my pay. I have been too happy to do the work.

Every good wish to you all.   *Aff'ly yours, O. W. Holmes*

Devon Lodge, 11.I.27

My dear Justice: . . . We were both rather tired after the exertions of moving in. So we went down last week to the Webbs for a couple of days, and had a most pleasant time. Their virtues, if I may so phrase it, have to be dug for; but I rate them high. They are open-minded, convinceable, eager for new knowledge, and warm-hearted. She has a curious love of religious mysticism and an unsatisfied appetite for religious ceremonial which baffle me a little, as also certain relics of society judgments of the eighties. For instance she regards Balfour as a significant person, apart from politics, where I should judge his work significant in a statesman but otherwise mediocre. We discussed all manner of things, agreeing that George Eliot was the greatest woman in the 19th century and that Mrs. J. R. Green was the best woman conversationalist of the last thirty years. We enquired why Haldane was so good at

---

[2] *Supra*, p. 253, Vol. I.

[3] In February 1927, a bill was enacted increasing the annual salaries of Associate Justices from $14,500 to $20,000.

most things and yet not superlative in anything and I heard, for the first time, the story of his engagement: the lady, a typical society butterfly, turned him down because the then reigning "great dame" Lady Londonderry sneered at him for not being a hunting man. Could anything be more English? . . . both Wallas and the Webbs have a vast sense of long and painful excursuses on things like the taking of notes, the method of personal enquiry, and so on which I believe to be sheer waste of time. . . .

And let me add one thing that has pleased me hugely. A year ago an Irish-American came to me and asked for the loan of ten pounds to get back to America. I liked something in his ways and risked it. Months elapsed and I entered the loan amid the great unpaid. Lo and behold comes back the ten pounds with an admirable letter on American conditions and a pound to give where I please in gratitude. Isn't that admirable?

Our love, as ever, to you both. *Affectionately always, H. J. L.*

Washington, D.C., January 18, 1927

My dear Laski: Your last joy-giving letter has had to wait two or three days for an answer because I have been so hard at work— my Sunday job having been to write a decision against a very thorough and really well expressed argument by two colored men —one bery black—that even in intonations was better than, I should say, the majority of white discourses that we hear. Your mention of Wodehouse led my wife to try, not yet successfully, to get *Piccadilly Jim*—but also to read to me *Mostly Sally*—which is good sport. *Leave It to Psmith* ("the P is silent" the hero remarks) made me roar. In fact Wodehouse is unsurpassed if equaled by anybody in power to make me guffaw. I note *Felix Holt.* Last night Redlich dined with us and was most agreeable. We talked for four hours which is more than I can stand without fatigue, especially after having listened to four hours of argument in court, but which did not bore me for a minute. Redlich is instructive, suggestive and personally pleasant—altogether a dear. I was delighted by his appreciation of you and Felix. He mentioned as to be read: Gilbert Murray's essays, *Tradition and Progress,* and *Felix Holt* may have to wait for that. You mention Seneca as one whom you enjoy. A morning's ramble through his letters gave me the impression of admirable platitudes of morality with good touches—as when he suggests to his younger friend, that perhaps it never has occurred to him that his slave may be a better man than he. But I decided to let him wait for better days. Of course I should like the portrait of Hobbes—but do you remember the very vivid and, for England, remarkably well-engraved likeness in the volume that you and Felix gave to me? I always have meant to

try to find out who could have done it. The date of the edition is
1750 and I should not have supposed that there was any English
line engraver that could have done it at that time—but my dates
are wobbly. I had not thought of Chamberlain's face as cruel—
but his daughter Miss Beatrice Chamberlain, whom I knew intimately, when she was talking of the conduct of England and met
an objection on the ground of morals, at times had a look of
cynical unscrupulosity that brought out a wonderful likeness to
her father. I think I had the cheek to quote Thackeray to her:
"At this moment her ladyship's resemblance to the late Marquis of
Steyne became positively frightful." This is after many years and
does not purport to be accurate. Zimmern sent me his *Third British
Empire* a month ago—and I haven't acknowledged because I do
not know where to address him—have you a notion? Also I have
not yet read the book. I should more readily if it dealt with the
Greeks.

Also a story, *Green Forest*, with kind remembrances from
Nathalie Sedgwick Colby—the authoress—who I find is wife of a
quondam Secretary of State[1] and whom I knew—temp. Wilson—
but why she should send it to me I know not. I suppose I must
read and write—thus runs the world away. I am not getting nug-
gets of wisdom from the arguments I hear or anything but practice
in English from the run of opinions that I have to write—yet I am
busy as I can be and am kept breathless till after dinner and solitaire. I agree with you as to *ennui*—and yet life strikes me sometimes as my hobby of prints does—a few superlatives and a finite
number of fairly interesting things. How can man take himself
seriously when his view of life changes as the wind is south or
west? However my view is cheerful now—and would be hilarious
were it summer—Rockport—in your little house with you.

                              Affectionately yours, O. W. Holmes

                                              Devon Lodge, 21.I.27
My dear Justice: I have had a week in bed with a nasty dose of
influenza; hence my silence. . . . I am in general rather appalled
by the vast aids to research in the social sciences which America is
developing. X writes to me that he has been given a fellowship
of 3000 dollars to write a report on the birth-control movement in
England; Frida, who is the Secretary of the labour party committee on the matter tells me that a full and adequate account of
it could be done in a couple of days. Y writes from Wisconsin to
say that he is to spend two years in Europe studying comparative
personnel administration in the public services. Now (a) the literature on all this is now so vast that it needs digest rather than addi-

---

[1] Bainbridge Colby, *supra*, p. 246, Vol. I.

tion; and (b) personal observation for two years is about ten times longer than the subject requires. I look down the long list of theses being done on these things in American universities and not more than two or three per cent of them seem to me more than the repetition of work already done or the elaborate proof of things too obvious to need proof. Meanwhile the things that really need research get neglected—partly because they are not easy, partly because they require not a peripatetic student armed, *cap à pie*, with letters to all the crowned heads of Europe and Asia, but a man in a room who knows his material and sweats blood to get an idea. But all this may be bad temper. All I can say is that I think the results attained by the new dispensation could be reached at one-tenth of the cost.

I had a good time of it in bed with books. First, I had a long pull at Trollope, always with delight even though I knew every taste of the liquor. Then, with the great interest, I read F. W. Hirst's *Early Life and Letters of Morley*. It's a little too long, as biographies usually are, but it kept me enthralled all the way through. I don't think Morley quite the size that Hirst as disciple does, *e.g.* I do not mention him with Burke. But he was quite certainly the finest Englishman I have known personally, and I think Hirst makes you see why. I was a little surprised at one or two things. Morley's immense admiration for Frederic Harrison means nothing to me. I never, to my knowledge, read a page by him that seems first-rate. And L. Stephen comes less into the picture than I imagined. I should have made a guess that on the side of religious belief Stephen had more influence on Morley than any other person, though less, of course, than the cumulative effect of his studies on 18th century France. And I had the same amazed sense I always have of the way in which obvious and banal speeches by politicians seem to each other epoch-making. That still exists, and I suppose the poor dears believe it. But I am sure that one of the results of being immersed in the actual conflict is to build things on personal influence of which the latter is the effect and not the cause. I don't deny, of course, that men influence events; but I think insiders tend to think that men are mountains when measurement over the whole map makes them molehills. What is above all curious in the book is the enchantment of Gladstone's personality. Even people like Huxley, who detested him, seem to have felt it; and I know no book which gives you any reason, except vigour of mind, to see in him anything that makes you feel any special moral or intellectual insight. All that he wrote is commonplace; and I cannot see that his speeches are in the same intellectual class as those of Bright. Indeed, the instinct of the contemporary working-man, who doubted Gladstone and clove to Cobden and Bright, seems to me thrice right. There is nothing in him of Lincoln's instinctive perceptiveness, or of the originality of people like Hamil-

ton. Yet, except Chamberlain, all of them are knocked over by
an hour of his company; and a great *gelehrte* like Acton never goes
into his presence except on his knees. What is the secret? . . .
And I read one novel which, on my knees, I pray you to read. It
is called *Jew Süss* and is by a German named Feuchtwanger. I take
an affidavit that it is the finest historical novel I have ever
read. . . .

Well, next time I hope to be about the world again and able to
write more sanely. Yet this, as you know, brings my love and greetings *more antiquo.*   *Ever affectionately yours, H. J. L.*

Washington, D.C., January 28, 1927
My dear Laski: When a man has been husy—pronounce hizzy—
which abridgement I use for hurriedly busy—he is cramped at
the end and can't expatiate at once—at least I can't. I think you
can, so that fact and the hope that I may not be too late to catch
tomorrow's boat—imagined by me, since before the war, to sail
on Saturdays—will lead me to be short. We have adjourned and
I am hoping for 3 weeks of leisure—though the C.J. dangles a
political case over my head. Fired by Gilbert Murray, Euripides is
on my table once more, and, who would have thought it? Ovid.
He, G.M., says such pretty things about him (O). I, with you, had
postponed Ovid to my Xth eternity and after I should have written
my work on Anthropology (1st Aeon)—mastered Mathematics
(2nd Aeon) and other unconsidered tasks accomplished, should
take up literature. The whole of which I suppose would take but
a few years.

I agree with you as to Balfour outside of politics—a very agreeable man but I thought his book one for ladies' centre tables. But
then I am afraid that I once told Bill James that his discourse on
free will would please the ladies and unitarian parsons. I remember once complimenting a young lady to Haldane, having understood that he was attentive to her, or had been, but he thereupon
spoke sardonically of how young women talked about books on
the strength of having read reviews, etc.

Again I agree with you on the *methods* business. I have no use
for them. Taking notes, keeping diaries, etc., etc., may suit me-
thodical minds, they don't suit me.

I told you how I liked to hear Mrs. J. R. Green praised. She is
a great friend of mine though it is long since I have heard from
her. When you see Nevinson again remember me to him. I envy
you for seeing him.

I have done nothing but write a little law, read a lot of applications for *certiorari* and opinions by others, etc., but hope to do
better by my next.

As I write this there is brought to me the life of Bernal Diaz del Castillo by R. B. Cunninghame Graham. Tommy Barfour lent it to me years ago, a chap that was with Cortez and tells a marvellous tale. To my joy it seems to have been reprinted though not marked 2d edition. As I remember it a priceless book.

Aff'ly yours, O. W. H.

Washington, D.C., February 4, 1927

My dear Laski: Your letter of the 21st reached me yesterday when I was distraught with details—paying my income tax, fussing about a registered bond, expecting your Ambassador[1] and his wife (pleasant creatures—she suggestive of Mona Lisa to me) at luncheon and a call to be made afterwards. This morning finds me free and serene. You speak of Wu—a letter a few days back informed me that he had been appointed judge of what seems an important local court[2]—so I expect that his yearnings will be appeased for a time. I do greatly desire success for him and have great hopes. He never mentions local disturbances. He seems to live in his world of thought. As to Frederic Harrison and Gladstone I agree with you. I talked with both of them. F. H. when I first saw him was a Comtist—I always supposed his good English was one cause of his standing. The only thing I ever learned from him was to turn from Hobbes to Bodin—but that was something—before the days of Figgis—*ni fallor*. Gladstone had a voice like Emerson's and in '66 seemed to me the one man who was like an American. He came out to meet you and had gusto—but, bar his financial speeches of which I can't judge, I never read anything of his that didn't impress me much as Roosevelt did when he ventured into the higher reaches. I seem to remember a discourse by T. R. which the N. Y. *Sun* pronounced great but of which Rémy de Gourmont made as it seemed to me deserved sport.[3] Possibly I have mixed up two deliverances but I am pretty sure that they were *eiusdem generis*. Also my Secretary who knows more about it than I, agrees, as I have every inclination to, with what you say about the expeditions of students for research, from here. He says they take any theme, the easiest, that will give them a visit to Europe.

I am rereading John Dewey's book—*Experience and Nature*—with the same opinion as before—but with some mitigation as to his style. There are moments that suggest that he could write well

---

[1] Sir Esme Howard (1863-1939), later Baron Howard of Penrith, was British Ambassador in Washington from 1924 to 1930.

[2] John C. H. Wu had recently been appointed a judge of the Shanghai Provisional Court.

[3] The reference is, perhaps, to Rémy de Gourmont's observations on Roosevelt's address delivered at the Sorbonne in 1910 during his zestful European trip; Rémy de Gourmont, *Épilogues, 1905-1912* (1913), 162.

—but then comes obscurity. Still there is very little that I have
not articulately grasped as I went along, though I shouldn't like
to be called on to recite. I think it a profound and illuminating
work. I am not sure that you would agree, but I shall stand firm.
But I get up rather late and go out to drive from 11:30 or 12 to
1:30 and am apt to get a snooze in the afternoon—and after 9 p.m.
play solitaire and listen—so I don't go ahead at your pace—even
if I could read as fast which of course I can't. I have a delightful
book on *Fishing from the Earliest Time* by William Radcliffe—
sometime of Balliol College, Oxford which I read some years ago
and which I may reread. G. Murray's stimulus was short lived. I
couldn't but believe that he read into the βακχαε things that weren't
there—and although he made me appreciate the reasons for
Ovid's long reign, a reading of one book of the *Metamorphoses* was
enough. I appreciate the felicities but I couldn't go on reading
silly stories merely because they had been taken seriously by people
—who couldn't get Dewey and who would have burned him if
they could have—or because they were a good lesson in style.

The time has come for me to go forth and so I will wind up
abruptly with eternally springing hope that this will go tomorrow
—and carry my remembrances.

Affectionately yours, O. W. Holmes

Devon Lodge, 13.II.27
My dear Justice: . . . I have had to be away at Oxford, Cambridge, Rugby and Nottingham . . . I was left with one or two impressions which I hazard for discussion. I am sure, first, that it is
excessively bad for dons to live the cloistered life. They lose all
sense of proportion and they get to loathe contradiction. Moreover
absence of contact with the great world outside makes them mag-
nify the inconceivably little into the enormously big. One don at
Oxford entertained me (quite unconsciously) for an hour with an
involved tale about a struggle with the University Press over the
size of Greek type in a forthcoming text of Lucian; . . . Of Rugby
and Nottingham where I had to speak to workers' classes I was
distressed by the tendency, especially of the university speakers, to
idealise the working man and to attribute to him virtues and interests in which other classes were held not to share proportionately.
It was, for instance, regarded as cynical on my part to suggest
that the main hope of the working-class was either unknown or
broadly a hope of ceasing to be the working-class. . . . My chairman, the professor of economics, was hugely cheered, for, as I
put it, offering Gardens of Eden for twopence a dozen; and my
denial of a royal road to learning was not popular.

In between, I have done a little dining. One most pleasant dinner

with the Swedish Minister[1] to meet Austen Chamberlain. The latter
is a curiously wooden person, who talks on stilts and never ceases
to be foreign minister. Ramsay MacDonald, who was there too,
shone by comparison. But what amused me most was Graham
Wallas's effort to explain to Chamberlain how he could improve
his thinking by exploring his foreconsciousness in the early morning. The scene was beyond words. Wallas in deadly earnest, Chamberlain without the remotest knowledge (a) of who Wallas was
(b) what his foreconsciousness was, and (c) anxious not to be
dragged into discussion of this deadly unknown, and Wallas determined that his victim should not escape.

. . . I am sending to you in April, my friend G. P. Gooch, the
historian, whose work you will know, but whose charm and sweetness you have still to taste. Wallas, by the way, leaves for America
on Tuesday and is, I believe, to live next door to you for some
months. Do look into his mind and tell me your thoughts.

Two items of news I reserve to the end. I may go out to Wisconsin in the spring of '28 for a couple of months; if so, I shall
have May in Washington and hereby provisionally engage your
evenings in advance. Second, you will be glad to know that Leslie
Scott has been made a privy councillor. I hope that is a prelude
to something more substantial.

My love to you both.   *Ever affectionately yours, Harold J. Laski*

Washington, D.C., February 25, 1927
My dear Laski: A letter, most interesting, as usual, comes from
you to enliven the first week of a sitting, in which as yet we have
encountered nothing very exciting. I should think that what you
say about the dons was human nature everywhere and marked in
England. I am more than pleased at your attitude about the working-man and the royal road to knowledge. The eternal effort to
discover cheap and agreeable substitutes for hard work and talent
has been the object of many sneers from me. I thought skirt danc-
ing when it appeared years ago a type. To evoke the hope that you
were going to see more the next high kick was to take the place of
the laborious gymnastics needed to make a *danseuse*. Some of the
modern painting strikes me in the same way—although I am told
that certain authors of what seem to me monstrosities are masters
of the whole business. Of course I have thought the same way as
to the working man. I am sorry at what you say about Austen
Chamberlain—I haven't seen him since he was young—and then
only casually. But his sister was a very dear friend of mine and I
should like to believe the best of him. The scene between Wallas

---

[1] Baron Erik Palmstierna (1877-1959) was Minister in London from 1920
to 1937 and author of works of political and religious subjects.

and him must have been amusing. I hope I shall see the former
—and also Gooch. I hope also that I shall be here to welcome you
in 1928—but as I shall be 86 about the time that this reaches you
I don't venture confident predictions. Since my adventures in philosophy and fishing I have read nothing and have tried to enjoy
a few moments of irresponsible idleness, driving and sleeping, but
I am afraid that I am industrious—an ominous tendency. My wife
is reading *Pickwick* to me, omitting the stories and my pleasure is
renewed. Next Monday I hope to fire off a few sardonic remarks
in a dissent on the Constitutional powers of the States,[1] beyond
that I am vacant. And I must stop and go to court.

Affectionately yours, O. W. Holmes

I thought to write more.

Devon Lodge, 24.II.27

My dear Justice: At last I can look forward to an uninterrupted
vista; last week-end, when I went again to Oxford, was the final
adventure away until next winter and I breathe again. It has been
interesting but tiring, and the great gain of an assurance that this
university is the place for me. All Souls, where I stayed this week,
is most pleasant and hospitable, but one gets really bored with
the continuous round of small talk about small persons, and the
deference paid to the good and great is a little painful. For example, at All Souls was Amery,[1] the colonial secretary; we were
talking of America and he expressed the view that it was nause-
atingly materialist and appealed to me. I said I thought, in that
respect, it was much the same as England or France, but being
richer could more obviously fulfil its desires. This was just like a
bombshell. A cabinet minister had been contradicted (which is
not done at All Souls') and the conversation was at once turned to
the memory of a late fellow on which there could be agreement! . . .

Our love *and* greetings to you both.   *Ever-yours, H. J. L.*

Devon Lodge, 5.III.27

My dear Justice: . . . Apart from this, the great experience of the
week has been reading Winston's two final volumes on the war.[1] I
hope greatly they will come your way, for I know nothing finer or
more revealing. He is, I guess, wrong about Jutland, and throughout he is over-rhetorical. But he makes you see the job of directing

---

[1] *Tyson and Brother* v. *Banton,* 273 U.S. 418, 445 (Feb. 28, 1927).

[1] Leopold Stennett Amery (1873-1955), politician, was Secretary of State
for the Colonies from 1924 to 1929.

[1] Volumes III and IV of Winston Churchill's *World Crisis* (1927) dealt
with the war years from 1916 to 1918.

the war in progress as no other work except Ludendorff that I have read. And he convinces me that in a democracy at any rate you can never get the right relationship between soldiers and statesmen. Either the former are too powerful and try to shape policy (which they don't understand) or the statesmen interfere with technical detail which is beyond them. You must not miss the great description of November 11, 1918 where Winston is gorgeously picturesque on waiting for Big Ben to strike the hour and the vast emotions aroused by the first stroke; of which the point is that Big Ben did not strike that day as it was being cleaned. Poor Winston! Huxley's "beautiful hypothesis killed by an ugly little fact." But he has written a very fine book.

. . . Did I, by the way, ever remark to you upon my pet thesis that one of the great lines in intellectual development (modern) is Spinoza—Lessing—Goethe—Carlyle and that this school converges with Montesquieu—Burke—Gentz—Savigny—Maine to form the philosophy and tactic of conservatism? A good deal, I think, could be usefully said by way of illustrating this: and it is surprising how little has been written to defend conservatism of recent times in a philosophic way. . . .

Ever affectionately yours, H. J. L.

Washington, D.C., March 17, 1927
My dear Laski: An answer to one letter was skipped and one that comes this morning must get but a hasty word. My birthday came in the middle of a lot of hard work and I haven't known which way to turn—let me get a new pen. You speak of lots of things that interest me—what you say of Winston (Churchill's?) book and the troubles between soldiers and statesmen, reminds of Patten (*Development of English Thought*) "the sensualist in the field is always at war with the Mugwump in the home office" [1]—I don't stop to verify but quote from recollection many years old. I always used to say that Fitzjames Stephen was an 18th century British controversialist, and he brings down his bludgeon with a whack. Carlyle I never think of except as an artist. He didn't care for truth as such, but only as it was pictorially available. As old James (the father of W. & H.) said of Mrs. Browning "She uses the name of the Divine Being as a pigment." As to the convergence you speak of to form the philosophy of conservatism, I listen with much interested silence.

I have had some cases that interested me—and a dissent in which I had a whack at "police power" and "dedicated to a public use"—as apologetic phrases springing from the unwillingness to

---

[1] In Patten's lingo the sensualists are the active men of strong conviction —the warriors, priests, and capitalists—while the mugwumps are the speculative and frail intellectuals—critics, not actors.

recognize the fact of power[2]—one upsetting a Philippine judgment declining to accept a British judgment in Hong Kong[3]—and one very plain one upsetting a Texas Statute forbidding negroes to vote at Democratic primaries.[4] I have been kept humming and still am —I can say no more now except that I am as ever

Aff'ly yours, O. W. Holmes

Some one wrote to me that it was said that I said I should not resign until God Almighty notified me—(which is a fiction of the papers), and asking what warrant I had for thinking there was one. I did not answer as I thought it impertinent.

Devon Lodge, 20.III.27

My dear Justice: . . . I met there a delightful old Canon who was at the meeting of the British Association at Oxford and heard Huxley smite Bishop Wilberforce.[1] He said that the sensation was beyond words, and that on him, as on many others, it was a revelation of moral power such as he has never seen again. The clergy, he said, were like an army in confused retreat, whose commander has failed them, listening to an exhortation from their enemy which they try not to believe is true. I had, also, a fascinating lunch with Winston Churchill where we fought over politics in solitude for three hours. Several things there interested me hugely. (1) The politician's assurance: if I could pronounce judgment on one thing with the same aplomb with which he settled a dozen, I should be very happy. There is not a trace of scepticism in his nature. (2) His sense of values. The scientist, the philosopher, the great artist, are for him children remote from the real paths of life. He has no sense at all of long-term influence. He feels that men don't go into politics for fear of failing there, not because they literally don't want to. (3) The rhetorical character of the political mind. It was very easy for him to slip from close argument into peroration and I was never sure that he really grasped the difference. I went, also, to an admirable lecture on "public policy" by Winfield of Cambridge, which contained one perfect sentence: "Public policy means the best judgment of distinguished men of the world as distinct from persons learned in the law; English judges have regarded

---

[2] *Tyson and Brother* v. *Banton,* 273 U.S. 418, 445.

[3] *Ingenohl* v. *Olsen and Company,* 273 U.S. 541. Holmes wrote for a unanimous court.

[4] *Nixon* v. *Herndon,* 272 U.S. 536 (March 7, 1927). Holmes delivered the opinion for a unanimous Court.

[1] The occasion was that on which Bishop Samuel Wilberforce (1805-1873), "Soapy Sam" to his contemporaries, sought to refute the impieties of Darwin before the British Association. Huxley, challenged by the Bishop to state whether the ape in his ancestry was on the maternal or paternal side, expressed his preference for descent from an ape to the ancestry of such a bishop as Wilberforce, with such vigor that Lady Brewster, in the audience, fainted.

their own views as the highest expression of the former category."
I met there Roche, J.[2] who is a charming person. He told me that
when he first read Cardozo on *The Judicial Process* it was a bombshell to him; he never realised that things like that went on in his
mind. Examination convinced him that they did and he began to
explore. At sixty he discovered Maitland and, as he put it, under-
went the phenomenon of conversion. I said I wished he would bite
the other judges. He replied that most of them were vaccinated
against the dangers of speculation by their careers at the bar. . . .

In the way of reading, I have mostly been confined to work.
But I read Felix's little book on Sacco and Vanzetti and thought it
a neat, surgical job. . . . I picked up the other day *Contarini
Fleming* which I had never read. Dizzy must have had a really
sublime contempt for the English nation to publish such stuff, or,
alternatively, the most weird attitude to himself of any man who
ever stood in the front rank. For it is the weirdest mixture of
Behmen,[3] Cagliostro, Byron, Rousseau, I ever looked at; and except
for the light it throws on Dizzy himself, entirely worthless. . . .

Our love to you both. I expect you are driving by the Potomac
to see the cherry-blossom.   *Ever affectionately yours, H. J. L.*

> *Washington, D.C., March 31, 1927*
> *My dear Laski:* Yours of March 20 just received and read and I
was just about to say I had a breathing moment in which to answer,
when, as I wrote your name a fat package came from the C.J. to
be read. But it shall not stop me. You are right in thinking that
I have been driving by the cherry trees and in one way and another trying to be unscrupulously idle for a few days. But it is almost impossible. When law makes no demand some bother of
business pops up. However all is going well enough.

Graham Wallas called here the other day and took luncheon
today. I find him a most pleasant creature—so pleasant that I
haven't inquired too curiously how much we have or have not
in common—in the way of opinions, beyond the general agreement of tolerant and civilized men. Don't talk to me of Huxley. I
thought him a boor on the only occasion when I saw him—I would
lock him up with Andrew Lang and a few others and put S.O.B.
on the door of the cell. *Per contra* Wallas lent me Cardozo's first
book and I read it and was reinforced in my conviction that he
(C.) was a sensitive, high-minded, delicate dear—but I think your

---

[2] Alexander Adair Roche (1871-1956), Baron Roche; Judge of the King's
Bench Division, 1917-1934; Lord Justice of Appeal and Lord of Appeal in
Ordinary, 1934-1938.

[3] Jacob Behmen (or Boehme) (1575-1624), mystical shoemaker whose
philosophy assigned to will a position of central importance and emphasized
the conflict between opposites, resulting finally in a new unity.

friend Roche, J. ingenuous if the book opened new vistas to him.

. . . [I] read a sentence by the Treasurer of the American Federation of Labor—that made my heart jump up with joy—and hope that it was true—"Labor and capital are now talking the same language—that of the 'informed economist' "—although he goes on that their differences are still acute. I haven't yet succeeded in getting *Piccadilly Jim.* I have received the *Life of Lord Bryce.*[1] I was fond of him and expect to find it interesting—but it came at a moment when it emphasized what I was reflecting—apropos of Pound—that knowledge is a dangerous diluent of thought. The poison of the sting is thinned out and made innocuous by too large an infusion of facts. One perfectly estimable side of Bryce left me cold—the pleasure he took in the society of admirable people like Charles Eliot who don't open the romantic perspectives of life—yet as I say that, I hesitate—for Charles Eliot wrote "the business of the scholar is to make poverty respectable" —a saying that has comforted me in my day—in the days when I lived on George Herbert's "who sweeps a room as for Thy laws" etc. and Browning's "Grammarian's Funeral." And didn't the good man when I wrote to him on his 90th birthday give me a kind of schoolmaster's summary of myself in four pages quarto—though I said don't answer. Let me walk delicately before the Lord— and it's a rum business—that of opening the romantic side of life. Some men who have done it for me would not be suspected of such a possibility by most of Boston. Old Norman[2] (you may have known some of the many sons whom I saw bear his coffin on their shoulders), a splendid old Philistine who had fought his way to wealth—Frank Parker[3]—the most squaretoed seeming of anglicised yankees—who had a green baize door to his office with "Mr. Parker" on it—was counsel for the Barings and the Cunard Co. etc.—but who had an inner fire that he didn't show often. Decidedly the men who have made life seem large and free would not always be picked out by the crowd.

I take it that Felix's book is a bit of heroism on his part—and I vaguely hear has brought criticism upon him. Naturally I can't talk about it—but it has left painful impressions. Disraeli I know more through Thackeray than himself—though I have read one or two of his things. I thought *Anna Karenina* the biggest ever when I read it—but was bored by *War and Peace.* I suppose I am too

---

[1] H. A. L. Fisher, *James Bryce* (2 vols., 1927).

[2] George H. Norman (1827-1900) of Newport, Rhode Island, had made a large fortune in civil engineering and the promotion of water works in the United States and abroad. Following Norman's death, Holmes is quoted as saying that few people he had known "have had so high a pressure of life to the square inch." Boston *Evening Transcript,* February 5, 1900, p. 10.

[3] Francis Edward Parker (1821-1886).

old now. They made quite a row on my birthday—which shows
that I am *really* old.   *Affectionately yours, O. W. H.*

Devon Lodge, 2.IV.27
My dear Justice: I got back yesterday from a memorable week in
Paris—one of the most intellectually exciting holidays I have ever
spent.[1] People, sights, books, all seem to unite to make things interesting. Of people there are some I must mention. At a conference
I met Jusserand with whom I spoke about you. He looked very fit
and eager, and is evidently most warmly esteemed. He wanted to
know all about my visit to you and how you both were and what
you were thinking about life. I met, too, André Gide, the novelist.
He is amazingly impressive, a queerly interesting mixture of the
Huguenot who has met Rimbaud and Mallarmé. Then, too, I had a
lunch with Briand[2] who interested me enormously. He lives in
the moment, and yesterday, with him, is ancient history which
only the archaeologist will study. He is supple as no persons existing elsewhere. He knows exactly what you want him to say and
is skilful in the art of pleasing in a quite remarkable degree. Also
René Lalou,[3] the critic, a kind of Faguet *de nos jours,* clever, witty,
and eloquent. One or two of his phrases, *"historiquement Platon a
eu une trop bonne presse"; "Bossuet a fait une religion pour des
rois"; "Le François est né malin et meurt sceptique au sein du bon
Dieu"* were admirable. I had all I could do to digest these experiences; and I recovered the sense that few peoples have the
French power to play with ideas. They are not, I think, originators;
but in subtlety and analytic power they are extraordinarily impressive. . . . I was struck in meeting the men of letters at the
degree to which they are bound up in groups and stick to them.
. . . One or two general things are worth saying, perhaps. One
gets the impression that the Church gains ground—especially among
the youth in the universities. The world in general is so confused
that they cling to it as an anchor. Also the degree of discredit into
which parliamentary institutions have fallen is as remarkable as it
is painful. To take a politician as dishonourable *a priori* is commonplace wherever one goes; and one hears continually of the need
"passer par quelque phase d'anarchie à une nouvelle synthèse."
On the other hand I am quite clear that France is on the verge of
a great intellectual renaissance. Granted the confusions of the
moment, it is the confusion of bigness. Valéry the poet, Gide the

---

[1] Laski's impressions of France are recorded in "A Little Tour of France,"
50 *New Republic* 292 (May 4, 1927).
[2] Aristide Briand (1862-1932) at this time was Minister of Foreign Affairs.
[3] René Lalou (1889-   ), author of *Histoire de la littérature française
contemporaine* (1923), and *Défense de l'homme* (1926).

novelist, one or two younger men like Dauden,[4] Giradoux [*sic*],
Lalou, are I think, the precursors of a great period. It may be that
I respond quickly to a sympathetic environment; but I should say
that the next ten years will give France a different intellectual
prestige from that of any other country. And in herself she is more
at peace. Most of the war-hate is dead; they laugh at us and you
instead of sneering; they dislike only Mussolini. Him they flagellate
in the comic press and the music-hall and, interestingly enough,
always as a threat to peace. I believe that they genuinely desire
European appeasement. . . .

Our love to you both.   *Ever affectionately yours, Harold J. L.*

                                                Devon Lodge, 15.IV.27
My dear Justice: I hope that by the time you receive this, you will
have had a call from Ramsay MacDonald; I wrote to him and to
Esme Howard that he should look in on you. For he is a likeable
fellow and I think you would have had a pleasant hour.

My main experience since I wrote you last has been a dinner
at which I sat next to a genius. He was, I gathered, a poet in his
second year at Oxford. He began by asking me if I liked his work;
I had, very humbly, to confess that I did not know it. "Perhaps
not," he said pityingly "as yet I have only done four things that
will live." Then a pause; silence from me; my poet, with an effort,
"But at my age Shelley had hardly done more." It is, I think, to
my credit that I took him seriously and asked him to summarise
his view of life. "The poet," he said, "is a reflection of the world-
spirit. When I write, I feel as though I carry all peoples and all
experiences in my womb." I said it must be a heavy burden. "Yes,"
he said, "I try not to be too conscious of my mission. I play bridge
for relaxation." He thought well of Dante and Shakespere. Homer,
and especially Virgil, were very overrated. Rimbaud was the greatest of Frenchmen—"I fancy myself a twin soul with him"—but
no German had ever written poetry. Goethe was without lyrical
powers. (He could not read German.) He would never marry. A
poet, like the bee, must sip from countless flowers; matrimony
must be a tie. . . .

I was depressed by the decision of the Massachusetts Supreme
Court in the Sacco-Vanzetti case.[1] Not only has Felix made me
feel that, at the least, a new trial was essential; but also the feeling
here is very deep that the whole thing is an injustice characteristic

---

[4] Not identified.

[1] On April 5 the Supreme Judicial Court of Massachusetts announced it
decision that it was powerless to review Judge Thayer's most recent action
in denying the defendants a new trial. On April 9 Judge Thayer sentenced
the two men to death.

of the American courts, and it is a thing difficult to combat. Frank,[2]
Mooney,[3] and this in fifteen years is unsatisfactory. It makes me
distrust the jury system were it not that Thayer, J. suggests that
the average judge is not a whit better. And it is especially disappointing to have it come in a state where judges are appointed
and not elected. . . .   *Ever affectionately yours, H. J. L.*

Devon Lodge, 23.IV.27

My dear Justice: It has been a busy week; for I have been roped
in to help the trade unions in their fight against this incredible
Bill of Baldwin's,[1] and most of my time has gone in conferences
with lawyers and politicians guessing at its legal consequences and
the best way to awaken a public opinion about the issue. It's
frightfully interesting; and not the least interesting side of it is
the lawyers' sheer ignorance of trade unionism. You may remember
an old plea of yours that lawyers should be taught political economy. That was never so forcibly brought home to me as now. . . .
The fight, I fear, will be very bitter, but if we lose the elementary
right of combination will go; and we shall be back in the old bad
days before the repeal of the Combination Acts. It's worth struggling against that.

. . . I expect with this letter you will receive my little book on
Communism. . . .

I hear with joy that you and Brandeis have dissented in a labour
case where emphasis was demanded.[2] I await the decision with
eagerness.

My love to you both.   *Ever affectionately yours, H. J. L.*

Washington, D.C., April 25, 1927

My dear Laski: It is ages since I have written—but I couldn't help
it. I have been very busy and last week was rather under the

---

[2] In August 1915, Leo Frank, a Jew who had been convicted of rape and
whose death sentence had been commuted to life imprisonment by the government of Georgia, was lynched. Over Holmes's dissent the Supreme Court,
in April 1915, on jurisdictional ground had refused to review the conviction
of the defendant; *Frank* v. *Mangum*, 237 U.S. 309, 345.

[3] Tom Mooney (1885-1942), on the basis of testimony known by the
prosecuting officers to be perjured, in 1915 was convicted by the California
courts of murder and sentenced to life imprisonment. It was not until 1939
that he was pardoned by Governor Olson and released from jail.

[1] On April 4 the government introduced its Trade Disputes and Trade
Unions Bill. Its most significant objectives were to make a general strike
illegal and to outlaw sympathetic strikes. After long and bitter debate the
Bill, with some modifications, became law in late July. Laski wrote of the
matter in "Mr. Baldwin attacks the Trade Unions," 51 *New Republic* 63
(June 8, 1927).

[2] *Bedford Cut Stone Company* v. *Journeymen Stone Cutters' Association*,
274 U.S. 37, 56 (April 11, 1927). Brandeis, J., with Holmes concurring,
dissented from the majority decision that under the Sherman act a strike
against nonunion materials was unlawful.

weather with my insides. As probably I have told you I have had
all forms of belly-ache known to the law except Asiatic *cholera*.
So I have to mind my eye. However it is all quiet along the
Potomac tonight (or more strictly, this morning).

Your Paris experiences are wonderfully interesting—what you
say about the literary groups falls in with an impression I got from a
book by a French interviewer in the time of Zola. The fierceness with
which each crowd spoke as if divided by a gulf when to me they
looked as like as Chinese—or had the same flavor throughout like
herrings in a box. As to a renaissance I heard a similar prediction
for this country the other day—that from the chaos of doubt and
ruins of the old times would arise a generation of philosophers
and poets. I am not quite sure—I think it was from Wallas. Wallas
has come here two or three times and I infer rather liked it as he
said that he should telephone on his return in May. He now has
gone to lecture elsewhere. My secretary thinks that he doesn't lecture as well as he talks. I of course have had no chance to hear
him *ex cathedra*—his talk is very agreeable. I have done nothing
but law—my opinion for this morning is held up by McReynolds
for a dissent. That which was given to me Saturday evening and
was written yesterday concerned the constitutionality of an act
for sterilizing feeble-minded people, with due precaution—as to
which my lad tells me the religious are astir. I have just sent what
I think to the printer.[1]

The Chief has given me a pretty interesting lot of cases this
term—and I have enjoyed writing them. I am always afraid that
he is considering my age &c. and giving me easy ones—but Brandeis seems to think not. Frankfurter's book on Sacco and Vanzetti
and the case itself has kicked up a commotion and Brandeis says
that Beacon Street is divided. Bishop Lawrence[2] and others of the
elect, like Charley Curtis (jr.) taking the side of the accused—
per contra Bob Grant (ex probate judge and author)[3] called yesterday and gave me a moderate statement tending rather the other
way. The wife appears and summons me to Court. Therefore a
premature *adieu*.   *Affectionately yours, O. W. Holmes*

Washington, D.C., April 29, 1927
My dear Laski: You have written delightfully interesting letters to
which you have received inadequate replies as I have fewer things

---

[1] *Buck v. Bell*, 274 U.S. 200 (May 2, 1927). Holmes, for a majority, sustained the constitutionality of Virginia's sterilization statute. Butler, J., dissented without opinon.

[2] *Supra*, p. 80, Vol. I.

[3] Robert Grant (1852-1940) was later named to the commission appointed by Governor Fuller to consider the application for the commutation
of the sentence on Sacco and Vanzetti. The commission recommended
execution of the sentence.

to tell and, as I wrote a day or two ago, have been driven hard and for a few days rather below par. I am all right now, but fate is plucking the leaves from the old tree rather fast. The day before yesterday came a telegram from Mrs. Beveridge telling of her husband's death that morning. And yesterday a letter giving me my first news of the death of Lady Castletown one of my oldest and most intimate friends.[1] Beveridge was a surprise although some years ago I got the idea from his doctor that he was running the machine too hard. I shall miss him until I am missed. Lady Castletown had had a stroke coming on top of other trouble so that her death seemed probably a release, but it makes a great gap in my horizon. It is a great fortune for me to have the friendship of some of you younger men. Tom Barbour turned up also two days ago far from well but he went on to Philadelphia yesterday and I hope will have no serious trouble. Apart from events all my ideas are in the law. I have had some rather interesting cases—the present one, as I believe I mentioned, on the Constitutionality of a Virginia act for the sterilizing of imbeciles, which I believe is a burning theme. In most cases the difficulty is rather with the writing than with the thinking. To put the case well and from time to time to hint at a vista is the job. I am amused (between ourselves) at some of the rhetorical changes suggested, when I purposely used short and rather brutal words for an antithesis, polysyllables that made them mad. I am pretty accommodating in cutting out even thought that I think important, but a man must be allowed his own style. At times I have gone too far in yielding my own views as to the reason for the decision. Years ago to finish a case that had been dawdled with for many months I struck out my reasons and put in what I thought at least inadequate and appear in the books as sanctioning what makes me blush.[2] This time, though I had said, Never again, I did the same thing in a milder form, and now as then have to accept criticism that I think pretty well justified. However, sooner or later one gets a chance to say what one thinks. I believe today is our last day of argument except one case on Monday. And the so-often-expected and near-coming leisure seems to be near at hand. Apart from the light stuff that I hear in the late evening I have read nothing, except at odd minutes to reread Murray's *History of Political Science,* which I believe you put me on to—a good book very ill written. I think I shall do some other rereadings when I get the chance. Fred Pollock's *Spinoza* for one and possibly a little of the old man himself. He comes nearer to me than most of the old. I am much pleased with your poet. The English are more ingenuous and innocent than we, even if capable of deeper abysses. And the par-

[1] *Supra,* p. 54.
[2] *Supra,* p. 124.

ticular swagger of poets as admitted to deeper intimacy with the cosmos than the rest used to aggravate and now amuses me. I gather that your lad was quite young. Probably he will get a jolt someday that may open his eyes. I should think you would be curious to look up his product.

How solemnly men have taken themselves. Theology has helped it. If there is to be the revival that you for France and Wallas for America predict, I hope that a corner-stone will be that speculatively man is interesting only as part of the cosmos, and that he cannot assume that he is specially needed as its confidential friend. The time for departure to Court has come and I must say *adieu pro tem.*   *Affectionately yours, O. W. Holmes*

Devon Lodge, 7.V.27

My dear Justice: Two most welcome letters from you. They remind me to adjure your abdominal organs to behave themselves. I write with the bitterness of one who has been for two days in a diarrhagic coma, the more intensely felt because each spasm has been disturbed by the telephone. But much of my pain disappeared on reading Felix's reply to that incredible Wigmore.[1] Nothing is more delightful than a really great surgical job. Certainly if I were Wigmore I would turn my attention to lesser artists in dissection.

. . . I add an attractive dinner I gave at the School to introduce Churchill to some of my younger colleagues. He was like a great actor playing a part. He did it supremely well, and, I think, enchanted them. But he left me convinced that a political career is ruinous to one's simplicity. He searched always to end a sentence with a climax. He looked for antitheses like a monkey looking for fleas. At one time he was so asseverative about loyalty to the state that I was tempted and asked him to define what he meant by the state. I then fully understood why a wise minister rarely answers supplementary questions in the House of Commons. But he is a good fellow, incurably romantic and an arresting mind. His tendency to classify into black and white arises, I suppose from his profession. All statesmen are theologians who have not taken holy orders.

. . . I must not forget to tell you that the other day at Haldane's—Mrs. Holmes, please, must hear this,—Lady Oxford was talking of eyes and said that in the '90's, you had a provocative gleam that might easily have tempted her had occasion offered; and old Lady Horner was emphatic in the same direction. I must

---

[1] The exchange of letters between Felix Frankfurter and Dean Wigmore appeared in the Boston *Evening Transcript* from April 21 to May 11. Wigmore's letters were infected by the petulance of a panicky patriot. See Joughin and Morgan, *The Legacy of Sacco and Vanzetti* (1948) 260-262.

say that these English friends of years ago have you most vividly
in memory. . . .   *Ever affectionately yours, H. J. L.*

Washington, D.C., May 12, 1927
My dear Laski: Bad days these for writing or reading (anything
but cases and *certioraris*) and I can't send more than a bulletin.
When I thought my work was done new stuff came pouring in
and there has been no rest. Your book on *Communism* came shortly
after your letter—and in crevices of time I have read half of it.
It seems to me, if I may say so, that your writing has improved
again and I find it deeply interesting, interesting not only in itself
but in suggesting the rationale of the differences between us. The
deepest no doubt turn on what we like, as to which argument is
useless—but there are also differences in theory. I have no respect
for the passion for equality, which seems to me merely idealizing
envy—I don't disparage envy but I don't accept it as legitimately
my master. If I am to consider contributions they vary infinitely
—all that any man contributes is giving a direction to force. The
architect does it on a larger scale than the bricklayer who only
sees that a brick is laid level. I know no *a priori* reason why he
should not have a greater reward. Kant did it on a larger scale than
the architect. But you know my views on that. I think the robbery of labor by capital is a humbug. The real competitors are
different kinds of labor. The capitalist by his power may turn a
part into directions that you deem undesirable—but if he does he
does it because he thinks a body of consumers will want the
product and he is the best prophet we can get. Some kind of
despotism is at the bottom of the seeking for change. I don't care
to boss my neighbors and to require them to want something different from what they do—even when, as frequently, I think their
wishes more or less suicidal. It is not really theory but a prophecy
that the crowd having got the power will use it to smash this
or that that lays the foundation for much of the fundamentally
innovating talk. I think it playing with fire and if I were not reduced to a nearly exhausted spectator, should say I will take what
precautions I can and abide the result—reminding you that it may
be you as well as it may be I that is hurt. I should rejoice if as
you say you had written over your heart *"Surtout point de l'en-
thousiasme."* I am amused by your currency man—I don't know
but they are the hatter-est kind of social tinkers. I wrote and delivered a decision upholding the constitutionality of a state law for
sterilizing imbeciles the other day—and felt that I was getting
near to the first principle of real reform. I say merely getting near.
I don't mean that the surgeon's knife is the ultimate symbol. Your
description of Lanfrey on the Churchmen has its parallels in every

cult. The abolitionists as I remember used to say that their antago-
nists must be either knaves or fools. I am glad I encountered that
sort of thing early as it taught me a lesson.

Well, dear boy, I wish I could go on but opinions and *certioraris*
are waiting to be attended to and this must let me out. My homage
to the missus.   *Aff'ly yours, O. W. H.*

Washington, D.C., May 20, 1927
My dear Laski: (1) Before anything else let me give you the re-
quested address of Mrs. Albert J. Beveridge—viz. #4164 Washington Boulevard, Indianapolis, Indiana, or at least that was it a few
days ago. I suppose from the papers that before long she will go
to Beverly Farms—Massachusetts.

(2) Insides all right. I hope yours are! . . .

I have had no leisure till the last two days when I have had
pleasant drives and read Lawrence's book—*Revolt in the Desert.*
I asked Wallas who has just been here at luncheon what the in-
ducement was. He spoke of it as a contribution to the war—which
of course—would make it perfectly intelligible—but I got the impression of a previously existing hobby. Probably I was wrong. I
haven't quite finished your book. You state the pros and cons
fairly—but with an implied sympathy for beliefs that I believe to
be noxious humbugs—that grieves me. I feel as if the *idem sentire
de republica* tended to become less keen between us. Either I am
wrong or your present associations and reflections are leading you
a little further in a direction away from our common ground.
Wallas is a very pleasant fellow. I do not feel as if increased
familiarity meant increased intimacy—but he is cultivated and says
a thousand agreeable and more or less suggestive things. What an
advantage all Europeans have in learning so much of our historic
environment through their eyes—not to speak of object lessons in
art &c. Of course faculty is more important than education but
certainly we are heavily handicapped. The melancholy of the
languid spring and of having finished work for the moment is upon
me. Luckily I no longer think such things important—as I don't
think man so, except from his own point of view or as part of this
universe. If the prophecy that Graham Wallas was mentioning of
the return of the ice cap in 1700 years may be accepted, perhaps
it would cool our enthusiasms.

The afternoon grist of duties comes in and I must turn aside to
opinions and letters to be answered. Then I will sleep and cheer
up.   *Aff'ly yours, O. W. H.*

Devon Lodge, 21.V.27
My dear Justice: Your letter was indeed a delight; and though I
should, I think, deny almost the whole of your economic diagnosis

as born of a philosophy contradicted by the whole trend of modern fact and analysis, I enjoyed every word of it. I add that it is at bottom the economics of the soldier who accepts a rough equation between isness and oughtness. I see no validity in such a creed except upon principles I would deny at the stake.

Life has been a little overwhelming this past fortnight. I have sat on a big civil service case in the Industrial Court which has so far occupied three days. I have been chairman of a Conciliation Court in the Co-operative Industry where, the case being left to me as independent arbitrator, I had the satisfaction of establishing the six-day instead of the seven-day week for milkmen—an obviously desirable change; and I have been acting as legal adviser to the trade unions on the present Trade Disputes Bill with the advantage of reciting judicial opinions to them and their opponents on the unwisdom of words like "intimidation" and "coercing the community" drawn from your old Massachusetts opinions. Also I had one great adventure with Frida which, psychologically, was most interesting. We motored to Cambridge for the day and, on the way back, skidded on a slippery road. The steering-gear went wrong and for one minute we found ourselves headed straight for a stone wall at the bottom of a ditch. It was certain death and in that one minute I found that I certainly thought of these things: (I) Was there any danger of Diana receiving a religious education from her grandparents? (II) If Frida survived me, would I leave enough to make her comfortable? (III) Who would succeed me in the university? (IV) What a pity I had not finished my book on French political ideas? (V) Would people remember to let Felix know what had happened? (VI) What a curious contrast between an hour ago in Cambridge and this moment. But just as everything seemed ended the car turned slightly and grazed the wall on its side instead of the front with the result that beyond a slight shock we were absolutely untouched and after changing a buckled wheel able to proceed home safely. It was intensely interesting even if uncomfortable; and I was struck by the rapidity with which the mind went on working, as also by the continuity of its operation. So far as I know consciously neither of us had any sense of fear; it was rather a sense of fate. The thing was there and one simply awaited the result like the fifth act in a drama.

We saw Chafee in Cambridge and hope to have him here next week. I had a good gossip with him about the Law School and found to my interest that he shares my doubts of Pound and the illusion of bigness. I also had tea with Lowes Dickinson and heard much of the problem of the unmarried don after he had passed the meridian—an interesting issue. Dickinson was very definite that the semi-monasticism of the older universities is a mistake. It may, he thinks, suit the great man with a 40-year *magnum opus* to finish.

But the average don is then conscious of powers that begin to sag a little, of new generations pressing on behind, of lonely evenings and lonelier vacations; above all, he said, of the inertness of an institutional routine instead of the freshness of a home.

One or two things I have read I must mention to you. A remarkable American book, which I beg you to take at all costs to Beverly Farms—*Main Currents in American Thought* by V. L. Parrington, 2 volumes (Harcourt) which is, I think, pretty nearly a masterpiece. It is learned, well-written, and most stimulating; and it makes America part of the world instead of an independent hemisphere. Do please read it and let me have your views. . . .

Ever yours affectionately, H. J. L.

Postscript, Washington, D.C., May 21, 1927
My dear Laski: Another day has come—I have finished your book and I don't feel quite so seedy as I did yesterday—wherefore this p.s. Of course I appreciate what you and Keynes say, that the Russian Communism is a religion and therefore cannot be expected to be just. But I don't see why sympathetic understanding should be confined to one side. Capitalism may not be a religion but it commands a fighting belief on its side and I don't at all agree to describing its tyrannies with resentment, as coming from bad men when you gloss those on the other side. I think that most of the so-called tyrannies of capital express the economic necessities created by the pressure of population—a pressure for which capitalism is not responsible and for which communism has offered no remedy. If I praised or blamed (which I don't) either one, I should blame the communists as consciously and voluntarily contemplating their despotism whereas on the other side it is largely unconscious and the automatic result of the situation. I may add that class for class I think the one that communism would abolish is more valuable—contributes more, a great deal more, than those whom Communism exalts. For as I said the other day, the only contribution that any man makes that can't be got more cheaply from the water and the sky is ideas—the immediate or remote direction of energy which man does not produce, whether it comes from his muscles or a machine. Ideas come from the despised *bourgeoisie* not from labor. With which I shut up and go for a capitalistic drive from which I hope some little joy.

We look at our fellow men with sympathy but nature looks at them as she looks at flies—and some of her dealings are hard but should not be attributed to those who from the accident of position happen to be her instruments. *Affectionately yours, O. W. Holmes*

Devon Lodge, 29.V.27

My dear Justice: Your letter was a delight indeed. And even though I see a real disparity between us on intellectual problems, I can't say I greatly mind. For your scepticism drives me back each time on first principle which is an admirable thing for me. A good deal of our difference is, I think, due to our different civilisations. You are living amid a system where the classic principles of capitalism still work successfully, I amid one where the growing inadequacy of that machine is most obvious. In the result you, broadly, are satisfied, I, broadly, dissatisfied with the classic economics. You see a general adequacy which makes you believe in economic liberty; I see a general inadequacy which makes me believe in economic equality. We are looking at different materials and drawing, naturally, different results from their contemplation. I add that I think you have not taken account of an immense new body of experience in economic matters, and that you do not allow enough for necessary modification of economic principle as it meets that new experience. Also, I think, you are over-occupied with pure theory and make quite insufficient allowance for a friction which makes pure theory relatively negligible in its operative influence. However, one day I shall set this all down at length in a short book and then, I hope, I shall drive *you* to revise *your* first principles. And I add (not without malicious joy) a reminder of your young friend's warning about building philosophies on fears rather than hopes.[1]

. . . I had a delightful lunch with Sankey, J. who told me a good story of ———— who has wangled himself—on what grounds I do not know—into being called a K.C. wherefore in the Temple, on account of his inability to get a brief, he is known as the "artificial silk." Sankey also told me that on a recent Assize he and his colleague dined with a *nouveau riche* who had gold plate on the table. The judges carefully refrained from comment and the host's face grew longer and longer. At last, when the ladies had left, the poor man could stand it no longer and burst out, "I suppose it would need diamonds before you gentlemen would lower yourselves to make a kind remark.". . .

I am sending you separately a little French book on beggars which may amuse you. . . .   *Ever devotedly yours, H. J. L.*

Washington, D.C., June 1, 1927

My dear Laski: Your letter is the last or last but one that will find me here if all goes as we expect. Boston 8th, Beverly Farms the Saturday or Monday following. Of course the first thing is your

---

[1] *Supra*, p. 50.

escape and your reflections in the moment of imminent death. They
do not surprise me as I have had several experiences of that sort,
and always have found that when you are in the trap it seems perfectly natural and you think on that footing. But it changes in a
flash if you see a chance to get out. You put well a philosophic
rather than economic difference between us. I do accept "a rough
equation between isness and oughtness," or rather I don't know
anything about oughtness except Cromwell's—a few poor gentlemen have put their lives upon it. You respect the rights of man
—I don't, except those things a given crowd will fight for—which
vary from religion to the price of a glass of beer. I also would
fight for some things—but instead of saying that they ought to be
I merely say they are part of the kind of a world that I like—or
should like. You put your ideals or prophecies with the slight
superior smile of the man who is sure that he has the future—(I
have seen it before in the past from the abolitionists to Christian
Science) and it may be so. I can only say that the reasoning seems
to me inadequate and if it comes to force I should put my [illegi-
ble] on the other side.

I am glad at what you say about Pound and his illusion of bigness. I never have contributed until a few days ago, when my
secretary said they have got Pound's money but really need some
to pay professors and do some building, whereat I sent $100—and
some doubts whether I was right—especially at this moment. I
understand that owing to the hold-up just before Congress adjourned and the failure to pass necessary bills our salary will not
be paid this month or next—so that I am calculating a little closely
so as not to have to borrow. I presume it will all come in later
with a rush, but the interruption is unpleasant.[1]

June 2. A new and pleasant day has come. My work is done and
I am divided between the business of packing one small trunk to
be sent to Beverly Farms and presently going out in a motor with
my wife. When in doubt let pleasure prevail over duty. One of
the ways in which I avail myself of my limited plutocratic advantages is to send my trunk by express rather than have the
bother of taking it with me and sending it on from Boston. Yet I
have scruples. I wouldn't, I think, smoke dollar cigars. To be sure
I am content with 12 cent ones, but I think I wouldn't even if I
wanted them, on the ground that I ought not to avail myself of
my power to levy that tax on the total stream of products. You
see we of the exterminand class have some conscience. I have had
my drive and luncheon at Rauscher's—as our women have left.
Do you know how beautiful the Potomac is? We often drive up to
the Chain Bridge—some miles up—cross and come down on the

---

[1] In March a Senate filibuster had prevented the adoption of the Urgent
Deficiencies Bill.

other side or return on our steps. I wish I could go on to Ball's Bluff where over 65 years ago I climbed those banks—but I doubt if I ever shall. 25 years of wishing have gone by—and it does not grow easier except in the roads and means of travel. In a few minutes when the victuals have settled I will turn to my modest packing.

I have made a note of your Parrington Book on *American Thought* for Beverly Farms. Also Morley's *Diderot*. So I shall have something to read at once beside my own volume of opinions which it is a first task to page and index. I am pleased with this year. Apropos of your talk with Dickinson about the dons, I think Leslie Stephen used to speak of those who lived on the reputation of a book that they were going to write.

Well—fire away my lad—I wish that we didn't diverge as much as we seem to—but I am afraid that I am no less convinced than you. Everyone thinks that he can account for the opposite convictions of his neighbor.   *Affectionately yours, O. W. Holmes*

Beverly Farms, June 14, 1927

My dear Laski: This paper marks the arrival at Beverly Farms and the receipt of a letter from you, which leads me to say a word more about our differences. I don't profess to know anything practically—theory is all that I can bring even to the law. But theory sometimes leads one to keep in mind fundamental facts that one more versed in detail may forget. You speak of an immense new body of experiences—Hum—have you had it? The modern books that I have read have seemed to me drool on their theoretic side. But if you should say that you are dealing empirically with an empirical case—I should listen respectfully. For I perfectly admit that if you have the power on your side and find that present arrangements cause you a discomfort that you can shift to somebody else, you probably will do so—and I should bow to the way of the world. I thought, however, that you also were theorizing—and stating or intimating things that you deemed ultimately desirable —and evidently what you desire and what I desire are appreciably different. So we will put up hedges to keep the unpleasing out of sight. When you write your book that you think can upset my theories I will read it—if I still am going—but you seem to be a trifle cock-sure.

I wish I had had your book-talk before I left Washington as I have a good book of which I forget the name, author and almost the theme, which deals with the rogues in literature. I'm afraid I shall not receive your little French book until I get back—as only letters are forwarded. I make a note of Helen Waddell *The Wandering Scholars* and will try for it. I couldn't set eyes on

Parrington while in Boston—it had been taken out from the Athenaeum. The Corner Book Store didn't have it and I didn't want to order it without inspection. I may try again later—but I want to begin and for a few days have no *pièce de résistance*. I brought down a little book, Pourtalès's *La vie de Franz Liszt*—which I haven't finished. The portrait of him as a young man is loathly—and I bet he didn't smell good—but Liszt and Wagner are noble and impressive. They care more for art than for themselves. Perhaps that is true of all who work with an ideal, and no doubt those gents are a little theatrical. I will wait until I finish the book to see what I think of the subject. I get the impression that the ladies who tumbled to him were facile, as were those of Casanova, given certain preliminaries—in his case music and fame. But I should judge that he did his anti-Malthusian damnedest—which reminds me Fred Pollock speaks of Saint Jane (Austen). I shall speak of Saint Malthus.   *Affectionately yours, O. W. H.*

Devon Lodge, 5.VI.27
My dear Justice: Since I wrote last, I have had a stroke of ill luck; for I had a bad dose of influenza—whence, I do not know—with the result that the last week has passed mournfully in bed. However, I am up and about again; and at least I have had a good dose of books in bed.

Of them the most interesting has been Gibbon whom I took in at the rate of a volume a day in Bury's edition. The effect is really overwhelming. He has a poise, a sureness of foot, and a rationality which make you forgive him everything. And the sweep of the thing is beyond words. I was very moved by Bury's notes; for he makes it clear that, the Eastern Empire apart, it is detail rather than principle that modern criticism corrects; and that, after 150 years, is a thing that cannot be said of any other eighteenth century work. . . .

I have been amusing myself, too, by reading a good deal of old Hobbes, with what pleasure you can imagine. One thing struck me most forcibly and that is that in explaining him nothing has been made in the books of the really obvious fact that his view of human nature is simply Calvinism set down in naturalistic instead of supernatural terms; and that anyone who reads the old Arminian controversy will perceive without much difficulty where he got his notions from—especially as we know how interested in it he was. And that leads me to the further reflection that not a little of

¹ Jean Mabillon (1632-1707), Benedictine scholar, challenged by Le Bouthillier de Rancé (1626-1700), the abbot of La Trappe, to defend the studies in which Maurists were engaged, published his *Traité des études monastiques* (1691) and *Réflexions sur la réponse de M. L'abbé da la Trappe* (1691-92).

the explanation of the Calvinist view is that it provided a basis for controlling human nature in that period when the exuberance of the Renaissance and the "follow your impulse" theories of Luther had released it from bondage and tended, accordingly, to make it a dangerous thing from the standpoint of government. Also I add the reflection that too much is made of the singularity of Hobbes's view. In the secular field abroad he is very akin in substance to La Rochefoucauld (whom he probably knew) and the Jansenists, whose works he had probably read. In fact I should like to see an essay on Hobbes's contemporaries pointing out how greatly he reflects a very general environment and transcends it only in his ability to get rid of a good deal of theological rubbish.

You can imagine that I was delighted to see that the Governor of Massachusetts had appointed a commission to enquire into the Sacco-Vanzetti case—Lowell, I imagine, would be fair; and I think you have some confidence in Judge Grant though I remember that at the time of the Harvard inquisition into me he tended to look upon radicals as noxious insects. The other man I do not know even by name.[2] But a reading of Felix's book ought to lead them to the salient points and result in a full pardon. It would be terrible to have an unsatisfactory ending with the Mooney case so recently before the attention of Europe.

I have been able to buy one or two pleasant things from catalogues. The nicest is a fine eighteenth century Locke in 4 vast quartos and bound by Roger Payne.[3] It looks most ample and the correspondence is singularly attractive on a big page with margins wide enough for annotation. Then I got, too, a 3 volume collection of the Remonstrances of the Parliament of Paris in the 18th Century which is extraordinarily revealing. For it shows conclusively how absolutely abhorrent to them was the Encyclopedist Movement. In their way these lawyers were as prejudiced, as narrow, and as ignorant as the priests. Their hostility to reform makes one wonder not why the Revolution came but however it came to be postponed for so long. . . .

My love to you both.   *Ever affectionately yours, H. J. L.*

Beverly Farms, June 16, 1927
My dear Laski: The little French book was sent on and I have just opened it and read your letter. Both delight me. I do envy your book hunting—and I sympathize with what you say of Gibbon although he told me nothing that I wanted to know. I was

---

[2] Samuel W. Stratton (1861-1931), physicist and President of the Massachusetts Institute of Technology, was the third member of the Advisory Commission which Alvan T. Fuller (1878-1958) had appointed on June 1.

[3] Roger Payne (1739-1797), London's eccentric bookbinder whose work was notable for the originality of its design.

equally impressed with his greatness and with the changes in the emphasis of our interests. On themes of perennial interest—the Roman Law—and Christianity—I should think from what I remember that he was behind the times, now. I have finished the little book on Liszt. You would read it in 2 hours. He was great in his treatment of Wagner, and women seem to have offered themselves to him up to the end. The writer treats him as a great originator in music. Of that I know not—but I do not believe that music is the highest expression of man. Do you? I have just received from the old Corner Book Store, Haskins, *The Renaissance of the Twelfth Century* and Morley's *Diderot*—I expect pleasure at least from the last. Haskins in his first few pages seems rather verbose in explaining that the changes of history are not accurately adjusted to centuries—but I have only peeked into him. Also I doubt if he writes very well—but eminent authorities are cited in the advertisement to show that he is a swell on his theme. Also the book is from the Harvard University Press. Why is it that the literary style is so different from that of talk? I am apt to hear the words as I read (which shows, I should think, that I am a slower reader than you) and the literary style makes them seem unreal. I don't see why men should not write in the same rhythm as they talk. Owen Wister once told me that a sentence of mine puzzled him until he read it aloud as he thought I should and then he understood it. Which I am far from quoting to my credit —but my prejudice remains.

I have received two copies of an English paper—*The Commonweal* [1] which no doubt you have seen, and which simplifies the problems of life. "The rent of land belongs to the people; the first duty of government is to collect it and abolish all taxation"— People for the most part believe what they want to—their postulates are rooted in their total experience and life. Those of us who flatter ourselves that we have intellectual detachment only get one story lower in our personality—and in the end are trying to make the kind of world we should like—I doubt if I should like the world desired by *The Commonweal*.

I haven't said a word about the great excitement of these parts —Lindbergh. What pleases me is that one hears no detracting word—genius provokes envy—but when a man bets his life on his own skill and courage and wins the bet against long odds no one can do anything but praise. We came away just before the Washington reception—our passage was engaged long beforehand and all arrangements made, so we didn't change. I am content to admire at a distance. I am as nearly idle as I can be—and enjoying beautiful days and beautiful country as much as it is in me to

---

[1] The periodical was edited by J. W. Graham Peace for the Commonwealth Land Party.

enjoy such things. Later I expect to diversify with *certioraris*. Them we have always with us.

Affectionately yours, O. W. Holmes

Devon Lodge, 28.VII. [sic] 27 [28 June 1927]
My dear Justice: It is good to know that you are settled in at Beverly F. and, as your letter suggests, in fine fighting trim. My mind at the moment is a little full of anxiety about Sacco and Vanzetti and I shall be glad when the next week is past and their future is certain. Otherwise my spirit has been given sustenance by the decision of the Government here to reform the House of Lords on the worst possible method.[1] That is one of the few subjects I really know something about and I can, I hope, add a little to political wisdom anent it. . . .

I had an interesting dinner here of half-a-dozen young Tories from the House which I wish you could have attended. Two of them were really able, and defended their creed with something of the gusto of Thrasymachus. Two were traditionalists who wanted the eighteenth century back and thought of the Rockingham Whigs as the best in English history. One was a fire-eating Fascist whose simple remedy for discontent was the wall and the firing-squad. The other was a Disraelite Tory who was nearer to me in sympathies than many of my own party and about as attractive as they make them. They were most pleasant lads who still retain a good deal of that *noblesse oblige* which is so very attractive at its best. . . .

My love to you both,   *Ever affectionately yours, H. J. L.*

Beverly Farms, July 1, 1927
My dear Laski: This morning there comes a delightful and desired letter[1] from you busy about many things to me as near idle as I can be. I have read little—the most serious book: Morley's on *Diderot*. Morley seems to me a razor not a sting—and the finest edge of his thought a little blunted by respectability. I did Haskins, *The Renaissance in the Twelfth Century*—a great wrong by the first impression that I told you of. I found him very interesting and instructive—although already it seems years since I finished

[1] In late June the government had indicated its intention at an early date to propose reforms in the constitution of the House of Lords. The plan as outlined would have reduced the size of the Upper House, made provision for the choice of a part of its members by the House itself, and given the reconstituted body a share in the enactment of revenue measures. To the Labour opposition, and to many Conservatives, the reforms as outlined seemed to be designed to frustrate democratic government and to serve as a means of forestalling socialism.

[1] Omitted from this edition.

the volume. Yet I believe my last letter—answering your last, was written as I was beginning it. It seems as if I had mentioned *The Road to Xanadu*—I can't have. I didn't read the whole of it but the best 100 pages, a search into the materials for "Kubla Khan" in what Coleridge had been reading is an admirable bit of work. Not a name, not a thought, hardly an adjective that is not traced, so that all that was needed was a dream, opinion and genius—and the writer fully appreciates the genius needed to produce the poem. Then a French tale—*La nuit kurde,* by Bloch—of which I do not see much use, depicting the melodramatic doings of a young warrior, of which it is enough to mention his emulating a spider by screwing a woman while he killed her by biting and, put in as an extra, chewing her throat. Then a few pages in a long book about a woman who writes would-be poetry and tales by the ouija board.[2] Pretty much drool to my mind—but exciting the admiration of the commentator. It is a comment on man—when he absorbs himself in a system or an atmosphere—Catholicism—Hegel—Spiritualism —it doesn't matter what, he soon loses all relation to outside standards, and becomes a satellite of the sun around which the system turns. I don't see how we can help smiling at ourselves—so arbitrary, irrational and despotically given are our ultimates. I feel as if I were wasting my patrimony when I am not producing articulate words and merely receiving impressions that lose their form when I turn my back. An artist would feel just the opposite— each yielding to a compulsion of nature as he yields to the outside world, and having no better justification than that he desires to live. Why? Why do I desire to win my game of solitaire? A foolish question, to which the only answer is that you are up against it. Accept the inevitable and do your damnedest. Meantime I do receive impressions in my daily drives that are full of charm and that at least enrich life if they don't enrich me. I can't get it quite straight in my memory whether Redlich came to us last winter— but I agree to all that you say about him. Frankfurter and Mrs. called the other day and gave me much pleasure. His *Progress Report of Harvard Survey of Crime and Law in Boston* impresses me greatly and makes me believe when heretofore I have been a sceptic. I should rejoice if he produced what promises (at least to my ignorance) to be a great and noble work. I had only a glimpse of Gooch and wished that I had seen more—but I suppose he was busy and so my talk ends in the doubtful hope that this will catch tomorrow's boat.   *Affectionately yours, O. W. H.*

Beverly Farms, July 8, 1927
My dear Laski: Your letter of the 28th comes this morning and

[2] Probably Walter Franklin Prince, *The Case of Patience Worth* (1927).

gives me the usual pleasure. I notice with amusement the innuendo in your remark that I seem in fine fighting trim. Really I almost have sunk from the world of ideas. I read little and for pleasure —a French life of Disraeli[1]—and *Coningsby*—the last as far as I have got gives me pleasure and recalls the departed splendors of which I caught some last glimpses—*e.g.* a lady driving in London with two outriders—on horses of the same color as those in her carriage. But I am peeping back into glory—as yesterday I began what I never expected to read, *The Story of Philosophy* by Will Durant. I had thought of him as a *vulgarisateur*, and how could one who calls himself Will write anything on philosophy that I should care to hear (notwithstanding the case of our dear Chief Justice). But he is uncommonly good as far as I have got. Which means that I think his account of Plato excellent. He brings out authentically the hints of future thought—better than I ever have seen it done. He passes rather more lightly than I should if I were introducing a young reader over the considerable infusion of twaddle—and the ease with which the "merciless logic" of Socrates very generally could be smashed. Also he tells the story interestingly. Graham Wallas did not exhibit that self estimate that you mention. Nor did I think of him as specially self-centred—though I am not surprised. He used to come in rather familiarly, although by appointment, to luncheon—I am afraid more because he liked the victuals and the atmosphere than for any special interest in what I had to say. We found him pleasant and companionable— which I dare say was a mutual impression rather than anything more considerable. Gooch, I think I told you only looked in for a fleeting instant. I won't read Beard—and possibly may accept your recommendation of Parrington's *Main Currents in American Thought*—or I may hold myself excused by having tried once to get it and failed. I don't hanker for it greatly. Your mention of your Chinese-philosopher brings up the thought of my friend Wu. I have not heard a word from him since the troubles in his neighborhood became acute and I am anxious. To return to Wallas— of course circumstances don't make great men (though talking of William Allen I once said "great places make great men")[2] but there is a French book of which Lester Ward gives an account, showing how large a proportion of the greater names in France came from Chateaux and university towns—the moral being that there *are* mute inglorious Miltons—and that opportunity may bring out or the want of it obscure the first rate. I could jaw with you with joy.   *Affectionately yours, O. W. Holmes*

---

[1] André Maurois, *La vie de Disraeli* (1927).

[2] *Speeches*, 51, 54.

Beverly Farms, July 23, 1927

Dear Laski: There are no such entertaining events, I fear, at this
end as those you tell me of. I received from the Clerk's office a
big bag of 31 *certioraris*—and I was willing to bet on my surviving long enough for it to be worth while to diminish the pressure
of next term by examining them now. I returned them this afternoon. Also I have been visited by counsel in two cases of men
about to be executed, seeking a stay until *certiorari* could be
brought. They both came from McReynolds' Circuit, and as the
first concerned two negroes who had been tried and convicted of
rape in a court room protected by machine guns I now suspect
that the lawyer wasn't very anxious to find McReynolds who dissented from an opinion I wrote in a somewhat similar case—but
I did not think of that at the moment and granted the stay with
a statement of the difficulties to be encountered further on.[1] I
wrote to McReynolds about it and had a very nice letter from
him this morning in reply. The second application I denied and
if the expected came to pass the petitioners were executed last
Monday.[2]

Cranks as usual do not fail. One letter yesterday told me that I
was a monster and might expect the judgment of an outraged God
for a decision that a law allowing the sterilization of imbeciles was
constitutional and for the part that I had taken in other decisions
that were dragging the country down. Then your friend (?—he
quotes you) Professor Borchard of Yale sent me reprints of learned
articles about the relation between states and law[3] that so far as I
read them I thought irrelevant to the decisions that I have written.
I told him that I rather thought that you agreed with me (when
the point I had to deal with was understood) and that if not I
should think that you are off your beat and had gone astray. He
seems a really learned man—but as he signed a brief which, if my
memory is right, sought to hold the Soviet government liable in
an action here for things that it did under its law in Russia[4]—I
venture to doubt his judgment.

I have been too busy to read much of anything. I have on my
table Spinoza's *Ethics* for rereading but haven't begun it. I think
I told you of my other books—except perhaps Lord Chesterfield's
Letters—a pretty good old sportsman—most of what he says and
copiously repeats is sound—though I think his prohibition of laughter is narrow, and nowadays his horror at the thought of his son's

---

[1] Not identified. The earlier case was, presumably, *Moore* v. *Dempsey*,
261 U.S. 86 (1923).

[2] Not identified.

[3] *Supra*, p. 121.

[4] The reference is probably to *Wulfsohn* v. *Russian Socialist Federated
Soviet Republic*, 266 U.S. 580 (1924), in which the Court dismissed the
writ of error to the New York Court for want of jurisdiction.

learning to fiddle would seem extravagant. I saw for the first time the other day a little theatre in the woods that enchanted me—built by an Englishman named Buswell—a man with good looks and flattering manners. His house is part of the structure which might be four hundred years old—and looks down on a charming fresh water lake that he created, and away over the woods before the Eastern Point of Gloucester and the sea. My wife thinks that she yielded to my desires as I believe that I repressed my doubts to please her in getting tickets for and going to a diminutive presentation of *Faust* (opera) last Wednesday evening. It was our first outbreak for years and whoever was guilty we enjoyed ourselves greatly. They were very considerate to me, or to my age and advantages—and a pleasing dame gave her hand down the steps. I am glad of what you say of the expressions of good will etc. to F. Pollock. I had just heard and had written to him. I understand all is going well. I hope so as he is a very dear friend. Once more forgive this paper.   *Affectionately yours, O. W. H.*

Beverly Farms, July 28, 1927

My dear Laski: You will have gone to the Continent if not returned from it, when this reaches England, but your letter deserves an immediate answer.[1] I stopped here to order *The Small Bachelor* from the Old Corner Bookstore. Wodehouse can make me do what Lord Chesterfield says a gentleman should not do, break from the well bred smile into the loud guffaw, and as *nil humani* &c. I do not eschew the laugh—good old boy, Lord Chesterfield. To read his letters puts Johnson in the wrong. I have just read another life —the third down here—after *Liszt* and *Disraeli*—that of John Sargent by Evan Charteris—which interested me by its subject and its author—and when I read it by its execution. I don't think Sargent himself, however, would have interested me greatly, had I known him beyond a visit to his studio with H. James.[2] He was musical, to be sure, and that may stand for complexities not otherwise manifest; but a man whose aim was to set down what he saw strikes me as a little too concrete for my more abstract taste. Now I have a volume of Everyman with a translation of Spinoza's *Ethics* which I am rereading at odd minutes. Of course his theological machinery seems to me *passé*, but his conception of the universe —his view of good and evil as human not cosmic formulae, &c. make him come home to me more than any philosopher of the past —even though he does think he has got God in a trap when he snaps logic on him.

---

[1] Omitted from this edition.

[2] See "The Letters of Henry James to Mr. Justice Holmes," 38 *Yale Review* 410, 432 (March 1949).

I envy you your purchases such as the first edition of Pascal's *Pensées*. If I weren't so old I should try to snap up a morsel here and there, but it seems foolish at my age—although I don't regard a moderate and intelligent avarice in the same way. I think I have observed before that I am trying to realize that a happy hour is an end in itself and does not need justification. So I oscillate between the extreme points of Rockport and Nahant and take in unimproving delight. I turned down by your house the other day in honor of you. I think it is unchanged, but that there are more structures in the neighborhood. I saw a paradise the other day. An English chap, good looking with conciliatory manners, having acquired cash, as I take it, built for himself a house and theater on an eminence in a wood from which you look down on a fresh water lake before it on one side—and in front, over the forest, the Eastern point of Gloucester and the sea. There is near a mile of wandering through the wood, a public park, before you reach this hall on the edge of it and feel as if it were fourteen hundred and something. Taking the look of this man and the theatrical characters &c. I should think that there might be wild moments there sometimes. I broke through all my rules and went with my wife to a miniature opera, *Faust,* and enjoyed it hugely. It looks as if before long we should have more places worth seeing here than in Europe—were it not for the fatal absence of history. But I recur to my axiom—that not only all society but most romance rests on the death of men—and where the most men have died there is the most interest. A good time to you and may Geneva not disappoint.

Aff'ly yours, O. W. H.

Grand Hotel de l'Abbaye
Talloire, Lac d'Annecy, Savoie, 9.VIII.27

My dear Justice: With us, as I expect with you, everything is obliterated except the decision of the Sacco-Vanzetti case.[1] Frankly, I do not understand it. The evidence, on any showing, seems to us at this distance incredibly thin. The whole world revolts at this execution; and it will remain, with the Frank case and the Mooney case, one of those judicial murders which make the mind reel. I agree fully with all that Felix says of Lowell in this case. Loyalty to his class has transcended his ideas of logic and of justice.

We stayed in the mountains a week. It was magnificent, but the height did not suit Frida with the result that we moved to this place which is adorable. . . .

Ever affectionately yours, H. J. L.

[1] On July 27 the Advisory Committee submitted its report to Governor Fuller, and on August 3 he announced that he found no justification for intervention to prevent execution of the death sentence. On August 23 Sacco and Vanzetti were electrocuted.

Beverly Farms, August 18, 1927

My dear Laski: A letter from you,[1] delightful as usual, shows you
on your vacation, and rather unusually, I should say, taking an
incidental pleasure in nature. You couldn't help it with Mont Blanc
in front. The Swiss mountains, as my father said to me before I
first went to Europe, stretch your mind. Meantime I am in the
main quiet here. But I have not escaped the Sacco Vanzetti case.
Stirred I guess by Felix, Arthur Hill has come in to the case and
last week appeared here with other lawyers and reporters tagging
on to try for a *habeas corpus* from me—relying on a case I wrote.[2]
They were here two hours and a half and said all that they had
to say and I declined to issue the writ.[3] I said that I had no authority to take the prisoners out of the custody of a State Court
having jurisdiction over the persons and dealing with a crime under State law—that the only ground for such an interference
would be want of jurisdiction in the tribunal or, as according to
the allegations in the negro case that I wrote where a mob in and
around the court ready to lynch the prisoner, jury, counsel and
possibly the judges if they did not convict, made the trial a mere
form. They said these facts went only to motives (I suspect having another Massachusetts case of mine in view) and what was
the difference whether the motive was fear or the prejudices alleged in this case. I said most differences are differences of degree,
and I thought that the line must be drawn between external force,
and prejudice—which could be alleged in every case. I could not
feel a doubt, but the result has been already some letters telling
me that I am a monster of injustice—in various forms of words,
from men who evidently don't know anything about the matter,
but who have the customary readiness to impute evil for any result
that they don't like. The house of one of the jurymen was blown
up two or three nights ago—and I was deeply touched on the
evening after Hill's departure to find Tom Barbour at my door
wanting to bivouak on my piazza against the chance of trouble.
Of course I said no, and I found later that he had just returned
from four nights in sleepers where he can't sleep as the berths are
too short for him, and was nearly worn out. Generous and gallant,
hein? The papers this morning say that Hill announces an intent
to try me again in connection with an application for *certiorari.*[4]
So I have no perfect peace. I believe I mentioned that I was reading—I now have read, Spinoza's *Ethics*—the most valuable result

---

[1] Omitted from this edition.

[2] *Moore* v. *Dempsey,* 261 U.S. 86, McReynolds, J., dissenting.

[3] Holmes's opinion of August 10 denying the writ of *habeas corpus* is in
5 *Record of the Sacco-Vanzetti Case* (1929) 5532.

[4] On August 20 counsel for Sacco and Vanzetti presented a petition to
Holmes praying for an extension of time for applying to the Supreme Court
for writs of *certiorari.* Holmes's opinion denying the petition is in 5 *Record
of the Sacco-Vanzetti Case* 5516.

a new article in my Bill of Rights viz: No man shall be held to
master a system of philosophy that is fifty years old. Comment. All
that any of the philosophers has to contribute is a small number of
insights, that could be told in ten minutes. But, especially if he
is a German, he has to make a system and to write a big book.
In 50 years, more or less, the system goes to pot; posterity doesn't
care for it—but you have to read the book to get the author's
aperçus—and novices think that the system is the thing and that
they must master it, whereas the old hand knows that really it is
simply working two tons of sand to get a tablespoonful of gold,
and probably he knew the substance of the insights as part of his
general knowledge, before. I care more for Spinoza's than for the
other old ones but I don't believe his postulates or yield to his
logic. What I care for is an attitude and a few truths that are
independent of his machinery. If I have said all this before, forgive
me. I have sent for two books by (Ludwig?) on *Napoleon* and
Kaiser Wilhelm. I think you praised them and John Morse[5] strongly
admired them. I being empty and lazy concurred. I have done
over 50 *certioraris* for next term. I shall send this to London as
safest.   *Affectionately yours, O. W. Holmes*

Hotel Victoria, Geneva, 19.VIII.27

My dear Justice: I need not tell you how much I sympathised with
your difficulties in the Sacco-Vanzetti case. I cannot see that you
had any alternative, and I suppose the event must move to its
tragic end. But I wish I could make people like Fuller realise the
immense damage his action has done to the good name of America.
This case has stirred Europe as nothing since the Dreyfus case has
done. And to me, at this distance, and with the reliance I have on
the substantial accuracy of Felix's picture, it seems that it is indeed
another Dreyfus case.

. . . I have seen a good deal of the League of Nations people
here, and found them very attractive, especially the German Dufour[1] and the Englishman Salter.[2] I heard, too, a dazzling address
by the Spanish critic, Madriaga,[3] which was, doubtless, persiflage,
but done with a grace and a verve which were most attractive.

---

[5] John T. Morse, Jr. (1840-1937), cousin and intimate friend of Holmes,
who wrote the first biography of Dr. Holmes, and was editor of and contributor to the American Statesmen Series of biographies.

[1] The reference is probably to Albert Dufour Feronce who in 1927 was
Under-Secretary General of the League of Nations.

[2] Sir Arthur Salter (1881-   ) at the time was Director of the Economic Section of the League Secretariat.

[3] Salvador de Madariaga (1886-   ), man of letters and diplomat, at
this time was director of the Disarmament Section of the League Secretariat.
His address to the Geneva Institute of International Relations in August
1927, is printed in *Problems of Peace, Second Series* (1928), 124.

The amusing (and amazing) thing to me is the vast population of Americans one sees. They are, literally, unending—professors of both sexes, travellers, business men. You are the conquerors of the world. These folk have an easy certainty of their position, a determination to know, a relentless obstinacy (especially the women) which leave me breathless. . . . But I have heartily enjoyed talking to the officials who are extraordinarily interesting from the very novelty and width of their experience. It is a new thing to watch a committee at work on which an Italian, a German, a Japanese and an Argentinian are all arguing. And I have had a jolly dinner here with my old friend Lowes Dickinson—whose books you know— and we dissected life as gentlemen should. He has a mellow sweetness about him that is irresistible; and if only he did not think Goethe's *Faust* the supreme human achievement, it would be difficult for us to disagree. . . .

My love to you both.   *Ever affectionately yours, H. J. L.*

Beverly Farms, August 24, 1927
My dear Laski: Your last letter shows you stirred up like the rest of the world on the Sacco Vanzetti case. I cannot but ask myself why this so much greater interest in red than black. A thousand-fold worse cases of negroes come up from time to time, but the world does not worry over them. It is not a mere simple abstract love of justice that has moved people so much. I never have read the evidence except on the limited points that came before me. As I remember the time of the trial I always have appreciated the difficulty in getting a dispassionate verdict when everyone was as excited as everyone was in those days. I also appreciate what I believe was the generous knight-errantry of Felix in writing his book. But I see no adequate available reasons for the world outside the U.S. taking up the matter and I think your public and literary men had better have kept their mouths shut. There were two applications for *habeas corpus* to me, the first presented by Arthur Hill, the last on different grounds the night before the execution, by other counsel,[1] both of which I denied, as I thought them beyond my power, on the case made. There was also an application for a stay until the full Court could consider granting of a *certiorari*, which also I denied, as I thought no shadow of a ground was shown on which the writ should be granted.[2] There was no way that I knew of in which the merits of the case could be brought before us. Of course I got lots of letters—some abusive, some precatory (and emotion from women) all more or less as-

---

[1] The published records do not contain this motion or Holmes's ruling thereon.

[2] See *supra*, p. 165, note 4.

suming that I had the power of Austin's sovereign over the matter. (Forgive my mentioning so contemptible a personage.) The most sensible talk I have seen was a letter by Norman Hapgood, who recognized the humbug of talking as if justice alone was thought of. Not having read the record I do not consider myself entitled to an opinion on the case—my prejudices are against the convictions, but they are still stronger against the run of the shriekers. The lovers of justice have emphasized their love by blowing up a building or two and there are guards in all sorts of places, including one for this house for a few days, which left to myself I should not have thought of.

A review of *Circus Parade* by Jim Tully in the *New Republic* begins "Jim Tully is so goddam hard-boiled that his spit bounces," [3] which made me guffaw when I read it and again when I remembered it in the watches of the night. The only reading I have is *Napoleon* by Ludwig, but I have to confess that his great Napoleon rather bores me. Living in a somewhat narrow groove I am not interested by men whose view of life does not interest me. I shall take refuge in some more *certioraris* that have come. Whether it was as my wife thinks the long jaw with Arthur Hill over the case or something that I eat, this being the time when I am likely to have a little trouble, I have been below par for a few days but I am on the up-grade with nothing more than the occasional discomfort of wandering zephyrs in the cave of the winds. I wish I had a book that hit me where I live. But all is for the best in the best of possible worlds.   *Aff'ly yours, O. W. H.*

Beverly Farms, September 1, 1927

My dear Laski: Your Geneva experiences are interesting and some of them amusing as you meant them to be. I am interested rather specially at Dickinson's opinion of *Faust*. It is a theme on which I am not settled. As to part 2 I hold my peace, silently not believing those who think it great. It seems to me that you can't rescue a drama that does not interest as such by asserting ulterior significances. If you put a thing in dramatic form your first obligation is to make it a success as a drama. My recollection is distant, but it is of a piece in which the artists happening to be available at the moment are introduced to do their specialties. Song and dance by Homunculus etc., etc.

The echoes of Sacco and Vanzetti grow fainter, but I got an abusive letter this morning and the police will guard my home at night for a day or two more. The *New Republic* had an article

---

[3] 52 *New Republic* 26 (Aug. 24, 1927).

that seemed to me hysterical.[1] My secretary[2] who turned up last
night and who worked with Felix thinks that he wisely dropped
the subject after the case was passed upon by the Governor's committee and that his general frame of mind is to drop the matter as
finished. So far as one who has not read the evidence has a right
to an opinion I think the row that has been made idiotical, if considered on its merits, but of course it is not on the merits that the
row is made, but because it gives the extremists a chance to yell.
If justice is the interest why do they not talk about the infinitely
worse cases of the blacks? My prejudices were all with Felix's book.
But after all, it's simply showing, if it was right, that the case was
tried in a hostile atmosphere. I doubt if anyone would say that
there was no evidence warranting a conviction, and as to prejudice
I have heard an English judge sock it to the jury in a murder case,
in a way that would have secured a reversal in Mass., if the jury
had not, as I thought rightly, corrected the prejudice of the judge.
As you know, I believe, I held that I had no power to grant a
habeas corpus and that I ought not to grant a stay, if I had power,
on an application for *certiorari,* as I thought there was no case
for the writ. I wrote an opinion on the spot, but left it open to
apply to another Justice. They then went to Brandeis who declined
to act on the ground that he had been too closely connected with
the case. My secretary says that thereafter a N.Y. paper called *The
Worker* had in its window "Brandeis, Pontius Pilate," and followed the analogy describing him as washing his hands of innocent blood, etc., etc. How can one respect that sort of thing? It
isn't a matter of reason, but simply shrieking because the world is
not the kind of a world they want—a trouble that most of us feel
in some way. Well, I shan't expect to bore you about this again.

  Not much else to tell. I have been seedy but am all right again.
Lady Bryce has been here and gone. I have read very little, Ludwig's *Napoleon,* nearly finished. Napoleon bores me. W. Lippmann's *Men of Destiny* came from him yesterday. I see admirable
writing in it. It winds up with a pretty thing to me when I was
75 [3]—*eheu fugaces*—that really touches me. Mighty good talk
about others so far as I have read. Also Diehl, *Figures byzantines,*
vol. I, borrowed yesterday and not looked at. I heard an interesting suggestion from him, that when the Crusaders took Constan-
tinople the people there regarded it as an incursion of barbarians.
Huns, who couldn't appreciate the beautiful Greek civilization.

Affectionately yours, O. W. H.

---

[1] Probably "The Ominous Execution," 52 *New Republic* 30 (Aug. 31,
1927).

[2] Arthur E. Sutherland, Jr., of Rochester, now Professor of Law at
Harvard; his father (1862-1950) was a Justice of the Supreme Court of
New York, 1906-1919.

[3] "To Justice Holmes," 6 *New Republic* 156 (March 11, 1916).

Devon Lodge, 2.IX.27

My dear Justice: . . . I found your very interesting letter about
Arthur Hill's visit when we came home on Monday. Of course you
had no alternative. If you sought to probe motive the state courts
would have no *raison d'être;* and though I think the decision a
tragic one, I see no other course. The negro case, obviously, is not
in *pari materia.*[1] The execution deeply affected me. We were in
Geneva when it happened. The riots there were very bad; and
both in Geneva and Paris the ill-feeling against Americans is obviously profound. What has angered thinking people most is the
incredible remark of Borah[2] that it would be "a national humilia-
tion if any account were given to European protests." As one
Frenchman said to me, "if we have to mobilise five thousand troops
to protect American lives and property, we are at least entitled to
consideration."

. . . A breakfast with Briand. He was very troubled by the
breakdown of the Anglo-American naval conference[3] and vehement
in his denunciation of naval and military experts. *"Ce bon Foch,"*
he said, *"pense que les frontières de notre France doivent être à
San Francisco à une côté et à Vladivostock sur l'autre."* . . .

Our love to you both.   *Ever affectionately yours, H. J. L.*

Devon Lodge, 24.IX.27

My dear Justice: . . . But some pleasant interludes. Last night we
had MacDonald to dinner and talked over the universe. He is a
fascinating creature. To watch him is like observing a really tem-
peramental prima donna. He is brilliant, jealous, eager for applause, quick, incoherent—the last person who ought ever to
lead a party. He dismayed me a little by his vivid certainty that
God is on his side; hardly less by his perception of politics as a
struggle in a theatre between contestants for the limelight. I was
amused, too, by his pose as a connoisseur of the arts—which
seemed to mean legislation against Romneys and Gainsboroughs
leaving the country; and I do not think he appreciated my remark
that I rather wanted legislation to make Goyas and Degas come in.
He spoke most warmly about America where he seems to think
the future of culture lies; and with the Calvinist's contempt for
Latin countries. I told him that he would have got on admirably
with John Adams and found Jefferson wanting in delicacy and
taste. Then, too, a dinner with Sankey to meet Scrutton L.J. Do

---

[1] *Moore v. Dempsey, supra,* p. 165.

[2] William E. Borah (1865-1940); independent Republican, ardent isola-
tionist, and United States Senator from Idaho, 1907-1940.

[3] The United States, Great Britain, and Japan had participated in a
naval disarmament conference at Geneva in June. It had broken up, however, without agreement.

you know the latter? I thought him quite one of the best minds I have met in many a day—quick, wide-reaching, passionate about his work. He appealed to me greatly by avowing a complete scepticism *in re* the greatness of Cairns and clinched my admiration by his remark that judges should learn more political economy. He told me that as a young man he met you at F. Pollock's in the 'nineties but only as an undergraduate meets a master—a great fellow. So too is Sankey who got off the remark that Mansfield made law with the air of Moses receiving the Tables from the Lord. And I lunched with Churchill who has been reading American history in the vacation and is full of envy of A. Hamilton. Nothing, I told him, better explains his own temper than that he should be unmoved by Washington and Lincoln, incapable of seeing anything in Jefferson, miss the significance of the West, and fasten on the one man in the record, who, with big purposes, was anti-democratic, anti-idealistic, and incapable of ultimate generosity. It was also an amusing index to the culture of our good and great that until he read Hamilton's life, he had never heard of Marshall C.J. and did not know that Madison was a President of the U.S. I went also to dinner to Arnold Bennett who was like a very clever *nouveau riche* asking you not to forget the power of the purse, even while he emphasised his contempt for mundane things. But he did interest me by explaining, as I thought with great power why, to a novelist, Dostoievski is by far the greatest man in his line and why the *Brothers Karamazov* is the proof of it. . . .

Our love to you both.   *Ever affectionately yours, H. J. L.*

Washington, D.C., October 9, 1927
My dear Laski: A delightful letter from you, 24th, deserves more than it will get—a too frequent happening. For until this moment I have been almost overtaxed. The usual business on arrival, but more than usual, with an overhanging atmosphere of *certioraris* filling every crevice, and an abnormal Washington heat that tackles the vitals. The result of everything was that at the conference yesterday p.m. we didn't finish the work and I have no opinion to write today—for which I am thankful, as it seemed too much. I shall have my hair cut and try to finish the *certioraris* on hand, knowing that a new lot will come tomorrow. My last secretary, Corcoran, was admirable in doing all that was possible to save me trouble and he seems to have imparted the ferment to the present one—Sutherland—son of a N.Y. lawyer and ex-judge. Of course I read nothing but records of cases. I am much interested by what you say of MacDonald, Churchill, Scrutton *et al.*—but the *Histoire de Jansénisme* must wait for better days. Montague's *Right off the*

Map?—possible—but I don't do much in present affairs outside the job. I remember reading Hauréau's book 1000 years ago—and being surprised to see how much Descartes owed to the scholastics —but in what particulars I have forgotten. There is a good article about Brandeis in the *Nation* of October 5 by Norman Hapgood.[1] I believe that Brandeis deserves all the praise that Hapgood gives him and I am glad to have him get it. There is inserted a sort of caricature sketch of B's face that I don't think pleasant, although by way of caricature it catches something of him. The brethren seem in fair condition except Sutherland, who is off for a month. I don't think there is any organic trouble—but he is rather down, I infer. I have not seen him.

My hair is cut with opposite effect to Sampson's [*sic*] but still instead of working all the afternoon I should like to lie down and sleep in spite of a long night in bed.

When we called on the President he asked me if I had enjoyed the summer. I said, Yes—towns that had celebrated their 300th birthday—noble cliffs—and broad beaches with young ladies who didn't wear trousers. He said when he reached my age perhaps he should notice them—and that ended my conversation with the Executive.

Now for the *certs.*—damn them!   *Affectionately yours, O. W. H.*

Devon Lodge, 15.X.27

My dear Justice: You must forgive my lapse in not writing last week; but I was in bed with a nasty dose of 'flu which made the reading of P. G. Woodhouse's [*sic*] *Sam the Sudden* the only bearable form of activity. But I am all right again; and if a little wan, still fit for the job.

. . . I won a guinea from Sankey, J. by predicting the new Appeal Judge (Greer, J.)[1] whom he proclaimed an impossible appointment. How goodly are thy tents O Jacob!

One or two nice things have come my way. I found in a French catalogue an excellent copy of Dreyfus-Brisac's great edition of the *Social Contract*—the one edition which (a) gives you a sense of its real relation to the MSS (b) the other parts of Rousseau which amend and illustrate it and (c) parallel texts from the other mighty which show definite parallelisms of thought. I have found it very useful. First it convinces me that near to Book III Rousseau changed his mind on much as a result of meeting Montesquieu. Second I think his attitude to religion and a good deal

---

[1] 125 *Nation* 330 (Oct. 5, 1927).

[1] Frederick Arthur Greer (1863-1945), first Baron Fairfield, Justice of the King's Bench Division of the High Court, 1919-1927, Lord Justice of Appeal, 1927-1938.

in particular of the *religion civile* was determined by a real acquaintance with Spinoza, and third I think that any effort to make Rousseau the author of a really consistent body of political doctrine is quite impossible. He is simply a great prophet in the same sense that Isaiah or Carlyle was a great prophet. Also I have been reading (to review) *The Correspondence of George III* [2] the last *roi de métier* we ever had and I find it most interesting. Character B, Brains E, obstinacy A+, ignorance D; yet, strangely enough, the letters show quite clearly that merely to remain for long at the centre of affairs gives an authority and a flair unmistakable even in a petty and stupid man. The misinterpretation of America is wonderful. Right on from 1765 he thought the Americans revolutionists—because they denied the validity of the Stamp Act. Yet to my thinking their view was much that of the Channel Islands today or of Ireland before the Act of Union and could have been supported by a very remarkable body of evidence. . . . And I went to the funeral of Mrs. H. G. Wells—a dear little soul with whom Frida and I have passed many a pleasant hour. If, by the way, you cared to write him a note I think he would like it much for he is very unhappy. (His address is Whitehall Court, London, S.W.1.) I know he cares much about you and would welcome a word of sympathy.

. . . I refused to go as a fellow to Oriel—after the freedom of London the narrow environment of an Oxford College would, I am sure, be intolerable, though, of course, the leisure would be attractive in its way. Frida interrupts me to insist that I must strongly recommend you both to read Walter Lippmann's book of essays which she says are admirable. I have not seen them yet, but she is a very good judge.

Our love to you both. I write amidst fog such as only England can create.   *Ever affectionately yours,* H. J. L.

Washington, D.C., October 28, 1927

My dear Laski: A delightful letter from you, just arrived consoles me by its explanations of delay, since I also have slipped a cog. I have been so pressed and oppressed by work that I simply haven't had a chance. But the weather is clearing—we adjourn next Monday and all my cases are written, up to date. Let me answer one or two items that you mention. *Imprimis*—I did read W. Lippmann's essays before I left Beverly and quite agree with your wife, uninfluenced, I swear, by the reprint of some words about me when I was 75. I thought the notices of Mencken and Sinclair Lewis A-1.

2. I will try to write a line to Wells—but one is so helpless on

---

[2] The review has not been located.

such occasions—the more so that the Godly common-places are not available, as he wouldn't want 'em and I could not use 'em.

3. I am glad you got your guinea, but it shows how old I am that the names now are all unfamiliar to me. Why don't they put in Leslie Scott?

4. Why do you call Carlyle a great prophet? Because he shows the influence of the Old Testament? He seems to me a man of imaginative humor who didn't care a damn for the truth except for its decorative possibilities and had no particular insight into it —present or future. Perhaps I go a little farther than my fighting line—but I indicate my animus.

I can understand you as to Rousseau although I doubt if prophet is the word that I should use, when I consider his reputed influence on what happened in France and his very manifest influence on German philosophy (Kant and Hegel).

I have read nothing except records and a short *Essay on Conversation* by Taft's brother and *The "Canary" Murder*—a good detective story. It amused me to see in the advertisements quotations from notices of a former and I presume similar work that spoke of it as not only a story but literature. This one has some slight affectations of culture done in French, put into the mouth of the detective—but seemed to me to want everything except the fundamental one—a real puzzle, the answer concealed to near the end, and things kept moving. I believe that in some past time I have heard of or even read works of literature but from September 30 to October 31 I have known and shall know nothing but law. I may have remarked before—but if so I repeat—that it is harder work to live at 86 than at 26—56 or 76, but still the gusto has not departed. My wife tripped and fell when she was out star gazing one night at Beverly and I don't think that she yet has recovered from the shock—but we went out early this morning and I took an hour off for an adorable drive in the Rock Creek Park. Don't tell me that you have to go north for brilliant color. It was an ecstasy. Brandeis generally comes with me as far as my house, driving home, and we go by the Potomac and around the Lincoln Monument, to get the wrinkles out a little. He is as good as ever. I owe a line to Frankfurter—I owe everybody—but hope is not dead.   *Affectionately yours, O. W. Holmes*

Devon Lodge, 23.X.27

My dear Justice: I picture you as a ghost, palely wan, wandering amid a vast ocean of *certioraris*. I hope you will emerge scathless, and not, like your most distinguished predecessor, disappear as the clock strikes midnight. . . .

I now end with my real story. I saw a pretty box in a second-hand furniture shop which (1 foot by 2 feet) seemed to me a kind of 17th century desk and Louis XIV in decoration. It was locked and there was no key. I asked the dealer the price and was told it was three pounds. I thought Frida would like it and brought it home as a present. We got in a locksmith to make a key and when this arrived it contained 80 uncut tracts of the Fronde— many of them really rare, and not one of them available in any modern reprint. Some were things I badly needed for my book; eleven are not at the *Bibliothèque Nationale* and 36 are not in the British Museum. Do you wonder I kept this to the end, or that for at least a month I shall go about with a light in my eyes?

Our love to you both.   *Ever affectionately yours, H. J. L.*

Washington, D.C., November 3, 1927

My dear Laski: The ghost that you say you picture is solidifying down a bit. I got through my work yesterday and through some business bothers today and when my nerves have quieted down I shall feel like a human being. I am doubting whether to say a few biting words in a dissent on the differences between a penalty and a tax, but don't quite know whether I shall take the trouble.[1] If I haven't acknowledged the things that you have sent me, I have appreciated them—and just now was rereading the admirable appreciation of Bossuet,[2] which makes me think of Racine about whom I once wrote to you. When one strikes fundamental differences of taste, especially national ones, one can but bow the head (keeping up inside a silly little desperate conviction that one is nearer the center of things than the other fellow). *We* think of poetry as uttering the unutterable, and don't care a damn for the most admirable lucidity as compared with the most confused hint at the infinite. So coming nearer to Bossuet we don't warm up to allegorical figures of Commerce and Plenty and other abstractions —and coming nearer still we prefer one touch of passion or of first-hand perception of truth to well modulated tremolo and majestic platitudes. But I dare say a noble oration might be made in defense of platitudes as against our transitory novelties, even though hot ones.

I wish we sympathized as much with regard to the social structure as we do in many of our literary and philosophical judgments. But I haven't your intellectual respect for Shaw. I think he is a mountebank—though a very gifted one and I don't care tuppence what he thinks. But I dare say I should like to see him. Your box story is beautiful—suppose the dealer should sue you for the value

---

[1] *Compañia General de Tabacos de Filipinas* v. *Collector,* 275 U.S. 87, 99 (Nov. 21, 1927).

[2] Laski had recently sent Holmes his "The Tercentenary of Bossuet," 17 Manchester Guardian Weekly 254 (Sept. 30, 1927).

of the contents that you have appropriated. I dare say your answer
would be complete—but an argument could be made. Suppose instead of pamphlets the contents had been current money—say
£1000—do you think that you could maintain a claim of title?
If I thought the difficulty serious I should not speak of it—but I
regard it merely as a slight stimulus to inquiry. I suppose that I
ought to give some time to a German essay which the writer sent
to me intimating that it was more or less inspired by my book and
was important, but there is so much bread in proportion to the
sack in most German theorizing that I shiver on the brink.

I wish I might hear something of Wu in China. My fears become
serious. I suppose you have not heard anything. I feel as if I
might be on the verge of culture in some form—at least when I get
through a little book *Rationale of Proximate Cause* by Leon Green,
Assistant Professor of Law at Yale—dedicated to the memory of
(a Texan?) John Charles Townes,[3] "Lawyer, Judge, Dean, Teacher
—He came nearer the ideal in each than any other man I have
known" &c and I never heard of the paragon. The author is a
cocky gent who dogmatizes about cases more than the notes in a
law student's Review—and thinks he is revealing more than as yet
I can see that he is. You tell of more interesting things.

Affectionately yours, O. W. H.

Devon Lodge, 5.XI.27

My dear Justice: I have had my annual dose of 'flu, which is the
reason for my silence last week. However, it has gone, beyond a
certain lassitude which is, I suppose, inevitable. And I have been
busy entertaining W. G. Thompson,[1] the Boston lawyer, whom
Felix sent to me. We both liked him greatly. I like that type of
Yankee simplicity and shrewdness. And he moved me much by his
account of your patience and helpfulness when he and Arthur Hill
interviewed you in August. . . .

We motored down to the Webbs for a day and had a good talk.
I had an amusing argument with her about the influence of aristocracy in England. I said that France and America had discovered
significances in social equality unknown here; and that the English
religion of inequality had plastered our cabinets with third-rate
men there for no other reason than care in the selection of their
parents. She disagreed; but not I think with cause. Then we had
Haldane to dinner and we fought with vigour over the allied question of the social influence of the monarchy. He tried to maintain
its value as an imposer of standards. We challenged him to pro-

---

[3] John Charles Townes (1852-1923), Texan practitioner and judge, and
teacher of law at the University of Texas.

[1] William G. Thompson (1864-1935) had been chief counsel of Sacco
and Vanzetti in the later phases of the case.

duce a single realm of life in which it had successfully done so; and I must say I think he made a sorry showing. Then a lunch with H. G. Wells who talked with unreproducible brilliancy about the modern novel. Dostoievski was, he said, the supreme practitioner, then he put Balzac; then George Eliot; then Fielding; then Turgenev. Of the Americans he put Hawthorne first, both for style and matter. He rated Henry James high but thought him bewildered by the convolutions of life with the result that he lost his way and never saw a man or a plot as an idea. We visited also Bernard Berenson the art critic. . . . Did you ever see him?

. . . I reread *Adam Bede* with infinite enjoyment, and Wells's *Tono-Bungay*, which I incline to think is the best of all his writings. And a reprint of pamphlets[4] gave me so much pleasure that I put a copy in the post to you. They are so short that you can read them in between arguments; and as some are old friends you will, I am sure, recapture some early moments of pleasure.

Our love to you both. I whisper that if some money comes in I have a half-formed plan of a month in America at Easter.

Ever affectionately yours, H. J. L.

Washington, D.C., November 16, 1927
My dear Laski: A good letter from you just opened and read. I am very sorry that you have been down and hope you will take care of yourself and be cautious for some time. I am glad that you liked Thompson the Boston lawyer. He made a very favorable impression on me. The further I get away from the S. & V. case the more I am convinced that it was hardly the occasion for kicking up a row that the facts did not justify. (I am not thinking of Felix's book.) *The New Republic* has seemed hysterical to me and when (if my memory doesn't deceive me) it talked of Governor Fuller's Sadic or Sadish thirst for blood I thought it ridiculous.[1] I am sure of the root of the adjective—after all liberals can talk twaddle as well as the old fogeys.

I had a fierce Sunday to do two cases—one a case that has been postponed because of doubts, the other an effort to escape by construction from declaring an act of Congress unconstitutional—Sutherland is ill and it looks as if I should have not less than 3 with me—as against the more arbitrary result.[2]

---

[4] *A Miscellany of Tracts and Pamphlets* (A. C. Ward, ed., 1927).

[1] Perhaps Holmes recalled an editorial comment of August 31, 1927, in which it was suggested that Governor Fuller and his advisory committee were "filled with an almost sadistic satisfaction" in seeing Sacco and Vanzetti as symbols of the poor and resentful classes in society.

[2] *Blodgett* v. *Holden*, 275 U.S. 142 (Nov. 21, 1927). In an opinion concurred in by three others, McReynolds, J., found portions of the Revenue Act of 1924 unconstitutional. Holmes, with Brandeis, Sanford, and Stone, JJ., concurring, found it possible so to construe the statute as to save its constitutionality.

Monday the work begins again and although I have had some heavenly days off I haven't had as many as I wanted, and I am not unreasonable in my demands, for I thoroughly enjoy the work when not too crowded.

I never wrote to Wells as you suggested. Somehow I did not feel familiar enough. Without somewhat personal relations it seems an intrusion to write to a man about intimate losses.

I have read nothing to speak of. I did reread Selden's *Table Talk* in Fred Pollock's new edition—with renewed appreciation of the shrewd sceptical old bird, who drew conclusions from his learning. I like your capacity for getting pleasure from all sorts of books. I read most of them I read with sweat upon my brow and noting how many pages there are and how far I have got. I think I mentioned Walter Lippmann's last volume as an exception. He is a born writer. How many big books I have read mainly to learn that I didn't believe them, because I was afraid to leave the fortress in the rear, although I was to find as I expected that the guns were wooden. But of course one learns something from them, even Karl Marx. Works intended for pleasure generally give me but a mitigated joy—*e.g.* your beloved (and F. P.'s Saint) Jane Austen. I imagine that I still could take pleasure in Scott, but I have been a little shy of later years. One big book of Dostoievski I didn't finish. I think it was called *The Idiot*—or some such name. It showed great gifts, no doubt, but I got enough. Ditto as to *War and Peace* though I finished it. I once read *Phineas* (*Phinn, Finn?*) with pleasure—but that was the end of Trollope.

If I am sardonic perhaps it is because a big filling has jumped out of my front tooth at a moment's pause from my writing so that I must haste to the dentist in the morning, just as I was promising myself to give him the go by. This world is transitory and a damaged judge is of little value. *Adieu* till next time.

Affectionately yours, O. W. H.

Devon Lodge, 13.XI.27

My dear Justice: This week has been rather saddened by the death of my brother-in-law. In a sense, it was a merciful relief. He had been wounded at the Somme in '16, and had been an invalid ever since, hardly knowing a day without pain. But death is always a stark fact, about which one can say nothing; and it is difficult for a complete sceptic like myself to bring any comfort in these matters to people who (Frida, of course, apart) want essentially confirmation in what you believe to be illusion. I at least could not bring myself to give it; and I found that I was on the margin of brutality in a way which was very painful.

That apart, I have been excessively busy. I had to write the

article on Bolshevism for the *Encyclopedia Britannica*,[1] and a
hellish job it was. They gave me 5000 words; and I found I had
committed the elementary sin of collecting enough material to
write five or six times as much with ease. The only comfort I have
is that I now move with assurance amid the mysteries of a hundred
sects all with uncouth names; and, as yesterday when lunching
with Churchill, an attack on Bolshevism generally can produce
from me one of those tantalising diversions into the particular so
irritating to . . . [one] who desires, quite naturally, to live on the
plane of the universal. Churchill, by the way, was most amusing.
After three years at the Exchequer he believes himself to be a
financier of genius with a full insight into the great mystery of the
gold standard. So I teased him gloriously by asking with the guile
of simpl[icit]y all sorts of elementary questions. What did he think
would happen if the South African gold mines doubled their output? Did he approve of Irving Fisher's theory of a compensated
dollar? Didn't he think the burden of proof was on those who accepted the quantity theory of money? If 4.86 is better than 3.19
for the pound sterling why is not 5 better still? He did not (neither
did I) know the answers; but all his satellites waited for papal
bulls which did not come. As all this came on top of a denunciation of the Labour Party for its inability to understand the questions the City has to face, I am afraid I thoroughly enjoyed it. I
add that I like him much; and I greatly enjoy his unique power
of convincing himself as he goes along by the sheer force of his
own eloquence. I was amused too by his obvious contempt for
most of his colleagues except Birkenhead; and his pity for Lloyd
George as a fellow adventurer whose boat has missed the tide. He
interested me much by the remark that to him as a young man Joe
Chamberlain seemed like an English Robespierre in the making;
and Haldane, who was there, added that Edward VII was always
a little afraid of Joe because of his radical activities in the 'eighties.
It was amusing to see at that table how much still the English
aristocracy is a close corporation. All of them were in some degree
related to each other (except Haldane) and they were discussing
the engagement of the Duke of Argyll's heir to the daughter of
Beaverbrook, the great newspaper owner, as a most distressing
thing. They make their small talk charming and very graceful; but
their ignorance is really colossal. Churchill had never heard of Port-
Royal; the lady next to me thought that the Richelieu of Louis
XV's reign[2] was the great Cardinal and was shocked by his *amours*
of which she had just read, as she thought, in reading about his
great-nephew; and another person there when Churchill spoke of

---

[1] 3 *Encyclopedia Britannica* (14th ed., 1929) 824.

[2] The Duc de Richelieu (1696-1788), Marshal of France, was the grand-
nephew of Cardinal Richelieu.

a visit he had received from a descendant of Madame de Staë.
looked so blank that I had to explain in an undertone. But they
know all the current books, or pictures or plays, about which there
is gossip. They have an absolutely immovable opinion of all the
politicians and the novelists and the painters. They are charming
people who do not know that other worlds exist, or that any car
compete with their own. One said of Esmé Howard, the Am
bassador, that it was a shame to send a decent fellow like that to
Washington. Another asked me if there were any decent historie:
of the United States; and a third opined that "those Yankee fellow:
want taking down a peg or two, you know." One lady said to me
that she was so surprised by Ramsay MacDonald's charming manners, "and his father, you know, was only a workman." I felt tha:
the times of Charles Greville were really less distant than one wa:
sometimes tempted to think. . . .

I do hope Mrs. Holmes has recovered from the fall. What you
say of Brandeis warms my heart; I know he on his side reciprocate:
it fully to you. When he writes to me he never fails to make you
the centre of what he has to say—always with a pride and affec
tion that are wholly delightful.

My love to you both.   *Ever affectionately yours, H. J. L.*

Devon Lodge, 20.XI.2:

My dear Justice: Let me begin with the bad news. The publishe:
of my *Communism* has gone bankrupt; with the result that instead
of the four hundred pounds he owes me (it has sold some forty
thousand copies) I shall have, I understand, about ten pounds. A:
I had counted on that for my American holiday at Easter, it means,
I fear, that I must postpone it until the French book is done. It is
I think, bad luck, to have written a "best seller" and then to be
deprived of the fruits thereof; but I see no other way of meeting
it except to shrug one's shoulders and go on to the next thing.
. . . I was glad to note that Felix had dedicated his book o:
your court with charm;[1] though I thought (not that I should say
so to him) that he had broken a butterfly on a wheel in devoting
400 pages to an analysis of what really was worth an article.

I have had a busy time since I wrote last. A jolly dinner with
H. G. Wells who gave forth judgments with vigour. Item, J. M
Barrie had never written a line worth a damn (warm consent)
item, Henry James spent his life pursuing a vain shadow; item,
Santayana had sacrificed essence to form; item, Herman Melville
was easily the biggest of all the Americans as Dostoievski of the

---

[1] Frankfurter and Landis, *The Business of the Supreme Court* (1927) wa:
dedicated "To Mr. Justice Holmes, who, after twenty-five terms, continue:
to contribute his genius to the work of a great court."

Russians. He was off to France for the winter and full of reckless gaiety so that the evening was a delight. I don't know a more stimulating fellow in England. Then dinner with Haldane at which Baldwin was the other—an amazing evening, with Haldane trying to make out (Great God!) that Gladstone was the most important Englishman of the 19th century. Baldwin and I argued in politics for Disraeli; in speculation for Darwin. But old Haldane was hearing the magic voice and the heaven-sent gesture and was immovable. Baldwin contributed the amusing fact that when a judgeship is vacant an average of 100 K.C.'s write in to explain their charms but when a Regius professorship is vacant he has to go out searching for news of the man. Modesty of the scholar, said I; no, said he, for most of those to whom it is offered think themselves too big for it.

. . . for the most part, I have been finishing an article on Bolshevism for the *Encyclopedia Britannica* and ploughing through dreary wastes of Bolshevist literature. No one, I fear can call it in the least exhilarating except the elect, and I, alas, am not of them. Did I tell you that I had traced the origins of the famous "Dictatorship of the Proletariat" to Babeuf? As that is Marx's chief claim to strategic creativeness, and as I dislike Marx intensely it gave me peculiar pleasure, as there is little doubt but that he had read Babeuf with great care. . . .

My love warmly to you both. I hope Mrs. Holmes has fully recovered from her fall.   *Ever affectionately yours, H. J. L.*

Washington, D.C., November 23, 1927

My dear Laski: Your old friend John W. Zane has written a book —*The Story of the Law*—and James M. Beck writes a letter of introduction. Beck, you may remember, is an ex-solicitor-general and thinks that only strokes of ill luck prevented his being Ambassador and on our Court. Zane has an irritating ability, at once undeniable and unsatisfactory. Evidently he has read a good deal, but he seems a *parvenu* in the world of intellect, from his arrogant dogmatism and, unless I am wrong, his somewhat painstaking introduction of quotations or allusions that he thinks you will not expect. The book is intended for popular reading and does not contain new ideas but it tells the story in an interesting way and with a sense of actuality. He begins with man in a pack and works down. Of course, there is more of the "would" in proportion to the "did" than we are accustomed to in these days. You remember how reconstructors of the past a century ago were accustomed to say that in the hunting stages men would do this and that &c. &c. Wells has begotten a progeny. We had the story of philosophy last summer and here the story of the law and there are others. Wells

I think produced a work of art. Whatever his faults of detail he makes you realize the world and the story of man as one—and realize something of what it was. This book so far as I have read has a similar merit in a less degree and is well qualified to make semi-civilized men out of the quarter civilized. But the conceit of the writer is amazing and I am sure that divine providence arranged that Beck should introduce him.

Nothing else to tell. We are sitting again. All my cases and a dissent are fired off and I begin fresh and empty. I have had nothing as yet that excited my enthusiasm—but there is a dim spark of interest in the meanest case. I had a letter from A. Hill saying that Frankfurter will write nothing more about Sacco and Vanzetti for a year. I hope it will be longer than that, as I think all those who were interested on that side seem to have got hysterical and to have lost their sense of proportion—but I don't refer to his book in saying that. He has published also a good one on *The Business of the Supreme Court*. He is so good in his chosen business that I think he helps the world more in that way than he does by becoming a knight errant or a martyr—though I don't undervalue or fail to revere his self sacrifice in his excursions and alarums. I might say something similar of another friend of mine.

Affectionately yours, O. W. Holmes

Washington, D.C., November 29, 1927
My dear Laski: Just as your letter came I received a parcel from the *China Law Review* with a judgment by Wu, of late date—and I suspect the address to be in his handwriting but he used to be an eager correspondent and he has been silent for more than a year, so that I don't quite know what to make of it as no written word explains. You speak of him in your letter which makes me mention him first. After finishing Zane's book of which I wrote to you I had a few hours which I filled delightfully with your *Miscellany of Tracts and Pamphlets*—very good reading—and if one used those methods, worth resorting to for new words or tricks of speech. My judgment of Zane was not changed as I read on. There were some things that seemed to me disproportionate toward the end—and renewed surprise at the boorish dogmatism of one who pauses in a history to reflect on the advantage of being born a gentleman. But the story interests and is made pretty real and actual, a grandchild of Wells's book.

I am truly sorry about the publisher of your *Communism*—in every aspect. As to Frankfurter's dedication, do you know that I didn't discover it till 3 days ago? A letter from A. Hill said something about the dedication which I did not understand—I looked at the book and had to cut that page, when lo! I was quite overcome. It touched and pleased me much.

Isn't it queer—what you tell me about the K.C.'s writing when a judgeship is vacant! I remember one or two cases of men who wrote on to Eliot—and then to Oxford—stating their claims to honorary degrees—I am happy to say in vain. As to your other themes, I remember years ago being moved by Barrie's *Window in Thrums*—and I have seen some of his short plays with sentimental emotion. I am inclined to agree about Herman Melville with considerable qualifications—and as to Gladstone. Little as I admire him in the higher intellectual spheres, I should have thought him more important than Disraeli. I am glad you can bore a gimlet hole in Marx, as I think him a humbug (I mean in his reasoning), and he almost beats Zane for patronizing side. . . .

Our cases haven't been specially interesting but we have one on where a man is going to try to make out that for a city to go into the gasoline business is *contra* the XIV Amendment. Also I hear that they have proposed a nationwide referendum on the drink question. I am amused at the recurring question as to Coolidge's meaning in saying that he didn't "choose" to stand for a third term.[1] I regard the expression as perfectly good English and presumably saying just what he meant. But those who justify it generally go no farther than to speak of it as a local usage. I must get 15 minutes reading—and I have barely time for it so I shut up. I think of things I want to say to you and forget them before the time comes to write.

Affectionately yours, O. W. Holmes

Devon Lodge, 3.XII.27

My dear Justice: If my memory serves me right, next Thursday is the 25th anniversary of your entrance into the Court. I need not tell you how warm my congratulations are, nor how affectionate. It has been a great thing for America in particular to have you there, and, in a larger sense, for the common law jurisdictions of the world. *Macte antiquae virtutis!*

I have had grimly busy days. A case at the Industrial Court, in which the briefs alone were a thousand pages, has occupied four long days; and we have still to finish conferences about it. And I have had three lectures to give of the irritating kind that one promises months ahead and forgets about until the night is on you. But much has been flavoured by a grand dinner at Sankey's to meet a number of deans and bishops. I have never before met the breed in bulk and a queer lot they are. First—their ignorance of their own ecclesiastical history is appalling; I talked of the Donatists and not one of them knew what Donatism was. Secondly they were all incapable of intellectual honesty. For example I asked

[1] On August 2, 1927, President Coolidge had released his famous brevity· "I do not choose to run for President in nineteen twenty-eight."

them if they thought anthropological discovery affected the place of the sacraments in theology, and they all said of course as regards Roman doctrines, but not on the Anglican side. Then we talked much of the next Archbishop and for them the essential quality they desired was *tact*; and tact meant what American politicians call "availability"—X would not do because he was labour; Y was too high; Z too low. A was ideal—very colourless but he had never spoken on dogmas and being 68 would not reign long enough to disappoint the younger men on the episcopal bench. I would not have missed the occasion for worlds; I left feeling like Voltaire. And as I left Sankey gave me a beautiful folio translation of Machiavelli (1675) which provoked a vast and bucolic dean to regret that it was a translation. He personally always read him in the original *Latin*. O God! O Montreal! Also let me chronicle an amusing dinner at which I sat next to a great lady whom I will not name. She had just come back from America. How distressing it was! So uncouth, so uncultured; rather like England before there were railways. The Americans were so conceited. They lacked an aristocracy to give them the grace of cultivated tradition. Thence to books. Did I know the works of Julia Freer[1] (do you?)? There was a great historian, learned and yet naughty! So many love stories. She adored love! There was no love in America; it was all money. England was losing ground because the working-classes wanted money just like the Americans instead of loving their betters as they did when the queen was alive. The Prime Minister ought always to be a peer—it gave confidence to know that one of the right kind was in office. In the old days peers were always Prime Ministers. I breathed the names of Pitt and Peel and Gladstone which she swept aside with the sublime ejaculation "*canaille*." I of course encouraged her by unconcealed admiration. She confided to me that her ambition had been a salon but the arts, alas, were dead. For instance only last month she had invited Kreisler to dinner and asked him to "bring his fiddle" to play afterwards and he refused. "These artists get so much money nowadays that they are getting above themselves." And the girls of today! Words failed her beyond the remark that of the daughters of her twenty closest friends not one was a virgin. I, of course, must know that. I disclaimed all knowledge as tactfully as I could. "Ah! but you are a man, and no man thinks of a woman except as an object of seduction." This from a hag of sixty with four chins and the dress of a girl of nineteen, the professional and permanent *ingénue*. I could have listened to her effortlessly all day; and she was so convinced that she was profound and important.

In the way of reading I have had little time for other than work —mainly St. Augustine. I wasn't very profoundly impressed, except

---

[1] Not identified.

by a certain unmistakable dexterity and fullness of mind—chiefly out of Plato and Cicero. He seemed to me to run away from all his real problems, and to lack altogether the ability to judge oneself that makes Spinoza so formidable an analyst. Curiously, I was less moved by the *magna opera* than by the letters some of which, *e.g.* No. 185, struck me as the work of a first-class administrator; and in general I offer the bet that there is no originality left in Bossuet after you have made your way through Augustine. He did have the effect on me of wanting to know more of Roman Africa which I have marked down as an enviable subject for leisure. The Zane you mention I do not know even by name, but I should like its exact title if you have it at hand. . . .

Our love to you both. *Ever affectionately yours, H. J. L.*

Washington, D.C., December 15, 1927
My dear Laski: My thanks for your references to my 25th anniversary. I think that I should have forgotten it had not Brandeis and a few others sent me kind remembrances and a little later Frankfurter's articles in the *Harvard Law Review*[1] reinforced his dedication—which I did not discover until a letter from A. Hill referred to it. You are better than usual, if possible, with your account of the Dean who reads Machiavelli in the original Latin, and the great lady with her penetrating criticisms of America and her revelations about her friends (and of herself). I haven't had time for reading yet, but I have got off my only opinion, a bothering one, and received it back approved from the Chief, Brandeis *et al.*[2] and have done my *certioraris,* so that now all that I have on my conscience for the next two weeks, is to try to make up my mind whether some gas rates are confiscatory[3] (Harlan used to call it confiscátory) and the dentist. At odd minutes I have read your little book of *Tracts and Pamphlets.* Among the later ones I was rather touched by Wesley and stirred by Tom Paine. I should have been slightly nauseated by Newman had he not been too remote for anything but curiosity. I haven't quite finished Kingsley, the only one not read. He makes me squirm, even while I dislike him as a wholesome parson imbued with convictions that I do not share. Zane's book is *The Story of Law.* John M. Zane, Ives Washburn, publisher, New York. You did know of him and were savage —I forget exactly the occasion. You will be pleased to know that he said in an article that anyone who thought my *Kawananakoa* v. *Polyblank* decision right might give up all hope of being a lawyer.

[1] "Mr. Justice Holmes and the Constitution," 41 *Harv. L. Rev.* 121 (December 1927).

[2] Probably *Equitable Trust Co.* v. *First National Bank,* 275 U.S. 347 (Jan. 3, 1928).

[3] The case has not been identified.

In this book he dismisses Plato as incredibly conceited, as formerly he dismissed all German law speculation (but that was during the war) and spit on his hand and wiped all the sequence from Hobbes to Austin off the slate. He never has told, so far as I know, what the great philosophy is that takes the place of all these—but I guess he thinks there ain't no such critter but just the sensible practising lawyer to be found in John M. Zane. He affects the tone of scholarship yet somehow seems to me a *parvenu* in the business. But I think he has told the story very well for its purpose. Perhaps you will regard it as an index that he seems to consider Vinogradoff as the great jurist of the century. Vinogradoff was learned, but so far as I have come in contact with his thought on legal themes it has not struck me as important. Do you agree? I am not malevolent in my attitude to Zane, but it tickled all that is evil in me to have him introduced and recommended by Beck. (There are many who suppose that Beck is a great constitutional lawyer.) I never read anything of St. Augustine except the *Confessions,* which interested me, though I couldn't recite very well on them now. You don't surprise me as to Bossuet, nor very much about Augustine, but on the latter I don't know enough to speak. I see no one except the JJ., and the rare caller who gets in, like your Ambassador and his wife, both of whom I like sincerely. I haven't yet got free from the cramp of continued application that I have felt ever since I have been here. I suppose I may live to expatiate free again.

My love to you all and a merry Xmas.   *Yours as ever, O. W. H.*

Devon Lodge, 12.XII.27

My dear Justice: . . . I was amused by your further account of Zane. It reminds me a good deal of a colleague of mine at McGill University who used to commence his courses on English Literature by explaining that attendance thereat did not constitute a personal introduction to him as a man of his birth and breeding could not possibly know students outside the lecture room. Only last night I was told of a young man who applied for the post of secretary to Curzon. The latter asked if he was married. "Yes" said the applicant. Curzon hoped his wife was a lady; if so when they were in want of an extra woman for dinner she might be put on the list of availables. The candidate thereupon abruptly explained that he was no longer a candidate. "Dear me," said Curzon, "do you think it fair to deprive your wife of the social opportunities she could have by dining with us?" Could the sublimity of insolence really go farther than that? . . .

I go North on Thursday for a week to give two lectures at Manchester University. Then home for Xmas and then a few days on the Continent before term begins. I think Antwerp, and if the money holds out, on to Amsterdam.

Our warm love to you both.   *Ever affectionately yours, H. J. L.*

Washington, D.C., December 24, 1927

My dear Laski: Your account of Curzon and the man who applied for the post of Secretary is striking and British. There was a simplicity and singleheartedness in Curzon's insolence that almost made it cease to be such—an English quality that to such a double-dyed sceptic as me is impressive. To be cock-sure is to have power. It comes in curious contrast to what I was saying yesterday to Brandeis. When we were boys we used to run tiddledies on the frog pond in the Common—that is jump from piece to piece of the ice, each being enough to jump from but sinking under you if you stopped. I said having ideas was like running tiddledies— if you stopped too long on one it sank with you. The thought was suggested to me by reading a collection of essays on *The Social Sciences and Their Inter-relations* edited by Ogburn and Golden-weiser—Houghton Mifflin & Co. The writers seem to take it for granted, as indeed do the scientific men whom I see, that the Spencerian straight line evolution is a dream—that there is no sufficient evidence that the matriarchate preceded the patriarchate (as a general fact) that the original promiscuity is an invention of the anthropologists &c, &c, &c. I think I will cease struggling and be an old fogey—for how the devil one can write decisions and do what the newspaper men call keeping abreast with the times I do not see. Before I forget it: Wu's name is John C. H. Wu—and his headquarters or address used to be 11ᵃ Quinsan Road, Shanghai —and a paper that I received lately containing a decision of his I think came from the same address. He was a member of the Shanghai Provisional Court. But if he is there and all right and if he sent me the decision I can't imagine why he has not written to me for so long. 11ᵃ Quinsan Road seems to have been the headquarters also of The Comparative Law School of China—Law Department of Soochow University—described on the title page of the *China Law Review*—Volume 1, 1922-24 as the publishers of the periodicals—with that address.

It is Christmas Eve and I am so interrupted and upset that I will not try to continue—except to send you every good wish. I have had two presents from disconnected men of a bottle of whiskey—which raises a misgiving in the mind of a careful observer of the Volstead Act but recalls the prayer Lead us into temptation.

Affectionately yours, O. W. Holmes

Devon Lodge, 28.XII.27

My dear Justice: . . . I thought Felix's piece in the December number of the *Law Review*[1] quite excellent in tone and temper, though he did not say one of the things I should have said, namely that comparing what you write with the judgments of Marshall you give a useful sense of a complex world into which with great effort a few sign-posts may be driven while Marshall always seems to suggest that the world is a damned simple place and he especially knows all about it. Somewhere lingering in me is a suspicion (dare I utter it) that Marshall is rather an overrated person and that he would have been much happier with sturdy Philistines like Field and Brewer and Peckham than with civilised creatures like you and Brandeis. I add that I was amazed by the article by Pound which followed on Felix's;[2] at first it didn't seem to me to mean anything and a second reading convinces me that if it does, what it has to say isn't particularly worth while. If ever a man lived beneath the tyranny of categories it is Pound, and the habit of thinking them realities seems to grow on him. A page of Morris Cohen is worth a whole article by him. . . .

May 1928 bring you both all that I am eager it should!

Ever affectionately yours, H. J. L.

---

[1] *Supra,* p. 185.

[2] "The Progress of the Law: Analytical Jurisprudence, 1914-27" (Part I), 41 *Harv. L. Rev.* 174 (December 1927).

VII

1928-1929

Devon Lodge, 8.I.28
My dear Justice: We got back yesterday from a divine week in
Antwerp. Talk of the best kind; food that even I appreciated as
different; two perfect etchings; and a host of old books the mere
finding of which was ecstasy. The man I enjoyed most there was
an old Belgian Jesuit who had been for nearly forty years a missionary in China. Religion had ceased to have much meaning for
him and he had, I think consciously, devoted himself to Chinese
anthropology. He was a brilliant fellow, with that suave sensibility which makes the Jesuits so much the ablest and most attractive of all the Catholics. I asked him how he had managed
to stay so long without being moved; he said that he always
arranged his diseases at a suitable moment. I asked, too, much
about his religious work. He said that he went over convinced
that he had a great mission and stayed convinced that he was
being humanised. Did he ever have religious doubts? Yes, but
when they came anthropology was an antitoxin. Had he ever seen
evidence that the Chinese were influenced by his teaching. Answer: a good Chinaman will not be harmed by Christianity, and
a bad Chinaman is less likely to starve if he becomes a Christian.
After all, he thought, it was good for China to know that Confucius and Lao-Tse had their European *confrère*. He objected to
no form of religion except Baptists; the latter he disliked because
they really thought their dogmas were important. The only Christian dogma to which he clung was the necessity of beautiful music
in the church positively; and, negatively, the aesthetic horror of
extempore prayer. . . . And I spent a day in the *Musée Plantin*
and sat in the chair where Lipsius corrected the proofs of his
texts with the fear of Scaliger's criticisms in his mind, not without emotion. The house we stayed in (an architect-friend's) was

itself a poem. Built in 1405, most of the original remains, especially its exquisite interior court, and its perfect Gothic façade.
Really it is a crime that you and I cannot have a month in Europe together so that I could show you my Paris and my Antwerp
and my patch of Prague that I would not change for the wealth
of the Indies.

Thanks for the address of Wu. I have written to Austen Chamberlain and asked him to make suitable inquiries discreetly and
you shall hear at once. The court I believe still functions which,
at least, means one has ground for hope. But in China just now
one ceases to expect anything but the worst.

I came back to a flooded London and a dinner party at Bernard
Shaw's where the guest was Chesterton. They both, I thought,
talked clever nonsense interminably under the impression that it
was metaphysics, and Chesterton acted as though the creation of
a paradox is proof of genius. Shaw (to speak in your private ear)
rather bored me. He talks as though he knows that Europe is
listening at the keyhole to what he says; and he has, consequently,
a reckless disregard for truth where this is in conflict with sensation that I really find a painful thing. And the adulation which
surrounds him is irritating beyond words. He says something
which makes you revolt; you contradict; and his audience looks
at you as though you had spat upon the Eucharist. When *e.g.* he
and Chesterton maintain that there has been no intellectual freedom in Europe since the middle ages what can you do except be
vehement. Yet with his audience that kind of cheap paradox is
greeted as an *ex cathedra* pronouncement from Rome. I am permanently anti-papal.

Our love warmly to you both. Please take great care in the cold
weather that I read of in Washington.

Ever affectionately yours, H. J. L.

Washington, D.C., January 11, 1928
My dear Laski: A double extra delightful letter from you this
morning—with . . . your astute remarks on Marshall. You may
recall on reflection that in *our Collected Legal Papers* we had a
few remarks on that sage—which led Roosevelt to doubt whether
I was the right man to appoint to this bench. I only think you
should not make it a trait of Marshall especially—it was the mark
of the time, a god-fearing, simple time that knew nothing of your
stinking twisters but had plain views of life. Story and Kent seem
to me similar in that way—and I never have noticed any marked
or extraordinary self-satisfaction to Marshall. They were an innocent lot and didn't need caviare for luncheon. I am all in the law
again and reading next to nothing. I do constantly miss my friend

Rice who was boss of the print department. That department offers a rather finite sphere of interest but there always was a little mystery of possible enchantment when I went over for a morning with him—and perhaps still more when I thought of going over without going. I haven't bought a print since he died —bar a Japanese trifle or two which I don't count.

Last night I set my wife to reading to us a Japanese woman's account of her bringing up and life that interests me much. (*A Daughter of the Samurai*—by Etsu Inagaki Sugimoto. Doubleday Page & Co.) Her account of one of the old Samurai after the new order had come in was like the most moving tales of the old French *noblesse*. She last sees him as doorkeeper in a shop, opening and shutting for those who in her youth would have touched the earth with their foreheads when he rode by—but with the same old dignity and little smile. My first Japanese student was like that. He was given 2 swords when he was 12 and told he could draw one when he chose but that if he did he must kill either the other feller or himself before putting it back.

As you say that you expect instruction from Zane by reason of what I said, I protest—I hardly think much instruction, but, as I said before, a realizing sense of the movement of the law—in a less degree the kind of thing done by Wells—and oh my lights —oh my liver—introduced to the public by that other great man Beck! I am pleased to notice how frequently our estimates agree.

Last night in my hour off after dinner, being unwilling to take up anything that I must finish if I began it, and having nothing particular in mind, I browsed a bit in the *Dictionary of Modern English Usage,* which embodies all my convictions so far as I have seen, and once in a while has a wrinkle that had escaped me—*e.g.* the distinction between "especially" and "specially"—but I think my instinct would have kept me right. It led to a misgiving for a moment after I had written especially on page 1 of this (last line) but I believe it is right.

You see how dry I am when I am in the Chamber of the Law, but I do wish you and yours all good things for the new year. It has begun pleasantly for me. Your address *Bridge* Place has given me a slight apprehension for you as to the floods but I hope an idle one.   *Affectionately yours, O. W. H.*

Devon Lodge, 21.I.28
My dear Justice: Your delightful letter of January 12 [*sic*] was very welcome; and I was glad that you did not feel unsympathetic to my heresies about Marshall. The floods here were pretty ghastly—in places like the desolation of a tidal wave. But the position of this house in a *cul de sac* renders it, luckily, remote

from any prospect of inundation. Two maids in the house of a
friend of ours—Haldane's niece—were actually drowned as they
slept in bed.

I have had a very busy time since term began. . . . Yesterday
I was at a board for over an hour which devoted passionate
energy to the question whether the title of a thesis should be
"Lord Odo Russell's Embassy in Berlin" or "Anglo-German Relations while Lord O.R. was at the Embassy". . . . On the whole
I am not very impressed by government by dons. They are remote
from life; they have what the Freudians call an "inferiority complex" about business; and that makes them wrangle interminably
about petty details without much regard to their importance.

You will have seen about Hardy's burial in the Abbey—to me
a melancholy spectacle. First the old man deliberately did not
want it; and second I object on principle to the Church getting
kudos from men who reject its doctrines. I never thought that
men like Shaw would take part in a ceremony which was built on
dogma Hardy spent his life in denying; but I suppose even a
neo-Jew like myself cannot quite grasp what burial in the Abbey
means to Christians. His death made me reread some of his
things. . . . *Tess* and *Jude* and *The Mayor of Casterbridge* were
assuredly in the great tradition.

In reading, I have had rather a jolly time. I read Paul Masson's
Religion de J. J. Rousseau, certainly the best explanation of him
that there is, and above all valuable because it makes so very
plain the relationship of R. to the religious reaction of Chateaubriand and his period. Then Miss Haldane's *Life of Descartes,*
good journeyman's work. It did not make me admire Descartes
unduly as a person—that cold self-centredness is singularly unattractive, and the tone of his letters to Christina of Sweden
makes one literally sick. Then I read the new volume of Queen
Victoria's *Letters,* which I do urge you at least to turn over if
they come your way. She was just like the popular conception
of the Kaiser except that she was the formal head of a system
able to neglect her opinions. Vicious, obstinate, ungenerous, the
creature of flattery, and with no power at all of self-criticism. If
Dilke and Chamberlain had known what she was saying of them
at the time, Republicanism in the eighties would have been a
serious business. . . .

I have bought, too, some pretty things. Two nice volumes of
Holbach go far towards making my set of him complete; and I
was tempted by, and fell for, the new national edition of Descartes in which I find the correspondence most attractive. . . .

We have hardly been out in the last fortnight through pressure
of work. But I have had a tea with Birrell and a dinner which
it may amuse you to hear of. Birrell was very full of a book by

Birkenhead called *Points of View*. "He thinks," said Birrell, "that
if he spits in the street men will think it the waters of Heaven."
He has satisfied himself that Demosthenes, Cicero, and Burke
combined to give him birth; and having satisfied himself that this
is so, he has compelled every half-wit in London to take him at
his own valuation. I said to Birrell that he seemed to feel very
strongly about Birkenhead. "Wouldn't you?" said Birrell. "I met
him on the street just now and the fellow had the insolence to
say that Lamb was not a loveable person." I wish I could reproduce the tone in which the words "the fellow" tumbled from
Birrell's mouth. Another great remark of Birrell's was that the new
school of poetry (the Sitwells *et al.*) seem to think that Apollo
played not the lyre but a brass band. At dinner I sat next to a
great lady whom I leave unnamed. She asked me if I were a
Theosophist and I said I was afraid not. Then for 20 minutes she
explained its glories to me and begged for my adhesion. She even
offered to meet me *on the astral plane* but not on Tuesdays and
Fridays when she had engagements. She told me that she vividly
remembered living in 16th century Italy where she was Lucretia
Borgia, and that in retrospect there was a cloying sweetness about
her sins. Afterwards, her husband asked me if she had told me
this; I had to admit it. "There have been moments," he said,
"when I wished I was the Borgian Pope." . . .

My love warmly to you both.

Ever affectionately yours, H. J. L.

Washington, D.C., January 23, 1928
My dear Laski: This begins a letter that I don't know when I
can finish seeing that I have a five to four case just assigned to
me in which I am the doubting fifth.[1] But I must say that you
stir depths when you speak of showing me your Paris and your
Antwerp. Also I am charmed by your old Belgian Jesuit and delighted at your experience with Shaw and Chesterton. I have told
you often that I didn't care what Shaw thought about anything—
that I regard him as he once described himself as a mountebank
—good to make you laugh but not to be taken too seriously.
When Chesterton tackles fundamentals he seems to me incompetent. When he utters paradoxical epigrams he amuses me—but as
to him also I don't care what he thinks.

'Tis done—my opinion has gone to the printer and I hope even
that it may convince Brandeis who took the opposite view. Two
generations ahead of me there was a well known lawyer in Bos-

---

[1] The case has not been identified; perhaps it was *Casey* v. *United States,*
276 U.S. 413, *infra,* p. 199.

ton, Charles G. Loring,[2] whom my mother-in-law pronounced a really good man because he never took a case that he didn't believe in—perhaps a more sardonic way of putting it would be that he believed in every case that he took. My senior partner[3] was a student in his office and one day Loring working on a brief said "I pursue this investigation with increasing confidence"—a good touch of human nature which I now illustrate, having convinced myself quite comfortably. Dear me—how can man take himself so seriously—in view not only of the foregoing, but of the fact that a change in the wind or the electrical condition will change his whole attitude toward life. Of course he can't help being serious in living and functioning, but I mean in attributing cosmic importance to his thought and believing that he is in on the ground floor with God. This interjection comes up to me so often that I can't help repeating it often as I probably have uttered it before.

I was amused last night by a number of the *Mercure de France* sent to me by Gerrit Miller[4] with an article intended to show that Casanova when he wrote his memoirs in his old life was an omnivorous reader, and as the reporters say in their rancid language— abreast of the times—that therefore various coincidences with a work by Diderot then attributed to the Chevalier de la Morlière, with Faublas and with Restif de la Brentonne, indicate that he had read the works referred to and heightened his memoirs with high lights from those sources.[5] If you are a Casanovan this may interest you. C's book did me good at a critical moment—just when I had got out my *Common Law* and had some symptoms that for the moment I mistook for a funeral knell. It is an amazing work as no doubt you know. There is also a queer article on Goethe which I hardly glanced at that interprets the seeming babble of the witch in *Faust* as a summary of mystic doctrine and I believe the key to the poem and to Goethe.[6] Probably I have told you, for you know all that I know, of seeing on the fences just after our war an advertisement ST 1860 X and saying and proving to myself that if one accepted that as a revelation of the ultimate secret one would be surprised at the corroboration that a fortnight could develop—which may be taken as an appendix to the second page of this letter.

---

[2] Charles Greeley Loring (1794-1867), enthusiastic conservative and leading member of the Boston bar whose energies were devoted almost exclusively to professional affairs.

[3] George Otis Shattuck (1829-1897); Holmes twice paid public tribute to Shattuck's memory: 14 *Proceedings of the Massachusetts Historical Society* (2nd Series) 367 (November 1900); *Speeches*, 70.

[4] *Supra*, p. 30.

[5] Edouard Maynial, "Les mémoires de Casanova et les conteurs français du XVIIIe siècle," 201 *Mercure de France* 112 (January 1928).

[6] Pierre Masclaux, "Le grand oeuvre de Goethe," *id.* 80.

Also I have bought the new edition of the Greville *Memoirs* and perhaps may read them and give serious thought a rest. They profess to be unexpurgated although abridged, and to contain much that was left out in former days on account of the Queen. But all reading is still in anticipation until the opinion is sent out. It is curious how many cases open some, little it may be, vista of legal speculation, if the general interests you more than the particular. I remember that the first time I was in London Henry Adams remarked that interest in general propositions means the absence of particular knowledge—a good caution for the young but not true throughout life. I am not afraid to confess the foible. My secretary[7] at this moment tells me of a little girl who told her mother that another little girl had white things in her head that bite—and her mother was alarmed, needlessly—she meant teeth. I had a drive in Rock Creek Park this morning, and walked down to the big open air bird cage. There is a new one now below it and two smaller ones—but *revocare gradus* and to walk back up the little hill I found a hardish job—age creeps on. It was delightful all the same. And so I wait for your next adventures.

Affectionately yours, O. W. H.

We have had almost no snow as yet—but February I always fear.

Devon Lodge, 28.I.28

My dear Justice: Today we got the distressing news that Felix's mother was dead, and I feel for him so deeply that I find this distance from him loathsome. Words of comfort on paper seem somehow to make one more conscious of isolation. I had a great affection for the old lady. She had such devotion to Felix—a sure way to my heart—such sterling commonsense and so vivid a personality. There stands out always in my mind a dinner with Gertrude King[1] when the latter was explaining her exploits in Russia. "And did you learn the language?", asked Felix. "Enough," said the great lady, "to get what I wanted in the shops." "Ah," remarked Mrs. Frankfurter, "when one has the money, one can buy in any language." Twelve years after that strikes a happy chord in my memory. . . .

I have been reading a good deal, though mostly in the line of work. One book—*Le rôle politique des protestants 1688-1715*— by Dedieu has been a revelation, for it shows that Bayle's very eminent adversary, the Calvinist minister Jurieu, was throughout the last twenty years of his life a spy in the pay of William III and Anne; which, naturally, makes one alter a good deal one's sense of his ideas and aims. I wish I knew whether Bayle had

---

[7] Arthur E. Sutherland, Jr., *supra*, p. 169.
[1] *Supra*, pp. 362, 428, Vol. I.

guessed this. It would give a very different colour to the famous *Avis aux refugiés* and his subsequent contortions if he had. Then I have been working rather hard at Babeuf for a school lecture and discovering that when one gets at the texts—now rare and almost irretrievable—a good deal of light is thrown on Marx's views about political tactics—that as he raped Saint-Simon for one set of ideas, so he raped poor Babeuf for others; and I can't find that he made even a passing reference of thanks for what he took. . . .   *Ever affectionately yours, H. J. L.*

Washington, D.C., February 5, 1928

My dear Laski: A most amusing letter from you of January 21 of academic discussions and government by dons—Hardy, and his burial in the Abbey—(I haven't read *Tess* or *Jude* and somehow shrink from them)—reading—Masson on Rousseau, then Haldane's *Descartes,* Queen V's *Letters*—(I dare say you are right about her —my prejudices are with you—but I suppose there is good to be said) etc.—purchases—and tickling tales of Birrell and the husband of the theosophic dame. I have no such yarns. Indeed my only gossip is from the Greville *Diary*—new edition. I don't like the mode of editing, or the sensational headings to chapters, but I am entertained by his disillusioned pictures of the Royal Family and the eminent statesmen of the time. He pictures most of them as dishonest and doing fishy things for office.

I made a mathematical conundrum in that connection: $X = >$ ∞—to find the number represented by X? answer No. 1. The old Duke of Wellington seems to stand highest in Greville's respect—*non obstant* some incapacities as a statesman. I didn't realize before the constant apprehension that George IV and William IV would fall into their father's malady. Indeed Greville seems to think that they did, more or less. Do you remember a sonnet written by a lady, I should guess near the time of Lord Melbourne (qu. Mrs. Norton? I think not) ending as nearly as I can remember "I had a friend who was all this—and more"? I have listened to a good deal of Miss Gertrude Bell's correspondence with pleasure—as perhaps I have mentioned. I had some good letters from her once—but only a few. But my wife turns back to Miss Kingsley[1] who is her pet. I saw her also once or twice, but when I was wanting to talk to some one else. Did I ever tell you of our converse? I said she was lucky to have seen the world before it was cut up into 5 acre lots—which seemed to be its destiny. "Oh, I don't know," said she, "Central Asia was easier to cross in Marco Polo's time than now." I wish now that

---

[1] Mary Henrietta Kingsley (1862-1900); scientist, traveler, and author of *Travels in West Africa* (1897).

I had made more of my opportunities. If I last a little longer I shall go into the last survivor business—and swagger on "I remember's." I have some good ones for this country—and some old English judges and generals—and Barry Cornwall[2]—who was a friend of Charles Lamb and went to school with Byron. Apropos of Lamb (and Birkenhead) you remember that Carlyle dismisses him rather contemptuously as a snuffy person—or something of that sort—and although I am far from justifying either B. or C. I suspect that there should have been drawbacks. I doubt if he or Dr. Johnson would have smelt good. It gave malignant joy to read (in Ste. Beuve?) of someone's saying that Louis XIV smelt like a *charogne*. He has a stout heart who when he visits a cathedral thinks more of that than of his pinching boots.

I am breathing free this Sunday p.m. I have readjusted an opinion to hold (I hope) the bare majority that I have on my side and have a week ahead before we sit. But one always has something to do and when I have I always am worried until it is done. I have a worrying nature—Brandeis says he has not. One generally can get the better of it if one happens to think of thinking about it. After reflection one can meet even great things calmly. The trouble with little daily fidgets is that you don't get beyond the bother of the moment. My rambling on in reply to your tales reminds of the story of Alcott going into a shop and wanting two yards of cloth: "I cannot give you money for it—as I do not approve of the use of it and have none, but I will converse with [you] to the value of the cloth." I hope you will not repine at the exchange.   *Affectionately yours, O. W. H.*

Devon Lodge, 7.II.27 [sic]

My dear Justice: A perfect delight of a letter from you yesterday reminds me of how much there is to say. The most pleasant thing that has happened since I wrote last was a lunch here with Siegfried Sassoon, the poet, and S. N. Behrman the American playwright. We talked for hours, and almost in all with assent. Sassoon, particularly, on the poets was extraordinarily interesting— especially his insistence that Poe and Emerson of all Americans had the purest lyric gift, and his contempt for the jingles of Kipling and his school did my heart good. And Behrman is a delight. A Harvard lad, in his simplicity, eagerness, unspoiltness, he reminds me a good deal of Felix. London has been lionising him, and his poise in the face of the dinners of the elect did my heart good, and I was especially won by his contempt (you will

---

[2] Barry Cornwall (1787-1874), the pseudonym of Bryan Waller Procter, poet, lawyer, schoolmate of Byron, and friend of the *literati*.

agree) for the supposed philosophy of Shaw and the sugar-and-cream of Barrie. . . .

And I end with a story. Theo Mathew[1] is the son of Mathew, L.J. and a witty junior at the Inner Temple. The other day, when lunching there, he found his usual table full of Hindus, negroes, Angolese and Chinese with one lone Englishman. Matthew walked up to him with outstretched hand saying "Dr. Livingstone, I presume?" Could perfection go further?

Our warm love to you both.

Ever affectionately yours, H. J. L.

Washington, D.C., February 18, 1928
My dear Laski: Two A-1 letters from you—one closely following the other and ending with the admirable tale of Matthew [*sic*]— I suppose it was his father that took me to Court one day to witness a trial before Sir A. Cockburn—in which M. was counsel on one side. Cockburn seemed to be busy correcting proof—it was supposed of his charge, in the *Tichborne* case, while the trial went on. I was much struck by the way it was conducted. One side stated the facts—the counsel on the other side at a certain point: "I shall have to trouble you to put on evidence upon that." If he did it didn't take long and Cockburn said he would direct a verdict. Thereupon one side said that he should like to be allowed to address the jury—which he did in a short argument—and then Cockburn charged strongly on the side for which he had been inclined to direct the verdict and the jury found accordingly without leaving their seats. Then one juryman stood up and said, "I understand"—(a certain fact, I forget what) to be so and so." "No, no, no" said the others—but he had put his finger on what seemed to me the point in the case—which I thought the judge and lawyer had overlooked. The jury put their heads together— discussed a little among themselves, and then brought in their verdict the other way—I thought rightly—with little help from Judge or lawyers. My memory may have distorted things, but that is the way I have remembered it for many years. I don't believe that I need to explain why it seemed to me to illustrate what Judge John Lowell[1] said to me when I was a young lawyer: "They do everything on honor in England." Well, this p.m., our last conference before going in again on Monday for 4 weeks of argument. I had but one case to deliver—a majority opinion of

[1] Theobald Mathew (1866-1939); son of Sir James Charles Mathew (1830-1908), judge in the Queen's Bench division. Versions of the son's wit were preserved in his *Forensic Fables* (1928) and their *sequelae*.

[1] *Supra.* p. 4, Vol. I.

no great interest—Brandeis dissenting[2]—but at the last minute
McReynolds said that he wanted to write something (against the
op.) and so it went over—it is rather aggravating to have things
hang up in that way because the Judge doesn't take the trouble
to be ready. He has three weeks of vacation for it. I tried to put
a shovel full of coals on his head by handing him my prospective
dissent where we stand 5 to 4 unless he changes his mind, and
where he has the majority opinion to write—which he has not
started on yet.[3] I despise the notion that I think some of the last
generation had that it was like opposing counsel in Court and
that it would be fine to spring something unforeseen on the other
side. I read them my views in another case[4] in which the following vote showed that I was in the minority but on which I will
have my whack if I live, if it is my last word.

Brandeis and I are so apt to agree that I was glad to have him
dissent in my case, as it shows that there is no preestablished harmony—I have had almost no time to read—having had two hours
of driving on pleasant days. I have finished Greville's *Diary* and
that is about all. I think I mentioned Demogue, *Notions fondamentales du droit privé*—which I was compelled to get hold of
by the remarks of Morris Cohen in an essay. Demogue is a good
man evidently—but for 100 pages he has told me nothing that I
didn't know—substantially—has illustrated to me that some problems are not dug down to the foundations as well as with us—
and yet I haven't the moral courage to stop—but feel obliged to
toil on through 559 more pages in a print that tires my eyes for
fear of missing something—or because I don't like to back out.
Your last letter but one was the first news I had had of the death
of Felix's mother. I referred obliquely to it in writing to him—
but could not do more.

I vehemently disagree with the "contempt for the jingles of
Kipling"—I agree that Kipling's attitude toward life seems to me
wanting in complexity and not interesting—but it will take more

---

[2] Holmes delivered no opinions on February 20. On April 9, Holmes
delivered the Court's opinion in *Casey* v. *United States*, 276 U.S. 413, which
had been argued on January 11. Dissenting opinions were delivered by
McReynolds, Brandeis, Butler, and Sanford, JJ. The majority sustained
provisions of the Anti-Narcotic Act which made the absence of revenue
stamps from packages of drugs *prima facie* evidence of unlawful possession.
The majority also found that the government was not chargeable with entrap-
ment of the defendant.

[3] Not identified.

[4] Quite probably *Black and White Taxi Co.* v. *Brown and Yellow Taxi
Co.*, 276 U.S. 518 (argued January 13 and 16, decided April 9, 1928).
Holmes in his dissent, concurred in by Brandeis and Stone, JJ., objected to
the theory that Federal courts in deciding common-law questions arising
within a particular state could decide the law as they saw fit, without regard
to state decisions.

than Sassoon to convince me that Kipling ought not to stir the
fundamental human emotions. I think he does—and that simple
thinkers often do. A student of mine long dead[5] spoke with contempt of the fighting lines in *Henry V*. His widow was a mainstay
of the sympathizers with Sacco and Vanzetti. I was not with him.

Aff'ly yours, O. W. H.

Devon Lodge, 20.II.28

My dear Justice: A letter from you[1]—as always a delight—reminds
me that nearly a fortnight has gone by since I last reported. In
mitigation, I plead the state of public business. I have had to
write a vast obituary notice of Asquith[2] for the Manchester
Guardian; sit twice on the Industrial Court; go to Oxford to lecture; and entertain twice for Hocking, the Harvard philosopher.[3]
Add to that a cloud of committees, and you will, I hope, accept
the explanation and say that there has been no contempt of court.

I was much moved by Asquith's death. He wasn't, I think, a
great man, for that word ought to be kept for the originator or
the man who profoundly changes by skill in adaptation; and beyond the limit on the House of Lords he was not, I think, the
author of anything big. But he brought qualities to politics which
are rare; absolute loyalty, supreme lucidity of mind, refusal to
truckle to the mob, and a sense of honour as exquisite as I have
ever met among politicians. He had the great defect of finding
decisions difficult. But he really was a great gentleman with less
of the rancour in his temper than any of the political breed I have
met. There is no one quite of his type left, and this new world
of a stunt press and a devotion to the slogans of the market-place
makes it difficult to hope for more of his kind. *Inani perfungor
munere.*

Oxford interested me a good deal, though in some ways it was
depressing. I was struck by the complacency of the dons and the
preciousness of the undergraduates. The former clearly thought
that the world was an oyster they had opened, and their ignorance was profound. They each had a little patch to cultivate and
they saw no reason to go outside it. And talk of America produced
the astounding view that the great Americans of today were Lowell and Murray Butler. I mentioned books like Parrington or
Beard in vain. When I was told that there was no great political
thought in America and summoned the period from 1780-1840 as

---

[5] Probably Glendower Evans (1856-1886), who had been a student in
Holmes's law office in the fall of 1881.

[1] *Supra*, p. 198.

[2] Lord Oxford and Asquith had died on February 15.

[3] William Ernest Hocking (1873-   ), Professor of Philosophy at Harvard, 1914-1943.

my compurgator and argued that only the greatest epochs could compete with it I was met with polite incredulity. And I was irritated by the immense volume of clericalism everywhere. Jesuits, Puseyites, Dominicans, Cowley Fathers, you met them at every turn. The times demand a Voltaire to show what the whole farce means. One college was rent in twain over the practice of auricular confession; another was passionately excited over the reservation of the Sacrament. Some men devoted their energies to preventing the scientists from having any more buildings in the Oxford Parks. Big sweeping views, a sense of the vastness of our problems, the excited hunt for novelty, these didn't exist. I tried names—Meyerson, Morris Cohen, Thibaudet; but they meant nothing. And I left feeling that the glories of London where one might be a small fish, but where, at least, the stream rushed by in the torrential excitement was worth a hundred Oxfords. The reply, I gather, is the virtue of the life contemplative; but that assumes the fact of deliberate reflection on great issues and of that I saw no wide evidence.

On the other hand I remark that Hocking is a ghastly bore. Right-minded, earnest, good, but he can say things like "the world needs peace" or, "Hegel is a very great man," or "the Gospels are exquisite" as though he were communicating new truth. Each idea of his comes out with a pleased self-regard as though it was a new law of gravitation; and when he told me that the League of Nations was very important, I felt I wanted to shriek. . . .

Of reading, I have done little that is worth report. . . . a book on the *History of Contempt* by Sir J. C. Fox really exploded Wilmot's case and gave me the pointers for a piece on constructive contempt which I have long been anxious to write.[4] Our English procedure whereby X and Y decide that Z has been unfairly criticised after a decision has been made and without hearing evidence opened the door, I think, to very serious abuses; and a recent case here (*R. v. the New Statesman*)[5] was little short of a scandal. . . .   *Ever affectionately yours, H. J. L.*

Washington, D.C., March 1, 1928
My dear Laski: Your letter 20.II.28 stirred my sympathies wondrously and made me wish I could be there or jaw with you. Your description of the dons of Oxford seems to me a description

---

[4] "Procedure for Constructive Contempt in England," 41 *Harv. L. Rev.* 1031 (June 1928). The case decided by Wilmot, J., was *Rex v. Almon,* Wilmot's notes 243 (1765).

[5] 44 T. L. R. 301 (1928). The King's Bench there held that newspaper criticism of judicial action could be punished summarily as contempt of court if the impartiality of an individual judge were questioned and if the criticism tended to undermine public confidence in the judiciary.

of the usual Englishman not enlightened by travel. To how many
the ultimate is "We don't do that in England." I grieve to hear
of the irruption of Clericalism. I had (too rashly) assumed that
the civilized man everywhere had a quiet substratum of scepticism even if he didn't show it. But isn't this at least largely true?

I have been staying at home this week with a cough that has
bothered me at intervals for many years. My doctor down here,
. . . died a few days ago—so I got the one who looks after the
C. J. (in his more general aspects—he says he has one for each
end)—and he is inclined to my opinion of the trouble and is trying some painting on my throat. I have hopes of relief—at all
events the spells pass away after a time. The cases are sent to
me and I shall send my votes (as we objectionably call them) to
the conference. As I get up latish I am kept pretty busy—but I
have had time for a little diary of Dr. John Ward who was Vicar
at Stratford-on-Avon a few years after Shakespeare's death—has a
few words about him and a number of shrewd remarks—a little
book, but worth looking through. Also Charles Francis Adams's[1]
Autobiography which I never read. He is brutal to himself and
his papa—but just—he saw pretty straight. It is curious to observe, alongside of his judgment of himself as not having excep-
tional gifts, the tone of importance that goes through the story—
and so dreary—those poor men were born without the capacity of
joy. I knew the whole lot pretty well—got much from them—
suggestiveness from Brooks—the best criticisms of some of my
speeches I ever had from anyone from Charles—and while Henry
chilled my soul when I came home tired from Court and stopped
in, to be told how futile it all was—he was grumblingly generous
to me when I first went to London, in the way of taking me about
—and when he gave up his Harvard professorship sent me a lot
of his books on early law. Ralph Palmer[2]—nephew or cousin of
Sir Roundell (as he was in my day) thought Henry a great
thinker. The whole lot certainly were unusual men. I may have
told you of Bill James coming back from meeting the three and
saying it was like meeting the augurs behind the altar and none
of them smiling. They seemed to stir him up as he also said,
"Powerful race, those Adamses, to remain plebeians after so many
generations of culture." This if taken seriously would be unjust—

---

[1] Charles Francis Adams (1835-1915); descendant of the presidential
Adamses; son of the American Ambassador to Great Britain during the Civil
War; brother of Brooks Adams and Henry Adams.

[2] Ralph Charlton Palmer (1839-1923), lawyer and man of affairs, had
become a close friend of Holmes during the latter's first visit to England in
1866. Palmer's father, George Palmer (1772-1853), was the uncle of Sir
Roundell Palmer (1812-1895), first Earl of Selborne, who was twice Lord
Chancellor, first from 1872 to 1874 and again from 1880 to 1885. Holmes's
friend had been secretary to Selborne during his second chancellorship.

because, though capable of queer things, they had an inward delicacy that was very far from plebeian.

I don't think I ever heard of Hocking—your account makes me chuckle. . . . I must try to remember to look into that history of contempt—I have dissented once or twice on that theme. You amaze me by saying, if I understand you, that criticism of an opinion or judgment after it has been rendered, may make a man liable for contempt. I thought that notion was left for some of our middle western states. I must try to get the book and the decision. Well—I have done as well as I can for a seedy worm (but nothing serious). My love to you all.

Affectionately yours, O. W. H.

Devon Lodge, 25.II.28

My dear Justice: Let me begin with my triumph. I have found, for six pounds, a copy of Althusius's *Politica methodice digesta* (1610) and it lies before me on the table as I write. I am immensely proud of it, as there seem to be seven copies only in existence and no other in private hands. It turned up in a Berlin catalogue, and after a moment's doubt whether it would not have been snapped up before I could reach it, I decided to telephone to Berlin. This I did, and, to my joy, there it still was. It is a beautiful quarto, vellum bound, with wide margins, and most exciting reading. I wish I could show it to you. But you will guess how my week has been sweetened by it.

Of other news but little. My nose is being kept to the grindstone rather more than I like and there are still three weeks before release comes. I slipped out to dinner last night and went to Haldane's. He had Barrie and Kipling there. The former hardly spoke a word, but sat like a grim mouse in a corner until it was time to go. Kipling literally amazed me. He took command of the talk (not an easy thing to do when Haldane is there) and laid down the law like a member of the Ku Klux Klan. I thought he had an essentially vulgar mind, incapable of any real finesse or delicacy; and his main reply to argument was a budgeoning "I don't agree with you" which was never accompanied by any effort to lay his mind alongside yours. I saw no power of reflexion, though there was a real gift of happy phrase. I suppose it is stupid to expect that a great story-teller should have other gifts than the power of telling stories, but I certainly expected something better than I encountered. Let me add, too, that he talked for applause in an irritating way. When he had said anything especially good he looked up as if waiting for you to clap your hands. Haldane amused me immensely. Much of what Kipling said was gall and wormwood to him. But he liked the idea of having him at his table and encouraged him to perform rather as a man persuades his dog to go through tricks for his friends. . . .

My love to you both.   *Ever affectionately yours, H. J. L.*

Washington, D.C., March 7, 1928

My dear Laski: A delightful letter from you to which I can answer but a word. Tomorrow is my birthday and already I am somewhat crowded. Also the doctor keeps me in the house—for a cough—nothing serious—same old trouble—but he insists on my staying at home. I do the same work here and am in all the cases that are being argued.

I am not impressed at what you say about Kipling. Many years ago I made up my mind that he did not interest me—that his view of the universe was too simple—and since then I thought that he had a breakdown. But as a story teller, and in spite of you, as a verse writer, I think he makes a direct appeal to the simpler emotions which we never are too sophisticated to feel when a man has the gift—as he has. Also, where Stevenson laboriously selects a word and lets you feel his labor, Kipling puts his fist into the guts of the dictionary, pulls out the utterly unavailable and makes it a jewel in his forehead or flesh of his flesh with no effort or outlay except of the pepsin that makes it part of him. But I thought he was finished years back.

I am tickled that you should have encountered the holiness of woman and been assured of it by herself. Lester Ward in one of his books intimates that she produced man to amuse her—having previously done very well without him to aid in continuing the race. With your belief in some apriorities like equality you may have difficulties. I who believe in force (mitigated by politeness) have no trouble—and if I were sincere and were asked certain *whys* by a woman should reply, "Because Ma'am I am the bull."

How fain were I to jaw with you but I must say good night. Tomorrow I am 87—and still Oliver asks for a little more—not that he is not prepared to shut up with good grace—but, apart from the pleasure of continuing as long as one can, to play one or two little fool games—the newest one to outlive Taney—(who died 87, 6 or 7 months old) remaining active—not that I really care a tuppence for that sort of thing.   *Aff'ly yours, O. W. H.*

Devon Lodge, 19.III.28

My dear Justice: . . . I had an amusing dinner at Haldane's last night, with Winston as the other guest. The latter being about to give birth to a budget was full of the vigour of intellectual pregnancy and gave us a list of the dozen greatest men in the

19th century. Characteristically it contained not a single scientist or thinker and so I drew him on to a discussion of their influence. It was really most illuminating. He had never read a line of Aristotle, Bacon, Hobbes, Descartes, Locke, Rousseau, Hume, Hegel, or Kant. He had read every line of Machiavelli, any printed volume summarising Napoleon's ideas, La Rochefoucauld, Stendhal (whom he greatly admired) and such like. Pascal and Goethe were hardly names to him; and of Montesquieu he knew only the lubricious *Temple du Gnide.* He watched my amusement with complete bewilderment and could not be made to understand that philosophy had the slightest relevance. When he had gone Haldane told me that years ago he had lent Winston Eckermann's *Conversations with Goethe.* It was returned in two days with the remark that he literally could not understand what they were talking about.

I went with Frida to another dinner that was amusing. I sat next to a retired judge of the county court who had been a distinguished wrangler in his day and thought this generation soft. He explained the things a wise man refuses to have any dealings with: (I) women (II) doctors (III) betting men (IV) clergymen (V) the Court of Criminal Appeal (VI) the Judicial Committee. Finding out that I was a university professor he explained (I) that no one ought to go to a university unless he knew the calculus (II) that the study of Laplace ought to be compulsory (III) that Newton was the greatest man, except Christ, who ever lived (IV) that all good mathematicians would make good judges. The greatest man he had ever met was J. J. Sylvester.[1] If Gauss[2] and Jacobi[3] were in hell he hoped to go there. He never read novels; but he found he had to give up the theory of numbers as a hobby for retirement as it made him too excited. He was really a charmer and full of a winning smile at his own absurdities which I found enchanting. He was 93, and only retired, he said, as a protest at the quality of the younger men who were being given him. "Nothing had gone right since Bowen died." . . .

My love eagerly to you both.

Every affectionately yours, H. J. L.

Washington, D.C., March 22, 1928
My dear Laski: You send me such interesting adventures with people and books that I feel like the often quoted Vicar of Wake-

[1] James Joseph Sylvester (1814-1897), English mathematician, Professor of Mathematics at the Johns Hopkins University and later at Oxford; founder of the *American Journal of Mathematics.*

[2] Karl Friedrich Gauss (1777-1855), German mathematician who made notable contribution to the theory of numbers.

[3] Karl Gustav Jakob Jacobi (1804-1851), Professor of Mathematics at Königsberg and expert on elliptical functions.

field "All one's migrations from the blue bed to the brown" or words to that effect. I write opinions, dissents, and examine *certioraris* and then begin over again. However, when I received a telegram on my birthday from my *quondam* brother Clarke—saying why not live and come with me to Rome and Athens or if you prefer to (some named paradise in the Pacific), I answer that not only Age with his stealing steps hath caught me in his clutch but the joys of sophistry beat scenery and the past. Are you not with me? I have this moment come to my first leisure for a long time, and I don't believe it will be leisure beyond the next mail. But I am cherishing hopes to finish that damned Demogue I told you of, I think—recommended by Morris Cohen. Also I have *Aperçu d'une théorie générale de l'état* an abridgement I gather by Hans Kelsen of a large work by him in German. God knows how little nourishment I get as a rule from such works —but I must look at it. Also Cohen sends me typewritten portions of a work—parts of which have appeared as articles, *Reason and Nature*—an essay on the meaning of scientific method, and dedicated to me—I am proud. Also (in the way of boasting) Ludwig—the author of the lives of Napoleon, Wilhelm II, Bismarck, etc. called on me some time ago and this week my driver, the faithful Charles, handed me a copy of the Washington *Herald* in which Ludwig seemed to have interviewed a number of our great men and wound up with a puff of me that I should blush to copy. Luckily, as I no doubt have said often, one who thinks of man as I do can't have a swelled head. Also, although I only glanced at the article, I had the impression that L. was saying soapy things about the whole lot of us, nevertheless, as I liked him when we talked, I was more than pleased to know that he had carried away an agreeable impression. Of course one runs through light things that don't add much to one's credit side in the intellectual world. I think I mentioned Charles Adams's *Autobiography*—last night I finished a pleasant volume of Thackeray's letters to Mr. Brookfield. His style soothes one's ear. But I made the reflection that no man of that time ever quite looked himself in the face, or was quite candid in his thought. I leave it as an impression—not amplifying. You speak of Russell's *Outline of Philosophy*—second thought suggests that this may be Bertrand in a book I've not heard of. I thought at first you had fallen on my friend of last summer, Will Durant's *Story of Philosophy* (fancy a man who calls himself Will writing on philosophy), an entertaining enough book—but one that I would spare you. I believe its success led him to think himself competent upon the theme and to write articles on serious subjects—I read a little of one and said no more for me, thank you. Things occur to me

to tell you, but I forget them before I write. I must away now—
and sooner than wait and resume, I will send this off.

Affectionately yours, O. W. Holmes

Devon Lodge, 27.III.28

My dear Justice: . . . Much the most interesting thing that has
happened since I wrote last has been a dinner at the House of
Commons where I met Sumner, the Lord of Appeal. He is an
amazingly powerful person, with a certitude on all matters, as
hard as nails, and with views compared to which those of Mc-
Reynolds can only be described as socialist. He interested me
enormously. He is widely read, a fine classical scholar, entirely
self-made, and yet completely deaf to external opinion. He said
for instance that discussion in the Court of Appeal was for him
a waste of time, he had made up his mind when he read the
brief. He attacked me for disbelieving in a second chamber and
insisted that no thinker of repute ever believed in single chamber
government. I instanced Franklin, Sieyès, Tom Paine, Bentham;
he swept them all aside and said that of all writers on politics
only Aristotle, Machiavelli and Hobbes really counted. His heroes
were Caesar, Napoleon and Bismarck, because they really knew
what they wanted. I said that was because they wanted only
what they knew and was an expression of their limitations. He
spoke warmly of your decisions but regretted a tinge of scepticism in them; a judge must bring down his fist with a thump. . . .

My love warmly to you both.

Ever affectionately yours, H. J. L.

Devon Lodge, 4.IV.28

My dear Justice: . . . You will like me to pass on the gossip, and
very pleasant it is, about Leslie Scott. He has gone out to India
as counsel to the Princes on a government enquiry and those not
very amiable gentlemen, being most anxious not to lose any further indicia of sovereignty, are said to have marked the brief fifty
thousand pounds with a hundred pounds a day refresher. I'm very
glad; for Scott has had a thin time this last few years and this
will certainly recoup his fortunes.

In the way of reading, my chief and quite unlimited joy has
been the complete works, recently reprinted in two volumes, of
Arthur Binstead, whom your London memories may enable you
to recognise as "Pitcher" of *The Pink'Un*. They are *Gal's Gossip*,
Pitcher in Paradise, et al.—quite wonderful reminiscences of the
demi-monde and racing sets of the 'eighties and 'nineties. Birrell

to whom I communicated my enthusiasm told me that he never wanted to meet anyone so badly as "Pitcher" and the latter would not because he never spoke to lawyers. But he once spent a weekend with Rosebery who was so tumultuously entertained that he had an inscription placed upon the seat that Pitcher occupied in his house. . . .

Here I must stop for I have to pack and get my boat-train to Paris within an hour. Frida is already down in Sussex and I hope tomorrow to start a real intellectual adventure.

My love warmly to you both.

Ever affectionately yours, H. J. L.

Washington, D.C., April 6, 1928

My dear Laski: You will get but a rotten reply to two good letters from you. I am very tired—I don't quite know why—partly, I suppose, the spring, which I always find hard here—and partly there has been almost no relaxation in my work during the recess, when you add in the letters and telegrams I had to answer after my birthday. I am tickled by what you tell me of Lord Sumner —I have seen other judges like that. I remember a son of Fitzjames Stephen who seemed to divide men into good and bad— and the bad were to be smacked. John Dickinson (author of *Administrative Justice and the Supremacy of Law* dedicated to Pound and Frankfurter) has sent to me a discourse *Working Theory of Sovereignty[1]* which respects you and criticises some of your views, careful, and I think perfectly correct to the point of obviousness. I infer from the inscription (MS) that he approves of *Kawananakoa* v. *Polyblank*—as who indeed that understands its limited scope, except your friend John M. Zane, does not— but he does not understand it I infer.

I think your answer to Sumner that his heroes knew what they wanted because they wanted only what they knew—an expression of their limitations—was admirable. I think I told you last summer that Ludwig's *Napoleon* didn't interest me because Napoleon did not, *i.e.*, in his view of life. By the by Ludwig was here— and made a short call on me—and later in the public prints, talking of those whom he had seen, used language that I should blush to repeat. He professed to think that I was It. Here the scepticism that Sumner regretted comes in handy. It shows a simple nature to be capable of a really believing conceit. Beck, Brandeis thinks and I incline to believe, is innocently *naif—non obstant* considerable intercourse with a hard and cynical world.

I have read almost nothing. I did read Demogue *Notions fondamentales du droit privé*—misled to it by words of Morris Cohen

[1] 42 *Pol. Sci. Qu.* 524; 43 *id.* 32 (December 1927 and March 1928).

in an article—a most respectable 669 pages of print not too legible at night and not a damned word from start to finish that I don't know or disbelieve—no doubt a little profitable emphases here and there—but it enraged me and kept me some time from reading a type-written skeleton of Cohen's book, parts in print and not reproduced, parts not yet set up, which so far as I could judge is truly admirable. He does not lightly yield to popular superstitions—though he made me shudder and wonder by saying that he believes in Natural Rights—I trust that it was but a *façon de parler*.

I have got two or three dissents for Monday next that I care about—but one in which I stated my differences from McR. in a few words,[2] Brandeis has taken up and worked out with such a mass of precedent that I should think McR. would feel as if a steam roller had gone over him. He in turn dissents from one of my decisions[3] as does Brandeis on other grounds and Butler—and I am not quite sure of my majority although not shaken. Also McR. keeps me waiting on his good pleasure to find out whether he will not change his vote (as we stupidly call it) where a change would leave me in a minority.

Meantime I have beautiful drives in the spring. Magnolias divine and today the cherry blossoms round the basin. So it is not all work.   *Aff'ly yours, O. W. H.*

Washington, D.C., April 17, 1928—Tuesday
My dear Laski: It is astonishingly hard to write down here—not that we have had a particularly hard lot of cases—rather the reverse—certainly so far as I am concerned—but the steady stream of *certioraris* seem to fill every crevice of promised leisure. A week ago I was more interested in delivering a dissent[1] of which I shall try to send you a copy tomorrow than in my judgments for the Court. I also dissented in another case in a few words—but Brandeis took the same theme up and put into his such a wealth of authority and such a lot of work that I should have been inclined simply to note my agreement with him had he not wanted me to remain articulate.[2] But we are drawing near to the end of arguments—two or at most three weeks including the present one —I believe is all. Your yarns about the ladies with rich sexual natures—I think this is the second one—seem to me almost incredible. I find it hard not to suspect you of embroidering—but

[2] *Untermeyer* v. *Anderson,* 276 U.S. 440, 446. The issue concerned the retroactive application of gift tax provisions of the Revenue Act of 1924.
[3] *Casey* v. *United States,* 276 U.S. 413 (Apr. 9, 1928); see *supra* p. 199.
[1] *Black and White Taxi* case, *supra,* p. 199.
[2] *Untermeyer* v. *Anderson, supra,* p. 209.

they make bully stories. I remember hearing of some dame who having a story to tell would ask—"Do you want it naked or will you have it clothed?"

I suppose you are back from Paris by this time—I envy you your excursions—and find it hard to believe that even little ones are at an end for me. My reason tells me that the fun can't last much longer—but it still is unabated and I don't encourage myself to dwell on the thought of *Finis*. Indeed yesterday I had a call from the prospective secretary of next year. When I have needed to enforce a little leisure on myself *ultra* the solitaire at 9 pm I latterly have taken up Disraeli's *Curiosities of Literature* which has been on my shelves uncut since I was a boy. I am inclined to add it to Pepys and Walpole's *Letters* as a good third when you don't want ideas and don't want to waste time. I just took up the Third Volume and have read a few pages at odd minutes now and then with much quiet pleasure. I have not your gusto over the printed word—but as I have told you am apt to read with a sigh and an eye to the number of pages. The other day Pound sent me the 4th edition of his *Outline of Lectures on Jurisprudence*—a prodigiously learned work—but I couldn't forbear saying to him that most of the authors that he cites, so far as I have read them, seem to me to write much drool for a few spoonsful of insight and that I doubted if most youngsters didn't get all the jurisprudence they needed if they studied law under a man with general ideas. Jurisprudence begins as soon as a man learns that the parcel-gilt goblet and sea-coal fire are not essentials of the alleged contract.

When the lamented Hough was alive and was chaffing a decision of mine to the effect that a boat of the U.S. was not guilty of a tort in running into another vessel—he said we don't talk of torts in Admiralty but of collision, and would I say that there had been no collision?—I wrote, alas just as he had died, that if he preferred to talk Basque instead of French and to deny himself the benefit of the wider generalizations of a more developed system it was all right but that having but one word for two ideas he must distinguish.[3] Collision in the sense of physical impact of course is not denied—but collision with legal responsibility—I certainly should deny. Collision might mean either—and I rather think Hough really was the victim of his own ambiguity. If I have told you all this before forgive me. Old men forget—and most men repeat. But this was a case where a little more jurisprudence was needed.

Wed. 18th. This morning a letter from Wu (I have had two or three now) telling of inquiry from Austen Chamberlain via

---

[3] See, *supra*, p. 418, Vol. I.

British consulate as to his whereabouts—on account of O.W.H. I thank Chamberlain via you. Wu seems troubled but does not give particulars—and his attitude is so adoring that it worries me. He wants to get a year over here and I believe Pound will offer him a scholarship though I doubt the wisdom of taking his hand from the plough. I should like to see him again before I die. I hope Paris was all you expected.

Ever affectionately yours, O. W. Holmes

Devon Lodge, 22.IV.28

My dear Justice: I came back yesterday from a divine fortnight in Paris—certainly the queen of all cities. . . .

You will remember that the publisher of Diderot's *Encyclopedia* got weary, at the end, of ecclesiastical opposition, and, to the great man's disgust cut out all the parts of articles which might give offence to the Jesuits. It has always been a problem where the original articles have got to. Some thought they had just perished; others that there [*sic*] were bought by Catherine II when she purchased Diderot's library. At the *Bibliothèque Nationale* there is an exhibition about the Revolution. I saw there a letter about Diderot which interested me. The name of the man who had lent it meant nothing to me, but, on enquiry, I found that he was Diderot's great-great grandson. I got an introduction to him and discovered that he had all the papers, as well as hundreds of unpublished letters of Diderot and his friends. But he was passionately religious, and pretty well divided between pride and shame in his ancestry. He did not think he ought to publish and raise the dust of an old controversy. *M. le curé* too thought the papers had better remain dead. I saw *M. le curé* who spoke vividly on the decay of the true faith, the *sottises* of those wicked men, Voltaire and Rousseau, the horrors of the Revolution, just as though he and I were *émigrés* talking over the causes of the terror we had just escaped. At least I was able to put the librarians on the track; and they are hopeful that they will persuade the old gentleman to part with his treasures.[1]

Then talk. I met Julien Benda, the author of *La trahison des clercs,* and had thoroughly enjoyable discussion of the growth of Bergsonism, and its disasters, the need to revive a faith in reason, the duty of defending Western civilization. Then Thibaudet the critic, who said many fine things; of Bourget that he had shown

[1] The papers in question, owned in 1928 by Baron Jacques Le Vavasseur, a distant relative but not a direct descendant of Diderot, are now in the Archives Nationales; they are inventoried in Herbert Dieckmann's *Inventaire du fonds Vandeul et inédits de Diderot* (1951).

how to make the ten commandments perfumed fiction for the drawing room; of Proust that he persuaded his readers that the infinitely little was infinitely important granted only that it was infinite enough; of Renan that his doubts were more powerful than the certainties of others; in every way an attractive personality. I met, too, Maurois, whose *Shelley* you may have read— a charming fellow, but quite obviously the man building his high-road to the academy and careful above all to see that there are no rocks in the way. And Mathiez, the historian of the Revolution, a great scholar, full of a great subject, and speaking of his material with a fire and enthusiasm that made one feel that there is no other subject save his. Of Taine, he said it was the finest autobiography in the French tongue; how curious that he should have chosen the French Revolution as the background of his narrative. He had a high regard for Mignet's old history, and a still higher regard for Acton; but he interested me enormously by saying that the work which had done most to give new impulses to the study of the Revolution in recent years was Kropotkin's *History* which, with grave faults and many inaccuracies, contained invaluable hints. He was a charming fellow, this Mathiez— the real *savant*, simple, unaffected, passionately sincere. As it was election-time I saw little of the politicians. But I went to lunch to the British embassy—a queerly artificial atmosphere—and met Briand there. Kellogg's note had just come,[2] and it was really amusing to watch the great man trying to convince himself that I was serious when I said that the note meant just what it said and that America was a pacifist people really believing that steps could be taken to prevent the recurrence of 1914. Really these politicians live in an unreal world. They exist by gossip, rumour, innuendo, suspicion; they have formulae, but not general ideas; perorations, but not serried argument. An hour of Morris Cohen's dialectic would reduce them to intellectual impotence. Give me the philosopher and the man of letters when you want to know whether the world is really moving!

The book-hunt was most profitable. New books apart, of which there were many I could not resist, I found Linguet's *Théorie des lois civiles*, which I think as powerful and more realistic than Montesquieu; a book curiously forgotten and rare, but about which I hope to make people really excited one day. . . .

Ever affectionately yours, H. J. L.

---

[2] The American Secretary of State, Frank B. Kellogg, had recently laid before the French government proposals for an international covenant for the outlawing of war. The negotiations which resulted ended in August with the signing of the General Pact for the renunciation of war. Laski wrote of "The Kellogg Plan and the European Powers" in 55 *New Republic* 143 (June 27, 1928).

Devon Lodge, 29.IV.28

My dear Justice: . . . I have been working this last three weeks at the economic side of L. XIV's reign; I find that it cost 50% of the product to collect the taxes, and that an average peasant paid over sixty per cent of his income in taxation. So that the revolution is so inevitable that I am sure the effective central problem is why it was postponed so long. I wonder how far Anglo-French Rivalry kept alive a national spirit which disappeared when peace gave the prospect of civil discord. But this is a mere *ballon d'essai* without much thought behind it.

I write on a perfect spring morning in the heart of London. And behind me on a small rose tree Frida planted to make the garage less human, a blackbird sings quite enchantingly; and by my feet the cat looks at me in agony because the window is closed at the top and she cannot interfere with the singing.

Our love to you both.   *Ever affectionately yours, H. J. L.*

Devon Lodge, 8.V.28

My dear Justice: . . . Of dinners, the most interesting was one given by Sankey. Haldane and Tawney were the other guests and we discussed the judge and his function for hours. I was astonished to find that whereas Sankey took the obvious and sensible view that judges inevitably legislate, even if it is what you have called "interstitial legislation," Haldane was insistent that they merely "declare" what is already law, and not the combined efforts of all of us could move him from that. It was amusing, too, to find how completely he and Sankey disagreed in their estimates of particular judges. Haldane seemed to look for what I may call a "man of the world" quality in their decisions; Sankey was more interested in the endeavour to make the case emit a big, working principle.

. . . Chafee sent me his new book,[1] and though bits of it seemed to me not worth reprinting, I thought it left a very charming impression of a mind at once liberal and distinguished; though I add that he makes the common error in the article on judges of thinking that the economic interpretation of history deals with individual motives. I do wish people would read the texts on which they comment. . . .

My love to you both.   *Ever yours affectionately, H. J. L.*

Washington, D.C., May 12, 1928

My dear Laski: It may be that age makes it harder, it may be the endless stream of *certioraris*—but I have found my work

---

[1] Zechariah Chafee, Jr., *The Inquiring Mind* (1928).

making it impossible for me to write as often as I should like to.
I should be very sorry if it led to my hearing less often from you.
However, the Conference this afternoon that left me tired left me
pretty well cleaned up—two opinions[1] and three dissents[2] to be
delivered next Monday and nothing undone except the delivery
of one 5 to 4 opinion which McReynolds, one of the 5, held up
at the last minute, two months or more ago, and keeps me
waiting on his lordly pleasure.[3] He does not share the opinion of
some of us that the work of the justices has the right of way and
should be considered before looking out for No. 1. He has me in
his hand as it depends on him whether what I wrote goes as the
judgment of the Court. There seems a preestablished harmony
between Brandeis and me. He agrees with all my dissents and I
agree with the only one that he will propound.[4] There has been a
succession of superlatively beautiful things here—each being an
event, beginning with the magnolias—but nature, jealous of allowing us the superlative degree, takes the life out of me, at
least, in the spring weather so that I take a somewhat languid joy.

I have read almost nothing—W. Lippmann's little book of
course—*American Inquisitors*. His writing is fly paper to me—if
I touch it I am stuck till I finish it. He writes so well—and sees
so much that it is difficult to put into words—I think he talks as
wisely as possible about our fundamentalism and modernism. My
wife has read to me (*pendente* solitaire) a good part of Mark
Sullivan's book—*Our Times*—a deuced clever evocation of the
past that I remember—and most of which you do. Also books of
flyers and one that Miss Gertrude Bell was to have written an
introduction for—had she not died—*The Marsh Arab* or some
such name. Incidentally, not for the first time, am I struck by the
courage of an Englishman going alone among a lot of savages that
would have liked to kill him. I suppose that in that and other
similar cases there is a good deal of confidence in the power of
the name of England, but there is a lot of courage too.

Your adventures in Paris were most interesting. Not for the
first time does your talk with Mathiez the historian of the Revolution suggest that one should read Kropotkin—I never did—but
Brandeis once told me suggestive things from him. Your names
are sometimes illegible—who wrote the *Théorie des lois civiles*

---

[1] *Ferry* v. *Ramsey,* 277 U.S. 88; *Larson Co.* v. *Wrigley Co., id.* 97 (May
14, 1928).

[2] *Long* v. *Rockwood,* 277 U.S. 142, 148; *Springer* v. *Philippine Islands
id.* 189, 209; *Panhandle Oil* v. *Knox, id.* 218, 222.

[3] Not identified; see, *supra,* p. 199.

[4] *King Manufacturing Co.* v. *Augusta,* 277 U.S. 100, 115 (May 14,
1928).

which makes me prick up my ears?[5] And what is your theory of
the difference between the French and English civil wars? Dear
me, how many things I want to ask or talk about—and I long to
see your book on the 17th century—but I agree with Frankfurter
who says he urged you not to hurry. Your *Grammar* seemed hurriedly written. You have much to tell but only a thing well told
lasts, and you have shown often enough that you can tell your
story well. . . . [I] wish I could think of things that you would
like. For want of other things I may venture to dispatch one or
two more dissents. I have told you I think that my last letter from
Wu spoke as if his life was in danger—I can't tell how seriously
to take it but it makes me uneasy. I begin to hope he will take the
year's scholarship that I believe Pound has offered him. I must
stop. I am a pretty tired old cove—but as ever

Affectionately yours, O. W. Holmes

Devon Lodge, 22.V.28
My dear Justice: . . . We have had Croly to dinner—a questioner
but not a contributor—and Abraham Flexner who is as delightful
as he is dogmatic. And I went to Allyn Young's to meet the German economist, Schumpeter[1] and was overwhelmed. He has
Felix's charm and brilliance, together with a power of analysis
that is staggering. His picture of the weakness of German politics
was as superb a conversational *tour de force* as I have ever heard.
If he goes to America again I shall certainly send him to see you;
I was quite literally entranced by him. Flexner, by the way, confirmed all my suspicions about such foundations as those of
Rockefeller. He has in his mind a "pattern" of what a university
institution ought to be; and he judges any particular university by
the degree of its conformity with the pattern. He made, however,
one admirable remark. He pointed out that in the nineteenth
century, when scientific discovery, political change, artistic evolution, were all on a Titanic scale the movements which deeply
impressed Oxford were without exception theological in character
—Newman, the admission of Nonconformists and so forth. That
is, I think, true, and worth while trying to explain. I think probably the reason lies in a kind of intellectual in-breeding that is
fatal to a proper appreciation of novelty. You see something of the
same thing in Harvard in the period before Langdell and in

---

[5] *Supra*, p. 212.
[1] Joseph Alois Schumpeter (1883-1950), whose career in economics began
in Austria, took him to a Professorship in Germany, at Bonn, from 1925 to
1932, and then brought him to the United States, where he became Professor of Economics at Harvard in 1932.

English Cambridge before they were shaken up by Clerk-Maxwell. . . .

Our love as always to you both.

Ever affectionately yours, H. J. L.

Beverly Farms, June 12, 1928

My dear Laski: There seems to be undue delay in the post. The last letter from you is dated 28.V.[1] To be sure it may have waited a day or two for my arrival last night. You ought to have received two or three of the little dissents that I scattered more copiously than I could wish this last term. But the Court has rendered some decisions that I deeply regret. Brandeis and I are together as we are so apt to be, by a sort of preestablished harmony. However it is over now and I am beginning to conceive the possibility of relaxation. Following your suggestion, which I should not have needed if I had known of the book I bought Russell's *Philosophy* —and following an older one of last year that I attributed to you I have bought Parrington's *The Colonial Mind.*[2] The something illegible of Cuthbert[3] had not reached these shores but is ordered, I believe. I wish I had kept a list of your recommendations as they came along—but some were off the beat to which in a general way I confine myself. While at the Touraine I read *Genghis Khan*—(by Harold Lamb)—an interesting picture of what a man can do with a moderate force that can get there quicker than the other feller. I was a little interested too by his indifference to life —at least to the life of other people—by way of antithesis to our sentimentalism. I am rather hard-hearted in theory and deal imaginary death more easily than I should find easy in the real case.

Yesterday morning before coming here I was taken over to the Gillette Safety Razor factory and was greatly impressed. You are familiar I suppose with the mechanism of modern great establishments. I am a child in most matters of practical business. Perhaps because I was a friend of Brandeis who used to be Gillette's counsel, I was presented with a parcel on leaving which flabbergasted me when I opened it. It was such a complete and pretty outfit of safety razor, blades, soap and brush in finest form. As yet I just own it as a miser, but in a day or two I shall begin to use it and cakes of soap will seem bristly compared with my face— a new comfort has set in, since in last September my secretary bought a safety razor and blade in a 10 cent store and gave them

---

[1] Omitted from this edition.

[2] The first volume of Parrington's *Main Currents in American Thought* (1927-30).

[3] Wodehouse, *The Clicking of Cuthbert* (1928).

to me. I am as converted as St. Paul—which reminds me—did I mention the seeming revivification, with reenforced arguments, of the notion that Jesus was a myth? It really sounds very plausible. To one who concludes from reading the story that one knows nothing certain of the sayings or character of Christ it doesn't much matter whether there was or was not a centre of radiant energy in the form of a man. Does it occur to you that there are more modern things in the *Bible* than in other ancient literature. I think "Father forgive them—they know not what they do"— beats all the classics. Think of those words being attributed to the supposed author of doctrine absolutely irreconcilable with such skeptic tolerance. Also "a thousand years are as a day in thy sight"—as embodying the possibility of the same period being an instant or an eternity according to the state of mind. It seems as if vacation had begun.   *Affectionately yours, O. W. Holmes*

Devon Lodge, 16.VI.28

My dear Justice: . . . I had Birrell to supper. . . . We agreed in thinking that the equation Gosse $= 0$ is an essential truth of the higher literary mathematics. . . . He told me . . . of Bob Romer[1] who, you remember, was senior wrangler, a remark to Fletcher Moulton, also a senior wrangler, who in a patent case was making some mathematical observations, "I do not think it advisable for my brother Moulton to recall the indecencies of our past when the junior bar is present." Don't you think that charming? . . .

Ever affectionately yours, H. J. L.

Beverly Farms, June 16, 1928

My dear Laski: A letter good as usual has just been forwarded from Washington. I shall not receive books or pamphlets until and (in view of age) unless I return there. I don't recognize the criticism on McReynolds for notes—that is Brandeis's *specialité* —which I criticized to him at the beginning, but which he sticks to and which certainly enables him to put in a lot of facts that no one but he could accumulate and which overawe me, even if I doubt the form. . . . As to the old age of nations I never could see much more than an *a priori* application of a superficial analogy. I daresay you propounded China. As to students, I of course approve scepticism—though I regret irreverence. Don't ask me to

---

[1] Some years after Sir Robert Romer (1840-1918) was advanced from the Chancery Division to the Court of Appeal in 1890, there were three Senior Wranglers on that court. Sir James Stirling (1863-1916) was Senior Wrangler at Cambridge three years before Romer and eight years before Fletcher Moulton.

disapprove of Ludwig—Einstein[1] sent me a German article by him, the other day, in which he said the best man he met in the U.S. was the oldest—"who but Lippo, I?" Ludwig must be all right.

As you see we are here—and have been since last Monday and I am as near bliss as I often get. I have read a little of Parrington —*Main Currents of American Thought*—with unmixed pleasure and instruction. Also a little of B. Russell's *Philosophy*—as yet without great edification although with pleasure—as he, so far, simply works out in more detail what one is in the habit of taking for granted. But I blush to admit that I know only by inference and only inadequate inference what Behaviorism is. I also have perused *But Gentlemen Marry Brunettes*—that nothing be lost.

But I am trying to take life easy—which I find hard. There always are things to do. However I have indexed my this term's volume of my decisions, and finished up—so far as my part goes, business that required attention. Yesterday afternoon we drove around the Cape and skirted the shores of your Rockport—everything was divinely beautiful. The sea its deepest blue—the quarries scarped omens of death—the long beach between R. and Gloucester beginning to look like a picture by Zamacois—picked out with figures of every colour—the roads through the foliage of June—and even the lilacs not yet quite gone—we have got the season at a little earlier stage than usual, this year.

I stop that I may creep out for a few steps in the fresh air and sunlight. During the winter I pretty nearly gave up walking—and now am making little attempts to revive the art.

Affectionately yours, O. W. H.

Beverly Farms, Mass., June 28, 1928
My dear Laski: It seems like resuming a long interrupted conversation to write to you from here. For though you have been delightful I have been no good until I reached this breathing place. I think I mentioned having at last taken Parrington—*Main Currents of American Thought*. Now I have read him and were you here we would jaw a volume. *Imprimis.* His work seems to me solid and probably as just as any one man would be likely to be. I felt as if I had seen the movement of New England as I never had seen it before. Yet I was conscious all through of an antagonism that would have reached issues had we both been articulate as to fundamentals. The dogmatic postulate implied in the word "exploitation" occurring on every page, and the sympathy that I infer with the church-descended talk of the transcendentalists as to the infinite value and potentialities of

[1] Presumably Lewis Einstein.

every human soul, got my hair up. I know that we are not at one on these themes—but I don't think that politeness requires me to disguise my opinion that the implications are noxious humbug. I will not amplify on that, but I can't retain my opinion. Some of his judgments do not commend my assent, but they are matters of detail. I am a long way off from believing that Thoreau was a thinker in any important sense. I am not surprised at what he said about my father, nor at his having missed what I think true, that although my father did not concentrate in his later days as he did when he wrote on puerperal fever, still he had in him a capacity for profound insight—that occasionally flashed out as I saw him. I think P's whole estimate of the federalist performance of making a nation in place of squabbling states is inadequate—&c &c. But in spite of all criticisms Parrington has instructed and stimulated me more than anything that I have read for some time.

We have paid our respect to Rockport which always moves me, and this morning have been at another moving spot, the old burying ground and lookout of Marblehead. One is in a different world, as one zigzaggles through the crowded streets, and pretty near heaven when one gets to the top of the hill where the old first settlers were buried and the point from which one gazes far out to sea. Within a rod or two of the top is the well by which the girl (Agnes Surriage) he made his mistress, and afterwards married, used to meet Sir Harry Frankland in the old days.[1] I guess the old Marbleheaders still stick to their traditions. I was told there of two old men talking of a third just dead whom one spoke of as of the place. "He wasn't no Marbleheader," said the other. "He was six months old before he came here." I have heard many yarns about them, which seem to show them as dogged as any Britons ever were. Of other books—a gentle yearning volume by Cardozo[2]—lovable creature I am sure. Stories by Owen Wister who is coming here for Sunday, and Bertrand Russell in process —not revelatory so far—though sound talk I doubt not. Many things in your letter give me pleasure—*inter alia*—Gosse—and the tale of Romer and Fletcher Moulton (at whose house I have fed and drunk well). It is a happy time here. Age has taken something from my capacity for delight but there is enough left for practical purposes.   *Affectionately yours, O. W. H.*

Beverly Farms, July 8, 1928
My dear Laski: A letter from you delightful as always comes this morning. Your *ennuis* (industrial court, examination papers, &c)

---

[1] In his poem "Agnes," Dr. Holmes wrote of the romance of Agnes Surriage, servant in the Fountain Inn at Marblehead, and Sir Charles Henry Frankland (1716-1768), Collector of the Port of Boston from 1746 to 1757.
[2] *Paradoxes of Legal Science* (1928).

have my sympathy. (I have received a first batch of *certioraris*.) Your pleasures and successes are my pleasures too. . . . Your German who wanted to explain your errors to you makes me realize the advantages of the blessed Atlantic upon which I look. You tell me of your birthday but don't tell me how old you are. *Please do*. My time since my last has been taken up in good part by the business incident to July 1, bills and accounts. I haven't read much—I think drives more important. After Parrington I did finish Bertrand Russell's *Philosophy*—devoutly as I believe him (*ex rel.* you and Cohen) to be a great mathematician there seems to me something wrong in his speculative apparatus. He spends infinite time on matters that I am quite ready to take for granted, and in his general views seems to me to wobble between reason and sentiment. I should suppose that he hadn't given up the notion that absolute truth is attainable, though perhaps I am wrong on that. I don't retain his book in articulate form in my head but only impressions which I couldn't refer to specific texts. Expound the merits to me if you think me blind. Owen Wister was here last Saturday—Sunday and we went through Rockport again. It always moves by its simple majesties of granite and ocean— and I always look over to where you were and wish that you were there again. If you were, no doubt you would put books into my hands—as it is, my only slight *pièce de résistance* is Morison's *Oxford History of the United States* lent to me by Miss Loring[1] the other day—as yet I have read but a few pages. Also I have partly read an account of *Russia after Ten Years*—report of the American Trade Union Delegates to the Soviet Union—optimistic, but intended to be fair. Perhaps it comes down to the question, as so many things do—of what kind of world you want. Personally I do not prefer a world with a hundred million bores in it to one with ten. The fewer the people who do not contribute beauty or thought, the better to my fancy. I perfectly realize that the other fellers feel otherwise and very likely would prefer to get rid of me and all my kind. Perhaps they will, and if they do I have nothing to say, except that our tastes differ. That is the justification of war —if people vehemently want to make different kinds of worlds I don't see what there is to do except for the most powerful to kill the others—as I suppose they did in Russia. I believe Kropotkin points out the mistake of the French Revolution in not doing so.

I have a line from Wu this morning. He is now engaged on a code—under government employment and has given up or was contemplating giving up his judgeship. His paper is headed Nationalist Government of the Republic of China. He proposes

---

[1] Katharine Peabody Loring (1849-1943), North Shore friend of Holmes, and sister of his associate on the Massachusetts Bench, William Caleb Loring, *supra*, p. 42.

to come over here in about a year, Pound having offered him a scholarship. I warned him that so far as seeing me was a motive, as he says it is, it wasn't safe to calculate so far ahead—but he replies that he hears (seemingly with belief) of a man who is 250 years old and in good health. I am afraid that the oriental criteria of evidence are not stringent. Tell your wife that though I don't often mention it I always put my faith in her to prevent your working your machine too hard. I have heard of men who exhausted their whole stock of vital energy in getting double firsts and did nothing afterwards. You have passed far beyond that stage, but I still fear that you run up bills against the end of your life. Remember the *Peau de Chagrin*. Another drawback to reading is slumber. I feel as if time couldn't be better spent, but you can't put it down on a list of things done.

Affectionately yours, O. W. Holmes

Devon Lodge, 7.VII.28

My dear Justice: A delightful letter from you breathes the peace of the country, and told me, as I hoped, that you had derived pleasure from Parrington. Of course he writes as a Southerner, with a permanent bias against the North. I, who believe most of the claims made for the South are either untrue or undesirable, remain unmoved by that side of him. But he has real intelligence and insight, and a delightful style.

We have had some pleasant days since I wrote lost. We celebrated my birthday with a party chiefly notable for talk from H. G. Wells which I shall not easily forget. Part of it was judgment of people—always quick and sober and vivid: of Galsworthy that he was always about to be an artist, but at the moment of insight a gift of unshed tears blurred the sureness of his vision; of Shaw that he wrote of government as though people had never cared for liberty; and of Henry James that he failed because he could never accept the possibility that life was simple. Then to my surprise he told us that he had been studying the art of prose and felt strongly that three English lawyers were among the great artists—Selden, Maitland, and Macnaghten—an interesting choice. And I was immensely touched by his kindness. I had a young Hungarian novelist here, on the verge of making his way. To watch Wells discussing his job with him, his patience, his tact and his discrimination were a real lesson to me in the greatness of a great man. I wish there were more like that. My young Hungarian said he felt, like Pizarro, that a new planet had swum into his ken. Then next day we motored down to the Cotswolds and spent a divine week-end in divine country. . . .

Our love to you both.   *Ever affectionately yours, H. J. L.*

Beverly Farms, July 20, 1928

My dear Laski: Whether this will get off in time to catch the evening mail and then be in time to sail from New York tomorrow I doubt—still more whether the effort can give you anything so interesting as your last. I didn't know Parrington was from the South. That explains some things. Your account of Wells has some little surprises in it. I didn't remember MacNaghten as a master of style and had not thought of Selden in that connection. There are fine and famous passages in some of the [illegible]. It gave me pleasure to hear of Wells's kindness and magnanimity. I don't know but you are right in calling him a great man. I have just received an account of the Cohen dinner[1]—to match you with a possibly great man on this side. It must have been very moving—and it is pretty to think of his old father and mother being there to see the triumph of their son. I notice that the toastmaster quotes Cohen as saying that Bertrand Russell comes nearest to being his philosophic God—and you seem to lean in that direction. I haven't got that religion from anything that I have read—and I did get pleasure from Fred Pollock a few days ago (writing of B.R.) "His theodicy so far as I make out consists in being angry with the gods for not existing, because if they did he would like to break their windows." I think that quite perfect.

I have finished the *Oxford History of the United States*[2] with continued pleasure and feel that I learned from it—incidentally to modify my old impressions of MacLellan and A. Johnson—at rare moments there is a pert turn in the end of a sentence—and sometimes hints at convictions I don't share. He seems (from a very few words) more than respectful to Christian Science.

One or two minor experiences—Owen Wister sent to me *The Sun Also Rises* by Hemingway—youngish American author, living in Paris, and I am told one of a gang that call one another great. Wister thought that when he left the garbage can he had a future. It is a queer thing—some rather every-day doings of people indicating no superiority of any kind, never expressing an idea—but conversing in the language of toughs, making up for their inability to find a discriminating word by "damned" and "hell"—all getting more or less drunk every day—with a hint of fornication, not overstressed—and yet one is interested. Mrs. Curtis suggests, because it is pure narrative which she said always interested—but rarely had been practised since Swift. That may

---

[1] In October 1927, Morris Cohen's students at City College had given him a dinner honoring his twenty-fifth anniversary as a member of the Faculty. Felix Frankfurter was toastmaster, and messages of affection and admiration from many distinguished persons were delivered. See Cohen, *A Dreamer's Journey* (1949), 148-149.

[2] By Samuel E. Morison.

be it, and anyhow I read on when so far as appeared I should have thought the *dramatis personae* in real life worse than bores. Item. A good article by Frankfurter on "Distribution of Judicial Power between United States and State Courts," [3] I should think he was doing a public good in tackling as he has an ungrateful and, but for him, tedious subject.

I now await from the Athenaeum a *Life of Villon*, said to be A-1 [4] and from the bookseller, Henry Osborn Taylor, *Human Values* (and something else that I can't read certainly) recommended by a professor whom I met the other day and who had been examining brains. He found no explanation in the brain of Morse of Salem—of his power to draw equally well with both hands—and I believe at the same time. [5] In short there was very little evidence of the localizing of faculties. You get a lot of things quicker than we do if we ever get them—but I am surprised to learn how many eminent writers of books &c &c there are here that I don't know about. I was frightfully impressed with the same thing on a larger scale when I read *These Eventful Years*. There promises to be enough to keep me busy during the short time that I have left. My love to you all.

Affectionately yours, O. W. Holmes

Devon Lodge, 23.VII.28

My dear Justice: . . . I had to go down to Bristol to speak on the "General Will" to the Aristotelian Society. I found myself in the midst of a gang of old-time Hegelians out for blood, including one passionate lawyer (a county court judge named Dowdall) [1] who said with, I am sure, perfect sincerity that he had met a general will six times in his life; and an ancient professor named Mackenzie [2] who said that the general will of America was permanently embodied in Woodrow Wilson's speeches. I enjoyed it in the way that one likes to strike a note of scepticism in a meeting where people are testifying to private revelation from on high; but I thought it rather a childish performance. Then three days at Oxford giving some lectures to five American students ensconced there for the summer. That I thoroughly enjoyed. They cross-

---

[3] 13 *Cornell Law Quarterly* 499 (June 1928).

[4] D. B. Wyndham Lewis, *François Villon* (1928).

[5] Edward Sylvester Morse (1838-1925).

[1] Harold Chaloner Dowdall (1868-1955), Judge of the County Court of Lancashire, 1921-1940.

[2] Probably Professor John Stuart Mackenzie (1860-1935); Professor of Logic and Philosophy, University College of South Wales and Monmouthshire, 1895-1915; author of *Outlines of Metaphysics* (1890).

examined me with machine-gun rapidity, and I felt at the end
that I had really earned my keep. . . . I met there Hardy the
mathematician.[3] He reminded me somewhat of Morris Cohen—
the same width of interest and razor-like mind, and his honesty
was remarkable. He said that England historically had only one
supreme mathematician in Newton and perhaps a dozen to whom
the word eminent was applicable, and he traced much of this to
our insularity on the one hand and bad academic methods on
the other. I thought his standards the kind of thing that makes one
inclined to creep into a hole and die there, but you could not help
being impressed because he so clearly felt that mathematics were
the most important thing in the world. Then a dinner with Sankey
to meet Scrutton, L.J. They speak of the latter as ill-tempered;
but I found him wholly delightful. . . . I gathered that he met
you once years ago on a tramp with F. Pollock, Leslie Stephen
and, if I have it right, Douglas Freshfield.[4] Finally I record a
dinner here for Neilson of Smith College,[5] an old Harvard friend,
who warmed my heart with a great account of Felix and comforted my fear that I may be wrong in refusing to give money to
the Law School by hinting that Pound has the illusion of bigness
in a dangerous degree. . . .

Sir, in answer to your enquiry, I beg hereby to state that I was
born on June 30, 1893. I have not ceased to talk, except at nights,
since about June, 1896.

Our love to you both.   *Ever affectionately yours, H. J. L.*

                                        Beverly Farms, August 13, 1928
My dear Laski: Your first vacation letter[1] has arrived and has
given me the usual pleasure. I have told you about Vondel, *quoad
nos,* before. My father amused himself with the thought that Vondel and Wendell might be the same and had his works and his
portrait (which I now have) by Janus Lutma engraved in a manner peculiar to Lutma—while I have Lutma by Rembrandt in my
dressing-room. So I am glad to hear that Vondel is the Belgians'
great man.

I have no great things to tell about myself. I am tired this
morning as we had a feller here for Sunday and more than an

---

[3] Godfrey Harold Hardy (1877-1947), Professor of Pure Mathematics at
Cambridge.
   [4] Douglas William Freshfield (1845-1934), geographer and mountaineer.
   [5] William Allan Neilson (1869-1946), President of Smith College, 1917-
1939, had been Professor of English at Harvard while Laski was on the
Harvard faculty.
   [1] Omitted from this edition.

hour and a half of talk takes it out of me. My wife if she sees
signs of fatigue always attributes it to the *certioraris*—I, not. But
I have done 125 and have told the clerk to send no more unless I
ask for them. If they have not tired me they have kept me from
reading more than a very little. I have on hand a book by one
Dill—*Roman Society from Nero to Marcus Aurelius,* which was
recommended to me and which has information that is for the
benefit of my immortal soul—and which therefore I expect to
finish—but which is almost the *ne plus ultra* of what I dislike as
writing. Fat and flabby adjectives—much repetition—the conventional attitude that any loose talk on Juvenal *et al* is *painful*—
deliquescent phrases about the corruption of the nobility by the
example of Nero and the others—Oh Lord—he makes me tired.
But as Sidney Bartlett[1] said of an argument by Evarts: "But
through it all there ran a vein of thought—attenuated at times to
be sure, but never wholly lost." (S.B. patronized everything
human). So I keep on. I read Lady Oxford's novel—*Octavia*—
and it made me a little sad—good hunting talk—and horses described in human terms. But the tale sounds to me as if years had
not added wisdom. Also some things by Ernest Hemingway that
I think I have mentioned.[2] Art shows in making you interested in
the picture of people doing and saying what in life would not
interest you in the least. I hope now to read a little more and
presently shall go to sleep over Dill. I am even thinking of taking
a book by your friend Trollope, perhaps *Barchester Towers,* and
seeing how I get on with that. Always there is imminent some
brief touch of the classics—but with them almost always the
feeling of wasted time. It would be a momentarily pleasant and
possibly a wholesome change to have two or three days come
when I didn't quite know what to do. There is always something
and partly from temperament it generally presents itself in the
light of a duty. You seem always to read no matter what with
gusto. I almost always read with a groan, a mark, and with a count
of the number of pages. Even my taste for novels like my taste
for meat has faded, although I still am all there on a real story of
the old fashion, not necessarily detective—provided there isn't too
much of it—as there was for me in *La guerre et la paix.* I suppose it is the Old Testament's grasshopper become a burden—
but cases don't, nor philosophical books that hit me. I wish I had
kept a list of the books recommended by you. Some shaft more

[1] Sidney Bartlett (1799-1889), for years a leader of the Boston bar and
an imposing figure on the profession's national horizon. Holmes spoke of
him briefly in his *Speeches,* 41.
[2] Holmes read both *The Sun Also Rises* (1926) and *Men Without Women*
(1927) during the summer of 1928.

lucky than the rest might seek my heart. Farewell—I am glad
you are having such a good time.*

Affectionately yours, O. W. Holmes

* Don't mistake me—I am.

Grand Hotel, Waulsort-sur-Meuse
Belgium, 13.VIII.28

My dear Justice: Life moves so peacefully here that it is difficult
to think I was ever caught in the whirlpool of term. I am having
the happiest possible time, enough reading and writing and talking
to make each of them specially attractive as it comes. This week
we have had with us James Ensor, I imagine the best of living
Belgian artists, a man of seventy and a great *causeur*. I have
enjoyed him hugely. To discover an artist whose God, so far as
he has one, is Henri Poincaré—is remarkable enough. But to find
him also a perfect tempest of ideas on everything is really exhilarating. He is that rare thing—an artist conscious of the need
to understand his own art. He pleases me by rejection of all effort
to distinguish between the highest forms of creative effort. That,
for him, is the attractiveness of Poincaré; he recognizes, he says,
in P's account of his scientific experience the same creative impulse which has led him to his own best pictures. And to hear
him on the Church in Belgium is a joy. He had not been to confession for thirty years when he married and the *curé* punished
him by refusing to allow him to enter the Church by the front
door. So Ensor marked his sense of the fitness of things by giving
the verger a hundred francs and the *curé* ten when he left. He
would please you by his enthusiasm for van Ostade. He puts Peter
Brughael at the head of all the Flemish school, and, to my surprise,
Memling very much in the second rank. And in his literary tastes
he is curiously classical. He sees things in Corneille and Racine
that literally do not exist for me; and, conversely, I cannot persuade him that there is anything at all in the poetry of the 19th
century romantics. He loathes Scott and Dickens and Meredith
and George Sand, and makes a God of Voltaire. It is curiously
fascinating to walk with him and watch how his eye fastens upon
a proportion in the landscape, an unexpected contour, some sudden cluster of flowers in one of the promontories of rocks in which
the district abounds. I would give much to bring him to I Street
and spend a night with you both. And Mrs. Holmes must know
that he cannot avoid a perfect passion for tiny, absurd, bizarre
ornaments. He wanders into shops and cottages and comes out
with little china dogs, or a cup with a scriptural illustration, or a
kind of sampler with verses telling the child its duty to God.
Altogether a splendid person.

In the way of reading, I have had a jolly time. The most interesting thing was Redslob's *History of the Principles of International Law* which illuminates for me a side of things I did not
know. What interests me especially is the number of really
second-rate minds who have had great influence in that subject. I
can't see that Puffendorf, or Wolff or Vattel, or Bynershöek, are
much more than, say, the average text-book writer in an American
University; yet each seems to mark an epoch in his subject. And,
intellectually, Grotius seems much more to have amplitude than
profundity. I should have said that Suarez or Franciscus de
Victoria in sheer rational power could have given him points every
time. . . .

Of other things, there is not much to tell. Once a week I have
been in to Dinant to get money from my bank; and I found there
some nice 18th century pewter bowls which pleased me since
Frida has a passion for ancient pewter. And I bought there also
a volume of Bernardin de S. Pierre's *Études de la nature* with the
name of Manon Phlipon on the title—the *bouquiniste* not knowing, or perhaps, not caring, that Manon Phlipon became Mme.
Roland and was certainly a lady worth knowing.[1] I add one final
experience that will interest you. We motored with a friend on
Friday to Bouillon[2]—the remains of Godfrey's chateau of that ilk,
and in the visitor's book at the inn under, I think it was 1873, I
saw the name of Henry Adams with the remark—"food excellent;
the light wines distinctly good." I fancy I can imagine his satisfaction at striking a note which left in at least one region the sense
that there had been a faint disappointment he was too stoic to
emphasise.

Our warm love to you both. I hope the heat wave of which we
read has left Beverly unmoved and unscathed.

Ever affectionately yours, H. J. L.

Beverly Farms, August 23, 1928
My dear Laski: This marks the moment when I have just finished
reading your portrait of Rousseau in the July *Yale Review*.[1] It is
beautiful and stirs me deeply. I wonder if in depths of your nature
that I have not fathomed there is a corresponding religious fervor
for some convictions, notwithstanding your formal scepticism. At

---

[1] Manon Phlipon Roland (1754-1793); Girondiste and revolutionary, whose
last words at the guillotine have preserved her name: "Oh Liberty, what
crimes are committed in thy name!"

[2] Bouillon, the "Key to the Ardennes" is the site of the remains of the
castle of Godfrey of Bouillon (c. 1060-1100), the leader of the First Crusade.

[1] "Portrait of Jean-Jacques Rousseau," 17 *Yale Review* (N.S.) 702 (July
1928).

all events your subtle appreciations go to my heart. None the less
do I repudiate the passion for equality as unphilosophical and as
with most of those who entertain it a disguise for less noble feelings. While I know very well that divinations *come before* proof,
yet I hate (intellectually) every appeal to intuitions that are
supposed to *transcend* reason, all the way down from Rousseau to
Bill James. But this is by the way. What I began I end with—
you have made a wonderful portrait that gives me delight.

I have had an unmixed vacation feeling since I sent back my
last batch of *certioraris*. I doubt if I shall send for more, lest I
should tempt destiny to snip my thread. If I made too much
preparation for the future, fate might like to wink and say: "Sold."
Perhaps my interjected protest was helped by my just having
finished a book I began some time ago—Dill—*Roman Society
from Nero to Marcus Aurelius*—(a dull, interesting work—like an
address to the jury in its eternal repetitions). While showing how
much there was alien to Christianity in the air, so that you almost
would think a sceptic was talking, he patronises it all from the
Christian point of view, as not having intuitions that I should
regard as products of ignorance, egotism, and conceit. As I have
said before I think man needs to learn to take himself less seriously when he attempts to philosophize.

Just now I have on hand Mallock's *Memoirs of Life and Literature*.[2] As in other books he makes me feel that I don't like him—
and at the point that I have reached he seems to wish to impress
you with what very exclusive society he frequented. Also I have
some stories by Chekov lent to me yesterday—and I have sent
for Petronius— but ὡς τάχιστα I purpose to read a novel of Trollope's—as a sacrifice to the Muses. Haldane's death[3] moves me—I
knew him since we both were relatively young—and I thought
him a great man—on the strength of his book about what he did
before the late war &c. My horizon grows pretty bare. I suppose
you will have got back when this arrives—I hope well and in high
spirits. *Macte virtute.*   *Aff'ly yours, O. W. H.*

Beverly Farms, August 26, 1928
My dear Laski: You keep me envying your power to read a book
in a wink and to remember what you have read. I suppose that
Petronius whom I have taken up just now could be swallowed in

---

[2] William Hunnell Mallock (1849-1923), man of letters and fashion;
author of *The New Republic* (1877), *The New Paul and Virginia* (1878),
and forgotten novels. His *Memoirs of Life and Literature* was published in
1920.

[3] Lord Haldane had died on August 19.

an hour. With a translation alongside it will last me several days.
To be sure, I hardly read at more than odd minutes. The dead
pen is generically of all time but specifically blunter and coarser
than what makes us laugh. Do you remember in *Verdant Green*
(itself I suppose now antiquated) the student overheard walking
up and down and chuckling at some wretched jest of Aristophanes? I believe I expressed my sorrow at the death of Haldane
in my last. The horizon narrows. I feel like the prisoner in the
room the walls of which draw nearer every day. That is true not
only of life but of vacation. In a month I shall be due in Washington. Today there is a dense fog and perhaps for that reason I
don't feel cheerful about it. Normally one is glad of vacation when
it comes and, in turn, glad to go back to work. Perhaps I should
feel better if I had read any book this summer that made a great
mark, or if it was a sunny day and the wind not from the South.
I have had no conversation to compare with your Belgian artists'.
An Indiana judge *et al.* lunched here on Friday, pleasant and
discreetly soapy, but nothing memorable.

One of the country people, or rather a couple, leave a mark.
He commands a vessel in the winter and works with his wife on
her flower garden in the summer. Last winter two voyages to
Buenos Ayres, etc. While he was away two police dogs that they
kept showed signs of trouble. She shoved her hand down the
throat of one thinking to relieve him, then the doctor said it was
rabies. I believe she is undergoing some treatment but didn't seem
worried at all—but the arches of his feet had given out on ship
board, and the rains had destroyed most of his wife's flowers, and
the authorities were taking a piece of his land that he wanted for
his road, and he was blue. I came to know them by stopping to
buy flowers at the roadside two years ago, and his melancholy
quite took hold of me. I worry easily. I don't know that I do more as
I grow older, but less things than that make me uneasy, even
a long communication from a crank among a series that the C.J.
would throw into the wastepaper basket. But I should give you a
wrong impression if I made you think that I was not happy in the
main. I have talked more about such things than you ever do. I
hardly know whether to apologise or to assume the privilege of
age. This letter was interrupted by a call from Reginald Foster.
Did you know him? A clever man, who like you reads, as he puts
it, down the page instead [of] across line by line like *nous autres,*
the worms. He like you reads Trollope recurrently, also Dumas
and Scott which last I have done in my time. Now I am expecting
a call from my *quondam* secretary, L. Curtis, who lost a leg in an
airplane accident while training for the war. Hard lines, which he

takes with admirable courage and good temper. I wish I had as interesting things to tell as you do.

Affectionately yours, O. W. Holmes

Beverly Farms, August 30, 1928

My dear Laski: Your letter came this morning and after returning from my drive I wrote to the Old Corner Book Store to see if they could get me in French or English Hazimeau's or Maziarani's or somebody else with a name looking like that (the first name illegible but immaterial), *History of English Literature*—thus having obeyed your behest.[1] It would make me easier to get an improving book. There has been a lack of them this vacation and while I more or less emulate older men who say they now read only for amusement, it is vain. I feel that I ought to be taking in fuel. Although I wrote lately I forget whether I mentioned that Dill the tiresome put me on to Petronius. I think I did. And that has a certain improvement in it as it suggests reflection, verified observations of others, and had a surprising number of quotable sentences, of which of course, I made no note. I do not greatly admire the writers of diaries and the economical noters of their happy thoughts and the felicities encountered in reading. *Ad interim,* I have read some stories by Chekov (qu.sp.?) well told but squalid—not the swinish instinct you attribute to Hemingway, but none the less displeasing to me. I am just rebeginning *Moby Dick,* which I surmise with your boatman of the Meuse to be great.

You rather seem to be defending Lady Asquith against me. Lord bless you—I know her pretty well and I think I appreciate her fine qualities as fully as anyone. The book however did not please me. Unlike you, though ignorant, I did enjoy the hunting and horse talk, but the emotional parts and the end seemed to me as if she had not learned by growing older.

Morris Cohen was here at luncheon yesterday and we talked for three hours plus and then at his suggestion I took a rest. I get tired with talking and normally consider an hour and a half my limit. I needn't say that I enjoyed it greatly. He said that he came back to the classics feeling as if he was wasting time with modern books. While I on the other hand always fear that I am wasting time if I dally long with the classics. He expounded an interesting theory of the Sadducees as the national party—the priests and upholders of the theocracy—the Pharisees as reformers, saying that every man might be his own high priest, but still upholding the ceremonial side—and Jesus, condemning the Pharisees

---

[1] Legouis and Cazamanian, *History of English Literature.* Laski's letter has been omitted from this edition.

more than the Sadducees, foreseeing the downfall of the theocracy (I forgot to ask him whether this attribution wasn't on the strength of words as to which one may take the liberty of doubting whether Jesus ever uttered them) and making it all a matter of the heart, or internal, not ceremonial. Also he had been rereading Kant's *Critique* with great admiration, while of course not accepting the structure. Cohen is a wonderful and noble creature. . . .

I thank you deeply for your encouraging words about resignation.   *Affectionately ever, O. W. Holmes*

Devon Lodge, 2.IX.28

My dear Justice: As you can imagine, I was deeply moved by Haldane's death; one does not dine with a man weekly for eight years without a sense of real affection for him. Heaven knows he had his faults; but he was generous, and warm hearted, and a very great organiser. I remember above all two things. First a talk with Haig in which the general insisted that Haldane alone had made the British army a really efficient instrument and, secondly, a talk with Haldane about amendments to the Trade Union Act of 1927 when he showed a fertility in inventiveness and a skill in drafting which were really incomparable. Only five weeks before he died Mrs. Asquith and Mrs. Webb—as different as chalk from cheese—had both said the same thing to me, that if they were in trouble they would go to Haldane before any other person. We all felt that about him. I add, what you will like to know, that he had immense respect for your work, and followed your decisions year by year with the fidelity of a man who knows the best when he sees it. He always asked for news of you and he always remembered the journey to America with you with quite special pleasure. *Inani perfungor munere.*

We came back last Wednesday from the Ardennes; and except for a week with my people in Manchester (whither I go tomorrow) the holiday is over. But it has been a great time, and I feel as fresh as paint. So much so that I almost begrudge the week up North as it interferes with a piece I have begun to write for the American Encyclopedia of the Social Sciences on the rise of liberalism[1]—a perfectly thrilling subject on which, I think, I can manage to say something new. I sat down to it with the kind of extra-thrill one gets when one feels that the job was really made for oneself; and I only regret that I can't have a real year of leisure to do it amply. . . .

Our love to you both. Don't do any more *certioraris* until you are back in Washington.   *Ever affectionately yours, H. J. L.*

[1] *Encyclopedia of Social Sciences* (1930) 103-124.

Devon Lodge, 18.IX.28

My dear Justice: I have been busy doing nothing this last ten days; hence an unusual silence. We went to Manchester to spend our annual week with my people and I find it impossible to write or think there. One lives in an atmosphere of such luxury that the main feeling which arises in me is that of the poor relation who ought to crouch in a corner. The vital questions turn either on market-movements in cotton, on which my stock of information is small, or on the comparative merits of Rolls-Royce against Daimler—upon which I probably know even less. Frida manages wonderfully by an assumption of knowledge about dress which I am confident she doesn't possess. I feel woe-begone, and count the hours until I return. We made up for it by a delightful week-end with the Webbs where we talked the political world round. Webb told me some interesting tales of Woodrow Wilson whom he visited thirty years ago as a professor at Princeton; and he wrote down in his diary that W.W. would like to be a Virginian Calvin if he got the chance, which was a good judgment for that early period. He told me, also, an amusing story of how Herbert Spencer appointed Mrs. Webb his literary executor just before her engagement; when it was announced that she was to wed the arch-collectivist he wrote warning her that if she persisted he would have to change his will; and his wedding present to them was a set, finely bound, of his writings against the state. We had a pleasant evening on Saturday when Russell came over. He talked, as always, brilliantly; and, I should have said, with less regard to the grim need for fact than any man I have ever heard. But when it came to judgments, his dismissal of Bergson was a superb piece of analysis, and his explanation of the significance of modern cosmology left me with the feeling that any really sensible person would specialise in astrophysics instead of a stupid subject like political science. . . .

I have three more weeks of peace; and I suppose you are just bidding farewell to the red-gold of New England autumn. Here we enjoy summer sunshine, and in Surrey, the beeches are still a vivid green.

Our love to you both.   *Ever affectionately yours, H. J. L.*

Devon Lodge, 9.X.28

My dear Justice: In the midst of term I cry unto thee. For a week I have been drowned amid students, of all colours and races and nationalities. It is exhilarating, but it makes me want to retire. If a kind American Foundation sent me a cheque for twenty thousand pounds I should take a cottage in Hindhead and write there for the rest of my life. But I am full of good works, and never, I think, nearer to salvation than just now. Which reminds me that we have a new member of the staff—a geographer— whose induction to our mysteries is worth recording. He is a fervent Baptist and at dinner was offered some port by Hobhouse. "I would sooner commit adultery" said the Baptist. "So would we all" said Hobhouse. Can you produce a finer retort than that?

As you can imagine, with term and its attendant committees I have had little space for other things. But I sneaked in a jolly lunch with Arnold Bennett who, *inter alia,* said (I) that the average of American fiction is, at the moment, higher than anywhere else in the world (II) that Dostoievski is the greatest novelist as a technician (III) that Proust is a snob writing for snobs and (IV) that he received an earnest letter from a clergyman urging him to write a novel helping God to the victory. A.B. replied that he had no knowledge of how to set about it, to which the reverend gent replied that if A.B. would supply the art he would supply the theology and that he would not ask for more than one-third of the profits. . . .

Of other things there is but little to say. Felix bombards me with literature upon the election campaign on which I have only the distinct impression that I like Smith and dislike Hoover; but upon his own activities he is silent and I am much more interested in them. One student who has come over from the Law School talks of him, to my joy, as easily the most respected teacher there. I have been interested, too, in a certain current of criticism that comes to me of Pound—how true I know not—but which in sum suggests the dawning sense that the mere amassing of materials and the refined separation of categories does not make a new jurisprudence. To one such I ventured the dictum that Morris Cohen was the outstanding legal theorist in America and found, to my pleasure, that a sense of this as a possible truth was not outside my visitor's powers of credence. But he queerly felt that poor Morris did not deserve the reputation I had given him because he had not written a *book.* My visitor, I add, spoke of anxiety felt at the Chicago Bar lest you be tempted to resign. He said he hoped you would go on without any fear that you had outstayed your welcome.

Our love to you both. Take care, please, and remember that life is even greater than *certioraris.*

Ever affectionately yours, H. J. L.

1729 I (Eye) Street N.W., October 11, 1928
My dear Laski: As a previous letter predicted, I, like you, have been filled with work till the cup overflowed. Unlike you I have had no amusing incidents to put a fizzle into it. I thought I had

done well in polishing off 125 *certioraris* in vacation. But when the term began there were near 250 and the Chief wanted to dispose of them all at once—with dramatic pauses in the announcement to meet the invincible scepticism of the Bar, that won't believe that we each and all examine every one. The result for me I have indicated. Some of the JJ. are ready—some worked late into the night, which I won't do, but I managed to be able to recite on all but 3—which didn't matter. Now we are hearing arguments, and the new *certs.* that came in on Monday are done. The papers got hold of the fact that this month I have reached a greater age than any judge who remained upon the Bench since the Court began—which has added letters to be answered to the other chores. It doesn't look much like reading your books at present. I have given a note of them to my secretary to be called to my attention if leisure comes. I have read your piece in the *Bookman.*[1] As you know I think you tend to confuse the necessary point of view taken by Courts (called Austinian by way of belittlement but really the only possible view for them) with ethical or social theory. As to this last you know that I also disagree. I don't know anything about the right of every man to an equal share on chances—that doesn't seem to me the order of the universe—and I am far from believing that man has in himself an independent fulcrum from which to react against that order. Of course it is open to you to prophesy that yours is the next step in the organic movement—but I don't bother much about prophecies as my time must be very short.

At odd minutes before and after coming here I have run through Philip Littell's *This Way Out.* He has an amusing pen and in his shorter pieces has written sentences worth a week off the end of one's life. This seems to me a little too much for the theme. It is Adam and Eve in the Garden—with diabolic accompaniments in the form of a parrot, called Paul, (Apollyon), a stork, &c with occasional messages from "Jovah"—it would seem incredibly blasphemous to a fundamentalist, and seems, as I said, a little too detailed for an outsider. It leads up to the discovery of the function of sex indicated and predicted but not indelicately detailed. There are very amusing touches. One of the Mephistophelians—Lucifer I think, takes a cigarette and lights it by breathing through his nose on the further end. Lucifer also gives an account of how he drafted a petition which 92% of the workers signed, and notwithstanding Jovah's reply that the works couldn't go on with the proposed hours, the new arrangement was made for 9 hours adoration instead of 12—and that fatigue, which formerly had set in at about the 9th hour, was virtually eliminated and production costs instead of increasing were low-

---

[1] "The Crisis in the Modern State," 68 *Bookman* 182 (October 1928).

ered by 7 4/10%—"a saving we passed on to the consumer. The
output was larger, the production was of better quality. Grade A
adoration was before long the order of the day and night."
Enough of this—I thought it might amuse you from one of your
cooperators in the *New Republic.* I don't see but that sheet has
become as frankly partisan as any party paper. But though Croly
is a thinker he is not a writer and I skip his pieces. Butler told
me a tale today that pleased me. Walker the mayor of New York
was asked to come to a meeting just about to take place. He said
he'd come if they wouldn't ask him to speak. They promised and
of course the promise was broken—so he rose and said "Ladies
and gentlemen, as Marcus Antony said when he entered the bou-
doir of Cleopatra, 'I didn't come here to talk.'" Apropos of what
you get about Lamb from Howe's *Life of Hazlitt* I dare say it is
true in a sense—and I dare say that Carlyle's description of him
as a snuffy, dingy, person is also true. So also I agree to any
language of delight in his essays or letters—yet when I went
through them I felt as I used to feel when working in the old
Law Library and saw the scenery that had charmed me on the
stage the night before run out through a slot in the wall and
loaded on a cart. But I have drooled long enough. Your letter
rec'd this morning was delightful.

Yours affectionately, O. W. Holmes

Washington, D.C., October 19, 1928
My dear Laski: Your report of your latest experience comes this
morning and brings the usual pleasure. The tale of your Baptist
colleague and the glass of port is superlative. I have heard nothing corresponding, even though it would call a blush to the cheeks
of innocence from *my* colleagues; though Sutherland and Butler
maintain a good average. The tension of work grows a little less.
I have written my first opinion and it has been approved by all
but Sanford who was the other way *ab initio.*[1] I felt a queer
nervousness until I got it back, lest it betray some symptom of
decline that I had not noticed. But I always have a nervous apprehension that someone will discover a chasm, until I get the
opinion back. For the moment I am cheerful. I am delighted at
what you were told about Frankfurter. My secretary[2] agrees, subject he says to a different kind of respect felt for Williston,[3]
which is easily understood. Williston is a delightful creature, and
admirable in the regular ruts. Frankfurter brings fire and invites

---

[1] *Maney* v. *United States,* 278 U.S. 17 (October 22, 1928).

[2] John E. Lockwood, now a practitioner in New York, had graduated
from the Harvard Law School in June 1928.

[3] Samuel Williston (1861-1963), beloved Professor of Law at Harvard,
1890-1938.

to new adventures. I have just run through a little brochure by Zimmern on *Learning and Leadership,* at the beginning with some coolness, at the almost indefinite Oxford exquisiteness and at the readiness of the scholar to offer schemes for the world, but in the end with delight in his discourse on the relation of ideas to action, a subject that always stirs me and on which he talks nobly. He is a fine creature, but I should doubt whether he had quite found his proper place in the world. Only a few days ago did I discover that you had sent me Bentham's *Comment on the Commentaries,* for which, warm thanks. No time to read it yet. A number of other books also encourage me. *Liberty in the Modern World,*[4] essays by people ranging from John Dewey and Chafee to Clarence Darrow. Lewis, *America, Nation or Confusion.* Sir Siraswamy Aiyar, *Indian Constitutional Problems.* What seems an entertaining little book sent by Mrs. Brandeis—*The Russian Land* by Albert Rhys Williams, etc. not to speak of articles including one on Legal Sciences by the, I suppose, great Kantorowitz.[5] Damn them all but one or two. You speak of Morris Cohen as an outstanding legal theorist. As you know I regard him with affection and reverence, but I hardly am aware of anything that I have felt to be a great contribution to legal theory. Like Henry Adams to someone who said that he had been with Charles and found him delightful—"You found Charles delightful? You interest me." I suppose I may as well make up my mind that I am an old fogey, and sit down, but there is little legal theory that strikes me as worth talking about.

One week more of arguments and then there may be some repose. I have not known this feeling since I got here.

Ever affectionately yours, O. W. H.

Devon Lodge, 16.X.28
My dear Justice: . . . Of news there is not a great deal, for the first fortnight in term is always swallowed up by students. But we had a jolly dinner on Sunday with Nevinson as the guest of honour (his 71st birthday) and as he gazed upon your photograph he said "Tell him that if ever my faith in the United States falters, I think of him and am comforted" which I report because I agree with it. And to tea on Sunday we had a Californian professor by the name of Kirk[1] (whom I know not otherwise) who said of you that for him and many of his colleagues your opin-

---

[4] *Freedom in the Modern World* (Kallen, ed., 1928).

[5] Herman Kantorowicz, "Legal Science—A Summary of Its Methodology," 28 *Columbia Law Review* 679 (June 1928).

[1] Probably William Kirk (1880-1959), Professor of Sociology at Pomona College.

ions were a source of permanent inspiration. So that you can feel how wide and deep is the sense of the ideas you have contributed to men of the most diverse experience.

The most interesting thing that has happened to me since I wrote last is for *your very private ear*. I got on Saturday a sudden summons to Downing Street and went quite bewildered as to its purpose. When I got into the P.M.'s presence he said with extraordinary kindness that he had followed my work with great care and wanted to offer me the secretaryship of the research committee of the cabinet with a salary about three times what I earn now. My breath was taken away and I said that I must have a day to think it over. After talk with Frida I went to see him this morning and declined it. For it would mean (I) that I could write no more (II) that I should research into things I might not believe in and (III) that my hands and tongue would be tied. He was extraordinarily kind and said he regretted it as much for his sake as any other, that Haldane had urged it strongly and that he knew no one more fit for the post. Then he urged me to go in for politics and tried to explain to me that I had a big career there. I was very moved by his kindness, but, of course, without a shred of doubt that what I am doing, especially with the independence it connotes, was five times more worth while than any official job. He could not have been more kind and I felt that after all the mere offer was some little justification of what I have been trying to do. I wish I could picture to you his extraordinary kindness both in what he said and the way in which he made his offer. But I'm quite sure I was right. It would be appalling to be silenced and not to be able to work with the people and the things I really care about. Liberty once felt is too precious to make it worth while to go into harness.

This little squeal of triumph must be forgiven me. I add to it (I know you will want to share in the things that please me) a letter from Meyerson, (the best of French philosophers) telling me that he had read what I wrote in the *Yale Review* about Rousseau and that he was really moved by it. I suppose all flesh is heir to flattery and I was enormously pleased. . . . And I mention because honour commands it one perfect book by E. Villey called the *Sources of Montaigne*. It is a superb *tour de force* for not only does it explain Montaigne as no other book I know but it is by a man blind from birth who is dependent absolutely on others both for reading and writing—an amazing record. . . .

I suppose when you get this you will be scrutinising a new President.[2] I am not greatly moved either way. I like Smith's

---

[2] On November 7 Herbert Hoover defeated Alfred E. Smith in the Presidential election.

speeches, and I dislike Hoover *quâ* person; and as Smith's election would please Felix I am for Smith. But that isn't very intelligent.

Our love heartily to you both.   *Ever affectionately yours, H. J. L.*

October 24, 1928
October 21, '61—(67 years ago) was Balls Bluff
My dear Laski: Your letter just come starts the day with joy. I am really delighted at the offer made to you by the P.M. You deserved the recognition and it makes me happy to know that you received it. I also confidently believe that you were right in declining, although I don't suppose my judgment to be worth much, except as to the general principles. I also am glad at the letter from the illegible French philosopher about your article on Rousseau. I wrote to you to this same effect some time ago. I was moved as he was. Also I thank you for the kind reports as to myself. Eternal doubt is the fate of old age unless it slumps into self-satisfaction! I suppose that I never shall see Nevinson again, but I wish that I might.

My wife showed me the other day an account of an interview with you—*inter alios*—in which you are reported to have said that you found President Wilson easy to work with. I did not know that you ever were in contact with him. When and what was it?

I have no reading to report except records. I wish that I could creep along upon—I can't say your tracks, for you fly—upon your lines of travel. There is a tale from Brandeis that Miss Norton (Charles's sister)[1] is or was (I think she is or was 90 or more) a great authority on Montaigne, as to whom you tell me a wonderful story and that this is a translation in 4 fat volumes with prefaces or headings or something supposed to be by her. But I don't want fat volumes or a translation. The book you mention I should like to see.

I am just in the suspense incident to having circulated an opinion in a case, where we stood 5 to 4 after a reargument.[2] I have not yet received the assent of my 4. V. and Br. have answered—the rest not yet. It is a case that could be decided either way but one in which most of the arguments against my view I thought drool. I hope I didn't show it too freely—but I am nervous.

---

[1] Grace Norton (1834-1926), author of *The Spirit of Montaigne* (1908) and editor of Montaigne's *Essays* (3 vols., 1925).

[2] *Boston Sand and Gravel Co.* v. *United States,* 278 U.S. 41. The majority held that under a special statute authorizing a particular claimant to sue the United States for the recovery of damages suffered in a collision with a naval vessel, interest should not be included in the award. Sutherland, J., delivered a dissenting opinion in which Butler, Sanford, and Stone, JJ., concurred.

I wish I could tell you some tales like those you sent me, but I am too much a recluse to hear any. How one is bothered by past civilities—people to whom one has been polite write that the Venerable Archdeacon A or the Chief Justice B is in one's neighborhood and that it would be nice if you were to do something. I just settle back and do nothing. The Supreme Court is called upon before it calls, and if and as they don't know enough to call I let them slide down the ringing grooves of time. But such things are bores and tax the nerves. Then a woman whose husband one knew once in some correspondence writes that she is ill and hard up and can't I contrive a plan for her relief. Answer no I can't—with a check, but it makes me uncomfortable for weeks.

I began this letter joyful this morning. I send it grumbling after a day in court but things are not going badly.

Aff'ly yours, O. W. Holmes

1720 I Street, N.W., November 13, 1928
My dear Laski: A moment's breathing space and I turn to you. We are adjourned and my work for the moment is done. My last case, given on Saturday evening (it now is Tuesday), has been written, printed, distributed and returned approved by all but one, who I don't doubt will approve it.[1] I have gone over the *Cert.*'s that will be presented when we come in next Monday and I have just this minute sent round a little dissent.[2] I can't think of anything more to do to make myself virtuous and disagreeable. I even have had time to read a good part of Warren's new book *The Making of the Constitution,* which is excellent, and so far as I can judge finally smashes the humbug talked about the economic origin of the Constitution. I thought Beard's book on that theme[3] a stinker, for all its patient research. For notwithstanding the disavowal of personal innuendo, it encouraged and I suspect was meant to encourage the notion that personal interests on the part of the prominent members of the Convention accounted for the attitude they took. Warren has the sense to realize that some men have emotions not dependent on their pocketbooks and brings out very forcibly what I don't doubt were the real dominant motives. Einstein (our minister) was here for a short call and away. He left a volume of *Sceptical Essays* by Bertrand Russell, which entertain so far as I have read, but seem rather light stuff. I suspect B.R. of being a sentimentalist disguised as a sceptic. E.

---

[1] *United States* v. *Lenson,* 278 U.S. 60 (Nov. 19, 1928).

[2] *Liggett Co.* v. *Baldridge,* 278 U.S. 105 (Nov. 19, 1928).

[3] Charles A. Beard, *An Economic Interpretation of the Constitution of the United States* (1913).

also left an account of Hoover written by himself (Einstein)[4] that made me realise that Hoover was very nearly, and not improbably quite, a great man. I was glad he beat Smith, though there has been a sort of fad among the New York highbrows (*New Republic,* Dewey, Cohen, FF *et al.*) to blow Smith's horn, on what seemed to me very inadequate reasons. But in these days *The New Republic* is a partisan like the rest, so far as I can see. My regard for some of its leading spirits makes me keep up my subscription but I should almost like to drop it. I shouldn't like to tell Frankfurter.

It's queer what an effect necessity and desperation have. This last case of mine, a little matter of statutes as to pay of some officer in the Navy, found me in hopeless confusion at the end of the arguments and at the conference, but after I was locked up with it and had to write it, everything seemed to clear up (as far as possible upon a matter inherently doubtful because of obscure language). As I have told you before, I dare say, when you go right up and grab the lion, the skin comes off and it is the same old donkey that you know so well.

Did I mention three little Chinamen making their appearance, sent by Wu? They came and sat silent in my library while I made desperate efforts to talk with them and to say something that they might care to hear. They are at the Washington University Law School I believe, and I feared that they didn't know very definitely what they wanted and weren't getting it. They vanished and I have heard no more. What the devil can I do in such a case? If you know, tell me. Little things worry and bother me I suspect more than when I was younger.

This book of Warren's will take the few hours that I have available, but I wish at such moments you were at hand to give me a hint. Russell has spoken so of Watson's *Behaviorism* that I feel as if I ought to read it at once, in spite of the prejudices that the title raises in my mind. Philosophy always has the right of way, the rest is incident, and *that* I don't believe, with which summary I bid you *adieu.*

How mistaken the notion that one ought to be doing something. It bothers me all the time, and when I take a drive through enchanting colors I find it hard to say to myself with conviction, this is life, this is self-justifying as an end. I don't feel quite right till I turn off a decision.   *Affectionately yours, O. W. H.*

Devon Lodge, 13,XI.28
My dear Justice: . . . I can't imagine where your reporter gets any connection of me with Wilson from. I saw him twice in my

---

[4] Lewis Einstein's "Hoover," 130 *Fort-Nightly Review* 577 (November 1928).

life: once in Washington in February, 1918 and once in Boston in March, 1919, in each case for an hour. I imagine the gent. has either got me mixed up with someone else or misunderstood some remarks of mine that I don't remember making. I add that I was (I have no right to be) a little disappointed in your presidential election. I was glad to see the solid South go at last,[1] and I assume that Hoover is a really able person. But I wish he had said something, for I like a bonny fighter in politics and there seems an unpleasant dourness about him which makes me a little uneasy. However, these things usually work themselves out. I should gather from Felix's lyric in the *New Republic* that he expected a very different result.[2] . . .

Our love to you both. Here it is as mild as June and roses are still being sold on the streets. I hope Washington bears that aspect.						*Ever affectionately yours, H. J. L.*

					1720 I (Eye) Street, November 23, 1928
My dear Laski: Your letter has just been read and I begin my answer at once—I have been shut up this week with a cold— merely in obedience to the doctor's caution. He said I could go to Court on Monday. Being rather seedy I haven't done much besides the cases sent home to me—as it generally is agreed that absent judges having the papers may take part in the decisions. But after finishing Warren's *Making of the Constitution* I did read Bertrand Russell's *Sceptical Essays*—amusing—but as I think I have said, never quite seeming to touch bottom philosophically. He put me on to Dr. Watson's *Behaviorism*—a very good book —though so preoccupied with resolving all our conduct into reflex reactions to stimuli, that he almost denies that consciousness means anything and that memory is more than a useless and misleading word. However much one may believe that men are automata one must recognize that what we call consciousness, memory &c. &c. are part of the phenomena—and we can't say that the phenomena would have been the same if those supposedly epiphenomena were absent. I now am in the middle of a *Life of Zola* by Matthew Josephson printed as No. 1 of Vol. 1 of the Book League Monthly. It was sent to me I suppose as an advertisement. It is very interesting—but not for the first time I find the French literary men unpleasing when seen close to—a sort of heroism in enduring squalor to be sure—but wilfulness and vanity getting into it—mean tricks of self-advertisement, and rather ill smelling. One can't but admire his force and courage in framing a great scheme and carrying it out—but at the same time one

---

[1] Largely because of the fact that Smith was a Roman Catholic much of the Democrat's Southern electorate had voted for Hoover.
[2] "Why I Am for Smith," 56 *New Republic* 292 (Oct. 31, 1928).

doesn't believe there was much real science or philosophy in framing it. As to the carrying out I can't recite as I've read but few of his tales. I used to say dull but improving—I now say I don't doubt improving but dull. I never realized before that Cézanne was a friend of Zola's youth. They seem to have drawn apart. Cézanne I imagine being a much more genuine idealist than Zola. Alas I have not seen enough of Cézanne's painting to have an impression of him. I shall try to see Nevinson's book. He left affectionate memories with us. Is his son still painting and successful?[1] It would be vain for me to try to follow the great procession of your reading. Even if I were not so much slower the court would take most of my time. . . . I forget now what the article was that spoke of you and Wilson. It had a series of interviews—one purporting to be with you and to the effect that I mentioned. I have not worried much about the election, but, as I told you, have the impression that Hoover is not impossibly a great man—I never saw him but once. He was not prepossessing —but as the talk went on for a few minutes he showed a penetrating eye for material facts and left me impressed. This was when he first appeared here on his return from Europe. When I came to your lectues on Stoicism and reading Seneca (my first impression was lectures on Stevenson and reading Samoa) I respect your poly-gluttony. Well, dear boy, I must go back to work. Your letters are an achievement.

Affectionately yours, O. W. Holmes

Devon Lodge, 20.XI.28

My dear Justice: . . . good talk with a German philosopher who told me that the main characteristic of the youth there today is the breakdown of Hegelianism. It is too strait, and too complete for the new generation. To me that is pleasant news; for I think the test of creativeness, at least in social questions, is anti-Hegelism. Indeed, I am sometimes tempted to believe that if one could work out its pedigree in detail, it would turn out to be a kind of stepchild of Calvinism in decay, and this isn't half so far-fetched as such a bald statement would seem to imply. I had also a very moving interview with a young Italian exile—a professor who had published a protest against being compelled to laud the "corporate state" of Mussolini. He was first dismissed; then nearly beaten to death in his own house by a gang of Fascist ruffians; and escaped by night over the Swiss frontier leaving everything he possessed to be confiscated. The problem is what to do with such men. I have got him a few lectures, but that

---

[1] Christopher Richard Wynne Nevinson (1889-1946).

merely keeps a transitory wolf from the door. I wish I could reproduce his description of that escape—the horror of sound, the dread of being caught by the beam of a passing car, the fear of the frontier guards, the sense that every passer-by must know who you are and can hear the beating of your heart. I made the poor fellow divinely happy by getting a friend of mine to make arrangements to take his *fiancée* out of the place by engaging her as his wife's lady's maid, and we hope that this will be effected in the next ten days. Certainly his experience makes you feel that the simplicity of 19th century liberty has much to commend it. I do not like, being old-fashioned, *étatisme* on the new model. . . .

Our love, dearly, to you both. I arouse your curiosity by saying that a really pleasant surprise is in store for you.

Ever affectionately yours, H. J. L.

Devon Lodge, 30.XI.28

My dear Justice: Let me begin with the fulfilment of a duty. I went on Wednesday to a lecture given by Leslie Scott (quite admirable) at the School of Economics. We had some talk of you and he charged me (a) to give you his love and (b) to tell you that he has been overwhelmed with this Indian Commission before which he is counsel, that as soon as it is over he will write to you.[1] . . .

In the way of entertainments I have not done very much. We had a pleasant dinner at Winston's but of that semi-official type where you get no intimate talk. I sat next to a Frenchman who had been in seven cabinets but had never held office for more than six months at a time. He amused me by talk of the severity of English morals. "I hear" he said, "that practically none of your statesmen has a mistress." I said I thought that was so. "Well," he said, with an inimitable shrug of the shoulders, "I have seen their wives, and I do not understand it." I went also to Grand Night at Lincoln's Inn—which I enjoyed greatly though the talk was rather too much in the realm of (to me) unknown legal incident. I was pleased to discover that to all of them F. Pollock was a kind of hero, held in real awe and reverence. The Prime Minister made a charming little speech and the Master of the Rolls a reply that would have been very effective if he had not learned the peroration off by heart. . . .

Our love, as always, to you both.

Ever affectionately yours, H. J. L.

---

[1] The Report of the Indian Statutory Commission, under the chairmanship of Sir John Simon, was issued in May 1930 (*Command Papers* #3568, 3569).

1720 I Street N.W., December 13, 1928

My dear Laski: Another letter today and the last one not answered! Well, I have been hard driven—and now am rewarded
with a hope of leisure in our adjournment, as my work is done.
I haven't looked at *Elizabeth and Essex*—but I may—and I feel
as if I should find your criticisms just and delicate—also I am
glad you saw Leslie Scott—a mighty good man. Why don't they
make him a judge? In connection with having finished my work
I forgot to mention that Brandeis looked in on me and said he
came to see how the leisure class live. Frankfurter lunched and
spent a good piece of the afternoon with me yesterday. He
seemed in fine condition. He is another who like you and to
some extent Wu (who has just printed a book of essays) amaze
me by the number of their swift penetrating contacts with such
a variety of subjects. I keenly enjoyed his visits. To put the
comble just before my supper this evening Dorothy Brown and a
clever young woman whose name I didn't get called here and I
had a brisk jaw with them. I don't see many people outside the
Court in these days. Another exception was the British Ambassador a few days ago, an old friend and a very sweet nature I
should think. He surprised me by asking me for my book of
Legal Papers—I guess on account of his son who though with
Morgan has not given up his interest in the law. Frankfurter's
wife and another have just edited the letters of Sacco and Vanzetti. I talked with him a little on the subject. He is convinced
of their innocence—but I was not convinced that too much talk
had not been made on the theme. The *New Republic* recurs to it
from time to time. But the *New Republic* strikes me as having
become partisan in tone of late—judging from an occasional
glance. It seemed to nag at Coolidge—and I rather think believes
a number of things that I don't. I come nearer to reading it than
I do reading any other newspaper—but I can't be said to read
that.

I went to the Congressional Library this morning and tried un-
successfully to get the *History of Political Thought in the XVI
Century* [J. W. Allen], that you recommended—and so fell back
on Legouis and Cazamian's *History of English Literature*—passages in which struck me greatly last summer. But I get little
time to read. Each day brings demands that take time. I was
pleased to learn the other day that Harcourt Brace &c. had sold
over 2500 copies of my *Legal Papers*—which seems to be doing
extraordinarily well—when the contents are considered. Apropos
of the German who looked so long at your library have you no
anxieties lest some such should whip a rare pamphlet into his
pocket? I keep my most thief-worthy volumes out of reach—so
far as may be. I wish I saw more of the illustrious to tell you

about and had your power to tell of the meetings, but if you
keep up relations with a recluse you must take the consequences.
                              Affectionately yours, O. W. H.
Vandevanter lent me the privately printed letters of Dickens to
(Miss Beadnell) the prototype of Dora in *David Copperfield* including later ones when their acquaintance was resumed—and
according to the editor she appeared in her later phase as Flora
(I think the name is) in *Little Dorrit*—Clennam's early love. I
think it a fishy business to print such things.

                              Devon Lodge, 16.XII.28
My dear Justice: If I guess aright, this should reach you about
Xmas day. It brings you both our warm affection and every sort
of good wish. I hope the cold has really gone. Brandeis writes
me that he has never known you in better form. . . .

   Of other things let us chant. I ask you to welcome with me
the advent to this house of a perfect copy of *L'Apologie de René
Herpin* which is Bodin's defence of his *République* and also the
discovery of a copy of the first edition of Pascal's *Pensées* for
ninepence, which I sold for eight pounds. I think I let it go too
cheap, but I did not desire the reputation of avarice. I have also
found a nice collection of French Utopias *circa* 1700—and they
interest me enormously not only because they are very good reading but also because they confirm a pet hobby of mine about the
influence of the voyages *e.g.* the Jesuit Relations on political
theory. It is clear that these things were well known to Rousseau
and profoundly affected him, as well they might. . . .

   In the way of reading there is not much to record. I have had
a good, stiff dose of Burke in preparation for a bicentenary piece
I have to write. How unanswerable he is, and how wrongheaded!
I re-read, too, Morley on him, with pleasure, but with less pleasure than I have known. I thought I detected a certain primness
of mind. Then, for work, I read Puffendorf who seemed to me
somewhere between fifth and sixth-rate; a reputation quite beyond my understanding. Dear little Wu sent me his volume of
essays and though I could not share all his enthusiasms (*e.g.*) I
am unmoved by Stammler and (*pace* you) Dewey's *Nature and
Experience,* I thought they showed a charming spirit and I was
glad to be able to write him a sincere note of congratulation.
And I must not forget to add that I was sent for review a volume
of Americana by various people called *The American Caravan*—
I read a good deal in the train and gathered from it that most
women around the age of twenty in New York cannot keep out
of strange men's bedrooms—an experience I never met in my day;
proof, I suppose, that new economic conditions rapidly change the

mores of a civilisation. Felix sent me the *Sacco-Vanzetti Letters* which his wife had edited. I do not think I should have printed so large a bulk. But even as they are, one cannot help being deeply moved by them, and they reinforce one's fear that a grave judicial error was made by the Massachusetts Courts—I need not say to you that I do not think your Court had a right to interfere. But if I were a Massachusetts judge I should not, especially as new facts emerge, feel very happy.

Chafee wrote me at length about Harvard. He was, gratefully to my ear, lyrical about Felix, and Brandeis writes to me that F. in his judgment [is] "the most useful lawyer in the United States". . . .

Love to you both.   *Ever affectionately yours, H. J. L.*

                              1720 Eye Street, December 29, 1928 [1]
My dear Laski: This will not be too late to wish you a happy New Year—or to express my happiness in thinking from your letters and what I hear that all is going successfully with you. I was delighted also at what you tell me in your letter (received a day or two ago) about Frankfurter—what Chafee and Brandeis say. I also am unmoved by Stammler but grieve that you are not hit by Dewey's *Nature and Experience.* Wu will be proud of your congratulations. His exaltation of me coupled with a letter that I received later, and that I considered one of the chief rewards of my life, make me feel as if I had finished, although I don't think it wrong in me to keep on at the work *non obstant* misgivings. There is no use in talking about that. One must make up one's mind as best one can. You speak of Morley's primness of mind which expresses well enough the quality that has limited my pleasure in his writing and led me to read him but rarely. It was a disappointment years and years ago after the first delight at meeting a civilized man to feel this limitation and to realize that he wasn't opening Paradise. I have had time during the recess to read the first volume of the *History of English Literature* that you put me onto—Legouis and 2nd vol. Cazamian. I read part of volume 2 last summer and was more impressed than I am by volume 1 though that is admirable and instructive. I should have liked to read in the authors referred to, as I went along, but I get too little time. I shan't attempt to finish volume 2 at present as a sitting begins next week, and I have lighter stuff, such as *Elizabeth and Essex*—uncommon good reading as Strachey always is. My Secretary gave me *The South Wind,* Norman Douglas, an extravaganza of which I should think there was too much, but I have read only a little. Christmas naturally is less

---

[1] A brief note from Laski, dated December 26, is omitted.

of an event with me than formerly but still, like every other damn thing it took time. And after this brief bulletin I must be off to a conference of the JJ.   *Affectionately yours, O. W. H.*

Devon Lodge, 29.XII.28
My dear Justice: I ought to have written you earlier, but I have had my annual dose of influenza, and that has meant a week in bed. However I am about again and rather rested than anything else; and tonight I go off with Frida to Antwerp for a week's real holiday.

The main experience in bed was the rediscovery of Thackeray. Granted everything that can be said against him (I) that he sniffles a little too much (II) that he has a grain of Podsnappery (III) that he lays on too thick the colours of vice and virtue, I hereby take solemn oath that he was a very great man. Item, he could by God, tell a story; item, he could make living creatures of flesh and blood; item, he was a great historian—where else in the world do Swift and Johnson and Richardson and Steele stand out so perfectly as they do in *Esmond and The Virginians?* No; it may not be fashionable, but I go bail for Thackeray. Second I desire to affirm that we talk much nonsense about the supreme aphoristic talent of the French. I conjure you to read Pearsall Smith's exquisite *Treasury of English Aphorisms,* and tell me if what you find there is one whit inferior to La Rochefoucauld or Pascal or Vauvenargues? That's a book, if you like! I desire further to affirm that I have discovered a great philosopher—Emile Meyerson whose *Explication dans les sciences* has revealed a new world to me. It's a world, if I make myself plain, for Sundays; but it is extraordinarily revealing, and it gives me the uncomfortable sense that the recent history of science makes Berkeleian idealism more satisfactory as an epistemology than any other view. I mean that admit the existence of a reality "out there," scientific discovery is, at bottom, simply a system of observer's patterns which at most have statistical validity. I add that Meyerson took me to Hume and I was more impressed by the sheerly devastating brilliance of his mind than I can ever remember before. And I wish I knew why the logicians have made so small an advance in the theory of induction. . . .

Our love to you both, and all good wishes for '29.
Ever affectionately yours, H. J. L.

1720 I Street N.W., January 11, 1929
My dear Laski: You have adventures even when in bed with the influenza—or just out of it. Apropos of your advertising friend I seem to remember that the sedate Croly in the *New Republic*

years ago spoke of advertising as a necessary and proper means
to success. (It may have been some understrapper but it rests in
my mind as from him.) You and I prefer the other way. I believe that advertising has become a science, on which Brandeis
could expound, having been counsel in former days, with psy-
chologic insight which it would be interesting to know. But I
settle more and more into ignorance—and in my brethren's talk
at luncheon am almost painfully impressed by my outsideness
from current affairs. We shall be powdering along for another
week and then have an adjournment. We have had nothing that
excited me very much, although one or two cases stirred up the
newspapers.

As to your Berkeleian idealism I suppose you know my short
formulas—I have repeated them often enough in talk and print.
I begin by an act of faith. I assume that I am not dreaming,
although I can't prove it—that you exist in the same sense that
I do—and that gives me an outside world of some sort (and I
think the *ding an sich*)—so I assume that I am in the world not
it in me. Next when I say that a thing is true I only mean that
I can't help believing it—but I have no grounds for assuming
that my can't helps are cosmic can't helps—and some reasons
for thinking otherwise. I therefore define the truth as the system
of my intellectual limitations—there being a tacit reference to
what I bet is or will be the prevailing can't help of the majority
of that part of the world that I count. The ultimate—even hu-
manly speaking, is a mystery. I don't see that it matters whether
you call it motion or thought or X—all we know of it is that it
is capable when tied in a certain knot of producing you and me
and all the rest of the show. Absolute truth is a mirage. Thus I
am indifferent to the Berkeley business. Also as I see no reasons
for attributing cosmic importance to man, other than that attaching
to whatever is, I regard him as I do the other species (except that
my private interests are with his) having for his main business to
live and propagate, and for his main interest food and sex. A few
get a little further along and get pleasure in it, but are fools if they
are proud.

Have I mentioned *South Wind*—by Norman Douglas? It is hard
to conceive writing or reading it—but when you do and don't ask
improvement but are content with a few hours pleasure I'm
blowed if you don't get it. I must turn back to the law.

Affectionately yours, O. W. Holmes

Devon Lodge, 15.I.29
My dear Justice: Your letter was doubly welcome, for it showed
that you were not troubled by the prevalent influenza. I have had

a dose of it (in Antwerp) and though I am back at work, it has left a certain deadness which is irritating. However, I am well enough content.

. . . Then I read and greatly enjoyed the whole of Darwin's correspondence. I lay my hand on my heart and say that there never was a more loveable great man—always modest, never aggressive, simple and kindly, and permanently open to new ideas. When you compare him as a person to Descartes or Newton or Leibnitz or Goethe he simply overtops them altogether. Really it is impossible to rate him too highly. I read, also, Vinet's *Études sur Pascal* which I conjure you to note for Beverly in the summer, an exquisite book. Probably he makes Pascal a little too Protestant but he is really inside that tortured being and if you do not know it I am sure it would please you greatly. . . .

With the beginning of term, I am hard at it on the usual lines. But I have a pleasant interlude on Thursday when I go off to Paris for a week-end to deliver a lecture at the Sorbonne. That, I hope, means a couple of days pleasant hunting in the book-shops. . . .

Our love to you both. Take care, don't get influenza, don't overwork and above all, don't let the notion of resignation cross your mind.   *Ever affectionately yours, H. J. L.*

1720 I (*Eye*) *Street N.W., January 27, 1929*
My dear Laski: A moment of leisure has come, not yet turned to much account, as it is beginning rather than ending. I have however read a detective story sent to me by Knopf—*Red Harvest*—by Dashiell Hammett—somebody shot on every page—and the narrative hero coming out unharmed and unhung when by probabilities he ought to have been finished one way or another—quite absorbing though suggesting doubts. Brandeis put me onto *King John*—Aeschylian lines as Swinburne says—curious that Shakespeare can't resist the word-quibbling which I suppose comes from *Euphues*. There are some lines of it in the beautiful tragic talk of Arthur to Hubert, when he is pleading for his eyes. That led to *Richard III*—rather amusing, his announcing himself as a villain at the start and giving you such doses of villainy straight along. (The editor of the reprint of the First Folio says "Villain" in the opening soliloquy means churl—I don't see why, quite—as he goes on to tell his acts and schemes.) The Bard seems lonely in his greatness. I don't make very much of his contemporaries—except Marlowe—who was the devil of a fellow. Also today I began Redlich's biography of the Emperor Francis Joseph—and am much interested. It occasionally is a little obscure because his familiarity with the whole business leads him at times to take a

good deal for granted. It isn't the kind of thing I like to read—it isn't in the line of my business and as well *Elizabeth and Essex*. I rather grudge time to personal histories—even when important. But what does it matter how I pass my time! I should be more sensible if I could loaf unscrupulously. You speak of answering many letters asking imbecile questions—I hand such letters to my secretary and tell him to regret that my duties don't leave me time &c. Autograph letters that don't enclose a stamp I tear up—arguing that if they don't care to pay two cents for my signature I don't care two cents to send it. I notice that many, I should think most of the stampless requests, come from intelligent young Hebrews—if I can judge by the names. I told my secretary to make a note of Vinet on Pascal—but the title does not draw me greatly. Apropos of what you say of Darwin (which I readily believe) it may interest you that a connection of mine, Clark,—has given comfort to the fundamentalists by publishing an article repudiating evolution as popularly conceived—and disbelieving in the missing link.[1] He is a distinguished man of science—and from past talks with my wife's nephew Gerrit Miller—another distinguished man of science—I gather that he shares the disbelief. He wrote an article some time ago discrediting the Piltdown man[2]—I believe generally accepted outside of England. Of course the chaps don't take theological views. Clark has published a schematism of development[3] which I don't understand and can't talk about but some competent people think he will stand beside Darwin some day. I think I mentioned a book on behaviorism once.[4] He seems to think that consciousness is shown to be a futile conception by the fact that no one tells or, he would say, can tell what it is. That seems to me silly. When I was a small boy my father taught me a philosophical lesson by asking me to tell him how salt tasted. You can't—and you can't tell a blind person how colors look. There are many questions to which you must know the answer at first hand or you can't know it. You don't disprove an ultimate by showing that I can't go beyond it. This detached reflection I interject for no particular reason—except my desire to mark my disrespect for what the writer thought a sockdolager.

Affectionately yours, O. W. H.

---

[1] Austin H. Clark, "Animal Evolution," 3 *Quarterly Review of Biology* 523 (December 1928).

[2] Gerrit S. Miller, Jr., "The Jaw of the Piltdown Man," 65 *Smithsonian Miscellaneous Collection*, no. 12, 1-31 (November 1915).

[3] "A New Classification of Animals," *Bulletin de L'Institut Océanographique*, No. 400 (1921).

[4] *Supra*, p. 241.

Devon Lodge, 5.II.29

My dear Justice: You must forgive my long silence. But the excuse is the good one that I have had a slight, but painful, attack of pneumonia which has badly embarrassed my time-table. I am much better, and back again at college; but I am going slow until I am really on my feet again. The nuisance of it is that I shall have to give up my cherished American plan for Easter—partly money, and partly the need to make up lost time. I hate doing it, for I had built enormously on the pleasure of seeing you and Felix. But if the decks are to be clear for action and I am ever to have leisure for my book I simply must have that Easter vacation as a locked-up recluse. Damn, and damn! Why are the days so short? . . .   *Ever affectionately yours, H. J. L.*

Devon Lodge, 12.II.29

My dear Justice: A delightful letter from you synchronises with my sense of complete fitness. I feel that I could leap over at any rate moderate sized hills. I was intensely interested by what you said of your scientists' attitude to Darwinism. I speak of course with ignorance and humility; but I have the sense first that the reaction against it is a little exaggerated and secondly that it remains profoundly unsatisfactory that it should not be able to explain (I) the origin of variation or (II) how a variation presented can, often enough, be of any utility for survival in its original stages. But granted all that, the fact that natural selection takes place seems to me solidly proved enough, and also that evolution is real, even though the details of the actual pedigree are much thinner and more uncertain than the original enthusiasts thought. And at any rate the supreme result of the seventy years since 1859 has been a body-blow to the Eternal from which he will find it difficult to recover. That is what really matters most. I remain permanently and impenitently anti-clerical. And the settlement of the papal question only makes me feel this the more strongly.[1] . . . I agree with Voltaire that there will be really no peace in the world until the last King has been strangled in the bowels of the last priest. I hope you warmly agree.

I must, next, let off my *cri de cour* [*sic*] for the temper boils within. I have had two literary adventures which make one foam at the mouth. In 1721 Lord Macclesfield was impeached for corruption. He was a great friend of Mandeville, the author of the *Fable of the Bees,* and all the latter's unpublished correspondence

---

[1] On February 11 the Lateran Treaty between the Pope and Mussolini had been signed. The Vatican received recognition of its claim of political sovereignty and the Italian state accepted the Roman Catholic religion as the sole religion of the state.

is in the Macclesfield archives. He wrote much to the continental philosophers and their replies are said to be there by the score. I wrote to Lord M. asking for permission either to see the papers or to have copies made, or even, if he wishes, to have them deposited at the British Museum for scrutiny. He wrote back two lines of refusal to say that a desire to see family papers on the part of an entire stranger seemed to him simply unnecessary intrusion. Next I discovered that a gentleman in Sussex possessed mountains of unpublished letters of Burke as also all the replies to Burke's pamphlets with his annotations thereon. I wrote and made a similar request and got a refusal on the ground that he did not desire publication. Can you imagine a more disgusting dog in the manger policy? The second irritates me more than the first for one of the things he has is Burke's copy of Tom Paine's *Rights of Man* which a friend of mine has seen literally covered with annotations from top to bottom. We ought certainly to have an Act of Parliament giving a right of entry to the Record Office to make copies of all historic papers after the lapse of seventy-five years. As it is, these two fellows could burn every page they possessed and no one could do anything. Let me add that I did not write out of a blue sky but obtained introductions in each case from personal friends of the two curmudgeons and then got those curt refusals. It really does make one angry.

. . . On Sunday Walter Lippmann and his wife came to dinner. I always like him, even though he lacks the charm of Felix and a certain moral fineness that Felix excels in. But he has great perceptiveness and sound judgment, though I think he needs to know a little more history and not to think that the next five weeks is what really matters. He told me the tragic news of poor Croly's illness, which he seemed to think would permanently incapacitate Croly. I never made much of his writing, but I always greatly respected his devotion and rectitude. They will find it difficult to replace him on the *New Republic*. . . .

Our love to you both. We are living amid arctic cold.

Ever affectionately yours, H. J. L.

1720 Eye Street N.W., February 15, 1929

My dear Laski: Your news is saddening and disquieting—you say you are better but are you taking all the proper precautions? I believe your wife can be trusted if you are obedient—but not all husbands are. I don't think you had mentioned to me your plan of a visit at this time but I had heard of it and was looking forward to it.

Your letter comes just at the end of an adjournment, when of course I am in a scrabble and so must cut this short. I haven't read a great deal. I think I mentioned looking through the *Malleus Maleficarum*[1] and the amazing introduction dated 1927 of the English translator. I am now just finished a little book of excerpts from Spinoza with some slight illustrations and an arrangement intended to elucidate.[2] It doesn't do me much good for Spinoza anyhow is rather tedious and I don't believe his postulates or accept his reasoning from them. It is his view of the universe that is the thing. He sees as I see it more nearly than any of the old that I can think of.

Redlich was here the other night and talked a steady stream for 5 hours which was rather long for me but full of brilliancy, fire, and amusement. He put me on to *À l'ombre de la croix* which I have read but a chapter of—but which won't take long— and I have another novel lent me by Gerrit Miller—*Dieu protège le Tsar*—L. Dumur—which he recommended to me to read I forget exactly *quo intuitu*—and this p.m. comes a volume from Felix—*The Bases of Modern Science* by J. W. N. Sullivan which I long to get at but which must take its turn—for tomorrow is a conference which so far as I can see must be followed by either an opinion or a dissent *per me* as my lord McReynolds may vote tomorrow. On Monday we begin a four weeks sitting—and there will be little reading I fear.

Did I ever mention *John Brown's Body*—a poem by Benét? A view of the Civil War—the last kind of thing that I want to read —but I was a good deal impressed by it. I am amused by your American exiles whom you saw in Paris—a strong presumption against them I should think—and interested by your recurrence to Thackeray. It may be age, or accident—or the small print but I find the old boys and pretty much all the new ones too long-winded for my impatience—yet I can read what sounds to me pretty drooly in Spinoza without discomfort—age I rather think draws some new lines.

Please remember that you have charge of an unusual and valuable instrument and take care of it. Tell your wife that I believe in and rely on her. Your little daughter must be quite grown up by this time—is she becoming a companion?

Affectionately yours, O. W. Holmes

Washington, D.C., February 22, 1929
My dear Laski: Your most interesting letter, received last night, raises a doubt in my mind. You boil with wrath that Lord

---

[1] *Malleus Maleficarum* (Rev. Montague Summers, tr., 1928) was a fifteenth-century treatise on witchcraft written by James Sprenger and Henry Kramer. The devout translator's belief in witches was no less intense than that of the original authors.

[2] *The Philosophy of Spinoza* (Ratner, ed., 1927).

Macclesfield would not let you see the Mandeville correspondence.
Is it not a case of literary curiosity against the feeling of family
privacy? I don't suppose that there is likely to be much philosophical importance in the letters. There may be matters bearing
on the character of an ancestor. While I incline to sympathize
with you, I should not dare to say that I thought Lord M. wrong.
The other case seems stronger for you—but even there I doubt
if it warrants more than vexation. I should hesitate to condemn
a man who refused to allow a picture to be photographed, even
though personally I might deem it more public spirited to allow
the photograph to be taken.

Next as to the views of my connection, Clark, on evolution. He
is a very considerable, very able, and very learned scientific man,
and knows what he is talking about. Of course his discourse was
laid hold of by the Bible men and I am afraid that he may have
thought of the publicity that that would give him—but I don't
suppose that he is any more a Bible man than you are—and
speaking ignorantly I take his view to be an outcrop of a different
scheme of development, which I don't pretend to understand. I
suppose that his belief is an extension of what De Vries showed
happens in some plants[1]—a sudden inexplicable jump. In an interesting book that Frankfurter sent to me lately, *The Bases of
Modern Science,* (J. W. N. Sullivan, pub. by Ernest Benn, London) I read that even among the mathematicians one theory now
offered is a theory of "emergence" by which "the properties of a
whole cannot always be deduced from the properties of its con-
stituents" and some of the evidences as to man that have been
relied on have been attacked. Some years ago my wife's nephew
Gerrit Miller, a really eminent scientific man published an elaborate examination of the Piltdown man relics and concluded that
they came from an ape (or some of them—I don't remember the
details). Of course the English stood up for their discovery but
my impression is that the weight of scientific opinion is with him.
Clark, (the man in question) I believe regards other supposed
exhibits of the missing link in the same way. I shouldn't think
that anyone except a man in the business could form an opinion of
any weight. We naturally incline toward anything that contributes
to ease of thought. The postulate of science is that everything can
be explained—but with the view of man that I take, this perfectly
well may not be so. I think it unlikely that we know anything
ultimate about the universe or have faculties that fit us to do more
than to adjust ourselves to it and to live. You, I suspect, have
more of a creed and empassioned enthusiasm than I have—

---

[1] Hugo de Vries (1848-1935), Dutch botanist whose experimental study
of evolution led to his formulation of the theory of mutation in *The Mutation Theory* (Farmer and Darbishire, tr., 1909-10).

though your creed is not the orthodox one. All the foregoing has
nothing to do with clericalism—I don't believe in it any more than
you—I think it childish—and yesterday just before I received
your letter I was hearing of a lady, speaking of Mussolini and the
pope, asking who cares about the Pope? At times I am a little
disturbed at exhibitions of ecclesiastical power, but I have such a
conviction that it is doomed that I don't care to hurry its fate. It
helps to keep order *ad interim*. I ought to add that my conviction
is only faith in the prevalence of reason in the long run (coupled
with indications on the specific points that have struck me) but I
am well aware how long reason may be kept under by what man
wants to believe. I do despise the Will to Believe.

Your faithfulness to the earlier generation—Thackeray—Trollope especially—always pleases me, while I share it but imperfectly. Since *Phineas Phinn,* 50 years ago, I haven't had the
courage to tackle Trollope. In my old age I am more bored by
novels than I used to be, while I am not bored at all by *The
Bases of Modern Science* or even by Spinoza—who, as I have
said before, although tedious and using premises and reasoning
that I disbelieve, sees the world as I do more nearly than any of
the old. I have just read a little book of selected translations,
because it was sent to me and had a recommendation by John
Dewey—another man who sees the world somewhat as I do. I
haven't heard of Croly's illness—I must inquire. We seem to agree
about him. I have a great respect for his intelligence but don't
willingly read his writing. I am availing myself of Washington's
birthday. We are sitting and having cases that I dislike about rates
and the Interstate Commerce Commission. I listen with respect
but without envy to questions by Brandeis and Butler using the
words of railroading and rate-making that I imperfectly understand. To be familiar with business is a great (secondary) advantage. Someone said of Brandeis, He is not afraid of a Balance
Sheet. His experience at the bar is an infinite advantage in many
cases. Butler has had something of the same, and Vandevanter
has land law and Indians at his fingers' end. McReynolds is the
boss in Admiralty because he has carried through a series of decisions that I don't believe in at all—although I don't [believe] he
had any special knowledge before his victories in that field.

I don't remember whether I have mentioned Redlich's being
here the other evening and discoursing as copiously and amusingly
as always. I read his *Francis Joseph* with profit to my prejudices.
We soon shall have the inauguration in which I shall endeavour
to avoid the death that it is apt to inflict on the old who sit out
of doors for the swearing in and address of the President. Four
days later I shall be 88 if I live till then. The straws gradually
accumulate on the camel's back, but only slowly I am glad to say.

You don't say, but I infer that all traces of the pneumonia have disappeared.   *Affectionately yours, O. W. Holmes*

Devon Lodge, 26.II.29

My dear Justice: Life flows on in the normal way, and I cannot complain of inertia. I have given a public lecture on Hobbes; I have written a long article on the danger of uniformity;[1] I broadcasted a long talk on Haldane's *Autobiography* and I am just finishing the notes on the six lectures I have to give next week at Geneva. And as I feel extraordinarily fit, I conclude that work is very good for me.

The most interesting thing I have done since I wrote last was a dinner at Winston Churchill's. It was good fun in two ways. First, I had a great scrap with him and an Admiral on the meaning of maritime rights. I maintaining the simple thesis that the British conception and the American merely derived from their different situations; they, poor souls, arguing with true English ὕβρις that the British view was essential to the safety of the world. May I whisper that Admirals may be great technicians but as students of logic they have a certain lack of profundity? Winston told us one glorious story. He reads all the letters sending conscience money to the exchequer. One enclosed a cheque for 22/6 and ran as follows. "Dear Sir, I enclose a cheque for the payment of a dog license for three years. You may say I have no dog: that is true. You may insist that I have never had a dog: that is also true. But I have a wife who is such a bitch that I feel morally obliged to accept the responsibilities of my position. Yours faithfully." And one brilliant remark was made there. We were discussing the suppressed novel *The Well of Loneliness* which deals with sexual relations between women and defends them. Winston asked if anyone knew the author and a young civil servant said he did. "What kind of a person is she?" "I should say," answered the civil servant, "that she is a self-made man." One thing, by the way, impressed me and that is the religiosity of naval men. There were three of them there, and they were all Bibleolaters if there was such a word. One told me quite seriously that during the war he always tried the bible for a text before issuing orders for the coming action. I could not think of any comment worthy of the occasion.

Reading, too, has been very pleasant. Haldane's *Autobiography* in which you, Felix and I have honourable mention, is very interesting reading. It brings out his great powers of work and

---

[1] Presumably "The Dangers of Obedience," 159 *Harper's Magazine* (June 1929); reprinted in *The Dangers of Obedience and Other Essays* (1930).

organisation, his essential kindliness, and a certain sweet vanity he had. It isn't, I think, the book of a first class mind but certainly of one who knew how to make the utmost of the ability he had. I hope you will have time to glance at it. Then I have read Zimmern's new book[2] which has much in it of extraordinary profundity. The essay on "The Prospects of Democracy" is really a masterpiece and deserves, I think, a quite special place in contemporary political literature. And a Frenchman Faÿ sent me a book called *The American Experiment* which while not always by any means first-class has again and again some really interesting *aperçus*. And a charming book on the French novelists from 1500-1800,[3] quite short but crowded with ideas and doing well what I have long wanted to see done—explaining the changes in the form of the novel in terms of changes in the social milieu of each period. And I add that Compton MacKenzie's *The Three Wayfarers* [sic][4] is a tip-top spy story which I earnestly recommend as an accompaniment to solitaire. . . .

I hope all goes well at 1727 [sic]. I am looking forward to Hoover's cabinet. Felix, I imagine, will be pleased at Stimson's nomination.[5]

Our love to you both.   *Ever affectionately yours, H. J. L.*

Devon Lodge, 16.III.29

My dear Justice: I got back from Geneva nearly a week ago to find myself in the midst of tragedy. My colleague Allyn Young died from pneumonia after only two days illness, and the world has lost a great economist and teacher and I a friend and colleague such as one rarely finds. I can't easily put on paper what a remarkable man he was. But his great quality was humanism—the ability to take difficult technical themes and deal with them not as a paper problem, but as they emerged into life with all its problems. His death makes me feel as though I had lost a limb, for ever since he came over from Harvard eighteen months ago he and I had fought every issue together on the same side. The tragedy is greater because his wife is blind and Frida and I have had the very difficult task of helping her, poor thing, to make arrangements for her return to America. You know how these things cut deep.

Geneva was extraordinarily interesting. The lectures went well, and I met every sort and kind of person. One or two you may

[2] *America and Europe, and Other Essays* (1929).
[3] Probably Frederick Charles Green, *French Novelists, Manners and Ideas from the Renaissance to the Revolution* (1929).
[4] *The Three Couriers* (1929).
[5] From March 1929, to 1933, Henry L. Stimson was Hoover's Secretary of State.

know by name. The outstanding one was Eugène Borel,[1] the
Swiss international lawyer, brilliant, witty, and altogether devoid
of the "professional" attitude one so often finds in the continentals.
I met, too, Struppe[2] [sic] the German lawyer, full of learning and
ideas but a much more formal type who never moved outside the
confines of his subject but talked extremely well within them.
And I enjoyed Anzilotti,[3] the Italian member of the International
Court, who, though much older, reminded me in his verve and
brilliancy, of Felix. I had breakfast with Stresemann,[4] the German
statesman, who struck me as subtle and shrewd, and honourable. I
add that I thought him without exception the ugliest man I have
ever seen. I had a brief talk with Austen Chamberlain[5] who said
he remembered you at their London house forty years ago and
that his sister never ceased to talk of you and her pleasure, which
I well understood, in your letters. Austen is very queer. He so
obviously means to do right and be kind but he has some defect
of personality which always, even when he is saying the kindest
thing, gives the impression of conscious superiority, so that, as
Titulescu, the Rumanian prime minister [sic][6] remarked to me,
you feel offended even when he is doing you a favour. Most of the
others I saw would not be names to you. But I must put on record
my sense of the high purpose by which all the officials of the
League are informed. It really is impressive to meet a real and
coherent zeal for a world-interest above the separate interest of
the different states there. The Polish delegate to the League put it
to me very well: he said he came there a fervent nationalist and
after three years of routine work he found himself writing home
to his government that certain policies he was asked to recommend were simply unfair in the light of European needs. . . .

I was enormously interested in your accounts of the critical
attitude to Darwinism. I met young Haldane[7] the other day and
put the substance of it to him and he said that most of the
younger biologists here would endorse it. He made the interesting

---

[1] Eugène Borel (1862-   ), Professor of International Law at th
Académie du Droit International and Swiss member of the Permanent Cour
of Arbitration, 1928-1946.

[2] Probably Karl Strupp (1886-1940), Professor of International Law a
Frankfurt, 1926-1933.

[3] Dionisio Anzilotti (1869-1950) was a member of the Permanent Cou
of International Justice from 1922 to 1930 and President of the Tribuna
from 1928 to 1930.

[4] Gustav Stresemann (1878-1929), as Foreign Minister of Germany from
1923 until his death in October 1929, rendered monumental services t
Germany in restoring her to the family of nations.

[5] Sir Austen Chamberlain was Foreign Minister in the Baldwin govern
ment.

[6] Nicolas Titulescu (1883-1941) at this time was Minister to England an
Rumanian delegate at the League; the Prime Minister of Rumania was Juliu
Manin.

[7] J. B. S. Haldane, distinguished biologist; nephew of Lord Haldane.

point that most Victorian science suffered from excessive simplicity and that now the balance is being painfully redressed. I
imagine there is truth in that; and I incline to think that the
process of redress will in the end be even more fatal to the religious outlook than was the case with the old frontal attack of
sixty-years ago. Though, obviously, there are dangers of religious
revival in terms of political tactics, as in Italy and in Spain; and'
it would be very interesting to measure the strength of religion
in England by seeing what happened to a political party which
came out definitely for disestablishment of the Church. I do not
know. Indifference grows by leaps and bounds; but the modern
electorate is very sentimental and I should not like to bet that the
indifference would reflect itself in the polls.

One piece of news will, I hope, please you. Yale University has
asked me to go there next March for three months. In principle I
have accepted, and if the finance turns out satisfactorily I shall
certainly go. You can imagine that the prospect of some week-ends
in Washington really attracts me. I long for some talk.

Our united love to you both. I am writing at a table covered
with snowdrops and daffodils. *Ever affectionately yours, H. J. L.*

1720 I Street N.W., March 17, 1929
My dear Laski: Pollock finds just fault with this paper—but I
haven't as yet succeeded in getting blocks that suited me as well
as the Capitol where we are furnished. So I allow my comfort to
prevail over other considerations. I have been under a pressure
that ceased only yesterday since my birthday—we were sitting
for arguments. I had two opinions to write and *certioraris* to
examine—and I have answered near 70 letters and telegrams. But
we are adjourned and my work is done. Only small items outside.
The only thing that I have read is an odious tale *Dieu protège le
Tsar*—L. Dumur—the first part battles that needed a map and
explanations to be more than a whirl of names, with too much
blood and guts—the last the doings of Rasputin with the highest
ladies in Russia—if true not well to tell—if, as I guess, the dream
of a writer seeking sensation, a dirty business—but it makes me
want to know something authentic about that seemingly unspeakable person. Like the life of Francis Joseph it makes one feel that
almost anything is better than to have the fate of an empire and
the best it holds depend upon the whim of a single incompetent
person.

Now I have for two or three hours a little book that Redlich
recommended—*L'ombre de la croix*—(J. & J. Tharaud) a strik-
ingly impressive account of the life of squalidly poor Jews in
Hungary—a life in which their religion plays an incredibly great

part. I think if the promised leisure keep on I shall read the
second edition of Dewey's *Experience and Nature*—partly re-
written. The publisher wrote to me that Dewey (whom I never
have seen) was much pleased at something that I wrote about it
to Wu—and that he rather indiscreetly published. You, I think,
got nothing from it—but it impressed me greatly. I must try to get
a look at Haldane's *Autobiography*—and I note what you say of
Zimmern's last book—and readily believe it. You don't mention the
name of the book on the French novelists—1600 [*sic*]-1800.[1] I
wish I had it just now—for it sounds about what I want. There
are moments when aimless repose or equally aimless wandering—
seem better than to have some damned end in view—even so
vague a one as improvement—but it is a frame of mind very hard
to get into when one is generally kept somewhat tense. Wouldn't
it be great if destiny should let me reach, if not 90 at least the
90th year, still working—not that it matters—but age makes
egotists of us all.   *Ever affectionately yours, O. W. Holmes*

Devon Lodge, 25.III.29
My dear Justice: Term being over, I am free again, and I feel
like a young ram upon the mountains. For next term is an easy
one, and I can really look forward to almost six months of safe
work. The last ten days have been very pleasant. A charming
lunch with the Swedish Minister,[1] at which Ramsay MacDonald
and Snowden were guests. It was a good political gossip which I
enjoyed less for the gossip than for the queer angle it threw on
the political mind. I should say that no politician lives more than
six or seven months ahead and that at least half his time he is talking to convince himself. He is curiously grateful when you can
give his argument philosophic form, and equally curiously eager
to give any argument special weight if it comes from a source he
approves. . . . I was entertained to lunch by the five senior
officers of the Army Class at the School—a delightful set of fellows. One had the V. C. with a bar and we made him tell the
story of their attainment. I wish I could describe the calm way
in which he described crossing no man's land under heavy fire to
put a machine gun which disturbed his wounded out of action. I
said "My God! I couldn't have done that," to which he replied,
"You couldn't have helped it; you'd have felt just like a nurse
who stops a noise that disturbs the children in the night-nursery."
They were adorable fellows, and their deference to me, men who
had seen service all over the world, made me feel strangely
humble. . . .

---

[1] *Supra*, p. 257, note 3.
[2] Baron Palmstierna, *supra*, p. 137.

In the way of reading I have not much to record. I read Winston's final volume with immense interest.[2] But he has a viciously rhetorical mind and you feel that he convinces himself by the sheer eloquence of his own voice. Still he has a great tale to tell and with all his defects it is quite impossible not to like him. . . .   *Ever affectionately yours, H. J. L.*

1720 I (Eye) Street N.W., April 2, 1929

My dear Laski: You deserve a better letter than you will get—for though we have been adjourned for weeks I am tired and haven't had much leisure. I find that I have examined 450 applications for *certiorari* this term—which means 30 days work. Apropos of what you say Haldane remarked about Victorian science, I thought that its oversimplification was generally acknowledged. I have seen it brought out so definitely in Anthropology and other matters of which I am least ignorant that I thought it had been a postulate.

The chief event here latterly has been the flowering of the cherry trees around the Potomac basin and the magnolias everywhere—I should say second only to the four greatest things I have seen on earth. Next to that I will put having read John Dewey's *Experience and Nature* for the third time. Just one idea running through the whole and I think that now I could sum it up. If reduced to not more than two pages it would be the profoundest *aperçu* of the universe that I ever have read, which of course means a strong tendency to agree with his insight. I was sent the *Yale Review* with your article[1] which seemed to me very able—but as you know some of your yearnings I don't sympathize with and almost believe noxious—but the crowd is with you rather than with me and I dare say you will smash a good deal that I should like to keep. But I don't feel so seriously about the human race as I once did. I am in pretty good shape—but my wife less so—however I think she is slowly improving from grippe and a succession of misfortunes. I got hold of a book yesterday on Rasputin which I shall look through, translated from German, by René Fülop-Miller. It seems to be impartial and I want to know something about him. Your *Yale Review* led me to think I should read *Le crime et le chatiment*[2]—and I have on hand a life of

---

[2] *The Aftermath* (1929) was the final volume of *The World Crisis*.

[1] "England in 1929," 18 *Yale Review* (N.S.) 417 (March 1929). Laski's article vigorously attacked the record of the Baldwin government and of the liberal opposition and urged that the first necessity was for the transformation of England into a social democracy.

[2] The suggestion perhaps came from Edith Wharton's "Visibility in Fiction," 18 *Yale Review* (N.S.) 480 (March 1929).

Herman Melville[3] and whether I shall do my duty or not I don't know. I mean now to take a nap.   *Aff'ly yours, O. W. H.*

Devon Lodge, 2.IV.29

My dear Justice: My days have been spent in the grim business of packing up poor Mrs. Young to return to America; and in sending off Frida and Diana for a month's holiday to Weimar, where Diana, who has a gift for languages, is to learn or begin to learn, German. So I sit here rather solitary and read and write until ten when I go off to bed with a novel unless some kindred solitary drops in for coffee. . . .

You will be amused when I say that the most interesting thing I have done since I wrote to you last week is to go to a funeral. The mother of my colleague Beveridge died and I went out of compliment. I was immensely struck by the fervour with which my neighbours (A. an eminent F.R.S. and B. a distinguished historian) participated in the service. They prayed, kneeled, sang hymns, etc. in a way that would have done credit to a revivalist. On the way back I asked them if they were Orthodox Christians. Each said no with emphasis. I then asked why the service had been so impressive to them. Each said the same thing that outside a church the whole thing is obnoxious but that inside some kind of childish memory takes possession of him, and he cannot resist the impulses it arouses. Our neighbour happened to hear the conversation and told us he was president of some secular society and yet found that on the great festivals of the Church he was uncomfortable if he was not there. To me it was nauseating to hear men and women thanking God for something that had hurt them like hell and taking comfort in the prospect of a future meeting in which 90 per cent of those present did not believe. Whether it is the aesthetic beauty of the tradition (to which, of course, I am a stranger) I don't know; but it is curious that I should be roused to intellectual indignation by something from which people who share my general intellectual outlook should derive emotional comfort. I should like to know what happens inside you in this realm.

. . . I have been reading some international law—mainly cases, but with one or two treatises like Westlake's. I am greatly impressed by Stowell and inclined to put Lord Parker very high indeed. But I am amazed at the intense nationalism of all these people. Natural law for Stowell meant so sweetly and naturally what an 18th century English gentleman who admired Mr. Pitt would approve. And, lastly, I have read Beard's big blast on American Civilisation (written with his wife) which I thought

[3] Lewis Mumford, *Herman Melville* (1929).

howed insight but was nowhere near so good as Sam Morison's
wo volumes and moreover written in an irritating journalese. . . .
                                        Ever affectionately yours, H. J. L.

                                        Washington, D.C., April 13, 1929
My dear Laski: Your page written from solitude comes on top of
an unanswered longer letter and I begin my reply when about to
go to a conference. Your companions at the funeral who took part
in prayer they didn't believe in, merely illustrate what I am
eternally repeating: that man is like all other growing things and
when he has grown in a certain crevice for say twenty years you
can't straighten him out without attacking his life. That is what
gives the power to churches that no rational man would deem
worthy of thought if he were growing free and had no past. You
know my oft repeated formula that property, friendship and truth
have a common root in time. I am not entirely insensible to the
effect of church ceremonies even now—though neither they nor
the patent fallacies in what they read from St. Paul interest me
very much—but I let time run over me till the show is over. But
f, as is unusual, the service is well done, and you are in a crowd
moved by emotion there is a contagion about it.

Now I have returned from the conference pretty well tired with
t, though afterwards Brandeis and I drove over to Georgetown
and home by a *circumbendibus* around the Cathedral, to see the
white and pink dogwood and wisteria that lined a part of our
road. The sights here are fleeting but they are superlative while
they last. What damned fools people are who believe things. A
case has gone over for further consideration, of a woman wanting
to become a citizen, but who, being as she says, more of a pacifist
than Jane Ad[d]ams,[1] has to explain that she would not fight for
the Constitution (or, as her counsel said, wouldn't do what the
law wouldn't let her do) and so opens to the Government a discourse on the foundation of the Constitution being in readiness
to defend itself by force &c. &c.[2] All 'isms seem to me silly—but
this hyperaethereal respect for human life seems perhaps the
silliest of all.

But I almost fear that I am impolite—for you are not without
your creed—to my regret. I haven't read much since my dash of
philosophy but I am engaged in Lewis Mumford's *Life of Herman*

---

[1] Jane Addams (1860-1935); social reformer, founder of Chicago's famous Hull House, who was a militant leader of the pacifist movement from
1915 until the time of her death; chairman of the Woman's Peace Party.

[2] *United States* v. *Schwimmer*, 279 U.S. 644 (May 27, 1929). A majority
of the Court held that Rosika Schwimmer's pacifism made her ineligible for
citizenship. Holmes delivered a dissenting opinion in which Brandeis, J., concurred.

Melville—which interests me much as a careful study of a man whom the writer believes great—but hardly less from the tone and attitude of the author. He despises the conventions of my earlier days but seems to me tied up in those of a later crowd. He looks down from a height on the America of the past and on the civil war—his *hauteur* toward the achievement of comfort imports a Tolstoy coupled with a Michael Angelo. He walks on lightning smitten peaks, but all samey—when I see a cove talking about the *malice* of the universe I feel pretty sure that I am with an anthropocentric who really thinks the world was made for man and has the old theological turn at bottom—and know that though he may puzzle he can not interest me. He does, however, with the rather pitiful story of Melville's life. I must leave Melville unticketed for the moment. I think he is great—but I think he also is anthropocentric—and therefore more busy with being gigantic than wise. I hope someone will tell me something about this chap Mumford. I think he must be one of a class—but as yet I don't get him exactly sized up. I merely doubt whether he is such a hell of a feller as he ought to be to carry so much side. The unconscious arrogance of your Arkansas student who did not condemn but pitied you is innocence compared with a full-fledged *New Republic* aesthete. Your man reminds me of a phrase—that a good fellow dead long ago used at times—"I pity and despise but do not hate you." But I must stop—to send this off.

Affectionately yours, O. W. H.

Devon Lodge, 3.V.29

My dear Justice: Consolation I cannot send, for there is no consolation in these moments of pain and loss.[1] But all the love that deep friendship can bring you I am anxious you should feel is yours. You know how big a space you both have filled in our hearts. It has altered the world for me to have known you; and I cannot easily bear the pain of thinking you are separated. She was always so good to me, and I learned almost the first time I saw her that she had, with all her reserve and reticence, a genius for affection. And to see you together was a lesson in the beauty of love. I know that things can never be the same for you again. But I want you to remember that your house was made by her for me as for others a place of loving pilgrimage and that while we live she will be remembered with deep affection. I can't say more, for I cannot write more. But think that I am with you in spirit and that my love for you will not grow dim.

Ever yours affectionately, H. J. L.

---

[1] Mrs. Holmes had died on April 30.

Devon Lodge, 21.V.29

My dear Justice: I am very anxious to have a word from you. But I do not want you to bother about writing just now. Would you therefore mind asking your young man to send me a couple of lines? I shall be on tenterhooks until I hear. I do wish more than ever I can remember that I could be with you these days.

I am, as you can imagine, wrapped up in the general election; and it is quite fascinating.[1] I have amused myself this time by speaking only for those candidates for whom I should be glad personally to vote, and certainly one cannot complain of lack of adventure. At Oundle, for instance, the whole school turned out in the market place to shout us down; but because I simply beamed with pleasure at the heckling they behaved like lambs to me, and for forty minutes I spoke in perfect peace to a thousand people who had come in the hope of a row. One great problem is to know what on earth one's questioners really want to know. For instance at Coventry a man asked me whether I did not think there was a grave decline of liberty. I said a decline but not grave. What did I propose to do about it? I said, with such composure as I could muster, that I proposed to do what I could to arrest it. He then thanked me, being obviously much relieved. Another man asked me if I did not think American prosperity a menace to the world. I said that on the contrary it was one of the hopes of the world and rebuked him for an attitude dead in 1789. The audience cheered wildly and he got up to apologise. Another fellow asked me if I could give him a guarantee that statesmen in the future would be of better principles than in the past. Another man wanted to know why there was a statue of the rebel George Washington in London while there was none of that great states-man, Lord Roberts![2] But in general the eagerness of one's audience to have facts and explanations, especially the women, is really very impressive. I believe that Baldwin will get a straight majority, though small; and all things considered I believe that this is the best thing that could happen. The great feature of the election is the fact that everyone has really ceased to be moved by Lloyd-George. That is really a triumph for English common-

---

[1] On May 10 the fifth session of the Parliament elected in 1924 came to an end and it was formally dissolved as from May 24. In the general election on May 30, Labour secured 287 seats, the Conservatives 261, and the Liberals 59. On June 4 Baldwin resigned as Prime Minister, recommending Ramsay MacDonald as his successor. MacDonald, despite earlier indication that he would not accept the office without a clear majority, did accept the Premiership.

[2] Frederick Sleigh Roberts (1832-1914), first Earl Roberts; field marshal, whose principal military services to the Empire were rendered in India in support of the "forward" policy, and in South Africa in bringing the Boer War to a successful conclusion.

sense. He plays the part of charlatan in a way that is quite unforgettable. . . .

Walter Lippmann sent me his *Preface to Morals* last week. I have been singularly moved by it. Though it hasn't originality, and doesn't deal with the big question of how disinterestedness is to grow, I thought it a superb definition of an attitude wholly sympathetic to me and written with a severe beauty quite beyond praise.

. . . at Helston [*sic*] in the Peterboro' division when I was speaking about the land problem I reminded them of how John Clare the poet[3] had protested there against the enclosure of commons. An old labourer applauded very hard and at the end came up to tell me that his grandfather had been imprisoned by the magistrates for taking round announcements of Clare's meetings. It is amazing to find how the events of a hundred years ago are still vivid traditions in rural England. They talk of the Tolpuddle Martyrs in Dorchester as though they were transported two or three years ago.[4] And if you mention them the chances are that a man will come up to you and say that he married the granddaughter of one "and the missus will be grateful for your kind words." It's a very moving thing.

But just now I shan't bother you with a long letter. Please take the greatest care of yourself. Your dissent in the valuation-reproduction case[5] alone shows how essential you are to the Court. But I do not need to ask you to have courage. That has been the principle round which you have built your life; and it is one of the roots of our pride in you.

Our deep love,   *Ever affectionately yours, H. J. L.*

May 23, 1929

Dear Laski: Please keep on writing to me and I shall get on to my pen before long. I am reconciled to my wife's death as the alternative seemed inevitably a life of nothing but pain. A companionship of sixty years is more than one can bargain for—a companionship that has made life poetry. If I can work on for a year or two more, it is well enough—and if not, I have lived my life.   *Affectionately yours, O. W. H.*

---

[3] John Clare (1793-1834), rustic poet from Helpstone whose poverty was the result in large measure of enclosure and who wrote frequently of its consequences, nowhere more effectively than in his satirical poem, "The Parish."

[4] In 1834 six laborers of Tolpuddle, Dorsetshire, were sentenced to seven years' transportation for having taken the oaths of membership of the Grand National Consolidated Trades Union. See Webb, *History of Trade Unionism* (1926) 144 *et seq.*

[5] Brandeis and Stone, JJ., had delivered dissenting opinions on May 20 in *St. Louis and O'Fallon Railway Co.* v. *United States*, 279 U.S. 461, 488, 548, in both of which Holmes had concurred.

Washington, D.C., May 30, 1929

My dear Laski: A dear letter from you has just come—you will have heard from me before this, but I reiterate: please keep on writing and I shall do the best I can. I don't lose my interest in my friends or affairs of the mind or in my job—although it may be, as I wrote to someone yesterday, like a man's beard growing after he is dead. My wife's death seems like the beginning of my own—but I am confused and hardly know what I think about anything. It hasn't prevented my writing. Frankfurter wrote to me highly praising something that I wrote in the midst of anxieties—and I have just turned off a dissent about the refusal to admit a pacifist to citizenship that Brandeis liked and joined in.[1] There seems to be a distinct compartment in one's mind that works away no matter what is going on with the rest of the machinery. I have been delayed in reading W. Lippmann's book but have it at my elbow, probably to be finished between here and Beverly—to which I go via the Touraine on the night of June 5—arriving Boston 6:50 AM and I hope Beverly Farms by Saturday. The women behaved like bricks and gave up their usual holiday at this time—go with me and straight on to B.F. where things will have been prepared for them and they will put on the finishing touches, and notify me. I have been reading a curious book called *The Confusion of Tongues*—by Charles W. Ferguson—an account of the best known come-out sects, Spiritualism—Theosophy—New Thought, Christian Science—Ku Klux—Mormonism, Mennonites —and other less known by name to me but he says maintaining great establishments—ending with the Atheists—(not the quiet scientific unbelievers but people on fire with the same enthusiasm as the others only with inverted values—or colors).

I don't remember whether I mentioned F. Hackett's *Henry VIII* which I agree with Frankfurter in thinking a masterpiece—but I am on the verge of shutting up and going north and am not available for consecutive thought. *Affectionately yours, O. W. Holmes*

Devon Lodge, 4.VI.29

My dear Justice: Your brave card gave me joy beyond words. *Macte antiquae virtutis.* You in any case could not want for courage. But you with memories of her are doubly armed.

I have, as you can imagine, been swept off my feet in these last three weeks. Thirty speeches, articles innumerable, my school work, and now the amusement of watching *de près* a cabinet in the making—it has been hard but interesting work. So far as I can see, it looks as though Sankey will be Lord Chancellor[1] and

[1] *United States* v. *Schwimmer, supra,* p. 263.
[1] Sir John Sankey became Lord Chancellor on June 8.

that gives me, as you can imagine, very special pleasure. It will amuse you to know (this absolutely, please, between ourselves) that MacDonald wanted me to go to the House of Lords as a debater for them. But I said (a) I haven't the money (b) I want my independence and (c) I am a scholar by vocation and not a politician. It is amazing to sit with MacDonald and watch what happens. People who hate him like poison send gifts and congratulations. They write pages to insist on their claims. When the leaders meet each has a list of his particular pets who think that they ought not to be overlooked. People who have never been Labour write to offer their help. It is all the most incredible picture of the lust for power that I have ever seen. . . . Nor must I forget to tell you of the lady who asked me in Dulwich whether a Labour government would base its legislation on the principles of Jesus Christ. I said that I thought this unlikely in the first five years, but that afterwards anything might happen. I add that the one thing that pleases me most in the defeat of Baldwin is the tolerable certainty of an improvement in Anglo-American relations. MacDonald is set on a term to this insane naval competition and a new agreed definition of freedom of the seas.[2] I am hopeful that all this may do immense good to the peace of the world. With England and America in harmony big things can be done. And I see no reason at all for the bickering of the last few years. At the same time I do regret the loss of Baldwin himself, for with many faults, he is a great gentleman and one of the cleanest fighters I have ever met in politics. . . .

I was made very happy by your dissent in the railway valuation case and the Rosika Schwimmer case. The former I know only by the decisions; the latter I thought an iniquitous injustice and I was proud of your dissent. I do hope the modern state is not going to become a medieval church.

Our love to you. Take great care *please*.

Ever affectionately yours, H. J. L.

Devon Lodge, 11.VI.29

My dear Justice: I expect you have now settled down to the peace of a Beverly summer; and I hope you are going to have Felix near at hand for talk. We have taken a house for August on the very top of the Surrey Hills—a part you may know as it is not three miles from Meredith's place at Box Hill. I am very content with it, as it has a good library and a study for me that looks out over

---

[2] In September, MacDonald announced that Great Britain would join the Five Power Conference on Naval Disarmament to be held in London in January 1930.

the hills to the sea and gives one the sense of being completely unconfined. I do wish it were August now.

The week since I wrote has passed very interestingly in watching from close at hand the making of the Cabinet. For me, as you can imagine, the chief joy is Sankey's appointment. He will be a really good Chancellor, for he has courage and integrity and wisdom. Most of the posts went by schedule; but I was very surprised by Webb's willingness to take office.[1] Evidently there is no *"nolo episcopari"* in politics, for only the day before he had insisted to me that he would not go into harness again. Two of my own colleagues at the School got office and one, at least, I was able to elevate from a very minor post to the undersecretaryship of Foreign Affairs.[2] I had a long talk with MacDonald on Friday about America; and there I really hope for a settlement of our quite unnecessary differences in a big and generous way. Henderson, too, who asked me for a memorandum took my points with admirable vigour and I think no effort will be wanting to end the present irritability.[3] I add as a footnote that the panting excitement of the aspirants to office made me grateful that I had not chosen a political career. To sit in the Prime Minister's room while he interviews the hopeful is like a meeting of assassins who have come armed with scriptural texts.

My days have been occupied with the grim business of writing memoranda for ministers. Of one great thing I am hopeful—that I shall get Sankey to set up a Royal Commission on Legal Education and see whether we cannot devote some of the immense funds of the Inns of Court to building a Harvard Law School in this country.[4] At present, as you know, the whole system of teaching law here is thoroughly bad; and the lack of any recognition for the barristers who become professors of law means that outside one or two posts like the Vinerian professorship the law teachers are a very inferior set of people who mainly teach because they cannot make a success of the bar. . . .

In the way of reading, I haven't very much to report. I have read an excellent *Life of Godwin* by Ford K. Brown (Dutton)

---

[1] Sidney Webb, shortly to become Baron Passfield, was Colonial Secretary in the MacDonald government.

[2] Mr. Hugh Dalton (1887-1962) held a readership in Economics at London University when he was made Parliamentary Under-Secretary for Foreign Affairs.

[3] Arthur Henderson was Foreign Secretary in MacDonald's Cabinet.

[4] It was not until August 1932 that Lord Sankey appointed a committee, under the chairmanship of Lord Atkin, to consider the possibilities of closer coördination between the work done by the Universities and the professional bodies, and further provision for advanced research in legal studies. Laski was a member of the committee. Its report was presented to Parliament in July 1934. *Command Papers* #4663.

written just at that level of irony that the subject demands. A
queer fellow, whom it is impossible to like or to admire; and yet
he must have had a power in him to move the world as he did.
The *Life* took me to *Caleb Williams* which I had not read in
years, and despite Mr. Brown who thinks it a minor classic, I
found it intolerable—*longueurs* unendurable in every chapter.
. . . I enjoyed, too, a book by my former colleague, Kingsley
Martin—*The French Liberal Tradition in the XVIII Century*—
which, without novelty, still puts old truths in an attractive way.
. . . I have, too, some doctoral examinations to go through. I
did one last week where the candidate had written on Montesquieu. . . . He made a great fuss about the separation of powers
so I read him an extract from your dissent in the *Jensen* case[5] and
asked him what he thought of it. His reply, I think, ought to be
classical "It is the business of judges to preserve and not to betray
the principles of the American constitution."

Our love to you. Keep well, and see plenty of friends.

Ever affectionately yours, H. J. L.

Beverly Farms, June 15, 1929

My dear Laski: Here I am—settled quietly—it is now a week
since I arrived. Everything is pleasant and I drive, see my friends,
and read a little and sleep in the process. Frankfurter and his wife
made a very satisfying call. He relieved my mind by telling me
that there was no danger of his leaving the Law School for
Chicago—which I had heard rumored. I have a faithful follower,
James Doherty, who thinks it his special duty to look after me.
Some of my wife's relatives thought it well that he should come
on to the funeral and he somehow established himself in charge
of a good deal and managed things admirably. He drove down
here with me last Saturday and didn't leave till Monday, after he
had taken me to walk and satisfied himself that I was safe—
solemnly exhorting me not to come to Boston without notifying
him. He seems to think that I oughtn't to be trusted in the streets
alone. I must tell you too that the moment he heard of my wife's
death the Chief Justice at once communicated with Arlington and
made sure that everything was ready. How can one help loving a
man with such a kind heart? I have a lovely spot in Arlington
toward the bottom of the hill where the house is, with pine trees,

---

[5] *Southern Pacific Co.* v. *Jensen*, 244 U.S. 205. Holmes had written one
of his most famous dissents in this case, denying that the states were powerless to make their Workmen's Compensation Acts applicable to shipboard
injuries suffered by longshoremen, and including his well-known aphorism:
"the common law is not a brooding omnipresence in the sky but the articulate voice of some sovereign or quasi-sovereign that can be identified. . . ."
Id. 222.

oak, and tulip all about, and where one looks to see a deer trot out (although of course there are no deer). I have ordered a stone of the form conventional for officers which will bear my name, Bvt. Col. and Capt. 20th Mass. Vol. Inf. Civil War—Justice Supreme Court, U.S.—March, 1841—His wife Fanny B. Holmes and the dates. It seemed queer to be putting up my own tombstone—but these things are under military direction and I suppose it was necessary to show a soldier's name to account for my wife.

Your last letter received yesterday—("4.VI.29") gave me the usual pleasure. I think you were entirely right in your answer to MacDonald, but not quite right as to Mrs. Schwimmer—I don't think the majority meant any more than that a person couldn't be attached to the principles of the Constitution if he didn't recognize that in case of need it must be supported by force, coupled with a recollection of the anti-draft talk during the late war. I couldn't help suspecting that their view was made easier by her somewhat flamboyant declaration that she was an atheist. I alluded to it discreetly without mentioning it, in what I said. (I was reading a book about the queer sects in the U.S., the last chapter of which was devoted to the Atheists, a society with a name, and pointed out that they were of the same timber as the others although inverted. The real solid unbelievers sit back with a smile—and are not 'asts for an 'ism.) After interruptions I have finished W. Lippmann's book. I was as much impressed as you were—and think it will hit a great many people where they live. I was delighted to hear from Frankfurter that it was having a great sale. I wrote to him—but I fear mainly repeated things that I have said many times before. My only criticism, which is not one really, would be to quote Twisden, C. J. in Saunders' Reports —"Twisden C. J. said to Mr. Saunders, 'Why do you labour so? for the Court is clearly with you.'"

By and by the *certioraris* will begin to come in—but I may keep them until my secretary arrives late in July—he is a great help. I am reading Isadora Duncan's life of herself which is worth reading—[three words illegible] and I have begun a *Life of Erasmus* by Preserved Smith—I am told that he believed nothing.

Ever affectionately yours, O. W. Holmes

Beverly Farms, Massachusetts, June 21, 1929
My dear Laski: Your letter, delightful as usual, stirs thoughts and recollections. As to the Commission on Legal Education I have no opinion, but I note that somehow you make good lawyers under the present system. I can't help remembering what I said as to

the President's Commission for enforcing the law[1]—on that also I
am ignorant—but I said long ago in a speech that for most of the
evil in the present state of the law I think the remedy is for us to
grow more civilized.[2] Your lawyers are educated in a more civilized *milieu* and whatever the system of teaching, they show it—
judging by the decisions that from time to time I read. The atmosphere is more important than the specific contacts. *Caleb Williams*
calls up my boyhood. I think my father thought it the most interesting novel in the world. I read it and have pretty well forgotten it—but I remember a criticism of De Quincey, that the
mystery was left unsolved because it had to be—no possible
dénouement would be adequate to the row that had been made
about it. I dare say I should agree with you if I read it now.

I hardly got the point of your doctor's candidate—as to the
duty not to betray the principles of the Constitution. I thought,
if I remember rightly, that I was standing in the ancient ways.
I haven't read much since Isadora Duncan—lent to me, by the
by, by that dear creature, Mrs. Beveridge. She seems to incline
to all the modernists—in art as in literature, which adds a spice
to our talk. I am just finishing another book that she lent me—
a life of Erasmus by Preserved Smith—interesting but not interestingly written—and now I have the Tom Barbour's (E. M.
Remarque) *All Quiet on the Western Front*—unexpurgated. I
understand that only an expurgated edition is commonly accessible here. You know perhaps how refined we are in Massachusetts
in the matter of morals in books! I haven't looked at it yet. I also
have a reprint of *Folkways*—by the later Sumner—a well known
professor of Yale. This Mrs. Curtis told me was more or less expurgated—but interesting—as yet also unexplored by me. I get
letters from time to time that leave me silent and abashed—
perhaps I told you that I answered one, that if the devil came
round the corner and said: "You and I know that that isn't true,"
I should believe him, but while he didn't appear in person it
fostered a hope that I had lived my dream. I am too much of a
skeptic to believe it fully—and I don't think it very important,
anyhow. I am conscious of the approach of the end—but I mildly
hope it may wait for a year and ¾ to take me into 90. My love
to you.   *Affectionately yours, O. W. Holmes*

Devon Lodge, 25.VI.29

My dear Justice: I hope all goes well with you; I read of heat

---

[1] In May 1929, President Hoover had appointed a National Commission
on Law Observance and Enforcement, of which George W. Wickersham was
Chairman. Holmes's comment on the Commission has not been identified.

[2] "The Use of Law Schools," *Speeches*, 38, 39-40.

waves in the Eastern States and almost perspire with you. Here
there are golden days—bright and cool so that it is really a pleasure to work. Certainly I seem destined to work—a huge mass of
exam papers, a number of doctoral examinations all clustered
together, and perpetual memoranda for one or other friends in
government. But it is all interesting and I do not complain, especially as the term ends on Friday and I am having a really
good time working a day in each week with Sankey and seeing
at first hand how the machine goes. My general impression is
definite that a real 18th century atmosphere still lingers over the
legal profession. Item a vacancy for a county court judgeship—
over 400 people write in to the L.C. to press their claims, de-
cayed silks, university professors, juniors who want a rest from
turmoil and so forth. A vicarage to be filled produced 300 letters.
Add to all this the people who send presents to the L.C. with
a view to prospective favours, the men who write asking that he
introduce them to the Attorney-General, others who want "silk"
and were passed over on a previous occasion, and one is really
startled at the extent to which, in this side of the work, patronage
lingers on. Then I read certain cabinet papers for him and I
should like to write an essay on what they imply. I reckon that
he would have to form a judgment on sixteen different subjects
which range from the recognition of Russia to the question of
whether the Trades Disputes Act of 1927 should be completely
repealed or merely amended. Sankey, thank heaven, is a real
glutton for work and I have only either to write a memorandum
or to indicate desirable sources of study and he is on to them
like a hawk. I have also had some pleasure in drawing up a
memorandum for the Foreign Office on the successor to Esmé
Howard. I mustn't speak about it, but you can imagine that it
was amusing to put into writing the qualities one feels that our
man at Washington ought to possess.[1] Felix, by the way, amused
me (between ourselves) enormously by writing to me urgently
to argue that the ideal Ambassador to appoint was A. N. Whitehead, the philosopher—who, to my knowledge, has never even
glimpsed that kind of experience and is one of the most practically disorganised men alive! I would about as soon think of appointing Morris Cohen your Ambassador in London. . . .

Of other things there is not much to tell. I got my Diderot and
my eyes dwell lovingly upon it as I write. I also got a beautiful
copy of Rousseau's *Social Contract* in the first edition as clean and
fresh as the day when it was printed, and an even more beautiful

---

[1] On December 31 Sir Ronald Lindsay (1877-1945) was appointed Ambassador to the United States.

Bodin—edition of 1591—bound by Derome in brown morocco.[2]
My love to you as always.   *Ever affectionately yours, H. J. L.*

Beverly Farms, July 9, 1929
My dear Laski: You have events and prominent people to write
about. I have only the quiet doings of an old would-be recluse.
But there hasn't been much recluse about it so far. People, all
friends, turn up nearly every day, oftener than I want, and are
apt to stay longer than I can well endure. An hour and a half—
two hours at the outside, is as much as I can carry off without
being tired—but last night one was here from 6 to after 10—
with no intermission except food. Well—I got a good night's sleep
and didn't get up till a quarter to 9. I think it will stop now. The
only fatigue for today is the dentist. But who does not tremble
before the dentist?
Reading has been less than I wished. I have just finished a
good book by the late Sumner of Yale, *Folkways,* the anthropological facts generally familiar but the conclusions and comments
showing his fierce incisors. He does despise and explode phrases
that serve as an excuse for not thinking. He speaks of the "jingle"
"government of the people, for the people, and by the people"—
which of course did not start from A. Lincoln. Also I read part
of a book and the summaries at the head of the remaining chapters by General Smuts—*Holism and Evolution*—in which I failed
to discover a new idea or anything to justify the General's evident belief that he is making a great contribution to philosophy.
Do you know by inspection or hearsay whether I am all wrong?
Barlow who was here Saturday-Sunday unearthed from my books
some short stories by "Saki"—that are very good and amusing—
and there has been other light stuff. The only interesting works
are the dull books. I am slow to take up a novel nowadays—and
I must look out for a *pièce de résistance.* I am like Dr. Johnson's
dull boy who hesitates between two books while the clever Laski
reads both. My routine you know. Mrs. Beveridge was here for
luncheon the other day and I took her over to Newburyport to
see the old house that perhaps you remember. We had a flattened
tire that made it rather long for me—but it was a success. One
day a delightful visit from Felix and his Mrs. I have not been
able yet to go through Rockport and wish that you were there—
but expect to soon.   *Affectionately yours, O. W. Holmes*
I hope you took to heart my remarks about civilization apropos
of your desired Commission on Legal Education.

---

[2] The Derome family, a French dynasty of binders, produced its greatest
figure in the eighteenth century when Nicolas Denis Derome, known as the
younger Derome, was master of the bindery.

Devon Lodge, 9.VII.29

My dear Justice: . . . I had a good day in Oxford, where I had tea with my old tutor Herbert Fisher[1] and heard some charming memories of you in the days when you frequented Leslie Stephen. I was interested by the effect of Oxford on Fisher after his years in politics. He obviously feels it a place of "small talk," intellectually constricting, and void of a big *ethos* of any kind. He made a strong plea for universities in great centres of population to make academic folk have contact with the big world. I am doubtful; but certainly some of the dons I saw were pathetically narrow in their outlook and did not seem to look beyond their own walled town. Then I went to a dinner of American professors in London and was interested by the contrast. The Oxford don is uninterested in the big world; the American professor is uninterested in the impractical. It was a curious experience to sit among men who spoke of men with money as the people who made universities great and to find a craving among them for the study of the immediate. Also I felt that they much too little realised what I may call the significance of the impalpable and were reaching out after a quite illusory quantitative exactitude which in the social sciences at least has hardly a title to serious consideration.

. . . I don't know if you ever read Alexander's *Moral Order and Progress* (1889)? I never had. I bought it cheap the other day and thought it in every way a most impressive performance —especially in its emphasis upon my pet theme that morality is necessarily social in character. . . .

I have now made all the arrangements for coming to America next year. I shall get to Yale the first week in March and stay until June. They give me only 3 hours work a week so I hope to invite myself to Washington with decent frequency. You can imagine how I look forward to talk.

Our united love to you. I hope all goes well. I read with dread of your heat-wave.   *Ever affectionately yours, H. J. L.*

Beverly Farms, July 19, 1929

My dear Laski: You never write an uninteresting letter and the one just received (9.VII.29) is no exception. But you speak of your pet theme that morality is social in character as if you were an exception. I thought that people who count generally held that opinion. I believe I have mentioned that recently I read Sumner's (late of Yale) *Folkways*—one of the main theses of which is that given certain *mores*, established by convenience, superstition, and what not else, the philosophers, accustomed to

---

[1] H. A. L. Fisher, distinguished historian, was in the House of Commons from 1916 to 1926.

them, proceed to demonstrate that the principles of conduct invoked are *a priori* necessities of human nature although in fact
only the outcome of particular habits of their community. I wish
I had you as near as Rockport (I drove round there the other
day) to give me a good *pièce de résistance* or two. The only one
I have now is Hermann M. Roth, *Der Trust in seinem Entwick-
lungsgang vom Feoffee to Uses* etc., which I read with a dictionary. It is only about 300 pages but I have little time and read
slowly. The author sent it to me last term, asking me to criticise
it. I had to tell him that I was 88, very busy, and read with some
difficulty, but I have got far enough to have written to him that
I was getting pleasure and profit from it. Naturally pleasure, as
he gives me full credit. It seems to me well done, though one or
two suggestions of his seem doubtful. I told him that for nearly
50 years I had been thinking on other themes. I have read some
light stuff, *e.g. Magie noire* by P. Morand and some short stories
by Saki which were in the shelves here but which seemed mostly
new to me when Bob Barlow unearthed them the other day.
Saki is often funny, but other tales have a streak of cruelty in
them, as does the French book. In my old age I prefer kindly
pleasant things. And some little poems by women, Elinor Wylie
et al. I preferred the *al.* to E.W. Little whiffs of semi-mystic
emotions over happenings of the earth, sea and sky with a touch
of sex, of course, in these days. I have heard women say that
women were coarser than men, possibly true. A dame occasionally
comes to luncheon with me, Mrs. Beveridge, (a dear, sad creature), Mrs. Curtis, Mrs. Codman, and men have come pretty frequently to call. I get tired after 2 hours. When Bob Barlow was
here for Sunday (a prescriptive right of his, I don't generally
want people for the night), W. Lippmann came in in the morning and was very pleasant. He seems like a real friend though I
see him very rarely. I received a communication in abstraction
the other day saying in part, "When mental strabismus causes
a jurist of supreme position and attainments and of illustrious
family to be under the hypnotic control of a shrewder fellow-jurist
whose every underlying line of action is to the end of world-
control by his race of atheism, free-love and anarchy the future
is indeed black for civilization." This is strictly between ourselves.
I should hate to have it come before the eyes of a shrewder fellow-jurist. I thought it best not to answer. Indeed it was in the
form of an ejaculation not addressed to me except on the envelope. You see how little I have to tell, I rejoice in the hope that
I shall live to my next birthday, March 8, and see you in Washington.   *Affectionately yours, O. W. Holmes*

Devon Lodge, 22.VII.29

My dear Justice: . . . a jolly dinner at the House with ten young
Tory members and Baldwin *père* who wanted to cross-examine
me about Labour policy. They were charming people and, as
always, I got on superbly with Baldwin who is a dear. (I wish
our own chief were as attractive.) I add a party here to which
about 70 people came. The most amusing moment, I think, a
fight between Arnold Bennett and H. G. Wells over the merits of
Aldous Huxley. H.G. insisted that he committed the first great
sin in being unable to tell a story and that he was pretentious.
Bennett said he was a great stylist in quest of material. They
fought like cats. I must tell you too of the young Jap who was
introduced by Frida to the Foreign Secretary and said with great
gravity that he hoped Mr. Henderson was not "bursted by the
explosion of responsibilities"—a new form of the time-honoured
phrase.

But it has not all been play. The Ministry of Labour sent me
down to Oxford to settle a builder's strike and later to Cardiff to
settle a threatened strike over an alleged wrongful dismissal. The
first was easy; but in the second I had to sit as a court for two
days, and to listen to excitable Welsh witnesses with the ther-
mometer at 90° is not an easy task. I had great difficulty too
when I ruled out evidence as inadmissible. The dismissal was for
alleged insubordination; and witnesses wanted to tell me everything about the man from the way he treated his wife to the
moral reputation of a sister who was a chorus girl; and bitterly
angry they were when I said I could not receive evidence on any
question except alleged insubordination. However, I got my way
and at least 1000 men are still at work which is the main
thing. . . .

Our united love to you. Keep well and don't do too much.
Please give my salutations to Mrs. Beveridge.

Ever affectionately yours, H. J. L.

Beverly Farms, August 4, 1929

My dear Laski: Your last letter is full of events and interesting
facts. You don't name the new novel by Wodehouse, but seeing
that in consideration of you, F.P. and Mrs. and Charley Curtis,
I have just taken *Emma* from the local library, I won't bother
for the moment. You see I don't have much time to read. The
occupations of idleness take time (driving, sleeping, solitaire, etc.)
and now just as my secretary and I had finished 79 *certioraris*
another bag full of them comes, the heap looks to me 30 or 20.
Also for my odd minutes I have Eddington, *The Nature of the*

Physical World which reminds of the little book *Eos* just read as it also provides for the end of the universe. I think the scientific men weak when they get into the realm of philosphy and in speculation as to beginning and end I think they are perilously near forbidden ground. I don't believe that we have any warrant for believing that we know cosmic ultimates and think therefore we had much better content ourselves with recognizing in good faith that we are finite creatures and can't formulate the infinite. Eddington thinks that blue and red are subjective facts but wave lengths objective, *i.e.*, that by translating our visual image into another he has reached a different sphere of being. I don't see it but I won't stop to criticize details. The book is very interesting, but I feel the omnipresent domination of what he is more accustomed to over his thought. (I am not quite sure that this hits what I have felt but it seems so at the moment). I have read some more Saki stories. He is an amusing and witty bird, but seems to live in the world of repartee and of fashion. It limits the interests of one to whom London society is not sacred, but it is entertaining. To how many Britons, "We don't do that in England," is the last word. I probably have told you of my wife's answer to this remark on one occasion, "That's why we came to this country." I would fain continue but a little cousin soon is coming to luncheon with a boy—and after them a dame, and I get very little repose though I long for it. My love to you all. I think of myself now as under the sword of Damocles and try to feel so, but I am afraid that daily interests interfere.

Affectionately yours, O. W. Holmes

As from Devon Lodge, 2.VIII.29

My dear Justice: . . . Life has flowed as rapidly as ever since I wrote last. Mainly—I need not say that this is between ourselves —I have been engaged in working with the Prime Minister on his American problem. It has been very interesting and I have great hopes of a successful issue. My main job has been twofold. First I have been trying to explain that the discussion of maritime law ought to follow and not either accompany or precede discussion on naval strength; this I think is now common ground. Second, I have been arguing that naval parity is a phrase which is elastic and not rigid. Our needs and yours being different, it is the technician's business to find formulae of transference in gun-power and torpedo power. The politicians must then agree on a total and leave each party free to work out what that total means in terms of its own view of its needs, the main safeguard lying in an agreement to communicate frankly the grounds of interpretation taken and the actual details of construction. The P.M.

has agreed to this and sent it on with approval to Hoover. The latter is being quite admirable, intelligent, perceptive, and properly urgent. So granted the will to succeed, I think the negotiations cannot easily fail and that when MacDonald goes over in October, he should find things very smooth.[1] I wish I could accompany him then. He was kind enough to suggest it, but I told him (I think wisely) that my one wish was to avoid anything which suggested an official connection with the government. As it was, I remain available whenever advice is offered, and, as he himself said, it is useful to have someone who is kept informed by him and can criticise without responsibility or subordination. . . .

We are going to be very happy here. The house is adorable, with a view of indescribable loveliness. It has a garden of thirteen acres full of flowers with a great mass of lupins and hollyhocks under my study windows. We are so high that from where I write, on a clear day like today, I can just see the sea, like a silver band on the horizon, though it is nearly 30 miles away. I am writing each morning and after dinner and playing in the afternoons and early evenings. With luck, and the vein, I hope to write my three Colver lectures for Brown (which I have to print)[2] and to get started on my Dodge Lectures for Yale. But the main thing is the sense of perfect peace here. Even the nearest house is over four miles away.

My love to you as always. I do wish you lived next door.

Ever affectionately yours, H. J. L.

Beverly Farms, August 11, 1929
My dear Laski: Your conversation between Wells and Bennett is interesting, though I don't value such wholesale judgments as the one you quote about *Moby Dick*, great though I think it. I am pleased at the "blasphemy of the successful bourgeois" and think you very well may be right about the unsuccessful men of letters, except that when I use the word in a derogatory sense, I say Egotist not Egoist. I shall try to get *La vie du droit* and I should send for Wodehouse's latest stories if I remembered their name, but Bob Benjamin, a former secretary, was here today and said he would send them on. I shall write for *The Case with Nine Solutions* by this mail.

I am drawing a free breath having sent back the last bag of cases (*certioraris*) all—123 in number—done up to date. Also I

[1] In October, MacDonald went to Washington for conferences with President Hoover concerning naval disarmament and other international matters of common interest.

[2] Laski was forced to abandon his intention of delivering the Colver lectures at Brown and the Dodge lectures at Yale. His *Liberty in the Modern State* (1930), however, was made up of the undelivered Colver lectures.

finished Eddington's *Nature of the Physical World,* interesting
and instructive, but which I should criticize much as I did Jeans's
Eos the other day.

F. Pollock walked into Sumner's *Folkways* in reviewer's fashion,
taking it as an attempt at anthropology and pointing out omissions
which I thought all wrong.[1] I take it merely as an illustration of
how much depends on *mores* and how propositions become obvious and universal by people being accustomed to their premises.
I think I told you of laboring with a dictionary over Dr. H. Roth,
Der Trust, in which he grovels and is polite to me, and of amusing leisure moments with Saki's tales which I still do. Also, *nè
fallor,* I told you of taking *Emma* from the library out of deference to my friends who love Miss Austen. I have been too busy
with law to read more than the first five chapters. If I spoke the
truth I *am afraid* that I should say (mind, I do not yet say it)
that I found it tedious twaddle. I want another serious book. I
don't know what. I wish I had the *Vie du droit* on hand this
minute for I suppose another bag full of cases will soon be here.
Rockport charms me as much as ever, and I don't think it notice-
ably changed, except that you are not there. FF was here and
gave me more facts I didn't know about Brandeis that made him
more than ever a great and good man.   *Aff'ly yours, O. W. H.*

> *Hurtwood House*
> *Albany near Guildford, 12.VIII.29*

My dear Justice: I cannot even begin to describe the indescribable peace of this place. Except for an occasional aeroplane, one
hears nothing of the outside world except by going to find it;
and you awaken in the morning to the thrush and the quiet plash
of a stream at the end of the garden. The result is that I work
marvellously here. I write all morning, usually getting five pages
done in three hours. In the afternoon we drive around, walk in
the early evening and read after dark. It is a great existence to
which I think I could devote myself quite easily for six months
in the year.

We have seen no one since we came here, except yesterday
when we motored over to the Webbs for tea. They were in good
form, and I was both amused and instructed. Amused, above all,
at their tales of difficulties among the wives of cabinet ministers
over the nice questions of precedence at court and over the eager
rivalry to arrange that their daughters shall be presented in due
form. Instructed by Webb's tales of cabinet technique I find myself amazed and disturbed by the immense discretion left to a
Minister in his department. Henderson for instance has just con-

---

[1] 2 *Holmes-Pollock Letters* 246 *et seq.*

cluded an epoch-making negotiation with the Egyptian Prime
Minister only one detail of which, and that by no means the most
important, was ever before the Cabinet;[1] and one begins to wonder, a little dizzily, what exactly collective cabinet responsibility
means. I was interested in another thing. I told Webb of several
young men in his department whose ability I knew at first-hand,
and suggested that he take the pains to meet them. Webb explained that he could not do that except by the mediation of the
permanent secretary. So I asked him what percentage of his officials he had met, and it appeared to be something like ten. Haldane used to take the most special pains to know everyone who
did important work for him. Webb seems quite content to know
only those selected out for him to meet. He agreed that it was
a wrong state of affairs, but seemed unwilling to take steps to
alter it. . . .   *Ever affectionately yours, H. J. L.*

                                   Beverly Farms, August 23, 1929
My dear Laski: In answer to your letter of laborious peace in the
country I have little to tell. Again I have finished the *certs.* sent
to me and now am 153 to the good. At odd minutes I am reading Allen, *Political Thought in the Sixteenth Century,* sent to me
by F.F., originally I think recommended by you, which seems to
me A-1, altogether admirable. In the crevices of the odd minute
Fish Preferred—which makes me smile but not guffaw. Perhaps,
as my secretary suggests, because I steal a quarter of an hour
from solitaire for Saki, whose 7 volumes I haven't quite finished.
Saki *laiquando* [illegible] but he bites. From time to time I see
Mrs. Codman, Mrs. Curtis and Mrs. Beveridge, and once in a
while others. But getting up comfortably and driving every afternoon and answering letters cut the day to pieces and time flies.
This month is always trying for me to keep well in, but I have
done it so far. I still get letters from lonely enthusiasts who shout
over my dissent in the case of a dame who was not allowed to
become a citizen because she was a pacifist. I had one this morning (also my D.C. tax bill, bigger than I hoped). I told one of
them that it was moral sympathy not legal judgment that led to
his encomiums. I have been interested in some modernist paintings. It seems to me that they have tried to think and thought
inefficiently. They say we don't compete with the photograph
but they admit in their practise some reference to the visible

---

[1] The negotiations between Henderson and the Egyptian Premier, Mahmud
Pasha, had resulted in specific proposals, to be submitted to both govern-
ments, under which British authority in Egypt would be greatly curtailed.
The hopes for settlement of outstanding differences were disappointed in
May 1930, when negotiations were abandoned as a result of disagreement
concerning the status of the Sudan.

world, and yet they put in houses and bowls that plainly won't stand up, and in that way, when seeking, as every work of art must, for an emotional response, begin by presenting an absudity that strikes us quicker than the remote harmony we are intended to feel, and interferes with their effect. They also say they are trying to express themselves, but they exhibit, and no one cares a damn about the personality of the painter, and it would be a pure impertinence to offer it for inspection. In fact, if they have any talent, they are trying to express something in nature that most of us fail to see, which is laudable and it is a pity to hamper the effort with absurdities.

Only a few days more than a month here and then, if I live, Washington.   *Affectionately yours, O. W. H.*

As from Devon Lodge, 28.VIII.29

My dear Justice: . . . Things here move peacefully to their appointed end. We go back to town on Saturday; a week there and then a week in Manchester—my annual offering on the parental altar. Then I go to Cardiff for, I expect, two or three days to arbitrate on a new wage-schedule for the shipyards; I hope to prevent a strike of five thousand men. But I am sorry to leave here, for its perfect tranquility has been quite exquisite.

We have not been entirely alone. Nevinson came over on Saturday for the day, and, as always with him, we had good talk. We agreed in disliking all the art for art's sake school on the twofold ground (a) that they don't know how to tell a story and (b) that they seem to view happiness as an indefinite extension of the genital impulse. We agreed also that Felix is the most remarkable person under fifty in America and that Hackett's *Henry VIII* is mostly brilliant eyewash, wholly lacking in the power to discriminate in the quality of the evidence he uses. N. by the way is probably going to Washington with MacDonald in October and looks forward, lucky fellow, to seeing you then. As soon as I am back in London I will send you a copy of his little pamphlet—*The English*—which is, I think, a charming piece of delicate irony. . . .

Our warm love to you. As I write, the horizon is so clear that I can just see the sun on the Channel nearly forty miles away.
                                Ever affectionately yours, H. J. L.

Beverly Farms, September 9, 1929

My dear Laski: A dear letter from you just received. I rejoice at the thought that I may see Nevinson and agree with you and his conclusions as to many of the modern painters and writers. I sometimes fear that my own evil nature suggests unfounded modernities. The new generation has discovered the act by which it came into being and is happy in the discovery. I am much interested in your criticism of Hackett's *Henry VIII*. I could not have made it, but I dare say you are right, though I don't know what, exactly, you have in mind. . . .

After finishing my *certioraris* for the present (I wrote to the clerk today to send me what more he has not later than the 18th, for the end approaches) and having read *Political Thought in the 16th Century* I begin to reread the French translation of *Anna Karénina*. (By the by I suppose the accent over the *e* merely indicates the pronunciation of the vowel, not the accent of the syllable?) I hate it; I dare say it is one of the greatest of novels, but I resent having my time taken up by the woes of a woman of society ideals and a man who has nothing but social and physical attraction. Vronsky seems to have been less of a person than Anna's husband, although the latter did have big ears. Then the little jealousies of Levine after his marriage annoy rather than amuse me. Altogether, now that I am ¾ through the book I wish it were in hell.

I don't know whether it is the extra pressure of the atmosphere on some of these damp days or the knowledge that I am near the end that makes me rather gloomy. I was going to say indifferent when I remembered that half an hour ago I was fidgeting over a question of investment and that I still want to write and read (solid books, not novels) if it is worth thinking about. One would like to have a glimpse of the meaning, or I know not what transcending meaning of the universe before one dies, but one who thinks as I do perceives that he has no right to make the demand, but should shut up and go under quietly like a good soldier. I am happy to get Swift's *Journal to Stella*, which I never read. Frankfurter and his Mrs. are expected here Thursday and occasionally a dame comes to luncheon. Otherwise all quiet on the Western Front.   *Affectionately yours, O. W. H.*

Devon Lodge, 4.IX.29
My dear Justice: This hot and noisy London is not pleasant after the cool and tranquillity of the country. But it has its compensations. I went this morning to an exhibition of a dozen Vermeers my delight in which I do not know how to express. The exquisite serenity and precision of line are perfect. I was literally overwhelmed with them—especially "The Little Street" and the "Music Lesson." I wish you could have been there to share them with me. Then I have had a jolly dinner with Tomlinson the writer. He is just back from Italy where he stayed in Rapallo. *Inter alios*

he encountered some of our best sellers, like Michael Arlen, who
were trying to convince themselves that they were great artists.
He said that their poses in public were beyond words. Arlen always explained, on the very slightest provocation, the pains of
composition. He could only write in one room; sometimes he had
taken a 'plane from Paris to London to put in a paragraph which
had moved him. Another gent. explained that he could only write
his poems while an electric piano played Beethoven sonatas.
There was also an Italian painter who could only paint in a
mauve room. Tomlinson said he never felt so normal in his life.
And Arlen told him that what his (T's) work lacked was the
power to put his hand on "the great pulse of London." He explained how at night he slept with open windows near Piccadilly
as the taxi-cabs made him feel nearer to London's soul. You can
see that people like you and I who write in ordinary rooms on
ordinary paper are really much too commonplace ever to have
anything real to say. Then I went to the wedding of a friend who
married the daughter of Forbes-Robertson, the actor.[1] I never saw
the theatre *in excelsis* as here. If you are a famous actress your
technique consists (a) in kissing your rival profusely and calling
her darling at every other word. (b) explaining that her dress or
hat is "quite too marvellous." (c) regretting that you did not see
her in her last show but everyone said she was "quite too marvellous." (d) What a pity that X ("I suppose he's quite our first
critic") hated the play; "did you choose it yourself, darling"? I
must add, so that you can the better appreciate my innocence,
that the lady next to whom I sat in the Church seemed to me
about 28-30; but such is the modern cosmetic art that I discovered she was in fact just on sixty. I had one amusing moment at
the reception with Bernard Shaw. He was explaining to an adoring audience that Ibsen did what had never been done before
by exploding the folly of obsolete pseudo-idealism. He asked me
to agree and I explained that I couldn't. He then explained to
the audience (suitably impressed) that I had the typical imper-
ceptiveness of the academic. So I thought the time for veneration
had passed and told the worshippers that even Shaw might have
been expected to know Cervantes. But as I think most of them
did not, probably the victory remained with him.

I am so glad you like Allen's book, which I thought really admirable. I am enclosing the notice I wrote of it in the *English
Historical Review* in the thought that it may interest for a moment.[2] Your "Saki" I do not know except by repute. I have been
in very different literary company—the classical international law-

---

[1] On August 31 Mr. James Hamilton and Miss Jean Forbes-Robertson,
daughter of Sir Johnston Forbes-Robertson, were married at St. Giles-in-the-
Fields.

[2] 44 *English Historical Review* 469 (July 1929)

yers of the 18th century. Sir, I beg to state with my hand on my heart that I cannot for the life of me see why Vattel or Wolff ever got a reputation. I think there is real mental power in Bynershöck; but the other two seem to me to have been just like what Nicholas Murray Butler is today—pompous, oily, and snobbish. Have you ever been driven to give them first-hand attention? I am not, God knows, proposing it; but I would like confirmation of my guess that they are nonsense in court dress. I have read a good book by E. Cannan—*A Review of Economic Theory*—a combination of historic analysis and argument you would like. Also a book by Jacques Rueff published by the new Johns Hopkins Law School called *From the Physical to the Social Sciences*. I can't say I was greatly impressed. It doesn't seem to me novel to say that the logic of the natural sciences is the only satisfactory method of analysis. It does seem to me futile to expect from the material of the social science principles like the laws say of physics; and even a science of politics like a Euclidean geometry would not tell me the "oughts" of desire. I mean that physics doesn't need a system of values; the social sciences do; and the attempt to build up analogies simply breaks down after the business of statement has been completed. But I must be wrong for I note as I write this that the book is enormously praised in the current *New Republic*.[3] . . .

My love to you deeply.   *Ever affectionately yours, H. J. L.*

Beverly Farms, September 15, 1929
My dear Laski: Such a nice letter from you on your return to London. You amuse me about the best sellers and their ways. I used to call them the unknown illustrious—people that the upper educated class never had heard of but that sold a million copies. I once devoted a little time to reading some of their books to try to discover the secret. My conclusion was: no style—no knowledge of life—no picture of character—but something doing all the time. And they were right, except to the sophisticated. I, the reader, am the hero and don't need to have him described—&c. &c. In my old age I somewhat sympathize with the barbarian and am amazed and bored by the hitches and troubles necessary to spin the story to a book's length. Your book *From the Physical to the Social Sciences* reminds me of early days at the dentists when I was recovering from chloroform, and found the secret of the universe in certain sounds, such as I got from striking saws of different sizes in my father's workshop. I said to the dentist, "I have effected the transition from the physical to the metaphysical." I have trouble in reading who the painter was who

_____
[3] Reviewed by C. J. Keyser, 60 *New Republic* 23 (Aug. 21, 1929).

pleased you—Veronese? Your remark about the "oughts" and system of values in political science leaves me rather cold. If, as I
think, the values are simply generalizations emotionally expressed,
the generalizations are matters for the same science as other observations of fact. If, as I sometimes suspect, you believe in some
transcendental sanction, I don't. Of course different people, and
especially different races, differ in their values—but those differences are matters of fact, and I have no respect for them except
my general respect for what exists. Man is an idealizing animal
—and expresses his ideals (values) in the conventions of his
time. I have very little respect for the conventions in themselves,
but respect and generally try to observe those of my own environment as the transitory expression of an eternal fact. I readily believe what you say about Vattel—and shall feel exonerated from
the duty of reading him as I was by Morris Cohen from Thomas
Aquinas. In your excellent notice of Allen you enhance my feeling that I ought to read Suarez—given me by Canon Sheehan
and pronounced by him an original thinker (but I didn't quite
trust his judgment). Well—the last two weeks of vacation promise to be busy. I have received our last bag of *certioraris*—and
the Law School wanted me to be painted by Hopkinson—full
length—to hang by the side of Marshall in a new reading room.
I am much flattered and the work begins tomorrow—and there
goes the leisure I had promised myself for the end. I have just
received *The Tragic Era* by Claude G. Bowers—an account of
Johnson and the times after Lincoln's death. The writer is a bitter partisan (democrat) but he tells the story in an absorbingly
interesting way. I believe he is going to write a life of Beveridge
—safe to be good reading. He seems to know all the dodges to
keep the reader intent. I shall go elsewhere for philosophic views
—and for general statements of fact that I believed. But the
burning problem now is shall I attempt to stand long enough to
be painted standing—and what will he do about my hair, which
I have not had cut for a good while—and there are many bothering doubts on varied themes which I omit. The morning paper
has a picture of Wu described [as] one of the foremost inter-
preters of oriental law to this world. So he is getting on.

Affectionately yours, O. W. Holmes

Devon Lodge, 16.IX.29
My dear Justice: . . . I looked through all the Manchester book-
shops in vain. Theology, sets of the mighty dead in full morocco,
and the lesser pornography. But I dug out a tiny pamphlet of
Buckle's which moved me greatly. You will remember Mill's discussion of the *Pooley* case in the essay on Liberty. Seeming [*sic*]

Buckle reviewed this in *Fraser* and Coleridge's son replied in a mean letter. Buckle replied in this little pamphlet and I must say that I think it is a really first-rate piece of polemical writing.[1] It led me back to his *History* and I was amazed again at his learning, without feeling that he is quite first-rate. J. M. Robertson tells me that I am wrong and that Buckle really was a supreme innovator. But I feel that he merely states eloquently a body of great platitudes none of which he can be said to have seen afresh. I like his anti-clericalism and his zeal for science; I like the body of incidental knowledge he accumulates; but I can't see greatness as a historian in the sense that Gibbon was great or, in the line he chose himself, the German scholar Burckhardt.[2] Have you any views?

I came back on Saturday to a jolly dinner with Nevinson who sails for Washington with MacDonald. He will only be there a week, but he is proposing to call on you one afternoon, so I am sure of direct news of you. He had a woman to dinner . . . an eminent pianist whom I wish you could have seen. Like all public performers who are women she is a professional languisher. She feels that life is a series of halts on the verge of elopements and I wish you could have watched her set her cap at me, S. K. Ratcliffe, *et al.* who were the guests. She started superbly with me by saying that when she read my *Communism* she felt I loved music from the movement of my sentences—pretty good. She told Nevinson that she is always reminded by him of a Bach fugue—really better. Shaw, she said, was like a Scarlatti prelude—Frida was nearly overwhelmed; I was really very good and told her that I felt musicians the natural judges of political science. She took it like a bird. Then on Sunday Frida had a party here for some continental members of the International Sexual Reform Congress which has been meeting here. I can't put on paper all the things that were said. A heavy German gentleman asked me who were the leading perverts among Labour politicians. A French lady asked me how long I had been married; I told her and she enquired whether I did not find sexual intercourse monotonous. I, poor thing, crept quietly away. Frida, poor child, who had given this party at B. Russell's request had even more difficult questions to answer. A Russian gent. told her that their auras corresponded and that they must meet alone. An American

[1] In 1857 Sir John Coleridge (1790-1876), with his son John Duke Coleridge, later Lord Chief Justice, acting as counsel for the prosecution, had sentenced Thomas Pooley to fifteen months' imprisonment for publishing a blasphemous libel. Buckle's first comment on the case was in *Fraser's* for May 1859 and is reprinted in 1 *The Miscellaneous Works of Henry Thomas Buckle* (Grant, ed., 1885) 75, 115 *et seq.*
[2] Jacob Christopher Burckhardt (1818-1897); Swiss cultural historian; author of *Die Kultur der Renaissance in Italien* (1860) and *Die Zeit Konstantins des Grossen* (1852).

lady hoped that Diana was being brought up to appreciate the
philosophy of nudity. Two hours of this were enough to make us
glad that the next meeting in London will be five years
hence. . . .   *Ever affectionately yours, H. J. L.*

Devon Lodge, 28.IX.29
My dear Justice: A delightful letter from you. And I have tried
to reply to it in the best way by giving my friend Lord Arnold[1]
an introduction to you. He is accompanying the P.M. on the great
tour and I think you will find him an interesting example of the
new type who has joined the Labour Party. He was a great friend
of Haldane's and is a thoroughly good fellow.

I have been very busy since I wrote last. Three grim days in
Cardiff arbitrating a strike took all the patience I have and was
a very difficult and delicate business. The two sides were so unpleasant to each other that at times I was in despair, and the
effect of being unable to have any private talk is a curious sense
of isolation. However, at the end they disagreed and accepted my
independent decision which I previously had worked out in great
detail. I came back on the train with three of the union's leaders
and had extraordinarily interesting talk. One of them was a passionate lover of Dickens and one responsive answer set him off
until he sounded almost like a lover with his mistress. Another
was a local J.P. and was so impressed by his own unfitness for
the work that he had actually got himself called to the Bar in
order to know what the law was about and not to feel that he
was merely the voice of his clerk. The third was an amateur
astronomer and to hear the reverence with which he mentioned
people like Leverrier and Adams[2] was really a pleasure. I had
three very revealing hours for they convinced me that the number of men who can be made to feel that leisure should be creative is much larger than our educational technique recognises.
All these men had gone to work at ten and eleven and all of
them had taken up intellectual pursuits out of a sense of want
through unsatisfied curiosity. I think it was significant that none
of them possessed a motor car, and that when they spoke of certain colleagues who did not share their tastes they said, "Oh yes!
Of course X devotes his evenings to his car" in a way that suggested definite incompatibility between the one and the other.
. . . We went also to a farewell dinner of the P.M., heard

---

[1] Sidney Arnold (1878-1945), first Baron Arnold, had joined the Labour
Party in 1922; in 1938 he resigned from the Party because of disagreement
with foreign policy.
[2] Urbain Jean Joseph Leverrier (1811-1877) and John Couch Adams
(1819-1892) almost simultaneously but quite independently determined the
existence of an unknown planet, Neptune.

some secrets, and watched with enormous interest the effort of under-secretaries to establish their future claim to cabinet position. MacDonald is charming in this kind of atmosphere. The vanity of the *prima donna* disappears, and he becomes a simple and interesting human being. . . . MacDonald, by the way, told a good story of a visitor to Frogmore, the royal mausoleum, who saw the tomb of the Prince Consort. "Who was he?" "The husband of Queen Victoria." "Yes, but what did he do?" "He was the father of King Edward, the Duke of Connaught, the Princess Royal, the Empress Frederick, etc." "Yes, but I mean what did he do in the daytime?" . . .   *Ever affectionately yours, H. J. L.*

Beverly Farms, September 29, 1929, Sunday
My dear Laski: You miscalculated a little, for your letter that expected to meet me in Washington was forwarded to me here and reached me yesterday. But tomorrow morning I do leave for Boston—and hope to be in Washington Thursday morning. I believe that I have told you that my expected last two weeks of idleness have been cut up by standing for a full length portrait by Hopkinson for the Harvard Law School. Hopkinson has a gift for catching a likeness and for vividness I think—and I am quite proud of his results. As to Buckle—it must be over 60 years ago that I read him—and I only have referred to him once, when writing about Montesquieu, to make sure of his having dwelt on climate. My general impression is like yours. I think on reopening him I found him abler than I had anticipated but I hardly had regarded him as a pathfinder although he more or less indicated the direction of future paths. Your musical dame and sexual reformers give me great pleasure—why am I denied these glimpses of a higher aether? To have a woman asking about your *medias res* is more amusing than ten *certioraris*. Your German historian Burckhardt I know not—ought I to before I die? As a result of the portrait I have read nothing since rereading *Anna Karenina* except part of Swift's *Diary to Stella*—not so good reading as Pepys and even perhaps a trifle squalid, but still interesting. I shall take it with me. Books like that and Pepys and Walpole's letters fill a niche in life very pleasantly.

I think that my wife's death, although I cannot regret it, because life would have meant suffering and pain, keeps the thought of my own before me, so that I want to add; if I am alive, when I say that I go to Washington Wednesday night. It makes me think of the time when all life shall have perished from the earth, and tests the strength of the only comfort I know—the belief that the I know not what, if it swamps all our human ultimates, does so because it is in some unimaginable way greater than they, which are only a part of it. But I also think that our demands for satisfaction are intensified by exaggeration of the belief in the unity of ourselves and a failure to see how they change in content and contour—as is natural if consciousness is only an electric illumination of cosmic currents when they make white light. Lord, Lord, I have said all this so many times before that I ought to be ashamed. But the thought must needs repeat itself daily and so the expression may be pardoned if not more than once a month. Also every litany has its repetitions.

I envy you your acquaintance with Birrell. I was just referring to a page in *Obiter Dicta* and found it hard to lay the enchanting volume down. Happy the man who can take books leisurely, like a soaking rain, and not inquire too curiously for the amount of fertilizer they contain. It takes robust and staying power to get adequate pleasure out of even the greatness of the past. It takes other and richer gifts to find all the good there is in the second rate. But I fear that I drool—farewell.

Affectionately yours, O. W. H.

Devon Lodge, 12.X.29

My dear Justice: I ought to have written to you last week; but I have been so driven and even pestered by students that I have just tumbled into bed o'nights. I have classes so large that they are almost nightmares, and graduates from half Europe have chosen to come and do research with me to say nothing of Indians and Chinese and Japs. It is only now that I have got things straight and can have a word with you.

I am intensely anxious to hear how you liked my political leader and also Arnold.[1] What they thought of you a cable from J.R.M. has told me; and I will not repeat it because it would make you vain. But at least I have won his gratitude by telling him what was the best sight in America today. I wish I could have been with you; and I dislike having to wait another fortnight before I can hear his tale of how you are and what you said.

Your dear letter from Beverly—written just before you left for Washington—moved me much. Please think all the time that though she is gone, there are one or two like myself to whom the fact of having you is a great part of the joy of life; I know that the day fourteen [*sic*] years ago when Felix took me to Beverly Farms is one of the three biggest events in my life. And I literally count the days until March when I can talk things over with you again.

---

[1] MacDonald and his staff had arrived in the United States on October 4. His conversations with President Hoover concerning naval disarmament took place from October 6 to 10, ending in satisfactory statements of accord. MacDonald did not in fact see Holmes; *infra*, pp. 291-92.

I have, as term necessitates, been hard at it indeed. Mostly it has been the grim business of political philosophy. I've been doing the Spanish theological jurists of the 16th century for my seminar—Soto, Suarez, Victoria *et al.* revelling in them and making an anthology of passages for the lads to read—great fellows they are, a little long-winded but subtle and noble-hearted. I put Suarez first, and I think that between Aquinas and Descartes he could claim to have about the best mind of all the people we know in these matters. Then, too, I have been slowly working through the classics of international law for my Yale lectures in April. Sir, may I say to you that Puffendorf is third-rate, Wolff fourth-rate, Thomasius seventh-rate, and Vattel elegant in a tenth-rate way. Why ever they became classics God only knows. And for amusement one or two things I must comment on. . . . J. M. Robertson, *A Short History of Morals*—simply admirable, with a brilliantly devastating analysis of the Christian ethic and some very good attacks on Plato. If this tempts you I wish you would say the word and I will send it. . . . I read with enormous pleasure *Mme. de Staël* by Lady Blennerhassett[2]—I gather one of Lord Acton's learned ladies—a first-rate job and a thoroughly interesting picture of a great epoch. I wish, by the way, that I could understand why literature went dead in France between 1780 and Chateaubriand; and I rather think the same is true in Russia since about 1910. With all her vanity and affection, she was a great woman. It's a good job that her mother didn't marry Gibbon after all. . . .

My love to you as always.   *Ever affectionately yours, H. J. L.*

Washington, D.C., October 16, 1929

My dear Laski: It seems a thousand years since I last wrote to you—but I have been immersed in the manifold tasks that beset one on arrival here at the beginning of the Term. I think I told you of the portrait I stood for before leaving—but not of my flying visit to the new Langdell Hall[1] while in Boston. I was tremendously impressed by it. I will not describe it for you will see it—but I doubt if there is anywhere so noble a recipient for teachers and students of the law. . . .

I didn't see the Prime Minister. The Ambassador wrote to me and I made an appointment for him to call but at the last minute he had to go to the White House and so I missed him. I was

---

[2] Charlotte de Leyden (1843-1917), German-born historian of French letters; her Irish husband, Sir Richard Blennerhassett, was a friend of Lord Acton's. Before her marriage to Necker, Madame de Staël's mother, Susanne Curchod, had been engaged to Gibbon, a commitment which Gibbon *père* could not approve. The son dutifully accepted the father's decision: "I sighed as a lover, I obeyed as a son."

[1] At the Harvard Law School.

sorry, especially because my wife had a great fancy for him because of his book, what she read about him, his looks, &c. However, I had a good call from the Ambassador (a dear good fellow) and your friend Lord Arnold who was very pleasant and
afterwards sent me a charming book: *Home* by Alan Mulgan, a
New Zealander—poetically rapturous about England. Of course
one smiles a little at his emotional responses more or less mistak-
ing themselves for critical estimates, but so far as I have read
I am charmed. But I have had no chance to read more than a
few inches of print other than legal records and arguments. I wish
I had had your letter before I saw Lord Arnold. It came just after
he had left.

I am interested by your labor leaders on the train—your reflections on leisure—and their reference to the others who devote
their evenings to their cars. I imagine that here at least there
would be a hundred after their cars to one after a book—a larger
proportion than that. Your Kelsen's *Hauptprobleme* worries me
—I fear that I ought to read it, and German does not come very
easy—supposing the work to be accessible, as it should be.

The last two days have been spoiled by the dentist, but I am
glad that I went to him. I told him I felt as I did when, after the
night in which I thought I was dying, the hospital man said that
I should recover and everything snapped back into life again. I
was rather in despair about my teeth—but though one has perished under the cutting and scraping—the rest seem to be coming out better than I feared, and I shall bet on them against my
body—*i.e.* I don't think that I shall die toothless—but there are
two or three days more when I must give an hour to him.

Brandeis, who seems in good shape, reminded me of a case
argued last term in which he said I should have to write a dissent. I looked at it and sure enough it is one rather specially in
my line on which I had and have decided views—one of those
cases in which it seems to one that most judges show limited
subtlety.[2] There are cases from time to time that strike bottom
notions and bottom notions often are very hazily held. I won't go
into it now, as I have had time to jot down a few sentences at
odd moments. I am keeping well and it looks now as I should be
alive when you come over—and if I am, no one will welcome
you more heartily than I shall.

I went over to Arlington a second time on Sunday (it is Wednesday now). The stone is up for my wife, and being in a military place had to justify itself by my name—so I see what the
passerby will read—Oliver Wendell Holmes, Captain & Bvt. Colonel—20th Mass. Vol. Inft'y. Civil War—March, 1841-   . I
wish you could see it for I think it is in as romantic a spot as

---

² The case has not been identified.

almost anywhere on the grounds. It looks as if a deer might trip
out and stop—but I don't want to exaggerate. At least the place
might have been much worse. It is time for me to stop. I feel an
affectionate thrill at the thought that perhaps I shall see you
again.   *Affectionately yours, O. W. H.*

Washington, D.C., October 23, 1929

October 21 was Ball's Bluff 68 years ago.
My dear Laski: Your letter came this evening—it is solitaire time
in 10 minutes but I must write a line. You put heart into me by
what you say—for though I can't quite believe such things I believe it enough to get happiness from it.

As to Robertson's *Short History of Morals* I wonder that you
ask me. It is the kind of book that I am keen to read—though I
should approach one written by an apostle or propagandist with
suspicion. Of course I should like it.

I looked at your Kelsen's *Hauptprobleme der Staatslehre*—but
it was too solid a lump of raw German for me—and it looked to
me as if he was somewhat like the German comic papers that
take you by both ears and shove your nose into a joke. I didn't
read half a page but it smelt as if he brought the German touch
to impalpables.

I revere your attack on Suarez *et al.* Canon Sheehan gave me
Suarez but I never have done more than peek into him. You
have infinitely more patience than I in reading books that tell
you nothing for the sake of the thoughts that you will contribute.
Yet I have done a fair share. If you make a volume of elegant
extracts I will read it if still alive and in possession of my wits.
There's lots more to say but I must go downstairs to my cards.
I have read nothing (bar records of cases) except *The Amazing
Chance* (Patricia Wentworth) which kept me interested though
it reminded me of Tom Appleton's remark about the statue of
Horace Mann in front of the State House—done by a sculptress
—"Man by Woman".

I am beginning to look forward to March for you.
                                          Affectionately yours, O. W. H.

Washington, D.C., November 22, 1929
My dear Laski: May this catch the mail, an inadequate answer to
two, as usual, unusual letters[1] from you, against which I can set
only a hasty scrawl and the volume of dissenting opinions.[2] Yet
I have been nearer to leisure than I often am—and yet again

---

[1] Omitted from this edition.
[2] *The Dissenting Opinions of Mr. Justice Holmes* (Lief, ed., 1929).

leisure is busier than business—endless bores by mail—people not
bores but who took time calling. I haven't improved my mind as
I should—unless by writing a short dissent from an opinion by
McReynolds in which I am alone—Brandeis and Stone concurring
in result of majority on grounds that I think not fairly open.[3] I
began Whitehead's *Process and Reality,* but apart from the fact
that I believe the line of thought would be one that I don't much
value if I understood it, I find W's vocabulary and mode of expression so difficult that I doubt if I understand anything I have
read. Yet he (W.) is an extraordinary man—talks and can write
with admirable clearness. I guess it is carrying over mathematical
habits into philosophical writing. It is a great humbug to say that
mathematics teaches accuracy or clearness of thought. That is
secured for you without effort because a is always a and $x = x$—
without any chance for an undistributed middle. So I have interrupted one whom by faith I believe to be a great and good
man to descend to easier levels—like Huneker's *Promenades of
an Impressionist*—which gives me pleasure after the ineffability of
the moderns. Also I was pleased by a side slash at T. S. Eliot
(poet and critic—did you ever hear of him—I am told regarded
by youth as its prophet) in a periodical *Life and Letters*[4] which
has good reading in it, and is sent to me by Richard Hale. I have
given up all subscriptions to periodicals and take *no* newspaper—
except by prescription, the *New Republic,* by curiosity, *Art*—a
modernist American quarto publication, oh yes and for merit, *The
Geographical Magazine*—though I haven't ever done much more
than look at the pictures—but I am not quite sure that that hasn't
stopped.

I was interrupted by a luncheon and a discourse to my secretary[5] on our wish for local color and the old notion that poetical
experience should always be in general terms—the notion of
France and England a hundred and fifty years ago—illustrated by
a passage from Dr. Johnson's *Life of Dryden* where he says that
every reader would wish every phrase of Dryden speaking of
Oakum Tarpaulins &c. apropos of the English ships after a battle,
struck out—or Legouvé in his Memoirs (60 years) when he says
that when his father in a play made someone answer a question
as to the hour: *"minuit"*—they feared a riot in the theatre—(*i.e.*
he should have talked tall) contrasting this with Brownell's "Bay
Fight" in which he uses oakum and boiling pitch with thrilling
effect. But probably I have said the same things to you.[6] It is an
old lecture.

---

[3] *Safe Deposit and Trust Co.* v. *Virginia,* 280 U.S. 83 (Nov. 25, 1929).
[4] F. L. Lucas, "Criticism," 3 *Life and Letters* 433 (November 1929).
[5] Alger Hiss, who had graduated from the Harvard Law School in June
1929, was Holmes's law clerk in 1929-30.
[6] See, *supra,* p. 56.

I think in these days often of the grace of an old man sitting in unproductive elegance awaiting death—but I can't do it. I should feel that I was wasting time. I am glad that I can't wrap myself in self-satisfaction as I have seen some do—but still people do and say pretty things to the old man—and they are not all damned fools. It eases the passage. My love to you all. *Aff. yrs., O. W. H.*

Devon Lodge, 17.XI.29

My dear Justice: Let me begin with my bad news first. I shall not be able to get to America in the Spring. My committee on delegated legislation is to begin taking evidence in February and will be hard at it until August, so of course I have to stay here and work at it. It is terrible luck; for I had counted more than I can say on seeing you and Felix and having real talk. It's also a serious financial loss to me, for I had reckoned on making about four hundred pounds which would have come very gratefully. But I saw the Lord Chancellor and the P.M. and they both insisted that I must stay as it is a good deal my special theme and they seem to build enormously on a good report from the committee. So there you are! I have written a pathetic apology to Yale, but I don't see that I have any alternative.

Feliciora canamus. I have been about a good deal this week. A jolly dinner at the Webbs to meet General Smuts. He is a fine fellow in most things, quick, vivid, shrewd. On the negro question he is very bad, talks like a Southerner of the 'fifties and seems not at all to realize that segregation is an impossible policy. But I should say that he is extraordinarily wide-minded on other things, possibly also a little "slim"; he struck me as curiously anxious to please. . . .

Our love to you—and forgive me.

Ever affectionately yours, H. J. L.

Washington, D.C., November 30, 1929

My dear Laski: It is a disappointment; but an earlier letter than this (17.XI.) had warned me that probably you would not come. I believe that I have remarked to you before that at my age 6 months is like an inch on a man's nose. But I will not bid you an eternal adieu, but simply turn my thoughts in another direction. I still may see you again, somehow, after all.

Work has begun again—I mean work-work, not leisure-work, which sometimes is the harder of the two. The first week, just finished, was mitigated by Thanksgiving and the fact that four cases running turned on a single point.[1] I am afraid I haven't made

---

[1] This may refer to the issues involved in *Safe Deposit and Trust Co.* v. *Virginia, supra,* p. 294, and *Farmers Loan and Trust Co.* v. *Minnesota,* 280 U.S. 204 (1930).

the most of my time—but I have read one book that I recommend:
Geoffrey Scott—*The Architecture of Humanism*—a short, well-
written exposition of various fallacies on the theme and a defense
of the Roman as against the Gothic product. Some years ago
Spengler on the downfall of the Western world cracked up the
Baroque, as a transition to music—and Scott does the same thing
on solid architectural reasoning. It is a pleasure to my ungenerous
soul to see Ruskin's pontifical dogmatizing kicked in the stomach.
I once believed all that Ruskin said and like a little revenge before
I die. Apropos of your Smuts I told you last summer that his effort
to philosophize seemed to me rather empty.

Your letter praising Hemingway came just two days after his
book had come to me from Owen Wister—an aftermath of a Sunday spent here—(to our mutual pleasure—I hope). I doubt if I
shall go as far as you do—but Hemingway must be a clever writer
for he interests me when I can't see any reason for it (in *The
Sun Also Rises*). Hemingway, I believe, is something of an athlete
and Wister writes to me has been hurt lately in a bull fight—which
seems good. I am told that he is one of the heroes of the young—
as T. S. Eliot has been. I don't yet see the need to get very excited about him—but it is well to keep one's mind open to the
fashions of the day. Every fashion is beautiful while it is the
fashion. My assignment has come from the Chief Justice and the
next words I put on paper must be the beginning of an opinion
—I hope to finish it on the Sabbath. My love to you.

Affectionately yours, O. W. Holmes

Devon Lodge, 9.XII.29
My dear Justice: . . . Your letter was a delight; and I was particularly gratified by your remarks on Whitehead's new book. I
was sent me for review and after going through it once I returned it. I can't say exactly that I could not make head or tail
of it. But I thought the price of admission excessive, and certain
parts, like the treatment of God, seemed to me as near intellectual
dishonesty as be damned. For Whitehead doesn't mean by God
anything that any theologian has ever meant, with the result that
he quite unjustifiably leaves an impression of a harmony between
science and religion which is only reached by making words, à la
Humpty-Dumpty, mean whatever he wants them to mean just by
paying them more. And the style seems to me excessively difficult.
No! I prefer ignorance if that is the cost of entrance to the philosophic fair. I wonder whether even such an admirer of his a
Felix would really justify this book.

I have been pretty busy this last fortnight. A speech to the
dining-club of the Civil servants on "A certain condescension in
civil servants"; a dinner with Snowden; a lunch with Webbs; and

a dinner at the Political Economy Club. Snowden was very interesting. He has a purely Victorian mind. The simple virtues, economy, chastity, etc. are absolutes for him and I don't believe his mind has ever wandered outside that realm. A certain absence of reading apart, talk with him is very like what it must have been with Mr. Gladstone. He spoke, for instance, of "the moral obliquity of George Eliot," and was insistent that the best social type is the contented workman who saves a few shillings a week. The Political Economy Club was also interesting. They discussed the coal crisis, and they were exactly like a body of people reading Darwin for the first time and being shocked at the abandonment of special creation. It was striking to observe how very much better the economists were than the business men. The latter were clearly unaware that they acted on assumptions, and as each of these was brought to light in discussion, its proponent promptly repudiated it with horror. What struck me very forcibly was that the business man does not seek any conscious body of principles. He clearly has a "flair" built on unconscious experience; and the attempt to make those "flairs" into a reasoned argument, (which may result in their destruction) simply makes him irritated. At the School one feature was amusing. Our guests were my two colleagues who have become ministers. The younger was so proud of it that he began by saying "how difficult it is to return to the smallness of academic life after participating in maintaining the peace of Europe" and proceeded quite solemnly in that vein for twenty minutes. . . .

Our love to you as always.   *Ever affectionately yours, H. J. L.*

Washington, D.C., December 18, 1929
My dear Laski: This will not arrive in time to repeat my wishes for a Merry Christmas but will I hope do so for a happy New Year. Yours marked 9.XII.29 came today and mentions themes for speech. Evidently you understand more than I do what Whitehead means to convey. I simply don't know what the words as he uses them mean. However, I think I am beginning to establish relations with him and I mean to read to the end, at rather rare and interrupted moments. If as I take it he conceives possible and probable another cosmic epoch with different ultimates, that falls in with my ways of thinking (as to the possibility at least). But I have got very little articulate from him so far, beyond a belief that perhaps it is important. Felix wrote that he gave it up.

It is interesting to think of your dining at the Political Economy Club. I went there with J. S. Mill and there were present Bramwell,[1] Cairnes,[2] Fitzjames Stephen, the blind Postmaster General

[1] George William Wilshire Bramwell (1808-1892), Baron Bramwell; judge of the Court of Exchequer, 1856-1876, and of the Court of Appeal, 1876-1881.

[2] John Elliot Cairnes (1823-1875); economist and effective advocate of

(who wrote on political economy or his wife did), Fawcett[3]—I couldn't think of his name—and curiously enough the talk then also was on Coal—whether the financial policy of England should be governed by the prospective exhaustion of coal in H years as predicted by Jevons (not, I believe, the political economist of that name).[4] I ventured a whisper to my neighbor that 90 years was too far ahead to take into account for such purposes—so many things might happen. I remember that Stephen went to sleep at the table.

As to the thinking of business men I used a phrase that has been a good deal repeated—the inarticulate major premise.[5]

I have encountered men like your colleague who having had a little to do with public affairs found it hard to take up the smaller interests of the law, etc. I want to say to them that everything in the universe is as interesting as anything else if you are able to see it as a coherent part of a possibly coherent whole—and if you don't see the universal in your particular, you are a manual laborer and it doesn't matter.

On your (a) and (b) for workmen if we would avoid social cleavage I feel some sympathy and some doubt—I am not well informed—but I think more men live an essentially animal life than you seem to think—and I know no *a priori* reason or necessity for their not doing so.

My secretary has been reading to me Tom Perry's letters[6]—he was a member of a dining club with H. Adams, Howells, W. James, and various others and a very amusing talker but you realize the slightness of his intellectual frame as he talks on—to John Morse[7]—Moorfield Storey[8]—W. J., S. Reinach[9] *et al.*—at the same time very pleasant for an idle hour. You mentioned some-

---

the Northern cause in the Civil War, he was an intimate friend of Mill and Fawcett and author of *Some Leading Principles of Political Economy* (1874).

[3] Henry Fawcett (1833-1884); blinded in a shooting accident in 1858, he became Professor of Political Economy at Cambridge in 1863, a member of Parliament from 1865 to 1874, and Postmaster General in Gladstone's government in 1880.

[4] It seems likely that Holmes's recollection was wrong; in 1865, a year before Holmes attended the dinner of the Political Economy Club, William Stanley Jevons (1835-1882), economist, published his book *The Coal Question: An Enquiry concerning the Progress of the Nation and the Probable Exhaustion of Our Coal Mines.*

[5] "The Theory of Legal Interpretation," *Collected Legal Papers*, 203, 209: "But although practical men generally prefer to leave their major premises inarticulate, yet even for practical purposes theory generally turns out the most important thing in the end."

[6] *Selections from the Letters of Thomas Sergeant Perry* (E. A. Robinson, ed., 1929).

[7] John Torrey Morse, Jr., *supra*, p. 166.

[8] *Supra*, p. 42.

[9] Salomon Reinach (1858-1932); French archaeologist; author of *Orpheus* (1909) and *Apollo* (1904).

time back, *Farewell to Arms*—by Hemingway. I couldn't quite use
the superlatives that you and some others have used about it—
but it has some thrilling power. The author interested me by the
wonder that he raised in my mind, especially by another book, *The
Sun Also Rises*—as to why and how he interests me—extremely
ordinary people and extremely ordinary talk (noted with great
intensity, I admit) and yet I read on. He certainly is something of
a writer—whether a very great one I still doubt—as I, with due
and sincere modesty, doubt about the great lights among the modernist painters—hastening to add that I have seen but little of
Cézanne—their goddest God. There is one of his things here that
an expounding admirer told me he had come to see more atmosphere and everything else in than in any other painting. I know
how dwelling with a great master is necessary to get hold of him
—and so bow my head—but I haven't seen it yet—and the dwelling may distort. Perhaps the admiration has a touch of what Tom
Perry talks about—the hatred of the 20th century for the 19th
just as the 19th despised the 18th. The reactions amuse and interest me. I think I told you how pleased I was to read Scott—
Architecture—cracking up Palladian and the Baroque and putting
a spear into the side of Ruskin.

I have just today circulated a dissent from an opinion by
McReynolds—on the taxing power of the States under the 14th
Amendment.[10] McReynolds has the popular side—but to my mind
it is another case of treating the XIV Amendment as prohibiting
what 5 out of 9 old gentlemen don't think about right. This is a
sequel to one that I fired off at our last day of sitting before the
present recess.

I think that perhaps I am more scrupulous than you in answering bores that bother me with letters, or more likely, am slower
in my work. I think that I feel the constant gnawing of time—my
secretary and servants treat me as if I were porcelain and should
chip if anything touched me—whereas I inwardly believe that I
can tumble (as I did last summer) without breaking. I could say
more on the theme but it isn't polite and I may have said it before.
The clock strikes 9. I must descend to solitaire—as an old couple
sitting near us at the Hague said as they left an evening concert
in the wood, "Goodnight pleasant people"—and I add, dear friend.
Affectionately yours, O. W. H.
A theatre manager in Boston said to Salvini:[11] "I say old man—
do you want to be billed as Mons. or Sig."—pronounce as written.
Do you prefer to be addressed as *Prof.* H.J.L.?

---

[10] *Farmer's Loan and Trust Co.* v. *Minnesota, supra*, p. 295.
[11] Tommaso Salvini (1829-1915), Italian tragedian.

Devon Lodge, 23.XII.29

My dear Justice: You will forgive the intermission of a week. Quite suddenly ten days ago the P.M. produced a huge document that Webb had circulated to the Cabinet and asked me to produce a critical analysis of it. The document turned out to be a proposed constitution for E. Africa in general and Kenya in particular; he gave me until this morning to get it done and if ever I have worked, I have done this last ten days. However I have enjoyed it; for I have slaughtered Webb out of his own mouth and produced an alternative which is, I think, fairly respectable. My one complaint is that Webb had 7 months for his job, and I only had ten days for mine; he, moreover, will defend himself in person in the Cabinet and I, poor soul, must depend on others to answer him back. Still, it was great fun and I do not think the Lord will hold my draft up against me at the judgment day. I observe that what Webb got into 74 folio pages I got effortlessly into eleven.[1] . . .

Private: I had got so far when the telephone went and I was summoned to see Sankey at his house. I find that I have got to write a memorandum on the place of an economic general staff in the structure of government. As I believe there is no place for it, and have so written at length in my *Grammar of Politics,* and as S. tells me that the P.M. thinks it one of the great ideas of all time, it looks as though I have a difficult task ahead. However, I have stipulated that it is not to interfere with Xmas, and my holiday, and perhaps in the excitement of the Naval Conference[2] I can be supremely critical without causing undue pain. I do wish politicians were not so surrounded with a chorus of adulation. Any fool could show that MacDonald's idea is administratively unworkable; but he invited a dozen economists and business men to discuss it, and as he indicated that he thought there was something in it, they seem to have persuaded him that it was to politics what relativity is to physics. And I, poor soul, have to provide the cold douche. It's a hard life.

I had a golden account of you from Nevinson who dropped in to tea this afternoon; and he gave me good news of Felix. It only made me resent the more this postponement of my visit. But Yale writes very charmingly that it may want me next year.

Our love to you in a quite special way for 1930.

Ever affectionately yours, H. J. L.

---

[1] The government's plan for the administration of East Africa was published in a White Paper in June 1930; *Command Papers* #3573, 3574 (1930).

[2] The Four-Power Naval Conference was scheduled to convene in London in January.

VIII

1930-1932

Devon Lodge, 18.I.30

My dear Justice: I ought to have written to you earlier. But when I got back from the Continent a week ago, I was caught up in a whirl of work from which I have only just emerged. I think I told you that I had at the zero hour to do a draft constitution for Kenya. I came back to find that Webb (who is Secretary for the Colonies) was bitterly hostile, that Sankey was all for my draft, and that there was a grand fight in the Cabinet. I had to prepare a vast memorandum to answer Webb's points, and, what with the inevitable labours of a new term, it has taken all my time. You will forgive. . . .

I got back on Thursday week and spent two days with my people in Manchester. I met Alexander the philosopher there and was delighted to find him wrestling grimly with Whitehead's new book. He says he is at the fifth reading and that light begins dimly to dawn for him. I have tried it twice; but I find it complicated beyond endurance and I am afraid that I am cowardly enough to take it for granted henceforth. Alexander says it is infinitely worth while whence I infer that I am mistaken. But Hume upset the world with a book I can understand as I move, and I don't see why Whitehead should not take the trouble to do the same. . . .

Our love to you. Brandeis writes us that he has never known you in such good form.　　　*Ever affectionately yours, H. J. L.*

Devon Lodge, 2.II.30

My dear Justice: I like the bust a great deal.[1] It is a little severe,

---

[1] A letter from Holmes in which he enclosed a photograph of a bust, probably done by Serge Konenkov, is missing. For a photograph of the bust see 31 *Col. L. Rev.* opposite 349 (March 1931).

and the curl over the forehead is somewhat exaggerated; those things apart, it has vividness and life in it. But you do not say who did it.

. . . I also had a good time at the Prime Minister's to meet the Frenchmen, Tardieu and Briand.[2] The first—did you ever meet him in Washington in the war—I thought brilliant. He is a little "slick," and nothing is really quite so clear-cut as he sees it. But for power of statement and incisive response I should rate him very high. Briand is, of course, incredibly subtle, Balfour with twice the charm, thrice the wickedness, and N-times the gentle malice. He seems to me rather exactly what Renan must have been like—delighting in nuances and the delicate art of putting pins into flesh too obstinate to creep. He said of Daudet the scallywag son of Alphonse (the great Monarchist Anti-Semite) that they let him return as the number of Jews in Brussels was not enough to cause him pain.[3] Of Paul-Boncour,[4] the socialist lawyer (who has the largest practice in France) he said that he was so eloquent that he was twice in danger of convincing himself; "luckily his wife is a practical woman." Of Lloyd-George he said that he makes one realise how much one must lose to be sincere. I am afraid that MacDonald lost most of this as he speaks no French, and to watch the genial irony in Briand's eyes when MacDonald uttered some idealistic *banalité* was a joy beyond words. . . . A malicious old devil, but extraordinarily fascinating. . . .

Our love, as always, to you. Don't, please, overdo it while the Chief is away.   *Ever affectionately yours, H. J. L.*

Washington, D.C., February 14, 1930
My dear Laski: To write to you I rise from a bed of pain—no—not exactly that, but from a reclining chair where I have intended to divide the afternoon between slumber and listening to Walpole's *Letters*—a most delightful occupation for the moments between vacuity and thinking. For I am resting after a slight bellyache and its concomitants last night, that I am inclined to attribute to over-wrought intensity of work earlier in the week. I had to write a letter of farewell to the late Chief Justice on behalf of us all,[1] and

---

[2] At this time André Tardieu (1876-1945) was Premier, and Briand Foreign Minister. They were attending the Naval Conference in London.

[3] Léon Daudet (1867-1942), Royalist editor of *Action française*, following his escape from prison had lived as a refugee in Belgium until January 1930, when the President of France, Doumergue, had pardoned him.

[4] Joseph Paul-Boncour (1873-   ), lawyer and statesman, later was Premier and Foreign Minister; author of *Entre deux guerres; Souvenirs sur la troisième République* (1945).

[1] On February 3 Mr. Chief Justice Taft had resigned from the Supreme Court. He died on March 8, 1930. For Holmes's letter see 2 Pringle, *The Life and Times of William Howard Taft* (1939) 1079.

at the same time felt bound to assign to myself a patent case that I thought no one wanted.[2] That doesn't sound much—but it was on my nerves until I got them both done. The answer came to me from the Chief today, this morning being the first time that he was well enough to sign since the day our letter was left at his house, and I have my opinion back from a majority agreeing to it. I guess the others will—and that the defeated side will apply for a rehearing hinting that we don't understand the patents and that the application will be denied in the belief that we damned well do. But I am just emerging to sunlight so to speak—and haven't done much. I have spent an hour or two on a French translation from German of Arthur Drews: *Le mythe de Jésus*. Within the last year or two I have read one or two other books on that subject which I am surprised to find that I have to take seriously. It is very interesting, although of course I don't care personally whether J. C. really lived or is the product of a Gnostic Myth. I have several things on hand when I can get at them—*inter alia* a volume of Henri de Régnier's poems—to see if I find in him what I generally miss in the poetry of the musoos.[3] But I shall not accomplish anything serious in my few free moments—even when I am relieved from presiding by Hughes who to my great satisfaction I learn today is confirmed by the Senate as C.J.

Extraordinary what people will say. Is it politics and dishonesty from a man who knows better—or credulous prejudice? A senator said to be able, &c., talked about Taft's resignation as compelled and part of a political job! Yet—by an unspeakable brutality there was in one or more of the leading papers a photograph of him caught between the train and his house—with every spark of intelligence gone from his face. He has recurrences when he is more or less himself, but I imagine has no prospect of life, or reason to desire it. Hardening of the arteries and other troubles, I understand. We shall miss him much——but I shall welcome Hughes as an old friend. I was too old to be thought of and I should not have wanted the place for the same reason. I have got beyond the time when anything that anybody can give me will satisfy or even gratify my ambition. The only thing that could be given at an earlier stage was opportunity and that I have had. I haven't yet heard whether you have received and like the photograph of my bust. I think it flatters and it certainly pleases me.

I read Bowers' *Tragic Era* last summer and probably mentioned it. Your comment is just, and all the villains are republican, and the south and democrats saints. I believe he is to write the life of Beveridge—and I am somewhat doubtful whether Bowers

    [2] *Minerals Separation Corp.* v. *Magma Copper Co.*, 280 U.S. 400 (Feb. 24, 1930).
    [3] The volume of verse by Henri de Régnier (1864-1936), symbolist poet, has not been identified.

will help Beveridge's fame. I have not yet seen Wu—who has been in Chicago and is now I suppose at the Harvard Law School. I gather that he has been warmly received and made a very good impression. I hope this will catch tomorrow's mail—but fear.

Ever affectionately yours, O. W. H.

Washington, D.C., February 27, 1930
My dear Laski: As usual your letter (17.II.30)[1] suggests many themes for discourse. As to Hughes I was more pleased by his appointment than I could have been by any other. I took luncheon with the President and Mrs. Hoover last Sunday and she told me that the President would have liked to appoint me &c. &c. but thought that I ought not to be burdened &c. &c. It is true that I did not want to be, and no longer care for anything that anyone can give me. I never did very much. I would rather, I say in all seriousness, have your article in *Harper's* than the Chief Justiceship.[2] That and a few other things like it are the only rewards except the work. I don't so much mind Hughes having left the Bench and coming back. Lots of our judges have had the presidential bee and as to appointments by way of promotion I should adopt no formula. I thought when White was appointed that every judge except McKenna and me with or without his concurrence had a claque that was urging his merits. If Hughes could have been appointed then as was expected (but it was said that the opposition was too great) I think the history of the Court's doings would have been better than it is.

Later—Coming home this p.m. Brandeis spoke of the beauty of your article—and others have done so. As I wrote to you before I shrink from speaking yet and almost from reading it—for fear that it should somehow vanish—or you take it back.

Wu is in Cambridge and has sent me his photograph and a bit of autobiography, compiled he says at the request of Wigmore. I felt bound to write to him a letter that may destroy his regard for me, noticing the good opinion he seems to have of himself and cautioning him not to take too seriously compliments paid more readily to a visiting foreigner than they would be to a chap working his way up from the bottom here. More especially did I end on that while philosophic generalization was the last reward of serious work it also saw the escape of people who weren't willing to tackle the details &c. &c. I may be all wrong—but I have felt as if he was dodging the grind of life and as if I shouldn't do the

---

[1] Omitted from this edition.

[2] Mr. Justice Holmes: For his Eighty-Ninth Birthday," 160 *Harper's Magazine* 415 (March 1930); reprinted in *Mr. Justice Holmes* (Frankfurter, ed., 1931).

square thing unless I said a word. But I hated to—perhaps he will absolve me from all further responsibility and repudiate me, my ways, works and machinery. I don't believe he will—but if he does, then I owe him no more. Poor little cuss—there is a *naiveté* in the way in which he repeats the not too many compliments that he has received, that rather goes to my heart. I think I may have mentioned *L'Homme blanc—Souvenirs d'un Pierrot—par Le mime Séverin*. That is the last illustration of the lesson I should like Wu to learn—the very severe training that Severin went through and believed necessary to become what he was—and clever young men and women in Paris that said, "Oh, no—feeling is the thing, and if you have talent you can do the trick." I did delight in Severin's scorn of such. Probably I have quoted to you the artist Bill Hunt's remark to a pupil: "Oh I see, you want to do something damned smart, right off."

We are sitting—and I have been busy from 9:30 to 6 which it now is. I propose now to extend myself in a reclining chair and let my secretary read Horace Walpole's *Letters*—from now till I sleep or go to dinner whichever first happens.

Affectionately yours, O. W. Holmes

Devon Lodge, 22.II.30

My dear Justice: If my reckoning is just, this ought to reach you in Washington on or about your birthday. So it brings you all sorts of affectionate good wishes from us both. If you will look in *Harper's Magazine* for March you will find my birthday present. I hope it will give you half an hour's pleasure. It was difficult to put the joys of fifteen years friendship into words; but I hope some faint emanation of my pride in you is there.

The week has gone abominably quickly. Monday night, a gloriously funny dinner at Sankey's to meet all the Labour peers; the S.G.[1] and I the only commoners present. Feelings on my part (I) that they are a damned poor lot as a whole (II) very conscious of their dignity (III) terrified that the Lords may one day be reformed and they disappear. The one really bright moment was when Earl Russel[2] said to me that Bertie (his brother) was not yet up to the family average in wives. He, I gather, has had three; and the last ("Elizabeth") refused to divorce him on the ground that it would be unfair to other women. I went also to a jolly lunch given to young Broglie,[3] the French physicist who got the

---

[1] Sir James Melville (1885-1931).

[2] The third wife of Earl Russell (1865-1931) was the Countess Russell whose novels were published under the pseudonym "Elizabeth."

[3] Louis Victor, Prince de Broglie (1892-   ), in 1929 had received the Nobel Prize in Physics for his formulation of the theory of the wave character of electrons.

Nobel prize. About a dozen were there, and I had the sense of being in quite a new world from our own. Immense ambitions freely expressed, but always selfless ambition; passionate reverence for a good piece of work; enormous pride in clarity; and utter lack of anything like worldliness. It was a great moral lesson to sit and take note of the types one saw there. They were all great men in that ultimate sense of having surveyed some fragment of the unknown horizon; and yet not one of them cared for the kind of glory by which the politician lives. A good essay lies buried in this theme. . . .

That, I think, is my tale for the moment. But the main thing is your birthday. We shall drink your health here in the one bottle of Clicquot 1911 we possess.

My love as always,   *Yours ever affectionately, H. J. L.*

Devon Lodge, 2.III.30

My dear Justice: Harpers were really wicked to send you an advance copy; I intended it to reach you on your birthday. Let me say only that if the article gave you half an hour's pleasure, I am happy indeed. It was a joy to write it, for I had long wanted to proclaim some such feeling from the house-tops.

The days have simply flown this last week. A visit to Oxford, a lunch with Dwight Morrow[1] (a good fellow), a dinner with Miss Haldane, and a reception at the Foreign Office, beside the usual round of work and committees have taken up time. Oxford was very pleasant. It was amusing to be treated as an "authority" by undergraduates and so to realise that my vanity was tickled; and I had some pleasant talk with Holdsworth who, if dull, is full of knowledge. I learned from him one tale which is a pearl of price. Jenks, whom you know, applied to Birkenhead when the latter was Lord Chancellor to be made a K.C. In reply, he got the following letter: "My dear Jenks, In 1897 you gave the present L. Chancellor a second in the B.C.L. In 1898 you gave a second also to the present Vinerian professor.[2] These are, I think, sufficient honours for a single lifetime. Yours faithfully, B". A superb letter, I think, which only Birkenhead would have the intolerable audacity to write. I saw also Herbert Fisher who told me (and it pleased me) that almost the last time he saw Leslie Stephen the latter told him that his happiest memories of America were some talks with you. Dwight Morrow I liked greatly, and he told me the secret history

---

[1] Dwight Whitney Morrow (1873-1931), lawyer, banker, and diplomat, had been made American ambassador to Mexico in 1927, where he had skillfully settled hostilities between the Mexican government and the Roman Catholic Church. At the time when Laski saw him in London he was attending the Naval Conference.

[2] Sir William Holdsworth.

of his Mexican negotiations which were genuinely medieval in character. . . .

I am sending you separately a little book on the Age of Reason in which you will find a lecture of mine.[8] Most of them, I fear, are pretty obvious; but I think you will find some novelties in the lecture on Holbach and Helvétius.

Our love to you. Keep well and let Hughes relearn the habit of work.   *Ever yours affectionately, H. J. L.*

Devon Lodge, 16.III.30

My dear Justice: I have had a busy time since I wrote last, including three days in Newcastle, arbitrating eight industrial disputes. I don't know anything quite so difficult as to sit for eight or nine hours without making any observation which indicates your point of view. But I got through them with the help of some novels, and came back feeling like a tired God. I have also spent some time helping a little at the Naval Conference. That led to a pleasant dinner with George Rublee[1] and Dwight Morrow who both gave me some pleasant personal news of you; and I went to see Briand for the P.M. and came away feeling that I had been talking to an incarnation of the whole eighteenth century. Briand is diabolically clever, utterly cynical, and with all that hideous French logic which so often and so utterly misses the point of life. He said many clever things, and he seized my own points with remarkable quickness. But he never sought *once* to relate his view to mine. We were always driven back to his premise which was a sacred cow not to be milked. I got, moreover, the impression that he was too old and tired to care very deeply what might happen. George Rublee, by the way, said one thing that interested me, that Stimson would have been much more valuable as a delegate here if they had brought along Felix as his aide; for Felix was the one person who could make Stimson a first class man by his own perceptiveness. Of other things, I have had two or three meetings of the Donoughmore Committee,[2] always interesting, and a discussion of the future of the Spanish monarchy with a group of exiles which was like nothing so much as a page out of a Dumas novel. I had Manley Hudson and Borchard (of Yale)[3] to lunch; the former I thought rather pompous and absurd, though he

---

[8] *The Social and Political Ideas of Some Great French Thinkers of the Age of Reason* (Hearnshaw, ed., 1930). The introductory lecture, "The Age of Reason," was by Laski. The lecture on Helvétius and Holbach was by W. H. Wickwar.

[1] *Supra*, p. 82, Vol. I.

[2] The Earl of Donoughmore was Chairman of the Committee on Ministers' Powers.

[3] *Supra*, pp. 121, 162.

passed some strictures on Pound which interested me; Borchard I
thought both learned and charming, and capable of passionate
feeling on the remoter issues as when he launched into a fierce
denunciation of Brandeis for his attitude to the declaratory judgment.[4] And, by the way, Brandeis sent along a charming St. Louis
journalist to see us (name, alas, forgotten)[5] who was a specialist
in Holmesian lore and would, I believe, have passed a joint examination from Felix and me—perhaps the supreme test. I must add
the visit of a Spanish professor who was researching into Tudor
England, felt it his duty to vindicate the character of Bloody-Mary.
I explained that I had not the least objection to his vindication of
her or anyone else. He then said that it was understood in Spain
that Englishmen felt very hostile to her and he did not want to
accept my hospitality under false pretences. Could anything be
more charming? Imagine my explaining to an American host that
I intensely desire to vindicate the memory of Chester Arthur and
must be received only on that understanding. It is at least a fine
gesture as an exordium.

   In the way of reading, there are one or two things I must mention. First, Maurois's *Byron* is both charming and competent and
I hope you will trifle with it. For me at least it explains one side
of B. I have never understood, namely his persistence in cruelty.
Its weakness is that it does not make you see why the kind of
man he draws should have swept over Europe like an event. Then
a book *Ne Obliviscaris* by Lady Frances Balfour which amused me
beyond words. She is the daughter of the Duke of Argyll who
wrote that *Reign of Law* which might compete for a place in the
list of the hundred worst books, and a sister-in-law of Arthur
Balfour. What is thrilling in the book is its tone. She always refers
to her father as his grace, to the Queen *et al.* in terms of Majesty.
She describes the people outside her cenacle of aristocracy as
"George Meredith, later well-known as a novelist," or "Rodin, who
obtained fame as a sculptor." She talks quite seriously of "Milli-
cent, Duchess of Sutherland who has a secure place in history as
a hostess" and of "one Richard Jebb who was admitted to society
on account of his eminence as a scholar." When an English aristo-
crat is an unconscious snob, she can, I think, make the art reach a
level to which no other people can even hope to attain. I spoke
of her to Mrs. Asquith the other day, and she told me that Lady

---

[4] In a number of cases Mr. Justice Brandeis had indicated that the judicial
power of the United States did not extend to the issuance of so-called declaratory judgments; see, *e.g.*, *Willing* v. *Chicago Auditorium Association*,
277 U.S. 274 (1928). Professor Borchard was a crusader for the declaratory
form of judicial relief; see his book, *Declaratory Judgments* (1934).

[5] Charles G. Ross (1885-1950) was chief Washington correspondent for
the St. Louis *Post Dispatch*, 1918-1934. In 1945 he became Secretary to
President Truman in charge of press relations.

F. never forgave her husband for admitting a "workman" to the
cabinet. The "workman" was Lloyd-George who at the time was
a solicitor. Evidently below the bar one ceased to be a gentleman.
Is it not as I say, superb? She remembers what she wore at dinners
and how she dealt with recalcitrant servants. If I could have forty
pages in the *Quarterly Review* about her and string some quotations together, I verily believe I could make her immortal. I also
read a book Sam Morison has edited on Harvard in the last half-
century[6] which brought back some very pleasant memories. I note
with interest that whereas Eliot seems to have found Harvard men
to build with, Lowell's Harvard choices have been people like
Harlow Shapley[7] and Haskins whom he has brought from outside.

I must add one thing upon which you are not to comment.
Brandeis and Cardozo, JJ. have written to me letters about that
Harper piece of mine which could not be more kind had I written
about them. And Miss Haldane wrote to me to say that her brother
would have endorsed every word of it.

My love to you, as always. *Ever affectionately yours, H. J. L.*

Washington, D.C., March 27, 1930
My dear Laski: You do write such delightful letters that I blush
to think what a poor return I have made. Especially in these later
days. But I am and have been pretty constantly driven. I have
had (*entre nous*) a most important case on the withdrawal of
water from the Great Lakes to write[1]—more *certioraris* than you
could shake a stick at—answers to birthday letters—more than
200 have been despatched—and every morning an hour's work
imposed on me mostly by bores. This morning just after I had sent
round my opinion the C.J. came in for me to write two little
fellows—as it seemed necessary from the division of the Court.
But I must at least begin an answer to one received this morning
with several matters that I can't keep quiet about—(1.) your admirable statement of "that hideous French logic which so often
and so utterly misses the point of life." I often have made the same
reflection less happily expressed. (2.) But before I go on let me
tell you with what delight I read your Introductory Chapter on the
Age of Reason. It is admirable. (2.) [*sic*] I was going to express
my joy over your Spaniard and his scruples about accepting your
hospitality until he had explained his attitude to Bloody Mary.
That and the enchanting account of Ly. Frances Balfour tend

---

[6] *The Development of Harvard University, 1869-1929* (S. E. Morison,
ed., 1930).

[7] Harlow Shapley (1885-　　　), the distinguished astronomer, had been
called to Harvard in 1921 from the Mount Wilson Observatory in California.

[1] *Wisconsin* v. *Illinois*, 281 U.S. 179 (April 14, 1930).

slightly to illustrate my axiom that a gentleman can't be a philosopher (or a philosopher a gentleman). But (3.) I didn't suppose
that it still was possible for anyone to write in the tone of the
lady as you quote her. The world changes very slowly—you optimists must remember it.

Just here Gerrit Miller and his wife came in and cut this short
for I want it to go in the morning. I feel as if I had not written
for a thousand years. I read to Miller the passage about Ly. F.
Balfour—saying as above that I shouldn't have thought it possible
—whereat he reminded me of an English translator of the *Malleus
Maleficarum* writing well after 1900 exactly as he might have
written when the original work came out. That also was incredible
but there it was. I must add that your article in *Harper* seems to
have made a stir among people who are impressed by the beauty
of the writing. The other day on motion of Mr. La Follette it was
printed among the Congressional documents.[2] I remember feeling
very proud when a speech of mine was printed there—but that
was on Cabot Lodge's suggestion—whereas I suppose La Follette
is a stranger to you as he is to me. Owen Wister was here on
Sunday and has sent me a life of Lafayette—2 vols. by Brand
Whitlock—which he found interesting. The Parker House sends a
history of itself with some old Boston in it that really drew me
from duty for a few minutes & Miller wanted to leave a book
about Casanova in London which I declined being too balled up
—I fear that you don't care for Casanova—one of the best of
books. Miller also showed me a lot of modernist etchings and
lithographs which didn't hit me hard—He said they were trying
to do something new—and that to repeat what had been done
was a bore. I told him I thought it better to keep on the old paths
unless one really had something new to say—which reminds me
of Joyce's *Ulysses*—of which I have read a few pages. I read in
the *New Republic* that Joyce was a great poet—or at least a poet.
He may be, but he has such an abnormal hankering for nasty
words and disgusting thoughts that I don't expect to read more
than a specimen. I should think there was something wrong in his
nut. But I *must* go to bed. Good night.

Affectionately yours, O. W. Holmes

Devon Lodge, 6.IV.30
My dear Justice: A delightful and welcome letter from you reminds me that I have not written to you since I returned from

---

[2] On March 8, following a birthday tribute to Holmes by Senator Walsh of
Massachusetts, Senator Robert M. LaFollette, Jr., of Wisconsin moved that
Laski's article in *Harper's Magazine*, "Mr. Justice Holmes: For his Eighty-
Ninth Birthday," should be printed in the *Congressional Record*. See 72
Congress. Rec. (71st Congress, 2nd Session), part V, p. 5008.

Paris. I had ten ecstatic days of sunshine there. Each day I hunted books; each night I dined and talked until the small hours. Except the politicians, whom I studiously avoided, I saw nearly everyone I wanted to see—Émile Meyerson, the philosopher, Lapradelle, the international lawyer, André Gide the novelist, Halévy the historian, and critics galore. The best night, I think, was one where I dined with half a dozen of the critics, and we fought the battle of romanticism all over again. You cannot even imagine the passion it engendered. That Racine and Bossuet and Boileau were the essential France; that Rousseau and Mme. de Staël and Hugo perverted the French genius; that only a return to the qualities of the 17th century can restore the greatness of France—these they maintained with a vehemence I cannot produce in it. I caused what I can only call consternation by arguing that classic and romantic are false antitheses—that each is a requisite of intellectual health, that romantic sensibility made men see beauties worth seeing and never before seen, that an affirmation of personal experience as valid against the tradition is one of the ways of adjusting that tradition to new wants which must find response. One excited soul got up and said I was a traitor to the Hellenic spirit —that I had been willing to *conspuer* the sacred beauties of France. Another argued that only by fidelity to the classic tradition could we distinguish between true and false, right and wrong, beauty and ugliness. For another still classicism was reverence, self-restraint, discipline; for another still, the monarchy and the church, parents of French glory. I asked if between 1830 and 1930 I could be given one Frenchman of genius who had dwelt in the classical tradition—answer in the negative. I said that if a century could not *create* in a tradition that meant its exhaustion as a vehicle of expression. Answer, let us be exhausted, but let us at least expel from our literature alien elements which corrupt the purity of our spirit. I wish you could have seen it all. Life being sacrificed to logic with a glorious disregard of everything significant in our time that made me feel as though I was dwelling with the last of the Mohicans. I was interested to find that Meyerson had a tremendous respect for Morris Cohen and an equal contempt for Bergson. And Gide tried to explain to me that James Joyce's *Ulysses* was a European portent; to which I replied that the willingness to write the vocabulary of the latrine in a book did not seem to me epoch-making. I was impressed by the universal commendation of Ernest Hemingway, whom all the critics I saw regard as the promise of America, with dos Passos a very close second. But what is striking, and, I think, a little painful, is that the American writers they know are chiefly what I may compendiously term the anti-Americans. People fifteen years dead they do not know at all; and people I regard as important, like Willa Cather, they do not

know because she only depicts America and does not criticise
it. Much the same is true of their attitude to ourselves. They translate the precious and the esoteric; they hardly know what is central and explanatory. Indeed I should be tempted to say that they
read foreign literature in order to thank God they are not as other
peoples are. But they retain a marvellous power of discussion for
the glory of discussion. They have their sects and chapels, but
they feel that intellectual differences really matter. That makes
them nearly as delightful as they are insular and wrong-
headed. . . .

Since then, I have been at committees and doing a good bit of
writing—all in a leisurely way. I dined the other night with
Dwight Morrow and we condoled over the fizzle of the Conference. . . .

Our love warmly to you. From now on I venture to resume
weekly discourse.   *Ever affectionately yours, H. J. L.*

April 18, 1930

My dear Laski: A wonderfully interesting account of your jaw
with the mussoos about classicism and romanticism, etc. Of course
they seem to me as to you ridiculous. But that we must discount,
for it means that you and I tacitly assume *our* aesthetic ultimates
to be valid against theirs. I think they are because I think them
founded on a wider view—but if the Frenchmen think not, we
can't patronize them before a dispassionate tribunal, although of
course we do between ourselves. I often think of the way our side
shrieked during the late war at various things done by the Germans such as the use of gas. We said gentlemen don't do such
things—to which the Germans: "Who the hell are you? *We* do
them." There was no superior tribunal to decide—so logically the
Germans stood as well as we did. That case reminded me of a
cause célèbre in a yearly collection that used to be put out by
Albert Bataille from the *Figaro.*[1] A duellist was tried on the ground
that he had done a forbidden thing—grasped his adversary's
weapon—and a lot of experts testified that that couldn't be done.
Then a lot of duellists went on the stand and said that is a fencing
school rule—when you go on the ground you go there to kill the
other man and may do what you can. Probably I have told you of
this a dozen times before, as it is a stock illustration of mine. But
to use another stock phrase inverted—you must deal with friends
as you do with great men and let them bore you if you want to
get the themness of them. I agree with your French philosopher

---

[1] Albert Bataille (1856-1899), journalist and reporter of criminal cases
tried in the French courts; his accounts of cases were republished in book
form.

whose name I can't read as to Cohen—and in a less certain degree as to Bergson. As to Ernest Hemingway, perhaps—Dos Passos I know only by name. Willa Cather I know only a little—by one book—name forgotten—that didn't impress me greatly.

As to the French critics feeling their intellectual differences—I remember a French book of interviews with the then young *littérateurs*—it must have been 20 years ago, for Zola was in it as an older man saying that these young sharks when they couldn't find anything else to bite devoured each other—well they all talked with ferocity as if they were divided by gulfs—and to me they seemed like smoked herrings in a box. They all tasted alike.

I am going on much as usual. Occasionally a dame feeds with me—preferably at luncheon as I am tired at night. Some time ago as perhaps I told you Mrs. Hoover came—*per quod* I had to break my rules and lunch with her and the President (no one else) and found it very pleasant. I have almost no time to read. I am much bothered by many letters that call for an answer to which they are not entitled. Just now I have a collection of essays called *Human Biology and Racial Welfare* that seems worth reading— though intolerably heavy to my hands, as cheap American books are. It seems to promise a good general view—beginning with Life in Space and Time—(the guess as to life on other bodies than the earth)—then Evolution traced biochemically—then the animal ancestry of man—the Evolution of the brain &c. &c. I think it will pay me. My sec'y has nearly finished reading aloud to me at the end of the day—*The Story of San Michele* by Axel Munthe. He is a real man I am told—and his tower of San Michele is very like a place that an Englishwoman whom I have met at intervals has told me about. I should think it might be truth in a haze. But I shall be glad to get back to my last volume of Horace Walpole. H. W. seems to have been a pretty good fellow and, in flashes, ahead of his time. But I must away from you—and turn to less intimate things.   *Affectionately yours, O. W. Holmes*

Devon Lodge, 19.IV.30

My dear Justice: A gloriously quiet week to record in which only one external event has happened. I went on Monday to hear Snowden introduce the Budget of which the essential feature was a small but (I think) inevitable increase in the income-tax. I wish you could have seen the House. It was packed like a sardine-tin, with a hum of eager expectancy the like of which one rarely sees as possible. The rich members sat as tho' they were going to hear sentence of death. The Labour people were like hounds in leash ready to dash into cheers at the slightest provocation. And the production of anger, sorrow, temper at a change which I can best express by saying that I shall pay about one hundred dollars more a year was, to me, quite amazing. I put the reflexion that I cannot understand why men are so anxious to die for the State and so angry if they are asked to give money to it, even for objects they know to be essential. Churchill, for instance, spoke to me in the lobby like a man who has heard that London has fallen. A young Tory said to me that four years more of this would ruin the empire. And all I heard was a rather dull and careful speech, with nothing dramatic in it, which made a difference of perhaps three per cent to the expenditure of anyone there with a thousand a year. Truly Madison was right when he said that the only durable source of faction is property. I asked Churchill, if he thought of taxation as a voluntary offering by the citizen to objects he felt inclined individually to support; certainly that was his attitude. Lady Astor, who is said to have a million dollars a year, was acting like a woman who has just heard that a defaulting solicitor has run off with all her money. . . .

I have read much these last days, but mostly the 17th century. At the moment, I am in the midst of an amusing and revealing literature, the imaginary voyages of the 17th century where people sought to criticise existing institutions by pretending to explain what they had seen elsewhere. It isn't exciting, except that it shows pretty obviously one of the vital sources of political romanticism, how profoundly the discoveries affected human imagination and how diseased was the society which issued inevitably in 1789. And I would like to write a little paper on the psychical effects of America before 1700, there is much to be said on that; how the reaction of what Europe thought America was sent out the immigrant with ideals which moulded American institutions themselves and made 1776 ultimately essential to the satisfaction of the human spirit. Then I have read the manifesto of that new humanism of which I gather Irving Babbitt is the high priest.[1] I have asked *Harper's* to let me write about it, and I hope they will, for it seemed to me even sillier than most religions. Why that type of cold, aesthetic renunciation (at a level of $5000 and up) should have any meaning for a factory civilisation I cannot imagine. And its humourless complacency, its plea for a self-chosen aristocracy, its sense of a high mission not open to ordinary men, its belief that it has rewon classic beauty, all this makes me a little sick. Incidentally, I am amused at its enthusiasm for French 17th century classicism. Apart from Corneille, La Fontaine and Racine, I doubt whether there was a single French poet of importance until the Romantic movement of the nineteenth century.

---

[1] Presumably *Humanism and America* (Norman Foerster, ed., 1930). The volume included "Humanism: an Essay at Definition," by Professor Irving Babbitt (1865-1933) of Harvard. *Harper's* published no essay on this subject by Laski.

There is not one great piece of political thinking, and the one great philosophic effort, Descartes, is, in a sense, the fount of romanticism by its insistence upon the validity of *my* experience as the sole source of my knowledge. These pale little prigs of professors in Princeton and Harvard and Virginia need a douche of cold water to make them use their minds seriously.

I have bought nothing since I got back from Paris, except a rather nice Spinoza in four volumes; and the letters are fascinating. I never, fool that I am, read them before.

Our united love to you. Keep well and take my new little book as evidence that you are never out of my thoughts.

Ever affectionately yours, H. J. L.

Devon Lodge, 26.IV.30

My dear Justice: I have felt almost on the way to you this week, for I have been busy arranging with Yale the courses I am to teach there next year, and I have got a real thrill out of it. Otherwise the time has been quiet and very pleasant: a little writing, much reading, and a jolly dinner. By the way, there will go off to you next Thursday a copy of my little book on Liberty. About Chapters I and III I expect only interstitial agreement from you; but on Chapter II I hope you will be my full compurgator.[1] What is really important is that you should feel that the book is, above all, the expression of an affection that only grows more full with the years.

First my dinner party. It was at Downing Street to meet some literary gents, and it so happened that it occurred on the day of the poet laureate's death.[2] Now three of them might well have thought themselves not ineligible for the post, and they did what you once described Henry van Dyke as doing—they strutted sitting. When one of them observed that the P.M. called me by my first name, he changed from complete ignoration of my presence to an almost pathetic agreement with every word I said. Ramsay spoke warmly of an article of mine; the poet spoke of it with ecstasy. Ramsay asked the source of a quotation which I supplied (some famous lines from Blake); the poet praised my marvellous memory. So it went on. Then, bashfully, another of them raised the question of who ought to succeed Bridges. Names were suggested and the P.M. asked my view. I spoke strongly in favour of abolishing the post as a stupid one and J.R.M. was obviously

---

[1] In the first chapter of *Liberty in the Modern State* (1930) Laski emphasized his familiar pluralistic thesis, acknowledging frankly that his was a doctrine of "contingent anarchy." The second chapter was a broad defense of libertarianism in matters of belief and the expression of belief. The third and final chapter, "Liberty and Social Power," urged that liberty can thrive only in a society in which there is equality.

[2] Robert Bridges (1844-1930) had been appointed Poet Laureate in 1913.

moved by what I said. I wish you could have seen the poet's face. He made a savage little oration to the effect that to destroy a tradition was like the ruin of a beautiful old building, that he was sure the P.M. did not share my vandalism and so on. I have never seen a man so embody hate. In fact Snowden said to me as we left, "Laski, if I were you, I would ask for police protection from that fellow until MacDonald has found his poet." The whole show was one of the very funniest things I have ever witnessed. . . .

Ever affectionately yours, H. J. L.

May 12, 1930

My dear Laski: You write books faster than I can read them. *The Dangers of Obedience,* I suppose, is ancient history to you by this time. I finished it a few days ago. I readmired the Rousseau and Machiavelli and believed without adequate knowledge what you say about foundations etc.[1] I always have viewed them with suspicion and many years ago when Dillon[2] sent me a speech accepting one of Carnegie's gifts wrote to him that *prima facie* a man who used his power to divert a considerable fund from the competition of the market was an enemy of his kind. You optimists tacitly postulate a dictator embodying your conception of what is best for the world. My only criterion is the *de facto* equilibrium of social desires. The first half of this is intended only for insult— in the hope of giving pain. What I put as an assertion is hardly more than a surmise. Of course as you know I have but partial sympathy with your equality business. This morning comes *The Socialist Tradition in the French Revolution*[3]—which I shall gobble before I sleep. It looks thrilling—to use your word. Yesterday I was notified of the sending of *Liberty in the Modern State*—not yet received. You keep me busy in my spare moments.

Also some ripping letters from you—the last enclosing one from my foster granddaughter. Please give her my love. If I could write as well as she does I should answer her directly—but I am instructed that adult education is needed for my chirography. My brethren habitually profess inability to read my script. I am delighted with your poets and the Laureateship. I rather incline to agree with you, that the institution might be dropped. I hardly believe that it will be. Your reflections on the income tax in

---

[1] In his essay "Foundations, Universities, and Research," Laski expressed much skepticism concerning the wisdom and fruitfulness of such enterprises in research as those fostered and directed by the large foundations and councils of social scientists.

[2] *Supra,* p. 237, Vol. I.

[3] The lecture, originally delivered at King's College, London, was first published as a pamphlet by the Fabian Society and was later republished in *The Social and Political Ideas of Some Representative Thinkers of the Revolutionary Era* (Hearnshaw, ed., 1931).

Supreme Court of the United States,
Justice's Chambers. May 12/30

My Dear Laski

Your *** books ***
than I can read them. The danger of
*** I suppose, is *** *** to you
by this time. I *** it a few days ago.
I read *** to Rousseau and Machiavelli
and believe without adequate knowledge
*** say about foundations *** I always
have *** them with suspicion and many
years ago when Dillon *** *** a *** ***
***ting one of Carnegie's gifts *** to him
*** *** *** a man to *** *** his ***
to *** a candidate *** *** the competition
of the market was an enemy of his kind.
Your optimists *** *** a dictator
embodying your conception of what is best for the
world. My only criterion is the de facto equilibrium of social *** The *** *** on this

Holmes to Laski, May 12, 1930

is intended only for insult - in the hope of giving pain. What I feel as an accusation is hardly more than a surmise. Of course as you know I have but partial sympathy with your Equality business.

This morning comes The Socialist Tradition in the French Revolution - which I shall gobble before I sleep - It looks thrilling - to use your words. Yesterday evening I was notified of the sending of Liberty in the Modern State - not yet received. You keep me busy in my spare moments.

Also, some rejoicing letters from you. The last enclosing one from my father & grandmother. Please give them my love. If I could write as well as she does I should answer her directly - but I am instructed that I dictate to our stenographer. My brethren habitually reproach an ability to read my script. I am delighted with your poster and its draughtsmanship. I rather incline to agree with you, but the inclination may be dropped. I hardly believe that it will be. Your reflection on the inclemency in another letter has my heartiest concurrence. (always excepted) I pay my tax bills more readily than anyone. The whole theory of money is one on which I get curiously deeply to me, I have wondered similarly at the readiness of otherwise honest people to dodge an attempt to exact the government out of dues when they come into port; I remember in

another letter have my heartiest concurrence. I always say that I pay my tax bills more readily than any others—for whether the money is well or ill spent I get civilized society for it. I have wondered similarly as to readiness of otherwise honest people to dodge or indeed to swindle the government out of duties when they come into port. I remember a classmate of mine, a comeouter, who probably thought himself a good example of the upward and onward, telling us with glee how he had defrauded the revenue coming into Boston. (We were on the same boat.) It made me gasp. Then I was more than interested by the German professor who had been sizing up America.

Apropos of the new humanism there was an article by Edmund Wilson in the *New Republic*[4] that I should think embodied your views. I do not know these seeming prigs—but I read the chaff and abuse of them with pleasure. Your "pale little prigs of professors" is A-1. I am ignorant as I say, but I propel them from my inner consciousness. I stop my comments to say that since the last sentence my secretary and I (with the faithful Charley who has driven me for more than a quarter of a century) have motored through the Soldier's Home and back by a *circumbendibus* through Rock Creek Park. The locusts are in bloom and the peonies are masses of perfumed purple—now turning a little with age. The weather is a little trying to me. But everything is most beautiful —*per quod,* reflecting that I had done nothing except take air, I said to my lad the last achievement is to enjoy without accomplishment. I find it hard.

My secretary has just telephoned to the Congressional Library to see if we can [have] L. Pearsall Smith's *Four Words*—that you mentioned. My opinions—only two rather trifling ones, but I suppose the last for this term[5]—have been written and approved— and I am for the moment up with the *certioraris.*

Berths to Boston for the night of June 4 bespoke [for] the whole crowd—the servants going up under my wing. It looks like the approach of breathing time—though there will be big mailbags of *certioraris* during the summer if I am there to receive them, as looks likely at this writing. Now I turn to some of the chores that are always on hand to be done.

Ever affectionately yours, O. W. Holmes

Devon Lodge, 10.V.30
My dear Justice: . . . For your private ear, I must tell you about the poet laureate. The P.M. had decided on Masefield from the

[4] "Notes on Babbitt and More," 62 *New Republic* 115 (March 19, 1930).
[5] *Eliason* v. *Wilborn,* 281 U.S. 457; *Barker Painting Co.* v. *Local No. 734, id.* 462 (May 19, 1930).

outset; but he had to let a decent interval elapse. The most incredible people wrote to him to emphasise their claims. A lady
poet wrote to exhort him to appoint her in the name of woman's
rights. John Drinkwater wrote to say that the P.M. might like to
know that he had just joined (the day after Bridges' death) the
Labour Party. Another gent sent him three specimen odes: 1.
funeral; 2. nuptial; 3. successful royal confinement to show him
how he would do the thing if appointed. Another poet wrote offering, if given the post, to do a philosophic-poetic account of the
Labour programme. And a well-known man of letters who is about
the best Tory-snob in London wrote to say that his advice was at
the P.M.'s disposal as he supposed that this was a realm in which
the P.M. had no experience. This gent., I may add, when he saw
the appointment wrote to congratulate MacDonald and added that
it was the name he himself would have suggested. As MacD. said
to me he probably wrote to Masefield claiming credit for the
appointment. It is a funny world, about which one really cannot
find one's way without a sense of humour. . . .

You must hear of Lord Birkenhead's dilemma. He has just published a Utopia which has had vast publicity. I read it and found
two passages taken verbatim from Haldane's *Daedalus*. I wrote to
the latter who, on careful comparison, has found forty-four passages of this kind and round this curious resemblance has written
a charming article suggesting that his book and B's are probably
based on a "Q" like Mark and Luke since it is impossible to suppose that Lord B. would plagiarise from a humble professor of
bio-chemistry.[1] We are waiting eagerly for Lord B's reply. It is a
warning to great men not, like him, to rely on ghosts but to write
their own books if they *must* write books.

Our love to you as always.   *Yours ever affectionately, H. J. L.*

Sunday evening, May 18, 1930
My dear Laski: In the great steeple chase after your pen I now
have read the latest—*Liberty in the Modern State*—and as it did
not bear your inscription I have written my name "from H.J.L."
with the date, that I might claim all the honor to which I am
entitled. You rightly divined that chapter 2 (I think it is) as to
Freedom of Thought commanded not only my sympathy but my
admiration. I may remark in passing that I think the argument for
free speech, devoutly as I believe in it, is not entirely easy. In
other cases, *e.g.* vaccination, when we know that we have the
power, want the end, and are convinced of the efficacy of the

---

[1] The comments of J. B. S. Haldane on Lord Birkenhead's *The World in
2030 A.D.* (1930) are found in his essay "Lord Birkenhead Improves his
Mind," in *A Banned Broadcast and Other Essays* (1946), 13.

means we don't hesitate very much over even conscientious scruples. Or at least I shouldn't. But as you leave worship free, when you become God, and dispose of large futures on formulas that I think fishy, I will hold my obeisance—can it be that I am in an unreasonably rebarbative condition? F. Pollock the other day, and again recurring to it, thinks that *The Testament of Beauty* by the late Laureate is a great philosophical poem. I admit that I read it under unfavorable conditions, but it seems to me the cosmos arranged to suit polite English taste, and by no means to be mentioned with Lucretius as it is by F. P. *Inter alia* I have read *The New Evolution-Zoogenesis* by Austin H. Clark, who married a dear little cousin of mine and in whom I therefore am interested. He like my (wife's) nephew Gerrit Miller is a very distinguished scientific man, rejects all missing links. He thinks there is not a particle of evidence that the great types of animal life did not start as distinct as they are now, and believes that the differentiation started with the primordial cell. I am curious to see how the book will be taken by the scientific world. The English I believe are pretty well committed to their Piltdown bones &c but I guess that Miller had a preponderant opinion on his side.

Also I read the little pamphlet on *Four Words* with pleasure—and have gone through a work by many authors dealing with man and the universe,[1] from the chance of other inhabited spheres to the details of the human body and the outlook for the future, at every point coming on mystery at the crucial point—incidentally one of those odiously heavy American books that contrast so unfavorably with the run of English ones. I suppose the paper is loaded with clay or chalk or God knows what.

This is all for the moment. We deliver some opinions tomorrow —but argument is over &c. I have bought tickets for the family for Boston the night of June 4. I wish I were going to see you. I shall drive through Rockport and glow and sigh.

Affectionately yours, O. W. Holmes

Devon Lodge, 18.V.30

My dear Justice: . . . Felix has worried me a little by sending me on a letter from Wu asking to be invited to give six lectures on legal philosophy to the university here. I have had to write and ask Felix to explain that the lawyers here, who have never heard of him, might ask him to lecture on China, but can hardly risk the other. I hope Wigmore & Co. are not spoiling him out there. His letter to Felix was almost like a royal command. He used always to sound so charming and modest that I was a little distressed by the peremptory character

[1] Presumably *Human Biology and Racial Welfare* (Cowdry, ed., 1930), *supra*, p. 313.

of his requirements. Have you seen him since he got to America?
And, between ourselves, do you think that what he has to say on
legal philosophy is really important? I thought his book of essays the
expression of a rare spirit, but no more. I do not want to disappoint
him. But, also, I do not want to recommend him to the lawyers and
leave them feeling they have wasted time and money in getting him
here. . . .

Our love to you and the very best of good wishes. You are, I
suppose, within a fortnight of Beverly?

Ever affectionately yours, H. J. L.

May 28, 1930

My dear Laski: A letter has just come from you after another not
answered that arrived on the heels of one that I had sent to you.
I have been and am so busy that I still should wait but for the
inquiry about Wu, which needs immediate attention. I am disturbed, almost distressed by what you say. While he was with
Wigmore he sent me some sort of autobiographical sketch, I think,
written in a tone that made me uneasy and I wrote to him about
it. But he is so ready to be humble that he disarmed me at once
I have done what I could to impress him with the belief that
philosophizing about the law does not amount to much until one
has soaked in the details—and have not disguised my fear that he
has chosen the primrose path in coming here at this time. He has
an instinct for philosophy and has read a good deal—but I wish
that he could wait until he had seen more of life. I doubt if he
yet distinguishes between what real contribution he may have to
make and the obvious, possibly expressed in a somewhat new form
I hate to throw cold water on anything that he wants—but
should not dare to say confidently that he could make any funda
mental revelation. Let me emphasize that I don't believe that the
swelling tone that you noted is serious. I guess that Wu is as ready
to despair as to assume a throne. I have seen him for a short time
only and then mainly in company and I think that he is the same
dear chap as always.

I have only had half an hour after supper (I don't call it dinner
any longer as the only scrap of meat that I eat comes at 1:30
to read. I have been reading unwillingly but with a good deal of
interest 2 volumes sent to me by Owen Wister—a life of LaFay
ette by Brand Whitlock—my notion of LaFayette, derived I sup
pose from Carlyle, had not been reverential. But the old boy did
stick to his convictions so magnificently, never yielding an inch
for royalty, mob, prison, or Bonaparte, that I feel a deep respect
—and that although he when young at least had incredible vanit
and cared more for the applause of the crowd than I should thin

possible for a wise man. He may not have been wise, but he was a gallant gentleman. As I read again about the time of the Terror I was reinforced in my feeling that the first of the primates was a good deal like the rest of them and as subject today as ever to herd movements. There is a good deal of sadness in old age, even if one has gaiety on top and an interest in the day. I was feeling finished when I got a letter from the ever encouraging Felix cracking up a dissent from an opinion of the majority by McReynolds, that put heart into me.[1] I was amused by McR.'s opening remark that all "with unclouded minds" could see &c. But to my regret I believe the phrase does not appear in the print. He readily lapses into a certain arrogance of tone—yet I believe him to be a man of feeling with a disguised tender side.

I want to run on but I must stop leaving many things untouched but always,   *Yours affectionately, O. W. Holmes*

Devon Lodge, 7.VI.30

My dear Justice: . . . In the way of reading there are some things you must read. Item One, a novel called *April Fools* by Compton Mackenzie, one of the funniest things I have read in years. The clergyman in it is worthy of P. G. Wodehouse at his most ludicrous. When I say that he proposed to write a play called *Thomas* and that as the curtain rises a cock is to crow thrice, you will see that it is a side-splitter. Item two, a *Short History of France* by Charles Guignebert which is the best short and critical survey—rather like George Trevelyan on England—I have ever read. The discussion on early French civilisation is peculiarly attractive. Item three—Trotsky's *Autobiography*. This I beg you to read. Nothing even approaches it either as explanation of Russia, its strength and weakness, or as a great and dramatic narrative. The book pulsates with excitement and I know nothing of the kind in years that has moved me so much. I challenge anyone to read his account of the capture of Petrograd by the Bolsheviks without a thrill, or his description of the negotiations at Brest-Litovsk without a desire to cheer. And apart from certain correspondence I know nothing which makes one see so clearly what a great man Lenin was or how small are the *epigoni* who have usurped his position. Do, do, read it and feel that the grandeur of romance on the heroic scale has not yet gone out of the world. Lastly, I must mention Mencken's *Treatise on the Gods*, which, with some faults of taste and temper, seemed to me to express incisively and sensibly the case against organised supernaturalism of any kind. . . .

[1] *Baldwin v. Missouri*, 281 U.S. 586, 595 (May 26, 1930).

Well—my love to you as always. Don't let either visitors or *certioraris* stand in the way of Trotsky and Compton Mackenzie.
Ever affectionately yours, H. J. L.

Beverly Farms, June 8, 1930
My dear Laski: It is a continual marvel to me how you find time to write to me such uniformly admirable and delightful letters when you have so much work to do. Two bodies perhaps can occupy the same place, but can you attend an arbitration, write a book and send off a letter all at once? Your letter[1] met me here on my arrival yesterday evening—the best of welcomes—and I am wallowing in comfort, though the weather is somewhat chilly and misty and I am staying indoors hoping to dodge a cold. The journey on is somewhat upsetting. Actually I have had a day of almost leisure and my secretary has read to me (1) *The Show Girl and her Friends* and (2) *Conversations of a Chorus Girl*—by Roy McCardell—an author of whom I never heard outside of this house but whose two booklets I read every time that I come here. I prefer them to the works of more famous authors. Before I left I let off a dissent on what sems to me the abuse of the "due process of law" clause in the 14th Amendment, as to which I have just come on some notice in the *New Republic* which I enclose as they copy what I say.[2] I regret being called the dissenting Judge in the papers for I don't like to dissent. But if one does one can talk more freely than when he speaks for others as well as for himself. Resolutions by a committee are always flat unless they put themselves into the hands of one man. I suspect that McReynolds may regard me as a bird that befouls its own nest, although nothing could be farther from my wishes or intent. We are on excellent terms together, but our notions are different. So that's that.

Later—My secretary this evening has been reading to me what you will more approve, some of Birrell's *Obiter Dicta*—mighty good reading they are—but I haven't passed so idle a day since I can't remember when. One of the pleasures of age is that occasionally some old lady that one hasn't seen for fifty or it may be more years, up and writes to one. I have had several such letters—and the day before yesterday in Boston called on one of them. I should not have known her but had a mighty pleasant talk with a civilized woman who has seen the world from China to Venice (if not Peru) and just before I left had a note proposing a call from one with whom I walked when she was a charming little girl to whom I told stories and who sent me a book mark that I was able to

---

[1] Omitted from this edition.
[2] 63 *New Republic* 82-83 (June 11, 1930). The comment was on Holmes's dissent in *Baldwin* v. *Missouri, supra,* p. 323.

tell her was still in Burke's *Works*. She is a grandmother and the mother of a Senator.[3] This drool that I am writing is better to go to sleep on than discourse on high themes—so I will go to bed now.
Ever your Affectionate O. W. H.

Beverly Farms, [Saturday] *June 21, 1930*
My dear Laski: Forgive this paper—it is so much more comfortable for writing than note paper and is the best that I can get here in a block. Obedient to your order I sent for and last night received Trotsky's *Autobiography* (off my beat, but I am reasonably obedient!). The Old Corner Bookstore did not have Compton Mackenzie's book and as somehow I doubted if I should find it as funny as you do I didn't press the order. At the same time I received Owen Wister's book about Roosevelt with some discourse on the people who used to get to the White House in his time including myself. I shall read that first, but it is easy doing. *Ad interim,* in my ¾ lazy and languid days my secretary has been reading aloud to me —some of the Restoration plays—Congreve and Van Brugh— rather rudimentary in their emotion, interest, and wit, with an absence of confidence between husband and wife that is surprising in our day, and I suppose stage rather than life. The Duke of Buckingham's *Rehearsal* seemed to me on a higher grade distinctly. He must have been a lively lad—to write that and run Lord Shrewsbury through.[1] As by-products—a book by Max Beerbohm, *Zuleika Dobson*—wit and good writing—but longer than the matter justified. Oscar Wilde's plays—mostly drool—but 2 or 3 good. One first class saying—a cynic—one who knows the price of everything and the value of nothing. And latterly Aug. Birrell's *Res Judicatae*—*Men Women and Books*—and now *Obiter Dicta*. They stand rereading well—but I had forgotten them. Why do you never mention him in these days? Have you cause to see him? He is a mighty pleasant embodiment of English discernment and prejudice —missing as I think the last word. It seems to me that there is a last spiritual touch that he cannot give, but a stout old Briton whom one respects. I spent some time on my friend Felix [*sic*] Warburg's account of the Federal Reserve System,[2] but it came hard to me because I do not understand the words or know the postulates. Yesterday Felix, Walter Lippmann and Judge Learned Hand came here to luncheon and gave me great pleasure. I said

---

[3] Mrs. William Bayard Cutting, mother of Bronson Cutting (1888-1935), Senator from New Mexico.

[1] George Villiers (1628-1687), second Duke of Buckingham, stormy statesman and sportsman of the Restoration, in 1667 killed the Earl of Shrewsbury in a duel and gave the widowed Countess, his mistress, shelter under his hospitable roof.

[2] Paul M. Warburg, *The Federal Reserve System, Its Origin and Growth* (1930).

to them that the best thing I could do was to die. Everything has
been so smiling to me this last year that I tremble, and fear that
I shall do some damned thing that will put a fly into the ointment,
but Hand replied, "All life is taking a risk. Go ahead and take it"
—and I thought he was right. But still I tremble. I am writing
hurriedly hoping to catch the presumed boat. I am a fool. I have
been thinking that today was Friday and that if I posted this about
3 p.m. it could go on the morrow. Still as I go out in a few minutes
to the p.o. I will send this off. I hate to have things waiting to be
finished. Yesterday I had also a visit from Wu and another Chinaman—who proposed to name a prospective building in Shanghai
for me and to use my name to invite subscriptions. I dissuaded the
former and denied the latter, and at once was impressed by the
good breeding of the East. They didn't tease or look sad. They
accepted my veto, remained pleasant and didn't stay too long. I
am easily tired in these days. At odd minutes I have reread some
chapters of Einstein's *Tudor Ideals*. They seemed to me very good.
They also had passed from my memory. It will be a shame if he
doesn't settle down to some solid work. I have exhorted him to.
I must go forth. My blessings on you—wonderful youth.

Affectionately yours, O. W. H.

My love to your family also—s.v.p.

Devon Lodge, 15.VI.30

My dear Justice: . . . The week has simply flown. I have been
busy writing some memoranda for the P.M. about India—a ghastly
problem of which the real essence is that we can't govern it and
it really is not fit to govern itself. Then a jolly dinner here for
Flexner who is a wise and able person. And much energy expended
in preventing Felix from coming here to dip his fingers in the
Zionist pie and create immense embarrassment. It seems to be one
of Brandeis's blind spots not to see that when the British government has a commission of enquiry in Palestine not even Felix can
get guarantees about policy until the commission has reported,
and that to send him here just now, instead of when there is a
document to discuss, would injure his prestige and waste his
time.[1] . . .

---

[1] The Shaw Commission which had been sent to Palestine to investigate
outbreaks which had occurred in 1929 had issued its report in March 1930,
recommending curtailment of Jewish immigration and new restrictions on the
acquisition of lands by Jews. Immediate protest by Zionist leaders was a
factor leading to the appointment of Sir John Hope Simpson as a Government Commissioner to investigate and report upon immigration and land
problems. His Report (*Command Papers* #3686) was published in October
1930, simultaneously with the issuance of the Passfield White Paper (*Command Papers* #3692), a document which was bitterly criticized by the
Zionists and others and which was substantially repudiated by MacDonald
in a letter to Dr. Chaim Weizmann in February 1931.

In the way of reading, one or two amusing trifles first. (a) Arnold Bennett's diary. This is worth turning over if only to see what a first-rate man of letters observes. Food, hotels, the manner of the idle rich, the quality of transportation, the manners of cinema directors. He seems to want to produce an atmosphere of extreme sophistication. He hardly mentions reading a book. He refrains from any political comment, whatsoever. Now and again he gets rightly lyrical over a Brueghel or a Donatello. But he is to himself above all a man of the world who can show the rich clubman of Pall Mall that Arnold Bennett knows the dialect of Belgravia just as well as anyone else. It's a queer ambition! . . .

Ever affectionately yours, Harold J. Laski

Beverly Farms, June 26, 1930

My dear Laski: Your letters are an education to poor old me—but if I tried to read all the books you exhort me to I should do nothing else—and already the first pile of *certioraris* looks at me from under the window. Why did you make me take up that damned Trotsky? I have not got through his education yet. If I sought only entertainment I should not complain—but biography is off my beat because of time. If I studied affairs as every one ought you would be right, but I now limit myself to a fraction of life. You speak of two books by Milt Gross. I know only *Nize Baby*—I read and reread that to my wife and we roared over it. Probably it was accident that I didn't mention it though I should not have been sure that it would amuse you. I must enquire about the second work—but I think he should be read aloud to be fully enjoyed. Frankfurter and Mrs. are coming here in an hour or two to luncheon. Your letter opens several themes for converse. I have been seeing rather more of people than I quite like. Over an hour and a half of talk tires me—and although every call has been pleasant I sometimes have to pay for them by a fit of coughing at night. Evidently when I was young I didn't learn to use my voice in the right way, and I am paying for it now. Wister's *Roosevelt* took only the leisure of a couple of days and naturally was very interesting to me. Incidentally he is more flattering to me than I could have dreamed that he would be. I hear a rumor that the book has been withdrawn from sale on some apprehension of libel. I don't know whether the story is true. Also Frankfurter sent me Edith Hamilton, *The Greek Way*—some discernment— more rhetoric, it seemed to me. Generalizations based on the distinction between spirit and mind seem to me nebulous. As you see I have not read a great deal, even for me. For you it all would be a bagatelle. But I have slept more than I have for many a year —and am apt to interrupt the improving in that way. My heart is heavy at the thought that the *certioraris* must begin again. I am so glad to think of you in your vacation in the quiet little town with bookcounters within reach. My love to you all.

Affectionately yours, O. W. H.

Devon Lodge, 28.VI.30

My dear Justice: Since I wrote last, I have lived in a whirl of examination papers, and if there is a more dismal occupation, I certainly do not know it. Now I have emerged, bloody but unbowed. And there have been examinations for Ph.D.'s, testimonials for students in search of a job, boards to appoint new professors, and all the intolerable accompaniments of a dying academic year. At least, it is now over; the captains and kings have departed. But one or two items will amuse you. The Commemoration ceremony, with Earl Beauchamp,[1] the university chancellor, as the set piece. He arrives in great state, with a train-bearer, and begins the proceedings by getting mixed up with his garments and falling over the trainbearer. Then he makes an hour's speech to the effect that if business men and universities get on well together, they are likely to get on well together. He himself is sure that they *can* get on well together if they do not fail to get on well together. He himself is a director of a public company and would like to say (with great impressiveness) that the business men he has liked, he has really liked. Some of them, of course, lack tradition. That is unfortunate; but a university can sometimes supply the absence of tradition in a self-made man's son, the kind of graceful charm he is glad to think the ancient families of England possess as their historic birthright. Can you beat it?

Then I have been busy writing memoranda for the P.M. about India. This is, I think, the biggest crisis in our colonial affairs since 1776, and likely to prove as difficult for the same lack of imagination. Simon has produced a very able report which has everything in it except an understanding of the psychology of the situation.[2] It is no use treating a great nationalist movement as though it consisted of men who have only to be told of the complexity of their situation to agree at once that Great Britain must go on governing them. It is queer how all Simon's defects come out in the document—it is brilliantly written, clear, logical, concise, but lacking in generosity, cold, even, in places, callous, and wanting in that power to make the reader feel he *ought* to go along with the writer which is half the art of writing documents

---

[1] William Lydon (1872-1938), seventh Earl Beauchamp, liberal politician and leader in London society; Chancellor of London University, 1929-1931.

[2] On June 10 and 24 the report of the Statutory Commission, under the Chairmanship of Sir John Simon, had been published. *Command Papers* #3568, 3569.

for government. I don't know what will happen to my effort. Mac-
Donald is not a courageous man, he is vain, and he wants to stay
in office. My fear is that India will become the Ireland of the next
generation—a prospect to me of unmitigated horror.

Then I have been working hard with the secretary of the Delegated Legislation Commission, getting out a kind of "heads of
proposals" report for discussion. It looks as though we might hope
for a large measure of agreement, and the conversion of Warren
Fisher,[3] the head of the Permanent Civil Service to my pet hypothesis that under all circumstances all questions of *vires* must be
decided by the Courts, a simplified procedure being invented for
the purpose, may even mean unanimity. I almost feel as though
things I have written to defend for years may come into the body
of a government document and even hope to get to the statute-
book. That will be worth all the labour these months have
cost. . . .

Ever yours affectionately, H. J. L.

Beverly Farms, July 10, 1930
My dear Laski: A letter from you brings the usual delight and the
usual regret that I have no incidents to match yours. The time
flies by as it does in a routine—at least if the routine is pleasant.
The accursed Trotsky still rides on my back—my secretary reads
him aloud to me—we are in sight of the end but over 100 pages
remain. I am interested enough not to be willing to throw the
book aside but I shall be glad when I am done with it. I don't
like him and the book seems to have a dominant purpose to blow
his own horn at the expense of Stalin. I feel the tone that I became familiar with in my youth among the abolitionists. He to be
sure takes his principles for granted. I should like to see them
stated. If he still believes in Marx I thought that *Capital* showed
chasms of unconscious error and sophistries that might be conscious. I think that the wisest men from Confucius and Aristotle
to Lincoln (if he is entitled to the superlative) have believed in
the *via media*. Of course that is unpopular in times of excitement
and once in a thousand times it is the extremists who get there.
But I have not had a very high opinion of the intellectual powers
of such extremists as I have known or known about. All of which
is painfully near rudimentary twaddle—but I say it because little
things once in a while make me wonder if your sympathies are
taking a more extreme turn as time goes on. I always am uncertain
how far Frankfurter goes. But I notice that he and you are a good
deal more stirred by Sacco and Vanzetti, who were turned into a

[3] Sir Warren Fisher (1879-1948); official Head of the Civil Service, 1919-
1939, and member of the Committee on Ministers' Powers.

text by the reds, than by a thousand worse things among the blacks. Indeed, so far as I can judge without having read the trial I doubt if those two suffered anything more from the conduct of the judge than would be a matter of course in England. It was their misfortune to be tried in a community that was stirred up, if not frightened by manifestations the import of which was exaggerated, and, without knowing anything about it, I presume that the jury felt like the community. I read an odious play by Strindberg the other day—*Countess Julie*—a countess who gives herself to a valet, and at the end goes out with a razor that he has handed to her, as the only solution. It made me think of modernist pictures —and seems like them to disregard the time rate of emotions. The most obvious come to you first and obstruct that which the author or painter wishes to excite. If you see that the clock in the picture will tumble over you feel that before you notice the elegance of the pattern of lines or the harmony of the color. In the play the hatefulness of the situation and the emergence of touches of brutal boorishness in the valet hit you quicker than the subtleties, and obstruct your appreciation of them—or at least mine. But I read nothing else until Trotsky is finished except a few pages of Mrs. Piozzi's *Anecdotes of Johnson* if I get into bed a quarter before 12. The secretary read a lot of Birrell earlier, as probably I told you. You haven't answered whether you ever see him now.

My reading propensities have, if not changed, intensified in the direction of subjects akin to my own and away from novels except funny or pleasant ones. I wouldn't touch the unnamed Russian one that you laid aside as too painful.

I am pleased at your prospect of prevalence in the Delegated Legislation Commission.

People believe what they want to—but the relative imminence of death brings me no dogma that might be pleasant. I see in myself a wave of the cosmos that is a little more phosphorescent— that carries consciousness—whatever may be the cosmic worth of consciousness—to a little higher than the average point before it disappears—but I see nothing else except the fact that the cosmos has that and presumably a good deal more among its possibilities.

Without much admiring Bergson I think his *Élan vital* was a good phrase—and so farewell for the moment.

Ever affectionately yours, O. W. Holmes

Devon Lodge, 14.VII.30

My dear Justice: . . . We spent a delightful day in the country with H. G. Wells. He was at the top of his form and discoursed *de omnibus rebus* in great style. A description of Henry James's style—an elephant of genius trying to pick up a pin; a memory of Oscar Wilde, shocked because his remarks at dinner had failed to shock his hostess; a wild attack on Roman Catholics in the Voltairean manner; a beautiful eulogy of Lincoln as one in whose presence even the elect feel humble. He has without exception the most active and stimulating mind I know. He isn't profound; but he knows that thought is important and he does passionately respect it. Moreover he has not only a really creative curiosity, but also something of the prophetic quality in him. And he is so receptive to ideas that he makes you feel that you are talking just about twice as well as you would ordinarily do. Then the French writer André Siegfried came to spend a day here. I liked him greatly. Like all Frenchmen, he sees things far too clearly in terms of predefined categories. But, he has great insight into big things. I liked, for instance, his argument that the English ideal of a gentleman has prevented us from doing much of the thinking we ought to have done. His description of Oxford as a place where there is more brilliant small talk and more jealousy of adult mind struck me as true and intimately connected with the first. He drew for me a quite extraordinary picture of the recapture of the French bourgeoisie by the Roman Church; and he said that even today your Catholic democrat, like the *politique* of the 16th century, accepts the lay state and protestantism *de facto* and not *de jure*. . . .

Next I must retail an incredible experience. You will have heard of Conan Doyle's death. The spiritualists organised a great service for their leader in the Albert Hall, so I went last night with Frida to listen. Imagine ten thousand people packed like sardines, a medium on a platform seated next to Lady Conan Doyle, with a black curtain with white stars behind. First a hymn or two beautifully sung by a hidden choir. Then a journalist explains what a great man C.D. was because he had faith. Then a request for a complete silence while the medium gets into touch with the spirit world. For an hour she gave messages to members of the audience. "There is a widow here whose husband passed over on July 11. He sends his love and hopes the children are well." Then the grand climax of a message to Lady Doyle. All the people seemed convinced. There were not tests of any kind, no attempt at control, and the attitude of the audience I can only describe as reverent excitement. To me, more incredible twaddle had never been talked even in the Albert Hall. England, my dear Justice; 1930; seemingly sane people, most of them well-fed and prosperous. In the admirable dialect of your native land, can you beat it?

. . . And for a bet I read *Clarissa* again and (whisper it low) was bored nearly to tears by it. I was lured into it by Birrell to whom I went to tea the other day. At eighty, he is as splendid as ever. He told me that he had just read for the first time the *Deontology* of Bentham. "I felt," he said, "as though I had been asked to masticate an icthyosaurus." He told me that he had been to hear an eminent pastor preach on drink and that he had to prevent himself crying out that Mr. Stiggins was a living portrait. He had also visited the National Portrait Gallery and saw with dismay that all the villains had the handsomest faces. He also concluded that had he been Nelson he would not have bothered with Trafalgar while he could have stayed with Lady Hamilton. He insisted that Bryce had more learning and less wisdom than any man who has been in a cabinet these hundred years! He spoke of a talk with Roosevelt in which the latter "used adjectives like hammers"; and his last word was that he liked a particular review of mine as I had learned the art "of using eulogy as invective."

Our love to you. In a fortnight we are off to the Moselle.

Ever affectionately yours, H. J. L.

Beverly Farms, July 27, 1930

My dear Laski: Your last letter looks me in the face—as always it gives me the keenest pleasure—and it shall not wait for an answer though I have received a sack of 74 *certioraris*. (I began on them at once yesterday, and have devoted a good part of this Sabbath to them—24 done—I hope to give my secretary pain on the morrow.) I was very glad to hear about Birrell. I have reread all his works that I have here—*Men Women and Books*—*Re Judicatae*—and 2 volumes, *Obiter dicta*—a typical and delightful Briton. I believe I had some particular remark that I wanted to make but I have forgotten it. Also I have read through Whitehead —*Process and Reality.* ⅔ I didn't understand definitely—I didn't know the words, and he thinks and writes like a mathematician. I got the drift, and felt somewhat remote because I cannot believe that human speculation about the cosmos is likely to amount to much. He seems to feel that he is in on the ground floor with God —which I cannot, either for myself or him. But I like very much that he, like Dewey, does not begin with the self-conscious ego. I was more impressed by Dewey in that way—and really much impressed. However, I can't recite on either—though for a few fierce days I could have on Dewey. My secretary read aloud Mencken's *Treatise on the Gods*—which, as I like M. in some other of his writing, I regretted to think 25 or 50 years behind the times. By the by he, as I should have done a year or two ago, treat with summary scorn the notion that Jesus is a myth—but two or three books French and English have made me more respectful to the belief. I have also listened to what seems to be a really

great novel, *My Àntonia*—by Willa Cather—turning the life of
early settlers on the prairie (in our time) so hard, so squalid, into
a noble poem. I do like an author who doesn't have to go to
London or Paris or Vienna to find his genius—but realizes that
any part of the universe can be seen poetically and takes what he
finds at hand and makes it blossom. I won't mention everything
that I have read but I got much pleasure from Owen Wister's
Roosevelt—which I got before it was called in, to change a few
pages that raised a question of libel. If I get into bed 10 or 15
minutes before 12 I allow myself to read until midnight and in
that way have reread Mrs. Piozzi's *Anecdotes of Johnson*, which
again I found well worth reading. I flatter myself that our times
wouldn't stand his boorish bullying, however great it might think
him—and so often wrong—in our view. There was something
beautiful in the old man, of course. I wonder if Eckerman's *Conversations with Goethe* still would interest. I think of getting hold
of them for my secretary to read aloud. He sits in the next room and
when there is silence here for a few minutes he appears and asks
How about Culture? (Of course with a smile.) I have taken no
part in and have seen next to nothing of our Tercentenary[1]—at
Salem there is rather a striking reproduction of the poor little
houses that John Winthrop found on landing or his company had.
They got some pretty good ones quite early. At Ipswich there is
one with beams that it would be hard to beat in England—if
memory does not deceive me.

Your H. A. L. Fisher made an address on The Bay Colony that
reads very well indeed. That was in Boston. I didn't hear it. Which
was your review that "used eulogy as invective"? It takes time
and a magnifying glass to get all the goodness out of your writing.
At first I thought it was "analogy" not eulogy and spoken of
Roosevelt—and was reminded of his remark that Brewer (who
had criticised him) had a sweetbread for a brain.

I can't read the name of your Frenchman André Siegf———?
My experience (little and long ago)—with mediums is like your
"incredible twaddle"—or as I say drool.

It is time for me to descend to solitaire. Habits are not unpleasant things for the old if not tyrannical. The day is apt to tire
me a little and I like the change—if I have a few minutes before
11—too short for a game I pull a book from the shelf on my right
—often the life of Miss Austen. I like to read about her even if
I don't adore.   *Ever affectionately yours, O. W. H.*

---

[1] The Commonwealth was currently celebrating the three hundredth anniversary of the founding of Massachusetts Bay Colony. H. A. L. Fisher, on July
15, had delivered at exercises on Boston Common an address published as
The Bay Colony, A Tercentenary Address (1930).

Devon Lodge, 26.VII.30

My dear Justice: . . . We had a jolly lunch on Thursday with Lewis Einstein, who is as charming as ever. My one fear for him is dilettantism. I wish he had something definite and continuous to do. I am trying to arrange that the University should make him an honorary lecturer in the hope that a course of lectures may pin him down to the writing of a real book. But he is amid the distractions of great luxury and social eminence, and I fear that he may be sucked into that amusing but futile vortex. (Can a vortex be amusing? I don't know!) Then a long dinner with Fleuriau, the French Ambassador.[1] He amused me much by saying that after six years he understood the English less than ever. "You are," he said, "more momentous about trifles than any people in the world." He told us how he went to see the Foreign Secretary at the House. On the way through the lobby he heard Baldwin say to a neighbour that "England was in real danger," and was distressed at Baldwin's tragic face. He mentioned this to the Foreign Secretary and asked what particularly was the cause of gloom. The Foreign Secretary electrified him by explaining that it was the position in the Test Match against Australia to which Baldwin referred. . . .

Our love to you both. I read with horror of your heat wave. I hope it did not disturb you.   *Ever affectionately yours, H. J. L.*

Beverly Farms, August 9, 1930

My dear Laski: You are the best correspondent I ever had. Each letter is interesting and is pretty sure to be a charming work of art. The only criticism I could make would be that you sometimes don't answer matters that hoped for an answer—but I have nothing of that sort in mind now. I don't always so fully agree with what you print, much as I admire some of it. That you know as to the equality business. I don't see any ground for your aspirations in the prospect of improved economic conditions for the many. That is I see no ground for the prospect. What I can see more clearly is the desire to get rid of a disagreeable contrast in position and public esteem—a desire for which I have little respect. What you say of sovereignty in the pamphlet received today[1] needs further reflection on my part. Off hand it seems an obsession grafted by Figgis and hardly a necessary part of your thinking. The other day Frankfurter brought over Cardozo (C.J. New York)—to my great delight. His face is sensitive, tender and strong—and such he is, unless I greatly err. He is one of the few who have said in print

---

[1] Aimé Joseph de Fleuriau (1870-1938) was French Ambassador in London from 1924 to 1933.

[1] Perhaps "Law and the State," originally published in 9 *Economica* 267 (November 1929); reprinted in *Studies in Law and Politics* (1932), 237.

and private the things that make my life seem worth having been lived—and that naturally made me the more rejoiced at the first chance I have had for a real talk with him. Felix seemed in first rate shape but kept in the background for the sake of his guest. My secretary is reading to me James Truslow Adams (no relation) on *The Adams Family*—which I find interesting—and at odd minutes I am rereading Maine's *Ancient Law* in Pollock's new edition. At times nowadays it seems a little thin—as an original effort. I am wondering whether I shall put my secretary to reading aloud Hooker's *Ecclesiastical Polity*. I never have read it and think it may be a required subject of examination at the Day of Judgment. There is a second breathing space after the second batch of *certioraris* (75) has been returned—but I live like the wild animals in continual terror for my life. It seems futile to write to you now, for I suppose you are *perdu* in Germany—but this may reach you in time. You will come back enriched no doubt as always— if not with 17th century pamphlets at least with some new experience. May it be joyful.   *Affectionately yours, O. W. Holmes*

Union-Hotel, Cochem, Germany, 2.VIII.30
My dear Justice: The address will tell its own tale. I write looking out onto a small range of hills completely covered with vineyards, and the swift-flowing Moselle crowned with old houses at my feet. To my right is a vast fifteenth century castle, so fortified, that it is difficult to see how Turenne could ever have taken it under Louis XIV if the inhabitants had food on the premises. There seems to be one winding path to it with gun-mounted walls at every turn. It is a marvellous sight, and I must try to get a photograph that will convey to you some idea of its beauty. The people are fascinating—solid German bourgeoisie, who eat and drink enormously, and look as though it is the unvariable rule at sixty never to gaze upon one's feet again. Certainly when I stand by some of them I feel as though I was a wan illusion of nature, a pure spirit seen darkly through a glass. But it is marvellous how they enjoy life. You see a stout grandfather holding up his wine to the light, and gazing upon it with a reverent ecstasy that can hardly be described in other than religious terms. Another thing struck me forcibly *en route:* if you look at the bookstalls on the stations, it is astonishing to see how much solid literature is sold. There are, of course, the inevitable Edgar Wallace, and the usual dubious magazines, but you see also in quite small towns, Goethe and Schiller, Ranke and Thomas Mann, to take names at random. I wonder whether I could buy say a Shakespere or a Bernard Shaw at the average London station. I was impressed, too, especially at Trier, by the experimental character of the architecture one sees.

It is clear that the Germans (I am told under Dutch and Swedish inspiration) are trying to do something new. It isn't massive, like American architecture. For instance the railway station here (a country market town of some three thousand people) is clearly an effort to express something that combines the fact that a railway is science with the fact that Cochem is old; and the result is something with an unexpected charm of its own. What one feels, even in the 24 hours since we arrived, is the power of this people, their energy, and drive and determination. They almost seem to play because they have measured the object which play can be made to serve. One other reflection. I have never before been in Catholic Germany. It is curious to see how Catholicism assumes a Germanic form. There is a dull heaviness in the crosses and Christs by the wayside which seems to ask you to believe that Christ was a good German burgher intent on his glass of lager after supper. When you see at the tenth century bridge here, a Christ with glowing red cheeks, it is difficult to remember that it advertises a religion and not somebody's beer. But I grow profane.

For the moment, no other news. But I want to send this word of greeting so that its very absence may assure you of our tranquil environment. Our love to you.   *Ever affectionately yours, H. J. L.*

Beverly Farms, August 18, 1930

My dear Laski: Your address, even if I were sure that I read it right, seems too uncertain in duration for me to risk a change from the one that you so admirably put at the head of your London letters. I cannot too highly praise your habit. It saves trouble invariably at this end. I meantime keep on in my routine. Latterly I have allowed myself the pleasures of irresponsibility—not bothered about improving my mind, but gone in for a good time. I did, to be sure, make my secretary read me one book of Hooker's *Ecclesiastical Polity*, which to my satisfaction had the passage that always is quoted [1] and that the Puritanical Austin calls Hooker's fustian. But having got his flavor I thought it would be a waste of time to read the rest. The appreciation of such an idle life in the *Essays of Elia*—just reread, goes far to justify me and I rather think that a little play with unstrenuous thought is civilizing in its way. I think I have mentioned the new edition of Maine's *Ancient Law*—almost as easy as, and akin to *belles lettres*—but perhaps not *God's Trombones*—poems by a negro sent to me by Cardozo, that wonderfully impress me. [2]

---

[1] "Of Law there can be no less acknowledged, than that her seat is the bosom of God, her voice the harmony of the world: all things in heaven and earth do her homage, the very least as feeling her care, and the greatest are not exempted from her power." *Ecclesiastical Polity*, Book I, Sec. XVI.

[2] James Weldon Johnson, *God's Trombones* (1927).

Just now my lad is reading to me from two, I believe out of many, volumes of Grant Duff's *Diary, 1886-8*—a light-weight, but with a lot of that agreeable cultivated English gossip that gives one entertainment if nothing much else. He says the true form of the saying of Oxenstierna is *"an nescis, mi fili, quantilla prudentia regitur orbis"*—citing as the original authority *Svensk Plutarch, II,* Stockholm 1826, p. 95.[3] I always have seen it in some different words—but I think it has an older origin. Do you know?

I had a letter from Leslie Scott today saying how much he liked you and enclosing the first day's proceedings in an arbitration between Lena Goldfields, Ltd., and the Russian Soviet Govt.—to which, it seems, the Soviet Govt. has refused to send its arbitrators alleging that L.G. had cancelled the whole agreement—but it is said that the agreement provides that in such cases the arbitration shall proceed.[4] The charges of L.G. sound not improbable to an outsider. I observe that the counsel for L.G. said that Stalin of whom Trotsky has so much to say, was the dictator of the U.S.S.R. I shall be interested to see the outcome. Ladies come here to luncheon and are always pleasant, though at times I am reminded of a line of one of the Darwins. "Next week looks very black—a pleasure for every day." Enough of gossip. I wish I could boast of some achievement, but I am having a good time.

Affectionately yours, O. W. Holmes

Union-Hotel, Cochem, Germany, 9.VIII.30

My dear Justice: Certainly this is very nearly a perfect place for a holiday. There is hardly any traffic, and the sheer silence, after London, is in itself most refreshing. And the surroundings are quite magnificent. At every bend of the river, the scenery is different, and there is a comfortable serenity about it which is most impressive. One or two things strike me which seem worth putting on record. If I had to put down the reasons for the success of Germany as a people, I should say, in this order, that they were first industry, second simplicity, and third organisation. Each of them in its way is astonishing. The ordinary man one meets is impressive neither in conversation nor knowledge. But he does his job with astonishing devotion; he is really proud of it as a job. He hasn't the Anglo-Saxon habit of knocking-off as soon as the clock strikes. Then he takes his pleasures very simply. They walk a little, drink a little, take obvious and obviously whole-hearted joy

---

[3] Sir Mountstuart Elphinstone Grant Duff, *Notes from a Diary,* 1886-1888 (2 vols., 1900), vol. II, p. 106.

[4] Sir Leslie Scott was the arbitrator named by Lena Goldfields Limited. After the refusal of the Soviet representative to participate in the arbitration, Sir Leslie, with Professor Stutzer as the neutral member of the Board, heard the case and entered an award in favor of the company in a sum exceeding £ 12,000,000. See 74 *Solicitor's Journal* 648 (Oct. 4, 1930).

in music and the theatre; but there are no signs of the complicated pursuit of complex pleasure such as you see so widely nowadays. This, for instance, is the most important place between Coblentz and Treves. There is no movie, two public-houses, a village orchestra (quite admirable), endless fishing, and a Saturday market which patently is an event in the lives of its participants. There is quite a good book-shop, and an even better music-shop; and the 17th century Town Hall is kept about as admirably as one could wish. The only disappointing feature is the Church. This is Catholic, and a quite charming 18th century building is ruined by the most vulgar collection of cheap statues I have ever seen in a public building. I spoke to the priest about it, and he clearly did not even understand that one could object to 14 plaster-casts (coloured) of Christ obviously turned out by mass-production and garish to the last degree. Then their organisation is remarkable. Whether it's the little steamer, or the ferry, or the village threshing machine, the people seem to fit into one another's needs remarkably. There are, of course, faults. There is a certain drab sameness about the talk you get. You don't find the individuality you always tumble upon in an English or American village. The people, like good Germans, are a little too respectful, and a little too neat and orderly. But they are full of common-sense. There is little or no bitterness about the war. The Republic is clearly firmly established; the only man who mentioned the Kaiser to me spoke of him as a figure of comic opera, and thought it a relief to be done with his theatrical gestures. They don't, indeed, like the French; but everyone to whom I speak takes the sensible view that one must either fight them or live with them, and that there is everything to be said for living with them. Let me add that the most impressive building in the town is the School, and that each morning at 7:30 two buses arrive to take the children to the nearest secondary school, and you will see why I am impressed by the communal virtues of these people. They know how to make defeat into victory by those solid virtues of patience, soberness, and hard work, which are, I think, about the best general qualities in the world. . . .   *Ever affectionately yours, H. J. L.*

Beverly Farms, August 22, 1930
My dear Laski: A letter from you admirably describing what you find your town to be came just after I had sent an answer to the one announcing your arrival. I have not much to tell of the interval. Mrs. Beveridge who generally accompanies her luncheon here, or shortly follows it, with a book, sent me *The Religious Background of American Culture* by Thomas Cuming Hall about three days ago and I have found it very interesting. His general

thesis is that far the most efficient cause of our development in the way of religion is not Puritanism properly so called but Wickliffe and the Lollards. The Puritans were in the Church and thought Church and State indivisible. The Lollards—the great mass of the poor in towns—were outside of the Church and hated its splendors as it hated the luxuries of the upper class in which they had no share. They had no central authority but independent conventicles which were a law unto themselves. They didn't care much for the sacraments but laid their emphasis on conduct. Being townspeople and having no share in the land they were no great hands at agriculture but found their chance in trade, shipbuilding, &c. He has to rely somewhat on the probability and conservatism of tradition (the same that is seen in children's games) —and in this point leads me to wish to see what authorities he finds to rely upon—and he repeats himself like a jury lawyer. But he quite stirs me up just as I was beginning to wallow in easy literature—*Essays of Elia*—Grant Duff *Notes from a Diary*—short stories by E. M. Forster.[1] Essays, *And Even Now*, by Max Beerbohm—none but the first hitting me very hard. Of course I have only given a hint at Hall. Mrs. B. says he was ordained a minister, and married her to her husband in Germany, and that he is rather a splendid fellow. He seems to have become a sceptic—I suppose too intelligent not to. He is described on the Title Page as Professor of English and American History and Culture—University of Goettingen—and writes with every appearance of very accurate knowledge and acute thoughts. Today I called on Mrs. Curtis to whom contrary to my practise I have read some passages (not confidential) from two or three of your letters—she appreciates them—then Mrs. Beveridge at luncheon—then a young lawyer who wanted to get some relief from me in a case on which his ideas were nebulous—and also, he more than implied, to see me. I sent him off seemingly convinced that he had no standing as yet for help from us—then a drive inland, as it is rather cold—then some reading of Hall by my secretary—then supper and now *you*. I think I quoted to you, but I quote again a gem from one of the Darwins—"Next week looks very black; a pleasure every day." I don't like to be hurried or crowded—but I need a *pièce de résistance* as well as light stuff in order to feel that I am accomplishing something. Why not be content with pleasure? I can't answer, except that by my experience in life and more by the temperament I get from my mother, without some feeling of accomplishment I feel as if it were time for me to die.

> *Affectionately yours, O. W. Holmes*

Apropos of children's games, my father interpreted some of their ways of counting—that carry their conservatism on their face—

---

[1] *The Celestial Omnibus and Other Stories* (1911).

One-er zol—Zua zol. Zigazol—Zau—&c. *i.e.—Un sol, deux sol, sex sol. Zehn.* Or cushy cow bonny let down your milk cushy cow let down your milk to me and I will give you a silver dee—c.c. couchez de'—[illegible].

Devon Lodge, 5.IX.30

My dear Justice: . . . I have been mostly busy on an article about Diderot for *Harper's*[1] which I have thoroughly enjoyed doing (I hope you will enjoy it later). It meant much re-reading; but when I came across the sentence "I would give ten Watteaus for one Teniers" I wished I could have shaken him by the hand. Did you ever look at his *"Pensées sur la nature"*? It is amazing what vistas they open up.

We had a surprise visit the day before we left Cochem from Z. Chafee at Harvard and some good talk with him. But his account of Pound disturbed me much; if it is only ten per cent true P. must have become impossible. And even Chafee's loyalty could not conceal the fact that all the people at Cambridge you and I care about are unhappy about him, especially Felix. It seems to be a very bad case of megalomania. But when anyone, like Pound, has written the same book seven times, one begins to suspect that something is wrong. . . .

One or two little things have pleased me and I put them down on the general principle that one should share one's pleasure. The *Berengaria* leaves tomorrow for New York with four of my young men on board, all the sons of working-class parents, two bound for professorships in Canada and two similarly in the U.S.A. Another of my young men has been given a fellowship at Oxford, and another one still a big job in the League. That kind of thing makes one feel that one doesn't sweat in vain. And I whisper in your sceptical ear that had there not been the artificial equality of free education they would probably have been clerks and grocers' assistants like their fathers. As a matter of fact any logical dissection of Holmes, J.'s "betterbilitarianism" [*sic*] would demonstrate that he shares these views with me.[2] . . .

Our love to you as always.   *Ever affectionately yours, H. J. L.*

Beverly Farms, Sunday, Sept. 14, 1930

My dear Laski: Two letters[1] from you within a week—the last (especially delightful) coming this morning and written from

---

[1] "Diderot: Homage to a Genius," 162 *Harper's Magazine* 597 (April 1931), reprinted in *Studies in Law and Politics* (1932), 48.

[2] Holmes's simplest definition of a "bettabilitarian" was: "One who thinks you may bet more or less on the universe." (Holmes to Felix Frankfurter, February 16, 1912.)

[1] The earlier of these has been omitted from this edition.

home. I, meantime, have been having the Pollocks here. They arrived last Monday after 9 p.m. having motored from N.Y. successfully to Boston but after that wandered for a wasted hour in the effort to find the North Shore. They left yesterday (Sat.) morning for a night at Chocorua—I know not where—thence to motor back to President Lowell next Tuesday and then home. Rather sporting for two so old people, both lame from broken legs, and Lady Pollock having also broken her right wrist. They were fully on deck and said that they enjoyed themselves. I think they really did. I had in some agreeable women for luncheon and a married couple for supper, and took them to drive to Gloucester and Marblehead. There was no chance to take them around Rockport. P. and I would take a short slow toddle in the morning—and while they were here I took a newspaper which at other times I do not and so have peace.

Naturally I haven't read much—a little Carlyle and De Quincey and now Eckerman, *Conversations with Goethe.* I have on hand the second part of *Faust* with Bayard Taylor's translation for another try at that. I am prejudiced against it. If a man chooses the form of a play, it seems to me that his first duty is to make it good in the external sense—*i.e.* to give it a coherent, interesting, easily intelligible movement. If it doesn't have that I don't care for inner meanings. Let the author put them in a treatise—but a play must in the first place be a play—not be a lord among wits and a wit among lords. I found myself repelled by the prophetic magisterial tone of Carlyle—especially as in some cases I thought he had no message to deliver. So far as my limited memory goes I don't agree with you and Diderot about Watteau and Teniers. I was much moved by the discourse of a former boss of the Wallace Collection (a very well known critic, now dead) standing in front of the Watteaus.[2] He became a different man as he showed Watteau looking on at but not sharing the gaieties and splendors. In a fortnight my vacation will be over, and I expect some *certs.* before then. I have done 175. The time has rushed by—old age and routine make time fly fast. I don't feel as if I had much to show for my quasi leisure, but a fairly long list of books read (long for me—not for you) looks respectable. I have kept very well—so far. My love to you all.

Affectionately yours, O. W. Holmes

Devon Lodge, 20.IX.30
My dear Justice: . . . for the first time since I left Oxford [I have reread] Lecky's *European Morals* which I think is really remarkable; I don't know anything since that touches it except per-

---

[2] Sir Claude Phillips (1848-1924), art critic, was Keeper of the Watteau Collection at Hertford House from 1897 to 1911.

haps Friedländer's *Roman Manners,* and that, of course, touches a much narrower field. Lecky made me doubt more than ever before whether Christianity was not almost wholly a deleterious influence. Certainly when it conquered it had lost most of the moral qualities which might have made it valuable. Then the translation of Max Weber's famous essay on *Protestantism and Capitalism.* It deserves its reputation, though I think there is a tendency in him to put the cart before the horse. I agree that the Calvinist conception of occupation as a "calling" was exactly what the new economic order needed; but I don't think it was conscious anticipation of need so much as an inevitable response to need. I mean that religions don't shape economic categories, they adapt themselves to them. But the essay is certainly a most brilliant and suggestive piece of work. . . .

I have still a fortnight before term begins; though Sankey tomorrow wants me to begin some delicate work for him in these Indian negotiations, and I am slowly drafting my part of the report on administrative law. Sankey, of course, is an angel to work for, he responds at once to suggestion, and he hasn't pride of authorship (that's the chief difficulty in working for MacDonald who in that respect is much like Wilson). But this Indian tangle is so complex that one is almost afraid to put suggestions on paper just because generalisations are so very difficult.

You, I expect, are beginning to count the days until Washington. I do hope the term will prove a happy one. One day at least I shall brighten before you. I have given a note to you to my friend Schacht, the late President of the German *Reichsbank,*[2] and possibly, the next President of the German Republic. He is a brilliant and attractive creature and I think will really interest you.

Our love to you. Keep fit and don't overdo it.

Ever affectionately yours, H. J. L.

Devon Lodge, 27.IX.30
My dear Justice: A delightful letter from you, telling me of the Pollocks' visit. It really is astonishing to hear of their courage in making, at their age, so astonishing an adventure. If I mistake not, it is now something like sixty-three years since you first met one another—a wonderful record.[1]

I have had a busy week. I had to write a long lecture, which I

---

[2] Hjalmar Schacht (1877-   ); in January 1930 Schacht had resigned the presidency of the *Reichsbank* in protest against the *Reichstag's* approval of the Young plan. In 1931 he made a lecture tour of the United States, and in 1933 Hitler restored him to the presidency of the *Reichsbank.*

[1] It is believed that Holmes and Sir Frederick Pollock first met in 1874; see John G. Palfrey's Introduction to 1 *Holmes-Pollock Letters,* xv, footnote 3.

will send you when printed, on justice and the Law, for which a
good gent. left thirty pounds a year to some society here.[2] Then
suddenly Sankey sent for me over the Imperial Conference[3] and I
have been doing memoranda for him ever since. The job has been
interesting beyond words; it has also made me a little Englander.
I never imagined that empire could be such a nuisance on points
of no real import *e.g.* what is to happen to the royal prerogative
in a Dominion if the King goes mad and a Council of Regency
has to be appointed? And I did not imagine, until I saw the letters,
that the King interfered so constantly on points which are bound
to raise grave difficulties for his government. I told Sankey that
the real lesson of this experience is the wisdom of the maxim *sol-
vitur ambulando* in matters of government. The lawyers sat down
and tried to define the British empire, which is *sui generis*, by
analogies drawn from dubious international law. In the result they
have raised questions of status and prestige which are all formidable and all meaningless, *e.g.* if the empire is now a union of equal
states under a single monarch, what is the standing of a Dominion
High Commissioner *vis à vis* a foreign ambassador. The real answer
is "Don't be silly." But these blessed legal civil servants have
drafted Acts and Orders in Council enough to make a wise man
shrink with horror into an early grave. I wish you could have seen
some of my marginalia; I think they were not unworthy of your
disciple.

A much pleasanter day was in the country with the Allen who
wrote *European Political Thought in the 16th Century.* He is now
working at a book on English ideas 1603-1660 and I went to have
a chat with him about it. We agreed that Hobbes is the genius of
the period, and, after him, a fellow called John Hall whom I discovered about 3 years ago.[4] We also agreed that Prynne is a vastly
overrated person in whom volume has been mistaken for insight
and learning. He puts Filmer much higher than I, and Cromwell
not so high; and I had a job to make him see the social significance
of the great movement for law reform under Cromwell. But it was
grand talk, and a good change from the meticulous dullness of the

---

[2] The lecture, delivered before the Ethical Union, is printed in *Studies in
Law and Politics* (1932), 276.

[3] The Imperial Conference opened on October 2. Though the Conference
gave its attention principally to current economic problems, its agenda included questions concerning the constitutional relationships of the members
of the British Commonwealth which were dealt with in the Report of the
Conference on the Operation of Dominion Legislation.

[4] J. W. Allen, *English Political Thought*, 1603-1660 (vol. I, 1938). The
John Hall referred to is perhaps the author of "The Grounds and Reasons
of Monarchy Considered" which was prefixed to Toland's edition of *The
Oceana and other Works of James Harrington* (1771). Hall, a contemporary
of Harrington's had died "before he was full thirty, lamented as a prodigy
of his age." *Id.,* p. xxv.

Imperial Conference. Then I went to a farewell dinner to the German Ambassador[5] at Downing Street. Bernard Shaw was there, and I came away with the impression that he felt that he was the guest of honour and rather resented the attentions paid to the poor Ambassador. He really is a poor creature for a great man— talks glibly of things about which he knows nothing. (*e.g.* reparations), lays down extravagant generalisations which he has never thought about, and is patently unhappy unless he is the centre of attention. A nice German there said to me that he supposed it was the artistic temperament; I said I thought in the non-elect, it was usually called bad manners.

I haven't as you can imagine, had much time for reading. But I have read a supremely interesting book by Namier on party politics at the accession of George III which makes one feel that, with all its ills, the present condition is admirable. George's letters to Bute are incredible; they are written with a degrading servility which makes his attitude to others, and his general attitude later, almost unintelligible. I may say that I think you did well to get rid of him; I wish we had. I read also Gandhi's *Autobiography;* and the best phrase for him that of Leslie Stephen for Robert Owen "one of those intolerable bores who are the very salt of the earth." His nobility of motive, his courage, and his simplicity, are all beyond praise. But he has no political sense whatever, his humility has that final arrogance which belongs only to the ultimately humble man, and he has that intimate communion with God which makes rational argument quite impossible. I can see that he presents any government with the problem that Christ would do; and no modern government dare repeat the Crucifixion. Incidentally this reminds me of a good remark of D'Abernon[6] to Stresemann at one of the disarmament rows in Berlin. The French made a great fuss about four guns they discovered. "What possible result," said Stresemann to D'Abernon, "could four bits of old iron have." "Remember," said D'Abernon, "the mischief brought by four nails at Jerusalem nearly two thousand years ago." I must add Sassoon's *Memoirs of an Infantry Officer*—a book with a wistful beauty quite beyond praise.

I have bought one pleasant trifle—a Machiavelli's *Discorsi* in the Aldine edition, bound, for some swell I should think, in a beautifully tooled morocco of about 1540. It is very attractive, and

---

[5] In June 1930, Dr. Friedrich Sthamer who had been German Ambassador in London since 1920, was succeeded by Baron Constantin von Neurath (1873-1956). In 1932 von Neurath became German Foreign Minister, holding that office under Papen, Schleicher, and Hitler. In 1946 he was sentenced to fifteen years' imprisonment as a war criminal.

[6] Edgar Vincent (1857-1941), first Viscount D'Abernon, was British Ambassador in Berlin from 1920 to 1926; author of *An Ambassador of Peace* (3 vols., 1929-31).

I picked up a nice set of Bynershöck in five volumes for two shillings.

I hope the journey to Washington was accomplished with comfort. You will not forget that I am dining with you on your birthday.

Our love and warm greetings for the term,

Ever affectionately yours, H. J. L.

Washington, D.C., October 9, 1930

My dear Laski: Your promise to dine with me on my birthday is delightful and all I can say is: May I be there to see. For although everything seems to be going well life seems precarious. If one has no illness it is so easy to fall and break a hip bone—but I don't worry, I only wonder. Your letters are full of interest as usual and I am rejoiced at what you say about Bernard Shaw—also I am thankful for the quotation from L. Stephen about Robert Owen—also D'Abernon to Stresemann about 4 nails at Jerusalem—but there is no end to the good things you tell me or say.

The term has begun. The first two weeks for *certs*. &c. not to speak of private work—acknowledging books &c. I was rather put to it to frame an answer to Milt Gross for *He Done Her Wrong; The Great American Novel with not a word in it—No music too* —I quote without the titles before me. We both are appreciators of *Nize Baby*. This, though it has fun, presents more difficulties. In your last but one you quote Alexander about Whitehead. About ⅔ of W.'s book I did not understand—but I felt a limit to my interest. Whitehead has, or seems to have, the mathematician's conviction that he can get in on the ground floor of the cosmos. It seems to me so unlikely that man should reach the cosmic ultimate that I don't care for such speculations. Of course I can't say that Whitehead hasn't uttered the last word—but I know no reason for believing that he has, and doubt if he or anyone else could offer one. I said to my secretary[1] the other day—(it pleased me and I'm not sure that I didn't tell you): "It would make one a little happier if God would come down and snuggle up to one and say 'Now I'm going to give you the real tip about the universe —and to show you that I'm the genuine thing I will do a little miracle for a starter.' Puff. 'You see you are in another world.' Puff. 'Now you are back again. Well, the correct tip is XXX. But don't tell it for they'd lock you up as crazy' "—I must stop but just a word about the *Nicomachean Ethics,* in the Everyman translation—read to me by my secretary—I sleeping when I saw fit. Of course I really revere Aristotle as a great man and saw some

---

[1] Robert W. Wales, presently a practitioner in New York City, was Holmes's secretary in 1930-31.

few evidences in the volume. I also understand that many things are formulated that were not in Aristotle's day. But for present purposes the book seems to me hopeless drool—I haven't read the like for years. If I am wrong indicate how and why.

Now I really must stop.   *Affectionately yours, O. W. H.*

Devon Lodge, 11.X.30

My dear Justice: You, I expect, like me, are now in the whirl of term. It has been hard work this week, for there has not only been the ghastly rush of students and committees, but, even worse, aid to Sankey on the constitutional side of the Imperial Conference. This last has been hard going, so infinitely complex and delicate, with the Irish and S. Africans making pretty little points of no special importance which have yet to be met. A good example is a four-hour discussion on the instrument to be used as seal for a Gov. General's appointment. Shall it be the great seal: Or the signet royal? Or shall the privy seal be used for this end? Or a plain wafer with the royal arms? When the legal mind goes into these mysteries, it gets much more excited than over large issues. I evolved, I think, a good solution. It horrified the lawyers, but it seems to have won a warm welcome from the politicians. It was, breathe it low, that no seal should be used at all. A document should be prepared saying "I George R etc. hereby appoint," he should sign it, and the Prime Minister of the Dominion concerned should countersign it in the presence of the Chief Dominion legal officer as his witness.[1] To think that grown men should quarrel over this kind of tripe in 1930.

I have had to go to various dinners to meet the Dominion premiers. The Canadian, I think, has brains;[2] he is vigorous, direct, and forcible. The New Zealand man hasn't even ordinary intelligence.[3] He can't follow an economic, much less a legal argument, and merely bleats. The Australian is a good, simple fellow who simply was not made for complex issues.[4] He told me that he was greatly impressed by the King's wit; I asked for a sample. "Well," he said, "the King said to me, 'I expect you will be pretty busy while you are here, Mr. Scullin.' 'Yes sir,' I replied, 'Conference all day and a dinner every night.' 'Well,' said the King (this is

---

[1] The final decision was that the commission of the Governor General should continue to be countersigned by the Secretary of State, who controls the Signet. See Berriedale-Keith, "The Imperial Conference of 1930," 13 *Journal of Comparative Legislation and International Law* 26, 35 (1931).

[2] Richard Bedford (1870-1947), first Viscount Bennett, was the Conservative Prime Minister and Minister of External Affairs, 1930-1935.

[3] George William Forbes (1869-1947), Prime Minister of New Zealand, 1930-1935.

[4] James Henry Scullin (1876-1953), Labour Prime Minister of Australia, 1929-1931.

the wit) 'you must be glad you haven't to eat two dinners.'" On the other hand I was greatly impressed by the Canadian Attorney-General [5]—Loring Christie ten years older in type—clear, succinct, and with a real flair for getting to the roots of the problem. . . .

Then [I have read] a first-rate book by Judge Parry (a retired County Court judge) on the law as it affects the poor—a beautiful piece of effectively simple humanism; and the autobiography of Wilamowitz the classical scholar, which is quite moving. . . . I must mention, too, an amusing novel of the life literary which I urge upon you as the accompaniment to solitaire—*Cakes and Ale* by Somerset Maugham. Please see that your secretary procures it for you without fail. . . .

Our love to you.   *Ever affectionately yours, H. J. L.*

                     Washington, D.C., October 24, 1930
My dear Laski: How many interesting and amusing things you always tell me. I am a little surprised by your high praise of Parry —the little that I have read of his writing has not impressed me. I sent at once this morning on reading your letter for *Cakes and Ale*, and it is to be read as soon as we finish *Humanity Uprooted* by Maurice Hindus which Brandeis put me on to. I am the minion of you children of the upward and onward in my reading—though I am not an upward and onwarder. I am kept at home today by the doctor because of a little cold but have hopes of being able to go out tomorrow to the conference of the JJ. This is the first week of arguments. I foresee some clashes of opinion and am wondering what turn our new member will take.[1] He makes a good impression, but as yet I have little notice of his characteristics. I may have remarked before that it is strange how many important modifications of the law McReynolds has been the mouthpiece for, including the overruling of a number of decisions written by me—without, so far as I can see, any more convincing argument than that he had a majority behind him. There are several points on which all that I can say is let those who have established the change say how far they will go. These local difficulties are not interesting, but they more or less occupy my mind and bother me.

Later. I have not attempted to work today and there is a horrid rate case on which I am ill prepared to recite.[2] But I have listened to more of *Humanity Uprooted*—a very interesting account of Russia by a Russian who returned from America to see how things were. His account of the Communists shows in the most extreme

---

[5] Hugh Guthrie (1886-1939).

[1] In June 1930, Owen J. Roberts (1875-1955) had been appointed to the Court to fill the vacancy resulting from the death of Mr. Justice Sanford.

[2] Perhaps *Beaumont, Sour Lake and Western Railway v. United States*, 282 U.S. 74 (argued, Oct. 20; decided, Nov. 24, 1930; opinion by Butler, J.).

form what I came to loathe in the Abolitionists—the conviction
that anyone who did not agree with them was a knave or a fool.
You see the same in some Catholics and some of the "Drys" apropos of the 18th amendment. I detest a man who knows that he
knows. I gather from the book and more from other sources that
the Communists have killed so far as they could those who did not
agree with them and want to kill the rest. They present a case
where I fail to see that war is absurd. When two crows deter-
minately wish to make different kinds of a world, if they come in
contact I don't see what there is to do but to fight. I must stop
—I am sorry to write a dull letter but I can't help it. I am not
sorry to think that I shall get my marching orders before long.

Ever affectionately yours, O. W. Holmes

Devon Lodge, 26.X.30
My dear Justice: Hectic days since I wrote to you last, beginning
with a telephone call from Felix in New York. Since then I have
been nearly run off my legs, trying to get the Prime Minister and
Webb to see sense about their policy.[1] I think the P.M. would be
all right if he were left alone; but Webb has the rooted and in-
curable obstinacy of the doctrinaire who, when he has arrived at
a position, can be more impossible in defending it than the least
practical man who has ever handled a practical policy. It is a bad
business, hardly compensated for even by the pleasure of hearing
Felix's voice three thousand miles away.

What else have I done? Tried to talk sense into Irishmen at the
Imperial Conference on the question of British nationality. *Quaere*,
does it really hurt Irish prestige, if a ship of British registry leaves
Dover with a crew containing one Irishman. The ship is wrecked
off Barcelona. The lifeboat takes the crew into harbour, and its
members call on the British Consul for means to return home. The
Irish say that an Irishman is humiliated by having to call on a
British consul. They would prefer him to be helped by any other
than a British official unless we can invent an adjective less historically offensive to their national pride. Can you beat that? Imagine calling a man "His Majesty's Consul for the Commonwealth
of Nations to which, *inter alios*, Ireland and Great Britain are
parties"? Certainly nationalism, like religion, is a source of intolerable difficulty in the modern world.

. . . I have dined with dusky Indian delegates to the Round
Table Conference.[2] . . .

---

[1] Presumably with respect to Palestine; see, *supra*, p. 326.
[2] The Round Table Conference convened on November 12. Its principal
concern was the demand of India for Dominion status—a demand which was
sympathetically received by MacDonald as Chairman of the Conference.

Our love to you warmly. Four months today I hope to land in New York.　　　　　　　　*Ever affectionately yours, H. J. L.*

1.XI.30

My dear Justice: A week of hard toil with amusing experiences to diversify it! Of interest, a lunch with the Prime Minister of S. Africa.[1] He is a most curious mixture of medievalism and modernity. When he talks of commerce, universities, or foreign affairs, he speaks like a man who is eager to be abreast of the last possible development. Speak to him of the native in Africa and it sounds just like a Southerner of the *Dred Scott* period defending slavery! Then a tea with Austen Chamberlain who spoke with feeling of your friendship with his sister. He is a curious type. He has at the bottom the feelings of a great gentleman, but all these are so plastered over with a stiff manner that unless you go on trying, when his real kindness becomes evident, you tend to think that he is just being rude and give up the effort to talk to him. I am inclined to guess that the statesman suffers enormously in ordinary life from the fact that he speaks from an artificial eminence. He is accustomed to giving orders; he does not easily argue; he isn't used to having his premisses examined. And he is, of course, surrounded with excessive adulation which makes him unwilling to realise that criticism need not proceed from hostility. That's what is so wrong with MacDonald, and what constitutes the great charm of Baldwin. You can talk to the latter as though he was a friend. With MacDonald, as with Wilson, unless you can convey your criticism in the form of eulogy, it is likely to do your cause more harm than good. I wish a technique could be invented for persuading statesmen not to live on a pedestal. Webb is suffering badly from it just now. He is literally shocked that I should criticise his policy for Palestine and he assumes that I can't really like him personally if he is not to be supported by me in his plans.

I have been reading a good deal. The first volume of Churchill's *Autobiography*—a good book, full of grit and courage. To himself he is amusingly Napoleonic and I think about as unpleasantly active as Roosevelt. One feels that he has never had half an hour's quiet reflection in his life; but he has certainly lived every minute of it. Then E. S. Montagu's *Indian Diary*—which I would like to make compulsory reading for all administrators. It reveals the physiology of empire amazingly, the isolating effect of ceremonial, the cringing influence on the subjects of an irresponsible government, the evil of routine. . . .

---

[1] General James Barry Munnik Hertzog (1886-1942), the South African Premier from 1924 to 1939, was attending the Imperial Conference.

Of other things, not much to report. But I must tell you that with the twenty-five dollars' royalties on *Collected Legal Papers* I have fitted up a miners' reading aide in S. Wales, where almost everyone is unemployed, with fifty volumes from Everyman's Library. Their gratitude was almost overpowering. On the whole I think the pleasure of giving pleasure is about the best thing that there is.

And I was pleased because on receiving the notification of my reappointment to the university for the rest of my days, the chairman of our governors wrote that "we build the next years of the School more round your work than that of any other teacher." That made me feel that, on the whole, it is probably better to go on with the hard work of teaching than my dream of a house in the country and endless leisure to write. But dreams are futile things!

My love to you as always.   *Ever affectionately yours, H. J. L.*

Washington, D.C., Nov. 10, 1930

My dear Laski: Although there has been no intimation from you I must assume that a big volume on *Les estampes de Peter Bruegel* comes from you. So I thank you for a renewal of the pleasures that I thought had died with Rice (former print boss in Cong. Library). I haven't yet quite finished my first examination—but I am much impressed and really interested. (I am not yet reconciled to Bruegel instead of Breughel). His "Devil's Progeny" lives as others that I remember do not. You believe 'em all. Also he was a surprisingly good landscape etcher, before the great advance with Rembrandt. B. had a fertile brain. I shall know more I hope soon.

I have written my first decisions for this term and expect from present appearances that they will go through.[1] Their only merit is brevity, I hope accurate and adequate—but somehow it put new life into me to write again.

I have received books and essays on legal themes from professors and others—more or less flattering to my vanity—but I was particularly struck by the tone of a N.Y. professor—Llewellyn, that I think I have noticed in one or two others.[2] They utter harmless things that I should not think could provoke antagonism, and that do not seem to me dazzlingly new, as if they were voices crying in the wilderness—or heroes challenging the world. I say to myself, "Why so hot?"

I am amused by your Irish and the British consul and your Italian lecturer and slightly tremble to hear you talk of "poor old

---

[1] *Klein* v. *Board of Supervisors,* 282 U.S. 10; *Sherman* v. *United States, id.* 25 (Nov. 24, 1930).

[2] Karl N. Llewellyn, "A Realistic Jurisprudence—The Next Step," 30 *Columbia L. Rev.* 431 (April 1930).

Scrutton" whom I haven't got over thinking of as a promising young man.

I read or rather listened to *Cakes and Ale.* I don't willingly read novels any longer but this seemed different. However, I thought the best thing in it was the end when Rosie explains the charm of Lord George: "He was always such a perfect gentleman." That I thought masterly—like the place in (*Man and Superman?*) where after the genius has explained that his engagement ends his performance and his sister calls him a brute—his girl says, "Never mind, dear, keep on talking"—or words to that effect.

Yours ever, O. W. H.

Devon Lodge, 22.XI.30

My dear Justice: I am ashamed of myself for so long a silence; but I have been simply overwhelmed and have hardly known where to turn. The P.M. dragged me in to try and help to arrange a *modus vivendi* between the British government and the Zionists, and I have been working at it like a slave. What with Webb's pedantic obstinacy and ambiguities, Felix and Brandeis's immovability, and the hectic indignation of the Zionists here it has been a grim business, and I don't know yet whether I have done any good. But much of it has been built upon letting every one talk to me about it and then acting as the honest broker between them, and they certainly *can* talk. I have spent a fortune in telegrams to New York, and at the end of each day I creep wearily to bed wondering if human nature is capable of mutual understanding.

Of other things, accordingly, not many. I am so glad you like the Breughel (note my spelling); I think I told you how enormously impressed I was by his paintings at the Antwerp exhibition. Then I have been helping a little with the Indian conference —mostly trying to explain the implications of federalism to them. They are queer people—a little extra dose of courtesy makes an absurdly great difference to their outlook, and the trouble with the British is the high degree in which they lack the imagination to see the importance of courtesy. Then I went up to Glasgow for a day to settle a strike and similarly to Manchester. The second I enjoyed, for I was able to give ten thousand men a week's holiday with pay annually and I really felt that the Recording Angel might accord that to me for righteousness. They were dairy workers who in the past had not even had Xmas day as a holiday thro' bad organisation in the industry. . . .

February comes closer and I am beginning to get really excited by its prospects. You will not forget that we dine together on March 8.

Our love to you.   *Ever affectionately yours, H. J. L.*

Devon Lodge, 30.XI.30

My dear Justice: A grand letter from you which warmed my heart.[1]
I was interested by what you said about the operations performed
on your draft decision. I yesterday presented a beautiful draft
memorandum to Sankey for the Indian comment; he accepted it
wholly except for two quite beautiful sentences which, if vigorous,
gave, I thought, point and colour to the whole. I did not fight for
them, but I felt like one of Brueghel's little devils. I hate this
process of emasculation to avoid offence. There are some interests
it is a public duty to offend.

I am still pretty busy on behalf of Felix and Brandeis.[2] Between
ourselves the latter is a *very* difficult person. He is intransigent and
dominating, and unnecessarily prone to read evil motives into obvious actions. Felix is like clay in his hands, and if it were not for
my deep affection for them both, I think I would have told them
long ago to go to hell and see what they could accomplish without
my intervention. I can't run daily to the Foreign Secretary because
Brandeis has doubts about a semicolon—at some point in a negotiation one has to assume that the cabinet really means what it says.
I did not realise before how curiously suspicious a nature Brandeis
has. He is extraordinarily profound in his insights, but, I should
have said, not quite human in his contacts, with the result that he
does not always see round a subject.

Of other things, the most amusing, I think, was a dinner last
night with half a dozen of the Prime Minister's colleagues, when
business was out of the way, and a good brandy had mellowed
them, they began dissecting him and it was like nothing so much
as a group of actors dealing with a successful rival. I gathered that
he was vain, arrogant, aloof, reserved, theatrical, over-subtle etc.
I asked why if he was all these things, they continued to work
with him; to which the pretty unanimous reply was that he was
really all right and that these were only surface defects. I asked
the First Lord[3] what he would take to be really serious ones. I also
went with Frida to a dinner to meet Virginia Woolf, the novelist.
She tickled me greatly; it was like watching someone organise her
immortality. Every phrase and gesture was studied. Now and again,
when she said something a little out of the ordinary, she wrote it

---

[1] The letter referred to is missing.

[2] The part which Mr. Justice Brandeis played in opposing the proposals
contained in the Passfield White Paper is briefly referred to in Mason,
Brandeis: A Free Man's Life (1946), 595. See, for a fuller account of the
matter, Frankfurter, "The Palestine Situation Restated," 9 *Foreign Affairs*
409 (April 1931); reprinted in *The Brandeis Avukah Volume of 1936*
(Rabbi Shubow, ed., c. 1932), 245.

[3] Albert V. Alexander (1885-   ), later Viscount Alexander of Hillsborough and, in 1963, the Earl of Hillsborough; First Lord of the Admiralty,
1929-1931; Minister of Defence, 1947-1950.

down herself in a notebook. . . . Really it was as good as an opera to see her put up a lorgnette and say in a coy whisper "You write?" "Yes." "Ah, I read so little—the effort of creation exhausts me." I wonder if you ever met her? She is L. Stephen's daughter by his second marriage.

. . . I read Owen Wister on T.R. . . . but with the feeling that the talent he depicts was that of a first-rate megaphone and not of a statesman. I accept the view that he talked well, adding that I never heard him do so in the half-dozen talks I had with him and that Wister reports nothing I could accept as proof. . . .

Our love to you. Please keep very fit until I get to Washington.

Ever affectionately yours, H. J. L.

Washington, D.C., December 19, 1930

My dear Laski: Belated best wishes for Xmas and the New Year and a word to say I have read your essay on "The Limitations of the Expert" with unqualified pleasure and agreement.[1] Many years ago Albert Nickerson,[2] long dead, a powerful Philistine with insight, said to me that a merit of the English government was that it had bodies of competent experts in the departments, but put a man of the world (or some such phrase) at the top—and I cannot help recalling as slightly relevant that with a similar idea in my head I said in my book that ignorance is the best of law reformers —a paradox looking your way. The discourse is admirable. My love to you all.   *Affectionately yours, O. W. H.*

Devon Lodge, 27.XII.30

My dear Justice: First of all, our loving good wishes to you for 1931. I hope it will bring you great happiness.

I have had very pleasant days since I wrote last. First of all a brief trip to Paris. . . . I came back to work, mostly with the Indians on behalf of Sankey. In that connection, we went to a great reception by the Secretary of India which, as a mere spectacle, I wish you could have seen. The robes and jewels of the Indians and their wives were like a Titian, a mass of superb, even dazzling, colour. The Indian problem goes slowly and with difficulty. How seriously the Moslems take themselves you can see from the fact that the Aga Khan, who, I gather has the blood of the prophet in his veins, is able to sell the water in which he washes to disciples in the East at so much a pint; and it is kept there in temples as

[1] 162 *Harper's Magazine* 101 (December 1930).
[2] See, *supra*, p. 320, Vol. I.

sacred! One or two of the Indians are really first-rate people, especially Sastri[1] whom I should reckon among the noblest men I have
ever met; but the depth of their religious fervour makes any plan
for effective justice between them a matter of extraordinary difficulty. Then I have had a further dose of Palestine which convinced me even more that Moses made a great mistake. I add that
your remark about Brandeis is certainly just.[2] Since these negotiations with the British government began I cannot remember one
telegram of his which has been really helpful. All statesmanship is,
after all, the power to compromise on inessentials; he digs himself
in on what are really matters of no consequence with the passion
of a tiger defending his cubs; and that makes him, in my judgment, much less effective on the big issues where he is really
entitled to care. He exercises a strange hold over Felix, for the
latter, who can usually be cool and independent, is in these things
simply an echo of L.D.B. He gives orders like an omnipotent Sul-
tan and negotiations do not come to a success in that way. Moreover he treats his fellow Zionists who differ from him almost as
criminals, and, as I think, gravely injures his own prestige by so
doing.

I was not much moved by White's remark on Jews which you
quote.[3] Taking them as a whole they seem to me very much like
other people. There is a small class of rich social climbers, the
type, I should guess, whom White knew, who are all that he says.
But they are a tiny class, and they have the inferiority complex
which comes from the horrid conjunction of great wealth and the
sense of uncertainty which comes from ostracism. I don't think one
can safely generalise about any people; Felix, Morris Cohen, Einstein, Julian Mack, don't fit into any box. I should say that White's
remark was less true than most. My difficulty with Jews is their
tough resistance to assimilation, their pride in being different, their
excessive sensibilities, their intellectual hubris. But I should certainly not accuse them of being selfish in any ordinary sense.

We leave tonight for a week in Antwerp with our Belgian artist
friends. It's always a jolly time and we look forward to it greatly.

Our united love and every sort of good wish.

Ever affectionately yours, H. J. L.

Devon Lodge, 10.I.31
My dear Justice: . . . I came back to the conferences on India
and Palestine and have been hard at work on both. The latter is

---

[1] V. S. Scinivasa Sastri (1869-1946), Indian statesman, was at the Round
Table Conference.

[2] The letter referred to is missing.

[3] Presumably the reference is to the same missing letter [A. H.].

all done except for formal registration; I hope Felix and Brandeis will be grateful for a job which has taken infinite pains and ought really to satisfy every decent aspiration to which they are entitled. The Indian show, at the moment, goes very well.[1] It has been a perfect delight to work for Sankey, hard though it has been. He not only takes one's points, but he treats one with an eager sympathy which is very moving, and he is always open-minded. On the whole I think the risks we take are right; certainly we could not have sent the Indians back with less. But there is still the difficulty of knowing what will be the attitude of India and the extremists when the draft is in shape. Anyhow, now that it all draws to a close I am glad to have had a hand in it especially as Sankey seems to feel that I have helped him. . . .

I'm also pretty busy with writing. An article for the *Yale Law Journal* was finished last night;[2] in case it is a secret of those young people I will only say that it left me not without admiration of your opinions during the last twenty-five years. Then a long article half-done on democracy for the new Encyclopedia of the Social Sciences, an interesting job to do, but irritating because of the limitations of space.[3] Most interesting of all, and already done, a piece on Woodrow Wilson for the March number of the *Forum*[4] (a journal I know not but which will, I hope, pay me $200) trying to estimate ten years after just where he stands and what he stands for. On reflection I concluded that his stature had diminished [and] that his social philosophy was out of date even while he was preaching it. But I must not anticipate what I hope you will read. . . .

Our love to you as always.   *Ever affectionately yours, H. J. L.*

Devon Lodge, 25.I.31

My dear Justice: I have almost begun to know what leisure is, now that the Indian Conference is over. It ended with a heavy burst of hospitality, in which the striking thing was a dinner given by the Indians to the P.M. I sat next to a Maharajah with an income of a million sterling a year, and if there is living a more banal idiot I have not met him. He was a most incredible fellow to watch. He had windows opened and closed simply for the sake of giving orders and drawing attention to himself. Then I was bidden to dine with another Prince who made no less than nine speeches in

---

[1] The Round Table Conference had made considerable progress towards its goal of establishing the principles upon which a federal constitution of India might be based.

[2] "The Political Philosophy of Mr. Justice Holmes," 40 *Yale L. J.* 683 March 1931).

[3] 5 *Encyclopedia of Social Sciences* (1931) 76-84.

[4] "Woodrow Wilson Ten Years After," 85 *Forum* 129 (March 1931).

one evening. Poor Sankey and the P.M. were bored to tears; I en
joyed the first five simply because one never knew just what he
was going to say next. Then I have been busy settling some co
operative disputes, a very interesting job. To compile wage-scale
in terms of a balance sheet is a good experience for a political phi
losopher, and as both sides went away satisfied I don't think I can
have done too badly at it. I went also to dine with the Webbs
Much good talk, especially from him on the pressure of tradition
in an office like his. But though he complained, I felt that, on the
whole, he welcomed its pressure because it saved him from the
labour of going at the facts for himself. I had a queer lunch with
Bertrand Russell. He wants a definite academic job. . . . He re
mains dazzling; but there has come into the tone of his mind a
curious and distressing cynicism which I should have said was the
worst possible attitude for one who wants to teach the young. And
I felt that he was prepared to give opinions without thought on
almost everything—not the outlook a man of his achievement ough
to have. He is very loveable, and obviously very lonely. But he
wants to have his cake and eat it . . . I must add a word about
a dinner with the German Ambassador who is extraordinarily able
and attractive.[1] He told us much about Holstein,[2] the *eminenc
grise* of the pre-war F.O. in Berlin; he had all sorts of black
mailing holds on people which made it dangerous to demand his
resignation. At last came a foreign secretary with courage and Hol
stein went. It was then discovered that most of his threats were
based on sheer intuition, and that he had a genius for scenting the
bad streak in a man's character; but he was quite unable, the
Ambassador said, either to tell a good man when he saw one, or
to trust anyone. Yet he was undoubtedly one of the people most
powerful in fixing German policy in Western matters. I collect one
phrase of his I liked—a description of Roosevelt in Berlin on his
visit to the Kaiser as "a corybantic Nimrod who always fired his
gun and mistook the explosion for a bull's eye."

. . . I urge you . . . to read a book by an old Harvard pupi
of mine, Crane Brinton, on the Jacobins; first it is dedicated to
me, which gave me the pleasure of satisfied vanity, and second it
really is an admirable study of what may be termed the mechanic
of a revolutionary organisation. Not even Aulard has made on
see quite so well how the thing really worked. I add the commen
that it is really a wonderful experience to see one's pupils becomin
people with solid achievement to their credit.

It is now only just over three months till I sail. I hope I ma

[1] Baron von Neurath, *supra*, p. 344.
[2] Friedrich von Holstein (1837–1909); his retirement from the Foreig
Office occurred at the time of the Morocco crisis, when Bülow, the chancello
resigned.

assume that we are going to dine in Washington on your birthday. Nothing else in my American visit matters quite so much as that. We all three send our love. *Ever affectionately yours, H. J. L.*

Devon Lodge, 7.II.31

My dear Justice: I have just passed the first really peaceful week in months, and it has really been a relief beyond words. I'm not sure that it isn't an oasis in a desert, for things seem to be looming up for next month. But at least it has been peace. Mostly I have been reading Tocqueville for a lecture I have to give next week at King's College.[1] It has been frightfully interesting. One of the problems one has to solve in the history of ideas is the changed attitude to America in Europe after 1800. Until then it clearly was paradise, and no one doubted that any Utopian ideal must be placed in America. After, and until Tocqueville no words were too harsh for it, and Europe wanted mostly to hear the kind of thing Basil Hall and Mrs. Trollope seemed to give. I think the reason is that America was democratic, that democracy meant 1789, and that the more it was attacked as democratic the more the "classes" could take comfort that in resisting popular reforms they were resisting democracy which threatened all decent ways of life. That's why I think Tocqueville so remarkable. Everything about him was patrician in temper; yet by a deliberate effort he made himself see the significance of the new world and appreciate its possibilities. With all his limitations, one could make out of his book a political anthology about as fine as any in the nineteenth century. I was amused to find in looking at the material a speech by Sir R. Peel urging Conservatives to read the book as a warning against democracy, mainly, I think, because the phrase "tyranny of the majority" which Tocqueville invented fell pleasantly on Peel's ear. It was also interesting to see how completely he had anticipated all that is good in the general part of Bryce's *American Commonwealth.* . . . I also re-read Maine's *Ancient Law,* and fell again under its inexhaustible charm. If I had to name a book to tempt the outsider into a sense that jurisprudence was a great subject I think I should ask him to read Maine and then deny greatness at his peril! . . .

I must end with a tale illustrating the glorious use of the British language by native Hindus. My friend Coatman[2] used to be inspector of prisons in India. Visiting the prison of Udaipur, he was

---

[1] Printed in F. J. C. Hearnshaw, *The Social and Political Ideas of Some Representative Thinkers of the Victorian Age* (1933), 100.

[2] John Coatman (1889-   ), after many years as a civil servant in India, had become Professor of Imperial Economic Relations at London University in 1930.

shown round by the Babu superintendent. They came to the condemned cell where a poor, shivering prisoner was crouching. Coatman asked about him. "He is to be hanged tomorrow," said the
Babu. Pause. "He is innocent." Pause. "That is why he looks so
peevish."

My love to you, my dear Justice. I wish I could drop in on you
for a talk.   *Ever affectionately yours, Harold J. Laski*

                                      Devon Lodge, 10.II.31
My dear Justice: Forgive my silence. I have been in bed with a
bad dose of influenza, and am only just about again. This is merely
to say that I leap at the chance of staying with you. I shall come
on March 7th and catch a late train to New Haven on the 8th. It
will be a joy beyond words to be with you.

Our love as always.   *Ever affectionately yours, H. J. L.*

        Yale Law School, New Haven, Connecticut, 2.III.31
My dear Justice: A very hurried note to ask whether it is all right
for me to turn up at 1720 on Saturday afternoon and stay until a
late train on Sunday night? I am more excited by the prospect of
this visit than anything I can remember in years.

My love as always.   *Ever affectionately yours, Harold J. Laski*

                                      Yale Law School, 16.III.31
My dear Justice: I ought to have written to you last week; but I
have been terribly driven and have not yet emerged from the
welter of correspondence this visit seems to entail. Yet I must put
on paper my joy at seeing you again. They were exquisite hours,
among the very happiest that I have ever known. And to have
been with you on that day will be a memory I shall always *cherish.*[1]
Forsan et haec olim meminisse juvabit. I wish I knew how to tell
you what friendship with you has meant to me. But it is one of
the things that lie too deep and too intimate for words.

The days pass very swiftly. It is extraordinarily interesting here.[2]
The level is not, I think, quite as good as at Harvard, especially
not in the Law School. But they are most attractive people, as
eager as could be, and I enjoy them. I don't know what they
make of me; but I seem to keep them excited, which is, after all,

---

[1] Holmes was ninety on March 8.

[2] During the second term of the academic year Laski gave two courses in
the Yale Law School: an Introduction to Legal and Political Theory, in the
first year curriculum, and a course in Administrative Law for advanced
students.

the teacher's main business. If I had to criticise I should guess two things (I) too much university interest in building and too little to [*sic*] men. (II) too much attention to points of administrative detail. They ask less, has X learned to think, than has X obtained a sufficient number of credits to entitle us to assume that he has learned to think. And this last involves a pretty vast structure in which the teacher gets buried unless he is painfully careful. The boys read too little for themselves, and what they read is too much in bits. The result is that they aren't accustomed to the job of tearing the heart out of a book or to thinking on their own. It may be that English experience gives me a wrong perspective of approach, but I should have said that my lads in London were much more critical and sceptical than the lads here because we throw on them a much greater onus of responsibility. . . .

My love to you as always. One of the best things about being here is the sense of your proximity.

Ever affectionately yours, H. J. L.

Washington, D.C., March 17, 1931
My dear Laski: Your letter gives me great happiness. Few things possible could give me so much. I will say no more except that it came just as I was asking myself whether it would not be better if I should die now—(without assistance from myself—*bien entendu*).

All my leisure time, *i.e.* all my time out of Court has been taken in writing letters and the end is not yet—but I have managed to write a little decision, distributed today and accepted by all but three not heard from yet. On Sunday the 15th most of my old secretaries turned up and made me a charming call. They proposed that next summer Hopkinson should paint a second portrait—half length, sitting—for the new Court house—which will not be much of a job and will be pleasant.

Of course your lads in London are more critical. They live in a thicker atmosphere of culture than any large body of men here— not only in the society they meet but in what comes through their eyes. Perhaps we spoke of that. I have read nothing but letters but have listened to the third volume of Parrington—posthumous about the rise of critical realism in the U.S. or some such title. There is a touch of radical dogmatism in his tone and speech—the catch words catch him—"exploitation"—"acquisition" &c. He cares most for those of his way of thinking—&c. &c. but he has a great deal of keen insight and I am sorry that solitaire going on while I listened, somewhat blunted the impression of his words. At the end of this week, or rather on the Monday following it, we adjourn for 3 weeks which will be a relief and let me catch my breath. Now I am panting all the time.

In my turn my love to you—always.

Affectionately yours, O. W. Holmes

Yale Law School, 23.III.31

My dear Justice: Your delightful letter gave me great joy. The boys, I gather, gave you their *Journal* on Saturday, where I hope you discovered my real birthday present.[1] One thing I must say. It was difficult to present the appearance of insight without the display of that intimate affection unsuitable for a learned journal. But I count on you to read between the lines.

I keep as busy as ever. I went to Williams and to New York— the latter particularly brightened by a long evening with Morris Cohen. I was immensely impressed first by his integrity of mind and second by his intellectual maturity. It is a great thing to meet that kind of mellow wisdom which handles ideas as tools and is not wedded to private dogmas. His insight is hardly less remarkable than his learning. I must add a word of a visit to his parents —two old Russian Jews well in the eighties. Neither speaks English and they have a tiny three room apartment on the East side. I told them of my pride in Morris and the esteem in which we all hold him. The old lady's ideas [*sic*] became twin fires as she said "I am poor and ill, but when I think of my son I bless America for making me the richest woman in the world." Do you mind if I envied America that? I also spent an hour with Walter Lippmann, but not very profitably. I think wealth has done two things to him. A goood deal of his sensitiveness has gone. He is interested in external things, queer little worthless comforts *e.g.* a bad display of temper because the servant forgot a cup of coffee he ordered. And he has arrived at the stage where he is not eager to take intellectual risks. . . . I found that he had ceased to read much outside modernities and he lacked a sense of perspective. He lives in the immediate moment and is not poised about it. . . .

And two other minor things. Wherever I go, I think I see a real intellectual renaissance in America. There is a spirit of critical enquiry abroad which it is quite refreshing, even exciting to witness. People are sceptical about inherited values—always the beginning of wisdom. Against it I put a curious passion for taking pleasure externally rather than internally. A man says at dinner "What shall we do tonight" not "what shall we talk about?" I wonder how few things like the radio and the motor car are responsible for that. Materialise the source of pleasure and you destroy the faculty for inner satisfactions. Wherefore you lose the

[1] See, *supra*, p. 355.

pleasure of reflection by asking others to do things and think things for you; and to the tired mind after a day in Wall Street it is the easiest way. But I am sure that mental breezes blow from within outward.

My love to you. The very thought of you as near is my main consolation at my distance from Frida and Diana.

Ever affectionately yours, H. J. L.

Yale Law School, 6.IV.31

My dear Justice: A delightful letter from you last week warmed my heart.[1] I am glad you liked the lads from the law journal. They came back lyrical with excitement, and each came alone to my room to give his separate version of the event.

Since I wrote last, my main experience, and fascinating it was, has been a week in the Middle West. I had not been there since 1915, and then only for two days in Chicago. This time I went to Chicago, Minneapolis and Columbus, and thoroughly enjoyed it. Impressions pour in on me so that it is difficult to select. First, I think, a most attractive simplicity in the people. It might easily be social crudity, but I am convinced it is not. On the contrary, it is a simple pleasure in simple things which I found charming. They are, of course, unsophiscated [*sic*] compared with the East, and curiously provincial. But there is a healthy earnestness about them which I could not but admire. Then I felt the immensity of distance from Europe. Our problems, clearly, do not even enter their consciousness. They are not reported because they do not interest. They are not even quite certain that the East really exists; and their minds are definitely turned Westward. Then I noted a curious faith in mass action, a sense that the more people are alike in taste and opinion and feeling, the better things will be. If a man wanted to condemn his neighbour the usual ground was the possession of a strong individuality. He was irreligious, or socialist, or pro-negro, or crazy about books and pictures, or did not go to the movies. It was a different civilisation from anything I have ever seen and I enjoyed every moment of it. You will, I hope, congratulate me on finding in Chicago Knolles' translation of Bodin (1616) a very stately folio, which belonged to Ellesmere the Chancellor, for ten dollars; I would cheerfully have paid seventy-five for it, as it gets increasingly rare. I lectured twice—once at Minnesota and once at Ohio State and perhaps because everyone was kind to me, I thought the standard there compared pretty favourably with Yale. I also spoke in New York with Redlich on parliamentary government to a show called the Foreign Policy

---

[1] The letter referred to is missing.

Association.[2] Redlich was charming, but suffered from the historian's fallacy that the *is* is the *inevitable*. Now I have peace until the week-end when I go to give a lecture at Bryn Mawr. I must add that wherever I went interest in your birthday was profound. I think it would make you really happy to find how widespread is the affection for you among men whom you yourself would respect. At Minnesota, for instance, the Governor,[3] a silent, able Swede actually unbent when I said I had been with you on your birthday and said that his party (farmer-labour) had a confidence in you which they extended to no other person on the bench. . . .

I expect you heard of Arnold Bennett's death. It moved me a good deal for I used to see much of him. He was a very generous soul, full of kindly wisdom, and I think three or four of his novels have a permanent place in English letters. He had taste, too, for pictures, wine and many other things. He first made me see the curious power of Gauguin and first made me realize the defects of Rodin. That's the worst of distance. It insulates you from talk which comforts one. If I could have half an hour with Frida or H. G. Wells and talk of him I should feel less lonely about it. For I cling to my friends.

Do you know yet when your Court stops for the term? I want, if I may, to have another week-end with you either at the end of May or early in June, whether at Washington or Beverly Farms as you think best. I can't, alas, do it before. But I must have one more glimpse of you before I sail.

My love to you as always.   *Ever affectionately yours, H. J. L.*

Washington, D.C., April 12, 1931
My dear Laski: To answer your last question first. We adjourn for the term on Monday, June 8 if nothing changes—and I should expect to head for Boston on the following Wednesday—June 10. Except on days too near departure and arrival to be consistent with making you comfortable, you always will be welcome. I should be much disappointed if we didn't have another time together.

The sittings begin again tomorrow, I believe with an important case between New Jersey and New York about taking water from a river[1]—in which the Chief can't sit and that I fear may mean that I shall have to take it to write—but I can't tell about that yet. I haven't had the leisure I hoped for—one never does—but still

---

[2] *The Decline of Parliamentary Government, Discussed by Harold J. Laski and Dr. Josef Redlich, March 28, 1931* (Foreign Policy Association, Pamphlet No. 74, 1931).

[3] Floyd B. Olson (1891-1936), Farmer-Labor Governor of Minnesota, 1930-1936.

[1] *New Jersey* v. *New York*, 283 U.S. 336 (May 4, 1931); opinion by Holmes, Hughes, C.J., and Roberts, J., not participating.

have had a little and some charming drives in the parks and by
the river. The apple blossoms around the basin are out today and
the place is packed with automobiles. Also some wonderful white
magnolias &c. but I am afraid such details don't interest you. My
secretary has just finished reading to me the *Maritime History of
Massachusetts,* an enchanting book. After ending it last night we
turned to your recommendation—Wodehouse—*Big Money*—and I
have roared over all that I have heard. I should think it was one of
W's best if it doesn't fall off. At odd minutes I am tucking in
Cohen's *Reason and Nature*—but that I must read to myself as I
get a chance. My only criticism so far is that when talking of particular impressions and universals, he doesn't think of the composite photograph—which seems to me more than an analogy—a
type of the process. These most frequently recurring elements
make coincidents and therefore deeper marks and you get a generalization mechanically achieved without any bother about particulars and universals.

I heartily agree with his repudiation of the irrationalists &c.—
but speaking only as a bettabilitarian and within the limits of our
very finite experience I have no faith that reason is the last word
of the universe. I know nothing about it. I have no prejudice
against a miracle—but I will bet a dollar to ten cents that any
miracle alleged to have occurred within the world of our experience didn't come off. I am sorry to have got only less than
half way through Cohen when the sitting begins again. I am much
interested by your impressions of the middle west. They sound
plausible. My secretary comes from there—but discloses from time
to time a critical judgment that I have not exactly measured.
Speech there, as elsewhere here, I think has degenerated—largely
through the obliteration of the consonants. Our crier opens court
excellently in other respects but he says The Unihd (this letter is
H) States of America.

My blessings on thee, lad. *Affectionately yours, O. W. Holmes*

Yale Law School, 20.IV.31
My dear Justice: A grand letter from you cheered me considerably,
for I have been feeling rather badly homesick and forlorn. Time
is a definite category at three thousand miles distance from Devon
Lodge; I realise the gay agony of devotion more than I thought
possible. But really I am having a most interesting time. I had a
great week-end in Philadelphia where I saw a superb collection of
French pictures in the house of one Barnes[1]—Renoirs and Manets

---

[1] Albert Coombs Barnes (1872-1951), inventor of Argyrol, educator, and
renowned collector of modern art.

which took my breath away and a Cézanne which was like a piece of the sun. . . .

You meanwhile are deciding I suppose whether New Jersey is to thirst or New York and whether that admirable young Mackintosh is fit to be the citizen of an America which digests Mr. Otto Kahn quite painlessly.[2] I am for Mackintosh on the admirable grounds upon which Sydney Smith defended Catholic Emancipation a century ago.[3] I expect you are finding constant glories in this superb spring. Even I notice the magnificence of the magnolias on every hand and the willows in their new green are singularly moving.

How would it suit your plans if I came down to Washington on Friday May 22nd and stayed until the Sunday? If that fits your household I needn't say that it would be grand for me.

My love to you as always.   *Yours ever affectionately, H. J. L.*

Yale Law School, 11.V.31

My dear Justice: I ought to have written earlier to tell you how glad I am that I may come on the 30th.[1] It will be the culmination of my stay here. I add that I shall try to steal one day with you in Beverly Farms before I leave on June 17 so that we can drive out together. *Haec olim meminisse juvabit;* but we can talk of this when I come.

I have been pretty busy since I wrote last. A week-end in Cornell, one with Felix, and four days giving the Weil lectures in North Carolina.[2] It has all been very exciting to me, though a little tiring. Cornell I shall long remember because I met there Carl Becker. He is really superb—a mature scholar, with a width of interest and a tolerant maturity that make talk a joy. And he shares my passion for the French 18th century, has the right contempt for Bossuet, and the proper realisation that Diderot is the biggest force of the age. N. Carolina fascinated me—an oasis of liberalism in the Southern desert. Here was a body of men who understand that ancient memories can be futile as well as precious and see the need for new thought and new energy. I must add that the Law School there was very good, and it was moving to me to see your

---

[2] In *United States* v. *MacIntosh,* 283 U.S. 605 (May 25, 1931), a majority of the Court held that under Congressional statutes relating to naturalization, an alien who was unwilling to take an oath of allegiance without reserving the right to decide for himself that a particular war was morally justified, was ineligible for citizenship. Holmes, Brandeis, and Stone, JJ., concurred in a dissenting opinion of Hughes, C.J.

[3] In Sydney Smith's *Peter Plymley's Letters* (1807) his plea for Catholic emancipation was based largely on the thesis that the enlightened self-interest of England required that Irishmen should be her friends.

[1] Two short notes, one from Laski of April 28 and one from Holmes of April 29, 1931 are omitted.

[2] Later expanded and published as *Democracy in Crisis* (1933).

picture (a photograph of the Hopkinson portrait) in the place of
honour over the Dean's desk in the faculty room. I liked the students too—lads with charming manners and an evident anxiety to
acquire not only information but the way of thought. Clearly the
South is in for a bad time unless it can tame to social purposes the
vast industrial revolution that is taking place there; and the impressive thing about the faculty is its sense that the university
must play its part in preventing the catastrophe of a hundred years
ago being repeated through absence of social purpose in the plan.
Of course the difference in temper from the North is astounding.
It comes out in the softness of speech, almost clinging manners,
the amazing and excessive deference to women, the tendency to
look backwards for inspiration, the sense that they are of different
clay from the Yankee. And I should have guessed that they suffer
much from intense religiosity which clouds their minds and makes
them feel that the Lord will provide without undue exertion on
their part. I also had (in New York) a most charming dinner with
Cardozo where we had much talk of you. He is a very beautiful
person with a combination of penetration and sweetness that are
unforgettable. Morris Cohen was there; and I much enjoyed
Morris's defiant dogmatism and the gentleness of Cardozo's footnotes of dubiety. Certainly he is among my half dozen American
candidates for my corner of heaven or hell. I met there, too, Jerome
Frank whose book I think you know. He is pleasant and earnest,
but, I should have guessed, rather a muddled person, though
attractive through it all. And I met Charles Burlingham[3] whom I
thought wholly delightful in every sort of way. His views on Felix
went straight to my heart.

   My love to you eagerly. I shall count the days till Washington.
                                    Ever affectionately yours, H. J. L.

                                    Yale Law School, 11.VI.31
My dear Justice: I have waited to write to you until I felt you had
really settled down in Beverly Farms. I need not tell you how delightful those two days were. I came to America primarily to see
you, for no friendship I have ever had has given me the same
beauty or exhilaration; and these two brief visits to Washington
have made me feel even more intensely what a happy day for me
it was when Felix brought me to Beverly on July 10, 1916. Thank
you again and again.

   May I raise one or two things that come out of our talk. (I) *À
propos* of the Bent book about you,[1] you will, I hope, send me a
few words saying that you agree that Felix is the best person to do

---

[3] Charles C. Burlingham (1858-1959), distinguished leader of New York's
admiralty bar and sage student of public affairs.

[1] In 1932 Silas Bent published his book, *Mr. Justice Holmes; A Biography.*

a really authoritative account. I build a great deal on this. (II) I think, too, that you should leave the bound volumes of your decisions and such papers to the Harvard Law School. That ensures their fullest use. (III) And the Poems to the Library of Congress. That is its proper home. (IV) But I want to have, at least for my own life, your copy of *The Common Law*.[2] That, with Maitland, was my first real introduction to scholarship, and it is full of precious memories for me. I should, when I die, put it in the Maitland Library at All Souls'. But, while I live, I want to have it as the embodiment of my own ideal of scholarship. Don't, please, think me interfering in putting down these things. You know the motive of affection from which they spring.

I have had some pleasant days lately. A charming visit to Eugene Meyer, where I saw a bust of his wife by, I think, Bourdelle[3] which was magnificent. Then two days in New York with a good dinner at Charles Burlingham's. Now I am clearing up here. Tomorrow I go off to Felix until Monday; then to New York (at the Commodore); and on Wednesday I sail on the *Aquitania*. I am very anxious to be home. The sense of being with Frida again is magical. But I hope Felix has arranged that we shall run over to see you while I am with him. Of course, as soon as I am home, I shall resume writing to you in the old way.

My best love, my dear Justice. I cannot put into words how precious are the memories you have given me.

Ever affectionately yours, Harold J. Laski

Beverly Farms, June 20, 1931

My dear Laski: When you left I wondered if I ever should see you again—but such inquiries are unprofitable. About that time I was feeling very feeble and finished—whichever way I look here there are only ghosts and memories. But whether I am recovering from more fatigue than I realized or what it is I don't know, but I am getting back something of a wiggle. People call—Mrs. Beveridge —sweet creature—with 2 fresh books from Paris—*L'âpre et splendide Espagne*—Camille Mauclaire—bully talk about pictures— and *Décadence de la nation française* (R. Aron and A. Dandieu) which the title makes me not want to read. The two JJ. Hand lunched here yesterday and were in better talking condition than I was.

Hopkinson who is going to do another portrait of me, sitting— probably not full length, is coming this p.m.—and I have driven to many of my favorite haunts—only to the outskirts of Rockport

---

[2] Holmes's last will contained no specific provisions on the matters referred to. Holmes's executor, however, gave the Justice's copy of *The Common Law* to Laski, and Laski in turn gave it to the Harvard Law School in 1940.

[3] Antoine Bourdelle (1861-1929).

as yet, the journey being a little long for me. I must try to resume a little walking. Now, I hope only for > 6 mos. disuse, I can go but a few steps. But the doctor looked me over and said arteries A-1—heart O.K. and urine satisfactory. Forgive these medical details. I still like to live though I awaited the doctor's answers I think without a quickened heart beat. We are rereading the *Romany Rye* having finished *Lavengro* and I have read a striking little book that I should like to hear you talk about: *The Impending Storm* by Somerset De Chaire—a boy of 18. To my ignorance it seemed remarkable.

The *certioraris* have not begun to come yet—and I am idle and worthless. I breakfast upstairs to avoid climbing, so far as I can —but this is under the dictatorship of Mary[1] who seems to think it a wrong to her if I do anything for myself.

Ever, dear boy, affectionately yours, O. W. Holmes

Beverly Farms, Massachusetts, July 25, 1931
My dear Laski: It is so long since a letter has come from you that anxiety begins to set in. But probably it only means that your hands were more than full on your return. I will wait, not speculate. With me things are going well. I think I must have been tired on my arrival here. I meditated on death—but I do so no longer. (I don't mean suicide, of course, but the imminent cloud.) I see slightly more people than I want to see but generally individually welcome, and my secretary reads copiously to me. The other day we finished *Our Mutual Friend* and now are deep in *Vanity Fair*. Separately I have tucked in Plato's *Laws* &c. &c. The *Laws* seem somewhat remote, but has fine *aperçus* in it, and is as despotic as even you could wish (if Laski were at the head). We have reread *Lavengro* and *The Romany Rye*—with somewhat abated enthusiasm. I was rather thrilled by Camille Mauclair—*L'âpre et splendide Espagne*—with fine talk about Goya, Velasquez and El Greco and about places and the moors. Also by V. Sackville-West —*All Passion Spent*. She is a very remarkable woman—when you take this—and her poem, *The Land*—and, unless I am confused, some book of travel in Persia[1] to say nothing of *The Edwardians*. Talking of books—I recur to some possible book about me after my death. While Felix seems to me the man for the law part I can't help thinking that there well might be another part dealing with the old Yankee that could perhaps better be managed by some other Yankee. I should think Palfrey would be good to advise with.

---

[1] Mary Donnellan was the devoted and imaginative manager of Holmes's household until his death.

[1] *Twelve Days; An Account of a Journey across the Bakhtiari Mountains in South-western Persia* (1928).

He is my executor and knows the ropes. I blush to assume so much interest in me—nor do I expect it—but I make the suggestion in case. I recall our times together with delight, and when I go through Rockport never fail to cast a reminiscent look down the road by the harbor side whence you radiated literature for two years. I like that drive superlatively but it is a little long for me.

I have pretty completely given up walking, and seem none the worse for it.

Now for *Vanity Fair*.   *Aff'ly yours, O. W. H.*

As from Devon Lodge, 6.VIII.31

My dear Justice: Let us resume operations! I should have been ashamed of so long a silence, had it not been that I knew you would understand. From the day (a very wonderful day) that I got home until we came abroad on July 31st my life was one mass of work. There were the royal commissions to which I belong.[1] Then Sankey roped me in to do a heap of things for him about the Indian Conference. Then university committees *ad nauseam;* and I who had hoped just nicely to avoid university examinations found that one of my colleagues had taken ill and I had to do my share after all. Indeed, I think I did more work in the month after I came home than I did during all the four I was in America. Now, however, it is really perfect peace. We came abroad just a week ago today, bringing the car with us and motoring on from Calais. A night at Rouen, one at Chartres, and after four days with some French friends near Tours, we are now staying for I expect about a fortnight at Amboise. We overlook the castle (a miracle) and the river and the views are quite beyond words. Each day we have motored genially round. The thing of all things that I have seen so far, after the Cathedral at Chartres, is Chenonceaux. That literally trembles with big moments. It is not only Renaissance architecture at its most efflorescent. The pictures, the situation, are all so completely blended into a harmony. And one understands better the spaciousness of the sixteenth century for having seen it. Only less lovely is Blois: the room there where the States-General of 1576 were held, and in which Bodin sat, is really a masterpiece of proportion made to produce the effect of massiveness. The whole countryside gives one a mass of ideas. It is clear, that in a full sense, a French nation, and nationalism, could not have been born. It is clear that these noblemen thought of themselves as each a state, going forward, if possible, but, if not, at least hanging on to what he held. It's also interesting to see how

---

[1] At this time Laski was serving not only on the Commission on Ministers' Powers but on the Departmental Committee on Local Government (see, *infra*, p. 439.

the province is in a literary sense still the underlying reality; the
department has all kinds of traditions, but it has not built itself
into the unconscious bones of the people. Yet now it is almost as
old as the province itself! It is amazing, too, to see a people to
whom equality means something so substantial as to the French.
Talk to the man in the garage, or the peasant in the field, and he
speaks to you with a vigour that is remarkable. At one little town,
Chançay, about six miles from here I saw the Mairie, with the
village registers going back in a complete series to 1573. I opened
up two historic years—1715 when L. XIV died and 1789. The
entry in the first among *"choses notables de l'année"* is that there
was a thunderstorm worse than any known since 1668, and in
1789 that the grapes (it is the Vouvray country) were of admirable
quality and brought a high price. That shows the truth of Jane
Austen who could write her novels without even a glimpse of the
Napoleonic wars. . . .

But America remains most vividly in my mind. It was one of the
supreme adventures I have ever had. Even now, I hardly begin
to realise how much I learned, and preciously. I thought on all
sides it was a richer civilisation than in 1926; and there was evidence and to spare of a growth of intellectual stature. One had the
sense that America was trembling on the verge of great discoveries
—that round the corner was the prospect of something of enormous
significance to civilisation. . . .

I came home to find Frida and Diana both well; and their welcome almost made it worth while to have gone away. In some ways
I find England very troubled and sad. She needs to make an
immense effort, and is rather like a patient to whom lethargy is
itself a source of pleasure. I have no doubt that at base she is
sound. But she needs to save herself by her energy and then, as
Pitt said, she may again save Europe by her example.

My love to you, dear Justice. Take care of yourself and be happy.
Ever your affectionate, H. J. L.

As from Devon Lodge, 15.VIII.31
My dear Justice: . . . The holiday proceeds peacefully. . . . The
vision of this endless procession of chateaux produces in me the
sense of the triumph of common-sense in the destruction of feudal-
ism. It is difficult to believe that the life of the common man could
have been endurable when the jurisdiction to which he was subject was so amazingly spasmodic in its operations. And one feels
intensely how great must have been the hatred of the peasants
for their masters when one reads in chateau after chateau that it
was pillaged and destroyed in 1789. I think too that the French
government deserves a tribute for the superb way in which it looks

after them. I have never seen restoration done with such delicacy and care, or rooms so arranged as to mesmerise the original idea of spaciousness.

. . . We have also spent a good deal of time with Chevalley, a friend of mine who is an old diplomat. He is fascinating—the best type of cultivated Frenchman. He interested me particularly in his power so to recite Racine that one sees a meaning of emphasis in simple adjectives due to their position which I had never seen before. . . . He is interesting, too, on the habits of the peasant. Himself the son of one, he says that he continually finds that they save despite themselves. The man who works for him will walk five miles to read a newspaper rather than buy one. He has never been to a large town save Tours, for the railway fare is more than fifty francs. Yet he is a peasant who owns his own house, fifteen hectares of rich vineyards and has something like twenty thousand dollars in the bank. His son and daughter work in the fields and except on Sunday and in harvest time never know what it is to eat meat. And this is characteristic of the whole neighbourhood. One old man even wore his wife's spectacles not, as he explained to Chevalley, that there was anything wrong with his eyes, but it would be such a pity to waste them. Harpagon must have lived here. Even the rich peasants' houses lack the most elementary sanitary accommodation; and I think an English or American Medical Officer would condemn in bulk the poorer houses as unfit for habitation. The infantile death rate is huge and the peasant reply is that one can always manufacture more children but that money spent is money wasted. Even agricultural methods are primitive. They prefer to kill themselves rather than spend money on modern machines. The result is that at forty all the women look old, and at sixty there is hardly a man not crippled by rheumatism. But they have their little plot of land and cottage and they seem very content.

We stay here until next Wednesday when I go off to Geneva[1] and Paris. Frida and Diana go in the car to Britanny and thence on to Antwerp where we meet. So I hope to give you news of significance when I write next week.

My love, as always,   *Ever affectionately yours, H. J. L.*

As from Devon Lodge, 26.VIII.31
My dear Justice: This is written in Antwerp where I have come on from Geneva and Paris. . . . I saw James Brown Scott [in Geneva] with French professors of international law eating out of his hand in the hope of a subsidy from the Carnegie Foundation. . . . Then

---

[1] Laski lectured at the Geneva Institute of International Relations on "The Theory of an International Society"; see *Problems of Peace* (Sixth Series, Laski and Zimmern, eds., 1932), 188.

a jolly dinner [in Paris] with G. Jèze, the French lawyer who has a happy name for Nicholas Murray Butler "Il Ponderoso" . . . I was going to stay in Paris until next week, but the English political crisis[1] resulted in some telegrams which take me home tomorrow and I am stealing unjustifiably two days here with our artist-friends on the way back. What I shall find I don't know; but all my sympathies are dead against the new government and I am praying that political differences won't, as they should not, make my personal relations with Sankey difficult. Things are clearly very confused and I dread a little the problems involved until, at least, the general election has cleared things up. Frida, meanwhile, has been motoring with Diana through Brittany and writes with ecstasy about the people and the churches.

My love to you as always. . . .

Ever affectionately yours, H. J. L.

Devon Lodge, 17.IX.31

My dear Justice: I was so grateful for Wales's letter;[1] and ever so glad that you feel better. All that you say of *Vanity Fair* commands my full-hearted assent with the note that one of the miraculous touches in literature is that brief word about Becky being heard weeping in her room at Miss Pinkerton's—but they were the tears of rage and not of sorrow. I've never understood why M. Arnold refused to agree that W.M.T. was a very great writer.

I have been busy beyond words with the political crisis here— working with Mr. Henderson morning, noon and night.[2] But it is not a thing to put on paper except to say to you that the spirit of this country is as fine and as sober as anyone could desire. In the front of danger, it is a great people, amazing in its power of self-control. Even in the very grave naval trouble[3] the good humour of the sailors was the main feature of the situation. I also have been

---

[1] On August 24, following a series of critical controversies concerning the economic crisis and measures to meet it, MacDonald tendered his resignation and that of the Labour ministry to the King. He was immediately asked to form a National Government. When the new Cabinet of ten was formed there were, in addition to MacDonald, but three members of the Labour Party, including Lord Sankey, who continued in office. On assuming office as head of the new government, MacDonald had indicated that when steps to meet the financial crisis had been taken, his National Government would be dissolved. It was not until October, however, that the dissolution of Parliament occurred and when it did, MacDonald appealed to the nation for a return of the National Government. That appeal was successful.

[1] Robert W. Wales, Holmes's secretary, 1930-31.

[2] Arthur Henderson had refused to follow MacDonald's leadership into the Nationalist government and was the principal spokesman of Labour's opposition to MacDonald's new policies.

[3] The Government's reduction of public expenditures, approved by Parliament in early September, included reductions in naval pay. This had led to such serious unrest that maneuvers of the Atlantic Fleet had been canceled.

doing a good deal at the Indian Conference. It was fascinating to
see Gandhi at work and try and penetrate his secret.[4] It comes, I
think, from what the Quakers call the inner light—a power of internal self-confidence which, having established its principles, is
completely impervious to reason. At bottom it is an incredible
egoism—what I think Canon Sheehan once described to you as the
arrogance of humility—sweetened by an indescribable sweetness of
temper. He is also an amazing casuist, with a Jesuitical love of
dubious formulae which would be amusing if it might not so easily
become tragic. But the drama of this wizened little man with the
whole power of the empire against him is a terrific spectacle. The
basis of it all is, I think, the power of an ascetic over Eastern minds
who resent the feeling of inferiority they have had for 150 years.
And to watch his people hang on his words, he who has neither
eloquence nor the gift of verbal artistry, is fascinating. Whether
we can come to terms with him, heaven alone knows; much depends on Sankey's negotiating ability. But at least I understand
now why Christianity in the first century appealed to the poor and
the oppressed. Through Gandhi the Indian ryot feels himself exalted, he embodies for them their own impulse to self-affirmation.
And another interesting side is the way in which he has become a
feature of English life—the crowd goes out to see him arrive in
his loin cloth and blanket as they might want to see Charlie Chap-
lin. Coming away from the conference yesterday I asked a workman craning his neck to see, what Gandhi stood for: "I don't know,
guv'nor!" "Then why do you come to see him?" "I always come
to look at the sights. Floodlighting yesterday, Gandhi today, it's
like a blooming festival." I don't think that even the prospect of
losing the empire would disturb the *sang-froid* of the man in the
street. . . .   *Ever affectionately yours, H. J. L.*

                                        Devon Lodge, 27.IX.31
My dear Justice: It was good to see your writing again.[1] I do hope
you will be really fit for the new term. Please take great care, and
do not overdo things.

I am leading a grimly busy life. Half the time I am a kind of
eminence grise for Sankey at the Indian Conference; the rest is
taken up with the political and economic crisis here. I interview
Saints like Gandhi, princes with unpronounceable names, and
Mohammedans who would cheerfully cut my throat in the name of
Allah. Gandhi is really remarkable; there is no difficulty at all in
understanding the veneration he inspires. He is quiet, precise, and

---

[4] Gandhi served on the Federal Structure Committee of the India Round
Table Conference, under the Chairmanship of Lord Sankey, at its September
session.

[1] The letter referred to is missing.

subtle, and there is an inner dignity about him which is of supreme quality. He isn't easy to negotiate with except on details; on those he is accomodating [*sic*] almost to an extreme. But on principles, he tends to put reason outside the pale and you can only counter dogma with dogma. The princes, with three exceptions, are a pretty poor lot. They are ill-educated, tyrannical, and with no conception of negotiation. They take you straight back to the days of the East India Company and make you feel that discussion with the likes o' them is folly and that one ought to act like a Warren Hastings with them. The Mohammedans are a poor lot in things of the mind, and their religious fanaticism is terrible. I guess, without evidence, that Pan-Islamic hopes are a huge farce in the East today and that behind their impossible demands are vague and terrible dreams. Poor Sankey! He and I both think a settlement possible. But what with Tory impossibilism on one side and Indian extremism on the other I fear that it is very unlikely. My prediction is a breakdown, Sankey's resignation, and three British army corps in India by Xmas. And this isn't the pessimism of a tired negotiator but a solemn estimate of the probabilities.[2]

You will know what vast events are taking place here. I will not comment on them except to say that if you want to see life at its most credulous just now the House of Commons lobby is the ideal place. If I see Henderson and say he is tired, by the time I get into the street, he is seriously ill. If MacDonald says a word to me, a lobby correspondent infers a coming rapprochement between him and Henderson. There is no rumour too wild not to be believed. From tales of immediate dictatorship downwards the buzzing goes on. If the events round which it centres were not so big with tragic destinies it would be a marvellous comedy. I have certainly been given a complete lesson in how miracles come to be accepted. And I beg you to double your regard for Gabriel Tarde. I undertake without effort to make ten members say the same thing in ten minutes, not because they believe it, or have stayed to examine it, but because someone has said authoritatively that it simply is so. A man started a rumour that twenty labour members were crossing the floor to support MacDonald. It was repeated with increasing emphasis until, at the adjournment, it was seventy members and four ex-ministers. I was even given the names of men with whom I had been sitting in committee that same evening drawing up the Labour programme for the imminent election as men certain to cross the House. Herbert Samuel went to see Mac-

---

[2] The first difficulties in the September meetings arose in connection with the problem of the rights of minorities, Gandhi and the Moslem leaders being almost hopelessly divided. In December the Conference came to an inconclusive and unsuccessful end. Lord Sankey did not abandon the government's policy with respect to India but remained in office until the Nationalist government was replaced by the Conservatives in 1935.

Donald in his room; ten minutes after he had come out, he told
his secretary that he would not be in the House any more that day.
Five minutes after that it was whispered everywhere that he had
had a quarrel with MacDonald and that his resignation would be
in the paper next morning. The actual truth was that he had a
slight attack of diarrhoea and had asked the Prime Minister to
arrange for someone else to answer the debate so that he could go
home. Now I say that in this atmosphere you have all the elements
which (I) explain miracles and (II) explain things like the touch
and go element in such coups as Thermidor or December 2nd,
1851. One literally can count on the fingers of one's hand those
who can keep calm in the atmosphere and refuse to believe without verification. When the crisis is over and there is normal life
once more (if there ever is) I want to put some reflections about
all this on paper. It is extraordinarily fascinating. It is the best
commentary I have ever seen on the meaning and worth of testimony when abstracted from the possibility of objective measurement. . . .   *Ever affectionately yours, H. J. L.*

1720 Eye Street N.W., October 9, 1931
My dear Laski: How long would you write to me if I do not go
through some form of reciprocation? I don't know that there's
anything the matter with me but I am not up to writing and so
far as may be make my secretary[1] take my place. We are doing
the usual work and arguments begin next Monday. Paltry personal
details prevail over world problems and cosmic questions. I have
lost two front teeth and can't get the dentist before Monday (it is
Friday now). The Bar Association Medal has come at last—frightfully heavy—I suppose with precious metal.[2] The enervating heat
of Washington has left me very languid. I infer that I must be
careful about my heart. My bed was moved downstairs at Beverly.
I don't worry—but my most willing activity is listening to my
secretary. Just now *Juan in America* (Eric Linklater)—well enough
—not very much. My affection for you is not flabby—everything
else is.   *Yours ever, O. W. Holmes*

Devon Lodge, 30.X.31
My dear Justice: I do hope you have cherished no hard feelings
against me. But I have had no moment since the election began
until now in which to do anything but its grim work. Three meet-

---

[1] Horace Chapman Rose was Holmes's secretary at the October term, 1931.
[2] At its annual meeting in September the American Bar Association had
conferred its annual medal on Holmes "for conspicuous service in the cause
of American jurisprudence." See 17 *Am. Bar Ass. J.* 715-717 (November
1931).

ings a night for a month, with India and teaching by day have
been a heavy toll. But at least the Tory victory has been so hugely
complete that I can hope for leisure from politics for pretty well
five years.

It has been a curious experience. I have never before seen a
whole people in a panic. They were, above all, terrified of a
German currency *débacle* here if we won, and all else was sub-
ordinated to that. So that one saw an atmosphere in which reason
had completely abdicated and no lie was too great to be believed.
I don't take our defeat tragically, even though I think five years
of Tory government a heavy price to pay for a moment's panic.
But five years is a small period in the life of a people. . . .

Most of my interesting experiences apart from the election have
come from the Indians. Sankey made me try to bring the Mohammedans to reason, and I had their leader here for hours trying to find a basis for discussion. But it was like talking to a wall.
His religion was ultimate truth, and he was never even willing to
find a plane of secular institutions which implied, so to say, a non-
theological society. It was like being taken back into Reformation
times. Then I had a long negotiation with Gandhi about the army.
Here we got somewhere by my discovery that one could separate
his rhetorical requirements from his actual. If I had had a free
hand I think a settlement would have been comparatively easy;
but, alas, the new political situation has hardened the mind of the
Secretary of State[1] and I think my long hours will probably go to
waste. The real tragedy of work like this is the sacrifice, on both
sides, of reason to prestige. At the back of the Secretary's mind is
the complex that the white man ought not to be asked to give way
to the black; and at the back of Gandhi's mind is the haunting
fear that the white man in India will always take a yard for each
inch of compromise. If ever one saw reason as the slave of the
passions it is in this realm. And I am terrified of failure which
means an India in flames in the next few years and out of that
tragedies too vast even to think of. What makes it so terrible is
that each side knows this as well as I and is yet so damnably obstinate that it will offer a holocaust to pride without a moment's
consideration of the cost. In a world like ours the only real thing
to be is a mathematician or a physicist to whose work the human
animal is irrelevant. . . .   *Ever affectionately yours, H. J. L.*

November 12, 1931
My dear Laski: It is so good to get a letter from you that it almost
becomes possible for me to write. I have been rather seedy since

---

[1] Sir Samuel Hoare (1880-1959), later Viscount Templewood, had become
Secretary of State for India in MacDonald's Nationalist government in August.

August, the month I always fear; but this little adjournment with my work done seems on the up grade. I don't feel tired all the time, as I did. My events apart from a short dissent from an opinion not yet seen if written,[1] are the books my secretary reads to me—some rather slight—Bliss Perry, *Emerson Today*—Bertrand Russell, *The Scientific Outlook*—Maurois, *Lyautey*, Birkenhead's potboiler—*Famous Trials of History*, Robertson *Fra Paolo Sarpi*—the book not much but the life most interesting—Sarpi seems to have been one of the greatest men that ever lived—Stevenson, Thackeray &c. I don't like Stevenson very well. Thackeray gives me new pleasure every time. Lately I have read to myself 2 vols. of *Lettres choises* of Voltaire. Not very delightful. A rather noticeable book Thomas Craven (of Kansas) *Men of Art*—a little conscious of culture—but really pretty good—and to me instructive. I try vainly at the Cong. Libr. for *Jill the Reckless*—but have got Mason, *The Paris Commune* which I expect to begin tonight or tomorrow. Tomorrow will be Brandeis's 75th birthday and the papers are or will be full of him. I have owed him much in the way of encouragement. He doesn't seem even to want it. Today I am listening to Arthur L. Goodhart, *Essays in Jurisprudence and the Common Law* with moderate pleasure. He seems to me not to get much above mediocrity, and makes one squirm by the constant respect and more, shown to Salmond, a pleasant gent, as I remember him at Judge Hitz's[2] house here some years ago, but not winged.

If you never read about Sarpi you had better—of course the book I read was by an unlimited admirer, a Scotch hater of the papacy (which gave Sarpi trouble) but I also marvelled.

I am not good for a long letter—to write one, that is—I am OK to receive one.

Yesterday I visited a fine new building next to the Congr. Libr. for an amazing collection of Shakespeare's works—70 or so of the first folios, to show all the corrections, and everything on that scale. Folger was the collector and left it to Amherst College with supporting funds. The books are not yet in—but are getting in.

Affectionately yours, O. W. Holmes

Devon Lodge, 14.XI.31
My dear Justice: I hope that the Vanguard Press has sent you the new volume of your decisions, and that it meets with your approval.[1] Of the Foreword, I will only say that it comes from the

---

[1] Probably *Hoefer* v. *Tax Commission*, 284 U.S. 206, 218 (Nov. 30, 1931).
[2] William Hitz (1872-1935), successively Justice of the Supreme Court, and of the Court of Appeals, of the District of Columbia, 1916-1935.
[1] *Representative Opinions of Mr. Justice Holmes* (Lief, ed., 1931), included a Foreword by Laski.

heart and that every word of it is instinct with affection for its
subject.

I have had a busy week—mainly academic and with the Indians
here. After all our efforts, the Conference has broken down,[2] and
I fear that with the turn of the year we are bound to be in for bad
times in India. It is a great tragedy, which makes me feel inclined
to curse religion—the real root of the problem—as a social disease.
I made an eleventh hour effort, at the joint request of Sankey and
Gandhi, to make the Mohammedans see reason. But it is impossible
to talk to men who believe themselves to have ultimate truth in
their possession, and my three hours were simply a dutiful wasting
of time. I blame MacDonald in part; for if he had been strong-
minded instead of weak and vain and indecisive I think he could
have compelled agreement. But he would rather go to Timbuctoo
than make up his mind upon a difficult subject. . . .

I had one intellectual pleasure I must put on record. I went on
Monday night to the University Law Society where F. Pollock read
a paper.[3] It was a remarkable performance. He never faltered for
a word and when the discussion was over he made a reply which
did not miss a point and, in his dry Pollockian way was as incisive
and direct as he must have been thirty years ago; and his familiarity with the recent literature I can only describe as astounding. I
went also to the inaugural lecture by young Plucknett, who used
to be at Harvard and has come on to us—an astonishing effort.[4]
The *pièce de résistance* was an entirely new theory of the Year
books which I shall not spoil by summary; you shall have the
lecture when we print it. To my mind, it was the best thing of its
kind done by an English academic lawyer since Maitland's inaugural lecture.[5]

. . . I read also a book on Lincoln by the poet (is he a poet?)
Edgar Lee Masters, which seemed to me simply a bad attack of
that terrible disease Lytton Stracheyitis—the notion that to write a
good biography all you need to do is to attack a great reputation
with shovelsfull of irony without any regard to the evidence. No
one can doubt Lincoln's greatness, I think, who looks at his changes
in Seward's dispatches. That is statesmanship if ever there was
such.

[2] See, *supra*, p. 373, note 2.
[3] "The Lawyer as Citizen of the World," 48 *L. Q. Rev.* 37 (January
1932).
[4] Theodore F. T. Plucknett (1897-   ) had been teaching legal history
at Harvard from 1923 to 1931, when he was called to London; author of
many works on English legal history; literary director of the Selden Society.
Plucknett's Inaugural Lecture, "The Place of the Legal Profession in the
History of English Law," was published in 48 *L. Q. Rev.* 328 (July 1932).
[5] "Why the History of English Law Is Not Written," 3 *Collected Papers
of Frederic William Maitland* (Fisher, ed., 1911), 488.

One nice purchase—a copy of the 1606 translation of Bodin—as new as on the day when it first appeared. It was amusing that the bookseller let me have it cheap—five pounds—because instead of the usual engraved title-page this copy has only a plain lettered one. This he regarded as a grave defect.

Our love to you. I hope you have the same succession of sunny autumn days as is being vouchsafed to us.

Ever affectionately yours, H. J. L.

Washington, D.C., November 21, 1931
My dear Laski: As you have discovered, it comes hard to me to write. The physical act comes hard. I don't know why or why I write smaller than I used to—but so it is. We come in next Monday. I have had a little feeling of rest and leisure though not much with 30 new applications for *certiorari* this last week, but I am in better condition than I have been, in August or September or most of October. My boy has read lots of books to me and I have done others by myself. I have this minute finished one by Virginia Woolf —*Mrs. Dalloway.* I don't care much for what I have read by her though I am deeply interested in her as Leslie Stephen's daughter. I suppose old age makes everything less pleasing to me than it used to be. There is a difference between 80 and 90. Just now my secretary is reading John Buchan—*The Blanket of the Dark*— but again I am not so interested as I hoped to be.

As I look back—Young, *The Medici*, and Robertson *Fra Paolo Sarpi*, both recommended by Brandeis, stand out—not for literary merit but for the amazement of the subject matter. Perhaps I might add Craven, *Men of Art*, which one hardly would have expected from Kansas. But, Lord, all the high aesthetes come from queer places nowadays. Parrington from Oklahoma (I believe he is dead) had a posthumous volume after his doing up our earlier efforts in a pretty smart way. I believe I have told you I can't see why they seem to take the author of *Walden* (I forget the name) so seriously.

I like what you say of Tocqueville and I have made much the same remarks about Maine's *Ancient Law* that you do.[1] I delight in your letters but as I have said I find it very hard to write.

Affectionately yours, O. W. Holmes
I think Brandeis has been repaid for the row that was made about his appointment by the volume of appreciation called out by his 75th birthday—and he deserves it all.[2]

---

[1] The references are perhaps in recollection of, or after rereading, Laski's letter of Feb. 7, *supra*, p. 357 [A. H.].

[2] See, *infra*, p. 398.

Devon Lodge, 28.XI.31

My dear Justice: . . . I spoke at the annual meeting of the National Birth Control Council on the desirability of scientific distribution of information on birth control by competent medical men instead of its furtive distribution by every sort of quack. I think that was sensible; and I was delighted when the *British Medical Journal* devoted a long leader to the wisdom of my remarks and the obligation of doctors to see that religious prejudice did not prevent people obtaining the best possible information when they wanted it.[1] . . .

In the way of reading. . . . A *really* good detective story by one Carr, called *The Lost Gallows,* published with you by Harpers, and, I think, guaranteed to intrigue and baffle. . . .

Here, for the moment, I must end. This week-end has to go to the grim and grave task of drawing up a report on the Home Office administration of alien laws. When one discovers that a little jack-in-office can stop an English woman married to an American from visiting her parents to exhibit their grandchild because the girl has a Russian name, as a civilised person one has got to act. So I went to the Home Secretary and threatened to start a press campaign. Now, for my sins, I have promised him a report on the general principles. But I've got that girl a visa for her passport and I feel that at least it is a tiny flower in the wreath of freedom.

Our love to you, as always. *Ever affectionately yours, H. J. L.*

Washington, D.C., November 27, 1931

My dear Laski: One of the greatest pleasures of my waning life is a letter from you. One came this morning. I am specially tickled by what you say of Lincoln's corrections in Seward's dispatches. I used to say that reading them had convinced me that Lincoln was a great man. Before that I had supposed and said that I was watching the growth of a myth. Apropos of the Bodin title page—when I was getting a first edition of *Paradise Regained* two copies were shown me—one scribbled all over the title page and others following by uninteresting remarks of some 2d rate 18th century man, the other clear, but perhaps cut ⅛ inch shorter, and therefore a guinea or two cheaper. I should have bought it if the dearer. It seemed to me a curious criterion. I am wandering and browsing in my reading—mostly by my secretary after working hours. Another of the books on Italian themes that

---

[1] In 2 *British Medical Journal* (1931) 1044 (December 5, 1931) there was a detailed account of Laski's remarks at the first annual meeting of the National Birth Control Association on November 23.

I have mentioned, suggested by Brandeis—*Isabella d'Este*—by Mrs. Julia Cartwright. I was pleased to learn that a beautiful familiar drawing by Leonardo was of the heroine—and also interested to see further evidence of the great place held in his day by Montaigne. I have three of the Mantegna Triumph Series. They have fine points but leave me rather cold—I see evidence that I haven't done him justice. I am reading to myself at odd moments Philip Schuyler Allen *Medieval Latin Lyrics*—Chicago University Press—which so far as I can judge is a contribution, but written disagreeably—to my taste. Miss Helen Waddell still holds the centre of the stage, so far as my knowledge goes. We read a recent book by John Buchan which didn't seem to me a success—*The Blanket of the Dark*—the name better than the tale. But I am afraid that there is no doubt that old age is dulling my taste for books as well as for food. I eat my meals with a pleasure that diminishes at each hour of the way, and books also find it harder to please—I also find it harder to write—partly eyesight, partly, I think, head. Living is harder work at 90 than at 80—but I hope you won't get tired of writing while I still can read and be thankful.   *Affectionately yours, O. W. Holmes*
I don't know how it is that I have failed to tell you how I am moved by your introduction to the book of my opinions. You make me happier than I can tell you. I don't want to talk about it.

Washington, D.C., December 3, 1931
My dear Laski: A delightful letter[1] from you this evening, bidding me tell my young man to write. Before this you must have had one or two from me. I don't know why it is that it comes so hard to me now, except that all life comes harder. I think that my usefulness is pretty much over and I am not sad. When the day's work is done my secretary from duty or devotion reads to me for an hour and a half before supper time and after it returns and reads again to say 10:30 when I go to bed. We have got through a lot. This p.m. 2 volumes Julia Cartwright *Isabella D'Este*—I think you must know a beautiful drawing in profile—with her hair down, by Leonardo da Vinci, and probably a portrait by Titian—I am quite charmed by the account—while the picture is so rich that it rather bores me. This, like the life of Sarpi, I owe to Brandeis who was lucky enough to spend part of his boyhood in Italy. . . . I may have mentioned Virginia Woolf—*Mrs. Dalloway* also not very pleasing to me—and your young man's book on the Paris Commune (Mason). I am afraid that old age makes me difficult. Books and victuals both find it harder to please. This seemed to me to be wanting in clearness of exposition. Some light

---
[1] Omitted from this edition.

things I don't mention *e.g.* like Buchan—*The Blanket of the Dark* —I found disappointing. Clouston—*The Lunatic in Charge* and another of the series made me laugh—not as much as your Jeeves man, but pleasantly. This evening I expect to begin—(we have read 2 or 3 pages) *Green Hell* by Julian Duguid which Lady Scott (Leslie's separated wife) asked me to read. So I dabble along—finding a sort of pleasure in life but expecting no more. 90 seems to have turned a corner. I am content however. Please don't let my flabbiness discourage your writing. It is one of my greatest pleasures.   *Affectionately yours, O. W. H.*

Washington, D.C., December 26, 1931

Dear Laski: It seems as if the shrinking of one's handwriting corresponded to a shrinking of one's being—both involuntary. I seem to be becoming a kind of well invalid. The faithful Mary the other day called in the doctor and he wanted me to go to bed. Things go very well if I don't try to accomplish anything—but I rather think the day of accomplishing is over. Like an invalid I talk about myself and my library is the field of my adventures. Philosophy and murder the main directions. You put me on to *The Lost Gallows,* which, when off the high horse, I do think A-1. For one thing it keeps the tone, throughout, and doesn't skip from tennis to poisoning a wife. To balance, a volume of John Dewey—obscure but always good.[1] . . . In short, leisure kept me busy with agreeable reading and slumber. But meantime a dissent that the ever active Brandeis put upon my conscience waits untouched.[2] I have said my say before and don't worry, but I suppose that shows my decline—I ought to.

Tell me if Addison Bridge Place is the echo of a tradition? as also Devon Lodge?

I was interrupted above. I believe I was going to say I don't know why it is a burden to write but latterly it comes hard. I hope it won't be so with you. I feel full of talk—but find it hard to drive the pen.

Ever affectionately yours, O. W. Holmes

Devon Lodge, 7.XII.31

My dear Justice: A grand letter from you! But I don't want you to bother answering my letters unless you feel like it. They will flow on and on irrepressibly, and independently of response.

---

[1] *Philosophy and Civilization* (1931).

[2] No such dissenting opinion has been identified. It is not unlikely that the case in question was *First National Bank* v. *Maine,* 284 U.S. 312 (Jan. 4, 1932), in which Holmes and Brandeis concurred in a dissenting opinion delivered by Mr. Justice Stone.

. . . [I have read] a volume of economic essays by Keynes—
Essays in Persuasion—which I thought quite masterly, technical
exposition so beautifully written that it was a joy just to watch the
movement of his mind even where one disagreed with him. One
essay—"The End of Laisser-Faire"—would I think have interested you greatly, for it is a wholly admirable pendant to your
dissent in *Adair* v. *U.S.* . . .

Most of the rest of my time has gone in Indian negotiation,
especially with Gandhi. What will come of it all, God only knows.[1]
I have been trying to stop it becoming a question of prestige on
either side, which, as in all nationalist issues, it has a tendency to
do. The trouble is that while I satisfy Sankey and begin to get a
move begun Sankey doesn't get his way with his colleagues in
the cabinet and it isn't at all easy to build up a coherent plan
which fits into one cabinet minister's instructions, and then find
that a large part of one's results are undone by the obstinacy of
another. Half the trouble with the Indians is a question of national
and racial pride. A good example is the army. Gandhi says "I
want control of the army; otherwise you don't give us responsible
government." The cabinet says "You are not ready for control; in
any case we can't put white troops under Indian control." I say,
"Let us begin with a preamble affirming Indian right to control
and then add that while an Indian army is being built up, the
following safeguards, a, b, c, d, shall obtain." Then I take back
the dangers, leaving all the rhetorical claims amply satisfied. This
contents Gandhi, and it satisfies Sankey who, being a sensible
man, doesn't mind leaving the other man the shadow, if he surrenders the substance. But the damned Tory Secretary of State[2]
gets on his hind legs and develops a prestige complex just as
footling as you can imagine, throws it all back into the melting
pot, and one has to begin all over again. Truly the way of the
negotiator is hard. I get loving words from Gandhi and Sankey,
and kicks from the rest; and the added joy of knowing that if
anything at all comes of it the credit goes to a government I
utterly despise. In one way it is, of course, extraordinarily interesting. The job of trying to bend the mind of a man who in his
turn influences the minds of millions in India is a fascinating
experience; and the intellectual effort of trying to discover middle
terms in the infinite series which prestige involves is a good
mental exercise. I have a high opinion of the subtlety of Gandhi,
and his charm is immense. But he is a ghastly faddist—and on

---

[1] Early in 1932 things went from bad to worse in India. With the revival
of the Congress policy of civil disobedience, Gandhi, who had returned to
India on December 28, 1931, was placed under arrest on January 4. It was
not until May 1933 that he was released.

[2] Sir Samuel Hoare; *supra*, p. 375.

economic matters he has literally not even the beginnings of realism. What the future holds for him and us I tremble to think. If he and Sankey and I were left alone for a week we could have solved the whole damned business and, I think, in a way that would have commended itself to most reasonable men. But, alas, that is not the way that things happen in politics. . . .

Ever affectionately yours, H. J. L.

Devon Lodge, 13.XII.31
My dear Justice: I imagine this will arrive in the proper time for our Xmas greetings. You know how warm and affectionate they are.

A letter from you, with much account of reading, was a great joy. I have had a busy week. Long interviews with the Indians; a couple of meetings of the committee on administrative law, now in its last sessions, I hope; a long dose of Sankey who (a) is unhappy in the government and (b) doesn't want to leave it and is therefore in that difficult frame of mind where a full sincerity is a dangerous luxury; a grim industrial arbitration where I had to reduce 2000 men's wages by 7 and ½% as an alternative to throwing them out of work altogether; and a dinner at Gray's Inn spoilt for me by sitting next to the Bishop of London who has that intolerable kind of unctiousness which makes you really want to vomit. When I hear men of his type speak of the "beautiful spirit of the poor" and the "noble sacrifices of our aristocracy" and the "devotion of the clergy to their Divine obligations" I really understand why the *tricoteuses* sat unmoved under the guillotine. However, I learned there one great story. At a Cambridge dinner the Master of S. Johns said that he dreamed he was present at the Day of Judgment. When the sheep had been divided from the goats, the late Master of Trinity (H. M. Butler)[1] arose from a prominent place among the sheep and without invitation spoke as follows: "I do not feel I can allow this great occasion to pass without extending to the Deity, on behalf of those present, and particularly for those among whom my lot has been cast, our sense of the admirable and, may I say, perceptive fashion in which a very difficult task has been performed. Not, indeed, that I am surprised; for there is a special sense of the word in which I may claim for the Deity the great privilege of being a Trinity man." Don't you think that is a really admirable example of dry academic humour?

. . . [I have been] reading J. M. Robertson's *Buckle and his*

---
[1] See *supra*, p. 126.

Critics which contains *inter alia* a savage and unjustified attack on L. Stephen. But I think the general thesis of the book wholly right *i.e.* that the explanation of history in terms of great men is foolish, and that one must penetrate to the reasons which permitted great men to succeed for *verae causae.* In fact, he made me feel that an argument like one of B. Russell's which I saw lately, that if 100 men like Descartes had perished *c.* 1600-1700 there would have been no such thing as modern civilisation is really futile. One can say that the one thing certain is that no man is indispensable to any movement; and that even Napoleon only shifts the axis a degree or so without altering its direction. . . .

Ever affectionately yours, Harold J. Laski

Devon Lodge, 29.XII.31

My dear Justice: Xmas has come and gone, and we are off to Antwerp this evening. I have had a pretty busy time as Leslie Scott kept us at the Administrative Law committee until Dec. 23, and owing to the illness of a colleague I suddenly had to do a long and complicated university report on academic policy—which I found very dull. However, it *is* done; and I can recite manfully on the needs of the university, supposing a millionaire to come along which he won't. And my great editor-hero C. P. Scott of the Manchester *Guardian*—the noblest journalist I have ever known—is dying and I have had at top-speed to write the kind of tribute which friendship demands on these occasions.[1] That is a curiously difficult decision to make. You don't want to write, because you feel the thing is too intimate for public utterance; but you feel that you must write to be sure that the just thing is said. I never knew a man more chivalrous than he, or with a finer sense of justice. He would fight at the drop of the hat. Only the other day he helped me with a grand protest against the foul action of Mussolini in dismissing all university professors in Italy who refused to sign a declaration of loyalty to the Fascist party. A man who will fight like that at eighty-six is worth having as an influence in public life. . . .

Our love to you, my dear Justice, and every sort of good wish for the New Year.   *Ever affectionately yours, H. J. L.*

Devon Lodge, 13.I.32

My dear Justice: I read in this morning's *Times* of your resigna-

---

[1] Charles Prestwick Scott (1846-1932) had been editor of the *Guardian* since 1872; he died on January 1, 1932. Laski's essay on Scott was in the *Daily Herald* for January 2, 1932.

tion.[1] I was not surprised, but deeply moved. And I will say no more than this that you will know how much of what you felt went through my mind and how wholly I was with you in spirit. . . .

My love to you, dear Justice. Be happy.

Ever affectionately yours, H. J. L.

My greetings for 1932 to Mary, please.

Washington, D.C., January 23, 1932

My dear Laski: I hope that I am not going to be confined to sending messages by my secretary, but for the time being at least I find it very hard to write. The doctor seems to think that I am better since my resignation and I really believe that I sleep better, though I don't care much for food. There has been a big chore answering letters &c. but my secretary has done most of it. He is angelic and reads to me even after supper, when he has no duty to be here. A good many detective stories; just now Lea's *History of the Inquisition of Spain*—which I always have meant to read. I think it a poor piece of literature. It does not marshal the facts in a luminous way, but it is very instructive. How can one care what people did who thought as men of the 16th and 17th centuries did about life and religion?

The President's secretary has repeated what the President did on my last birthday—sent me a great package of mounted clippings from the newspapers. I can't take such things very seriously, but I really have been surprised by the semblance of popularity. (I did not mean to let egotism get beyond the first page—but the little devil slipped between my fingers.) I am open to suggestions for reading as I don't expect to have much else to do indoors. When the weather permits there is pleasure in driving out for an hour or two in Virginia or Maryland. One might go to the Congressional Library and turn over a portfolio—but I lack the energy to follow up suggestions of others than those I ask for about books. Frankfurter was here at luncheon last Sunday greatly to my delight—though I didn't get as much time with him alone as I could have wished. And people do come in and call, being warned I think by my watchful parlor maid and secretary not to stay too long. In short I am pretty idle and find it easy to be so for I am tired. This poor little missive must stand for a letter from me. My energy gives out. I do hope that you won't be discouraged from writing to me. Your letters help to keep me alive.

Affectionately yours, O. W. Holmes

---

[1] On January 12 President Hoover announced Holmes's retirement from the Supreme Court.

Devon Lodge, 30.I.32

My dear Justice: Ten days of hard work since I wrote last. First this incredible government decided to abandon the doctrine of collective cabinet responsibility,[1] and I had hurriedly to write a long appendix to a booklet I am publishing very shortly on the crisis; then Mr. Henderson asked me to help him with his Presidential speech to the Disarmament Conference at Geneva,[2] and, of course, for such an occasion I had to sweat blood to see that the thing was really well done; then I have done a big industrial arbitration which involved trying to understand the boot and shoe industry and settling six separate schedules of wages. So, that, altogether, I have had the feeling that I have earned my keep.

But, mostly in trains, I have read one book which interested me enormously. It is called *American Literature* and is by a man I never heard of named Blankenship. He deserves a medal. There are things from which I fiercely dissent *e.g.* the emphasis on Cabell, whom I believe to be a mere faker, as an important figure. But all in all it is a model of what such books should be—as good in its way as Lanson's *History of French Literature*. It has learning and wit and incisiveness. Now that Parrington is dead, that fellow takes his rank at the very head of the American critics. I do hope it will come your way for I know nothing even to compare with it in its field. I read also an admirable book on France by E. R. Curtius, the late German Foreign Minister. It is rather Germanisch in the sense of searching for quintessences, to which light and shade are sometimes sacrificed for the sake of the thesis. But I don't know a better book to use for explaining what the idea of France is in the history of the last three hundred years. I have also been reading—for a book review—some of Dryden's plays. And I was led by them to the thesis that the difference (Shakespere apart) between English and French tragedy is that in the former incident is the source round which the treatment coheres while in the latter the essential action takes place in the mind. The result is that with Dryden you are always the spectator *at* the drama while with Corneille or Racine you are an actor *in* it. The editor of this new edition amused me mightily. He begins by attacking all his predecessors as worthless; I supposed that to be true until he turned on W. P. Ker who, whatever his sins, was

---

[1] On January 22, members of the Cabinet being in disagreement on fiscal policy, it was announced the four ministers were to be permitted in Parliament to oppose the proposals of their colleagues. See Laski, *The Crisis and the Constitution: 1931 and After* (1932), Appendix, p. 59.

[2] Arthur Henderson was President of the Conference for the Reduction and Limitation of Armaments, an agency established by the League of Nations. Its first meeting was held in Geneva on February 2, 1932. Henderson's opening speech is in I *Records of the Conference for the Reduction and Limitation of Armaments* (Series A, 1932), 39.

not lacking in scholarship. So I spent a little time comparing the editions and found (it makes a good sentence) that the first thirty [sic] footnotes of the two editions coincide[3]; and I think that is one up to Ker. . . .

My love to you, my dear Justice. You are never long absent from my thoughts.   *Ever affectionately yours, H. J. L.*
Please give my warm greetings to Mary.

Devon Lodge, 16.II.32

My dear Justice: I begin by congratulating you on Cardozo's appointment.[1] Nothing, I think, can more securely measure the sense we all have of your place than that he should be your successor. I know it will give you pleasure. And it gives a great tradition security. I could throw my hat to the sky.

. . . I wish, in your leisure, you would write a short paper for our School journal on "The Judicial Process." It needs someone of your authority to end this humbug of the judge as a soulless automaton whose mind and heart are silent when he performs his operations. And I should of course be proud beyond words to have a paper from you in the journal I edit. If you say you are too old to write, I reply first that this is untrue and second that Ranke (bless his memory) began to write his *Weltgeschichte* when he was eighty-nine.[2] Indeed I wish you would put down on paper your reflections on legal philosophy for us. It would be a grand and exciting legacy fifty years after *The Common Law* to say what has happened to the ethos you then discovered in it.

I was so glad to have your letter. As long as you feel fit and go on reading I feel as though a special sun was still shining.

Our love to you.   *Ever affectionately yours, H. J. L.*

Devon Lodge, 23.II.32

My dear Justice: . . . I had an amusing dinner with Lady Astor, where I sat next to the journalist Garvin. You do not know what journalism can do by way of breeding egoism until you have met him. He does not indicate opinions; he pronounces oracles, and they are sometimes quite marvellous *e.g.* "The essence of the Chinese problem is their lack of the British sense of right and

---

[3] The reference is presumably to the six-volume edition of *Dryden's Dramatic Works* (1931-32), edited by Montague Summers. Laski's review has not been identified. W. P. Ker (1855-1923), literary critic and historian at the University of London, was the editor of *The Essays of John Dryden* (2 vols., 1900).

[1] On February 15 President Hoover nominated Cardozo as Holmes's successor; the Senate confirmed the nomination on February 24.

[2] Ranke in fact was eighty-five when he began his *Weltgeschichte*.

wrong." "Lincoln represents the manifest destiny of the ordinary
American at his best." I do not argue with such men. Duty demands that you draw them on and obtain the maximum delight
from their majestic progress. "Never," said he, "have I ever felt
so conscious of the hand of God in British destiny as I did when
the government decided upon a protective tariff." Imagine this
vast voice booming these gigantic conclusions to twenty people
who only by effort can prevent themselves from collapsing in
quite helpless laughter. Then Frida and I went to a jolly party at
the Russian embassy, where we met old George Moore, whom I
had never before seen. He is a different type of egotist—the
esthetic type who broods on his own introspective results. He told
me he had never published any book until he was sure (I) that
it was in its way perfect (II) that it had a definite contribution to
make to aesthetic technique. He thought Hardy, Meredith,
Dickens, Fielding, unreadable. There were exquisite moments in
Flaubert and Pater; Balzac could observe, but could not omit.
Poets who battled with life lost their purity of gesture. He regretted that I wrote about politics. "You have," he said, "a clear
gift of pointed phrase. Why waste it on so low an object." He had
once been invited to meet Bismarck but felt that his nerves could
not stand it. On the other hand the mere presence of Manet in a
room gave a sense of exhilaration. He was interested in the new
Russia as he felt that new and keen impressions could be gained
there. He had a happy life by always denying the reality of what
displeased him; so, he said, he could always suppress a critic who
disliked his work. A very happy old gentleman, conscious that he
was a classic, and talking, I am sure, in the hope that his auditors
kept notebooks so that the torch of his wisdom could be handed
down the ages. He asked me, with a graceful gesture, whom I
admired most of living novelists, making an effective pause for the
reply. But I took a moment of artful reflection and said "P. G
Wodehouse" which completely disconcerted him as he felt it
quite out of keeping with his character to descend to argue with
one whose tastes were so wholly unseemly. Frida said it was like
watching a minuet on a canvas of Watteau to listen to him, and I
think the comparison is not inapt to the scene. . . .

We all send you our love as always. And please remember my
remark last week that if some of your leisure went to written reflections on the foundations of law it would be a great day for all
of us.   *Ever affectionately yours, H. J. L*

Washington, D.C., Feb. 24, '32
My dear Laski: Of course the nomination of Cardozo delights me
I hear that the committee reports unanimously for confirmation. I

can't suppose there is any doubt. (Later) I hear he is confirmed. I have no news but books—McDougall, (I believe a successor of William James), *World Chaos,* led me to Whiting Williams's *Mainsprings of Men*—emphasizing at not too great length the weight of the imponderable, with working men as with others— these two by myself. My boy is reading to me a translation of *The History of World Civilization* by a German—Schneider— Frankfurter put me on to it. I rather doubt if it is worth the trouble. He seems to think that the Germans do or have done all that is worth doing—so much so that when my lad read a sentence about something done by a German poet, Kleist, I thought he was presenting the son of God in a new light.

Much to my regret we have finished the 6 volumes of Sherlock Holmes. So much better than his successors. I have made a note to inquire about some books mentioned by you. Also I thank you for your *Studies in Law and Politics.* I don't always agree with you but I generally do and admire the learning and power of your presentation. Brandeis has been having trouble with his throat, which has cut down his calls, but he was here a few days ago and I don't think the trouble serious.

(Later) I have got Nevinson's *Goethe* from the Library. I would rather read it than Schneider—who lays down as facts matters of neolithic religion and many others with an absolutism that provokes doubts akin to those I used to feel when White in an opinion pronounced some generality as obvious. Also a book of likenesses *Drawn from Life* (the title) coupled with interviews— one of me *inter alios*—not bad. I remember the author, S. J. Woolf, as pleasant.

Lest I forget it Mary wanted very particularly that I should tell you how pleased she was by your remembering her and your message. You have stood very high in her opinion since you were last here (very likely earlier, but it has been brought to my attention lately).

Feb. 26. I go out to drive in a few minutes but must not keep this note of affection longer.   *Affectionately yours, O. W. H.*

Washington, D.C., March 18, 1932
My dear Laski: You are in the middle of affairs and I am out of them altogether. I find idleness life-giving—I get up late—have a motor drive—this morning to Mount Vernon and back in an hour and a quarter—easily brought down to an hour. After luncheon my secretary reads to me and people call. I write the few letters that I attempt. I find these come hard as I have told you before. Don't let it stop your writing, I hope, though I hardly have the right to ask. My lad read to me C. D. Broad—*The Mind and Its*

Place in Nature. I found it difficult to follow and not worth bothering about—though he is sharp enough. All manner of other things. We are just finishing *The Double Heart* about Mme. de l'Espinasse—rather good and written as if the author, Naomi Gwladis Royde-Smith had had some experience in the business.

Wigmore has praised Stimson's *My United States* but I hardly believe him. The "my" excites my prejudice—*et superest ager* as ground for criticism, for Stimson is clever and can be very agreeable[1]—perhaps I may venture on. His name reminds me of the Secretary of State who comes here from time to time and who certainly is very pleasant. Your pamphlet on the Crisis and the Constitution has come and I am reading it. Also Keynes, *Essays in Persuasion*—gifted cove—I suspect dogmatic and unprepossessing but seeing things.

In short you amaze me by your activities and help me to realize that I am finished—but I hardly do. I still enjoy life—but I must shut up.   *Affectionately yours, O. W. Holmes*

Devon Lodge, 26.III.32

My dear Justice: This is the first breathing space I have had for a fortnight. A visit to Glasgow, a sojourn in Manchester, and a long industrial arbitration for the Co-operative people have overwhelmed me. The latter at least had the merit (I should have said the last) that for the next month I shall be able to recite backwards the wages and hours of the boot and shoe operatives of England.

At least I have had time in trains and in dingy hotels at night to read. . . . I . . . enjoyed a *Life of Robert Emmet,* the Irish revolutionary, by R. W. Postgate. It is an extraordinarily moving tale, and explains the character of Anglo-Irish relations with great ability. Also it told me a thing I never knew before that McNally,[1] who always appeared with J. P. Curran in the trials of their patriots as their junior counsel, was throughout a spy in the pay of Dublin Castle. He even communicated to government the information afforded him by Emmet in their relations as client and counsel. That eighteenth century Ireland leaves a taste in one's mouth nastier than any other episode in modern British history. Postgate tells the story admirably—no eloquence but a simple record of fact which is twice as damning as adjectival emphasis would have been. And he makes it clear that once any government neglects profound grievance there is no infamy to which it will not be driven to stoop in order to conceal the wrong it is doing.

---

[1] Frederic Jesup Stimson (1855-1943), author, lawyer, and diplomat.
[1] Leonard MacNally (1752-1820) was informer against many other revolutionaries than Emmet.

. . . I press again my yearning that some of your leisure should go toward writing at your ease—especially on the foundations of law.

Our love to you as always. *Ever affectionately yours, H. J. L.*

Devon Lodge, 3.IV.32

My dear Justice: Your letter was very welcome. Be sure that I shall go on writing. For it's the next best thing to talking to you, and so long as I have an occasional note from Eye Street to say that you are well I am more than content.

I have had a really pleasant week, free from all cares except a couple of lectures to workingmen. The latter were interesting as there was a strong group of communists among them, and answering their questions was a grim job. It amused me to watch their anxiety to make the best of both worlds *e.g.* (I) how dare the bourgeois state suppress working-class freedom of expression (II) Russia is entitled to suppress bourgeois freedom of expression because that threatens her safety. Pressed by me on the lines of *cet animal est méchant*, the answer was that the proletariat being, historically, the rising class, it is entitled to different principles. I had a happy time with them. Otherwise, I have been reading quietly, writing a little, and seeing friends at dinner. Last Monday we spent with Sprague, the American adviser to the Bank of England. He was very gloomy about the outlook, mainly because it seems so difficult to persuade the nations that freedom of trade is their one secure road to survival. And I could not, I fear, comfort him. Then an amusing lunch with Garvin the journalist who was so magnificently *ex cathedra* in his pronouncements that I told him he could make a fortune by giving lessons in the nature of infallibility to prospective papal candidates.[1] Some of his judgments were too magnificent not to quote. (I) Every American feels instinctively a special kinship with the English people. (II) What has made Great Britain what she is is the fact that her business men have always been passionate idealists. (III) In the last nine months there has been a moral renaissance in England—otherwise the income-tax returns are inexplicable. (IV) The special mission of England is to assure fair play by and among the other nations. Imagine these judgments delivered by a great bull of a man, without a smile, and with the earnestness of a prophet in ancient Israel. Then I went to dinner with old Birrell, now over eighty, and had, as always, a delightful time. He began by saying that he was in sackcloth and ashes. He had always unduly belittled Matthew Arnold. He now

---

[1] Laski wrote of Garvin in the *Daily Herald;* reprinted in 341 *Living Age* 514 (February 1932).

thought him a great essayist and a great poet. He regretted the
revival of Tennyson, who was a poet for milkmaids—pretty verse
meant to be hymned by a choir in a country church. He though
Hazlitt remained the supreme *causeur* among essayists and "My
first acquaintance with poets" his supreme *causerie*. He asked me
why it is (I could not answer him) that conveyancers, who have
so marvellous an experience of precision in English, almost always
write books which are heavy and confused in style. The only
exception he knew was Challis on *Real Property* which had, he
thought, exquisite limpidity. He thought criminal lawyers had a
good sense of humour probably by compensation as a refreshment from their job. He talked a good deal about Sir William
Anson whom he compared to an ostrich—in the distance the body
looked most dignified, but when you got near the head was buried
in the sand. I told him some tales of Vinogradoff and he said
that Maitland once brought V. to dinner to Morley's. The latter
said something about chancery lawyers and this started off V. on
a monologue about the early history of chancery which lasted for
half an hour. They all looked on helplessly until he finished when
Morley broke in with some talk about an aphorism of Goethe's
which led V. into another vast monologue on the influence of
Goethe on Russian philosophy. Birrell in despair led the conversation round to electoral talk (the election of 1895); but this
only started off Vinogradoff on the philosophy of English freedom and its probable relation to the Protestant tradition. Birrell
said that Morley was furious, Rosebery aloof in aristocratic *hauteur*, and Maitland grinning like an Italian circus man whose
well-intentioned bear has got off the chain and really thinks he
is pleasing everybody by gloomy pawings among the audience.
Can't you see the picture? . . .

Ever affectionately yours, H. J. L.

Washington, D.C., April 9, 1932

My dear Laski: Your letters are such a pleasure to me that I tremble to think of their being interrupted by my failure to come up
to them. You will remember and allow for my difficulties. *Inter
alia* I have gone back to Virgil. A few years ago I reread the
Eclogues, the *Georgics* and the first six books of the *Aeneid*. I
like to have a translation on hand and had none after book 6.
Now I have one and my secretary reads the English while I read
the Latin. But this is at odd moments—a break in the serious
business of murder cases—but alas there are few good ones.
Sherlock Holmes is not equalled by later tales. I think you recommended the best: *The Lost Gallows*—(Carr). That keeps the
tone throughout. I reread *The Moonstone* (W. Collins) the other

day and thought it the best of all. Of course I read your political pamphlet with proper awe in the presence of things I know not of. I am insisting to myself that I have outlived duty and have a right to be idle. I greatly enjoy being so. The notion of writing recollections and reflections I abhor. I might attempt a statement of law in my own terms—with no rights or duties, but I have only a few sentences in my head and I don't want to work. Is not a man of 91 free? Cheer me up and don't give me any damned exhortations. But I am very grateful for recommendations for reading—not in German except in extremest exigency. English much preferred because mainly I am read to by my secretary. It would be good, if you made a little list. But I have no right to bother you and don't mean to. A good many people come in the afternoons. The other day for the first time of recent days Mrs. Longworth (Alice Roosevelt) very pleasant—and at intervals several good-lookers. 7 cherry trees have come out around the Potomac basin—but today when they should be expanding it rains hard—and I fear the result. I do so enjoy the successive flowerings of the spring. I am afraid you don't care quite so much for them. No high thoughts for today—but affectionate ones from
Your affectionate O. W. H.

Devon Lodge, 17.IV.32
My dear Justice: I got back yesterday from ten most happy days in Paris. The first three I spent with the International Institute of Public Law. Of those I met there, Kelsen of Cologne, certainly the first German jurist of the day, was the most interesting. A profound philosophic mind, quick, agile, and widely read. He interested me greatly by his comments on our friends. Pound he rated on the whole low; "a mass of undigested learning," he said. He thought well of Morris Cohen with the limitation that he had an evil tendency to score dialectic points. His great God was Maitland whom he—wisely—never ceased to praise. He knew you well through the German translation of *The Common Law* and asked why so few of your successors at Harvard had seen the necessity for pursuing your combination of the comparative-historical method with a system of hypotheses. Of the others I liked much a Spaniard who was no great shakes but most charming and at dinner gave me a great account of the night of the King's abdication when they did not know from one hour to another whether he would go without bloodshed or not.[1] . . . I also had dinner with our Ambassador,[2] a clever fellow but something of a

---

[1] King Alfonso had left Spain in April 1931, following a bloodless revolution by the Republicans.
[2] William George Tyrrell (1866-1947), first Baron Tyrrell, was British Ambassador in Paris from 1928 to 1934.

Metternich, with his nose in all sorts of dark corners sniffing for scents which are not there. I thought the France he knew gravely limited in character; and if I were our Foreign Office I should feel very unhappy at the limitations upon the kind of opinion upon which he could report. He was, also, far too anti-German for my liking, in that sense rather a hang-over from a dead age. . . . *Ever affectionately yours, H. J. L.*

Devon Lodge, 23.IV.32

My dear Justice: A grand letter from you followed on the heels of mine going Westward. You ask for names of books—and I assume that you want a combination, like Artemus Ward, of amusement and instruction. I read this week a life by Ernest Kantorowicz of *Frederick II* (*Stupor Mundi*) which I think would tickle your palate; and a really amusing and exhilarating study of *Mme. de Staël* by R. McNair Wilson which set Frida and me discussing for hours. Then I got much instruction from an admirably written book on Hume by John Laird which I commend very warmly—not the usual academic angle, and, in addition, some fresh and original material. I have also read with great interest a new life of *Fontenelle* by J. F. Carré (Alcan) which I think would give you a good deal of interest. It explains awfully well the transition between the 17th and the 18th century; and it shows—a thing one too little realises—how profound was the naturalistic and humanist tradition which went on growing from Rabelais to the philosophers behind the elaborate façade of the classical tradition and the religious revival. It is a rather big book, but I think one can honestly say that there isn't a word in it unnecessary to the purpose. In the way, also, of what the French call the *"vie romancée"* I enjoyed a life of Brissot de Warville by J. F. Primo—really amusing, full of novelty to me, and a very striking picture of the journalistic *dessous* of the 18th century. The only defect is a tendency on the author's part to be somewhat excessively intimate with his reader, rather like a man who *will* whisper in your ear instead of speaking to the company at large. But emphatically a jolly book about a really interesting creature.

As this has been the last week of my vacation I have spent it idling very pleasantly. We went to hear a discussion on the state of the world by eminent economists and business men which amused me greatly. One man read out a programme of the measures necessary for salvation and explained that it was impossible to hope they would be carried out. Another saw the only hope in Russia which he had not visited and did not propose to visit

in case he suffered disillusion. Then came the *pièce de résistance*
in which a most eminent business man explained that the woes
of the world had come because we had forgotten Christianity;
by which it appeared, to our astonishment, that he meant the gold
standard. Then an eminent economist suggested (I) that America
should go Free Trade (II) that the world should disarm and
(III) that the working class should accept a thirty per cent cut
in wages. At that point we went home feeling, as John Bright
once said, that the worst of great thinkers is that they will not
think greatly. We also had one of the most amusing dinners I
have had in many a day with Behrman, the American playwright.
He has been working at Hollywood and his picture of its habits
was just one glorious farce. He told us how a film company decided to do a movie for children. After various attempts none
of their scenario writers could do an adequate dialogue. So a man
was got in from another Company on the condition (I) that he
was to have two thousand dollars a week for writing the scenario.
(II) As the other writers had made their efforts towards the text
their names were to appear with his on the screen; in consideration of which, as he was to do the work, he was to receive an
extra 500 dollars a week. When the first night came, to his utter
amazement, his name was the only one on the screen and not
one word of the text was his! He told us also how his company
had bought the screen rights of an English play for one hundred
thousand dollars; when they got it over, they realised that as all
its episodes represented English history it would not be very intelligible to an American audience. So they decided to scrap
everything but the title and to fill it in with episodes from American history instead. After dinner he introduced us to a "star" who
was in the hotel. She asked me what I did. I explained. She said
"Gee! Isn't that a job that taxes your bean?" I said modestly that
I did my best. She then said "Gosh! I guess I should register
fatigue," and then lapsed into complete and panicked silence. I
wish I were an artist and could draw for you the marvellous
expression of pained astonishment on her face. . . .

Our love to you.   *Ever affectionately yours, H. J. L.*

Washington, D.C., May 3, 1932
My dear Laski: The only things of which I can tell you are books
that I have read or more or less listened to. One of the last is
Spengler's 2 volume (translated) *The Decline of the West.* I read
volume 1 with a dictionary when it came out, but the translation
makes it easier—though it is not always easy—and comparisons
with the State of Egypt under the —th Dynasty, Rome under —,

Arabia in X A.D. &c &c convey nothing to me. He certainly is an able and learned man—but I can't measure his pretentions. In view of his suggestion that philosophy is the insignificant reaction of a given personality, varying with the makeup, I hardly understand his ambition to make the philosophy of Germany—and I hardly can doubt that he has an abnormally swelled head. Have you views about him? We have just begun McIlwain's *Growth of Political Thought in the West*—sent by Felix. Stories by Locke who I think has some charm. Yesterday we drove out to an apple orchard with 7000 apple trees in flowers—which was pretty fine. And today at last Cardozo (my successor) came to luncheon—with his beautiful face and nature. So I idle along and expect to go to Beverly Farms on June 8. They have been putting an elevator into my house there—so that I still can sleep upstairs and shan't have to receive people in my bedroom. I think more or less on death but don't worry and seem at present likely to last for some time.   *Affectionately yours, O. W. Holmes*

Devon Lodge, 8.V.32

My dear Justice: . . . I have had one of those busy weeks upon which one looks back at the end and wonders to what exactly it amounts. Committees, lectures, the Indian students annual dinner, the dinner of the Rational Press Association. The latter was made interesting by a really fine speech from J. M. Robertson who contributed to me really fascinating memories of Kingdon Clifford and Bradlaugh. I should much like to know where the militant secularism of the working-class, to which Bradlaugh used to appeal, has gone. So far as I can make out that kind of fighting spirit, which used to read Tom Paine's *Age of Reason* by the hundred thousand, makes little appeal. Yet the need for a militant temper in the religious field is just as great as ever. If the fight is stopped for one day whether in education, or Sabbatarianism or what not, you find the clergy creeping back to its old positions. Robertson's picture of Bradlaugh hissed in the House of Commons by men who later fought for the honour of being pallbearers at his funeral was very arresting. He also told how, as a young man, brought up in a pious Scottish home, he had heard Kingdon Clifford lecture to a workingmen's Sunday lecture society and came away feeling that a new universe had opened before his eyes. It was impressive to hear him say that no man he had met since seemed to him to have embodied so completely the ideal of the scientific temper as Clifford. Robertson, then a printer's apprentice, wrote to him for books and advice on study; and for three years Clifford directed his reading as a teacher might the work of a disciple for this unknown boy whom he was never actually to meet. The story moved me profoundly; the kind of thing that gives an extra sweetness to life. . . .

Our love to you.   *Ever affectionately yours, H. J. L.*

Washington, D.C., May 15, 1932
My dear Laski: My secretary tells me that by a rough calculation we have read 4,500,000 words since we got here—some of them just buzzed through my head. Do speak ill of that accursed Spengler, *Decline of the West*. It is not lawful to know as much as he assumes to know. *Per contra* this p.m. we began Sir A. Salter—*Recovery* which I like very much—though I don't think the now unfashionable *Laissez-Faire* has been disposed of yet.

Wodehouse is a joy every time—we even have reread some volumes.

I expect to go to Beverly Farms on June 8—and drive there at once from Boston on the 9th. I suppose I shall find an elevator put in. I am not allowed to walk upstairs. I am enjoying my idleness vastly. I think of death, but don't worry.

Affectionately yours, O. W. Holmes

Devon Lodge, 16.V.32
My dear Justice: . . . Abraham Flexner came to dinner and we had a grand talk out of which two main themes emerged which are, I think, worth putting down: (I) the harm done to education by Dewey and his followers in telling teachers that the child ought to study the thing it finds pleasant, which has the result of making effort seem an evil on the ground that it is unpleasant. In the result the student fails to learn the need of that organised concentration of mind which gives understanding because as soon as it is difficult it becomes unpleasant. (II) We agreed also that the main difference between people lies in the capacity for abstraction. The weakness *e.g.* of the uneducated lies in the fact that they see all problems in terms of persons. So that a quarrel or a dislike makes them the enemy of an idea where education ought to reach that point where the personal can be transcended into an abstraction, *e.g.* I remain a Republican even though Mr. Hoover did not make me a member of the Law Enforcement Commission; or, "I do not condemn American civilisation" (the keynote of most comment at this moment) even though I am horror-struck at the Lindbergh tragedy.[1]

In the way of reading, some interesting things. McIlwain's book, which the *Harvard Law Review* sent me,[2] is *very* good; less

---

[1] The kidnapping of the Lindbergh child had occurred in March; on May 12 the child's body had been found.
[2] Reviewed by Laski, 46 *Harv. L. Rev.* 345 (December 1932).

I think in the earlier than in the later period. Its weakness seems to me the separation of a body of doctrine from the living world to which it belonged; and, at times, an excessive interest in minutiae to the exclusion of the big problems. Sometimes, also, I disagree with the emphasis. I should, for instance, give more space to the Counciliar movement than he on the ground that though the movement did not give birth to new ideas it gave first-rate significance to views which were of little importance when they were first put forward. I think he is very good on Fortescue, and quite unquestionably right as against Holdsworth on Hobbes. Altogether I should regard it as the most important book of its kind since Gierke, and a credit to American scholarship. . . .

Ever affectionately yours, H. J. L.

Washington, D.C., May 25, '32

My dear Laski: Your letters do give me much pleasure. One to-day in which you say much the same things that I had been thinking about McIlwain's book—especially the end better than the beginning; excessive interest in minutiae &c, &c, but on the whole a creditable book. Sir ——— Salter's book, *Recovery*, impressed me but didn't move me to such intelligent scrutiny as it deserves. Two good books by Tomlinson about 1) the wilds of the Amazon[1] and 2) the Islands near Borneo or Sumatra.[2] Clive Bell, *An Account of French Painting*, a Japanese story.[3] . . . I am just finishing a book on Sam Houston—(Texas) partly squalid but impressive[4] &c. &c. I got a heavenly drive—before luncheon. A good letter from F. Frankfurter today pleasing me much by showing that Brandeis and Mrs. B. were pleased by a few words of introduction to a book about him I wrote[5]—and speaking in a high hearted way of the effect of the hard times on our young men. I don't know why writing comes so hard to me these few last weeks—I suppose it is old age—but I can no more. . . .

Affectionately yours, O. W. Holmes

Devon Lodge, 29.V.32

My dear Justice: I was amused and pleased with your account of your strivings with Spengler. I read him when he first came out, and thought him pretentious and absurd. Of course I can't check

---

[1] H. M. Tomlinson, *The Sea and the Jungle* (1923).

[2] *Tide Marks* (1924).

[3] Lady Muraski, *The Tale of Genji* (Waley, tr., 1925).

[4] Marquis James, *The Raven: A Biography of Sam Houston* (1929).

[5] *Mr. Justice Brandeis* (Frankfurter, ed., 1932). Laski reviewed the book in 72 *New Republic* 50 (Aug. 24, 1932).

a good deal of his learning, *e.g.* in the history of architecture or of mathematics. But I could not bring myself to believe that history repeats itself upon a morphological pattern and I felt that the book belonged to the category I always suspect which seeks for scientific laws in a material not susceptible to that kind of expression. As I see the historical movement, decline and improvement are the products of a large number of incommensurable factors—technological changes, the birth-rate, immersion in luxury, power to postpone immediate consumption, effective control of vested interests, wisdom in government, etc. and I doubt the power to build prediction on their operation. So I simply assume that you are entitled to relief from headaches upon the simple basis that Spengler belongs to those people like Mme. Blavatsky[1] whom one assumes to be outside the realm of necessary experience. . . .

We are living here through a period of grim pessimism—worse than anything I have known. The dark outlook in Germany, the black prospect in the Danubian states, the failure of America to recover, and the danger of war in the Far East raises awful questions of economic collapse. Our people are making a mess of it. They lack courage and faith in big principle and we seem to be drifting rather helplessly to disaster. No one seems to nail his colours to the mast; and if I had to find a metaphor I should say that statesmen look like nothing so much as squirrels running round a cage. Unless I gravely miss my guess the foundations are being laid of a position out of which, all over the world, there is no egress save through social conflict; and the price we may have to pay for that is hardly likely to be worth the results.

Our love to you. I hope this will find you pleasantly installed at Beverly, and with the new lift adding to your ease.

Ever affectionately yours, H. J. L.

Devon Lodge, 4.VI.32

My dear Justice: . . . I have been busy colloguing with the French socialists for our labour party on their line of action in this crisis.[1] It was an interesting job—not easy. They are a curiously divided lot—some admirable, some about as Chauvinistic as Roosevelt or Lodge. They seemed divided into those who would like to see Germany ruined politically and damn the economic consequences and those who realise that the world market means

---

[1] Helena Petrovna Blavatsky (1831-1891), wandering theosophist, founder of the Theosophical Society; author of *Isis Unveiled* (1877).

[1] On June 4 Edouard Herriot had formed a government of Radical-Socialists from which the Unified Socialists under Léon Blum were excluded.

that a ruined Germany means in the long run a ruined France.
I was amazed at the intensity of their dislike for America. Mainly
of course their attitude is based upon sheer ignorance. The
America they know is tourist America—rich, careless, dominating. Their knowledge is made out of a composite picture built
on the stock yards, the skyscraper, Rockefeller, Capone and the
Lindbergh tragedy. They know little or nothing of American literature (or any other except their own). They believe she is entirely materialistic; and an hour's speech from me on the America
they did not know I can only describe as a real revelation. But it
does make one feel that, with all their great qualities, the insularity of the French is something like a danger to the world.
For the assessment of national motives is at bottom the thing that
forms the stereotype out of which foreign policy emerges. . . .

Our love as always.   *Ever affectionately yours, H. J. L.*

Devon Lodge, 28.VI.32
My dear Justice: Of course the supreme event of the day is Felix's
nomination;[1] compared to it little things like the Presidential election pale for me into insignificance. I am more overjoyed than I
can say, even though I suppose confirmation to be uncertain and
that, like Brandeis sixteen years ago, he will go through a grim
time. But I am so glad this recognition has come to him; and I
get peculiar pleasure from the fact that it is just fifty years since
your nomination to the same court. I don't know any better way
of celebrating that great anniversary. I do hope his friends will
work their hardest to put the thing through. . . .

Our love to you, as always.   *Ever affectionately yours, H. J. L.*

Beverly Farms, July 10, 1932
My dear Laski: Every letter from you is a book—those from me
are merely petitions for another. Life goes on very pleasantly. I
delight in this place with its early associations—but most of my
friends are dead. . . . John Morse is as alive as ever at 92 ½—
and took luncheon with me yesterday. I go around by Rockport
once in a while and sigh for you. The place is not much changed,
I think. Books, Morton *In Search of Ireland*—the Beards' *Rise of
American Civilization*—good. James Truslow Adams, *The Epic
of America*. I don't care much for it. Hardy's, *Dynasts*, I don't
care much for it—all mitigated by Wodehouse, *passim.*

The excitement has been the nomination of Frankfurter for the

---

[1] On June 22 Governor Ely had nominated Felix Frankfurter as Associate
Justice of the Supreme Judicial Court of Massachusetts. In July the Governor
announced that Professor Frankfurter refused to accept the nomination.

Supreme Court of Massachusetts. I hear tell he is disposed to decline. I thought he couldn't after so much talk and his ensuing silence. But I believe he wrote at once and that the silence rests with the Governor. Brandeis I hear is against his taking the place —but it is a mystery to me and I await developments. I hardly know what I should advise if asked.[1] It is curious that the Sacco and Vanzetti business has left such deep prejudices. I dare say you know more than I about the whole matter.

You see with what difficulty I write. I hope that will not stop you. For I am as always your affectionate   *O. W. Holmes*

Devon Lodge, 12.VII.32

My dear Justice: I have had a fortnight of hard extra work which has prevented me from any serious correspondence. Sankey finished the draft of his Indian Constitutional Bill[1] and called me in to comment. The result was the need to write a series of memoranda on his proposals which were literally done with sweat and blood. It was all very interesting, but very grim; the more especially as I don't think the measure will satisfy Indian demands and is cluttered up with all kinds of checks and balances which seem to me to reproduce the worst features of the worst modern constitutions.

But there have been some compensations. We had Alvin Johnson[2] to dinner and had good talk with him on the present position of social studies in America. He interests me. It takes about an hour to stoke him up, and he is then rather like an artichoke which you have to strip leaf by leaf in order to reach the heart. But he has most sterling commonsense and is wholly without malice. Then a good dinner with Sir Maurice Amos, who leaves me breathless. In the course of two hours he moved through the canonical doctrine of marriage to the significance of the seal in contract, to the diffusionist controversy in anthropology, the danger of principle in politics, the value of the snob to a social system, why judges die from arterial sclerosis, the virtues and de-

---

[1] Some months earlier, Holmes had written to Governor Ely expressing the warmest opinion of Professor Frankfurter's capacities. After Governor Ely's nomination was announced, vigorous opposition to the appointment was expressed by ex-Governor Fuller, who charged that Professor Frankfurter was "an open sympathizer with murderers" and expressed the fear that if the nomination were confirmed he saw "no reason why murder should not flourish here in Massachusetts"; New York *Times,* June 23, 1932, p. 23, column 2.

[1] The Government's proposed bill contemplated the inclusion of provisions providing for provincial autonomy and for the federation of Indian states and provinces.

[2] Alvin Saunders Johnson (1874-), economist and Director of the New School for Social Research, 1923-1945.

fects of the English nobleman with special reference to Eustace
Percy, Bertrand Russell and the danger of life on the heights, and,
as a final dish, why *Love's Labour Lost* is Shakespere's most
admirable comedy. He always talked with persuasive vehemence
and never without knowledge. As a sheer exhibition it was quite
marvellous. Then a dinner with Low[3] our most famous cartoonist
in which one incident is worth recording. He explained that he
saw Ramsay MacDonald today as a quite different person from
when he began to caricature him ten years ago. We asked why;
and he proceeded to draw six pictures of J.R.M. on the menus
in which he began with a dreamy idealist, continued with a man
trying hard to make himself look important, and ended up with
a face that had exchanged nobility for slyness, and left one with
a sense of profound distrust. A Tory M.P. who was at dinner said
he thought them the best biography he had seen. I wish you
could have seen them, merely as a piece of draftsmanship. They
were cruel in their intensity of perception; but they were simply
masterly.

My mind of course dwells very much on what is going to happen to Felix. Thompson[4] wired me that F. is now himself the
difficulty and that Brandeis is against his acceptance. I think
Brandeis is wholly wrong. First I don't believe any man ought
to evade vital responsibility. Then it looks to me as though the
nomination ought to be, as with yourself and Cardozo, the step-
ping stone to Washington. Indeed Brandeis made me rather angry
by his attitude for exactly the same was said to him in 1916 about
his own nomination by Wilson and I gather that he did not hesitate at all. It is terribly trying to be at this distance where I can't
urge Felix to what seems to me the quite obvious line of duty for
him to follow. . . .

Our love as always.   *Ever affectionately yours, H. J. L.*

Devon Lodge, 23.VII.32
My dear Justice: . . . I have had a terribly busy time—as always
just before I get away. I have done two long and difficult industrial arbitrations in Manchester, the kind of thing in which you
have to grasp complicated masses of controversial statistics and
settle schedules of wages. Then I have had some long meetings
with Sankey, partly over Ireland,[1]—a terrible and stupid problem

---

[3] David Low (1891-   ), caricaturist and cartoonist for British papers,
principally the *Evening Standard*.

[4] William G. Thompson (1864-1935), Boston lawyer who had been
defense counsel in the later stages of the Sacco-Vanzetti case.

[1] In June and July there was vigorous disagreement between the British
government and the government of the Irish Free State, culminating in the
withholding of land annuities payable to Great Britain and the retaliatory
imposition of duties on Irish imports.

—and partly over our committee on legal education which is now all ready except for the actual letters of invitation; it's a funny thought that it should have taken me three years to convince him of the need for an enquiry of this sort. Then I have been busy with examiner's meetings—always a grim job—and the hateful task of writing a 4000 word article for Alvin Johnson on liberty,[2] and trying to say in it what one really needs ten times the space to say adequately. However, it is nearly done; and a week today as ever is we depart to the peace of Cornwall. I am more anxious about getting away than I can remember.

I went to one dinner which is worth recounting. It was the annual feast of the law teachers and I was very interested by the speeches. They were of two kinds. One lot—very well typified by Holdsworth—went on the lines that the law teacher ought not to encourage criticism of the judiciary and its decisions in an age of scepticism, and produced the effect of a desire on his part to fall flat on his face before a law lord. The other—typified by my friend Gutteridge—argued that the essential task of the teacher of law was a critical one; that he ought to make the law schools the centre from which juristic principle is born.[3] And I was struck by the fact that in this lot the names occurred over and over again—Holmes, Maitland, Pollock, Eugen Ehrlich, Demogue, and that, quite clearly, this attitude was the dividing line between the younger men and their elders. There were over 200 teachers of law there; and, Oxford and Cambridge apart, it was clear that Harvard was the ideal at which they aimed. Queer that after fifty years since Maitland delivered his inaugural address at Cambridge[4] nothing serious should have been done to realise his quite moderate ideals.

I had to learn from the *New Republic* that Felix had declined the Mass. Supreme Court.[5] I assume, at this distance, that he knows best. But I was a good deal disappointed, for I felt (a) that one ought not to decline that kind of post except on grounds beyond dispute and (b) that five years of that court might well prove the direct high-road to Washington when Brandeis goes, which is, of course, where I want him to be. It's an immense satisfaction to know that the opposition to him collapsed. But, as I say, at this distance I do not assume a title to judge. I only hope that he will not regret the choice he has made. Felix was made to have a big field in which to play. . . .

Our love to you as always.   *Ever affectionately yours, H. J. L.*

---

[2] 9 *Encyclopedia of Social Sciences* (1933) 442.

[3] See *Journal of the Society of Public Teachers of Law,* 1932, p. 67.

[4] Why the History of English Law is not Written," 3 *Collected Papers of Frederic William Maitland* (Fisher, ed., 1911), 488.

[5] 71 *New Republic* 247 (July 20, 1932).

As from Devon Lodge, 11.VIII.32

My dear Justice: I expect you will hear of Graham Wallas's death.[1] He was on holiday near us here, and developed quite suddenly a fatal attack of uraemia. I shall miss him sorely. He was always full of ideas, he had humour, and sensitiveness. Above all things, he was a great teacher. All over the world there are first-rate people in the social sciences who owe their original impulse to work to him; and I don't think a man could wish for a finer epitaph. And two of his books did a big job. I don't think it is too much to say that his *Francis Place* made the rewriting of a big period in English history inescapable; and a good many books have been written since out of its suggestiveness. *Human Nature in Politics* also created a tradition; and I think it would be possible to show that people like Walter Lippmann have built their reputation out of developing its ideas. He had warm affection and admiration for you, and I don't think we ever met this last dozen years without my being minutely questioned by him on what I knew of your activities. His death is a big gap among my friends. . . .

Well—these holiday letters are mere paralipomena—a greeting rather than an account. You know that they bring you my love.

Ever affectionately yours, H. J. L.

Devon Lodge, 27.VIII.32

My dear Justice: I got home this afternoon from one of the best holidays I have ever spent. And it ended with an amusing day which may interest you in the telling. Frida and I motored over to lunch with Bertrand Russell some twenty miles from us. He was in great form. He began with a passionate attack on the modern physicists. Subjective idealism, as preached by Jeans and Eddington, is simply part of the technique of theological reaction. It postulates comfortable inferences and finds their truth in the applause with which they are received. No science can ever be properly understood until it is conceived in its social setting. Newton did his work in England because a man of his type could not have found a favourable environment (as the experience of Galileo showed) in France or Germany or Italy. Those who seek to hand over the control of life to scientific experts ought to remember that Laplace, Lagrange and Legendre, probably the most brilliant mathematical trio a given age has ever known, united to reject Fourier's classical papers as ridiculous when these were submitted to the French Institute. Free will is a doctrine born in part out of man's desire to be master of his fate, and in part

---

[1] See Laski, 4 *New Statesman and Nation* (N.S.) 199 (Aug. 20, 1932).

of his eagerness to prevent God from being identified with the devil. Every age needs its Dreyfus case to persuade men to remember the limitations of human justice. The surest sign that a man is unimaginative is when he takes the idea of progress for granted. Business men's success is incredible until we remember that they have only one another to compete with. I select, of course, and abbreviate; but I hope I have said enough to show that we had a thoroughly enjoyable afternoon. . . .

My love to you. I hope you are as fit and brown as

Ever affectionately yours, H. J. L.

Beverly Farms, Massachusetts—September 1, 1932
My dear Laski: A succession of delightful letters—but I no longer can give them adequate answers. I simply can't write more than a few hesitating straggling words—I suppose it is old age, and the worst feature of it so far. Your last with your notice of Graham Wallas came today. You give me so much pleasure that I do hope you will continue even though it becomes more and more unilateral. Most of my reading is done by my secretary aloud to me. We have just finished the *Life of Beveridge.* What a glutton for work B. was—and altogether a pretty big fellow. I didn't realize how many things he had up his sleeve when he was talking to me. His boastfulness was innocent and ready to accept correction. The biography seems to me to be much better than a political book—*The Tragic Era*—that the same author, Claude Bowers, did before. Beveridge had sound theories about writing and lived up [to] them. He took endless trouble. His travels in Europe and interviews with most of the important people are interesting. In short I have been reliving with him for a week and absorbed and moved by it.

Felix and his wife come here to luncheon from time to time. I can't help feeling as if his declining the Mass. Supreme Judicial Court was a mistake, but he and Brandeis know better than I do.

Yesterday I went over to the Richard Curtises[1] to see the eclipse, which I did, but somehow was far less impressed than I was when my wife and I went to Norfolk, Va. to see one 30 years ago. That was my only approach to seeing people except in this house. Tomorrow I expect Mrs. Beveridge for luncheon the first time down here, the next day Greenslet[2] the publisher

---

[1] Richard Cary Curtis (1894-1951), son of Holmes's old friend, Mrs. Charles P. Curtis, and brother of Charles P. Curtis, Jr.

[2] Ferris Greenslet (1875-1959); for many years he was director and editor at Houghton, Mifflin Company, and as such was a close friend and adviser of Senator Beveridge.

&c. Idleness suits me—with a pleasant secretary for companion. I should like to write more but I can't.

Affectionately yours always, O. W. Holmes

Devon Lodge, 10.IX.32

My dear Justice: . . . The most interesting thing in Manchester was a long talk with Alexander the philosopher. I wish you could have heard it, for I am sure that you would have been largely in sympathy. He denounced Hegel and all his followers as having led a reaction which destroyed the promising rationalism of the 18th century. He set out a theory of ethics which won my heart because it went back to Adam Smith and made the judgment of goodness the result of a sentiment of approval towards the act involved, and hence enabled the experience of society to be the largest factor in producing the attitude men take to good and bad things. I confess I can see no other approach which does not, in the end, become either theological or purely personal in character. He told me a very interesting tale about B. Russell and the British Academy. In 1920 he proposed Russell for the philosophic section. This was rejected on the ground that as Russell had just been divorced, he was not a fit person to be a member. This year he proposed him again; and though all the philosophers were unanimous that it would be a disgrace not to elect him the council, on moral and social grounds, preferred a quite second-rate Oxford don. Can you beat that? Alexander said that all the people concerned agreed that Russell was by far the most distinguished philosopher in England. But those who did not object to his divorce (1932 please note!) objected to his political views and vice-versa. I said to Alexander that on those terms if I were he I should resign from the Academy in protest; that once Russell's intellectual pre-eminence was admitted the academy disgraced itself by allowing any personal questions to enter in. But this was too heroic a gesture for him. He thought that he might bring the members round to sanity by staying inside. . . .

Our love to you as always.   *Ever affectionately yours, H. J. L.*

Devon Lodge, 9.X.32

My dear Justice: I am ashamed of myself for the long interval since I wrote; but I have really been terribly driven. A visit to Manchester to see my people; a visit to the miners in Northumberland; three days of industrial arbitrations; a long job in connection with the dispute between this country and Ireland;[1] and

---

[1] On October 5, Mr. de Valera participated in conferences in London with British representatives concerning outstanding issues between the two governments. Negotiations which followed between October 14 and 16 quickly broke down.

the grim toil of the beginning of term (I interviewed 168 students in a fortnight)—these are my excuses. But now that the routine is in full swing again I hope to return to my decent habits.

In the way of news I have little to record. Our politics, like yours, go from bad to worse. We ignore common sense in the pursuit of a stupid economic imperialism which denies every rational economic principle; and in matters of social constitution we are now reaping the evil fruit of our class-ridden society. It is becoming terribly true that our governors speak in terms which mean less and less to the multitude. I am finally convinced that a civilisation dominated by business men is incapable of statesmanship. Their habits and motives are not wide enough for the task of a democracy; and the economic world they make gets into relentless contradiction with the political. The result is that the vested interests of the one deny the established expectations of the other; and the thing moves with an almost awe-inspiring determination to catastrophe. I don't say that is for today or tomorrow; I do prophesy that the basis of common agreement is in process of disappearance. It is a tragedy; but it is a tragedy implied logically in the facts. . . .

Our love as always to you both. Please keep fit and well, as the first vacation when I have sixty pounds or so to spare I shall run over to see you.   *Ever affectionately yours, H. J. L.*

Devon Lodge, 15.X.32

My dear Justice: . . . I went . . . to an amusing lunch with H. G. Wells. He and I maintained against the company that in the next generation there was going to be a great intellectual renascence in the United States—that the present coincidence of scepticism, material difficulty, absence of overmastering tradition, faith in experimentalism, made it probable that new views and new creativeness were far more likely there than in England or Western Europe. He interested me much by his fervid praise of Dos Passos and Sinclair Lewis, and we agreed that people like Willa Cather mark the attempt of any sensitive mind in a critical period to try and find a private hole in the ground. Wells remains the most alert mind I know, quick, sensitive, eager to see the light on the horizon and its significance. He has grave faults of temper, especially his insistence that his private scheme of values is the quintessence of universal experience. But he is a mind unafraid and unwilling ever to bow the knee to the conventional mythologies which are always so comfortable to those who fear the need to think anew. . . .

Our love to you as always; and don't be too disturbed by Mr.

Hoover's imminent disappearance from public life. If Frank Roosevelt makes Felix Solicitor-General, I will forgive him everything!   *Ever affectionately yours, H. J. L.*

Devon Lodge, 30.X.32

My dear Justice: A fortnight of grim labour with one or two pleasant interludes. The most amusing, I think, was a dinner with H. G. Wells who was in great form; or perhaps I ought to say that he damned all the things I like to damn. He made a furious attack on James Joyce as, effectively, the annihilation of rationality; he went for a D. H. Lawrenceite by urging that no one has the right to make his private emotions the measure of the universe. And he and I went for a Frenchman who was anxious to explain that America was materialistic where France was the spiritual guardian of civilised values. Then I went to dinner with Slesser L. J. and had a good night of legal talk. It was amusing to find that his two other guests had just discovered the Harvard Law School and were eager to explain how much more important it was than Englishmen realised. And their views of American law were funnier than I can put into words. They had found a volume of Cardozo in the Inner Temple and evidently felt about it the same wondering admiration as you or I might feel if we ran across a copy of Descartes in the *hinterland* of Manchuria. One of them was a son of old Lord MacNaghten who is now a K.B. judge; and he was so full of distress when I propounded the view that the law of torts was expressive of a certain framework of economic conditions. When I mentioned your "inarticulate major premise," he explained to me with something like passion that he had no such premises, that he "simply applied the law, looking neither to the right nor to the left." I suggested that his mind might be slightly more complex than he knew, to which he retorted that he was a simple and honourable man and that no damned nonsense about complexity was going to obscure his motives. "I never give a decision," he said "unless I can find a case to support it." I asked him if he had ever read Maitland to which he replied that he read Pollock who was very good, especially in his book on Contract, but in his "humble submission" Maitland was not a lawyer at all, but a poet. Don't you think that is a superb way to take life?

. . . I read Walter Lippmann's selected editorials, which he sent me. I didn't think they stood republication very well. They lacked body, and the power to take a long view. The style is, of course, simply admirable; but they are very emphatically the work of a journalist who wants to get an immediate audience, rather than of a thinker who reflects for the few hundreds who are seeking the way to penetrate to foundations. There is a desire to please which I found myself resenting. . . .

Our love to you unchangeably. I hope Roosevelt is elected and that he makes Felix Solicitor General. Then I shall believe in a divinity which shapes our ends!

Ever affectionately yours, H. J. L.

Devon Lodge, 5.XI.32

My dear Justice: . . . I have been having some interesting correspondence with Mrs. Asquith over a review I wrote of her husband's biography. She tells me one thing that is, I think, an interesting commentary on the habits of the politician. When Asquith had his final quarrel with Lloyd-George the two men to whom he gave his greatest confidence on the Tory side were Curzon and Balfour who were his most intimate friends. They were profuse up to the very last day of Asquith's government in protestations of loyalty to him, and of dislike of L-G in whom, they insisted, they had had no confidence; but twenty-four hours later they were both members of L-G's cabinet and Curzon was especially loud in his protestations that L-G was the only possible candidate for the Premiership. The more there emerges about those days, the worse the intrigue seems to be by which L-G got the supreme place. And as a commentary on the poison of power I know little comparable, except perhaps the folly of Hoover's last few speeches, to what men were then prepared to do in order to keep their place. Mrs. Asquith says that she is now convinced that under a mask of bland indifference Balfour had a quite insatiable appetite for office, and that this was true of him down to his very last days. Blessed indeed are they who find no satisfaction in that particular kind of ambition.

I haven't read much this week as I have been busy trying to find out the limits of a search warrant. Our genial police authorities have been going into communist headquarters, taking everything they could lay their hands on, and then founding indictments on the scraps they pick up.[1] To me, perhaps wrongly, that seems exactly the kind of thing the General Warrants case was intended to prevent; and I know that your Court has been adamant against it. I fail to find any authority which entitles them to act in this way, and though the Communists are not a very friendly type, it seems to me a public obligation to assure them

---

[1] Certain aspects of the matter referred to were later dealt with in the Courts: *Elias* v. *Pasmore*, [1934] 2 K.B. 164. Horridge, J., in his judgment conceded broad powers of search and seizure to the police. See, further, *The Law of Public Meeting and the Right of Police Search* (prepared by a Committee of the Haldane Club; New Fabian Research Bureau Publication, No. 13; 1933).

adequate legal treatment. So if my researches prove me to have reason on my side, I propose to give the Attorney-General something to think over in the next few days. Really it is painful that one should have to re-establish elementary constitutional propositions nearly two hundred years after they have been regarded as well settled.

My love to you. Keep well, and read *The Cask* by Freeman Crofts!   *Ever affectionately yours, H. J. L.*

Washington, D.C., Nov. 7, 1932

My dear Laski: In spite of all that I have written about not writing it makes me very uncomfortable to remain silent long. I am still pursuing idleness, largely in the form of murder stories, and very little serious reading of any kind. The chief recent exception, Walter Lippmann's *Interpretations* which I read with modest admiration. I don't feel excited over the approaching election —I should think that the President had little political judgment, but I should vote for him if I had a vote—vainly I presume— the indications seeming to be for Roosevelt. Brandeis gave me the idea that Felix was in the inner circle of R. advisers, but does not believe that he would take the Solicitor-Generalship. I think it would be queer to turn down a seat on the Mass. Supreme Bench for a Solicitor-Generalship. Perhaps the perspective has changed and I am an old fogey.

In the way of murder I like what I have read of John Dickson Carr—(author of *The Lost Gallows*).

Owen Wister sent me a poem by Robinson Jeffers—*Thurso's Landing*—some marks of power in it, but I don't care for it— though the advertisements tell me that Jeffers is the greatest living American poet.

Also G. Miller (nephew) leaves for me to sample T. Dreiser: *An American Tragedy*—but I don't mean to read it.

I have seen most of the judges but I feel very remote from the business. A Chinaman called the other day—and wanted to see you when he went to London (soon). I rather liked him—but held out no more than that I would mention his name when I wrote—Mr. Liang—Yuen Liang.[1]

This doesn't call on you to do anything. You see I can't write —except to say   *Ever affectionately yours, O. W. Holmes*

Devon Lodge, 12.XI.32

My dear Justice: Well! We watched the presidential election with almost the same excitement as Americans themselves. Felix, I sup-

---

[1] Yuen-Li-Liang (1904-   ), law professor and diplomatist, had recently been a teaching fellow at the Harvard Law School.

pose, is delighted. I have a sense of relief at Hoover's defeat; but though I greatly like Frank Roosevelt, I am not able to feel enthusiasm at his victory. I thought he fought a second-rate campaign, evasive and timid; and I am no admirer of most of the people on whose advice he is going to depend. And I don't see how a Democrat, with Bryanism and Hearstism and such-like excrescences to consider, has got much chance of being decisive or courageous. I shall watch with enormous interest; but I suspect that this is in fact a pill to cure an earthquake.[1]

I have had a busy week. The most interesting thing in it was a dinner party of economists at the School—all experts of the first order. What emerged was that there was no single issue on which any three out of the twelve were prepared to adopt the same principles or causal explanations; and when they approached agreement, the kind of proposal they made would require a revolution to make it possible for the politician to implement it. I came away feeling that *expertise* is a very small item in common sense; and that statesmanship is a kind of divine intuition which hasn't got much relationship to *expertise*. There was not one of the twelve whom I should have wanted as a colleague in a cabinet; each could analyse, not one of them could propose. The most distinguished of them was a German who said that the British cabinet should (I) get rid of the export trades that were not paying (II) force unemployment up to five millions (III) smash the trade unions (IV) and so force wages on to a competitive basis. I said that if the Prime Minister tried to put his policy into operation he would fill all the jails in Great Britain with trade unionists and have to use the troops to prevent them being freed by indignant mobs. Did the economists think that desirable? He thought it would be lamentable. I asked if he thought a policy with such lamentable consequences was practical. He thought perhaps not. I then asked his alternative, and he said he had none. Don't you think I may be forgiven if I feel that experts need a course of training in common-sense?

Of reading I have something to tell. I have thoroughly enjoyed our Winston Churchill's *Thoughts and Adventures*. He is a most exhilarating fellow. I doubt whether he even knows what is meant by an inarticulate major premise. I suspect that, like Theodore Roosevelt, his ideas are the outcome of physical rather than mental exertion. But if there is danger, he is in it. If there is action he is at the centre. He is incapable of reflection or of second thoughts. But he is a grand fighting animal and I think you would enjoy every page of his book. Even when he describes his pleasure in painting you feel that for him the canvas is a battlefield. . . .

---

[1] A comment by Laski on Roosevelt's victory was published in the *Daily Herald* and was reprinted in 343 *Living Age* 386 (January 1933).

I have had one amusing book adventure. I went to Derby last Saturday to make a speech. Coming out of the station I found a market—a sight I can never resist. I found a bookstall in it, and on the bookstall a mass of *Mazarinades*, some of them really rare, and all of them in first class condition. I asked the price and was told I could have them for three-pence a piece or seven and six for the lot. So I bought the lot and got thereby a really precious addition to my library. . . .

My love to you. Keep well and read Henry Wade—*The Murder at the Duke of York's Steps.*   *Ever affectionately yours, H. J. L.*

Devon Lodge, 19.XI.32

My dear Justice: . . . My most interesting adventure this week must remain a secret between us—but it was really interesting. Some writing of mine[1] had been much discussed in the press and the King's secretary asked me to go and see him and have a talk on the functions of the monarchy. I did so and we walked around the problem for two hours. Charming as he was, I left him a convinced republican. He made me feel (I) that the King's power, though intangible, is immense (II) that he is the vital pivot, and almost necessarily so, in a constitutional crisis, (III) that the sources of his opinions are drawn from so narrow a circle of experience that he cannot adequately estimate the claims of novelty in matters of social constitution, (IV) that he regards his formal powers as contingently active for emergency purposes. In other words, in a big fight the Crown would almost certainly be on the Tory side, and if it assumed a constitutional form the monarchy could be precipitated with its immense social prestige into politics. He picked my brains with skill—not least about America and Frank Roosevelt. But he didn't *know* things. What he had was, so to speak, the best gossip; and I felt that it was an inadequate basis of policy-formation that he should be so limited. I liked him greatly, and was convinced of his benevolent intentions. But he knew only one world and he did not even know that he lacked the key to the other.

Of other things, there is less to say. An amusing dinner with Bernard Shaw, at which I met J. M. Barrie. He reminded me of sugar and water dressed up to look like champagne. A curious effort to be winsome which left one feeling that he was a case of arrested intellectual development. Shaw talked well, especially

---

[1] Perhaps *The Crisis and the Constitution: 1931 and After* and "Labour and the Constitution," 4 *New Statesman and Nation* 276 (Sept. 10, 1932). The article urged that large-scale constitutional changes would have to be effected were the Labour Party to return to power committed to an effective program of socialism.

about the immense effect on our times made by the decline in religious belief as one of the big factors for instability. A hundred years ago men looked to heaven for consolation for the errors of this world; now they reject heaven and this world has, somehow, to make its peace with them. He also made the interesting remark that Ibsen wrote the best stage dialogue since Molière, that he had the supreme gift of the theatre which consists in giving every actor a first-rate entrance and exit. He thought—Barrie dissenting vehemently—that Galsworthy was important as a social document rather than an artist. He understood the Englishman of decent habits and cultured mind who has a family-place, seven thousand a year, and a butler who stands by the tradition; but he can't understand why that type does not necessarily impress the English multitude, still less the foreigner. I think that a very fair picture, though I think the pre-war Galsworthy saw deeper than him of the post-war period. He has a kind of intellectual arteriosclerosis. . . .

My love to you dear Justice. Keep well. Isn't it grand about Felix's appointment to Oxford?[2]

Ever affectionately yours, H. J. L.

Washington, D.C., November 23, 1932

My dear Laski: If you keep a list of your charities—my name should lead all the rest.

A letter received a few days ago revives memory of cases we had on the limits of authority under search warrants. I think Butler expounded and I will try to add the name of his case if my secretary can find it. I am rather infirm for a search. *Marron* v. *U.S.*, 275 U.S. 192.[1] I have an impression there are others— but I have not thought of law for nearly a year.

As to the election if I had a vote it would have been for Hoover—without enthusiasm—Roosevelt when I knew him struck me as a good fellow with rather a soft edge, years ago.

Thank you for book recommendations—some of which at least I shall follow. I have read very little serious reading—(good life of J. Q. Adams by a son of Champ Clark—you wouldn't think that name could produce so good a one). But I almost have given up the effort after improvement and seek mainly amusement and

---

[2] In 1933-34 Felix Frankfurter was George Eastman Visiting Professor at Oxford University.

[1] In an opinion by Butler, J., the Court unanimously held that, although general search warrants were outlawed by the Fourth Amendment, federal officers might, without a warrant, and incidentally to effecting an arrest, search the premises on which a crime was in process of commission and which were under the control of the criminal.

repose. I hope you didn't despise my flabbiness—but I am rather flabby.

You will have heard of Lowell's resignation.[2] Tom Barbour called last night just after the radio had brought the news. I thought he was the proper successor but he didn't want it—and is wrapped up in the Agassiz Museum of which he is head. I see the papers mention Charley Adams—I should suppose he would be A-1. Brandeis doesn't approve the suggestion of Felix for Attorney-General or Solicitor-General and I guess that he is right.

You see how hard I find it to write—my affection is unabated—but I can no more. *Please* keep on writing to me.[3]   O. W. H.

Devon Lodge, 27.XII.32

My dear Justice: You will have thought hardly of me for my silence in three weeks. But I got dragged into the India Conference by Sankey and had a grim time trying to be useful—five or six hours a day.[1] And though in one sense I learned much—particularly that politicians are a race apart—I ended believing that imperialism has a curve of its own the line of which moves quite independently of past experience. I spent days trying to drum into his obstinate head that as long as thirty thousand Indians, including Gandhi, were in jail, no one would look at the Constitution and that the part of wisdom was to grant an amnesty before it was exacted. Not a step have the Government taken; and I think so far as common sense is concerned I might have saved my breath to cool my porridge. Sankey is prodigal in assurances that he agrees with me but gets nothing done. The last quality of a politician is the courage to take risks, and it is certainly the most urgent.

My great news you may have heard by way of Felix. I have accepted an invitation from Yale to give the Storrs lectures at the Law School,[2] and I shall come over for about a fortnight after March 17th. I haven't got my dates here quite settled yet, but, please, assume that I shall look in upon you about the first week in April. I needn't tell you how thrilling it will be for me to see you again; that is really the point of the whole adventure. And please be very fit so that we can have the maximum of talk. It's

---

[2] As President of Harvard.

[3] This is the last letter from Holmes to Laski which has been preserved.

[1] The Third Round Table Conference had convened in November and closed on December 24.

[2] Laski's four lectures at Yale were on "The Economic Basis of Law"; they were not published.

ntolerable to have to wait ten weeks for this joyful consumma-
ion. But even ten weeks must pass somehow or other. . . .

My love to you dear Justice. Please count the days until the
nd of March.   *Ever affectionately yours, H. J. L.*

IX

1933-1935

Devon Lodge, 6.I.3

My dear Justice: Your telegram for 1933 gave me enormous pleas
ure; and I need not tell you how warmly it is reciprocated. My
mind is full of the anticipation of seeing you in about eleven
weeks from now. It will be a red-letter day for me.

We came back this morning from a very pleasant week in
Antwerp—mostly full of talk with artists. I saw there one thing
you would, I think, have enjoyed—a very remarkable exhibition
of Rops' etchings. Some were wicked; some merely unpleasantly
obscene; but their power and purity of line were really amazing
I was interested, too, in a long talk with Ensor, now the leading
artist in Belgium, and some say in Europe. He was particularly
interesting about English art. He is absorbed by Turner and Con
stable whom he rates very high; for all the rest he appears not
to give the Duke's two-penny damn. Of the Americans he had
literal worship for Whistler and a high regard for the impres
sionist Sisley.[1] Sargent he regards as no more than a fashionable
trickster who had learned the technique of being impressive with
out being profound. He was, of course, an enthusiast for the
Dutchmen; but he had some interesting special views e.g. that
El Greco and Goya were above Velasquez, and that after the
period of da Vinci Italian art had become so conventionalised
that none saw things definitively for himself. He was a gay, bril
liant creature, with a hatred for art dealers which was gloriously
funny. . . .

Another interesting afternoon was a visit to a village where re

---

[1] Alfred Sisley (1840-1899), French landscapist, who was much influ
enced by Monet and Renoir.

416

ently the Virgin Mary is said to have appeared to five children.
fter investigation the Church was inclined to doubt the miracle.
ut the local landowner, who is also the hotel proprietor, is very
ious and brought pressure to bear to prevent the scepticism from
ecoming too positive. The result is that in less than a month he
as reaped a harvest from tourists who haunt the grotto in the
vening in the hope of a further appearance. I add, as a piece
f social history, that drink is sold on the steps of the Church,
nd that the children involved are already set apart for the re-
gious life. Do you wonder that the atmosphere made me feel
nat there is much to be said for the anti-religious campaign of
oviet Russia? My friends of Antwerp all took it with bitter in-
ignation. They said that the effort involved in fighting the church
: every stage was intolerable and that in a Catholic country only
rastic social surgery could deal with its poisonous results. The
ttle I saw of this profiteering in miracles and its accompanying
ysteria made me feel they may be right.

My love and warm good wishes for '33.

Ever affectionately yours, H. J. L.

Devon Lodge, 21.I.33

My dear Justice: It looks as though we shall sail on the *Majestic*
n March 15; and I shall propose myself for a visit shortly after
e get settled in Cambridge where we propose to stay until I
ave to go on to Yale. I need not tell you how excited I am by
he prospect. It's more than I ever hoped to manage.

. . . I had dinner with Arthur Henderson, our late Foreign
ecretary, and learned much about the inner history of our crisis
f last year.[1] He made it clear to me that my own much-criticised
uess that the King was largely responsible for what occurred was
mply justified; and he wholly rebutted the allegation that Ameri-
an officials of the Federal Reserve Bank had interfered. Some
f his tales of MacDonald I must tell you when we meet; they
onfirm my impression that the politician is normally ruined not
y the pressure of his work but by the influence of the adulation
f his immediate environment. He spoke with great warmth of

---

[1] Arthur Henderson in October had resigned as Leader of the Labour Party
ollowing the action of the annual conference of the Party in adopting a reso-
ution committing it to a program of forceful socialist legislation if it should
btain office. The "crisis" of 1932, to which Laski referred, was presumably
he split in the Nationalist government which had led to the resignation, in
eptember, of ten Ministers who refused further to continue in a government
ommitted to the policy of governing through a ministry which had agreed
o differ. See, *supra*, p. 386. Other critical issues of the year had concerned
nemployment relief and the means test, the failures of the Disarmament
Conference at Geneva to which Mr. Norman Davis was Chief United States
Delegate, and the termination in December of the Hoover moratorium on
he payment of war debts.

Stimson as direct, sincere, and really eager for the big thing; and
with something like affection for Norman Davis. For John Simon
he had complete contempt.[2] Simon, he said, is a man with a big
mind on a small point and a small mind on a big one. He made
me feel pretty hopeless about the present international situation
not because he himself was hopeless but because the grounds of
his own faith in improvement seemed to me so fragile. But I have
rarely met a finer energy of character devoted to high ends.

I am busy trying to get a draft of lectures done for Yale
though I do not propose to write them out seriously until the
long vacation. I am going to talk about the economic basis of
law; and, as I hope, to talk sound commonsense of which you
will approve the method but not the result.

Our love to you as always.   *Ever affectionately yours, H. J. L.*
Don't omit to read F. Pollock's brilliant little paper in the January
L.Q.R.[3]

Devon Lodge, 19.II.3
My dear Justice: Your brief note moved me profoundly.[1] You can
imagine how eagerly I look forward to March. It lights up the
whole horizon.

The last week has been pretty full. Quite the most interesting
experience was a long talk at the House of Commons with an
eminent minister about America. I never quite realised before the
importance of imagination. He had a debt-plan and I think he
sent for me in the hope that I would give him unctuous confirmation. I had to say (I) there really is an American point of view
which you had better try to understand (II) you must not think
even to yourself, that Great Britain has been called by God to act
as his instrument and (III) the easier you make it for the President to command your point of view the more rational your proposals are likely to be. I assure you, with my hand on my heart
that all this came to him with the force of novelty. He saw the
economic devastation of this country; he was quite unable even
dimly to realise what it was like with you. . . .

Our love to you. Please be fit and well for the end of March
     Ever affectionately yours, H. J. L.

Devon Lodge, 4.III.3
My dear Justice: If I judge correctly the mysteries of the post
this ought to arrive just after your birthday. It brings you our love

---

[2] Sir John Simon was Foreign Secretary at the time.
[3] "The Snail in the Bottle, and Thereafter," 49 *L. Q. Rev.* 22 (January
1933).
[1] The letter referred to is missing.

and every sort of good wish. It is thrilling to think that in about
three weeks I shall be presenting them in person. I need not tell
you how I am looking forward to that.

I have been terribly busy since I wrote to you last. When one
has to go away, all the concerns of the world seem to fall on one's
head. I have had some public lectures, some talks on the wireless, two long cases on the Industrial Court, and a heavy spate
of work at the School. Somehow or other, in between, I have had
to find time to get my Yale lectures done. But they almost *are*
done, though I have found them a job. I must say one of the most
interesting experiences in doing them has been the completeness
of my discovery (you and I always agreed on that) that Pound
really is second rate. First I am dismayed by the inability on his
part to distinguish one idea from another, or a good authority
from a bad. Then I am surprised at his inability to distinguish
between description and cause. Then, I am baffled by the way in
which he makes his historical account lead up to categories and
then uses the categories as an explanation of the histories he has
summarised. And he so often can't see things that are just under
his nose. It is clear for instance that the common employment
doctrine arises out of the major premises of judges in a *laisser-
faire* society and is part of the mental climate of a society in
which capitalism is arrogant and determined in the protection of
its interests. Pound won't have this because it gives too much
away to the economic interpretation of law, which he dislikes. So
he tells one cumbrously that this won't do, and puts forward instead a theory of the ideal of free contract as its explanation.[1]
Could anything be more puerile? Of other things I have read, or
reread, with great pleasure Mathiez's *French Revolution,* and an
admirable book on the *cahiers* of 1789 by Chassin called *"La
génie de la R.F."* which is quite first-rate. Also as the Spanish
Government has asked me to lecture in Madrid in June I have
begun to read some Spanish history and law which is complicated
but worth the price of admission. It also pleased me by showing
clearly that a people always pays dearly for the acceptance of
religious domination. The fear of the Lord is the end of all wisdom is what the preacher really ought to have said.

We have had one or two jaunts. We went to dinner to Bertrand
Russell. . . . The most interesting thing was his vivid praise for
Leibniz whom he seemed to put above nearly all philosophers
except Plato. Then he spoke with great indignation of the metaphysical efforts of physicists like Jeans and Eddington which he
(I think rightly) denounced as unscientific humbug and pointed
out that the really first-rate people like Einstein and Max Planck

[1] See Pound, *Interpretations of Legal History* (1946 ed.), 109-111.

had definitely separated themselves from any such pronouncements. He gave us a most amusing account of his introduction
into the House of Lords where he was greeted as though a kind
of minor devil had wandered in by mistake. Another interesting
thing was a dinner at the Soviet Embassy.[2] I sat next to one of
those typically English aristocrats who will dine anywhere so
long as it is sure to be in the *Times* next day. She began by
telling me that she had been at the Palace the night before—if
the Bolsheviks had only had a good Tsar in Russia it all might
have been so different. Then she said that the crisis in America
was due to the fact that there were no old families to whom the
people could look for guidance. I ventured a hint of doubt whereupon she said that her view was that there was too much mingling
of classes in the modern world and that this gave the people the
idea that their views were important. Then she confided to me
that "friends in the know" had told her that a monarchical restoration in Germany was certain. She thought it very fine as it
would stabilise things. I asked her why and she said, "Well, because you know there simply must be stability." Then, sighing as
she gazed at the table, she thought it so terrible that the magnificent caviare we were eating was largely at the disposal in Russia
of people who didn't have the hereditary palate to appreciate such
delicacies. At this I laughed outright, I fear; and she said she was
afraid I was one of those terribly sceptical moderns who did not
realise that artistic taste was a function of ancient title. I asked
her if she liked the Velasquez opposite—a great thing from the
Hermitage. She then said she adored the Italian School. She added
that the King of Spain had a fine taste—did I know that good
shots were invariably first-rate judges of pictures? I said that might
be a good reason for making the annual rifle champion of the
army a director of the National Portrait gallery but this did not
commend itself to her. Then she told the Ambassador that Lenin
was a wicked man but she forgave him for his bravery; and the
Ambassador gravely said he would report the fact of her forgive-
ness to Moscow. Later he told me that her husband had been
one of the main organisers of anti-Russian propaganda in London
until he had been made a guinea pig director of a company
which traded with Russia and became an enthusiast who continually asked for free trips to the Caucasus "to inspect how our
fellows are doing." O God, O Montreal!

My love to you, dear Justice. Please keep very fit these next
weeks.   *Ever affectionately yours, H. J. L.*

---

[2] Since November 1932, Jean Maisky had been the Soviet Ambassador in
London.

192 Brattle Street, Cambridge, Mass., April 3, 1933
My dear Justice: The most important thing is to say that I propose, subject to your approval, to arrive in Washington on Sunday, April 16th and to have lunch and dinner with you that day. I must, alas, leave on Monday morning for New York and home. You will tell me whether I am to stay with you: that is exactly as you (and Mary) find it convenient. I can perfectly well put up at the Powhatan.

The ten days since we landed have been absorbing. Save for a day in New York we have been constantly with Felix here, and it has been a liberal education. He is in magnificent shape, full of drive and electric energy. And there is a mature wisdom about him which, without being new, is newly refreshed. I did not know how profoundly my emotional loyalties were engaged to him until these days.

Our plans are simple. We stay here until Thursday; then Amherst where I have promised Stanley King to talk to his lads;[1] then Yale for a week where I blow off steam about the law; then to you as the climax of a month brimful of stimulus. Do I need to tell you with what joy I look forward to those hours.

My love and my homage.

Ever affectionately yours, Harold J. Laski
I insist that your young man[2] answer this.

Devon Lodge, 7.V.33
My dear Justice: I have no words to express the joy I had in those hours with you. They were the kind of thing that gives life its richest flavour, and they remain with me as the climax of a month of days as happy as any I can remember.

Indeed I have never had a time so exciting and so stimulating as this last visit. Partly, no doubt, this was due to the incredible kindness of Americans. You are certainly a generous people with an hospitality that goes beyond anything I have elsewhere known. But I found also that my ideas were enriched in a way that leaves me full of anxiety to get leisure (not, alas, until August) to work out something of what I have learned. And it was grand to find that the old friends remain so completely friends. The relation with you and Felix above all is, my home apart, about the most precious thing there is in my life. It expresses poorly what I want to say; but you will understand what lies behind it.

---

[1] Stanley King was President of Amherst College.
[2] Holmes's secretary at the time was Donald Hiss, who had graduated from the Harvard Law School in 1932.

Since I came home ten days ago I have been plunged into a whirlpool of work. Mainly it concerns this quite terrible German situation, and the vast academic problem it has created.[1] It is so large and so tragic that the problem is to know just where one can begin. I have got my colleagues by a unanimous vote to give up five per cent of their salaries for three years to form a fund for endowing fellowships for the dismissed people; and now I am trying, with the assistance of other professors, to get all the British universities to follow the same road. It looks as though we may be successful; and if so I hope that we in England can take care of about one hundred of them. No doubt France and America will take a similar line; and it may well be, if we show energy and resolution, that we can make this German tragedy a turning-point at which men make a determined stand for intellectual freedom indifferently to the views in which it results. The letters I have from Germany are just horrible. It is as though a whole people was luxuriating in sadism. There is neither respect for persons nor for ideas. Mild liberals go out just as much as Jews and socialists. There has been nothing like it since the aftermath of the Revocation of the Edict of Nantes.

. . . Last night we went to a dinner with Sprague, the Harvard economist, who is now the technical adviser to the Bank of England. We had grand talk about the state of the world, pretty pessimistic, I fear, but the kind of talk which gives one wide perspectives. He was terribly disturbed by the American decision to inflate and I, who am hardly less so, found myself in the unwanted role of explaining the President with vigour to his most technically equipped critic. Did I by the way say to you in Washington that my main American disappointment was Walter Lippmann? He seemed to me to have worn terribly thin, and to be pontifical and dogmatic in realms where his knowledge and insight were lacking. I mention him because last night he was described by Sprague in vitriolic terms; and as Walter is now one of the main voices of American conservatism this attack from the inner citadel of financial orthodoxy interested me profoundly. . . .

Always yours affectionately, Harold J. Laski

Devon Lodge, 13.V.33

My dear Justice: A week of hard work, and of quite heart-rending visits from German academic exiles each with a tale of brutality beyond words. I think we are now moving rapidly towards an

---

[1] During April the Aryan decrees had been promulgated, ousting all Jews from their positions in the civil service, the academic world, and professional life.

ffective relief organisation for them, and some of the "stars" we
ave already managed to take care of; but it is the future of the
oung men that disturb me, and it isn't easy to see one's way.
et for the price of one second-class battleship one could assure
at for many years to come.

I have seen people endlessly all week. The most interesting talk
as with Stafford Cripps, the deputy-leader of the Opposition,
ho is an ex-Solicitor General and a great friend of mine. I was
nterested to find how eager he was for law reform on a much
ider scale in England—especially of the hierarchy of appeals, the
evision of the law of evidence, and the deliberate cheapening of
he cost of litigation. And he was emphatic that of the younger
awyers many are as eager as some of us outside the profession,
hat the opposition comes from the Bench, which dislikes the idea
f change, and the leaders of the bar who find things quite alright
s they are. He told me a good story of a lawyer who asked Alver-
tone, C. J. if he ever read books on jurisprudence. "No," said A,
I find that commonsense is all that is necessary." The lawyer
entioned in succession Maine, Dicey, Pollock, to find that Alver-
tone had never read a line of any of them and thought "the
terary line" was alright for the man "who couldn't make a success
t the bar." He also told me that he once quoted in Court *Mar-
ury* v. *Madison* to illustrate a point about the Australian Con-
titution and found that one noble lord had never heard of Mar-
hall and was inclined to dislike an attempt to introduce "foreign
urists" into a respectable court. . . .

Here, as you can imagine, we feel as though we were living on
he edge of a volcano. With the breakdown of Geneva,[1] and the
adness of Hitler, there is a general atmosphere of unreason
bout which is a kind of cynical revival of the war-psychology.
ew people even pretend to themselves that war can be avoided
nless there is a rapid and widespread recovery of trade and the
hadow of its coming looms over everything. There is a nervous
ension in the air which gives to rumour and unreason an authority
hey have not had for fifteen years. It is a grim spectacle to see—
ke nothing so much as watching the suicide of a culture which,
ith all its faults, has really represented about the best that hu-
an nature has so far been able to accomplish. It seems stupid to
estroy the foundations when one can with goodwill and deter-
ination reconstruct the house. But I have never realised so
ividly before the grim hold that a regime has upon its votaries,
nd how difficult it is to persuade them that there are times in the

---

[1] Despite a British effort in March to save the faltering Disarmament Con-
erence at Geneva no effective progress was made, and energies were dis-
racted by Mussolini's effort to secure a four-power pact, which was con-
luded in June.

history of the human race when it becomes a necessity to recon
sider first principles intelligently. Heaven knows what is to be th
outcome of it all; but I understand, for the first time with sym
pathy, why Candide was content to cultivate his garden.

My love to you as always. Please let me know when you mov
to Beverly Farms.   *Ever affectionately yours, Harold J. Lask*

Devon Lodge, 21.V.3
My dear Justice: The week has gone by almost before I ha
adequately realised it had commenced. The main thing is that w
have now really made a start towards helping the dismissed Ger
man professors. Next week we issue an appeal for a national fund
signed by every figure who matters at all in English academic life
and my colleagues at the School have made a start towards givin
the appeal reality by subscribing from the salaries of the staff
thousand pounds a year for three years. It's going, of course, to b
a big job, as there are already over two hundred people dismissed
But I hope all this will give a lead, and that between England an
America we shall make Hitler and Co. realise that freedom o
thought still remains a matter of importance if only to a significan
minority.

The most interesting thing I have done this week was to g
with Frida and Diana to a party given by some musical friends o
theirs. If you wanted proof that this was a pluralistic world tha
evening certainly provided it. Of the two dozen or so people ther
I doubt whether there were five who knew that anything existe
outside of music. All the values were musical; and one pianis
after having ascertained that I played no instrument asked m
with sincere bewilderment what I did with my time. I sat nex
to a German girl who sang really superbly. She did not know th
names of Roosevelt, Trotsky, Bacon, Spinoza, Rousseau; but sh
could tell you the biographical details of even the most mino
German musicians of the last two hundred years. I told Frid
that she had given me one of the most healthy experiences I ca
remember. I learned why the things that make me glad or angr
fail to make any serious impact outside a very narrow circle; an
why governments so rarely encounter resistance even to thei
major stupidities. Not the least interesting moment was when
asked a quite eminent musical critic if he thought that one coul
detect the strains and stresses of the present time in music that i
now being written. He obviously hardly knew what I was talkin
about and when I developed the theme he grew quite excited a
though he had been put on the track of a really important dis
covery. . . .

Roosevelt did a great job by his appeal on disarmament.[1] Heaven alone knows what will emerge from the present mess in Europe. But at least I think the possibility of salvation has been brought closer by his action.

I am off to Geneva for a few days on Saturday to lecture to the University. Meanwhile, my love to you as always.

Ever affectionately yours, H. J. L.

Devon Lodge, 13.VI.33

My dear Justice: It was grand to have word from you. But I don't want you to feel any compulsion to write. I can go on quite happily telling you what things drift my way so long as it interests you to hear them.

I am just back from ten very good days in Geneva. I lectured there at the University, and in the intervals between lectures saw my friends. The outstanding fact there was the isolation of Germany—one felt it pervade the whole atmosphere. They were like men living under a cloud and trying vainly to act with bravado in order to show that they do not care. But I thought it interesting to notice that during the sitting of the League Council, at which German treatment of the Jewish minority in Upper Silesia was condemned, the German delegate had to relight his cigar eighteen times to keep it going. I had some pleasant book-hunts there, and had one find that pleased me much, a copy of Blanqui's *La patrie en danger* in which the old revolutionary wrote a dramatic inscription. I also found a bookseller who had Gibbon's library for sale practically intact. He had found it in some Swiss Chateau where it had lain undisturbed for nearly 150 years.

I came back to a busy time—examinations and a good deal of quiet work in the background over the World Economic Conference.[1] I went to its opening which was rather pathetic. Some kind, insignificant words from the King and a futile speech by Mac-Donald. Your Secretary of State has made a very good personal impression. But I felt convinced that any great hopes from the Conference are doomed to disappointment. These big shows only succeed where the conference itself registers the result of precise and detailed preliminary work. Here, this is absent; and the field to be covered is so wide that it will, I fear, end like that of 1927 with a body of pious resolutions about which no one will do anything.

---

[1] On May 16 President Roosevelt had addressed fifty-four nations, appealing for disarmament and a new nonaggression pact.

[1] The World Economic Conference met in London from June 12 to July 27. The Secretary of State, Cordell Hull (1871-1955), headed the American delegation.

This apart, I have been busy with the dismissed German professors. After long efforts, I have persuaded our governors to take on three of them, one of whom the jurist Kantorowicz, I expect you know by name at least. It's a tragic business seeing them especially the younger men, and telling them one after another that you fear there is no opening. Some of them seem to me so first-rate, both in mind and temper, that I cannot even begin to understand how anyone could regard them as other than an honour to their country. And the distress is widespread. I have as you know, very little money; but I have felt that self-respect made it necessary for me to spend three hundred pounds of my own in relieving necessitous cases. Heaven only knows what the future holds for the children of these people—most of them quiet, inoffensive scholars whose only ambition was the chance to go on quietly with their own work.

You ask me about John Strachey's book—*The Struggle for Power*. My view of it is that on the critical side it is full of good things. I agree with his broad picture of the drift of civilisation. But on the positive side I disagree. I see no reason why there should necessarily be a communist victory. The breakdown seems to me more likely to result in a dark age of dictatorships without principle than in the triumph of any coherent body of principles. But that this civilisation drifts chaotically to its destruction seems to me the inescapable implication of the facts. Its contradictions cannot be resolved without an overturn of its foundations. Our business is to think out the planning of a new order. But there will be blood and tears before we attain it.

I have done a good deal of reading these days. First and foremost, I place Lauterpacht's *Function of Law in an International Community* (Oxford) one of the ablest legal books I have read in many a day. It's a little long and a little heavy, but a grand piece of work. Then a very interesting little book by Ensor called *Courts and Judges,* also an Oxford book, which is a comparative essay on the judicial systems of England, France and Germany, the kind of book I wish could be widely read by Judges. And through Felix I read Max Lowenthal's *The Investor Pays,* an exciting account of the receivership of the St. Paul R.R. in which the habits of Kuhn, Loeb emerge as the kind of thing making a communist philosophy seem intelligent and beneficent. And Lewis Einstein sent me his *Divided Loyalties.* I found its first part enchanting; after that I thought it somewhat tailed off. But it remains an admirable piece of work, admirably written.

I send this to Beverly in the belief that you must be there. I hope you will have the happiest of summers. I wish I could wander in to discuss once more the eternal verities.

Our love to you.　　　*Ever affectionately yours, Harold J. Laski*

Devon Lodge, 8.VII.33

My dear Justice: I have been rushed off my feet these last weeks so that I have hardly known where to turn. First, and most difficult, there has been a constant stream of German academic exiles, who have needed advice and money and all other sorts of aid. They are, as you can imagine, poor, bewildered people, who hardly know where they are; and merely to explain their own pathetic prospects to them without depriving them of hope is a bitterly difficult business. Then one of the blessed government committees on which I sit assigned the drafting of its report to me; I did not mind that so much as the endless time spent in discussing my draft with the members mostly on quite unimportant minutiae. Then I have had examinations and a series of committees of the Labour Party; and, as the *comble* of everything (this between ourselves) I got into the job of reconciling Litvinoff and Simon over the imprisoned engineers in Russia;[1] and though it came off really admirably it was a grim and exhausting process. I hope I am pardoned in the light of this programme.

One or two things are worth recording. A very pleasant dinner with H. G. Wells, at which, among others, was Walter Lippmann. It was curious to see him there. As an oracular monologist he was impressive; so soon as he was cross-examined *e.g.* by a great civil servant like Arthur Salter he emerged as feeble and vacillating. He did not really know; he had a body of prejudices, largely gained at second-hand, which he expresses so felicitously that only discussion reveals their very substantial weakness. Then an amusing lunch with the Webbs at which she tells Litvinoff that the reason the Russians are succeeding is because they have a religion. Litvinoff: "If you are using that word in an atheistic sense, Mrs. Webb, I think you are quite right." I also had Siegfried, the French publicist, to dinner. He is a very clever fellow. But he arrives at his conclusions by the most drastic selection of evidence I have ever seen a man attempt. His theories about America, for example, are true between Iowa and Arkansas for one set of premises, and for about two square miles of New York for another set. Whatever does not accord with them is rejected as atypical and therefore useless. But he is very able and pertinacious; and then summarising what he has heard in the form of a sweeping generalisation. Only I wish I felt as certain about my own specialism as he does about other people's. One or two things he said

---

[1] In March, six officials of the Metropolitan-Vickers Company had been arrested in Moscow, charged with sabotage. Five of the accused had been convicted in April, two being sentenced to imprisonment and three being sentenced to deportation. Sir John Simon, throughout the episode, had led the Parliament to take stern measures of economic reprisal. In June, Maxim Litvinoff, the Soviet Foreign Minister had come to London to the Economic Conference. On July 1, after negotiations with Sir John Simon, he announced that the two imprisoned Britons would be released.

amazed me *e.g.* that Brooks Adams was the most important American publicist since Hamilton, and that office confers less dignity of stature in U.S.A. than in any other great state. And I must not omit a visit from the Belgian socialist professor Henri de Man[2] who gave me a better description of Germany by comparing Hitler with Joseph Smith the Mormon than anyone I have met in these last weeks. . . .

I go off to Spain next Sunday for ten days; then back to Cornwall where we shall be for the whole of August. So I hope to get a genuine rest to be fit and active for Felix's arrival in September.

My love to you. Keep well and remember me warmly to Rockport.

Ever affectionately yours, H. J. L.

As from Devon Lodge, 6.VIII.33

My dear Justice: I came back from Spain last Monday after a fortnight there. It was a great adventure. I liked the people, and the scenery, and the atmosphere. The people were the English "gentleman" of legend—dignified, self-respecting, taking life as an exercise in leisure, and not a mean and petty thing we are to scramble through as we can.

. . . I had a very interesting time with the Prime Minister, Azaña,[1] a fine fellow, honest, strong, and with a resonant anti-clericalism that went to my heart. I liked immensely, too, the Foreign Minister, Dos Rios, lately a professor of law, and widely read.[2] He had that kind of generous-hearted liberalism which sprang from the best of the French Revolution. It was very interesting to see the consciousness in these people of being responsible for the making anew of a great nation. Heaven only knows what chance of success they have. My own temptation is to believe that, sooner or later, they will give way to Fascism; that their special brand of liberalism will be crushed between the pressure of two extremes. At least I felt confident that there was no danger of a return to Alfonso XIII. They are done for good with that particular brand of impotent hypocrisy. . . .

---

[2] Henri de Man (1885-1953), sociologist and socialist, Professor of Social Psychology at Brussels University; during the Nazi occupation of Belgium he renounced socialism and supported the Nazis. After liberation he was sentenced to twenty years penal servitude.

[1] Manuel Azaña (1880-1940) had been Premier in the Zamora government since 1931; on September 8, 1933, he fell from office, returning, however, as President in 1936. He provided ineffective leadership to the Republican government in the Franco rebellion and fled to France in 1939.

[2] Fernando de los Ríos (1879-1949), formerly Professor of Law at the University of Madrid, had been Minister of Justice and Minister of Education before taking over the Foreign Office in May 1933; in the later stages of his career he was Spanish Ambassador in Washington and, finally, Professor of Political Science in the New School for Social Research.

This is written from Cornwall where we are staying, as last
year, until the beginning of September. I am doing a little work
each day; but the country is so lovely, and the weather so perfect,
that I succumb too often to the fatal charm of idleness.

My love to you, dear Justice. Take care of yourself.

Ever affectionately yours, H. J. L.

As from Devon Lodge, 12.VIII.33

My dear Justice: A week of perfect peace—beautiful weather, no
telephone calls, and only a small discussion with a group of unemployed men at a camp to disturb me. Apart from reading and
driving, I have been working slowly at a paper on Brandeis for
Harper's—a kind of portrait of the man and his significance.[1] It
has interested me a good deal to work at it, and I think the necessity of straightening out my own ideas has made me understand
him better than I ever did before. The three things that emerge
for me are that he is really a Jeffersonian Democrat, trying to use
the power of the State to enforce an environment in which competition may be really free and equal; this I take to be an impossible task. Secondly, his method of analysis does magnificently
relate law to the life of which it is the expression; third his
criterion for all action is an ethical individualism. I take him to
be intellectually, as to ends, a romantic anachronism, but as to
methods a really significant figure in the Court. I doubt whether
he would have had the influence he has exerted if there had not
been your thirteen previous years there to form the channel for its
reception. But, granted that, I conclude that his contribution has
been that of a good and big man. A prophet, I suspect, rather
than a judge; a grand player for a side in which he believes both
disinterestedly and with all his might.

. . . I send you my love and the news that Diana next October
begins life at the School of Economics. Imagine that!

Ever affectionately yours, H. J. L.

Devon Lodge, 9.IX.33

My dear Justice: I have been back here not quite a fortnight,
though with an intermission in Clay Cross, helping Arthur Henderson with his bye-election, and one in Manchester to see my
people. I have been pretty busy, mainly getting a long article done
for a joint book with some friends (I hope to send it to you next
month) on the prevention of war,[1] and in helping these poor devils
of German professors who are now more numerous and more

---

[1] "Mr. Justice Brandeis," 168 *Harper's Magazine* 209 (January 1934).
[1] *The Intelligent Man's Way to Prevent War* (L. Woolf, ed., 1933).

tragic than ever. (Just as I write comes a telephone message to say that the historian Mendelssohn-Bartholdy[2] has been dismissed). It is a terribly grim world, in which, so far as Europe is concerned, I fear that Benesh is right in saying that war or revolution are the alternatives. The British government is completely supine. We can't even get them to raise the question of the treatment of the Jews at the League; MacDonald simply argues that it is a domestic German problem in which he has no right to interfere. Yet a generation ago, I do not doubt that Europe would have made the same magnificent protest they did against the Russian pogroms. Now we seem to regard it as something it is unnecessary to concern ourselves with. I wish I could tell you of the intensity of persecution there—torture, suicide to escape torture, murder; and yet the world is content to look on as though this may be regarded as part of the life of a civilised community. . . .

Our love to you as always. It is very pleasant to be home.

Ever affectionately yours, H. J. L.

Devon Lodge, 24.IX.33

My dear Justice: . . . It has been a crowded fortnight. The most interesting experience was a lunch at which H. G. Wells spoke on Intolerance—one of the ablest pleas for free discussion I have ever heard. I had very good talk there with Lord Horder,[1] who is not only our best general physician, but also MacDonald's specialist and an old friend of the P.M. He told me that twenty years ago he told MacDonald he had a superb constitution and that all his illnesses were a defence-mechanism to escape from some decision he wanted to avoid. He said that MacDonald's health is an almost exact function of the state of politics; he can be made ill whenever a difficulty occurs that he doesn't want to meet by sheer auto-suggestion, and no amount of persuasion is then effective. I also spoke at a vast protest meeting for the victims of Hitlerism. I wish you could have seen it. The thing that impressed and depressed me there was the sense that all over the world we are building parties who have not only ideas but ideas stirred into action by the grimmest of all passions—hate and revenge. To sit next to a German woman whose husband, a trade-union official, was literally beaten into pulp in front of her eyes was to realise the kind of future Germany is preparing for itself when Hitlerism breaks down. Last night I took the chair at a

---

[2] Albrecht Mendelssohn-Bartholdy (1874-1936), historian of modern Germany, in 1933 was awarded a lectureship at Balliol College, Oxford; author of *The War and German Society: The Testimony of a Liberal* (1937).

[1] Thomas Jeeves Horder (1871-1955), Baron Horder; distinguished physician to kings and statesmen.

centenary celebration of Bradlaugh—a very interesting occasion. But the most interesting thing was the history of the effort to have a ten-minute speech on the radio about him. After three months of negotiation the B.B.C. agreed that he should be mentioned on condition (I) that they chose the speaker (II) that his work for birth-control should not be mentioned (III) that he should be called a "freethinker" and not an atheist. Their original proposal, which the committee of course refused, was that they should discuss him only in relation to his fight for admission to the House of Commons. It is an interesting reflection on the power of organised religion that it should be able to get a religious service broadcast every day and three times on Sunday, and that when a really big person like Bradlaugh is to be commemorated its pressure should be sufficient to make the soft-pedal essential even to the mention of his name.

This reminds me that I have been reading with great interest a book by J. F. Hecker called *Religions and Communism* in Russia. This persuades me very convincingly that nowadays the main root of religious power is property and that once this basis goes, the power of the Church goes also with a bang. Aulard showed this was true of the French Revolution; and a very interesting book by an American named Bakke on the unemployed has just been published in which the author, whom I should judge to be a mild Liberal, says that organised religion in England, the Catholics apart, has no influence whatever on the lives of the working-class who regard it as simply an instrument intended to promote acquiescence in an established order. . . .

Books to buy I have not seen lately, at least at reasonable prices. I did see a grand copy of the Ellis and Spedding edition of Bacon, which I coveted, but the bookseller did not realise that this is a period of economic crisis and spurned my offer. However, tomorrow I go to Oxford (actually to discuss with Lady Margaret Hall the prospect of Diana going there next year[3]—imagine that!) and I hope to be more fortunate than I have been for some time.

My love to you as always.   *Ever affectionately yours, H. J. L.*

Devon Lodge, 10.X.33

My dear Justice: My main news is to tell you that we have seen Felix at Oxford, and he seems happy and comfortable there. He has a house like a small palace, all complete with servants, and from what I gathered his reception has been particularly warm. He and Marion both look very fit, and I think that if he does not try to do too much he will have a restful and creative year. You

---

[3] In 1938 Diana Laski received her B.A. degree from Lady Margaret Hall, Oxford.

can imagine what a joy it was to have first-hand news of you.

Term has begun, and, at present, I am simply drowned in a perfect ocean of students. One or two look promising, and I believe that I can get something started with them. I was amused by a Nazi student from Berlin who asked me whether I was a Jew, and, on learning that I was, explained that he could not work under me. I sent him along to a colleague who told him that, for his subject, (the sources of Hegel's philosophy of law) I was the only person from whom he could get help in England. So he complained despairingly that all the people who might help him in Germany had been dismissed and when he came to England for help he was assigned to someone with whom he dared not work! I was sorry for the lad, but his dilemma was really comic.

I have been up to Edinburgh. . . . In the evening I spent an hour at a vast meeting to commemorate the centenary of Charles Bradlaugh. When I left to catch my train an old gentleman came to me and said that as a boy of eighteen he had dined at James Russell Lowell's to go on with the latter to hear Bradlaugh speak; it was, I think, sometime in the late seventies. He also told me that in 1885 he heard Leslie Stephen speak to an ethical society, in Glasgow, and tell them that when America passed through a great economic crisis she would, with her energy and resilience, set an example in constructive determination to the whole world. I think that is a pretty piece of prophetic insight.

In the way of people, the most interesting thing to tell you of was a long dinner alone with Sankey. He wanted to consult me on the queerest problem I ever encountered. Perhaps you know that in the general economy move our judges' salaries have been cut ten per cent and there has been deep resentment about it owing to the doubt whether this is constitutional. One judge is so indignant that he has refused to pay his super-tax and challenged the revenue people to sue him for it. The latter appealed to Sankey who, on my advice, replied that as a judge he could not advise on whether a prosecution should be instituted or no: that was a matter for the Attorney General as the legal adviser to the government. So there the matter stands, about as curious a position, I think, as has ever turned up under our system of government.[1] I was interested also when I went to our Royal Commission on legal education and examined Lord Justice Greer to drive him into admitting that there was no serious legal education attempted by the Inns of Court. When I suggested that their vast

---

[1] The reduction of salaries had been voted in 1931; in July 1933 the judges had filed a memorandum with the House of Lords urging that their salaries should be restored. When their petition came before the Lords in November, Sankey, the Lord Chancellor, opposed the judges' petition, citing numerous prior instances on which the salaries of judges had been reduced. The Chancellor's position prevailed.

funds might not unjustifiably be used to create jointly with the universities law schools which might rival Harvard he said that he had often thought this might be a good thing to do but the Inns were terribly conservative and would resent the suggestion that the time for change had come. Practically he said in terms that the time for change had come but that one must force it on the lawyers if one wanted to do anything. A queer position to take up, which I think made his fellow-lawyers there pretty uncomfortable. . . .

Our love to you, dear Justice. Please keep fit and well for I want to come over to see you next year.

Ever affectionately yours, Harold J. Laski

Devon Lodge, 28.X.33

My dear Justice: I have been very driven these last weeks. A big bye-election in my own constituency here (which we won with a resounding majority) and the endless process of German refugees —a pitiful tale has taken up all my time. But I have managed to see something of Felix, and the first thing I want to tell you is that he and Marion are both well, and that (as was to be expected) he is a resounding success at Oxford. Not only has he a great crowd to his lectures, but he has made a very real impression on the dons; and I hear from all quarters the kind of accounts of him that warm a friend's heart. You and I, of course, knew that it would be so in a civilised place. But the unanimity and depth of conviction is a pleasant thing to hear. And I find him (need I tell you?) as electric as ever. In a grim and angry world it is good to have him alive.

I have been doing so much that I hardly know what to pick out to amuse you. But I think you would like most to hear of a very jolly lunch I had with Lady Oxford the other day. First let me say that she enquired with great warmth after you: "an old love of mine." Then we agreed on many things worth recording. First that Arthur Balfour masked a passionate love of power beneath a mask of nonchalance. We agreed that Lloyd-George was incapable of common honesty but that he was certainly the cleverest politician that this country has known since Disraeli. We scrapped pleasantly about America. For the most part the Americans she admires—like Theodore Roosevelt—I regard as tinkling cymbals; and though I admire Henry Adams's *History of the United States* I think his *Autobiography* a sophomore performance, full of the false profundities of which one ought to cease to be capable at twenty-five; but she thinks it a really great book which, *mirabile dictu,* she puts among the great autobiographies. For a woman of nearly seventy, she is an amazing creature—vivid, absolutely fearless, and with a pungency of utterance that is quite unforgettable. I had also a very interesting dinner with the German dramatist (now a refugee) Ernst Toller. He, too, is an unforgettable person, exquisitely simple, and, in the best sense, a free spirit. It was grand to meet a man who has my view of Heine as the finest soul in German letters. We agreed that though Goethe was the profounder man you cannot love him as you love Heine; not least because the latter knew how to hate his enemies. It was wonderful to see the complete absence of bitterness in Toller though he has been two years in prison and twice sentenced to death. He takes all this as the incidents of a career in much the same kind of way that one might take a poor reception for a book. I heard him tell of his experiences in prison and especially of the warden's slow conversion to the idea that he was not a criminal, but a man who happened to think differently from the existing *régime,* and the awkward realisation that differences in ideas ought not to involve cruelty of treatment. He pleased me too by his vehement denunciation of Shaw as a man who was never concerned to respect personality. That, after all, is the secret of a respect for freedom. For if, as Toller said, you are willing, as Shaw is willing, to impose your ideas on the world you take the right to persecute in your stride; and at that point it is clear that you lack sufficient confidence in the claim of personality to respect to be willing to argue with it. Once that is your position the line between your outlook and the Inquisition becomes terribly thin.

Of books the main thing I must do is to urge you at least to look at *Three Cities* by Sholem Asch—a translation from the Yiddish. I think it belongs naturally to the class of Dostoievsky and Tolstoy—the account of the Revolution, especially its pictures of bewildered adjustment to the unknown are, I think, not unworthy of the battle pieces of *War and Peace.* Then I read Winston's first volume on *Marlborough*—a really brilliant piece of special pleading, too special, I believe, as you can't make any statesman of that period into the saintly statesman for the simple but sufficient reason that no one is saintly in an age when men are gambling for their heads. I also read an old book—Tyler's *History of the Literature of the American Revolution* with great pleasure. There were Kings before Agamemnon Parrington.

My love to you dear Justice. Keep well. I shall send Felix back to you refreshed and eager. *Ever affectionately yours, H. J. Laski*

Devon Lodge, 17.XII.33

My dear Justice: I am afraid you have put me among the damned. But the truth is that I have been so drowned in work that I have hardly known where to turn. I have had a vast and difficult report to write for a government committee to which I belong; and what with German refugees, the Industrial Court, an article for the *Atlantic*,[1] and the normal academic work, I have only just been able to meet the problem of time. However, term is over; the worst pressure has relaxed; and I turn to you at once with the assurance of pardon for my sins.

I must give you news of Felix first. There is no doubt that he has made a profound impression. I hear that alike from dons and students in Oxford; and the others he meets, here and elsewhere, are all captured at once by his personality. And I think it has done him good. He looks rested and peaceful. He has a sense of perspective about things born of distance; and I think we shall return him to you in the summer with, so to say, increased horsepower. I need not tell you what a joy it is to me to have him here. We manage to see each other about once in ten days; and I get from him the old electric stimulus in a fully satisfying way. And I observe with special pleasure that he has the same effect on the best of my colleagues.

Things political are pretty bad with us; no one is deceived by the temporary turn in trade. And the new Germany is a terrifying portent—brutal, beastly, and belligerent. Some of the men who have come to me for help are figures of world-wide distinction now almost destitute. Others for whom I have been seeking help are in concentration camps; one man, for instance, is a specialist in ancient Chinese history and is there for having expressed sympathy with Chinese communism as the way of life most suitable to their historic conditions. The whole thing, not least the Reichstag trial,[2] is a perpetual nightmare; and the sense of helplessness one has as chaos comes ever more near is a grim experience. I have never seen a whole continent before drift with open eyes into a dark age.

Your secretary[3] sent me a charming letter the other week with an emphatic request for books. There are a few I want to urge on you which combine pleasure with instruction. First and foremost I put the *Age of Johnson* edited by Turberville (Oxford Press). I think you will find the chapters on travel, art, architecture, lawyers, booksellers and authors not less enchanting than I did. I have also enjoyed the new Lytton Strachey essays.[4] With one ex-

---

[1] "The Roosevelt Experiment," 153 *Atlantic Monthly* 143 (February 1934).

[2] The trial of Van der Lübbe and the four Communists, Torgler, Dimitroff, Popoff, and Taneff was currently in process before the Leipzig High Court, ending in the conviction of Van der Lübbe.

[3] Mark De Wolfe Howe, the scholarly editor of the first edition of these letters and Holmes's biographer, was Holmes's secretary at the time, having graduated from the Harvard Law School the preceding June [A.H.].

[4] Lytton Strachey, *Characters and Commentaries* (1933).

ception I don't think they are of the calibre of his first books; but
they are an expression of a first-class mind working with first-class
material. Then I enjoyed Brinton's *English Political Thought in
the XIXth Century*—clear-headed, very well written, and with a
(to me) pleasing ironic power; he is particularly good on Coleridge, Bagehot, Kingsley, Newman and T. H. Green. Of novels I
have had little experience these last weeks, though I read on a
night-train to Newcastle a good detective-story (I almost feel your
secretary's shudder) by Agatha Christie called *The Death of Lord
Egerton.*[5] And I emphasise again the quality of Sholom Asch's
Three Cities which I believe belongs with the stuff to which quite
permanent quality attaches.

I have had no chance to hunt books; and catalogues, for the
most part, have been either too expensive or barren. I did find a
very nice set of the *editio princeps* of Descartes; and a rather rare
volume of old Dean Tucker's tracts; but they can't be put in the
first class. My chief experience is a different one. There was a
famous early English socialist named Bray who, in the 'thirties,
published a *Labour's Wrongs and Labour's Remedies* which is a
classic of its kind. Nothing is known of him save that book. But
last week but one I was doing an industrial arbitration in Leeds
and wandered into the public library. I found there a mass of
papers relating to him which had remained untouched for nearly
forty years. It appears that about 1840 he got sick of failure and
migrated to Boston where he had a brother who was comfortably
off. The brother wrote home regularly to his mother in England
and from these letters one can reconstruct nearly fifty years of the
socialist brother's life. The letters were left to the library by some
donor and as the librarian had never heard of Bray he did not, of
course, know anything of his significance in the history of Marxian
socialism. But at least he catalogued the collection under the
name, and now we have made a grant to a clever young student
of mine to go and see what he can do with the manuscripts.

One other tale I must tell. A poor German scholar came over, a
man who had written good, if not first-rate books, and is about
75 years of age. He explained that for years he had wanted to
write a history of English political economy before A. Smith; he
had lost everything; did I think I could get him a grant to cover
his living costs for two years while he slaved at its completion.
With the caution of experience I asked him how much he wanted
to be comfortable. He said if he could have thirty shillings a week
he could manage very well. I got him two pounds and had difficulty in persuading him that he would not be extravagant in
taking it.

---

[5] This title has not been identified; perhaps the reference was to *Lord
Edgware Dies* (1933).

This should arrive by the New Year. It brings you my love, dear Justice, and warm good wishes.

Ever affectionately yours, H. J. L.

Devon Lodge, 26.XII.33

My dear Justice: I have had two days real holiday, and I almost begin to feel that I know what the quiet peace of scholarship is again. For I turned to 17th century French political thought and worked at a little book published anonymously in 1657 and called *Le politique du temps.* It is usually attributed to a writer under the Fronde named Davenne and all the pundits ascribe it to him like a flock of sheep. When I read it, I thought it seemed familiar, and after a morning's digging I discovered that it was a reprint of a pamphlet written about 1573 and published in the famous collection of Simon Goulart called *Mémoires d'état sous Charles IX.* Alas! the pleasure of original discovery isn't mine as Moreau the bibliographer noticed this in 1849.[1] But it is an interesting comment on the habits of historians that a book which is clearly sixteenth century in character should have taken them in. Obviously each copies the other's footnotes eagerly and embellishes them. The last of them describes it as the "ablest and most typical of the Mazarinades." I think it is really a good example of the vice of specialism. The modern people know their own little period and nothing else, so that the most elementary deception, even when it is a deception on its face, takes them in.

Then I have had a week of early bed with a huge dose of Gibbon; it is, I think, about seven years since I took a good look at him. He seems to me greater than ever—and Chapters XV and XVI [2] are greater in their power of erosion by irony than anything Voltaire or Holbach ever did. I am a little baffled as to how a man as selfish, as pompous, and as self-satisfied as Gibbon could have written so great a book. Incidentally, it seems to me that the clue to his whole atmosphere is partly in Bayle (who still needs *the* book to be written on his influence) and partly in Hume's essay on Enthusiasm which is surely the basis of the temper of those two chapters. I thought, too, that chapter 44 remains the supreme general account of Roman law.

I had also one good book hunt which was grand. Imagine a shop in a cellar in a slum near Houndsditch. The books were without order in vertical columns on the floor. The man might have been the offspring of a marriage between Fagin and Mrs. Gamp; for he was in a kind of perpetual moisture from gin, and he

---

[1] C. Moreau, *Bibliographie des Mazarinades* (vol. 2, 1850), p. 361.

[2] "The Progress of the Christian Religion" and "The Conduct of the Roman Government towards the Christians."

constantly shot round corners of the shop as though on guard to
see that one stole no books. I found all the contemporary pamphlets on the general warrants case, three of them being the personal
copies of Lord Camden and though they are not annotated, they
are underlined so that one can almost see the path his mind
travelled in writing *Entick* v. *Carrington*.[3] I also found three contemporary replies to Rousseau, and a nice little lot of anti-philo-
sophic pamphlets of the 18th century; but best of all I got for
seven shillings the complete set of Fréron's *Année littéraire*, much
the best of the anti-Voltaire journals of the age of Louis XV. Altogether I suppose I spent thirty shillings, and the effect produced on the bookseller was as though he had been visited by
J. P. Morgan. I was so dirty when I left that I asked him if I
could wash my hands. He took me down to his bedroom which
consisted of (a) a chair loaded with old novels (b) a camp-bed
covered with early nineteenth century plays and (c) a chest containing a vast collection of scrap-books and keepsakes mostly of
the time of George III. From under the bed he produced what I
first thought was a soup-tureen but which was in fact a utensil
for more private purposes. This he filled with water from a tap
in the yard, then from his waistcoat pocket he brought out a small
piece of soap, and, as a kind of climax to the whole, he took the
pillowslip off the pillow to provide me with a towel. Why go to
the Gobi desert or to Tibet for adventures? Is it not invariably
true that they lie at one's door? I knew exactly what the lower
reaches of Grub Street were like in the 18th century. I add that
I do not need to assure you how thoroughly I enjoyed myself.

By the time this comes out the January number of *Harper's*
should be out. Will you ask Mr. Howe to get you a copy and read
you a piece of mine there on Brandeis? I am anxious to know what
you think of it as it represents a real effort to paint the inside of
a really interesting character.

Felix and Marion came down for the night last Wednesday—
both well *and* very happy. I have never seen him look so well or
so peaceful. Oxford clearly gives him a real rest and he will be
physically a different person on his return to you.

I read the other day an interesting little book which is worth
noting—*Burke and Coleridge* by Alfred Cobban. It is the best
discussion I know of the lines of thought out of which conservatism as a real philosophy developed. You can see in it where
Hegel, Savigny and Maine all came from. And in a very different
line I read a Xmas present *Six Elizabethan Tragedies* by Webster,
Marlowe *et al.* which has a good critical introduction by the editor

---

[3] 19 State Trials 1030 (1765); Lord Camden held in that case that
seizure of books and papers taken while a defendant charged with sedition
was being arrested, was unlawful at common law.

George Rylands. His tracing of the line of descent of Tennyson's best passage in "Maud" is a beautiful piece of criticism, and the comment, in the last sentence of the introduction, is really quite masterly.[4] I also re-read Matthew Arnold's *Friendship's Garland* with infinite amusement and very considerable admiration. I gather that it is the fashion nowadays to decry Arnold as a critic; but I must say with emphasis that I know no one writing who has quite his body of ideas or his power of social insight. On the whole I think the Victorians did as good a job as any other age; and the present tendency to think them stuffy and complacent misses, I think, somewhere about two-thirds of the story.

My love to you as always,   *Ever affectionately yours, H. J. L.*

Devon Lodge, 6.1.34

My dear Justice: Your secretary's note was very welcome. As I told him, it looks as though I can get over to America in January of 1935; so please keep really fit for then. And I need not tell you how glad I was to know you liked my piece on Brandeis. It took much time, and I was not without anxiety about the result. . . .

We see Felix and Marion pretty continuously. There isn't much doubt that this adventure is doing Felix a world of good. He has lost the sense of strain he had when I was in America in the spring, and is getting a new perspective and peace of mind which are very good for him. And he is doing a very good job in making the elect realise the importance of America and the inner significance of the Roosevelt experiment. I need not tell you what a joy it is to have him on hand.

Our love to you as always.   *Ever affectionately yours, H. J. L.*

Devon Lodge, 28.1.34

My dear Justice: A long tale of work! and I don't see hope of a real leisure period until some of my lectures end in about a month from now. However I have finished one vast government committee and got out its report,[1] and a labour party committee on constitutional change seems also to be within sight of its goal. But it is hard work and I really long for the leisure to do some of my own writing.

Everything, however, goes well. I manage to see Felix about

---

[4] "The authors I have chosen are the six trials into a pathless jungle where sooner or later every reader loses his way." George Rylands, *Elizabethan Tragedy: Six Representative Plays (Excluding Shakespeare)* (1933), xix.

[1] The reference is probably to the *Report to the Minister of Health by the Departmentmental Committee on Qualifications, Recruitment, Training, and Promotion of Local Government Officers* (32-306), dated January 10, 1934, of which Laski was a member.

once a week, and to draw the refreshment you would expect from him. He is very fit and happy, and the change, clearly, is doing him a world of good. And as his house has become a kind of Mecca for the people doing law at Oxford I think he is really exercising some influence there—a real achievement as that is no easy thing in a place so self-sufficient as Oxford.

There are some books I want to recommend to you. First a French one—*Propos de littérature* by Alain. It has detached brief essays on Montaigne, Pascal and the like, and a remarkable power of hitting the jugular which would please you. Then an admirable book of critical essays by F. L. Lucas, a Cambridge don. He is specially good on Proust, and on modern criticism. One of the essays in which, *inter alios,* he tilts at T. S. Eliot and Herbert Read, the high-priests of the moderns seems to me done in the grand style or pretty near it. I also greatly enjoyed a little *Life of Milton* by Rose Macaulay, somewhat in the Lytton Strachey manner but built on a very real knowledge and full of *aperçus.* And, above all, I recommend J. E. Neale's *Queen Elizabeth* which is not only a work of great scholarship but also of real art. If I were reviewing it, I should say that the view taken is too simple, too much a study in blacks and whites, that the case against Mary Stuart isn't so clear, and that the Essex episode is far from being as simple as he makes it. But all in all it is a grand piece of portraiture a hundred times better than any other, and the proof that the real scholar can do the popular book on the big theme very much better than the elegant trifler who sits down to do a Freudian analysis upon the basis of a recovery of his schoolboy knowledge.

I have read other things without emotion. Eustace Percy's solemn pronouncement[2] seemed to me pontifical mysticism without power to distinguish between the essential and the unimportant; and I really don't believe, despite his persuasiveness, that Mussolini has discovered a new discipline which, by scotching political ambitions in the masses, enables them to devote their leisure to the discovery of their souls. . . .

The atmosphere here is very grim. Hitler grows worse; and it is evident enough that the long-term prospects for peace are bad. He has shown that persecution, ardently enough pursued, can in fact break the spirit of a people, and all its consequences are those pointed out by Aristotle in the fifth book of the *Politics.* Roosevelt and Russia seem to me the only two countries in the world where something is being done about which men are entitled to hope. We are in a bad way. There is no energy and no clarity of purpose. The government has nothing to say and its opponents lack the courage to say the things that need to be said. It is a tragedy, because among the masses is a confused stirring of

[2] Lord Eustace Percy, *Government in Transition* (1934).

pirit which could be turned to great ends under adequate leader-
hip. As it is one feels drift, complacency and apathy. Great things
o not, Micawber-like, turn up in civilisations; you have to go
ut and search for them in the high-ways and bye-ways. But I
o not see the politicians who are making the search.

My love to you as always. *Ever affectionately yours, H. J. L.*

Devon Lodge, 3.II.34

Ay dear Justice: The main thing of which to tell you this week
; Felix's address to the Institute of International Affairs—a body
.alf-eminent, half-expert to which it is far from easy to speak. It
.vas a discussion of the Roosevelt experiment and the Constitution,
.nd I thought it about as masterly a job as I have ever heard. He
.ad great clarity, simplicity, and directness. But, even more, in
.he discussion, in which there was much criticism and no little
.ostility, he really scored a triumph. He knew, of course, infinitely
.1ore than his critics; but to keep the audience in a mood where
:s sympathy was always on his side, and to show tact, and charm,
.nd discretion in keeping the ball rolling always to your oppo-
.ents' goal isn't easy; but Felix did it like a great artist and I
.at there, as you would have done, bubbling with pride. It's not
.verybody who can make an audience feel that *e.g.* poor Bernard
'haw is, of course very bright and brilliant as a rule, but that this
; one of his off-days, and the lecturer, who is a very kind person,
; letting him off nicely because he is an old man. I wish you
.ould have heard it and rejoiced with me in its consummate
.1astery and artistic excellence. . . .

Of reading there is not much to tell. I have been busy with
.olitics since I wrote last for causes with which you would emo-
.ionally agree and intellectually disapprove. The most interesting
.art of it has been arranging a private discussion between the
.tussians and Lord Cecil to see whether common ground for com-
.non action cannot be discovered to ward off the very real danger
.f a European conflict. I don't know yet where it will lead; but
.t least it is effort in a very good cause. And then I have been
.usy trying to raise money for some German academic exiles, and
.n persuading our never-to-be-sufficiently damned emigration peo-
.le not to put obstacles in the way of some of the poor devils
.rying to earn a living. My own feeling is that the kind of dip-
.omacy this type of effort involves is a fascinating combination
.f persuasion and blackmail. You tell the minister he is a great
.1an in one breath, while, in the other, you explain that if he
.loes not think your way you are going to make his name stink
.n the nostrils of all decent-minded people. He did give way and
.o five of them have jobs which will at least keep body and soul

together for them. I hope this will be accounted unto me for righteousness on the day of judgment!

My love to you.   *Ever affectionately yours, H. J. L.*

Devon Lodge, 1.III.34

My dear Justice: First of all, and above all, a very happy birthday. I wish that I could have dropped in for lunch. There is so much to tell that needs talk rather than the written word that the insulation of distance is unpardonable.

Life is terribly hectic. But oases like Howe's very kind last letter are welcome indeed. I'm glad you liked my article on Roosevelt. Whether he wins or loses I think it is one of the essential pieces of political courage in modern times; and it is absence of courage in democracies that is proving their destruction. And I am glad you liked my friend Neale's book on Elizabeth. I thought it was a pretty good example of the professional proving that, at least now and again, there is something to be said for knowing a subject before you write about it.

There seems no limit to the things I have been doing. Meetings to secure the release of Dimitroff (the world seems a cleaner place now that he is free),[1] meetings to protest against the wickedness of Austrian fascism and its massacre, the electoral campaign over the London County Council,[2] beside the endless stream of academic work. It is a grim time to live in with values all confused and doubtful, and most people afraid to speak forthrightly about anything. I fear we are in for an iron age in which the chances of decency will be small; and it is not going to be easy for those of us who think that the claims of reason against passion are paramount. But I suppose no civilisation can confront its most basic problems without uncovering the naked savage in man. Decency seems to be a very thin and fragile covering at best.

In the way of reading there are several things I want to recommend. Ernst Toller's autobiography *I Was a German* is a beautiful book the charm of which will, I am sure, capture you as it did me. I was impressed also by Charles Beard's *Idea of National Interest* which I thought a most useful disentanglement of a complex notion. I also enjoyed a volume of critical essays by G. W. Stonier called *Gog and Magog*, and another very amusing collection by Ivor Brown called *I Commit to the Flames*. These, I think, all have the right mixture of light and idea which you require

---

[1] Georgi Dimitrov (1882-1949), following his acquittal of the charge of firing the Reichstag, went to Russia.

[2] Laski was elected Alderman of the Metropolitan Borough Council of Fulham.

More solid but illuminating is Alexander's *Beauty* which would I think interest you for its account of the artistic process and the relation of value to beauty.

Felix and Marion flourish. He goes ahead like a house on fire and I think makes an impact everywhere such as you and I would wish. Of his Cambridge lectures a colleague wrote me "that quite unquestionably they were the most distinguished performance in Cambridge in years," and a talk on the wireless enchanted Diana not less than Frida, both of them grimly critical judges.

I must not omit my pet discovery of the moment; one day, if I get a fortnight of real leisure, I will write it all out in detail. I have found that Sieyès's constitution was built almost wholly on Spinoza's *Tractatus politicus.*[3] I have found 26 separate institutions so identical down to minutiae that the resemblance must be born of influence. Of course I can't prove it in the full sense. But I think I can show that the identities are too great to be capable of explanation on grounds of chance. And another curiosity has come my way. The conspiracy of Rohan against Louis XIV for which the former was executed[4] produced a plan of constitutional reorganisation for France which also has many resemblances to Spinoza's ideas. Now I find that Rohan's adviser was Van den Ende who taught Spinoza Latin and I wonder if (a) that is the source of the connection and (b) if Spinoza who corresponded with V. der E. to the end of his life was cogniscant of the plot. It is a pretty mystery story, unworked out, so far as I know.

Well—again a happy birthday, and my love as always.

Ever affectionately yours, H. J. L.

Devon Lodge, 16.XII.34
My dear Justice: I will not apologise for my long silence. I merely ask a generous man to forgive. I now resume in the old style and with undiminished affection.

It is a terribly busy year. Academic business apart, I am trying my hand at being an alderman on our local borough council. Partly I am trying to make its public libraries be what they ought to be; and, partly, I am trying to reorganise the local civil service on lines which will give it some drive and efficiency. It's a dog's work; but I think it is worth while. And I have written a book which I hope to publish in April,[1] which won't, I fear, be popular

---

[3] Abbé Joseph Emmanuel Sieyès (1748-1836); his first contribution to constitutional theory was in his pamphlet, *Qu'est-ce que le tiers-état?* (1789); his greatest, was his draft of a perfect constitution after the *coup d'état* of Brumaire.

[4] Louis de Rohan (1635-1674), the scandalous Chevalier de Rohan, after his conspiracy with the Dutch was beheaded by Louis XIV. Franz van den Ende was also executed for his participation in the same conspiracy.

[1] *The State in Theory and Practice* (1935).

with the eminent but is at least as realistic an account of what the state is like as I can get down on paper. It all takes time; and as I am drowned amid students, especially the poor devils of *émigrés* from Germany, I do not always know how to avoid being overwhelmed.

It is a bad Europe just now. I don't agree with the alarmists who see war just round the corner. But the seeds of war are there, and they are sprouting. And I don't think it can seriously be denied that Fascism grows. One sees it gaining ground month by month in France, and Hitler's grip on Germany is at present unbreakable. Our government is a bad show, with no real foreign policy, no power to co-operate with America (the one thing that should be the pivot of any sane British policy) and with no mind to embark on any creative domestic adventures. I think myself that we shall have a general election next July, and I hope then that there will be a better House of Commons.[2] But as things are the case for representative government goes by default. People learn from inaction to doubt Parliament's power to tackle things decisively, and you find, too widely and too unnecessarily, a temper of apathy that bodes ill for a political democracy. We need leadership and we are not getting it. That, I think, is always a bad state of affairs. I feel as I travel around that I understand the epoch which led to the French Revolution. We need a remaking of foundations, and that is an adventure which the guardians of the old order are not prepared to attempt. The great consolation, of course, is reading and work. Some books have recently appeared which I should like very warmly to recommend. Have you read Crane Brinton's *Decade of Revolution* (Harper)? I think it a brilliant panorama, scholarly, detached, imaginative. I hope you will persuade your secretary to embark upon it. And I enjoyed Croce's *History of Europe in the 19th Century* (Harcourt). It is a little too "liberal" for me; but is a profound book, with style and colour in it. And I do beg you to read H. G. Wells's *Autobiography*. I don't put it in the class of S. Augustine or Rousseau. But it is not much below them—a really truthful picture of an extraordinarily fertile mind. It is terribly interesting, too, as a picture of the inherent weaknesses of the intellectual, his vanity, his inability to cooperate, his lack of the power of endurance and persistency which alone gets things done. Wells is like a butterfly which flits from one flower to another, never staying long enough at any to sense its beauty. But it is the tale of a big man who has had his insights into the universe. In the way of fiction I can only recommend the new Wodehouse *Right Ho, Jeeves* which is in the supreme tradition. A really good detective story has not come my way for months.

---

[2] The next General Election did not occur until November 1935.

All your friends are well. Pollock I have not seen, but I have
met those who have and they give a picture of unfailing vigour.
I did meet Leslie Scott, busy and well. I have seen a little of
Bertrand Russell. . . .

I miss Felix greatly, as you can imagine; he lent a special charm
to Oxford and almost galvanised it into life. He appears to retain
deep faith in the New Deal—more, I imagine, than I can permit
myself. But he can't outdo me in admiration for Roosevelt as a
person even though I don't believe he can succeed. America excites us all as never in my lifetime. Even at this distance one has
a sense of something big being tried; and the superiority of effort
to our policy of do-nothingism is immeasureable. I was glad to see
that Harvard's new President did not shrink from making clear his
attitude to Pound. There is one of your real victories, for I remember that as far back as 1916, when Felix and I were still
under the spell of his learning, you were sceptical of its significance. You were right and we wrong . . . I hear occasionally
from Brandeis, and he never fails to give me news of you.

I must not omit to tell you that one of my great pleasures in
these last months has been J. B. Atlay's *Victorian Chancellors*.
Have you ever read it? The chapters on Brougham, Campbell,
and Westbury are superb. And the story of the latter meeting
Mme. de Genlis who informs him that she keeps all her male
books in one bookcase and her female books in another, to which
he replies "Ah, madame, you do not then propose to add to your
library" is alone worth the price of admission.[3]

I give you warning now that early in April I hope to descend
on you. I propose to take off a month in America and I needn't
say that a visit to 1720 is an essential object of my programme.

Our love to you. This letter ought to arrive about Xmas. I hope
it will bring you peace and energy for the new year.

Ever affectionately yours, H. J. Laski

Devon Lodge, 24.XII.34

My dear Justice: This is one of those grim weeks in which you do
an accumulation of irritating nothings, which keep you busy with
no results to show. I have been buying Xmas presents, examining
Ph.D.'s, trying to persuade the Lord Chancellor to abolish imprisonment for debt,[1] correcting the proofs of my book, and doing

---

[3] The editor has not found the anecdote in Atlay's volumes.
[1] In July 1934, the Home Department had submitted its *Departmental
Report on Imprisonment by Courts of Summary Jurisdiction in Default of
Payment of Fines and Other Sums of Money* (*Command Papers* #4649). In
1935 legislation was adopted, along the lines recommended in the Departmental Report, curtailing substantially the power of courts to imprison
debtors; 25 & 26 Geo. V, c. 46.

a chapter on committee government for a volume to celebrate the centenary of the Municipal Corporations Act next year.[2]

I have found some nice books, if rather out of the way. They are more or less contemporary criticisms of Grotius, works of the natural law school which culminated in Thomasius in the 18th century. I found them in Edinburgh where I had gone to give a lecture. And at four shillings a volume I thought them cheap and interesting. Also I picked up a very nice letter, seven pages long, of old Jeremy Bentham. It is a draft of a petition to the Prime Minister about Panopticon, a preparation on his part to try and get his money back. The old man sputters sparks admirably, with hints at a conspiracy of the great to prevent him from receiving compensation. Evidently he did not send it. But it is pleasant to see how human he was.

In the way of reading a number of things worth comment. You will not read the selected *Correspondence of Marx and Engels*. But they are very interesting letters. The two are unpleasant— acrid, contemptuous, harsh. They are not very good (who is?) at short-term political prophecies. But in long-term diagnosis they deserve a medal; and there is a letter from Engels on the basis of social change to one Schmidt which deserves to be called really masterly.[3] Then I have read a book by an American scholar, Miss Whitney, on *Primitivism and the Idea of Progress in the 18th Century* which deserves high marks. She is a little *simpliste* as (forgive me!) some of the Americans tend to me [*sic*]. If a man like Adam Ferguson,[4] for instance, runs the ideas she is looking for her critical faculty deserts her, and she shouts a eulogy instead of recognising him for the pinchbeck Montesquieu he was. But she has dug up well a mass of to me unknown stuff, some of it really significant. Then a charming book on Condorcet by one Schapiro of New York. Even he cannot make him more than very good second-rate. But he has painted his picture well, and the book sustains interest all the way through. All this, say you, is very highbrow stuff, suitable only to those relentless academic people who spend their lives in that state of resentful coma they too easily regard as research. Like Ireton, you demand more blood, and, by God, sir, you shall have it. I commend to you two shockers and one "straight" novel. The first are (I) *The Sittaford Mystery* by Agatha Christie, good at least in the sense that my villain was a blameless innocent at the end; and (II) *He Laughed*

[2] "The Committee System in Local Government," *A Century of Municipal Progress, 1835-1935* (Laski, Jennings, and Robson eds., 1935), 82.

[3] Engels to Conrad Schmidt, October 27, 1890, *Karl Marx and Frederick Engels: Selected Correspondence 1846-1895* (Torr, ed., 1934), 477.

[4] Adam Ferguson (1716-1816), Scottish historian and philosopher; author of *Principles of Moral and Political Sciences* (1792), *Essay on the History of Civil Society* (1762).

at Murder by Richard Keverne, which is the thriller rather than the detective story proper, but well-written and with those breath-taking moments wholly appropriate to quiet lives like yours and mine. The straight novel is *Elizabeth* by Frank Swinnerton which both Frida and I thought charming—characters alive, no damned Joyceism or Eliotism or any of those new modern patterns which I find so abhorrent. And I commend a volume of short stories by Winifred Holtby called *Truth is not Sober* as the ideal accompaniment for solitaire. They are not only witty: they are also malicious. I take it that you will find an invitation in the emphasis of those adjectives.

Of people there is not much to tell. I had lunch with Lady Oxford, who enquired eagerly after you. She is as brilliant as ever, with a certain mellowness which is attractive. I find Elizabeth (Bibesco) a little trying. She is so full of what she said to eminent men in far-off places about nothing in particular that you can't help feeling that you are listening to extracts from a velvet-bound diary of a highly artificial society to which you have no desire to belong. Mackenzie King, the Canadian liberal leader, was there.[5] I thought him dull and unctuous, continually emitting truisms with a heavy air of profundity *e.g.* "on the American continent Mr. Roosevelt is undoubtedly a popular figure." There were moments, my dear Justice, when I felt it quite difficult to be polite. I went also to a dinner at the Russian Embassy where I met the aviators who had rescued Schmidt and his colleagues from the ice-floes by which they were imprisoned.[6] They told one of those heroic stories in the face of which one is simply silent because words are meaningless in relation to adventures of that kind. I had the same emotion that one has in reading the diaries of Captain Scott on his last expedition. And I must record the visit of a Chinese who came to ask me to lecture in Pekin. He was uncertain of his English and therefore asked permission to read what he wished to say. He began "O most eminent professor" in superb oriental style, compared me with Hegel, Marx, Proudhon, F. H. Bradley, Bosanquet and Lester Ward, and ended by saying that, "were you to come generations of Chinese students yet unborn would greet you as their father." Now what do you make of that? I could not tell him that it was a direct invitation to break the sixth commandment, and I could not make my secretary (who is terribly young) refrain from giggles. But at least

---

[5] William Lyon Mackenzie King (1874-1950); Prime Minister of Canada, 1921-1930, 1935-1948.

[6] In March and April Russian planes had rescued Professor Otto Schmidt and his 101 companions who had been stranded on an ice pack northwest of the Bering Strait for some two months after the sinking of the Soviet ice-breaker, *Chelyuskin.*

you will admit that this is one of the minor compensations for the pursuit of an academic career.

My love to you as always, dear Justice. Please keep fit and well.

Ever affectionately yours, H. J. L.

3.I.35

My dear Justice: Your telegram warmed my heart. And I found it on returning from Antwerp to an empty house sixteen hours late through fog in the Schildt. That was a real welcome.

I wish you could have been with us in Antwerp. First there was a marvellous exhibition of Brueghel and James Ensor (please get from the Library of Congress the *Catalogue raisonée* of his etchings) which was a feast. Then I met an old Jesuit there who was a trump. He had been forty years out in China and had come home at eighty five to finish a grammar of Chinese dialects in comfort. I hope I explain myself when I say that he was one of those Jesuits who had ceased to be interested in dogma and was simply a civilised gentleman. His consolations in China were (I) Seneca—the most human, he thought, of all philosophers; (II) Tacitus who saw more deeply into the habits of rulers than any other writer, and (III) Gibbon (in a Flemish translation) because Gibbon belonged to "the best of all centuries when men still hoped to make reason triumph over passion." He told marvellous tales of heroism among simple people—the peasant who carries his wife fifteen miles to a hospital to be confined; a doctor who walks all night through the snow to attend a village stricken with fever; a village of poor folk who all subscribe to send a bright lad to Pekin because he showed aptitude for letters and maybe would become a sage bringing honour to the village. I saw in him that kind of wisdom which is born of infinite loneliness and infinite understanding. He said that what impresses him in the Europe he has recovered is that it expresses so exactly Goethe's word *Sehnsucht*, which I translate by the Scottish "wearying"—a sense of longing for things it knows to be good yet does not know how to attain. He said fine things like his belief that the best type of human being is he who consciously surrenders power over other beings lest he be poisoned by pride of authority. I have rarely met anything so impressive as the old fellow, and he was as physically beautiful as he was spiritually exquisite.

In the way of reading, I have not much to tell. I reread Zimmern's *Greek Commonwealth* there and thought it better than ever before, with a sigh in remembering that he will never write such a book again. I read Brandeis's new volume,[1] powerful and

[1] *The Curse of Bigness; Miscellaneous Papers of Louis D. Brandeis* (Fraenkel, ed., 1934).

e expression of a noble passion, but, to me, unsatisfying because
was like the pronouncement of a believer in the Ptolemaic as-
onomy that the new Copernican world will not do. There's noth-
g at all in this desire to return to the simple verities of Jeffer-
nian Democracy. Then I read the new translation of Engels's
euerbach, which you will not read, but which is, especially in
s treatment of the social sciences masterly, not least in its em-
hasis (which O.W.H. will consider sympathetically) that the
ue to legal doctrine lies in its economic context. And I re-read
anity Fair which I thought nearly A-1 though I resented some
the not quite open moralising, and Trollope's *The Way We
ive Now* which I thought definitely remarkable, even, in its way,
n the level of all but the very best of Balzac. (There is no
igher praise.) Frida, I add, read for the first time Zola's *Germi-
al* and ordered me to put in a special word that it was immensely
npressive. I did not think so ten years ago; but I might revise
y view today. I also read on the boat *After Strange Gods* by
. S. Eliot which I thought artificial and snobbish and devoid
f any real insight even though I know I ought not to speak of
eminent a minor prophet in this way.

I combed Antwerp for books, but in vain. But tomorrow I go
Paris for the week-end, and I hope for victories over the mon-
rous regiment of *bouquinistes* who will not bring down their
rices even in this time of crisis. It breaks one's heart to get a
atalogue which contains an unpublished letter of Voltaire all
bout Hume and D'Alembert and Rousseau, seven pages long. I
m in favour of a state right of eminent domain in these matters.
nd I noticed in a sale that a collection made by Lanson of those
naginary voyages I collect so assiduously was bought by a Greek
nillionaire who specialises in the manufacture of date boxes. Sir,
hat makes for Bolshevism! He has from a scholar's energy the
ruits of a lifetime's collection which he buys to have a social
achet. It will not do!

I am having an amusing time with the Lord Chancellor just
ow trying to prevent him putting an age-retirement for judges
nto his new Bill. I note with amused pleasure that some of the
est work in the law is done after 75; that as a rule the younger
inglish judges have not been the most successful; that the older
udges are not a whit less radical than the young. (It isn't so
vith statesmen.) But it is good for Sankey to be hot and both-
red.

My love and every sort of good wish.

Ever affectionately yours, H. J. L.

20.I.3

My dear Justice: At least my brother's visit to America brough
me personal news of you. I was grateful for that. And I wa
pleased to find that he emerged therefrom with a healthy respec
for all those in Washington to whom my affection is vowed.

The first week of a new term is always irritating. You are a
half-cock instead of in the middle of a routine. But this week ha
been notable for at least one thing. A German student of min
read in my seminar a paper on Ames[1] which I thought a master
piece. I don't know what you would have made of it, as I, curi
ously, have never heard your view of Ames. I am an anti, on th
ground that though, clearly, he had real learning, he had no gen
eral principles by which that learning was informed. This lad, a
émigré, took on the job in his stride, and speaking from notes
did as clear and concise a piece of demolition, as I have eve
heard in a seminar. I don't expect it would have pleased Feli
to whom Ames is still a hero; but I thought it among the two o
three best academic experiences I have ever had.

Otherwise it has been the usual kind of week, enlivened only b
a political meeting at Canterbury in which I had the unusual ex
perience of having the Dean for my chairman. He was so kin
about me in his opening remarks that I told him it only remaine
for me to speak with the archbishop in the chair for my critic
to detect the sprouting of my wings. And I went to dinner wit
Sankey to hear the long tale of his woes. Lawyers are bad peo
ple who don't show an appropriate interest in law reform. I tol
him to introduce his reforms first and consult the profession afte
wards. And it was amusing to hear his account, for it showed tha
there are just the same evils at our Bar as in yours only that w
manage to gloss them over with a subtlety from which you ar
(wisely or unwisely) wholly free. I think Sankey not wholl
happy; and I should guess that he finds his seat in the cabine
less and less satisfactory. It is his own fault; for he should hav
had the courage to resign when the P.M. began to side-track hi
activities. . . .

One other tale I must tell. A colleague of mine was speakin
with some sharpness of Ramsay MacDonald's new passion for th
rich which expresses itself especially in a friendship for Lor
Londonderry, "Ah!" he said, "MacDonald has still to learn tha
you cannot sing the Internationale to the Londonderry air." I
wish I had said that.

My love to you as always.   *Ever affectionately yours, H. J. L*

[1] James Barr Ames (1846-1910), legal historian and Dean of the Harvar
Law School, 1895-1910.

29.I.35

My dear Justice: It was good to have news of you from your
young man.[1] I hope he will not mind every few weeks sending
me a word. I value it greatly.

I have had a busy week. A visit to Swansea, where I had to
make a speech. A mass of committee meetings, all of them necessary, but (I think) most of them insignificant. And students! On
the average my secretary tells me that I interview fifteen each
day and the variety of need, from a simple bibliography to a
request for a subject for a book is a grim business. Add to that
lectures, and the need to get some real work done, and I think
on the whole I am entitled to my holiday in America.

I had one meeting last week that would have amused you. In
the public libraries of the borough I am having special rooms
constructed as special reading rooms for children. I put forward
my estimate which was fiercely attacked by the opposition. A
bluff real estate deal [*sic*] explained that he must oppose it as
he thought separate rooms for children wanton extravagance. I
pointed out that this was now standard library practice: 26 out
of 28 London boroughs had them already. Then a gallant rear-
admiral said that he observed from the figures that I proposed
to spend three thousand pounds on rebuilding and six hundred
pounds on equipment. This was an unpardonable waste of the
ratepayers' money. He must, in his conscience, make his protest
against it. I thereupon interjected that if the gallant admiral would
be so kind as to refer to the estimate again I thought he would
agree that the three thousand and the six hundred to which he
referred were square feet and not pounds. After that my estimate
(which was in fact for four hundred pounds) went through without any further criticism!

In the way of reading one or two things are worth recording.
A (to me) unknown P. G. Wodehouse called *Uneasy Money*
which I thought in the classic tradition. A very good and very
short book called *Morals and Politics* by E. F. Carritt which puts
the general problem with point and acuteness. A symposium
called *The Meaning of Marx* edited by Sidney Hook which contains a brilliant essay by him for most of which I would go bail
and one by Morris Cohen upon which I would be prepared to
attack him for very nearly every sentence.[2] Then a quite marvellous attack on Russia by one of these economists whose writings
are really an account of the mental limitations of the expert.[3] He

---

[1] James Henry Rowe, Jr., had come to Holmes as his secretary in October
1934.

[2] "Why I Am Not a Communist," *The Meaning of Marx* (Hook, ed.,
1934), 91.

[3] Boris Davidovich Brutskus, *Economic Planning in Soviet Russia* (with a
Foreword by F. A. Hayek, 1935).

defines economics as the alternative choice between scarce means to achieve maximum satisfaction. He seeks to explain marginal utility (he is a German). The English workman, he says, with an air intended to show you what a finely realistic observer he is, gladly gives up his third or fourth glass of beer to buy himself a frock coat or an evening dress for his wife. I suppose there are still people who have inherited a frock coat from their Nonconformist grandfathers, but they must be marvellously few. And the book is introduced by my eminent colleague Hayek (of whom Keynes admirably said that he has the most distinguished muddlehead in Europe) with a preface explaining that the great value of the book is its author's special knowledge of the habits of the working class! Oh God, oh Montreal! I don't wonder that the public does not take the economists very seriously. For lectures I must add that I have re-read Rousseau's *Confessions*, once again with infinite admiration for its art and its general truthfulness. With all his frailties he was a supreme artist. The description of meeting the girls in the cherry-orchard is surely among the dozen most exquisite idylls in literature. . . .

We all send our love. As an incident I add that I thought Cardozo had much the best of the argument in the oil case.[4]

Ever affectionately yours, H. J. L.

17.II.35

My dear Justice: I have been over half England since I last wrote to you, speaking at Bristol, Swansea, Burnley and Durham for a cause you would not bless to audiences you would have found exciting. Imagine near Durham speaking to 300 Dalesmen who come in from the hills with their storm-lanterns and their sheepdogs and sit there grim and gnarled asking one questions for two hours with never even a grunt to display their feelings. Or the old man at Bristol who asked me what I thought of Carlyle. I expressed a qualified admiration. He struck his stick on the ground and exclaimed with a vigour I cannot convey, "Sir, he teaches a man the glory of self-respect."

In the way of reading I have some recommendations. If you have not read it, I think you would enjoy *The Roman Hat Mystery* by Ellery Queen; at least it baffled me completely as neither of my candidates was finally arrested. Then a superb little book *Ethics and Politics* by E. F. Carritt (Oxford) which analyses the

---

[4] *Panama Refining Co.* v. *Ryan*, 293 U.S. 388 (Jan. 7, 1935). A majority of the Court, over the dissent of Cardozo, J., determined that there was an excessive delegation of power in those sections of the National Industrial Recovery Act under which the President had prohibited the transportation in interstate and foreign commerce of petroleum products produced in excess of state quotas.

main theories of their relation from Hobbes onwards with a clarity
and skill which leave me envious. And I have had joy beyond
words in the three volumes of Diderot's letters to Sophie Volland.
There is one of the half-dozen most attractive human beings in
the record—all the qualities one wants from hatred of unnecessary
pain, through fire in the belly, to that penumbra of decent vulgarity that is a necessary part of the whole man. His descriptions
of the dinners at Holbach's are simply enchanting. I have also
read with profit, not unmixed with pain, Commons' *Institutional
Economics*. His own theory seems to me bunk; but his accounts
of Locke, Turgot, and Adam Smith do, I think, throw genuinely
new light on the ideas of each by the manner of his approach to
them. Finally I beg to recommend a novel about contemporary
Italy called *Fontamara* by one Silone which is superb. The ability
to make a farcical comedy the vehicle of simply first-rate political
satire is rare indeed; and this comes off with a vigour and gusto
that will delight you. Please do not fail to have it as your accompaniment to solitaire.

I must tell you, too, of a night in Oxford. Imagine the high
table at Christ Church in which the guest is flanked by the professor of pastoral theology. . . . The guest asks what exactly pastoral theology is: before he can reply, a young don across the
table defines it as "the study of foot and mouth disease in the
clergy." Then a discussion of the government and the queer relations of MacDonald to the Tories. "Ah," said my young don,
"he cannot go on trying to sing the Red Flag to the tune of the
Londonderry Air." A little later the talk turned to the sins of a
youth in the college named Price who, being drunk in charge of
a car, when charged at the police station agreed that he was
drunk and with great vehemence offered to fight any constable
who thought him sober. "In fact," said my young don, "Price
ceased to pay to virtue the homage of hypocrisy." And all this in
one evening from a lad whose specialty is vector analysis. I did
not previously believe the young mathematician had so much
blood in him.

In the way of book-hunting I have not much to record. I found
some nice sixteenth century criticisms of Machiavelli which I was
glad to have, and a small collection of pamphlets on the law of
libel in the 18th century—the issues which led up to Fox's libel
act. But at present the depression has led to a lull in the book
world and apart from the obvious rarities things are not being
bought and sold. All this reminds me of a pleasant book I do not
think I have ever mentioned to you—*Confessions of a Bankrupt
Bookseller*. It is a good picture of an attractive type which I enjoyed greatly. After all a good bookseller, even though he only

pays five shillings in the pound, is pretty nearly the noblest worl of God.

We are at the moment in one of those minor crises in politic which always emerge when the sands of a government are be ginning to run out. I don't think it means a general election jus yet. But it is most interesting to see the men who hope for a return begin to burnish their armour and prepare the ground fo fighting alliances. Eustace Percy for instance is beginning to an nounce his claims and it is good fun to watch his anxiety to b in the light sufficiently to prevent the danger of his being over looked once more.[1] But he is not alone. Politicians who have bee silent ever since 1931 begin to whisper that they have don enough to warrant consideration. I can't help feeling that exhibi tionism is an integral part of the politician's equipment. That an the power to improvise sincerely are the essence of the breed Lord Horder, the physician, said, I thought, a good thing th other day when he remarked that the politician who succeeds i the man who convinces himself by his own perorations.

I have booked my passage on March 20th—so I shall be i Washington sometime in the first part of April. I have promise to be in Illinois on April 10-11 and in New York on Mondays But I am going to leave 3 or 4 days for a sight of the New Dea and I shall assume that I may come along to see you on each o them.[2]

Our love to you as always. I do not need to tell you that th book you will get next week brings you all and more of the ol affection.   *Yours devotedly, Harold J. Lask*

[1] When MacDonald resigned in June 1935, Lord Eustace Percy becam Minister Without Portfolio in Baldwin's Cabinet.

[2] Holmes died on March 6, 1935.

Biographical Appendix

Adams, Brooks (1848-1927), descendant of Presidents. His forebodings of doom found justification in a cyclical and cynical interpretation of history which he formulated in *The Law of Civilization and Decay* (1895). He was as distinctively a Bostonian and as uncompromisingly an Adams as his better-known brother, Henry, whom he idolized—in that devotion rising above the rebellious skepticism which sharpened his judgment of his own world and its aspirations.

Alexander, Samuel (1859-1938), beloved Professor of Philosophy at Manchester from 1893 to 1924. Save for his one large work, *Space, Time, and Deity* (2 vols., 1920), Alexander's distinguished contributions to philosophy were principally in essays and lectures. His metaphysical affiliations were with Spinoza, with the realists and theists; in his ethics he was an evolutionist, and in aesthetics he was greatly concerned with the psychology of artistry.

Ames, James Barr (1846-1910), beloved Dean and Professor of the Harvard Law School. As teacher he made of the case method of instruction a success which its founder, Langdell, never achieved. As scholar he is best known for his numerous essays on English legal history and his many case-books on various branches of the law.

Amos, Sir Maurice Sheldon (1872-1940). Following his years of judicial service in Egypt, Amos became a frequent adviser to the British government in matters of foreign law and international affairs. After the publication of his principal work, *The English Constitution* (1930), he became Quain Professor of Comparative Law at University College, London.

Astor, Nancy (1879-   ), Viscountess. American zest, Virginian charm, and marriage to Lord Astor facilitated an energetic career as suffragette, conservative member of Parliament, explosive friend of the great, and intemperate enemy of intemperance. With humor and pride she has told her own story under the somewhat possessive title *My Two Countries* (1923).

Aulard, François Alphonse (1849-1928), founder of the *Société de l'histoire de la Révolution* and masterful editor of forgotten records of the Revolution. His own interpretations of the Revolution, though frankly partisan, were so infused with enthusiasm and so firmly grounded in scholarship that they commenced a new era in the historiography of the Revolution. His greatest single work was the *Histoire politique de la Révolution française* (1901). His passionate disagreement with Taine's despairing interpretation of the Revolution was most fully expressed in his *Taine: Historien de la Révolution française* (1907).

Austin, John (1790-1859), follower of Bentham and father of the modern school of analytical jurisprudence. In *The Province of Jurisprudence Determined* (1832) he sought to define the boundaries between "law strictly so-called" and "law by analogy." By his process of definition he determined that his province of jurisprudence should be that of "law strictly so-called," wherein every positive law may be seen to be a direct or circuitous command of a sovereign. This discarding of morality and the law of nature was, needless to say, a repudiation which critics of the analytical school have been unwilling to accept.

Bagehot, Walter (1826-1877) economist, whose training in the law and intimate relations with leaders in political and intellectual affairs gave to his writing in political science (*The English Constitution* and *Physics and Politics*) and economics (*Lombard Street*) an effective vitality. Admiring the deferential strain in British character and seeing the social value of dullness as contrasted with originality, he was no radical in his politics and was an ardent and able spokesman for that political liberalism and institutional conservatism which marked the age of Victoria.

Bayle, Pierre (1647-1706), French philosopher who turned from Calvinism to Catholicism and returned again from whence he started. His *Dictionnaire historique et critique* (1696) became the model of Diderot's *Encyclopédie* in an age of enlightenment for which Bayle might have had small sympathy. Though he rejected the all-sufficiency of reason, considered that man's nature is essentially evil, and in politics was timidly conservative, in his *Dictionnaire* he indulged an ingenious talent for irreverent paradox which was the admiration of the *philosophes* of the eighteenth century. Voltaire spoke fairly of him: "Bayle is the first of logicians and sceptics. His greatest enemies must confess that there is not a line in his works which con-

tains an open aspersion of Christ tianity; but his warmest apologist must acknowledge that there is no a page in his controversial writing which does not lead the reader t doubt, and often to scepticism." See herein, Jurieu, Pierre.

Beck, James Montgomery (1861 1936), lawyer and politician whose service as Solicitor General of th United States in the Harding admin istration was followed by a career i Congress from 1927 to 1934. H most pretentious work, *The Consti tution of the United States* (1922) stimulated Thomas Reed Powell devastating sketch of constitutiona pontification in 33 *New Republi* 297 (Feb. 7, 1923).

Becker, Carl (1873-1945), Professo of History at Cornell. His greates contributions to the history of idea were *The Declaration of Independ ence* (1922) and *The Heavenly Cit of the Eighteenth Century Philoso phers* (1932).

Bell, Gertrude Margaret Lowthia (1868-1926), traveler, renowned let ter-writer, and expert on the antiqui ties and immediacies of the Middl East. Through scholarship and devo tion she did much to interpret an direct the course of history in Meso potamia in the years following th First World War. *The Letters o Gertrude Bell* (2 vols., 1927; Lad Bell, ed.), edited with great dis cretion if not excessive prudence were published shortly after he death.

Berenson, Bernard (1865-1959) American-born art critic, whose lif in Italy contributed to the distinctio of his many works on the Italia painters. He has told the story c his life in art in *Sketch for a Se Portrait* (1949).

Beveridge, Albert J. (1862-1927) Following his energetic career a Senator from Indiana and leader c the Progressive Republicans, he pro fessionalized an aptitude for histor and wrote his monumental *Life c John Marshall* (4 vols., 1918-19) Thereafter he turned to the task c writing a four-volume biography c Lincoln, but died when his work wa but half completed. Holmes's associ

'on with him was as a summer
ighbor on the North Shore of
assachusetts.

veridge, Sir William (1879-   ),
ter first Baron Beveridge; econo-
ist, civil servant and, from 1919
1937, Director of the London
hool of Economics. His lifelong
ncern with problems of unemploy-
ent led to his most famous achieve-
ent—the Beveridge Report of 1942,
which he set forth proposals for a
heme of social insurance, a plan
hich in many of its essentials was
opted by the Labor Government
tween 1945 and 1947.

rrell, Augustine (1850-1933), law-
r, statesman, and essayist. In pub-
e life he was a loyal supporter of
ladstone and held the presidency
the Board of Education in the
ampbell-Bannerman government. As
ief Secretary for Ireland from
)07 to 1916 he followed the suc-
ssion of Morley and Bryce, doing
s duties charmingly but so casually
at he failed entirely to foresee the
aster rebellion. His political career
ded, he returned to a quiet life of
tters in Chelsea. He told his own
ory in *Things Past Redress* (1937).

osanquet, Bernard (1848-1923),
nilosopher and political theorist who
ve a Hegelian interpretation to
ousseau's "general will." Through
etaphysical inquiry he discovered
e moral person of the state and
signed to it an unlimited authority
r which it compelled the individual
realize his freedom. In coloring
ne supremacy of a state's authority
ith the virtue of moral truth he
elieved that he had not taken from
e individual liberties which he
ight legitimately seek to retain. His
ost important work in political
eory was *The Philosophical Theory
the State* (1899).

ossuet, Jacques Bénigne (1627-
704), Catholic theologian who be-
eved that the drift of his age to-
ard rationalism must be stopped by
storing the philosophical credit of
ovidence and of miracle, and by
e reconversion of Protestants. In
s political writing, while denying
Louis XIV the special grace of
bitrary power and to the people
y natural rights, he acknowledged
that the King's authority was as
absolute as were his rights divine. As
theological controversialist he succeeded in effecting the Papal con-
demnation of Fénelon's quietism. His
fame as preacher rests principally on
the magniloquence of his funeral
orations.

Bowen, Charles (1835-1894), Baron
Bowen. At the bar and on the bench
he retained the graceful literary talent which marked his early contributions to the *Saturday Review*. His
subtle and sensitive genius was
largely wasted on the jurymen of
the Queen's Bench, on which he sat
from 1879 to 1882, but refreshed
and vivified the Court of Appeal, to
which he was advanced in 1882.
The opinions which perhaps most
fully reveal the quality of his mind
and of his style were those which
he delivered in *Mogul Steamship
Company v. McGregor*, 23 Q.B.D.
598 (1889) and *Maxim Nordenfeldt
Gas and Ammunition Co. v. Nordenfeldt* [1893] Ch. 630.

Bradlaugh, Charles (1833-1891),
self-made atheist and missionary of
doubt who saw a natural alliance between political republicanism and
theological radicalism. He succeeded
in his effort to force a respectable
society to make itself ridiculous by
prosecuting and persecuting him.
Elected to Parliament in 1880 he
finally prevailed, five years later, in
his effort to be seated despite his
atheism.

Bradley, Francis Herbert (1846-
1924), principal figure in the English philosophical movement away
from empiricism and utilitarianism
towards an idealism largely Kantian
and Hegelian in inspiration. In metaphysics his inquiries led him to the
Absolute, a superrelational reality
beyond the reach of experience yet
imperfectly manifested in the appearance with which experience is
concerned. His metaphysics and his
distrust of an optimistic empiricism
led him in political theory to the
belief that the individual must recognize his social station and find his
freedom in participation in the life
of the moral organism known as the
state.

Brandeis, Louis Dembitz (1856-
1941). His service on the bench of

the Supreme Court of the United States from 1916 to 1939 followed a distinguished, successful, and vigorous career at the Boston bar. The high morality of his mind and his deep concern that the state's efforts to improve the lot of man should not be frustrated by constitutional abstractions made him an influence of profound importance. Frequently associated in dissent from the views of a majority of their Brethren, Holmes and Brandeis differed greatly in their temperaments, their political convictions, and their basic interests, yet were devoted friends and allies in their search for truth.

Brissaud, Jean-Baptiste (1854-1904), Professor of Law at Toulouse. Brissaud's greatest work of historical scholarship was *Cours d'histoire générale du droit français* (1904). His philosophic inclinations were utilitarian and scientific, and his concern as legal historian was with the institutions which surround and shape the law, rather than with its content. His perspective was European, not merely French, and he did much to further the comparative method in the study of legal history.

Brunetière, Ferdinand (1849-1906), militant critic, historian of ideas in French literature, and champion of the classical tradition. Brunetière discovered the sources of modern pollution in the Enlightenment, and made it his special responsibility to assault its progeny, the scientific naturalism of Zola and Anatole France. His ultimate conversion to Catholicism concluded a lifelong search for the security of a disciplined tradition. His greatest work was *Études critiques sur l'histoire de la littérature française* (8 vols., 1880-1907). Laski included a telling summary of Brunetière's traditionalism in *Authority in the Modern State* (1919) 171 *et seq.*

Bynkershoek, Cornelius van (1673-1743), Dutch judge and jurist whose *De domino maris dissertatio* (1702) became one of the classics of international law. Less philosophically inclined than Grotius, he gave larger emphasis to such positive sources of international law as custom, treaties, and Roman law than to the law of nature.

Cardozo, Benjamin N. (1870-1938 one of the greatest of American cor mon-law judges. He sat on the Ne York Court of Appeals from 1914 1932, when he was named Holmes successor on the Supreme Court the United States by President Ho ver. The sensitivity of his temper ment, the delicacy of his mind, ar his profound concern with the ph losophy of law and the responsibili of judges were shown not only in h judicial opinions but in his extr. judicial writings, such as *The Natu of the Judicial Process* (1922) ar *The Paradoxes of Legal Scien* (1928).

Cecil, Lord Robert (1864-1958), fir Viscount Cecil of Chalwood; co servative statesman whose greate efforts were in the cause of worl peace and the League of Nations. **I** 1937 he was awarded the Nob Peace Prize.

Clarke, John Hessin (1857-1945 Following a career at the Ohio b. he was appointed United States Di trict Judge for the Northern Distri of Ohio by Woodrow Wilson i 1914. In 1916 President Wilson el. vated him to the Supreme Court the United States to fill the vacanc resulting from the resignation Charles Evans Hughes. Mr. Justic Clarke resigned from the Court i 1922 in order to devote his energi. to the cause of world peace and tl League of Nations.

Cohen, Morris Raphael (1880-1947 American philosopher whose devote friends Holmes, Laski, and Fel. Frankfurter found in him the sam qualities which made him a pr. foundly influential teacher of man generations of students at City Co lege, New York. His skeptical bent **i** metaphysics did not destroy a pas sionate conviction that man's ult mate reliance must be on reason c qualify the conviction that logic and mathematical relations have r. ality. His *Law and the Social Orde* (1933) contained his essays on leg. philosophy, a group of writing which had greatly influenced th thinking of American judges an lawyers. The story of his person. and intellectual life is told in h. autobiography, *A Dreamer's Journe* (1949).

Cole, G. D. H. (1889-1959), economist and political scientist whose innumerable writings on economic and political problems have had a significant influence on socialist thought and the policies of the Labour Party in the last thirty years. Neither these works nor his teaching at Oxford prevented him from collaborating with his wife, Margaret, in the writing of a five-foot shelf of mystery stories.

Curzon, George Nathaniel (1859-1925), Marquess Curzon of Kedleston. His arrogant conservatism combined with political ambition made him see British imperialism as a "majestic responsibility." As Viceroy of India he took the vision seriously and exercised his responsibilities with such majestic luxury and administrative capacity that he antagonized nearly all with whom he had dealings. Foreign Secretary in the Coalition Government of Lloyd George and in Bonar Law's cabinet, he ended his career having, in the words of Harold Nicolson, "achieved successes rather than success."

Demogue, René (1872-). Best known for his *Notions fondamentales du droit privé* (1911), Demogue was Professor of Civil Law and Criminal Law at Lille. Philosophically he was affiliated with the pluralistic school of which Hauriou and Duguit were the best known spokesmen. Impatient of abstractions, he demanded of positivists a larger concern with ends of law than they had previously shown; sympathetic with the efforts of rationalism he was willing to recognize the law of nature if it was seen to be an ideal rather than a positive body of law.

Dicey, Albert Venn (1835-1922), Vinerian Professor of English Law at Oxford. Through his Stephen blood and personal friendship he was closely associated with the intellectual and political leaders of his day. His notable contributions to law and jurisprudence include his Introduction to the *Study of the Law of the Constitution* (1885) and *Lectures on the Relation between Law and Public Opinion in England during the Nineteenth Century* (1905).

Dickinson, G. Lowes (1862-1932), historian, political scientist, and philosopher whose academic post at Cambridge was the center from which his humane and sensitive intelligence made its influence felt throughout the world of letters. He was intimately associated with the London School of Economics as lecturer on political science from 1896 until 1920. E. M. Forster has painted an unforgettable portrait of his friend in *Goldsworthy Lowes Dickinson* (1934).

Dilke, Sir Charles Wentworth (1843-1911), Second Baronet; politician and author, whose political loyalties embraced both radicalism and imperialism. As President of the Local Government Board from 1882 to 1885 he rendered invaluable service to Gladstone, but his effective public career was brought to an end by a notorious divorce case in which he, without justice, was implicated.

Duguit, Léon (1859-1928), Professor of Constitutional Law at Bordeaux. In a series of volumes on public law and jurisprudence Duguit developed the thesis that the state is beneath the law, has no claim to sovereignty, and lacks the personality attributed to it by classical legal theory. On the basis of these principles Duguit asserted that the state is legally responsible for its wrongful acts and that the stuff of law is to be found not in rights, but in duties. He found that the requirement of social solidarity was the driving influence in modern law by means of which the interests of state and individual were reconciled and adjusted. In 1919 Laski and his wife published a translation of Duguit's *Les transformations du droit public* (1913) under the title, *Law in the Modern State*. Laski's later, somewhat more critical estimate of Duguit's philosophy of law is to be found in *Modern Theories of Law* (Jennings, ed., 1933) 52.

Eddington, Sir Arthur (1882-1944), Cambridge astronomer whose large contributions to a science for the experts was followed by a series of works in which its mysteries were made comprehensible to laymen. His efforts to reconcile science and religion and to justify his belief that the realm of physical science is subjective are to be found in his *Nature of the Physical World* (1928), *Science and the Unseen World* (1929), and *The Philosophy of Physical Science* (1939).

Ehrlich, Eugen (1862-1922), Professor of Roman Law at the University of Czernowitz. Ehrlich was the European leader of the modern sociological movement in jurisprudence. His most influential books were *Grundelung der Soziologie des Rechts* (1913) and *Die juristische Logik* (1918). He found in the inner order of such social institutions as the family, the corporation, and the labor union the basic facts of law which, through the state's legislation and the decisions of courts, takes on the form of legal propositions. His emphasis upon the dichotomy between the living law, created by society, and the rules established by statute or decision for deciding lawsuits had considerable influence on English and American jurisprudence and methods of legal study. Ehrlich's philosophy of law was related, of course, both in fact and in theory, to the pluralistic strain in modern political theory as represented by Hauriou in France and Laski in England. The *Grundelung* was published in translation as *Fundamental Principles of the Sociology of Law* (Moll, tr., 1936).

Einstein, Lewis (1877-1949), American diplomat and scholar. His most important foreign post was that of Minister to Czechoslovakia from 1921 to 1930. His principal historical works are *Tudor Ideals* (1920) and *Divided Loyalties* (1933). His intimate friendship with Holmes is recorded in their extensive unpublished correspondence.

Faguet, Émile (1847-1916), critic and literary historian whose sympathies were those of a cool-headed liberal and whose insights into the character of the great writers of France made his criticism as useful to the historians of ideas as to the historians of letters. His great works of criticism were his *Histoire de la littérature française* (2 vols., 1900-1901) and *Politiques et moralistes du XIXᵉ siècle* (3 vols., 1890-1899).

In his later years his concern was principally with the political and intellectual problems of his own day, as in his *Le liberalisme* (1902) and *L'anticléricalisme* (1906), in which he sought to defend the middle way between Traditionalism and Jacobinism.

Figgis, John Neville (1866-1919), churchman and historian. Concerned primarily with assuring churches adequate freedom, Figgis insisted, with Gierke, that each group in society has a personality of its own and an inherent liberty of growth. He had great influence on the movement in English political theory towards pluralism. His most important works were *From Gerson to Grotius* (1907) and *Churches in the Modern State* (1913).

Fisher, H. A. L. (1865-1940), Warden of New College, Oxford, historian, and statesman. In politics his most important services were rendered as President of the Board of Education in the Lloyd George ministry from 1916 to 1922. Of his many historical works his most important was his *History of Europe* (3 vols., 1935). His principal biography was *James Bryce* (2 vols., 1927).

Flexner, Abraham (1866-1959), teacher and constructive critic of American education whose industry did much to persuade the great philanthropists to be far-sighted in their generosity, particularly to the advancement of medical education. He has told his own story in *I Remember* (1940).

Garvin, J. L. (1868-1947), thunderous editor of the London *Observer* and a forceful influence on British conservatism. His achievements, outside journalism, were principally those of writing the official biography of Joseph Chamberlain and editing the fourteenth edition of the *Encyclopaedia Brittanica*.

Gierke, Otto von (1844-1921). His great concept of *Genossenschaft*, as a Germanic principle of coöperative association, was at the foundation of his theory that the corporate body is not, as the Roman law considered it to be, a *persona ficta* but a real group person, created not by the state but by social action. Made familiar to English and American scholars by Maitland, Gierke had great influence on pluralistic theories of the state, though those who admired the depth of his scholarship and the massiveness of his *Genossenschafts theorie* did not accept his ultimately Hegelian view that all groups in a society are subordinate to the will of the state.

Gray, John Chipman (1839-1915), Professor of Law at the Harvard Law School from 1869 to 1913. A master of the law of property and an active practitioner, Gray concerned himself, somewhat impatiently, with the larger problems of jurisprudence in his *Nature and Sources of the Law* (1909). He there insisted that all theories of sovereignty are inadequate which deny or do not recognize that judges are makers of the law and as such exercise a larger share of sovereign power than do legislators. "The law of a great nation," he said, "means the opinions of half-a-dozen old gentlemen . . ."; a proposition which played a significant part in initiating the American movement towards a so-called "realist" school of jurisprudence.

Green, Thomas Hill (1836-1882). Rebel against English empiricism, he taught a doubting generation that idealism in philosophy does not, of necessity, mean conservatism in politics. His political theory emphasized the dependence of the individual upon the whole and found that the ideal of freedom may be achieved only in fulfillment of the general will as expressed in the authority of the state, and, so expressed, sanctioned by the inherited tradition of morality. His most important work in political theory was *The Principles of Moral Obligation* (1888).

Hackett, Francis (1883-1962). Irish by birth and education, he came to the United States in 1901, where he drifted into journalism. He was on the editorial board of *The New Republic* in its early years. After 1922 he was a free-lance writer. He has written of certain aspects of his life in *I Chose Denmark* (1940).

Hamilton, John Andrew (1859-1934), Viscount Sumner. Judge, successively, of the King's Bench Division and of the Court of Appeal from 1908 to 1913, he became Lord of Appeal in Ordinary in 1913. One of the great judges of his time, he will be remembered as much for the style of his opinions, salted with touches of cynicism, as for the wisdom of his judgments.

Hand, Learned (1872-1961), Federal District Judge from 1909 to 1924 and Circuit Judge in the Second Circuit from 1924 to 1951. One of the great figures in American law, his special distinctions were not dissimilar to those of Holmes, in their graceful mingling of literary gifts with a philosophical if skeptical enthusiasm.

Harrison, Frederic (1831-1923), critic and man of letters. The Positivism of Comte became his religion and he its leading British missionary. His active pen and multifarious interests produced a series of short biographies; a historical romance, *Theophano: The Crusade of the Tenth Century* (1904); and a volume of critical essays, *Studies in Early Victorian Literature* (1895).

Henderson, Arthur (1863-1935), labour leader and statesman. In his early years Henderson played a critical part in the formation of the Labour Party, and later became Home Secretary in MacDonald's first government. His greatest concern then and thereafter was with international affairs and led to his becoming MacDonald's Foreign Secretary in 1929. When the National government was formed in 1931, Henderson joined the opposition. In 1934 he was awarded the Nobel Peace Prize.

Hirst, Francis W. (1873-1953), publicist and economist, long associated with the London School of Economics. His enthusiastic Liberalism is recorded in his *Early Life and Letters of John Morley* (2 vols., 1927). His recollections of his friendships and youthful association are found in his volume of reminiscences, *In the Golden Days* (1947).

Holbach, Baron von (1723-1789), German-born contributor of scientific articles to the *Encyclopédie*. His most vigorous philosophical energies, in *Le système de la nature* (1770) and *Christianisme dévoilé* (1767), were devoted to attacking not only Christianity but the natural religion of Voltaire. It was not surprising, perhaps, that Voltaire described *Le système de la nature* as execrable in morality and absurd in physics.

Horner, Sir John (1842-1927). He and his wife, Lady Horner, were the intimate friends of many of the leading figures in British political and intellectual affairs, and members of that elect circle known as "The Souls." Their daughter Katherine in 1907 married Raymond Asquith. There are frequent references to Sir John and Lady Horner in Spender and Asquith, *Life of Lord Oxford and Asquith* (2 vols., 1932) and *Richard Bendon Haldane, an Autobiography* (1929).

Hough, Charles Merrill (1858-1927), Federal judge, first on the District then on the Circuit Court in New York. His special competence was in Admiralty.

Hughes, Charles Evans (1862-1948). After serving with distinction as Governor of New York, he became an Associate Justice of the Supreme Court of the United States in 1910. In 1916 he resigned from the Court to become Republican nominee for the Presidency, being defeated by a narrow margin when Wilson was reëlected. In 1930 he was named Chief Justice of the United States by President Hoover, retiring in 1941. A great judge, and among the greatest of Chief Justices, his strength of character and intellect made an indelible impression on his times and on the institutions with which he was associated.

Hunt, William Morris (1824-1879). Born in Vermont, he nurtured his artistic spirit in Europe, where he became a disciple of Millet. Returning to the United States in 1855, he became the Newport teacher and friend of William and Henry James and of Holmes. His later years in Boston found him the inspiring teacher of the young and the ardent supporter of modernism in art.

Inge, William Ralph (1860-1954), Dean of St. Paul's, 1911-1934, teacher, scholar, and essayist. In 1911 Asquith, then Prime Minister, persuaded Inge to move from his academic post as Professor of Divinity at Cambridge to the Deanship of St. Paul's Cathedral. Thereafter his pithy observations on affairs brought upon him, and perhaps earned for him the title of "the gloomy Dean." His studies of mysticism and of Plotinus were his greatest achievements in scholarship.

Jeans, Sir James Hopwood (1877-1946), physicist, astronomer, and mathematician. His name, like Eddington's, is generally known not only for his skillful efforts to make science comprehensible to laymen, but for his formulation of a philosophy which found a place for religion in a scientist's view of the universe.

Jenks, Edward (1861-1939), teacher and historian of law. His academic career began at the University of Melbourne and took him successively to Liverpool, Oxford, and London. From 1903 to 1924 he was Principal and Director of Legal Studies of the Law Society and from 1924 to 1929 held the chair of English Law at the University of London. His most useful book was *A Short History of English Law* (1912).

Jurieu, Pierre (1637-1713), Protestant theologian, controversialist, and defender of the Huguenots. His early friendship with Bayle ended in bitter disagreement. Jurieu, believing that Bayle was the author of the anonymous *Avis important aux refugiés sur leur prochain retour en France* (1690), in which Protestant proclivities for intolerance were vigorously attacked, replied in his *Examen d'un libelle contre la religion, contre l'état et contre la révolution d'Angleterre* (1690). Modern scholarship is generally persuaded that Bayle, while not the author of the *Avis,* could not escape responsibility for its publication. (See Tilley, *The Decline of the Age of Louis XIV,* 1929, 378-379). Jurieu's later attacks on Bayle led to Bayle's dismissal from his professorship at Rotterdam.

Jusserand, Jean Jules (1855-1932), diplomat and scholar who was French Ambassador to the United States from 1902 to 1915. His principal works of literary criticism concerned English literature.

Kelsen, Hans (1881-   ), father of the so-called Vienna School of jurisprudence. He has been Professor of Law at Vienna and many other European universities and is presently lecturer on International Law and Jurisprudence in the Department of Political Science at the University of California. His "pure science of law" makes the analytical method omnicompetent in jurisprudence, insists that the legal rule is concerned with what shall be, not with what ought to be, yet makes law a normative science. The State, in Kelsen's eyes, is an expression for the unity of the legal system, and is ultimately superior to the law. The essential elements of his philosophy are found in his *Allgemeine Staatslehre* (1925).

Ker, William Paton (1855-1923), Professor of English Literature at University College, London, from 1889 to 1922, and Fellow of All Souls from 1879 until his death. Ker's learning in comparative literature was extraordinarily wide and his relatively short list of published works only suggests the breadth of scholarship of which innumerable students were the beneficiaries. Author, *inter alia,* of *Epic and Romance* (1897) and *Collected Essays of W. P. Ker* (Whibley, ed., 1925).

La Bruyère, Jean de (1645-1696), essayist and defender of the ancients whose barbed portraits of his contemporaries in his *Caractères* (1688) gave pain to the subjects as intense as the pleasure which it gave to the audience. Master of style, he preserved in his method and his mood the tradition of the seventeenth century and satisfied the taste of the eighteenth.

Lang, Andrew (1844-1912), knowledgeable journalist and man of letters whose archaeological wanderings were more those of a folklorist than of a scientist. His talent for fugitive verse grew into a fugitive

competence in many fields—fiction, history, psychical research, and sport all engaged his versatile enthusiasm.

Langdell, Christopher Columbus (1826-1906), Dean of the Harvard Law School, 1870-1895. His conviction that the life of the law was logic, not experience, led him to his great discovery—the case-method of legal education. In the hands of his successors the method contributed strength to the conviction of Holmes that the life of the law has not been logic; it has been experience.

Leroy, Maxime (1873-1957), sociologist and historian of French socialism. His important works include *La loi, essai sur le théorie de l'autorité dans la démocratie* (1908) and *Histoire des idées sociales en France* (2 vols., 1946, 1949).

Mack, Julian W. (1866-1943), Federal judge whose distinguished services on the District Courts and Circuit Courts of Appeal covered the thirty years between 1911 and 1941. For many years he was an active leader of American Zionism, and in numerous public offices advanced the cause of civil liberty and the public's welfare.

McKenna, Joseph (1843-1926), Associate Justice of the Supreme Court of the United States, 1898-1926. A Catholic, he came to the Court after a political career in Congress, a Federal circuit judgeship, and a brief term as President McKinley's Attorney General. If settled conviction which may form the basis for predicting a judge's decision is a fault in the judicial temperament McKenna could escape that criticism, for his constitutional opinions, though frequently strong, were constantly variable. The occasional flowering of his conservatism into an effulgent fear of change—as when he determined that the Federal Employers' Liability Act was unconstitutional— did not prevent an independent mind from showing statesmanship.

McReynolds, James Clark (1862-1941). Appointed to the Supreme Court of the United States by Wilson in 1914, he contributed little wisdom, much conservatism, and unparalleled ill temper to the deliberations of the

Court. Holmes, however, found lovable qualities behind the jagged and irascible surface.

Maitland, Frederic William (1850-1906). Trained in the law, Maitland in 1884 abandoned his career as conveyancer to become Reader in the History of English Law at Cambridge, and four years later Downing Professor. His contributions to the legal and institutional history of England were of unequaled brilliance, mingling literary style, philosophic insight, and detailed learning with such graceful ease that few of his readers have failed to fall victims to his charm. He influenced Laski's political thought principally through his Introduction to a substantial portion of Gierke's *Political Theories of the Middle Age* (1900).

Masterman, C. F. G. (1874-1927), journalist and liberal politician. He successively was literary editor of *The Speaker* and of *The Nation*, and held important posts in the government before the First World War.

Mathiez, Albert (1874-1932), learned disciple of Aulard and sympathetic historian of the Revolution. In his principal work, *La révolution française* (3 vols., 1922-27), he developed a socialistic interpretation of the Revolution.

Mommsen, Theodor (1817-1903), historian of ancient Rome, active liberal politician, and Professor of Ancient History at Berlin. All of a scholar's learning and much of a journalist's enthusiasm combined to make his *Roman History* a great achievement. His later works, even more monumental in their scholarly dimensions, were a vast edition of the *Corpus inscriptionum latinarum* and his *Römischen Staatsrechts* (a part of the *Handbook of Roman Antiquities*, written with Joachim Marquardt, 1812-1882). The latter work has been described as "the greatest historical treatise on political institutions ever written."

Nevinson, Henry Woodd (1856-1941), traveler, man of letters, and journalist. His talents as war correspondent were far greater than those of a mere reporter and made him a military historian of consider-able stature. The record of his life in journalism and pursuit of lost causes is found in his trilogy of *Changes and Chances*.

Primrose, Archibald Philip (1847-1927), fifth Earl of Rosebery; statesman who was Gladstone's Foreign Secretary and briefly succeeded his chief as Prime Minister in 1894. Thereafter he became the leader of the imperialist wing of the Liberal Party, but when the policies of that wing were overridden and Campbell-Bannerman became Prime Minister in 1905 he retired from politics. Thereafter he gave his energies to public address and to the pursuits of a cultivated leisure.

Proudhon, Pierre Joseph (1809-1865), French socialist who stirred Marx with his declaration that "property is theft" and antagonized him by repudiating the dictatorship of the proletariat. His conviction that federalism would be the greatest instrument for achieving justice was the reflection of his dislike of strong state authority. His theories became an important element in the dogma of the syndicalists of a later generation.

Pufendorf, Samuel (1632-1694). In his efforts to formulate a theory of the law of nature he so skillfully mixed the divergent views of Grotius and Hobbes that a view of his own was the result. He pictured the world with which the law is concerned as peopled with moral beings acting not only in response to the instinct of self-preservation but by reason of sociability, and emphasized the rights of the individual against the state. The source of international law he discovered neither in treaties nor in custom, but in a law of nature more rational than divine.

Redlich, Josef (1869-1936), Professor of Public Law at the University of Vienna, statesman, and learned student of the English government. His greatest contributions to scholarship were *The Procedure of the House of Commons* (1908) and *Local Government in England* (Hirst, tr., 1907). In 1925 he came to the Harvard Law School as Professor of Comparative Public Law. His qualities as teacher and scholar are described by Felix Frankfurter and Charles C. Burlingham in 50 *Harv. L. Rev.* 389, 392 (January 1937). Rice, Richard A. (1846-1924), Professor of Art at Williams College until 1911. He then moved to Washington and in 1912 became Chief of the Division of Prints in the Library of Congress.

Robertson, John Mackinnon (1856-1933), radical freethinker, politician, and academically unaccredited scholar of the humanities. His "militant unorthodoxy" was expressed in many journals but was shown to be buttressed by extensive learning in his *History of Free Thought* (2 vols., 1936), and *A Short History of Christianity* (1902). Laski contributed a short biographical sketch of Robertson to *The Dictionary of National Biography, 1931-1940* (Legg, ed., 1949) 736.

Rosebery, Lord. *See* Primrose, Archibald Philip.

Rutherford, Sir Ernest (1871-1937), Baron Rutherford. Born and educated in New Zealand he became one of the great physicists of his times. His academic career was at McGill, Manchester, and Cambridge. His great discoveries in physics concerned radioactivity and the structure of atoms.

Sanford, Edward Terry (1865-1930). Advanced by President Harding to the Supreme Court of the United States from the Federal District Court in Tennessee, Sanford was a colorless colleague of Holmes's from 1923 to 1930. His tranquil inclinations were conservative, yet he joined with Holmes and Brandeis in a number of their important opinions on free speech.

Sankey, John (1866-1948), first Viscount Sankey; successively Judge of the King's Bench and of the Court of Appeal between 1914 and 1929; and Lord Chancellor from 1929 to 1935. At the bar he had been a master in the field of workmen's compensation and by his distinguished service as Chairman the Coal Mining Commission of 1919 had shown the capacity to make an acute intelligence the instrument of progress. It was no surprise, there-

fore, when he became Chancellor in the Labour Government of 1929.

Scott, James Brown (1866-1943), Professor of Law at Illinois, Columbia, and Chicago, and authority on international law. He held many governmental posts in connection with foreign affairs, and from 1907 to 1924 was editor of the *American Journal of International Law.*

Scott, Sir Leslie (1869-1950), Lord Justice of Appeal from 1935 to 1948. His life was devoted more to professional than to political affairs, but his professional services to the state were many. He and Lady Scott were intimate friends of Holmes.

Scrutton, Thomas Edward (1856-1934), Justice of the King's Bench, 1910-1916, and of the Court of Appeal, 1916 to 1934. His genius as practitioner and as judge was in the field of commercial law; an irascible, ill-mannered temperament was somewhat softened with the years and at no time was so dominant as to prevent his being a great lawyer and a great judge.

Selden, John (1584-1654), lawyer and historian. Like Coke, he put his immense learning to the service of constitutional government, but, unlike Coke did so with gracious discretion. His numerous contributions to legal history were of such substantial importance that Maitland, the greatest of legal historians, named the Selden Society in his honor.

Simon, Sir John (1873-1954), first Viscount Simon; conservative Liberal, who held many high offices of state and served as Lord Chancellor from 1940 to 1945. His legal capacities were acknowledged by all; his political judgment was mistrusted by those who thought appeasement of Hitler a mistake and doubted whether the rearmament of Germany would make for peace.

Smuts, Jan Christiaan (1870-1951), South African soldier, statesman, and philosopher. His youth was spent in the military service of the Boers, his maturity in the service both of Great Britain and of his own people, with the public's gratitude for these latter services more prevalent abroad than at home. Following the First World War he put his hopes in the League of Nations. His lifelong interest in philosophy produced one piece of work of some importance—*Holism and Evolution* (1926).

Snowden, Philip (1864-1937), Viscount Snowden; Chancellor of the Exchequer in each of the MacDonald governments. His socialism, which came to him more from study than from experience, being of a different brand than that of the trade unionists, did not always fit with theirs, and made it comparatively easy for him to remain with MacDonald's National Government in 1931, when the Trade Unions refused to do so.

Soto, Domingo de (1494-1560), Spanish jurist, who sought, in his most important work, *De justicia et jure* (2 vols., 1553-54), to translate Thomistic ethics into principles of the legal order.

Stammler, Rudolf (1856-1938), whose neo-Kantian philosophy of law emphasized the collective interests in a community of free-willing men and accepted as absolute "the principles of just law." If, as Geny charged, he failed to inform us what law is "just" and showed a greater skill in juggling abstractions than in establishing criteria of judgment, he did, despite the sterility of his basic effort, succeed in reminding judges of their creative responsibilities in guiding the judicial process. He also persuasively supported the thesis that the content of the law of nature is variable and changing. His most important works were *Lehre von dem richtigen Recht* (1902), (published in an English translation under the title *The Theory of Justice*, Husik, tr., 1925), *Wirtschaft und Recht* (1896), and *Lehrbuch der Rechtsphilosophie* (1922).

Stephen, Sir James Fitzjames (1829-1894). Lawyer, judge, and publicist, he was the forceful brother of Sir Leslie Stephen. In affairs his greatest achievement was as successor to Sir Henry Maine as legal member of the Council in India. That experience converted him to the cause of codification and nourished the doubt whether the optimism of Mill, in so far as it affected political principles, was acceptable. The result was the publication of his *Liberty, Equality, Fraternity* (1873). That work, together with his *History of the Criminal Law* (3 vols., 1883), reveal more fully than any other of his writings the vigor of his mind and the breadth of his scholarship.

Story, Joseph (1779-1845), Associate Justice of the Supreme Court of the United States from 1811 to 1845. Appointed to the Court by Madison he became as ardent a defender of national power as his Chief, John Marshall. His extraordinary energies were such that while serving on the Court he was also a member of the law faculty at Harvard and the author of ten large treatises on various subjects in the law. The utility of these volumes as reasoned, if somewhat uncritical compendia of cases and principles, was enormous and they had an influence equal to if not greater than Story's judicial opinions.

Suárez, Francisco (1548-1617). In answering such Protestant theorists of the Reformation as Althusius, he revivified the Thomistic version of the law of nature and made the last great contributions to scholastic philosophy. His political theory reëmphasized the medieval doctrine of popular sovereignty as a limitation on the power of kings.

Sumner, Lord. *See* Hamilton, John Andrew.

Taine, Hippolyte (1828-1893), critic and historian whose misanthropic positivism led him to see man as a "dismal gorilla" and whose respect for the fruitfulness of inequality led him to condemn the objectives and the achievements of the French Revolution. In his chief historical work, *Les origines de la France contemporaine* (6 vols., 1876-94), he was immersed in the tragedies of a modern France which had not enjoyed the buoyant successes of Victorian England, and became in the words of Professor Gooch, "a pessimist in a passion." The greatest influence of Taine as historian was on the conservatives who, abandoning his positivism, shared his regret that the Revolution had occurred.

Taney, Roger Brooke (1774-1864), Chief Justice of the United States from 1836 to 1864. Coming to the Supreme Court as Marshall's successor, he showed himself to be a judge of extraordinary competence well qualified for the succession. The perspective of time has made his one great error—his opinion in the Dred Scott case—seem less significant than it did to earlier generations, which saw it as a primary cause of the Civil War.

Tarde, Gabriel (1843-1904), French social psychologist. In his best known work, *Les lois de l'imitation* (1890), he sought to uncover the laws of repetition, by which he conceived that most actions of most men are determined. In all his work he was more concerned with concrete instances than with large abstractions. Tawney, R. H. (1880-1962), economic historian and publicist, long associated with London University and frequently called to the public service. Of his many works the best known, perhaps, are *Religion and the Rise of Capitalism* (1926) and *The Acquisitive Society* (1920).

Vattel, Emmerich de (1714-1767), Swiss jurist. His great work on international law, *Le droit des gens* (2 vols., 1758), found the basis of international law in principles of utility which were the postulates of reason. He sought to find legal doctrine which would make war unlawful, but was compelled to acknowledge its legality when it was waged for the enforcement of customary duties and treaty obligations.

Vauvenargues, Marquis de (1715-1747), soldier, moralist, and epigrammatist. It was largely owing to the friendship of Voltaire that the Marquis, becoming an invalid, turned to letters as his occupation. The most important result was his *Introduction à la connaissance de l'esprit humain* (1746) with its accompanying maxims.

Vinogradoff, Sir Paul (1854-1925), legal historian of Russian birth who became Professor of Jurisprudence at Oxford in 1903, succeeding Sir Frederick Pollock. His greatest discovery was the manuscript of Bracton's *Notebook* and his most important

piece of historical writing was *Villainage in England* (1892). His Oxford seminar produced the Oxford *Studies in Social and Legal History* (9 vols., 1908-27), under his editorship.

Wallas, Graham (1858-1932). In his early years Wallas was intimately associated with Shaw and Webb in the Fabian Society. Later he became one of the organizers of and early lecturers at the London School of Economics and Political Science, filling its first chair of political science from 1914 to 1923. His earliest book, *The Life of Francis Place* (1898), was an important addition to knowledge of the history of the British labor movement. In his later works he endeavored to build a science of social psychology in the hope that political theory might be freed from the grip of intellectualism. *The Great Society* (1914) was a book of enormous influence in revealing the relationships between psychology and political science and in suggesting how fruitful the scientific temper might be when applied to the problems of political theory.

Ward, Lester Frank (1841-1913), American sociologist whose most important work, *Dynamic Sociology* (2 vols., 1883), was written while he was a civil servant in Washington engaged in scientific research and before his appointment as Professor of Sociology at Brown University. His sociological theory emphasized the capacity of man by conscious effort to improve the human lot and through that emphasis served effectively to refute the evolutionary determinism of Spencer. From an early date Holmes was an admirer of Ward's writing.

Wigmore, John Henry (1863-1943), learned Dean of the Law School of Northwestern University. His monumental treatise on *The Law of Evidence* (3rd ed., 10 vols., 1940) is one of the great classics of Anglo-American law. His close friendship with Holmes survived the strain to which it was subjected by Wigmore's petulant postwar patriotism which found Holmes's tolerant views on free speech intolerable.

Wister, Owen (1860-1938), lawyer, novelist, grandson of Fanny Kemble, and, above all, Philadelphian. A vigorous admirer of Theodore Roosevelt's vigor, he was best known, perhaps, for his novel *The Virginian* (1902). His friendship with Holmes began when Holmes was on the Massachusetts bench and Wister was a law student at Harvard.

Wu, John C. H. (1899-   ), jurist, judge, and intimate friend of Holmes. The original story of their intimacy is revealed in the letters of Holmes to Wu, first published in the *T'ien Hsia Monthly* for October 1935, later reprinted in Shriver, *Justice Oliver Wendell Holmes, His Book Notices and Uncollected Letters and Papers* (1936), 151 *et seq.* Dr. Wu has written of his own life, of his friendship with Holmes, and of his conversion to Roman Catholicism in *Beyond East and West* (1951).

Zimmern, Sir Alfred (1879-1957), historian, classicist, and student of foreign affairs. He held many academic posts in Great Britain and the United States, and participated in such international enterprises as the League of Nations and UNESCO. His most important piece of scholarship is *The Greek Commonwealth* (1911).

Index

MARK DEWOLFE HOWE is Professor of Law, Harvard Law School. Mr. Howe has for many years made the life and work of Justice Holmes the object of his scholarship. He has in progress the definitive biography of the Justice, of which two volumes have appeared: *The Shaping Years 1847-1870; The Proving Years 1870-1882.* Mr. Howe has also edited the *Holmes-Pollock Letters,* Holmes' *The Common Law,* and *The Occasional Speeches of Justice Holmes.* In addition to the numerous works relating to Holmes, Mr. Howe is also the compiler of *Cases on Church and State in the United States.*

314 TAXES INCREASED! EFECT
    WILLING TO DIE FOR STATE, NOT PAY FOR

Atheneum Paperbacks

Government and Public Affairs

Economics and Business

History and Societal Studies